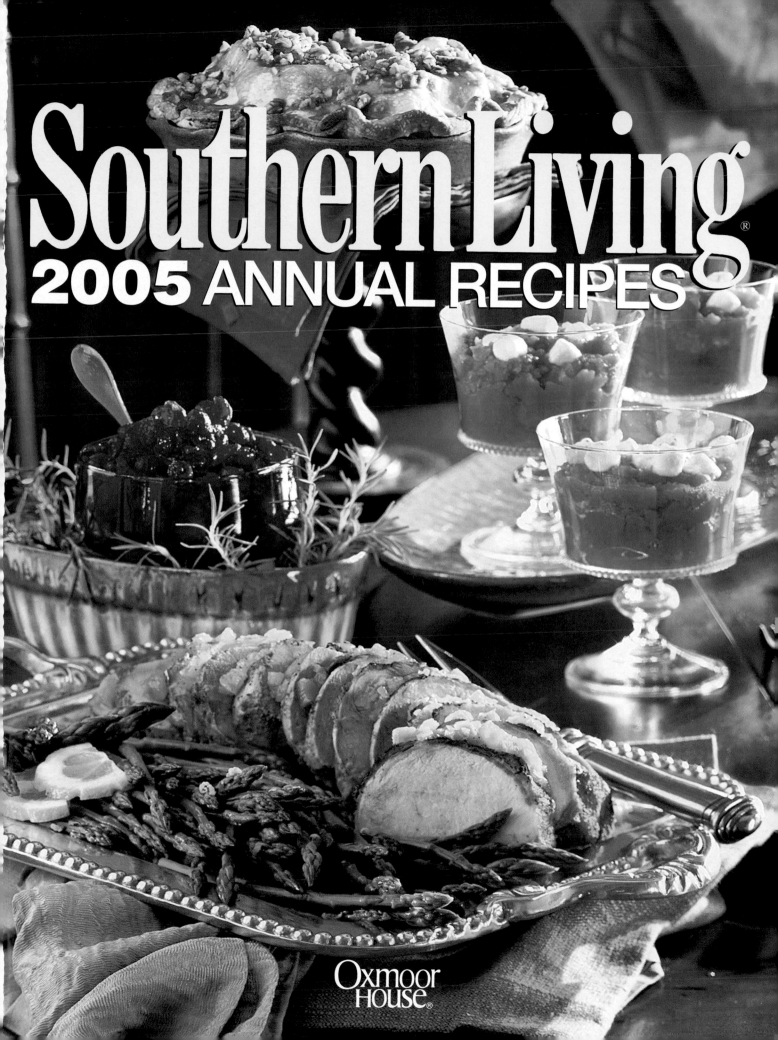

Southern Living

2005 ANNUAL RECIPES

Oxmoor House®

meet the *Southern Living*® foods staff

Dozens of recipes go through our Test Kitchens each day, where they are evaluated on taste, appearance, practicality, and ease of preparation. On these pages, we invite you to match the names and faces of the people who test, photograph, and write about our favorites (left to right unless otherwise noted).

▲ (seated) SUSAN DOSIER, *Executive Editor;* SCOTT JONES, *Foods Editor;* (standing) SANDRA J. THOMAS, *Administrative Assistant;* CHARLOTTE LIAPIS, *Editorial Assistant;* LYDA H. JONES, *Test Kitchens Director*

◄ (seated) VANESSA MCNEIL ROCCHIO, *Test Kitchens Specialist/Food Styling;* JAMES SCHEND, *Assistant Test Kitchens Director;* (standing) MARIAN CAIRNS COOPER, ANGELA SELLERS, ALYSSA PORUBCAN, PAM LOLLEY, *Test Kitchens Staff*

(clockwise from top left) ►
KATE NICHOLSON, *Associate Foods Editor;* VICKI A. POELLNITZ, *Assistant Foods Editor;* SHIRLEY HARRINGTON, *Associate Foods Editor;* JOHN MCMILLIAN, *Assistant Recipe Editor;* DONNA FLORIO, *Senior Writer;* CHARLA DRAPER, MARY ALLEN PERRY, SHANNON SLITER SATTERWHITE, *and* HOLLEY JOHNSON, *Associate Foods Editors;* ANDRIA SCOTT HURST, *Senior Writer*

best recipes of 2005

Not all recipes are created equal. At *Southern Living,* only those that have passed muster with our Test Kitchens staff and Foods editors—not an easy crowd to please—make it onto the pages of our magazine. Members of our Foods staff gather almost every day to taste-test recipes to ensure not only that they're reliable, but also that they taste as good as they possibly can. Here we share this year's favorites.

◄Strawberry-Citrus Chicken Salad *(page 84):*

This refreshing salad gets its zing from a drizzle of vinaigrette made with strawberry preserves, balsamic vinegar, and crushed rosemary.

◄Uptown Collards *(page 21):*

Long, slow cooking matched with a seasoned broth brings out the assertive flavor of this Southern gem.

◄Dark Chocolate Mousse with Raspberry Sauce *(page 31):*

Dish up some decadence with velvety-smooth mousse crowned with raspberry sauce.

◄Chicken Pudding *(page 22):*

Good, simple ingredients like chicken and vegetables form layers of flavor in this comfort food standout.

◄Butternut Squash-Parsnip Soup *(page 32):*

With its eye-catching color and rich flavor, this silky soup proves that elegant doesn't have to be fussy.

◄Cream Cheese Banana-Nut Bread, plus variations *(page 27):*

One speedy-to-mix batter with several different toppings produces moist and tender breads that will melt in your mouth.

◄Double Citrus Tart *(page 55):*

A zesty blend of orange and lemon juices creates the sunny flavor of this showy dessert with a gingersnap crust.

▲ Chocolate-Coffee Cheesecake With Mocha Sauce *(page 316):*

This melt-in-your-mouth dessert received rave reviews and $100,000 from the judges at our annual Cook-Off. For more winning recipes, see page 315.

◄ Strawberry Smoothie Ice-Cream Pie *(page 89):*

Fresh strawberries, blueberries, and bananas atop a waffle cone crust make biting into this luscious dessert a dreamy experience.

◄ Hush Puppies *(page 99):*

Substituting beer for milk adds tang to these Southern specialties. And you're just 6 ingredients from lip-smacking goodness.

◄ Avocado Soup *(page 200):*

It takes just 15 minutes and a blender or food processor to whip up this buttery smooth soup.

◄ Field Greens With Roasted Bacon-Wrapped Pears *(page 230):*

Enjoy the taste of fall with this beguiling blend of mixed salad greens and pears tossed with a drizzle of spicy apple-ginger vinaigrette.

◄ Spiced Soufflés With Lemon Whipped Cream *(page 255):*

Follow our seven foolproof tips to whip up this elegant dessert that's a sure party pleaser.

◄ Layered Sun-dried Tomato and Basil Spread *(page 275):*

A wreath of rosemary sprigs garnishes this makeahead appetizer that tastes as good as it looks.

◄ Crispy Brown Sugar Bacon *(page 283):*

Twisting the bacon before cooking ensures a texture that's crisp on the ends and chewy in the center.

◄ Chocolate Fudge Cheesecake *(page 288):*

A velvety cream cheese mixture nestles between a rich brownie crust and an irresistible chocolate glaze.

▶ **Sweet Potato Biscuits** (*page 22*) Wake up your taste buds with these comfy-cozy treats warm out of the oven slathered with butter or jam.

▶ **Easy Pan Biscuits** (*page 26*) Lemon-lime soft drink is the secret ingredient in these biscuits. And just 3 other ingredients complete the recipe for a quick treat anytime of the day. Talk about easy!

▶ **Southwest Fried Oysters** (*page 48*) This heavenly half shell gets its crisp, flavorful crust from a combination of buttermilk, cornmeal, and a skillful blend of spices.

▶ **Jalapeño Hush Puppies** (*page 99*) That zip that you taste comes from the magic potency of a seeded and diced jalapeño added to this fried favorite.

▶ **Coconut Cream Pie** (*page 110*) Nothing says Southern graciousness more than a slice of coconut pie. And with just 10 minutes of prep time, no one will guess how easy it is to make this rich, fluffy dessert

▶ **Vietnamese Fajitas (Bo Nuong Xa)** (*page 117*) Grilled Flank steak chilled in a delicious marinade and bundled with vegetables and fruits in spring roll wrappers make up this Vietnamese specialty.

▶ **Raspberry-Buttermilk Sherbet, plus variations** (*page 133*) This frosty, fruity recipe boasts a short ingredient list and easy preparation. Three variations let you take advantage of summer's bountiful berry crop.

▶ **Southwest Breakfast Strata** (*page 136*) Sausage, vegetables, cheese, and eggs poured over tortilla pieces provide the great texture and flavor of this make-ahead casserole that bakes to a bubbly finish.

▶ **Herb-and-Garlic Goat Cheese Truffles** (*page 143*) You'll love every buttery mouthful of these bite-size party pleasers laced with chives and basil. Promise!

▶ **Lemon-Rosemary Mayonnaise** (*page 144*) Discover how, in mere minutes, you can transform store-bought mayonnaise into this flavor-packed condiment.

▶ **Big "D" Smoked Baby Back Ribs, Paul's Pork Ribs Rub, Paul's Barbecue Sauce, and Big "D" Smoked Chicken** (*page 174–175*) Taste for yourself what our Foods staff deemed as "the best barbecue sauce we've ever had" from the recipe of North Carolina native Paul Bender's ribs and chicken accented with a dry rub.

▶ **Sweet Spice Blend and Sugar-and-Spice Nuts** (*page 274*) Use this easy-to-make spice blend to create all kinds of delicious recipes including an addictive snack mix that's made with your favorite combination of nuts.

▶ **Praline-Pecan Cakes** (*page 286*) Perfect for holiday gift-giving, this recipe yields 9 (5-inch) loaves that can be frozen for up to 1 month.

▶ **Sour Cream Cake Batter** (*page 286*) It takes just 15 minutes to whip up this versatile batter that can be used to make cakes in a variety of flavors and pans.

▶ **Praline-Pecan Brownies, Caramel-Coconut-Pecan Brownies, and Peppermint Brownie Tarts** (*page 288*) Use our decadent Chocolate Fudge Brownies recipe to make a chocolate sampler with these festive treats.

All of our winning recipes in Cook-Off 2005 received our highest rating as well. These recipes begin on page 315.

ISBN: 0-8487-2893-9
ISSN: 0272-2003

Printed in the United States of America
First printing 2005

To order additional publications, call 1-800-765-6400.

Congratulations!

As a buyer of *Southern Living*® *2005 Annual Recipes,* you have exclusive access to the *Southern Living*® Web site on America Online. Simply go to www.southernliving.com.
   When prompted, log on with this Web site access code: **SLAR2893**
   Effective until December 31, 2006

Southern Living®
Executive Editor: Susan Dosier
Foods Editor: Scott Jones
Senior Writers: Donna Florio, Andria Scott Hurst
Associate Foods Editors: Charla Draper, Shirley Harrington, Holley Johnson, Kate Nicholson, Mary Allen Perry, Shannon Sliter Satterwhite
Assistant Foods Editor: Vicki A. Poellnitz
Assistant Recipe Editor: John McMillan
Test Kitchens Director: Lyda H. Jones
Assistant Test Kitchens Director: James Schend
Test Kitchens Specialist/Food Styling: Vanessa McNeil Rocchio
Test Kitchens Staff: Marian Cairns Cooper, Rebecca Kracke Gordon, Pam Lolley, Alyssa Porubcan, Angela Sellers
Administrative Assistant: Sandra J. Thomas
Production and Color Quality Manager: Katie Terrell Morrow
Photography and Cover Art Director: Jon Thompson
Copy Chief: Dawn P. Cannon
Copy Editor: Leah Dueffer, Cindy Riegle
Senior Foods Photographers: Ralph Anderson, Charles Walton IV
Photographers: Tina Cornett, William Dickey, Beth Dreiling
Senior Photo Stylist: Buffy Hargett
Photo Stylist: Rose Nguyen
Assistant Photo Stylists: Lisa Powell, Cari South
Photo Librarian: Tracy Duncan
Photo Assistant: Catherine Carr
Assistant Production Manager: Jamie Barnhart
Production Coordinators: Christy Coleman, Paula Dennis
Production Assistant: Allison Brooke Wilson

Oxmoor House, Inc.
Editor in Chief: Nancy Fitzpatrick Wyatt
Executive Editor: Susan Carlisle Payne
Copy Chief: Allison Long Lowery

Southern Living® *2005 Annual Recipes*
Editor: Susan Hernandez Ray
Copy Editor: Donna Baldone
Assistant Editor: Terri Laschober
Director of Production: Laura Lockhart
Books Production Manager: Greg Amason
Production Assistant: Faye Porter Bonner
Publishing Systems Administrator: Rick Tucker

Contributors
Designer: Nancy Johnson
Indexer: Mary Ann Laurens
Editorial Consultant: Jean Wickstrom Liles

Cover (clockwise from top): Chocolate-Red Velvet Layer Cake, page 287; Praline-Pecan Cakes, page 286; Fluted Chocolate-Red Velvet Cake, page 287

Page 1 (clockwise from front): Balsamic-Browned Butter Asparagus, page 260; Apricot Glazed-and-Spiced Pork Loin, page 259; Quick Orange-Cranberry Sauce, page 270; Praline-Apple Pie, page 251; Maple-Sweet Potato Casserole, page 245

contents

3 Best Recipes of 2005

9 Our Year at *Southern Living*
10 Favorite Columns at a Glance
12 Cook's Chat

15 january

16 Family Friendly
18 Family Game Night
19 *Quick & Easy*
   Fast Meat-and-Sauce Meals
20 *Top-Rated Menu*
   Chili Tonight
21 Greens Made Simple
21 *Taste of the South*
   Hoppin' John
22 Down-Home and Delicious
23 The Comfort of Cider
24 Everyday Choices
26 *What's for Supper?*
   A Cozy Breakfast
27 *Food and Hospitality*
   Banana-Nut Bread
28 *From Our Kitchen*

29 february

30 *Healthy & Light*
   Good-for-You Chocolate
32 The Kitchen: Recipe for Style
34 *What's for Supper?* Pot Roasts
36 Keep It Casual
41 One Dressing, Three Salads
42 5 Money-Saving Menus
44 Banana Bonanza
45 Ham and Beans
46 *Top-Rated Menu*
   Table-to-Table Dinner
47 Oysters
49 *Quick & Easy* Pasta Suppers
   Ready in Minutes
50 *From Our Kitchen*

51 march

52 *Healthy & Light*
   Season's First Grilling
54 Laid-back Sunday Dinner
55 Hooked on Catfish
56 Good for the Soul
58 *What's for Supper?*
   Tex-Mex Tonight
58 Family-Favorite Casseroles
59 Add Zest With Lemon

60 *Food and Hospitality*
   Entertaining That's Simple
61 Fruity Thirst Quenchers
62 Irresistible Ice-Cream
   Sandwiches
63 You'll Love this Easy-Does-It
   Cake
64 *Top-Rated Menu*
   March Madness
64 Ready, Set, Serve
66 Bake These Southern Sides
67 *Quick & Easy*
   Speedy Steaks Fried Right
68 Freshen a Menu With Herbs
69 *Taste of the South*
   Rémoulade Sauce
70 *From Our Kitchen*

71 april

72 Easy Menu for Passover
82 Flavor Lamb With Fresh Herbs
83 Make Bread in the Mixer
84 *Food and Hospitality*
   Grilling Smarter
85 Stir Up Some Veggies
86 Cut Up a Pineapple
87 Milk and Cookies Anytime
88 *Quick & Easy*
   Family Weekend Breakfast
89 Good to the Last Bite
90 Savor Easy Pot Roast
91 Start With a Slaw Mix
92 *What's for Supper?*
   Have a Deli-Style Dinner
93 Stuff a Dozen (or Two)
94 To Market, To Market
96 *Top-Rated Menu*
   New-Fashioned Luncheon
   Party
97 Speedy Appetizers
98 Lunch in the Lowcountry
99 *Taste of the South* Hush Puppies
100 *Healthy & Light*
   Italian Made Fresh
102 *From Our Kitchen*

103 favorites

104 Mid-Atlantic Flavors
106 Shortcuts to Top-Rated Cakes
108 Mountain Country Recipes
110 A Southern Sampler
111 Lowcountry Cuisine
112 Comfort Food, Delta Style
117 Food You'll Yee-Haw Over

118 Bayou Cooking
120 A Taste of Sunshine

121 may

122 Start the Party in the Kitchen
124 Secrets to Great Seafood
124 Keep That Knife Sharp
125 Coleslaw Three Ways
126 *Healthy & Light*
   Taste the Goodness of
   Grains
127 Exceptional Eggplant
128 Dill-icious Ideas
129 Make Ahead and Marinate
130 Easy Beach Menu
131 *Quick & Easy*
   Ready-to-Assemble Meals
132 Enjoy Fresh Strawberries
133 Chillin' Out With Sherbets
134 *Taste of the South*
   Chocolate Nut-Pies
134 Tea Is the Key
136 Pamper Mom With Breakfast
137 A Taste of Honey
138 *Top-Rated Menu*
   Southwestern Starters
139 Skillet Suppers
140 *What's for Supper?*
   Dish Up Pasta
141 Savor Sweet Onion Sides
142 Lunch on the Go
143 Cheesy Bites
144 *From Our Kitchen*

145 june

146 Serve a Pretty Salad
148 Growing Made Simple
157 Easy Icebox Pies
158 Great Time Get-together
159 Avocados for Any Occasion
160 *Quick & Easy*
   Take Five for Sides
161 Guilt-Free Comfort Food
162 *What's for Supper?*
   Barbecue Spuds
162 Hot Off the Grill
164 *From Our Kitchen*

165 july

166 Barbecue Buddies
168 Cherry Jewels
169 *Healthy & Light*
   Simple and Fresh Brunch

170 *What's for Supper?*
　　Quick Catfish Tonight
171 Potato Salad Like You've
　　Never Had
172 Summer Living®
　　Special Section
172 Savor a Sunset Supper
174 Backyard Smokehouse in
　　Dallas
176 Add Flavor With Goat Cheese
177 Summer-Fresh Produce
178 Gather for a Blueberry Bash
180 Casual Outdoor Get-together
181 Bake Up Some Fun
182 *From Our Kitchen*

183 august
184 Cast-Iron Chefs
186 Pasta: Toss It and Love It
188 *Top-Rated Menu*
　　Favorite Picnic Food
193 *Quick & Easy* Speedy and
　　Scrumptious Desserts
194 *Healthy & Light* Smart Eating
　　Starts With Good Taste
196 *Taste of the South*
　　White Barbecue Sauce
197 *What's for Supper?*
　　It's on the Grill
198 *From Our Kitchen*

199 september
200 Casual Family Gathering
202 4 Speedy Suppers
204 Menu With a View
205 *Top-Rated Menu*
　　One Sauce, Three Meals
206 *What's for Supper?* Try Greek
　　for a Fresh Change
207 Blend the Easy Way
207 *Quick & Easy* Better Mac and
　　Cheese, Please
208 *Healthy & Light*
　　Simple Southern Salads
210 How Sweet It Is
211 Bake Sale Treats
212 Easy Game Day Get-together
213 COOKING SCHOOL®
　　Special Section
213 Quick-and-Easy Favorites
214 Dinner and a Movie
215 Fruit and Spice Make It
　　Nice
217 Weeknight Wonders
219 Girls' Night Out
220 Southern Hospitality With
　　an International Accent

222 Soccer Night Solutions
222 Tweens' Turn to Cook
224 *From Our Kitchen*

229 october
230 Try a Taste of Fall
232 It's Great Pumpkin
233 Oven-Roasted Goodness
234 *Taste of the South*
　　Make a Batch of Texas Chili
235 Warm and Hearty Stews
236 Cooking Up Cabbage
237 Supper Tonight
238 *Healthy & Light*
　　The Season's Best Spices
240 *Top-Rated Menu*
　　Savor a Fall Breakfast
241 *What's for Supper?*
　　Keep on Grilling
241 *Quick & Easy* Fast Asian Fare
242 *From Our Kitchen*

243 november
244 Gather Together
246 *What's for Supper?*
　　Love the Leftovers
247 Simple Southwestern
　　Casserole Starts the Fun
248 *Top-Rated Menu*
　　Easy, Elegant Dinner
249 Make-Ahead Appetizer
250 Cook With Confidence
251 Stir-and-Bake Breads
252 *Quick & Easy* Microwave Magic
253 Deep Chocolate Brownies
254 Soup for Supper
255 Soufflés: Here's the Trick
256 *Healthy & Light* Good News:
　　Five-Ingredient Southern
　　Recipes
257 Enjoy a Cup of Hot Tea
258 HOLIDAY DINNERS® Special Section
258 Pack-and-Go Supper Club
260 Three Yummy Desserts
270 Kitchen Shortcuts
270 Ultimate Mashed Potatoes
272 Gather Around the Table
272 Bake the Best Cheesecake
274 Party Flavors in a Flash
274 Hats Off to This Celebration
276 A Buffet Built on Comfort
278 We're Glad You're Here
280 Cheers to an Easy,
　　Gorgeous Party
282 Pop the Cork
282 At Play in the Kitchen
284 *From Our Kitchen*

285 december
286 Can't-Miss Cakes
289 *Healthy & Light* Lightened
　　and Luscious
290 Fix and Freeze Ground Beef
291 Winter Fruit Salads
291 Special-Occasion Salad
292 Stir Up a Quick Side
293 *Quick & Easy*
　　Fast Dishes for Busier Days
294 Spice Up Your Christmas
296 CHRISTMAS ALL THROUGH THE
　　HOUSE® Special Section
296 Beautiful Buffets
300 Garlands and Goodies
306 Come Over for Coffee
307 Have a Cookie
309 *Top-Rated Menu*
　　Simply Splendid
310 Make-Ahead Appetizers
311 Hearty Casseroles
312 *What's for Supper?*
　　Crusted Baked Chicken
313 Fresh Ways With Cranberries
314 *From Our Kitchen*

315 *Southern Living®* 2005 cook-off winners
316 Grand Prize Winner
316 Southern Desserts
318 Healthy & Good For You
320 Easy Entrées
322 Your Best Recipe
324 Kids Love It!
325 Brand Winners

331 Christmas bonus
332 Our Editors' Favorite Holiday
　　Recipes

336 indexes
336 Menu Index
341 Recipe Title Index
346 Month-by-Month Index
352 General Recipe Index

368 favorite recipes journal

Southern Living®

Dear Food Friends,

As I write this, we are three weeks out from Hurricane Katrina. The overwhelming abundance pictured in our magazine plays out in stark contrast to the needs of victims who lost everything. At this time, we speculate more than 50,000 subscribers were affected by the storm. We are contributing our resources and asking our fellow Southerners to join us in reaching out to all those affected.

"May all our kitchens serve as places of comfort and hope."

At our tasting table last week, we nodded in unison as one editor commented on the healing, soulful power of food. At that time, several members of the *Southern Living* staff were housing family evacuated from the storm; others were anxiously awaiting news of loved ones from which they'd received no word. Everyone was trying to decide what the most meaningful, hands-on way of helping was—in addition to contributing to the Red Cross.

I have always found hope in stepping up to the stove. Whether I'm making creamy mashed potatoes or a simple pot of soup, sharing food with another person is a transformational act, a gift often taken for granted. In this time of rebuilding, my prayer for each of us is gratitude in moments of bounty and generosity in response to need—from the elderly neighbor next door to the newly relocated evacuee. May all our kitchens serve as places of comfort and hope.

Sincerely,

Susan Dosier

Executive Editor
susan_dosier@timeinc.com

favorite columns
at a glance

Each month we focus on topics that are important to our readers—
from Southern classics to fast dinners to delicious menus.

>>top-rated menus

■ Invite your friends and family over for **Chili Tonight.** Cold winter nights call for a menu of Chunky Beef 'n' Tomato Chili, Quick Creamy Vegetable Dip, and Parmesan Cheese Breadsticks (page 20).

■ Host a **Table-to-Table Dinner** where guests rotate dinner spots and enjoy a menu that includes Festive Pork Roast and Roasted Baby Vegetables (pages 46–47).

■ As the basketball championships heat up, celebrate **March Madness** with a few winning recipes. Enjoy the games with Slow-Cooker Barbecue Beef Sandwiches, Buffalo Wings, and Chile-Cheese Logs (page 64).

■ Entertain the girls at a **New-Fashioned Luncheon Party** with Apricot Bellinis, Cucumber-Dill Rounds, and Smoked Turkey Tetrazzini (page 96).

■ Add a little flair to your next get-together with these **Southwestern Starters.** Meaty Empanadas, Cinco de Mayo Shrimp Cocktail, and Armadillo Eggs will all be a hit with your guests (pages 138–139).

■ **Favorite Picnic Food** such as Honey-Pecan Chicken Strips, Old Bay Shrimp Salad, and Bacon 'n' Honey Onion Potato Salad lets you enjoy summer nights with friends (page 188).

■ Enjoy **One Sauce, Three Meals** with a Cajun-Shrimp-and-Crab Sauce that can be served with grits, pasta, or rice. Round out a dinner or lunch meal with Sautéed Green Beans and Lemon-Blueberry Layered Dessert (page 205).

■ Whip up a Savory Ham-and-Swiss Breakfast Pie and Orange Syrup mixed with yogurt and Mixed Fruit Granola to **Savor a Fall Breakfast** with friends (page 240).

■ Celebrate the holidays with an **Easy, Elegant Dinner** of Rosemary-Thyme Rib Roast, Potato-and-Gruyère Casserole, and Strawberry-Cranberry-Orange Salad (page 248).

■ Throw a **Simple, Elegant Gathering** with a few carefully chosen items. Serve a menu of Blue Cheese Biscuits, Beef Tenderloin With Horseradish Cream, and Mulled Pomegranate Cider (page 309).

>>taste of the south

■ **Hoppin' John** (page 21) Tradition holds that this hearty Lowcountry dish brings good luck when eaten on New Year's Day.

■ **Rémoulade Sauce** (page 69) Southerners have adopted this tangy French classic as their very own.

■ **Hush Puppies** (page 99) This fish-fry and barbecue staple is made from a six-ingredient batter.

■ **Chocolate-Nut Pies** (page 134) Celebrate a Kentucky tradition by serving these easy-to-make desserts.

■ **White Barbecue Sauce** (page 196) This robust, mayonnaise-based condiment got its start in North Alabama.

>> quick & easy

■ Stir up tasty one-pan entrées with no fuss and little muss (page 19).

- Toss together these easy pasta suppers that are ready in the time it takes to boil water and cook the pasta (page 49).

- You're gonna love these affordable steaks fried just right (page 67).

- Weeknight meals are made easy with these breakfast recipes that you can serve anytime (page 88).

- Speed up supper with these time-saving recipes that use store-bought bread products as a base (page 131).

- Complete your supper with these sensational side dishes that boast short ingredient lists (page 160).

- Indulge in some scrumptious desserts that start with a simple hot fudge sauce (page 193).

- Ten minutes are all you need to stir up the sauce for a comforting mac-and-cheese dinner (page 207).

- Use some tongue-tingling ingredients to put together a tantalizing Asian stir-fry (page 241).

- Speedy Lasagna solves the dinner dilema, and the microwave makes it happen (page 252).

- Time-saving convenience products make it easy to get tasty sides on the table in a hurry (page 292).

>> what's for supper

- For a quick supper that uses on-hand ingredients, try serving breakfast (page 26).

- These slow-cooker recipes let you come home to a warm supper (page 34).

- Add some spice to your dinner with a Fiesta Salad loaded with fresh flavor (page 58).

- Hit the deli counter for a super-good and super-simple sandwich supper (page 92).

- These comforting pasta dishes will have your family begging for second helpings (page 140).

- It's hard to beat this twice-baked potato full of tangy, tender chopped barbecue (page 162).

- Enjoy a catfish supper that starts on the cooktop (page 170).

- Throw some pork chops on the grill for a speedy weeknight meal (page 197).

- Grill some flank steak and whip up some make-ahead sauces and salad all with a Greek accent (page 206).

- Don't let a little autumn nip in the air stop you from firing up the grill for a great weeknight supper (page 241).

- Turn holiday leftovers into divine new recipes (page 246).

- Make a delicious and versatile crusted baked chicken and a few easy sides for a weeknight meal or company supper (page 312).

>> healthy & light

- Satisfy your desire for something chocolate with a small serving of these delicious sweets (page 30).

- Fire up the flavor with these hot dinners from the grill (page 52).

- The aroma of wholesome, fragrant ingredients sizzling on the cooktop will convince your family that they'll find the best Italian dinner in town at your house tonight (page 100).

- Try these fresh ideas to get more whole grains in your next meal (page 126).

- We've revised these classic morning favorites to lower the calories and fat but keep the rich flavor (page 169).

- Deliciously good-for-you recipes inspire smart choices and fit perfectly into the new *Dietary Guidelines for Americans 2005* (page 194).

- Try these updated Southern classics that boast simple preparation as well as shortened and lightened ingredient lists (page 208).

- Give some sweet and savory dishes a tasty boost by adding nutmeg, cinnamon, allspice, and cloves (page 238).

- Taste and ease inspire this menu of five-ingredient recipes (page 256).

- These *Southern Living* traditional entrées boast luscious flavor with less fat (page 289).

cook's chat

Our readers chat online about what they think about our recipes and how they use them. Here they brag about some of their favorites.

>> appetizers and beverages

Buffalo Wings, page 64—"It's an easy and great tasting recipe. This took what I thought would be an expensive and complicated dish to simple and easy."

Chile-Cheese Logs, page 64—"My friends and I love this spread! I get requests to bring this to get-togethers now. I omitted the pecans."

Cheese Wafers, page 97—"Super easy and delicious! It always gets rave reviews when I make it for parties, especially wedding and baby showers. The ground red pepper gives it a little kick."

Frozen Blueberry Margaritas, page 179—"This is so good. I will be making this again. I had a group of girls over for dinner and everyone raved about this refreshing summer drink."

>> soups and stews

Chunky Beef 'n' Tomato Chili, page 20—"I loved this recipe and can't wait to make it again!"

Avocado Soup, page 159—"I went to a dinner party where this was served and ate 2 servings. I fixed it myself and ate it with just Italian bread as a meal 3 nights in a row. It's terrific for summer meals."

Frogmore Stew, page 111—"I took a chance and made this for the first time for a shrimp boil party. I made a double batch and it was a huge hit! It was so easy to make. I even used the uneaten potatoes for potato salad the next day and that was a big hit!"

>> entrées

Chicken Pudding, page 22—"This recipe is a lot of work, but it's delicious! I fed it to children and adults, who all loved it. It's excellent comfort food. I made it over 2 days, which made it easier, and put it in 2 dishes. I served it with carrots and a spinach salad, which made a pretty plate. Also, the stewed chicken was a breeze to shred, and the leftover broth is worth saving for other uses."

Lexington-Style Grilled Chicken, page 54—"This chicken was wonderful! It came off the grill very juicy and with just the right kick of spice. I used boneless, skinless chicken breasts and halved the marinade for four breasts."

Traditional Crawfish Étoufée, page 56—"This is so good. I did substitute red bell pepper because we do not care for green peppers. Also, you might want to start with half the amount of Cajun seasoning and red pepper and add more to taste. It tasted just as good warmed up the next day."

Smothered Enchiladas, page 59—"This recipe was really easy to make and tasted great! It was a really basic meal and individual enchiladas were easily packed for lunch the next day. (It was also tasty when reheated in the microwave.) It is not for dieters, but I think could easily be modified with light ingredients and still taste wonderful."

Chicken-Fried Steak, page 67—"I had never cooked this before, but have had it in restaurants several times. This is far superior to any restaurant recipe. It was quick and easy to prepare and was so good. I followed the recipe exactly and served it with mashed potatoes and steamed broccoli."

Old-Fashioned Meat Loaf, page 95—"Very tasty! We really enjoyed this recipe.

I cooked mine a little longer, since we like it well done. Next time, I will make two smaller meat loaves."

Smoked Turkey Tetrazzini, page 96— "Great recipe! The wine cooks off but leaves a wonderful taste behind. Definitely go for smoked turkey instead of plain. I used whole wheat fettuccine and left out the mushrooms, and it still turned out great! Good served cold or hot. Easy for me to make, even with an infant and a preschooler to keep track of these days!"

Broiled Mahi-Mahi With Parsleyed Tomatoes, page 130— "I made this recipe because I had all the ingredients on-hand, including vine-ripened tomatoes from my garden. I wasn't expecting it to be exceptional, which it turned out to be (even my two-year-old liked it). I used fresh basil rather than parsley, and it was reminiscent of a fresh marinara sauce. Very quick and healthy for an after-work meal."

One-Pot Pasta, page 202— "This recipe is easy! The kids loved it and begged me to store the leftovers (a first!) for lunch the next day. Serve with a Caesar salad and garlic bread for a complete quick and easy meal."

>> burgers and sandwiches

Balsamic-Blue Cheese Portobello Burgers, page 53— "This is delicious and very easy. I love the balsamic flavor from marinating and it is enhanced by the balsamic-mayo. The blue cheese puts it over the top! Yum-mm!"

Pesto Focaccia Sandwich, page 131— "I made this recipe for a tailgate party and it was great. I used the focaccia bread. It was a hit with everyone and deemed 'a keeper recipe.'"

Bacon-Pimiento Cheese, page 142— "Mmmm...good and easy to make. I used whole wheat bread for the sandwiches. The bacon makes all the difference."

Spicy Cheddar-Stuffed Burgers, page 163— "We made these burgers for Father's Day

and they were a big hit—these burgers are huge! We had them with a baked potato salad, which complemented them very well."

Open-Faced Monte Cristo Sandwiches, page 222— "This sandwich just melts in your mouth. Every ingredient works together and not against each other. It will leave you begging for more."

>> salads

Spinach-and-Strawberry Salad, page 55— "This salad is delicious. Everyone wanted the recipe. The dressing is wonderful! I will definitely serve this again and again. Be sure to use baby spinach."

Tomato-and-Cucumber Salad, page 69— "This recipe is absolutely terrific. My husband, who typically is not a big fan of salads, raved about this dish. It was also good the next day when I ate it for lunch. This dish is definitely a 'keeper.' "

Hot Tomato Salad, page 129— "What a great treat for my lady who just loves tomatoes and loves hot spicy food. She was in heaven. Great with a side of bread and a cooling tall glass of homemade lemonade."

Chicken-and-Strawberry Salad, page 132— "I served this at a bridal shower last night and everyone wanted the recipe! Can't wait to make it again!"

Chinese Cabbage Salad, page 142— "This recipe was extremely good and easy to make. I used coleslaw mix instead of Chinese cabbage, and diced red onions instead of green onions. It's great for family dinners; it makes enough leftovers to take for lunch. I would highly recommend it!"

Bacon Potato Salad, page 171— "My family loved this potato salad, even my husband who grew up in eastern North Carolina and only wants what he calls "Southern" potato salad. I did, however, leave out the pimientos. That would be a bit too much change for my husband. I found that the flavors blended well overnight, and we had no problems eating the leftovers."

>> sides

Three-Cheese Pasta Bake, page 54—
"This is delicious and it makes a lot! I added a large bag of frozen broccoli florets to the pasta as it boiled. I would probably add red pepper and mushrooms the next time, but it really is very good just the way the recipe is written. It's a good substitute for lasagna at a potluck."

Sweet Corn Pudding, page 66—"This is a very good side for barbecue and spicy foods. It may be a bit sweet for some tastes. I found it easy to fix and it reheats for leftovers perfectly."

Potato-Stuffed Grilled Bell Peppers, page 123—"This dish is very tasty. It's also good with other cheeses such as Muenster or Monterey Jack. Excellent as a reheated leftover—reheat in the microwave or conventional oven."

Feta-Stuffed Tomatoes, page 148—"We absolutely love this dish. The recipe just came out last month and we've had it numerous times already. We are feta-cheese lovers, and the fact that this dish is healthy was just a bonus. It's simple to prepare, but different enough to change up a boring menu. I've made it for company as a side with some grilled chicken and steamed asparagus and it was liked by all."

>> breads

Cream Cheese-Banana-Nut Bread, page 27—"This is absolutely the best banana-nut bread I have ever tasted. I just made the basic recipe as a loaf and my husband loved it! He wants me to make it all of the time to take to work. It's so moist and even better the second day."

Lemon-Walnut Tea Bread, page 59—"This bread was very easy to make. The lemon flavor was excellent. It turned out exactly as I expected. I made it for an afternoon tea for a gathering of "Red Hat" Ladies. Everyone enjoyed it and said it was delicious. I definitely would make it again but the next time I'll use artificial sweetener and egg substitute and leave out the nuts so that my husband who is on a special diet can enjoy it, too."

Caramel-Apple Muffins, page 210—"These muffins were a huge hit in my house! They are delicious! I did add more cinnamon however. These are the perfect fall treat!"

>> desserts

Dark Chocolate Mousse With Raspberry Sauce, page 31—"This is easy to make and is absolutely wonderful, especially when you consider the low-fat ingredients!"

Double Citrus Tart, page 55—"This tart was wonderful—similar to a Key lime pie, only better. It was very easy to prepare and the presentation was stunning. I've made it twice now and I will make it again!"

Pig Pickin' Cake, page 63—"This dessert is a favorite from my childhood! It's perfect in the hot summer because it's so cool and fruity and not too heavy. I always prepare this for summer barbecues."

German Chocolate Cake, page 107—"Holy-moly! One of the best cakes I've ever had—period. I made it for my dad's birthday because it's his favorite cake. I was scared it wasn't going to taste like the original version, but it was so much better. The frosting was incredible, too. What a hit! Everyone loved it—especially my dad. I will make this anytime I have to bring a dessert somewhere—it will knock everyone's socks off!"

Pineapple-Apple Bread Pudding With Bourbon Sauce, page 119—"I love bread pudding. This is how I remember my grandmother making it when I was growing up in Tennessee."

Favorite Chocolate Chip Cookies, page 142—"What a great cookie! Perfect consistency. I used only half the recommended amount of semisweet chocolate chips. I will definitely make this again. It's a perfect cookie for an afternoon snack or when you're in the mood for something sweet."

Zesty Lemon Pie, page 157—"What a delicious and easy pie to make. Because it makes two pies it's great for potlucks, etc. It was the perfect dessert for a hot summer night. This will become a staple in my recipe box!"

january

16   Family Friendly *Solutions for the dinnertime blues*

18   Family Game Night *Plan a special evening of food and fun*

19   Quick & Easy Fast Meat-and-Sauce Meals *Stir up tasty one-pan entrées with no fuss*

20   Top-Rated Menu Chili Tonight *Warm up with a bowlful of this seasonal favorite*

21   Greens Made Simple *Enjoy these Southern gems slow-cooked*

21   Taste of the South Hoppin' John *Good eats steeped in tradition and lore*

22   Down-Home and Delicious *Simple and good ingredients yield great flavors in Mama Dip's Kitchen cookbook*

23   The Comfort of Cider *Soothing sippers for cool winter nights*

24   Everyday Choices *Take small steps toward better health*

26   What's for Supper? A Cozy Breakfast *Eggs solve the supper scramble*

26   Food and Hospitality Banana-Nut Bread *One batter, four toppings, unlimited melt-in-your mouth taste*

28   From Our Kitchen *Grilling sandwiches, panini presses, and more*

Family Friendly

Even when you're time challenged, you can still enjoy full-flavored meals at home.

Dinner Fast and Fresh

Serves 6

Shredded Grilled Tilapia Tacos with
Fruity Black Bean Salsa and Sweet-and-Spicy Slaw

Ginger-and-Lemon Fruit Salad

Lemon-and-Dill Green Beans

Lime-Grilled Portobello Mushrooms

Two-Color Rosemary Roasted Potatoes

Doris Pulido of Houston had a case of the bland dinner blues. That was until we arrived for a flavor and nutrition makeover. Her goal was to prepare bold-flavored dishes not too high in calories that did not require a big time investment. "My kids think what I cook is boring unless I make rich, creamy Mexican dishes," she says.

As a registered dietician, Associate Foods Editor Joy Zacharia's job was to create simple, grill-friendly recipes and to teach Doris how to prepare them. Joy aimed to include plenty of colorful, cancer-fighting, heart-healthy veggies and fruits. In less than two days, Doris learned how to infuse fabulous flavor into meats, seafood, vegetables, and fruits with a few spices, seasoning mixtures, and marinades.

SHREDDED GRILLED TILAPIA TACOS

family favorite • fast fixin's

Prep: 10 min., Grill: 6 min.

Use two forks to pull apart the fish for this family favorite.

- **1 tablespoon ground chipotle seasoning**
- **1½ teaspoons ground cumin**
- **½ teaspoon salt**
- **6 (6-ounce) tilapia fillets**
- **2 tablespoons olive oil**
- **1 teaspoon grated lime rind**
- **2 tablespoons fresh lime juice**
- **Vegetable cooking spray**
- **12 corn tortillas**
- **Fruity Black Bean Salsa (recipe at right)**
- **Sweet-and-Spicy Slaw (recipe on facing page)**
- **Fresh lime wedges**

Combine first 3 ingredients. Rub seasoning mixture evenly over fillets. Stir together oil, grated rind, and juice; rub over fillets.

Arrange fillets in a grill basket coated with cooking spray.
Grill over medium-high heat (350° to 400°) 3 minutes on each side or just until fish begins to flake with a fork. Cool slightly. Shred fish. Spoon 2 to 3 tablespoons fish into tortillas, and top with Fruity Black Bean Salsa and Sweet-and-Spicy Slaw. Serve with a squeeze of fresh lime juice. **Makes** 6 servings.

Per serving (including slaw and salsa): Calories 358 (25% from fat); Fat 10g (sat 1.9g, mono 4.7g, poly 2.1g); Protein 44g; Carb 23g; Fiber 3.2g; Chol 118mg; Iron 1mg; Sodium 486mg; Calc 75mg

---

FRUITY BLACK BEAN SALSA

family favorite • fast fixin's

Prep: 15 min.

The fat in this salsa comes from avocado, a great source of monounsaturated (good) fat. It helps increase your HDL (good) cholesterol level and decrease your LDL (bad) cholesterol level.

- **1 (15-ounce) can black beans, rinsed and drained**
- **1 small papaya, peeled, seeded, and cut into ½-inch cubes✻**
- **½ red or green bell pepper, seeded and chopped**
- **1 large ripe avocado, cut into ½-inch cubes**
- **2 jalapeño peppers, seeded and minced**
- **¼ cup chopped fresh cilantro**
- **1 teaspoon grated lemon rind**
- **2 tablespoons fresh lemon juice**
- **1 tablespoon honey**
- **½ teaspoon salt**

Combine first 6 ingredients in a glass bowl. Whisk together rind and remaining ingredients in a small bowl, and drizzle over bean mixture. Toss gently to coat. Cover and chill salsa until ready to serve. **Makes** 7 (½-cup) servings.

✻Substitute ½ (24-ounce) jar papaya available in the produce section of your supermarket for fresh, if desired. If you can't find papaya, substitute 2 ripe mangoes, cubed.

Per serving: Calories 88 (40% from fat); Fat 3.9g (sat 0.5g, mono 2.4g, poly 0.5g); Protein 2.5g; Carb 14g; Fiber 4.3g; Chol 0mg; Iron 0.8mg; Sodium 296mg; Calc 25mg

SWEET-AND-SPICY SLAW

family favorite • fast fixin's

Prep: 8 min.

- **1 cup reduced-fat sour cream**
- **2 tablespoons rice wine vinegar**
- **2 tablespoons pineapple or orange marmalade**
- **½ teaspoon salt**
- **¼ to ½ teaspoon dried chipotle seasoning**
- **1 (16-ounce) package cabbage slaw mix**

Whisk together first 5 ingredients in a medium glass bowl until blended. Add slaw mix, tossing to coat. Cover and chill until ready to serve. **Makes** 12 (½-cup) servings.

Per serving: Calories 53 (46% from fat); Fat 2.7g (sat 1.7g, mono 0.8g, poly 0.12g); Protein 1.9g; Carb 6g; Fiber 0.8g; Chol 7mg; Iron 0.3mg; Sodium 119mg; Calc 46mg

GINGER-AND-LEMON FRUIT SALAD

family favorite • fast fixin's

Prep: 20 min.

If you can't find ripe mangoes, use refrigerated mango slices found in the produce section of your supermarket.

- **2 large Gala or Fuji apples**
- **2 large mangoes, peeled**
- **2 large red Bartlett pears**
- **2 large navel oranges, peeled**
- **1 fresh pineapple, peeled and cored**
- **¼ cup fresh lemon juice**
- **2 tablespoons honey**
- **2 teaspoons finely grated fresh ginger**

Cut first 5 ingredients into bite-size pieces; place in a large bowl. Whisk together lemon juice, honey, and ginger. Drizzle over fruit mixture, tossing to coat. Cover and chill until ready to serve. **Makes** 16 (1-cup) servings.

Per serving: Calories 78 (2% from fat); Fat 0.2g (sat 0g, mono 0g, poly 0.1g); Protein 0.7g; Carb 21g; Fiber 2.7g; Chol 0mg; Iron 0.2mg; Sodium 2mg; Calc 18mg

LEMON-AND-DILL GREEN BEANS

family favorite • fast fixin's

Prep: 15 min., Cook: 13 min.

To lighten further, use 1 tablespoon reduced-calorie margarine and 2 tablespoons almonds, chopped. The original version's fat percentage appears high because most of the calories come from the nuts and margarine (green beans are very low in calories). Almonds contain heart-healthy fat, protein, and fiber.

- **2 pounds fresh green beans, trimmed ✱**
- **2 tablespoons reduced-calorie margarine**
- **1 teaspoon minced garlic**
- **2 tablespoons chopped fresh dill or 2 teaspoons dried dill weed**
- **½ teaspoon salt**
- **½ teaspoon freshly ground pepper**
- **1 tablespoon fresh lemon juice**
- **½ cup whole almonds, chopped**

Cook beans in boiling water to cover 8 minutes or until crisp-tender; drain. Plunge into ice water to stop the cooking process; drain.

Melt margarine in a large nonstick skillet over medium-high heat; add garlic, and sauté 1 to 2 minutes. Add green beans, dill, and next 3 ingredients; sauté 1 to 2 minutes or until thoroughly heated. Remove from heat; sprinkle evenly with almonds. **Makes** 6 servings.

Note: For testing purposes only, we used Planters Salted Almonds.

✱ Substitute 2 (16-ounce) packages frozen green beans for fresh, if desired.

Per serving: Calories 143 (60% from fat); Fat 9.6g (sat 1.3g, mono 4.9g, poly 1.9g); Protein 4.3g; Carb 11g; Fiber 5.5g; Chol 0mg; Iron 1mg; Sodium 224mg; Calc 102mg

Healthy Benefits

■ Beans and other legumes are rich in soluble (dissolves in water) fiber. A ½-cup serving of cooked beans provides 4 to 10 grams of fiber (adults need 20 to 35 grams per day). Soluble fiber helps lower bad (LDL) cholesterol, reducing the incidence of some heart diseases. It also helps regulate blood sugar levels, making it an excellent nutrient for people with diabetes. Oats, barley, and citrus fruits also contain soluble fiber.

■ Iron plays an essential role in getting oxygen from the bloodstream to every cell in your body. Low iron can lead to anemia, weakness, and infections. Besides liver, the best source of readily absorbed iron is lean beef, such as flank steak. Nonmeat sources of iron include fortified breakfast cereals, spinach, beans, and pumpkin seeds. Iron from these sources isn't absorbed as well, but when enjoyed with vitamin C-rich foods such as bell peppers and citrus fruit, iron absorption increases.

■ Eat *at least* five servings of veggies and fruits daily. Here's why: Produce is rich in selenium and vitamins A, C, and E—powerful antioxidants that protect your body's cells from damage caused by smoke, pollution, sun, etc. They also keep your immune system healthy, reducing your risk of cancer and other diseases. To learn more about how foods and their nutrients protect your health, visit the American Dietetic Association's Web site at **www.eatright.org.**

LIME-GRILLED PORTOBELLO MUSHROOMS

family favorite • fast fixin's

Prep: 15 min., Grill: 14 min.

> **6 portobello mushroom caps**
> **1 tablespoon olive oil**
> **1 teaspoon salt**
> **1 teaspoon pepper**
> **1 teaspoon grated lime rind**
> **2 tablespoons fresh lime juice**
> **Vegetable cooking spray**

Scrape gills from mushroom caps using a metal spoon; discard gills.
Rub mushrooms evenly with oil; sprinkle evenly with salt, pepper, and rind. Drizzle with lime juice, tossing to coat.
Grill, covered with grill lid, on a grill rack coated with cooking spray over medium-high heat (350° to 400°) 5 to 7 minutes on each side or until tender. Cut into strips, if desired. **Makes** 6 servings.

Per serving: Calories 56 (42% from fat); Fat 2.6g (sat 0.3g, mono 1.8g, poly 0.2g); Protein 1g; Carb 4g; Fiber 1.1g; Chol 0mg; Iron 0mg; Sodium 393mg; Calc 2.5mg

TWO-COLOR ROSEMARY ROASTED POTATOES

family favorite

Prep: 20 min., Bake: 45 min.

> **2½ pounds sweet potatoes, peeled**
> **1 pound red potatoes**
> **Vegetable cooking spray**
> **2 tablespoons olive oil**
> **1 tablespoon chopped fresh rosemary**
> **½ teaspoon salt**
> **½ teaspoon pepper**

Cut sweet potatoes and red potatoes into 2-inch pieces. Place on a jellyroll pan coated with cooking spray. Drizzle potatoes with oil; sprinkle with rosemary, salt, and pepper, tossing gently to coat.
Bake at 450° for 35 to 45 minutes or until golden brown, gently stirring potatoes once. **Makes** 6 servings.

Per serving: Calories 230 (20% from fat); Fat 5g (sat 0.7g, mono 3.6g, poly 0.6g); Protein 4.4g; Carb 43g; Fiber 6.2g; Chol 0mg; Iron 1.6mg; Sodium 252mg; Calc 65mg

Family Game Night

Create a game night for your family to enjoy a special time together. Before the games begin, make a quick stop at the grocery store for some family-friendly snacks. These clever pickups can be made in advance and are perfect for a themed party or for a casual night at home.

CHECKERBOARD CHEESE SANDWICHES

fast fixin's • make ahead

Prep: 30 min.

You can also serve this cheesy filling as a dip with fresh veggies and crackers. To make ahead, layer the sandwiches with damp paper towels in an airtight container and store in the refrigerator up to six hours.

> **1 (10-ounce) block extra-sharp Cheddar cheese, grated**
> **1 (10-ounce) block Swiss cheese, grated**
> **1¼ cups light or regular mayonnaise**
> **1 (4-ounce) jar diced pimiento, drained**
> **1 teaspoon dried onion flakes**
> **¼ teaspoon freshly ground pepper**
> **20 thin white bread slices**
> **20 thin wheat bread slices**
> **Garnishes: grape tomatoes and black olives, secured with wooden picks**

Stir together first 6 ingredients. Spread half of mixture evenly on half of white bread slices; top with remaining half of white bread slices. Spread remaining half of mixture evenly on half of wheat bread slices; top with remaining half of wheat bread slices. Remove crusts with a serrated knife; cut each sandwich into 4 squares. Arrange, stacked in pairs, on a serving plate in a checkerboard pattern, alternating white and wheat.

Successful Cooking Tips

- Rub lean meats such as pork tenderloin, flank steak, or chicken with spice rubs, or marinate them; freeze in zip-top freezer bags. When thawed, meats will be perfectly seasoned and ready to go on the grill.
- A good knife is a sharp knife. Visit **www.cutlery.com** for information about sharpening knives. A chef's knife is ideal for most chopping needs. Use a paring knife for coring and peeling fruits and veggies.
- Flatten thick boneless chicken pieces with a meat mallet for more even cooking. When you pound them, the flesh becomes more porous so it absorbs additional seasonings from rubs and marinades.
- Use a zester to remove the fragrant rinds from oranges, lemons, and limes to add flavor with virtually no calories. Look for one in the kitchen gadget aisle of department stores, or visit **www.kitchengizmo.com.**
- Cutting meats into wafer-thin slices and threading them onto skewers allows for quick cooking as well as fabulous flavor. Marinades and spices come in contact with every surface, making each bite delicious.
- Keep dinner interesting by trying one new recipe each month.
- Sneak in the veggies and fruit. Doris says her kids won't automatically grab a piece of fruit out of the fridge or fruit bowl. Entice kids and grown-ups by preparing a fresh and delicious fruit salad. This is a great snack or dessert. Stirring colorful peppers and beans into salsa offers another opportunity to add vegetables.

Garnish, if desired. **Makes** 80 mini sandwiches.

Note: For testing purposes only, we used Pepperidge Farm Very Thin White and Wheat Bread.

DONNA W. LANEY
MONROE, NORTH CAROLINA

DOMINO COOKIES

family favorite • make ahead

Prep: 20 min., Bake: 15 min. per batch

**1 (18-ounce) package refrigerated sugar cookie bar dough
Semisweet chocolate morsels**

Roll half of dough into a 10- x 6-inch rectangle on a lightly floured surface. Cut into 12 rectangles, and place 2 inches apart on a lightly greased or parchment paper-lined baking sheet. Score each rectangle in the center crosswise with a knife. Press chocolate morsels, points down, into dough, forming domino dots. Repeat with remaining dough.
Bake at 325° for 10 to 15 minutes or until edges are golden. Slightly cool on baking sheets; remove to wire racks and cool completely. **Makes** 2 dozen.

quick & easy
Fast Meat-and-Sauce Meals

Get supper on the table in a hurry with a sauté. This method of cooking food is done in a skillet over direct, moderately high heat. Keep the food moving, much like a stir-fry. Have all your ingredients ready before you turn on the stove, because once you start, it goes really fast.

BALSAMIC GARLIC-AND-HERB CHICKEN THIGHS

family favorite

Prep: 10 min., Cook: 23 min.

Put the noodles on to cook when you start the chicken so that everything's done on time.

**¼ cup all-purpose flour
½ teaspoon salt
½ teaspoon pepper
8 skinned and boned chicken thighs
2 tablespoons olive oil
1 cup dry white wine or chicken broth
¼ cup balsamic vinegar
1 (10-ounce) can diced tomatoes and green chiles, undrained
1 (1.6-ounce) envelope garlic-and-herb sauce mix
½ cup sliced green onions (about 4)
Hot cooked egg noodles**

Combine flour, salt, and pepper. Dredge chicken in flour mixture.
Brown half of chicken in 1 tablespoon hot oil in a large skillet over medium-high heat 4 minutes on each side. Remove chicken from skillet. Repeat procedure with remaining chicken and oil, reserving drippings in skillet.
Add wine and vinegar to skillet, stirring to loosen particles from bottom of skillet; cook 2 minutes. Stir in tomatoes and green chiles and garlic-and-herb sauce mix until combined. Return chicken to skillet. Cook, uncovered, over medium heat 5 minutes or until done. Stir in ¼ cup green onions. Serve over hot cooked egg noodles; sprinkle with remaining ¼ cup green onions.
Makes 4 servings.

Note: For testing purposes only, we used Knorr Garlic Herb Sauce Mix, which can be found with the Italian sauce mixes in the pasta aisle of the grocery store.

JUDY ARMSTRONG
PRAIRIEVILLE, LOUISIANA

STEAK-AND-SPINACH SALAD WITH HOT PAN DRESSING

family favorite

Prep: 15 min., Cook: 20 min.

Serve with your favorite crusty garlic bread.

**1 (1½-pound) top sirloin steak
½ teaspoon salt
½ teaspoon freshly ground pepper
1 teaspoon butter, divided
1 teaspoon olive oil, divided
2 medium portobello mushroom caps, sliced (about 1½ cups)
2 teaspoons minced garlic
½ cup red wine
½ cup beef broth
¼ cup balsamic vinegar
1 (6-ounce) package baby spinach
2 plum tomatoes, sliced
1 small red onion, thinly sliced
½ lemon
⅓ cup crumbled Roquefort cheese**

Sprinkle steak evenly with salt and pepper.
Heat a large nonstick skillet over medium heat for 2 minutes. Melt ½ teaspoon butter with ½ teaspoon oil. Add steak, and cook until well browned on 1 side, about 6 minutes. Turn steak, and cook 3 more minutes (rare), 4 minutes (medium-rare), or 5 minutes (medium). Remove steak from pan, and set aside.
Melt remaining ½ teaspoon butter with ½ teaspoon oil in skillet over medium heat. Sauté mushrooms and garlic 4 minutes. Stir in wine, broth, and balsamic vinegar, stirring to loosen particles from bottom of skillet. Bring to a boil; reduce heat, and cook 4 to 5 minutes.
Toss together spinach, tomatoes, onion, and hot mixture in pan; divide evenly among 4 plates. Squeeze lemon, drizzling juice evenly over top.
Cut steak into ½-inch slices, and arrange over salads. Sprinkle cheese evenly over top. **Makes** 4 servings.

LAURIE CONRAD
MANASSAS, VIRGINIA

Chili Tonight

Serve up a bowl of this soul-satisfying favorite.

Prep: 10 min., Chill: 2 hrs.

Chili Night

Serves 6

Chunky Beef 'n' Tomato Chili

Quick Creamy Vegetable Dip with assorted vegetables

Parmesan Cheese Breadsticks

Cold winter nights beg for chill-chasing meals. Chili is a great option, and large chunks of ground beef make our Chunky Beef 'n' Tomato Chili similar to a stew. Crackers are fine on the side, but yummy Parmesan Cheese Breadsticks offer a tasty alternative and are a snap to prepare. Last but not least, Quick Creamy Vegetable Dip and assorted fresh veggies add the perfect cool contrast.

CHUNKY BEEF 'N' TOMATO CHILI

Prep: 20 min.; Cook: 1 hr., 25 min.

Turn up the heat in this chili with a splash of chipotle hot sauce.

- 1 pound ground round
- 1 (14.5-ounce) can diced tomatoes with green peppers and onions
- 1 (14.5-ounce) can diced tomatoes with zesty mild green chiles
- 1 (10-ounce) can condensed beef broth
- 2 garlic cloves, pressed
- 3 tablespoons tomato paste
- 1 tablespoon chili powder
- 1 teaspoon ground cumin
- ½ teaspoon black pepper
- ½ teaspoon ground red pepper
- 1 (15-ounce) can light kidney beans, rinsed and drained
- 1 (15-ounce) can dark kidney beans, rinsed and drained
- Toppings: chipotle hot sauce, shredded Cheddar cheese, chopped green onions, Quick Creamy Vegetable Dip

Cook beef in a Dutch oven over medium heat, stirring occasionally into large chunks, 10 minutes or until no longer pink. (Do not stir beef into crumbles.) Drain and return beef to Dutch oven.
Stir both cans of diced tomatoes and next 7 ingredients into browned beef; reduce heat to medium-low, and simmer, uncovered, stirring occasionally, 1 hour. Stir in beans, and simmer 15 minutes. Serve with desired toppings.
Makes about 6 (1⅔-cup) servings.

QUICK CREAMY VEGETABLE DIP

make ahead

Prep: 10 min., Chill: 2 hrs.

- ½ cup mayonnaise
- ½ cup sour cream
- ¼ cup drained, chopped jarred roasted red bell peppers*
- ¼ cup finely chopped onion
- ¼ cup finely chopped green bell pepper
- ½ teaspoon salt
- ⅛ teaspoon garlic powder
- ⅛ teaspoon pepper
- ⅛ teaspoon hot sauce
- Baby carrots, celery sticks, radish slices

Stir together first 9 ingredients in a medium bowl. Cover and chill at least 2 hours. Serve dip with baby carrots, celery sticks, and radish slices. **Makes** about 1½ cups.

*Substitute 1 (2-ounce) jar diced pimiento, drained, if desired.

CHARLOTTE GUTTORMSEN
TITUSVILLE, FLORIDA

PARMESAN CHEESE BREADSTICKS

fast fixin's

Prep: 15 min., Bake: 10 min.

- ½ cup freshly grated Parmesan cheese
- ¼ teaspoon paprika
- ⅛ teaspoon ground cumin
- 1 (11-ounce) can refrigerated breadsticks
- 3 tablespoons melted butter

Combine first 3 ingredients in a shallow dish.
Unroll breadstick dough, and separate into 12 strips at perforations. Gently pull each strip to a length of 12 inches. Brush both sides of each strip with butter; dredge in cheese mixture. Twist each strip, and place 2 inches apart on lightly greased baking sheets.
Bake at 400° for 8 to 10 minutes or until golden brown. Serve warm or at room temperature. **Makes** 12 breadsticks.

Greens Made Simple

Collard and turnip greens are revered Southern gems. In the kitchen, their assertive flavors are best matched with long, slow cooking and a seasoned broth (usually containing bacon or ham).

The younger, smaller greens you find in your garden or at farm stands are more tender and less bitter than more mature greens found in grocery stores. If you do buy them from the supermarket, avoid greens with large, leathery leaves that are withered or have yellow spots.

Whether fresh or prepackaged, always wash greens thoroughly. And, remember, greens cook down considerably, so a good rule of thumb is that 1 pound of raw greens yields about 1½ cups cooked.

UPTOWN COLLARDS

Prep: 30 min., Cook: 1 hr.

Southern Living Editor in Chief John Floyd recommends adding your favorite white wine to turnip and other tender greens. A bowl of these Southern favorites will get your year started right. (pictured on page 39)

- 7 pounds fresh collards
- 1 medium onion, quartered
- 1 cup water
- 1 cup dry white wine
- 1 tablespoon sugar
- 1 tablespoon bacon drippings
- 1 red bell pepper, diced

Remove and discard stems from greens. Wash leaves thoroughly, and cut into 1-inch-wide strips; set aside.
Pulse onion in a food processor 3 or 4 times or until minced.
Bring onion and next 4 ingredients to a boil in a Dutch oven. Add greens and bell pepper; cook, covered, over medium heat 45 minutes to 1 hour or until greens are tender. **Makes** 8 to 10 servings.

JOHN ALEX FLOYD, JR.
TRUSSVILLE, ALABAMA

WILTED GREENS AND RED BEANS

Prep: 15 min., Cook: 22 min.

- 2 (1-pound) packages fresh turnip greens
- ¼ cup diced country ham
- 1 tablespoon olive or canola oil
- 1 (15¼-ounce) can red kidney beans, rinsed and drained
- 2 tablespoons red wine vinegar
- 2 teaspoons granulated or brown sugar
- Pepper sauce (optional)

Remove and discard stems from greens. Tear into ½-inch pieces.
Sauté ham in hot oil in a large skillet over high heat 2 minutes or until browned. Add greens, beans, and vinegar; cook, stirring often, 15 to 20 minutes or until greens are tender. Sprinkle with sugar. Serve with pepper sauce, if desired. **Makes** 4 to 6 servings.

WOLFGANG H.M. HANAU
PALM BEACH, FLORIDA

taste of the south
Hoppin' John

We discovered lots of differences in our search for the definitive recipe. Black-eyed peas are just one kind of dried peas popping up in recipes. Some recipes call for cooking the rice and peas together, while others suggest spooning the peas over a mound of hot rice. Some folks prefer a creamier, stew-like consistency over drier versions. But regardless of whether the cook uses salt pork, a ham hock, or bacon, pork is the primary flavoring agent.

The hearty combination first emerged on Lowcountry rice plantations. Abundant Carolina Gold rice and field peas recreated the rice-and-pigeon pea combination familiar to West African slaves, who were hungry for the comforting flavors of their homeland.

As for lore, well, there are many stories regarding the origin of the name Hoppin' John. One of the more popular theories suggests it's a Southernization of *pois à pigeon* (pwah ah pee-ZHAN), which is French for pigeon pea.

Tradition holds that when eaten on New Year's Day, Hoppin' John brings good luck. The rice signifies abundance for the coming year, while black-eyed peas are thought to bring wealth in the form of coins. Pork also plays an important role in the dish. Hogs can't look back, so pork represents the future.

After testing a range of recipes, we settled on one that originally appeared in *Civil War Cooking: The Confederacy* (Capstone Press, 2000). This recipe gives you an authentic taste of Hoppin' John in all of its delicious glory.

HOPPIN' JOHN

Soak: 8 hrs., Prep: 10 min., Cook: 2 hrs., Stand: 10 min.

- 1 cup (8 ounces) dried black-eyed peas
- 10 cups water, divided
- 3 bacon slices
- 1 small onion, chopped
- 1 green bell pepper, chopped
- 1 cup uncooked long-grain rice
- 1½ teaspoons salt
- Garnishes: green onion pieces, tomato wedges

Place peas in a Dutch oven or large saucepan. Add water to cover 2 inches above peas; let soak 8 hours. Drain peas, discarding water.
Bring peas and 7 cups water to a boil over medium-high heat in Dutch oven. Reduce heat to medium, and simmer, uncovered, 1½ hours or until peas are tender.
Cook bacon in a large skillet 5 minutes or until crisp; remove bacon, and drain on paper towels, reserving drippings in skillet. Crumble bacon.
Sauté onion and bell pepper in hot drippings in skillet over medium heat 5 minutes or until tender. Add vegetable mixture, remaining 3 cups water, rice, and salt to peas. Cook, covered, over medium heat 20 minutes or until rice is tender. Remove from heat, and let stand, covered, 10 minutes before serving. Sprinkle with crumbled bacon. Garnish, if desired. **Makes** 4 to 6 servings.

Down-Home and Delicious

The comfort food you love is easy to fix. This inspiring Carolina cook will make a believer out of you.

Mildred Council. Mama Dip, as she is known, is the owner of Mama Dip's Kitchen in Chapel Hill, North Carolina. She's also a best-selling cookbook author. Mama Dip even started her own version of Meals-On-Wheels in the 1970s—delivering hot packaged dinners around the neighborhood to the housebound, to those who couldn't afford electricity, and to kids who had no adult supervision.

Associate Foods Editor Mary Allen Perry has always loved Mama Dip's ability to render great flavors from simple and good ingredients. For these recipes, Mary Allen tested and adapted some of Mama's favorites from her book, *Mama Dip's Kitchen* (UNC Press, 1999). You can also visit Mama Dip's Web site at **www.mamadips.com.**

SWEET POTATO BISCUITS

family favorite

Prep: 20 min., Bake: 15 min.

Depending on the moisture content of sweet potatoes, you may need to adjust the quantity of milk, adding the remaining ¼ cup. Eat these warm out of the oven with butter or jam.

> **2 cups cooked, mashed sweet potatoes**
> **½ cup butter, melted**
> **1 to 1¼ cups milk**
> **4 cups self-rising flour**
> **⅛ teaspoon baking soda**
> **3 tablespoons sugar**

Stir together sweet potatoes, butter, and 1 cup milk until well blended. Add flour, baking soda, and sugar, stirring just until dry ingredients are moistened. Add remaining ¼ cup milk to moisten dough, if needed.

Turn dough out onto a lightly floured surface; knead 8 to 10 times. Pat or roll dough to a ¾-inch thickness; cut with a 2-inch round cutter. Place biscuits on lightly greased baking sheets.

Bake at 400° for 15 minutes or until golden brown. **Makes** about 3 dozen.

CHICKEN PUDDING

family favorite

Prep: 30 min., Cook: 1 hr., Bake: 55 min., Stand: 10 min.

> **1 (5-pound) whole chicken**
> **4 carrots**
> **4 celery ribs**
> **1 large onion, quartered**
> **1½ teaspoons salt**
> **1 teaspoon pepper**
> **6 tablespoons butter**
> **1 tablespoon chicken bouillon granules**
> **1 teaspoon poultry seasoning**
> **¼ cup shortening**
> **2 cups self-rising flour**
> **¾ cup milk**
> **3 large eggs, lightly beaten**
> **1 cup coarsely crushed saltine crackers (about 24 crackers)**
> **1 tablespoon butter or margarine, melted**

Combine first 6 ingredients and water to cover in a large Dutch oven. Bring to a boil over medium-high heat; reduce heat, and simmer 1 hour or until tender. Remove chicken, and cool.

Pour 6 cups broth through a wire-mesh strainer into a large bowl, discarding solids. Reserve remaining broth for later use. Whisk 6 tablespoons butter, bouillon granules, and poultry seasoning into strained broth until smooth; let cool.

Cut shortening into flour with a pastry blender or fork until crumbly. Add milk, stirring just until dry ingredients are moistened. Spread dough to a ½-inch thickness on a lightly greased baking sheet, forming 1 large hoecake.

Bake at 400° for 25 minutes or until golden brown. Cool on a wire rack; break into pieces.

Skin, bone, and coarsely chop chicken. Layer chicken and hoecake pieces in a lightly greased 13- x 9-inch baking dish. Whisk together broth mixture and eggs; pour over chicken and hoecake pieces.

Stir together cracker crumbs and 1 tablespoon melted butter; sprinkle evenly over chicken mixture.

Bake at 375° for 30 minutes or until golden brown and set. Let stand 10 minutes before serving. **Makes** 10 to 12 servings.

TOMATO CASSEROLE

family favorite

Prep: 10 min., Bake: 40 min.

This is a classic Southern flavor combination. The sugar forms a nice caramel crust on the tomatoes.

> **2 (14½-ounce) cans whole tomatoes, drained and coarsely chopped**
> **1½ cups soft white bread cubes (about 3 slices)**
> **¼ cup butter, melted**
> **¼ cup firmly packed brown sugar**
> **¼ teaspoon pepper**

Stir together all ingredients. Spoon into a lightly greased 9-inch baking dish.
Bake at 400° for 35 to 40 minutes.
Makes 6 servings.

GREAT NORTHERN BEANS WITH TOMATOES

family favorite

Prep: 5 min.; Cook: 2 hrs., 10 min.

- 1 pound dried great Northern beans
- 7 cups water
- ¼ pound salt pork
- 1 teaspoon salt
- 1 (14½-ounce) can diced tomatoes, drained
- 1 tablespoon molasses

Rinse and sort beans. Bring beans, 7 cups water, and salt pork to a boil in a Dutch oven over medium heat. Cover, reduce heat to low, and simmer 2 hours or until beans are tender, adding more water as needed to keep beans moist. Remove salt pork, and stir in remaining ingredients. Simmer, covered, 10 more minutes. **Makes** 6 to 8 servings.

COCOA BREAD WITH STEWED YARD PEACHES

family favorite

Prep: 10 min., Cook: 30 min.

More like a chocolate gingerbread without the ginger, this incredibly light bread is perfect topped with stewed fresh or frozen peaches or apples.

- 1 cup boiling water
- ½ cup butter or margarine, melted
- ½ cup molasses
- ½ cup sugar
- 2 large eggs, lightly beaten
- 2 cups self-rising flour
- ½ teaspoon baking soda
- ¼ cup unsweetened cocoa
- 1 teaspoon ground cinnamon
- Stewed Yard Peaches

Whisk together first 4 ingredients in a large bowl; let cool. Whisk in eggs. **Sift** together flour and next 3 ingredients; whisk into molasses mixture, whisking until smooth. Pour batter into a greased and floured 8-inch square pan.

Bake at 350° for 30 minutes or until a wooden pick inserted in center comes out clean. Serve with warm Stewed Yard Peaches. **Makes** 6 to 8 servings.

STEWED YARD PEACHES:

fast fixin's

Prep: 10 min., Cook: 15 min.

- 6 cups sliced, peeled peaches *
- ¾ cup sugar
- ½ cup water

Bring all ingredients to a boil in a 3-quart saucepan over medium heat, stirring gently until sugar dissolves. Reduce heat to low, and simmer 10 minutes. **Makes** 6 to 8 servings.

***** Substitute 2 (16-ounce) bags frozen sliced peaches, thawed, or 6 cups sliced, peeled apples for fresh peaches, if desired.

The Comfort of Cider

Nothing beats a mug of hot apple cider on a cool winter evening. We've added a little sugar and spice to these beverages, most of which can be served hot. Look for clear apple cider so your drinks won't be cloudy. For a chilled alternative, try Spicy Sparkling Punch (on page 24), made with red cinnamon candies. Pour these soothing sippers in an insulated bottle for any outdoor event.

HONEY-APPLE PUNCH

fast fixin's

Prep: 5 min., Cook: 15 min.

- 2 cups apple cider
- 2 cups cranberry juice
- ⅓ to ½ cup honey
- 1 (3-inch) cinnamon stick
- 4 lemon slices
- 4 whole cloves

Bring all ingredients to a boil; reduce heat, and simmer 10 minutes. Remove lemon slices and spices. Pour into mugs, and serve immediately. **Makes** about 4⅓ cups.

LAURA MORRIS
BUNNELL, FLORIDA

HOT SPICED LEMON-APPLEADE

fast fixin's

Prep: 10 min., Cook: 15 min.

- 2 cups water
- ⅓ cup sugar
- ¼ teaspoon ground cinnamon
- ¼ teaspoon ground nutmeg
- ¼ teaspoon ground allspice
- 2 cups apple cider
- ⅓ cup fresh lemon juice

Bring first 5 ingredients to a boil in a large saucepan; reduce heat, and simmer 10 minutes. Stir in apple cider and lemon juice, and cook until thoroughly heated. Serve hot. **Makes** 4½ cups.

SIBYL WHITE
WOODSTOCK, GEORGIA

CITRUS CIDER SIPPER

fast fixin's

Prep: 10 min., Cook: 20 min.

- 1 orange, sliced
- 1 lemon, sliced
- 1½ teaspoons whole cloves
- 3 (3-inch) cinnamon sticks
- 1 gallon apple cider
- 2 cups fresh orange juice
- ½ cup fresh lemon juice
- Garnishes: cinnamon sticks, orange rind curls

Bring first 7 ingredients to a boil in a large Dutch oven. Reduce heat, and simmer, stirring occasionally, 10 to 15 minutes. Remove fruit slices and spices. Serve hot. Garnish, if desired. **Makes** about 18½ cups.

SPICY SPARKLING PUNCH

make ahead

Prep: 5 min., Cook: 7 min., Chill: 2 hrs.

- **2 quarts apple cider, divided**
- **1 (4-ounce) package red cinnamon candies**
- **1 (48-ounce) bottle cranberry juice**
- **1 liter ginger ale, chilled**

Heat 2 cups apple cider in a small saucepan over medium-high heat; add red cinnamon candies, stirring until melted. Cool.

Pour mixture through a wire-mesh strainer into a 1-gallon container. Add cranberry juice and remaining 6 cups cider. Chill at least 2 hours. Add chilled ginger ale just before serving. **Makes** 18 cups.

DEBBIE MCLAURIN
ETHELSVILLE, ALABAMA

APPLE TEA

make ahead

Prep: 5 min., Stand: 5 min., Chill: 2 hrs.

For a quicker iced beverage, omit the sugar, add cider and spices to premade sweetened tea from the grocery store, and then chill.

- **4 cups boiling water**
- **8 regular tea bags**
- **2½ cups apple cider**
- **¼ cup sugar**
- **6 whole cloves**
- **2 (3-inch) cinnamon sticks**

Pour 4 cups boiling water over tea bags; cover and let stand 5 minutes. Remove and discard tea bags. Pour tea into a 2-quart pitcher. Add cider and remaining ingredients, stirring until sugar dissolves. Serve warm, or chill at least 2 hours, if desired. Remove spices before serving. **Makes** about 6½ cups.

Everyday Choices

Take small steps toward better health with these simple eating solutions and good-for-you snacks.

Being healthy doesn't mean you have to run 10 miles a day or give up your favorite foods. There are lots of little things you can do to improve your health without drastically changing your lifestyle. Follow these tips to see how making simple changes can increase motivation and maintain balance in your life. Read on for quick and nutritious snack recipes.

Choose wisely

With all the hype about what to eat these days, it's nearly impossible to get through a meal without feeling guilty—not to mention the pressure from tracking carbs and fat grams. If math is not your forte, stop counting, and repeat: "There are no bad foods, just bad choices." These guidelines show that you *can* enjoy the foods you love while still eating healthfully.

■ Eat smart carbs, such as fiber-rich, whole-wheat breads and pastas. Fiber not only lowers cholesterol, but it also increases satiety and reduces the tendency to overeat. Look in the pasta aisle for 100% whole-wheat semolina spaghetti and other varieties.

■ Get your daily dose of vitamins and antioxidants this cold-and-flu season by eating a combination of at least five fruits and vegetables a day. Add berries to cereal, or make a yogurt-fruit smoothie. Having trouble getting the kids to eat their veggies? Add chopped zucchini and squash to their favorite spaghetti casserole, or drizzle a cheesy sauce over steamed broccoli.

■ Choose nutrient-dense snacks that give you more energy and keep you satisfied throughout the day. Eat a handful of heart-healthy nuts or trail mix instead of reaching for potato chips and candy.

BANANA-BERRY SMOOTHIE

fast fixin's

Prep: 5 min.

Freeze leftover fruit to use in shakes, smoothies, or any blended treat.

- **1 cup low-fat plain yogurt**
- **3 cups frozen strawberries**
- **2 bananas, coarsely chopped**
- **¾ cup fat-free milk**
- **¼ cup crushed ice**
- **¼ cup honey**

Process all ingredients in a blender until smooth. Serve immediately. **Makes** about 5 cups.

Calories per 1-cup serving: 168 (5% from fat); Fat 1g (sat 0.6g, mono 0.25g, poly 0.1g); Protein 4.8g; Carb 38g; Fiber 3.14g; Chol 3.7mg; Iron 0.91mg; Sodium 53mg; calc 153mg

LESLIE MEADOWS
MONTGOMERY, ALABAMA

Healthy Benefits

■ A diet moderate in monounsaturated fat, such as that found in nuts and peanut butter, and low in saturated fat helps reduce the risk of heart disease.

■ Walking just 20 minutes burns about 100 calories.

■ As part of a healthy weight-loss plan, increasing your dairy servings to three or four a day can help you lose significantly more body fat than by cutting calories alone, research indicates.

BERRY-AND-SPICE WHOLE-WHEAT MUFFINS

family favorite

Prep: 15 min., Bake: 21 min., Cool: 5 min.

- ¼ cup firmly packed light brown sugar
- 1 tablespoon all-purpose flour
- 3 tablespoons chopped pecans
- 1 tablespoon butter, melted
- 1 cup all-purpose flour
- 1 cup whole-wheat flour
- ¼ cup sugar
- ¾ teaspoon baking powder
- ¾ teaspoon baking soda
- ½ teaspoon ground cinnamon
- ¼ teaspoon ground allspice
- 1 egg
- 1¼ cups buttermilk
- 1½ tablespoons vegetable oil
- 1 cup fresh or frozen blueberries

Combine brown sugar, 1 tablespoon flour, and pecans in a small bowl. Stir in melted butter; set aside.

Combine 1 cup all-purpose flour, whole-wheat flour, and next 5 ingredients in a large bowl; make a well in center of mixture.

Stir together egg, buttermilk, and oil; add to dry ingredients, stirring just until moistened. Fold in blueberries.

Spoon about ⅓ cup batter into each of 12 lightly greased muffin cups. Sprinkle batter evenly with reserved pecan mixture.

Bake at 375° for 19 to 21 minutes or until lightly browned. Cool in pans on a wire rack 5 minutes. Remove from pans, and cool slightly on wire rack. Serve warm. **Makes** 1 dozen.

Calories per muffin: 168 (26% from fat); Fat 5g (sat 1.2g, mono 2g, poly 1.4g); Protein 4.2g; Carb 28g; Fiber 2g; Chol 21mg; Iron 1.2mg; Sodium 151mg; Calc 61mg

How Do Your Servings Size Up?

Did you know that a jumbo bagel may equal up to 6 servings of bread? Let's face it, many of us are overeating simply because our portions are too big. In fact, we've become so accustomed to larger serving sizes that feeling full requires more food—and unwanted calories. The good news is that we can easily adapt to smaller serving sizes and still feel satisfied if we practice a little portion control.

- **Grains and breads** (6 to 11 servings a day): ½ cup cooked cereal, brown rice, or whole-wheat pasta; 1 cup ready-to-eat cereal; 1 slice sandwich bread
- **Meats and other proteins** (2 to 3 servings a day): 1 (2- to 3-ounce) chicken breast or lean pork chop (about the size of the palm of your hand); 1 egg; ½ cup cooked beans; ⅓ cup nuts; 2 tablespoons peanut butter
- **Vegetables** (3 to 5 servings a day): 1 cup raw leafy vegetables; ½ cup cooked vegetables; 4 grilled asparagus spears; ¾ cup vegetable juice
- **Fruits** (2 to 4 servings a day): 1 small apple, banana, or other whole fruit; ½ cup berries; ¾ cup 100% fruit juice
- **Dairy** (2 to 3 servings a day): 1 cup low-fat milk, yogurt, or cottage cheese; 1 (1.5-ounce) slice cheese

Note: Number of servings depends on individual calorie needs and activity levels.

Keep a Food Diary

Most of us are not aware of how much we're eating on a daily basis, according to Dr. John P. Foreyt, a clinical psychologist, expert in diet modification, and professor at Baylor College of Medicine in Houston. "In order to change your eating behavior," says Dr. Foreyt, "you have to know what your eating behavior is."

- Documenting everything you eat in a food diary is one way to observe habits and patterns that you may not otherwise notice. Not surprisingly, many diary keepers find that they are eating more than they should. Though seeing your food summary on paper may be a painful discovery, Dr. Foreyt says it can prompt change. "Self observation raises awareness about daily habits and encourages discipline and control."
- First, choose a favorite journal or notebook, and write down the general times of all your meals, snacks, and drinks, leaving space for extra nibbles. Take your diary with you to each meal, and simply document what and how much you ate. (Figuring the amount of food on your plate can be tricky, so follow the guidelines above on serving sizes before estimating.) After one week, review your diary, and take inventory. Then, make moderate changes, such as eating one more vegetable or walking 20 more minutes a day.

A Cozy Breakfast

Scrambling for a quick supper? Try eggs.

Breakfast for Supper

Serves 6

Cream Cheese Scrambled Eggs

bacon or sausage

fresh fruit

Easy Pan Biscuits

iced coffee

CREAM CHEESE SCRAMBLED EGGS

fast fixin's

Prep: 10 min., Cook: 6 min.

We used a heat-resistant spatula in preparing the eggs. A turning spatula will work too.

- **8 large eggs**
- **¼ cup milk**
- **½ teaspoon salt**
- **½ teaspoon pepper**
- **1 tablespoon butter**
- **1 (3-ounce) package cream cheese, cut into cubes**
- **⅓ cup chopped fresh basil (optional)**
- **Garnish: fresh basil sprigs**

Whisk together first 4 ingredients.
Melt butter in a large nonstick skillet over medium heat; add egg mixture, and cook, without stirring, until eggs begin to set on bottom. Sprinkle cream cheese cubes over egg mixture; draw a spatula across bottom of skillet to form large curds.
Cook until eggs are thickened but still moist. (Do not stir constantly.) Remove from heat. Stir in chopped basil before serving, if desired, and garnish, if desired. **Makes** 4 to 6 servings.

Note: To lighten, substitute 2 cups egg substitute for eggs and 3 ounces light cream cheese for 3 ounces regular cream cheese. Proceed as directed.

LIBBIE SEUSS
MEMPHIS, TENNESSEE

Sausage-Egg Soft Tacos: Prepare Cream Cheese Scrambled Eggs as directed, substituting 1 seeded and chopped jalapeño pepper for chopped basil. Sprinkle 6 (8-inch) flour tortillas evenly with 1½ cups shredded colby-Jack cheese. Top one half of each tortilla evenly with Cream Cheese Scrambled Eggs and 1 (16-ounce) package cooked, drained, and crumbled ground pork sausage. Sprinkle evenly with ½ cup shredded colby-Jack cheese. Fold tortillas over filling. Serve with sour cream and salsa. **Makes** 6 servings. Prep: 20 min., Cook: 15 min.

EASY PAN BISCUITS

fast fixin's

Prep: 15 min., Bake: 15 min.

- **2 cups all-purpose baking mix**
- **½ cup sour cream**
- **6 tablespoons lemon-lime soft drink**
- **3 tablespoons butter, melted and divided**

Stir together first 3 ingredients; lightly flour hands, and divide dough into 20 equal portions. Shape each portion into a ball, and place in a lightly greased 8-inch square pan. (Dough portions will touch.) Brush with half of butter.
Bake at 425° for 15 minutes or until golden brown. Brush evenly with remaining half of butter. Serve immediately. **Makes** 20 biscuits.

Note: For testing purposes only, we used Bisquick All-Purpose Baking Mix and Sprite (do not use diet).

AZINE G. RUSH
MONROE, LOUISIANA

food and hospitality
Banana-Nut Bread

The cream cheese in the banana bread batter provides a melt-in-your-mouth texture and a slightly tangy flavor.

Banana Basics

Let the bananas for this bread get ripe, almost black or very speckled. It takes a week to go from green to ready. To hasten ripening, place bananas in a paper bag with a bruised apple. Once ripe, refrigerate or freeze unpeeled bananas in zip-top freezer bags; thaw before mashing. We tried to freeze mashed bananas, but once thawed, they were watery. A 6-ounce unpeeled banana yields about ⅓ cup mashed banana.

CREAM CHEESE-BANANA-NUT BREAD

family favorite

Prep: 15 min., Bake: 1 hr., Cool: 40 min.

Warm bread is yummy, but to get perfect slices, let bread cool 30 minutes, and cut with a serrated or an electric knife. Extra-ripe bananas are the secret to the sweetness in these breads.

- ¾ cup butter, softened
- 1 (8-ounce) package cream cheese, softened
- 2 cups sugar
- 2 large eggs
- 3 cups all-purpose flour
- ½ teaspoon baking powder
- ½ teaspoon baking soda
- ½ teaspoon salt
- 1½ cups mashed bananas (1¼ pounds unpeeled bananas, about 4 medium)
- 1 cup chopped pecans, toasted
- ½ teaspoon vanilla extract

Beat butter and cream cheese at medium speed with an electric mixer until creamy. Gradually add sugar, beating until light and fluffy. Add eggs, 1 at a time, beating just until blended after each addition.

Combine flour and next 3 ingredients; gradually add to butter mixture, beating at low speed just until blended. Stir in bananas, pecans, and vanilla. Spoon batter into 2 greased and floured 8- x 4-inch loafpans.

Bake at 350° for 1 hour or until a long wooden pick inserted in center comes out clean and sides pull away from pan, shielding with aluminum foil last 15 minutes to prevent browning, if necessary. Cool bread in pans on wire racks 10 minutes. Remove from pans, and cool 30 minutes on wire racks before slicing. **Makes** 2 loaves.

WILLIE MONROE
HOMEWOOD, ALABAMA

Toasted Coconut-Topped Cream Cheese-Banana-Nut Bread:

Prepare and bake bread or muffins in desired pans. While bread is baking, stir together ¼ cup butter, ¼ cup granulated sugar, ¼ cup firmly packed brown sugar, and ¼ cup milk in a small saucepan over medium-high heat; bring to a boil, stirring constantly. Remove from heat. Stir in 1 cup sweetened flaked coconut; 1 cup chopped, toasted pecans; and 2 teaspoons vanilla extract. Remove baked bread or muffins from oven, and immediately spread tops with coconut mixture. Broil 5½ inches from heat 2 to 3 minutes or just until topping starts to lightly brown. Cool in pans on wire racks 20 minutes. Remove from pans, and cool 30 minutes on wire racks before slicing.

MARY HAWKES
PRESCOTT, ARIZONA

Orange-Pecan-Topped Cream Cheese-Banana-Nut Bread: *(pictured on page 37)*

Prepare bread batter as directed, and spoon into desired pans. Sprinkle 1 cup coarsely chopped, toasted pecans evenly over batter in pans. Bake as directed. Cool bread or muffins in pans 10 minutes; remove from pans to wire racks. Stir together 1 cup powdered sugar, 3 tablespoons fresh orange juice, and 1 teaspoon grated orange rind until blended. Drizzle evenly over warm bread or muffins, and cool 30 minutes on wire racks.

Cinnamon Crisp-Topped Cream Cheese-Banana-Nut Bread:

Prepare bread batter as directed, and spoon into desired pans. Stir together ½ cup firmly packed brown sugar; ½ cup chopped, toasted pecans; 1 tablespoon all-purpose flour; 1 tablespoon melted butter; and ⅛ teaspoon ground cinnamon. Sprinkle mixture evenly over batter. Bake and cool as directed.

Peanut Butter Streusel-Topped Cream Cheese-Banana-Nut Bread:

Prepare bread batter as directed, and spoon into desired pans. Combine ½ cup plus 1 tablespoon all-purpose flour and ½ cup firmly packed brown sugar in a small bowl. Cut in ¼ cup butter and 3 tablespoons creamy peanut butter with a pastry blender or fork until mixture resembles small peas. Sprinkle mixture evenly over batter in pans. Bake and cool as directed.

Cream Cheese-Banana-Nut Muffins:

To bake muffins, spoon batter evenly into 24 paper-lined muffin cups. Bake at 350° for 25 minutes or until a wooden pick inserted in center comes out clean. Cool in pans 10 minutes. Remove from pans, and cool completely on wire racks. **Makes** 24 muffins.

Test Kitchen *Notebook*

"I love how life works out in the long run. I wasn't gung-ho on banana-nut bread when given this story. It always seemed to confuse me. Was it a dessert? A snack? Or, in the case of one recipe-gone-bad in my kitchen—a doorstop? Yet, one bite of this recipe, and I turned into a cheerleader for the plain loaf. Then, each of the four fabulous toppings sent me into orbit. Could it get much better? Yep, with a fifth topping to choose from. I've had this one tucked in my hip pocket since testing, waiting for just the right time to share it with you—like now! Enjoy."

Toffee-Topped Cream Cheese-Banana-Nut Bread: Prepare bread batter as directed, and spoon into desired pans. Stir together 3 tablespoons melted butter, ⅓ cup plus 3 tablespoons all-purpose flour, ⅓ cup firmly packed light brown sugar, ¼ teaspoon ground cinnamon, and 2 (1.4-ounce) chocolate-covered toffee candy bars, finely chopped. Sprinkle evenly over batter in pans. Bake and cool as directed.

Shirley Harrington
ASSOCIATE FOODS EDITOR

from our kitchen

Quick and easy to make, the new grilled sandwiches are big on nutrition and flavor. Whole grain breads filled with a hearty mix of lean meats, melted cheese, and fresh vegetables make a terrific meal anytime of day—and with a nonstick surface, you can cook up a crisp, golden-brown crust using little or no added oil.

The popular Italian-style sandwiches known as panini are prepared in a special grill press that eliminates the need for turning. When we gave one a try in the Test Kitchens, it was a huge hit. The top and bottom heating units cook sandwiches quickly and evenly, compressing and searing the bread to create distinctive ridges. Floating hinges accommodate thick-sliced breads and rolls, as well as meats and vegetables.

We tested dozens of different sandwiches, using all sorts of flavorful breads and fillings. Smoked chicken and fontina cheese layered with fresh spinach, red onion, yellow bell pepper, and plum tomatoes on a crusty Italian ciabatta roll is one of our favorites. You'll find all the ingredients in the supermarket deli and produce section—just choose any combination your family enjoys.

Hot Off the Press

Panini presses are available in a wide range of prices (from $40 to $400 or more), but you don't need to pay a fortune for a good one. Look for panini presses in specialty stores and discount department stores that carry cookware. A Krups Panini Press, shown at right, sells for around $80 (**www.williams-sonoma.com**). For a quick grab-and-go breakfast, stack slices of colby-Jack cheese, Granny Smith apple, and cooked bacon on whole grain bread. Assemble sandwiches the night before, and store in zip-top plastic bags; they'll be ready to grill first thing in the morning.

Tips and Tidbits

Grilling Sandwiches

■ If you don't have a panini press, place the sandwiches in a hot skillet and press with a smaller heavy pan or clean brick wrapped in aluminum foil. Cook until the bread is golden brown; then turn and continue to cook until the second side is golden brown and the cheese is melted.

■ For a super-crisp crust, lightly coat bread with vegetable cooking spray or brush with a mixture of melted butter and olive oil before grilling.

■ Grill sandwiches over medium to low heat rather than high so the bread doesn't burn before the cheese melts.

■ Oval-shaped plum tomatoes are a flavorful choice for the winter months, and their meaty texture holds up well when heated. Try them in a sandwich with fresh mozzarella and basil or cool-weather greens such as spinach and arugula.

■ For easy entertaining, select an assortment of colorful containers and trays, and set up a sandwich bar, letting guests come up with their own creative combinations. Use decorative place card holders to identify the different ingredients for the sandwiches.

■ Pantry items such as roasted red bell peppers, green chiles, artichoke hearts, and olives are all delicious additions to grilled sandwiches. Try a bold and sassy salad dressing in place of mayonnaise. Experiment with flavored mustards and pestos, or drizzle on some spicy peanut sauce. Layer on a chutney-cheese spread or a chunky homemade salsa—the possibilities are endless.

february

30   **Healthy & Light** Good-for-You Chocolate *Rich treats to indulge your sweet tooth*

32   **The Kitchen: Recipe for Style** *Several families share some of their kitchen updates and their favorite dishes*

34   **What's for Supper?** Pot Roasts *Let your trusty slow cooker whip up some mouthwatering meals*

36   **Keep It Casual** *Enjoy some make-ahead Valentine's nibbles before a night out on the town*

41   **One Dressing, Three Salads** *A homemade vinaigrette made with fridge and pantry staples couldn't be easier—or more delicious*

42   **5 Money-Saving Menus** *Budget-friendly dinners your family will love*

44   **Banana Bonanza** *Tempting recipes showcase this fruit's natural affinity for dessert*

45   **Ham and Beans** *Get your pot ready to cook up some ultimate comfort food*

46   **Top-Rated Menu** Table-to-Table Dinner *Host a progressive dinner at your home*

47   **Oysters** *Discover heaven on the half shell*

49   **Quick & Easy** Pasta Suppers Ready in Minutes *Cook the noodles, sauté a few ingredients, and toss together for a simplified meal*

50   **From Our Kitchen** *Speedy suppers, bagging bargains, and more*

Good-for-You Chocolate

Indulge your sweet cravings with recipes showcasing this rich, dark treat.

This may be the best news you've read all day. Chocolate, especially the dark variety, is good for you. It contains more cacao than milk chocolate and doesn't have added milk solids. And because it's such a boldly flavorful treat, you can savor and enjoy it in small portions. We used eating chocolates, not baking chocolates, in these recipes.

CHOCOLATE-CINNAMON BISCOTTI

Prep: 20 min., Bake: 43 min.

Enjoy this biscotti with your favorite snuggling-weather beverage.

⅓ cup butter, softened
½ cup firmly packed brown sugar
½ cup reduced-calorie sweetener
1 tablespoon instant espresso granules
½ cup egg substitute
2 cups all-purpose flour
1½ teaspoons baking powder
½ teaspoon ground cinnamon
⅛ teaspoon salt
1 cup (about 4.5 ounces) finely chopped premium dark chocolate
½ cup chopped walnuts, toasted (optional)

Beat first 4 ingredients at medium speed with an electric mixer 2 minutes or until well blended. Add egg substitute, beating until well blended. **Combine** flour and next 3 ingredients; add to butter mixture, beating at low speed just until blended. Stir in chocolate and, if desired, nuts. **Divide** dough in half; shape each portion into a 10- x 2-inch log on a lightly greased baking sheet. **Bake** at 350° for 23 to 25 minutes or until firm and lightly browned. Cool on baking sheet 5 minutes. Remove to wire racks to cool completely. **Cut** each log diagonally into ½-inch slices with a serrated knife, using a gentle sawing motion. Place slices on ungreased baking sheets. **Bake** at 350° for 7 to 9 minutes; turn cookies over, and bake 7 to 9 more minutes or until cookies are browned. Remove cookies to wire racks to cool completely. **Makes** about 2½ dozen.

Note: For testing purposes only, we used Equal Sugar Lite, Café Bustelo Instant Coffee (Espresso), and Ghirardelli Dark Chocolate.

Per cookie (with nuts): Calories 107 (42% from fat); Fat 5g (sat 2.3g, mono 0.8g, poly 1.1g); Protein 1.9g; Carb 15g; Fiber 0.6g; Chol 6mg; Iron 0.8mg; Sodium 57mg; Calc 23mg

Per cookie (without nuts): Calories 94 (35% from fat); Fat 3.7g (sat 2.1g, mono 0.6g, poly 0.2g); Protein 1.6g; Carb 14g; Fiber 0.5g; Chol 6mg; Iron 0.8mg; Sodium 57mg; Calc 21mg

DARK CHOCOLATE-ALMOND CRISPS

make ahead

Prep: 20 min.; Chill: 4 hrs., 10 min.; Stand: 10 min.; Bake: 15 min.

2 ounces premium dark chocolate
6 tablespoons butter, softened
¾ cup sugar
1 large egg
¾ teaspoon vanilla extract
¼ teaspoon almond extract
1½ cups all-purpose flour
¼ cup Dutch process cocoa
½ teaspoon baking soda
⅛ teaspoon salt
¼ cup chopped almonds, toasted

Microwave chocolate in a small glass bowl at MEDIUM (50% power) 1 minute or until softened, stirring once; stir until chocolate is smooth. **Beat** butter and sugar at medium speed with an electric mixer until fluffy. Add egg and extracts, beating until blended. Add melted chocolate, beating until blended. **Sift** together flour and next 3 ingredients. Add half of flour mixture to butter mixture, beating at low speed just until combined. Add remaining flour mixture, beating just until combined; stir in almonds. Divide dough in half, shaping into 2 flattened discs. Wrap each disc in plastic wrap, and chill at least 4 hours. Remove 1 dough disc from refrigerator; let stand 10 minutes. Turn out onto a lightly floured surface, and roll to ⅛-inch thickness. Cut dough with a round 2½-inch cutter; place rounds 2 inches apart on parchment paper-lined baking sheets. Chill prepared baking sheets with dough rounds 5 to 10 minutes or until dough is firm. Repeat with remaining dough. **Bake** at 350° on center oven rack 13 to 15 minutes or until centers are firm. Cool on baking sheet 2 to 3 minutes. Remove to wire racks to cool completely. Store in an airtight container up to 1 week. **Makes** about 2 dozen.

Note: For testing purposes only, we used Ghirardelli Dark Chocolate and Hershey's European Style Dutch Processed Cocoa.

Per 1 crisp: Calories 104 (41% from fat); Fat 4.8g (sat 2.5g, mono 1.3g, poly 0.3g); Protein 1.6g; Carb 15g; Fiber 0.8g; Chol 17mg; Iron 0.6mg; Sodium 50mg; Calc 4mg

Dark Chocolate Mousse With Raspberry Sauce

make ahead

Prep: 10 min., Cook: 11 min., Stand: 45 min., Chill: 2 hrs. *(pictured on page 40)*

- **2 (3.5-ounce) bars premium dark chocolate, coarsely chopped**
- **¼ cup sugar**
- **2 tablespoons butter**
- **½ cup egg substitute**
- **¼ cup fat-free milk**
- **1½ cups fat-free nondairy whipped topping**
- **Raspberry Sauce (optional)**
- **Garnishes: fresh raspberries, dark chocolate shavings**

Cook first 3 ingredients in a heavy saucepan over low heat, stirring constantly, until chocolate melts.

Whisk together egg substitute and milk. Gradually whisk about ½ cup chocolate mixture into egg mixture; add to remaining chocolate mixture, stirring constantly. Cook mixture over low heat, stirring constantly, 5 to 8 minutes or until thickened. Remove from heat; transfer to a small nonmetallic bowl, and let stand 45 minutes.

Fold whipped topping gently into cooled chocolate mixture until blended. Spoon evenly into 8 stemmed glasses; cover and chill 2 hours. Top each serving with 2 tablespoons Raspberry Sauce, if desired, and garnish, if desired. **Makes** 8 servings.

Note: For testing purposes only, we used Lindt Excellence 70% Cocoa Dark Chocolate.

Per serving: Calories (with sauce) 252 (42% from fat); Fat 11.8g (sat 6.6g, mono 0.9g, poly 0.4g); Protein 3.6g; Carb 37g; Fiber 2.4g; Chol 11mg; Iron 1.6mg; Sodium 60mg; Calc 21mg

Raspberry Sauce:

fast fixin's

Prep: 5 min., Cook: 4 min.

- **1 (10-ounce) package frozen raspberries in syrup, thawed**
- **1 teaspoon cornstarch**
- **2 tablespoons sugar**

Process raspberries in a blender until smooth, stopping once to scrape down sides. Press mixture through a wire-mesh strainer into a small saucepan, using the back of a spoon to squeeze out juice. Discard pulp and seeds. Whisk in cornstarch until mixture is smooth; whisk in sugar.

Cook over medium heat, stirring constantly, until mixture boils. Boil 1 minute, stirring constantly; remove from heat, and cool. **Makes** ⅔ cup.

Per (2-tablespoon) serving of sauce: Calories 40 (0% from fat); Fat 0g (sat 0g, mono 0g, poly 0g); Protein 0.2g; Carb 10g; Fiber 1.3g; Chol 0mg; Iron 0.2mg; Sodium 0.3mg; Calc 4mg

---

Chocolate's Good Stuff

- A typical dark chocolate bar contains significantly fewer calories and carbs than milk chocolate.
- Although it contains saturated fat that's believed to increase LDL, or "bad," cholesterol, new studies reveal that dark chocolate doesn't raise LDL levels. Its high stearic acid content is actually thought to lower serum cholesterol levels.
- Dark chocolate contains magnesium, known to regulate blood pressure, reducing the risk of heart disease. Magnesium also helps to metabolize the sugar in the chocolate—a good double whammy.
- Cacao beans (which chocolate is made from) have the highest levels of antioxidants of any known plant source. Antioxidants suppress free radicals, which can damage healthy cells in your body. Dark chocolate has the highest level of cacao solids of any chocolate, making it the healthiest, disease-fighting chocolate choice.

Test Kitchen Notebook

A small serving of Dark Chocolate Mousse With Raspberry Sauce is all you need to satisfy your desire for something creamy and rich. Like crunch? The Chocolate-Cinnamon Biscotti are a dunker's delight. Serve them with coffee or hot tea. We think these recipes will be the best-tasting dark chocolate sweets you've ever had.

Joy Zacharia

ASSOCIATE FOODS EDITOR

Dark Chocolate Sauce

fast fixin's

Prep: 10 min., Cook: 3 min.

Whip up some of this rich sauce for an impressive way to dress up store-bought ice cream, cake, or pie.

- **8 ounces premium dark chocolate, coarsely chopped**
- **¼ cup half-and-half**
- **¼ cup fat-free half-and-half**
- **Angel food cake squares (optional)**
- **Fresh whole strawberries (optional)**
- **Fresh banana slices (optional)**

Place chocolate in a medium bowl.

Cook half-and-half and fat-free half-and-half in a small heavy saucepan over medium heat until mixture steams and bubbles form around edges.

Remove from heat. Pour hot half-and-half mixture over chocolate, stirring constantly until melted and smooth.

Serve immediately with cake squares, strawberries, and banana slices, if desired. **Makes** 8 servings.

Note: For testing purposes only, we used Ghirardelli Dark Chocolate.

Per (2-tablespoon) serving of sauce: Calories 157 (59% from fat); Fat 10.2g (sat 5.9g, mono 0.3g, poly 0g); Protein 1.6g; Carb 19g; Fiber 1.4g; Chol 7mg; Iron 1.2mg; Sodium 11mg; Calc 15mg

Per (2-tablespoon) serving with 1/12 of angel food cake, 4 strawberries, and ½ banana: Calories 307 (31% from fat); Fat 10.4g (sat 5.9g, mono 0.3g, poly 0.1g); Protein 4.3g; Carb 55g; Fiber 5.8g; Chol 7mg; Iron 1.9mg; Sodium 224mg; Calc 65mg

The Kitchen: Recipe for Style

Our Homes and Foods departments joined forces to create a combination of designs and flavors sure to whet your appetite.

Some folks savor delicious foods, while others crave rich design over haute cuisine. Whatever side you fall on—we have a sweet treat for you. Along with mouthwatering recipes, you'll find some great tips for creating charming cooking spaces.

Cottage Charm

Shannon and Scott Satterwhite turned a small, dark kitchen into a cheerful place to prepare meals. During the week, the couple shares cooking duties, but on weekends they prepare food that can be frozen and reheated on weeknights.

Cottage Solutions

- The Satterwhites removed two layers of vinyl flooring to reveal the original hardwood floors.
- They created cafe curtains from simple napkins.
- To enhance the cottage theme in the kitchen, the couple installed a beaded-board backsplash. It's relatively simple to install and offers a less expensive option to a tile backsplash.

OPEN-FACED PHILLY SANDWICHES

Prep: 15 min., Cook: 29 min., Broil: 3 min.

This recipe is great by itself, but you could add a salad or home fries for a side dish.

    2 (8-inch) submarine rolls, unsliced
    ½ pound boneless top round
        steak
    2 tablespoons Italian dressing
    ¼ teaspoon dried crushed red
        pepper
    2 tablespoons butter
    1 large onion, thinly sliced
    1½ cups sliced fresh mushrooms
    1 green bell pepper, cut into thin
        strips
    1 garlic clove, pressed
    2 (¾-ounce) slices provolone
        cheese

Make a 1½- to 2-inch deep vertical cut around outside edge of each roll, leaving a ½-inch border. Remove tops of rolls, and discard. Hollow out about 1½ inches of each bread roll, forming a boat. Set boats aside.

Cut steak diagonally across grain into ⅛-inch-thick strips; place in a small shallow bowl. Add dressing and crushed red pepper, tossing to coat; set aside.

Melt butter in a nonstick skillet over medium-high heat; add onion and mushrooms, and sauté 15 minutes or until onion is golden brown. Add bell pepper, and sauté 8 to 10 minutes or until bell pepper is tender. Add garlic, and sauté 1 minute. Remove mixture from skillet, and set aside.

Stir-fry steak mixture in skillet over medium-high heat 2 to 3 minutes or until steak strips are no longer pink.

Fill bread boats evenly with layers of steak mixture and onion mixture; top with cheese.

Broil 5½ inches from heat 3 minutes or until cheese is lightly browned. **Makes** 2 servings.

PORK-AND-BLACK BEAN SOUP

family favorite

Prep: 15 min., Cook: 33 min.

For a stewlike consistency, you can increase the amount of barbecued pork in the recipe by one pound.

    ¼ cup sour cream
    2 tablespoons chopped fresh
        cilantro
    1 small onion, chopped
    2 tablespoons olive oil
    2 garlic cloves, minced
    3 cups chicken broth
    3 (15-ounce) cans black beans,
        rinsed and drained
    1 (10-ounce) can diced tomatoes
        and green chiles
    1 teaspoon ground cumin
    ½ pound shredded barbecued
        pork
    2 tablespoons fresh lime
        juice
    Shredded Cheddar cheese
    Garnish: cilantro sprigs

Stir together sour cream and chopped cilantro. Cover and chill until ready to serve.

Sauté onion in hot oil in a Dutch oven over medium heat 7 minutes or until tender; add garlic, and sauté 1 minute. Stir in broth and next 3 ingredients. Bring to a boil; reduce heat, and simmer, stirring often, 15 minutes.

Process 2 cups bean mixture in a food processor or blender until smooth. Return bean puree to Dutch oven. Stir in pork, and simmer 10 minutes. Stir in lime juice. Top each serving with shredded cheese and a dollop of sour cream mixture. Garnish, if desired. **Makes** 8 servings.

Cooking With Color

Kerri Ann Chambless painted yellow everywhere in her kitchen, making it a sunny spot for her family of four to share meals and conversation. To get young children out the door with their stomachs full, Kerri Ann focuses on heartier foods such as egg sandwiches and waffles topped with fruit and granola. She also relies on convenience products. Here are some of her family-pleasing recipes.

SOUTHWESTERN BBQ CHICKEN PIZZA

family favorite • fast fixin's

Prep: 5 min., Bake: 10 min.

Using prepared chicken and commercial pizza crust gets this recipe on the table in only 15 minutes.

- 1 (16-ounce) package prebaked Italian pizza crust
- ½ cup barbecue sauce, divided
- 2 (9-ounce) packages already-cooked Southwest-flavored chicken breast strips, chopped
- 1½ cups (6 ounces) shredded Mexican four-cheese blend
- 2 tablespoons chopped fresh cilantro

Place pizza crust on a large baking sheet or pizza stone; spread ¼ cup barbecue sauce over crust.
Combine remaining ¼ cup barbecue sauce and chicken in a bowl, coating well. Spoon chicken mixture over crust; top with cheese and cilantro.
Bake at 450° for 10 minutes or until cheese melts. **Makes** 4 to 6 servings.

Note: For testing purposes only, we used Boboli pizza crust and Tyson Southwest Seasoned Chicken Breast Strips.

PATRICIA ANN GROVER
RICHBORO, PENNSYLVANIA

LEMON-POPPY SEED MUFFINS

freezeable • make ahead

Prep: 10 min., Bake: 20 min.

Make these ahead, and freeze up to 1 month, if desired. Thaw muffins at room temperature 2 hours.

- 2 cups all-purpose flour
- 1½ tablespoons poppy seeds
- 1 tablespoon baking powder
- ½ teaspoon baking soda
- ¼ teaspoon ground cinnamon
- 1½ cups buttermilk
- 1 large egg, lightly beaten
- ⅔ cup firmly packed light brown sugar
- ½ cup butter, melted
- 1 tablespoon grated lemon rind

Combine first 5 ingredients in a bowl; make a well in center of mixture. Combine buttermilk and next 4 ingredients; add to dry ingredients, stirring just until moistened. Do not overmix.
Spoon batter into greased muffin pans, filling two-thirds full.
Bake at 400° for 18 to 20 minutes or until lightly browned. Remove from pans immediately. **Makes** 18 servings.

WALTON TURNAGE
ALBUQUERQUE, NEW MEXICO

Decorating Solutions

- Use different types of lighting, such as suspended halogen lights and lamps, for a cozy feel.
- Add instant appeal by applying an antique glaze or stain over white cabinets.
- Choose synthetic flooring and countertops that mimic more expensive natural products.
- Got a neutral kitchen? Give it an instant dose of bright color by painting dining chairs or stools red or by topping them with red cushions.

Dreamy Kitchen

With five grandchildren and a flurry of people to entertain, Carolyn and Joe Dorris's kitchen needed a makeover. One necessity was a large island. The island serves multiple functions: separating cooks from guests, working as a bar for parties, and providing a buffet for family meals. The island is fitted with a cooktop and raised vent, and below there's plenty of storage space for pots and pans. A built-in warming drawer is perfect for cookies and breads. A granite countertop wraps around the kitchen and reaches to the island to unite the space.

Carolyn enjoys cooking—especially baking with her grandchildren. Following are some of her crowd-pleasers.

CHEESE RING

make ahead

Prep: 15 min., Chill: 2 hrs.

Serve this easy-to-make appetizer at your next family get-together or dinner party.

- 2 (8-ounce) blocks sharp Cheddar cheese, finely grated
- 1 small onion, grated
- 1 garlic clove, pressed
- 1 cup pecans, toasted and finely chopped
- ¾ cup mayonnaise
- ½ teaspoon hot sauce
- ¾ cup strawberry preserves
- Assorted crackers
- Garnish: fresh whole strawberries

Stir together first 6 ingredients. Shape mixture into a 6-inch ring with a 2-inch center on a serving platter. Cover and chill 2 hours.
Fill center of ring with preserves before serving. Serve with assorted crackers. Garnish, if desired. **Makes** about 20 servings.

CAROLYN DORRIS
CALERA, ALABAMA

MEATY CHEESE MANICOTTI

family favorite

Prep: 15 min., Cook: 20 min., Bake: 30 min., Broil: 3 min.

An 8-ounce package of manicotti shells has 14 shells; a couple may break, so we count on using 12 shells in this recipe.

- **1 (8-ounce) package uncooked manicotti shells**
- **½ pound hot Italian sausage**
- **½ pound ground round**
- **1 medium onion, chopped**
- **½ cup dry white wine**
- **2 cups whipping cream**
- **1 teaspoon dried Italian seasoning**
- **½ teaspoon salt**
- **½ teaspoon pepper**
- **1 (14½-ounce) can diced tomatoes with basil, garlic, and oregano, drained**
- **2 cups (8 ounces) shredded mozzarella cheese**
- **¾ cup shredded Parmesan cheese**

Cook pasta according to package directions; rinse in cold water. Drain. Place in a single layer on a wire rack; set aside.

Remove casings from sausage, and discard. Cook sausage, ground round, and onion in a large skillet, stirring until meat crumbles and is no longer pink. Drain and set aside.

Add wine to skillet, stirring to loosen browned bits; bring to a boil. Add whipping cream and next 3 ingredients; reduce heat, and simmer, stirring often, 15 minutes or until thickened. Remove from heat; cover and set aside.

Combine meat mixture, tomatoes, and mozzarella cheese. Spoon mixture evenly into 12 manicotti shells; arrange shells in a lightly greased 13- x 9-inch baking dish.

Bake, covered, at 350° for 20 minutes. Uncover and pour cream mixture evenly over shells; sprinkle with Parmesan cheese. Bake, uncovered, at 350° for 10 more minutes. Broil 5½ inches from heat 2 to 3 minutes or until cheese is lightly browned. **Makes** 6 servings.

TRACI MEADOR
HERMITAGE, TENNESSEE

what's for supper?

Pot Roasts

Hands off! Let the slow cooker do the cooking.

There's nothing better than coming home from a long day at work or play to find a warm supper waiting for you. With a minimum of prep time, a pot roast made in the slow cooker couldn't be easier. Here are two perfect-for-the-season recipes and a quick rundown of what's new with slow cookers.

ITALIAN POT ROAST

family favorite • make ahead

Prep: 15 min.; Cook: 6 hrs., 40 min.

Chuck roast is one of the most economical cuts of beef for pot roast, but it's a high-fat choice. Substitute eye of round (which is more expensive) or English shoulder roast for a lower fat choice.

- **8 ounces sliced fresh mushrooms**
- **1 large onion, cut in half and sliced**
- **1 (2½- to 3-pound) boneless beef chuck roast, trimmed**
- **1 teaspoon pepper**
- **2 tablespoons olive oil**
- **1 (1-ounce) envelope dry onion soup mix**
- **1 (14-ounce) can beef broth**
- **1 (8-ounce) can tomato sauce**
- **1 teaspoon dried Italian seasoning**
- **3 tablespoons tomato paste**
- **2 tablespoons cornstarch**
- **2 tablespoons water**
- **Hot cooked egg noodles**

Place mushrooms and onion in a 5½-quart slow cooker.

Sprinkle roast evenly with pepper. Brown roast on all sides in hot oil in a large Dutch oven over medium-high heat. Place roast on mushrooms and onion in slow cooker. Sprinkle onion soup mix evenly over roast. Pour beef broth and tomato sauce over roast. Cover and cook on HIGH 5 to 6 hours or until meat shreds easily with a fork.

Remove roast from slow cooker, and cut into large chunks; keep warm.

Skim fat from juices in slow cooker; stir in Italian seasoning and tomato paste. Stir together cornstarch and 2 tablespoons water in a small bowl until smooth; add to juices in slow cooker, stirring until blended. Cover and cook on HIGH 20 to 30 more minutes or until mixture is thickened. Add roast pieces back to slow cooker. Cover and cook until thoroughly heated. Serve over hot cooked egg noodles. **Makes** 6 servings.

Two Slow-Cooked Meals

Cowboy Pot Roast with creamy-style deli coleslaw and Texas toast or Cheese-and-Onion Cornbread

Italian Pot Roast with green salad or Caesar salad (use a bagged salad kit) and buttery garlic bread

For dessert: Drizzle fresh Red Delicious apple and Bartlett pear slices with a little lemon juice, and sprinkle with cinnamon and sugar.

COWBOY POT ROAST

family favorite • make ahead

Prep: 15 min.; Cook: 6 hrs., 30 min.

Browning the meat before slow cooking enhances both the appearance and flavor of the meat.

- 1½ teaspoons salt, divided
- 1½ teaspoons pepper, divided
- 1 (14.5-ounce) can petite-cut diced tomatoes, drained
- 1 (10-ounce) can diced tomatoes and green chiles, undrained
- 1 onion, cut into 8 wedges
- 1 tablespoon chili powder
- 1 (2½- to 3-pound) eye of round roast, trimmed
- 2 tablespoons vegetable oil
- 2 (16-ounce) cans pinto beans, drained
- 1 (15-ounce) can black beans, drained
- Pickled jalapeño pepper slices (optional)

Combine 1 teaspoon salt, 1 teaspoon pepper, and next 4 ingredients in a medium bowl.

Sprinkle roast evenly with remaining ½ teaspoon salt and ½ teaspoon pepper. Brown roast on all sides in hot oil in a large Dutch oven over medium-high heat. Transfer roast to a 5½-quart slow cooker. Pour tomato mixture over roast. Cover and cook on HIGH 5 to 6 hours or until meat shreds easily with a fork.

Remove roast from slow cooker, and cut into large chunks; keep warm.

Skim fat from juices in slow cooker. Mash 1½ cans (about 2¾ cups) pinto beans; add to slow cooker, and stir until combined. Stir in black beans and remaining ½ can pinto beans. Add roast pieces back to slow cooker; cover and cook on HIGH 20 to 25 more minutes. Top each serving with jalapeño pepper slices, if desired. **Makes** 6 servings.

SABRINA DANA
NORTH RICHLAND HILLS, TEXAS

CHEESE-AND-ONION CORNBREAD

family favorite

Prep: 10 min., Bake: 24 min.

- 2 (6-ounce) packages buttermilk cornbread mix
- 1 cup (4 ounces) shredded Cheddar-Monterey Jack cheese blend
- ¼ cup chopped green onion tops
- 1 tablespoon butter
- 1⅓ cups milk

Combine cornbread mix, cheese, and green onions in a large bowl; set aside.

Heat butter in an 8-inch square pan in a 450° oven 3 to 4 minutes or until melted and lightly browned. Tilt baking pan to coat bottom with melted butter.

Add milk to cornbread mixture, stirring just until blended. Pour batter into hot baking pan.

Bake at 450° for 18 to 20 minutes or until golden and cornbread pulls away from sides of baking pan. **Makes** 9 servings.

Note: For testing purposes only, we used Martha White Buttermilk Cornbread Mix.

What's New in Slow Cookers

Programmability and versatility are the buzzwords when talking about the next generation of slow cookers. To check out a few, we looked to Rival, the manufacturer who debuted this appliance more than 30 years ago.

Catching everyone's eye was the **VersaWare slow cooker** ($49.99-$59.99) featuring an extreme temperature stoneware insert. You can brown food—meat for spaghetti, roast, etc.—in the insert on your cooktop; the insert will go in the oven too. After any prep work is done, place the stoneware insert into the slow cooker base for traditional slow cooking. You can also prep a recipe and hold it in the insert in the fridge; just pop it into the slow cooker before you leave for the day.

The first-ever programmable slow cooker, Rival's **Smart-Pot** ($39.99-$49.99) was introduced just a few years ago. Just push the touch pad to scroll through the timed cooking options. Select the 4- or 6-hour cook times, and the unit automatically cooks on HIGH temperature. To cook on LOW temperature, program the time for 8 or 10 hours. A warm setting comes on at the end of the cook time. Foods may be kept warm for up to 4 hours. This is available in both a 5- and 6-quart size. A 5-quart slow cooker is ideal to feed a family of four, while a 6-quart slow cooker is enough for a family of six.

For the top-of-the-line Rival programmable slow cooker, look to the **Recipe Smart-Pot** ($39.99-$69.99). You can set the cook time in hour and half-hour increments, and it automatically switches to warm once time's up. It also contains a 200-recipe, categorized database. A simple push of an arrow on the touch pad allows you to scroll through the ingredients and procedure for each dish. If you aren't in the market for recipes, then take a look at their countdown programmable unit—the screen displays the hours and minutes remaining in the cook time. It also will go into a warm mode when cooking finishes. All stoneware inserts in the programmable models are now dishwasher safe too.

There are many more brands and models from a variety of manufacturers hitting the stores. As with any purchase decision, you'll want to do some comparison shopping and a thorough reading of the manufacturer's features and directions before making your selection.

Keep It Casual

Toast Valentine's Day with friends before a big night out.

E legant doesn't have to be fussy. Just ask Warren Brown. This busy owner of CakeLove, the award-winning Washington, D.C., bakery, uses make-ahead recipes with flavors that dance on the palate.

CREAMY RASPBERRY BITES

Prep: 35 min., Cook: 10 min.

This simple platter of Creamy Raspberry Bites makes a stunning presentation.

- ½ cup fresh or frozen raspberries
- 5 egg whites
- 1¼ cups sugar, divided
- ¼ cup water
- 1 pound unsalted butter, softened and cut into 1-inch pieces
- 4 cups fresh raspberries

Process ½ cup raspberries in a blender or food processor until smooth, stopping to scrape down sides. Pour through a wire-mesh strainer into a bowl, discarding solids. Set aside.
Beat egg whites at high speed with an electric mixer until stiff peaks form. Gradually add ¼ cup sugar, beating at low speed until blended; set aside.
Cook remaining 1 cup sugar and ¼ cup water in a heavy saucepan over low heat, without stirring, until sugar dissolves and a candy thermometer registers 248° (about 10 minutes). Remove from heat.
Pour hot sugar syrup in a thin stream over egg whites, beating constantly at high speed for 5 minutes. Gradually add butter pieces and raspberry puree, and beat frosting mixture at medium speed 2 minutes or until creamy.
Spoon frosting mixture into a 1-quart zip-top plastic freezer bag or piping bag. Seal freezer bag, and snip a tiny hole in 1 corner of bag. Pipe a small amount into hollow end of 4 cups fresh raspberries. **Makes** 8 to 10 servings.

Note: Frosting mixture can be stored in an airtight container in the refrigerator for up to 1 week. To soften for piping or spreading consistency, place in a glass bowl; microwave at HIGH 45 seconds. Whisk and then microwave 30 more seconds. Whisk until smooth.

Creamy Berry Ladyfingers: Prepare frosting as directed. Pipe frosting on cut sides of 1 (3-ounce) package ladyfingers, split, and top evenly with 2 cups sliced strawberries. Dust with powdered sugar. Prep: 35 min. **Makes** 24 servings.

Sparkling Sips

Here are a few sparkling wines that deliver great taste and value.
- Prosecco di Valdobbiadene, Mionetto, Italy
- Prosecco di Valdobbiadene, Rustico, Nino Franco, Italy
- Brut, Reserva, Jaume Serra, Spain
- Brut Classic, Domaine Chandon, California
- Blanc de Blanc, Domaine Ste. Michelle, Washington

Worth the splurge:
- Brut, S. Anderson, California ($28)
- Carte Classique, G.H. Mumm, France ($35)
- Étoile Brut, Domaine Chandon, California ($35)
- Brut Royal, Pommery, France ($35)
- Grand Brut, Perrier Jouët, France ($40)

BUTTERNUT SQUASH-PARSNIP SOUP

make ahead

Prep: 15 min., Bake: 45 min., Cook: 40 min.

- 1 (3- to 4-pound) butternut squash *
- 1 Granny Smith apple, peeled, cored, and quartered
- 2 tablespoons butter
- 2 tablespoons olive oil
- 1 large sweet onion, chopped
- 3 parsnips, peeled and chopped * *
- 1½ teaspoons salt
- 1 teaspoon pepper
- 5 cups low-sodium fat-free chicken broth
- ¼ cup whipping cream
- ⅛ teaspoon paprika
- ⅛ teaspoon ground cumin
- Garnishes: sour cream, paprika

Cut squash in half; remove seeds. Place squash, cut sides down, and apples on a lightly greased aluminum foil-lined baking sheet.
Bake at 400° for 45 minutes or until squash pulp is tender. Remove from oven; cool. Scoop out pulp, discarding shells.
Melt butter in olive oil in a large Dutch oven over medium heat; add onion and next 3 ingredients, and sauté 20 minutes or until onion is caramel colored. Add squash, apple quarters, and chicken broth, and bring to a boil. Reduce heat to medium, and simmer, stirring often, 10 minutes. Remove from heat; cool.
Process squash mixture, in batches, in a blender or food processor until smooth, stopping to scrape down sides. Return to Dutch oven. Stir in whipping cream, paprika, and cumin, and simmer 5 to 10 minutes or until heated. Garnish, if desired. **Makes** about 6 (1-cup) servings.

*Substitute 3 (12-ounce) packages frozen butternut squash, thawed, if desired. For testing purposes only, we used McKenzie's Southland Microwaveable Butternut Squash.

* *Substitute 3 carrots, peeled and chopped, if desired.

Orange-Pecan-Topped Cream-Cheese
Banana-Nut Bread, page 27

Southwest Fried Oysters, page 48

Lemon-Apple Coleslaw, page 44

Dark Chocolate Mousse With Raspberry
Sauce, page 31

One Dressing, Three Salads

A homemade vinaigrette made with fridge and pantry staples couldn't be easier—or more delicious.

There are plenty of good bottled dressings on your supermarket shelves, but their flavor won't compare to this easy-to-prepare, fresh-tasting vinaigrette. It's so adaptable that we paired it with three different salads. Feel free to drizzle it over your favorite salad ingredients, alongside steamed artichokes or asparagus, or even use it as a marinade for chicken.

CIDER VINEGAR-HONEY DRESSING

fast fixin's • make ahead

Prep: 10 min.

- ½ cup cider vinegar
- 3 tablespoons honey
- 1 teaspoon grated lemon rind
- 1 tablespoon fresh lemon juice
- ½ teaspoon salt
- ¼ teaspoon freshly ground pepper
- ¾ cup extra-virgin olive oil

Whisk together first 6 ingredients until combined. Add oil in a slow, steady stream, whisking until combined. Store in an airtight container in the refrigerator up to 1 week. **Makes** 1½ cups.

NORA HENSHAW
OKEMAH, OKLAHOMA

MARINATED POTATO-APPLE SALAD

make ahead

Prep: 20 min., Cook: 40 min., Cool: 10 min., Chill: 1 hr.

The tangy sweet dressing marries chunks of apple and potatoes into a memorable new salad.

- 2 quarts water
- 2 teaspoons salt, divided
- 3 pounds unpeeled red potatoes
- 2 large Granny Smith apples, cut into bite-size pieces
- 2 celery ribs, chopped
- ½ small red onion, thinly sliced
- ⅛ teaspoon ground red pepper
- ½ cup Cider Vinegar-Honey Dressing, divided
- ¼ cup chopped fresh parsley
- Bibb lettuce leaves (optional)

Bring 2 quarts water and 1½ teaspoons salt to a boil in a Dutch oven; add potatoes, and return to a boil. Reduce heat, and simmer 30 to 40 minutes or until potatoes are tender. Drain; cool 10 minutes.
Cut potatoes into ¼-inch-thick slices, and place in a large bowl. Add apples and next 3 ingredients. Drizzle with ¼ cup Cider Vinegar-Honey Dressing, tossing gently to coat. Cover and chill 1 hour. Drizzle with remaining ¼ cup dressing, and sprinkle with parsley and remaining ½ teaspoon salt just before serving, tossing gently to coat. Serve on Bibb lettuce leaves, if desired. **Makes** 6 to 8 servings.

MOZZARELLA, AVOCADO, AND TOMATO SALAD

fast fixin's

Prep: 15 min.

- 1 head Bibb lettuce
- 2 large avocados, sliced
- 4 plum tomatoes, sliced
- ¼ teaspoon salt
- 1 (8-ounce) package fresh mozzarella cheese, sliced
- ½ cup Cider Vinegar-Honey Dressing
- ¼ teaspoon freshly ground pepper
- French bread slices (optional)

Arrange lettuce leaves on a serving platter; top with avocado and tomato. Sprinkle evenly with salt; top with cheese slices. Drizzle evenly with dressing, and sprinkle with pepper. Serve with bread slices, if desired. **Makes** 4 to 6 servings.

EASY SPINACH, PEAR, AND BLUE CHEESE SALAD

fast fixin's

Prep: 15 min.

- 3 large pears, peeled and thinly sliced
- ¼ cup orange juice
- 1 (10-ounce) package fresh baby spinach
- 1 (4-ounce) package blue cheese, crumbled
- ½ cup coarsely chopped pecans, toasted
- ¼ teaspoon freshly ground pepper
- ½ cup Cider Vinegar-Honey Dressing

Toss pear slices in orange juice; drain, discarding juice.
Place spinach on a serving platter or in a large bowl. Top with pear slices. Sprinkle evenly with cheese, pecans, and pepper. Drizzle with dressing. **Makes** 6 to 8 servings.

5 Money-Saving Menus

Make nearly a week's worth of meals for about $5 each.

To read more about our cost-cutting secrets, turn to "From Our Kitchen" on page 50.

Budget-Friendly Menus

Serves 4

Meatloaf With Green Chile-Tomato Gravy

Garlic Mashed Potatoes

Sautéed Squash and Carrots

Lemon-Garlic Roast Chicken With Sautéed Green Beans

Cornmeal Pudding

Baked Chicken Breasts

Pasta Pancakes and Gravy

steamed fresh broccoli

Pan-fried Pork Chops With Onions

Cheddar Cheese Grits

Fresh Spinach-and-Apple Salad With Cinnamon Vinaigrette

Cornmeal-Crusted Catfish Nuggets

Oven-Roasted Potatoes

Lemon-Apple Coleslaw

When our editor asked the Foods staff to come up with five meals that would serve four people for less than $25, we wondered if such a challenge was even possible. At $1.25 a serving, the prospects seemed slim—but with a little planning and some smart shopping, we surprised everyone with family-pleasing favorites such as baked chicken and pan-fried pork chops.

To read more about our cost-cutting secrets, turn to "From Our Kitchen" on page 50.

MEATLOAF WITH GREEN CHILE-TOMATO GRAVY

family favorite

Prep: 15 min., Bake: 45 min.

- **1½ pounds ground chuck**
- **½ cup soft breadcrumbs**
- **1 small onion, minced**
- **¼ cup ketchup**
- **1 large egg, lightly beaten**
- **2 tablespoons Worcestershire sauce**
- **1½ teaspoons salt**
- **½ teaspoon pepper**
- **Green Chile-Tomato Gravy**

Stir together first 8 ingredients in a large bowl just until combined. Shape into 4 (4-inch) loaves, and place in a lightly greased 13- x 9-inch baking dish.

Bake at 350° for 45 minutes or until meat is no longer pink in center. Serve with Green Chile-Tomato Gravy. **Makes** 4 servings.

GREEN CHILE-TOMATO GRAVY:
fast fixin's

Prep: 5 min., Cook: 6 min

Melt 2 tablespoons butter or margarine in a large saucepan over medium heat; add 2 tablespoons flour, stirring until smooth. Cook, stirring constantly, 1 minute. Add 1 (14½-ounce) can diced tomatoes with green chiles, ½ cup ketchup, and ½ cup water; cook, stirring often, 3 to 5 minutes or until thickened. **Makes** about 2 cups.

GARLIC MASHED POTATOES

family favorite

Prep: 15 min., Cook: 20 min.

Cook 3 pounds baking potatoes, peeled and quartered, and 1 teaspoon salt in boiling water to cover 20 minutes or until potato is tender; drain. Coarsely mash potatoes with ⅓ cup butter, softened; ½ cup milk; 2 garlic cloves, pressed; and ½ teaspoon each of salt and pepper. Transfer potatoes to a serving bowl, and sprinkle with ½ cup shredded sharp Cheddar cheese. **Makes** 4 servings.

SAUTÉED SQUASH AND CARROTS

family favorite • fast fixin's

Prep: 10 min., Cook: 10 min.

- **2 tablespoons butter**
- **½ pound zucchini, sliced**
- **½ pound yellow squash, sliced**
- **4 carrots, sliced**
- **½ teaspoon seasoned salt**
- **¼ teaspoon pepper**
- **¼ cup chopped fresh parsley**

Melt butter in a large skillet over medium-high heat; add zucchini and next 4 ingredients, and sauté 8 to 10 minutes or until tender. Stir in parsley. **Makes** 4 servings.

LEMON-GARLIC ROAST CHICKEN WITH SAUTÉED GREEN BEANS

family favorite

Prep: 10 min.; Bake: 1 hr., 15 min.;
Stand: 10 min.; Cook: 7 min.

- 3 tablespoons chopped fresh parsley
- 2 tablespoons butter, softened
- 2 tablespoons olive oil
- 2 teaspoons grated lemon rind
- 2 garlic cloves, pressed
- 1 teaspoon salt
- ½ teaspoon pepper
- 1 (4-pound) whole chicken
- 1 (16-ounce) package frozen whole green beans
- Salt and pepper to taste

Stir together first 7 ingredients. Starting at neck cavity, loosen skin from breast and drumsticks by inserting fingers and gently pushing between skin and meat. (Do not completely detach skin.) Rub half of butter mixture evenly under skin.

Tie ends of legs together with string; tuck wing tips under. Spread remaining half of butter mixture over chicken. Place chicken, breast side up, on a lightly greased rack in a lightly greased shallow roasting pan.

Bake at 450° for 30 minutes.

Reduce heat to 350°, and bake 45 minutes or until a meat thermometer inserted into thigh registers 180°. Cover chicken loosely with aluminum foil to prevent excessive browning, if necessary. Remove chicken to a serving platter, reserving drippings in pan. Cover chicken with foil, and let stand 10 minutes before slicing.

Bring pan juices to a boil in a large skillet; add green beans, and cook 5 to 7 minutes or to desired degree of tenderness. Season with salt and pepper to taste. **Makes** 4 servings.

CORNMEAL PUDDING

family favorite

Prep: 5 min., Bake: 45 min.

Whisk together 1 (20-ounce) tube frozen cream-style corn, thawed; 2 large eggs; ⅓ cup cornmeal mix; ½ teaspoon seasoned salt; and ¼ teaspoon pepper. Pour mixture into a lightly greased 1½-quart baking dish. Bake at 350° for 45 minutes or until golden brown and set. **Makes** 4 servings.

BAKED CHICKEN BREASTS

family favorite

Prep: 5 min., Bake: 35 min.

Sprinkle 4 bone-in chicken breasts with seasoned salt and pepper to taste. Place in a lightly greased 11- x 7-inch baking dish. Bake at 375° for 35 minutes or until done. **Makes** 4 servings.

PASTA PANCAKES AND GRAVY

family favorite

Prep: 15 min., Cook: 10 min.

- 2 (3-ounce) packages chicken ramen noodle soup mix
- ¼ cup vegetable oil, divided
- 2 tablespoons all-purpose flour
- 3 large eggs, lightly beaten
- 1 small onion, diced
- ½ cup chopped fresh parsley
- 2 tablespoons soy sauce
- 1 garlic clove, pressed

Cook soup according to package directions; drain noodles, and set aside, reserving broth.

Whisk together 2 tablespoons oil and flour in a saucepan over medium-high heat; cook, stirring constantly, 1 minute. Add reserved broth, and cook, stirring constantly, 2 to 3 minutes or until thickened. Set gravy aside, and keep warm.

Stir together cooked noodles, eggs, and next 4 ingredients. Heat 1 tablespoon oil in a large skillet over medium-high heat. Spoon noodle mixture by ½ cupfuls into hot skillet, and cook, in batches, 1 to 2 minutes on each side or until golden brown, adding remaining 1 tablespoon oil as needed. Serve with warm gravy. **Makes** 4 servings.

PAN-FRIED PORK CHOPS WITH ONIONS

family favorite • fast fixin's

Prep: 10 min., Cook: 20 min.

- 4 (6-ounce) bone-in pork chops
- 2 teaspoons Creole seasoning
- ¼ cup all-purpose flour
- 2 tablespoons vegetable oil
- 3 medium onions, sliced
- ½ cup water

Sprinkle pork chops evenly with Creole seasoning; dredge in flour, shaking off excess.

Cook pork chops in hot vegetable oil in a heavy skillet over medium-high heat 1 to 2 minutes each side or until golden brown. Remove from skillet, and keep warm.

Add onions and ½ cup water to skillet, stirring to loosen particles from bottom of skillet; sauté 10 minutes or until golden brown. Return pork chops to skillet; reduce heat to low, cover, and simmer 5 minutes. **Makes** 4 servings.

CHEDDAR CHEESE GRITS

family favorite • fast fixin's

Prep: 5 min., Cook: 15 min.

Bring 2 cups milk and 2 cups water to a boil in a 3-quart saucepan over medium-high heat. Gradually whisk in 1 cup uncooked quick-cooking grits and 1 teaspoon seasoned salt. Cover, reduce heat to low, and simmer, stirring occasionally, 10 minutes or until thickened. Add 1½ cups shredded sharp Cheddar cheese, 2 teaspoons Worcestershire sauce, and ½ teaspoon ground red pepper, whisking until cheese melts. **Makes** 4 servings.

Fresh Spinach-and-Apple Salad With Cinnamon Vinaigrette

family favorite • fast fixin's

Prep: 10 min.

- 2 medium apples, thinly sliced
- 6 cups torn fresh spinach
- ¼ cup honey
- 3 tablespoons vegetable oil
- 2 tablespoons cider vinegar
- ½ teaspoon dry mustard
- ¼ teaspoon ground cinnamon
- 1 garlic clove, pressed
- ⅛ teaspoon salt

Combine apples and spinach in a serving bowl. Whisk together honey and next 6 ingredients until well blended. Pour mixture over salad, tossing gently. Serve immediately. **Makes** 4 servings.

Cornmeal-Crusted Catfish Nuggets

family favorite • fast fixin's

Prep: 10 min., Cook: 10 min.

Stir together ¾ cup cornmeal mix, 2 tablespoons paprika, 1½ teaspoons seasoned salt, and 1 teaspoon pepper in a large shallow dish. Dredge 2 pounds catfish nuggets in cornmeal mixture; coat lightly with vegetable cooking spray. Cook catfish nuggets, in batches, in a hot nonstick skillet over medium heat 2 to 3 minutes or until golden, gently turning to brown each side. **Makes** 4 servings.

Oven-Roasted Potatoes

family favorite

Prep: 10 min., Bake: 30 min.

Cut 4 medium baking potatoes lengthwise into 8 wedges. Drizzle with 2 tablespoons olive oil, and sprinkle with 1 large garlic clove, minced; 1½ teaspoons dried Italian seasoning; ¾ teaspoon salt; and ½ teaspoon pepper. Toss to coat. Arrange potato wedges in a single layer on a lightly greased baking sheet, and bake at 450° for 30 minutes or until wedges are golden brown and tender. **Makes** 4 servings.

Lemon-Apple Coleslaw

family favorite • make ahead

Prep: 15 min., Chill: 1 hr.

- 1 small cabbage, shredded (8 cups)
- 2 apples, chopped
- 2 carrots, shredded
- ⅓ cup mayonnaise
- 1 tablespoon sugar
- 2 tablespoons minced onion
- 1 teaspoon grated lemon rind
- 2 tablespoons fresh lemon juice
- ¼ teaspoon salt
- ¼ teaspoon pepper

Combine cabbage, apples, and carrots in a large bowl.
Whisk together mayonnaise and next 6 ingredients; toss with cabbage mixture. Cover and chill 1 hour. **Makes** 4 servings.

Banana Bonanza

With a sweet, tropical flavor and creamy texture, this humble yellow food is most often enjoyed straight out of hand. However, when cozied up with classic partners such as chocolate, caramelized sugar, or peanut butter, the results are sublime. We're certain you'll agree after one spoonful of the Peanut Butter-Banana Pudding or Brown Sugar Bananas.

Peanut Butter-Banana Pudding

make ahead

Prep: 10 min., Cook: 25 min., Chill: 4 hrs.

This recipe originally appeared in our pages almost 10 years ago. This time we added chocolate wafers, and it's never been better.

- 1 cup sugar
- 3 tablespoons all-purpose flour
- Dash of salt
- 2 large eggs, lightly beaten
- 3 cups milk
- 2 tablespoons butter or margarine
- 1 teaspoon vanilla extract
- ½ cup creamy peanut butter
- 1 (9-ounce) package chocolate wafers
- 4 medium bananas, sliced and divided
- 1 (8-ounce) container frozen whipped topping, thawed
- ½ cup unsalted dry-roasted peanuts

Combine first 3 ingredients in a heavy saucepan; whisk in eggs and milk, and cook, whisking constantly, over low heat until thickened (about 25 minutes). Remove pan from heat, and stir in butter and vanilla. Set custard aside.
Spread ½ teaspoon peanut butter between 2 chocolate wafers, forming a sandwich; repeat with remaining peanut butter and chocolate wafers.
Place sandwich cookies in the bottom of a 3-quart bowl; top with banana slices. Pour custard over bananas; cover and chill 4 hours.
Spread whipped topping evenly over custard, and sprinkle with peanuts before serving. **Makes** 8 to 10 servings.

Brown Sugar Bananas

fast fixin's

Prep: 10 min., Cook: 10 min.

Try this decadent recipe spooned over your favorite pound cake or ice cream.

> ¼ cup butter
> 4 medium bananas, peeled and sliced
> ½ cup firmly packed brown sugar
> ½ cup cane or maple syrup
> ½ teaspoon ground cinnamon
> ½ cup whipping cream, whipped
> ¼ cup sweetened flaked coconut, toasted

Melt butter in a large skillet over medium-high heat. Add sliced bananas and next 3 ingredients; sauté mixture 5 minutes or until sugar melts. Top banana mixture with whipped cream and toasted coconut. **Makes** 6 servings.

Banana-Mocha Shake

fast fixin's

Prep: 5 min.

> 3 medium bananas
> 2 cups coffee ice cream
> 1 cup milk
> ¼ cup chocolate syrup

Process all ingredients in a blender 1 minute or until smooth, stopping to scrape down sides. Serve immediately. **Makes** 4 servings.

Ham and Beans

These comfort-food recipes use the overnight soaking method for dried beans. But if you're pressed for time, use the quick soak method detailed in the box below.

Ham-and-Bean Soup

Prep: 15 min.; Soak: 8 hrs.;
Cook: 1 hr., 35 min.

Freeze leftover ham bones until ready to use in this flavorful soup.

> 1 (16-ounce) package dried great Northern beans
> 3 cups chopped cooked ham
> 1 large sweet onion, diced
> 2 garlic cloves, minced
> 2 tablespoons olive oil
> 1 ham bone
> 2 (32-ounce) containers chicken broth
> ½ teaspoon dried crushed red pepper
> Cornbread Croutons

Sort and rinse beans. Place in a 6-quart Dutch oven; add water 2 inches above beans, and soak 8 hours. Drain.
Sauté ham, onion, and garlic in hot oil in a Dutch oven over medium-high heat 5 minutes or until onion is tender.
Add beans, ham bone, broth, and pepper. Bring to a boil; cover, reduce heat, and simmer, stirring occasionally, 1½ hours or until beans are tender and soup has thickened. Serve with Cornbread Croutons. **Makes** 3 quarts.

CORNBREAD CROUTONS:
Prep: 30 min, Bake: 10 min.

Prepare 1 recipe (enough for 6 servings) cornbread mix according to package directions.
Cut baked cornbread into 1-inch squares, brush with melted butter, and place on a baking sheet. Bake at 350° for 10 minutes or until golden brown.

Baked Beans and Ham

Prep: 15 min.; Soak: 8 hrs.;
Cook: 1 hr., 5 min.; Bake: 1 hr.

> 1 (20-ounce) package dried 15-bean soup mix
> 4 cups water
> 2 (8-ounce) smoked ham hocks
> 1 large sweet onion, diced
> 2 cups chopped cooked ham
> 2 tablespoons vegetable oil
> 2 cups ketchup
> 3 tablespoons brown sugar
> 2 tablespoons spicy brown mustard
> ½ teaspoon salt
> ½ teaspoon dried crushed red pepper
> ¼ cup bourbon (optional)

Place beans in a Dutch oven; add water 2 inches above beans, and soak 8 hours. Drain.
Bring beans, 4 cups water, and ham hocks to a boil in a Dutch oven; cover, reduce heat, and simmer 1 hour or until beans are tender. Drain. Remove beans; set beans aside. Remove ham hocks, and let cool; chop meat, discarding skin and bones.
Sauté onion and 2 cups ham in hot oil in Dutch oven 5 minutes or until onion is tender. Add beans, reserved meat from ham hocks, ketchup, next 4 ingredients, and, if desired, bourbon to Dutch oven.
Bake, covered, at 350° for 1 hour.
Makes 6 to 8 servings.

Sorting and Soaking Beans

To sort beans, pick out any foreign substances such as small stones and soil particles.

For quick soaking, add 6 to 8 cups water to 1 pound dried beans in a Dutch oven, and bring to a boil. Cover and cook 2 minutes; remove from heat, and soak 1 hour. Rinse and drain; cook according to recipe directions.

PINTO BEANS, HAM HOCKS, AND RICE

Prep: 10 min., Soak: 8 hrs., Cook: 3 hrs.

To reduce the fat in this recipe, cook the ham hocks, covered, in 2 quarts of water a day early; chill overnight. Skim the congealed fat from the chilled broth before adding beans and other ingredients; then cook as directed.

1 (16-ounce) package dried pinto beans
2 (10-ounce) smoked ham hocks
2 quarts water
1 teaspoon salt
½ teaspoon pepper
1 cup uncooked long-grain rice
1 large green bell pepper, diced
6 green onions, chopped
2 cups chopped cooked ham (optional)

Sort and wash beans. Place beans in a Dutch oven; add water 2 inches above beans, and soak 8 hours. Drain.

Bring beans and next 4 ingredients to a boil in a Dutch oven; cover, reduce heat, and simmer, stirring occasionally, 2½ hours or until beans are tender.

Stir in rice, bell pepper, and green onions. Cover and simmer 20 minutes or until rice is tender. Remove ham hocks, and let cool; remove and chop meat, discarding skin and bones. Stir in chopped meat from ham hocks and, if desired, 2 cups chopped ham. **Makes** 6 to 8 servings.

RAY HATTON
GRAND PRAIRIE, TEXAS

---

top-rated menu

Table-to-Table Dinner

One house and one host offer a fun evening.

There's no denying that progressive dinners are trendy and fun. Host one that all takes place at your home. Using two tables, guests rotate dinner spots after each course. It's a clever way to introduce your couple friends to each other.

FESTIVE PORK ROAST

make ahead

Prep: 15 min.; Chill: 8 hrs.; Broil: 5 min.; Bake: 1 hr., 30 min.; Stand: 10 min.

Cook the roast beforehand, taking it out as guests arrive. Reheat the sauce for the roast in a glass dish in the microwave before serving.

1½ cups dry red wine
⅔ cup firmly packed brown sugar
½ cup water
½ cup ketchup
¼ cup vegetable oil
4 garlic cloves, minced
3 tablespoons soy sauce
2 teaspoons curry powder
1 teaspoon ground ginger
½ teaspoon pepper
2 (2½- to 3-pound) boneless rolled pork roasts
4 teaspoons cornstarch
1½ cups water

Combine first 10 ingredients in a large shallow dish or zip-top plastic freezer bag; add pork. Cover or seal, and chill 8 hours, turning occasionally.

Remove pork from marinade, reserving marinade to equal 2½ cups, adding water if necessary. Place pork on a rack in a shallow roasting pan lined with aluminum foil.

Whisk reserved marinade into cornstarch in a small saucepan. Place pan over medium-high heat, and bring sauce to a boil, whisking constantly. Cook, whisking constantly, 2 to 3 minutes or until thickened. Remove and reserve ¼ cup sauce. Set remaining sauce in saucepan aside.

Broil pork 6 inches from heat 5 minutes. Pour 1½ cups water into pan. Reduce oven temperature to 325°, and bake 1 hour and 15 minutes to 1 hour and 30 minutes or until a meat thermometer inserted into thickest portion registers 155°, basting with reserved ¼ cup sauce during the last 15 minutes. Remove roast, and let stand at least 10 minutes or until meat thermometer inserted into thickest portion registers 160° before slicing. Serve with remaining warm sauce. **Makes** 8 to 10 servings.

MARY FRANCES GRIFFIN
COLUMBUS, MISSISSIPPI

Along the Southeast coast, oysters steamed over a blazing fire provide cause for celebration. Mid-Atlantic residents favor fritters and oyster stew to chase away winter's chill. Gulf oysters, which account for two-thirds of the nation's 750-million-pound harvest, set the taste standard by virtue of sheer numbers.

So take time this month (perhaps the best of the year for enjoying oysters) to schedule a small feast. Following are a few recipes to get you started.

ROASTED BABY VEGETABLES

Prep: 20 min., Bake: 40 min.

For even roasting, all vegetables should be cut to about the same size. Put them in the oven when you take out the roast.

- 1 pound baby beets with tops
- ¼ cup olive oil, divided
- 1½ tablespoons chopped fresh rosemary
- 1 teaspoon coarse-grained sea salt, divided
- ¼ teaspoon pepper, divided
- 8 shallots
- 1 pound baby carrots
- 2 medium-size sweet potatoes (about 1½ pounds), peeled and cut into 1-inch pieces
- 1¼ pounds turnips, peeled and cut into eighths
- Garnish: fresh rosemary sprigs

Cut tops from beets, leaving 1-inch stems. Peel beets, and cut into quarters. Place on a 12-inch square of aluminum foil. Drizzle with 1 tablespoon olive oil; sprinkle with rosemary, ¼ teaspoon salt, and ⅛ teaspoon pepper. Fold up foil sides, forming a bowl. Place foil bowl in 1 end of a large roasting pan; set aside.
Peel shallots; cut in half lengthwise.

Toss together shallots, carrots, potatoes, turnips, remaining 3 tablespoons oil, remaining ¾ teaspoon salt, and remaining ⅛ teaspoon pepper. Place in remaining end of roasting pan.
Bake at 450° for 30 to 40 minutes or until tender. Garnish, if desired. **Makes** 8 servings.

Oysters

Southerners love the taste and lore of oysters. We treat them with reverence, displaying a nearly cultlike devotion.

Nonetheless, oysters are unlikely culinary icons. They're not exciting to catch, as fish are, nor do they beckon like a shapely crimson tomato. Once you have stabbed, pried, and muscled your way into an oyster's shell, you discover that eye appeal is not one of its qualities either. If there were no one around to tell you how terrific oysters taste, why would you bother?

Fortunately for oyster lovers everywhere, some hungry Neolithic-era soul *did* bother, and humans have been eating these briny bivalves ever since—nowhere more faithfully than in our region of the country.

SCALLOPED OYSTERS

Prep: 15 min., Chill: 8 hrs., Stand: 30 min., Bake: 30 min.

- 1 quart fresh oysters, undrained
- 2½ sleeves rectangle buttery crackers (about 66 crackers), crushed
- 1 teaspoon salt
- 1 cup butter, melted
- 1½ cups half-and-half
- 1 teaspoon Worcestershire sauce
- ½ teaspoon freshly ground pepper

Drain oysters, reserving ½ cup oyster liquor (liquid from oyster container).
Place cracker crumbs in a large bowl; sprinkle evenly with salt. Drizzle butter over crumbs, tossing to combine.
Whisk together ½ cup reserved oyster liquor, half-and-half, and Worcestershire sauce.
Place one-third crumb mixture evenly in a 2-quart baking dish; top with half of oysters. Sprinkle with ¼ teaspoon pepper. Pour half of cream mixture evenly over oysters. Repeat layers, ending with crumb mixture.
Cover and chill at least 8 hours.
Let stand at room temperature 30 minutes before baking. Bake at 350° for 30 minutes or until bubbly. **Makes** 8 servings.

Note: For testing purposes only, we used Keebler Club Original crackers.

JANICE BRAGG
SCOTTSBORO, ALABAMA

SOUTHWEST FRIED OYSTERS

chef recipe

Prep: 20 min., Chill: 2 hrs.,
Fry: 3 min. per batch

Selects are fairly large shucked oysters—the perfect size for frying. *(pictured on page 38)*

- **2 pints fresh Select oysters, drained**
- **2 cups buttermilk**
- **1 cup all-purpose flour**
- **½ cup yellow cornmeal**
- **1 tablespoon paprika**
- **1½ teaspoons garlic powder**
- **1½ teaspoons dried oregano**
- **1½ teaspoons chili powder**
- **1½ teaspoons ground red pepper**
- **½ teaspoon dried mustard**
- **½ teaspoon salt**
- **½ teaspoon ground black pepper**
- **Vegetable oil**

Combine oysters and buttermilk in a large shallow dish or zip-top plastic freezer bag. Cover or seal and chill at least 2 hours. Drain oysters well.

Combine flour and next 9 ingredients. Dredge oysters in flour mixture, shaking off excess.

Pour oil to a depth of 1 inch in a Dutch oven; heat to 370°.

Fry oysters, in batches, 3 minutes or until golden. Drain on paper towels. Serve immediately. **Makes** 4 to 6 servings.

KEVIN WILLIAMSON
CHEF/OWNER, *RANCH 616*
AUSTIN, TEXAS

Fried Buffalo Oysters: Prepare Southwest Fried Oysters as directed, omitting chili powder. Stir together ½ cup melted butter, ½ cup hot sauce, and 2 tablespoons fresh lemon juice. Pour butter mixture evenly over hot fried oysters. Serve oysters with Ranch dressing and celery sticks on the side.

Fried Buffalo Oyster Po'Boys: Prepare Fried Buffalo Oysters as directed. Split 4 French bread rolls. Spread 1 tablespoon mayonnaise evenly on cut sides of rolls. Place ¼ cup shredded iceberg lettuce and one-fourth of Buffalo Oysters on bottom halves of rolls; cover with roll tops.

But Are Oysters Safe?

Cooked oysters are generally safe to eat. Raw oysters, though, can harbor a variety of ills, among them Norwalk virus, which causes stomach upset, and hepatitis (though such occurrences are extremely rare). In the last decade, a naturally occurring bacteria *Vibrio vulnificus* has caused serious illness and death in a number of people.

The seafood industry has come up with ways to treat raw oysters to kill the bacteria, called post-harvest processing or PHP. Oysters can be frozen, treated with hydrostatic pressure, or pasteurized. Oysters treated this way are designated virtually bacteria-free by the FDA. If you are concerned about eating raw ones, ask your seafood market to order post-harvest processed oysters. In a restaurant, ask if the oysters have been post-harvest processed. If not, order cooked oysters instead.

OYSTER STEW

chef recipe

Prep: 15 min., Cook: 30 min.

Using smaller oysters in a stew allows them to be more evenly distributed than large ones. Oyster liquor is simply the juice that is in the oyster shell, which they are packed in. Be sure to use shucked oysters before the sell-by date on the container.

- **1 (12-ounce) container fresh oysters, undrained**
- **2 tablespoons butter**
- **1 tablespoon canola oil**
- **1 small onion, chopped**
- **1 medium carrot, diced**
- **2 celery ribs, chopped**
- **½ cup white wine**
- **4 cups whipping cream**
- **2 medium Yukon Gold potatoes, cut into 1-inch cubes**
- **1½ teaspoons salt**
- **½ teaspoon freshly ground pepper**
- **2 plum tomatoes, chopped**
- **8 bacon strips, cooked and crumbled**
- **Chopped fresh chives**

Drain oysters, reserving liquor (liquid from oyster container); set aside.

Melt butter in canola oil in a Dutch oven over medium heat; add onion, carrot, and celery, and sauté 5 minutes or until tender.

Add wine and reserved oyster liquor; simmer 5 minutes, or until reduced by half. Stir in whipping cream, cubed potatoes, salt, and pepper; simmer 15 minutes or until cream is slightly thickened and potatoes are tender. Add oysters, and cook 3 minutes or just until edges begin to curl; stir in tomatoes.

Remove from heat, and serve; sprinkle each serving evenly with crumbled bacon and chives. **Makes** 4 servings.

CHEF DALE REITZER
ACACIA RESTAURANT
RICHMOND, VIRGINIA

Pasta Suppers Ready in Minutes

This month we've gathered a variety of recipes as alternatives to weekly spaghetti night. The ingredient lists aren't long, and most of the dishes are ready in the time it takes to boil the water and cook the pasta.

CHICKEN AND BOW TIE PASTA

family favorite

Prep: 10 min., Cook: 30 min.

Cooking the pasta in the same water that the chicken was cooked in gives the noodles extra flavor—and makes cleanup easy.

- 1 quart water
- 4 skinned and boned chicken breasts, cut into bite-size pieces
- 8 ounces uncooked bow tie pasta
- 1 cup chicken broth
- 1 celery rib, chopped (about ½ cup)
- 1 small onion, chopped (about ½ cup)
- 1 (10¾-ounce) can cream of mushroom soup, undiluted
- 1 (8-ounce) package pasteurized prepared cheese product, cubed

Garnish: chopped fresh parsley

Bring 1 quart salted water to a boil in a Dutch oven. Add chicken, and cook 12 minutes or until done. Remove chicken from water with a slotted spoon. Add pasta to water in Dutch oven, and cook 10 minutes or until tender; drain. Keep warm.
Heat ¼ cup broth over medium-high heat in a Dutch oven; add celery and onion, and cook 5 minutes or until tender. Stir in chicken, soup, cheese, and remaining ¾ cup chicken broth, stirring until cheese is melted. Toss with pasta; garnish, if desired. Serve immediately. **Makes** 4 servings.

Note: For testing purposes only, we used Velveeta for pasteurized prepared cheese product.

LORAINE CARDER
CUMMING, GEORGIA

SHRIMP AND PASTA WITH CREOLE CREAM SAUCE

family favorite

Prep: 10 min., Cook: 18 min.

- 1½ pounds unpeeled, medium-size fresh shrimp *
- 2 teaspoons Creole seasoning
- 12 ounces uncooked penne pasta
- 2 tablespoons butter or margarine
- 4 green onions, sliced
- 2 garlic cloves, minced
- 1½ cups whipping cream
- 1 teaspoon hot sauce
- ¼ cup fresh parsley, chopped
- ½ cup (2 ounces) freshly grated Parmesan cheese

Peel shrimp, and devein, if desired. Toss shrimp with Creole seasoning; set aside.
Prepare pasta according to package directions; drain. Keep warm.
Melt butter in a large skillet over medium-high heat; add shrimp, and cook, stirring constantly, 5 minutes or just until shrimp turn pink. Remove shrimp from skillet. Add green onions and garlic to skillet; sauté 2 to 3 minutes or until tender. Reduce heat to medium; stir in cream and hot sauce. Bring to a boil; reduce heat, and simmer, stirring constantly, 8 to 10 minutes or until sauce is slightly thickened. Stir in shrimp and parsley. Toss with pasta. Sprinkle evenly with Parmesan cheese. Serve immediately. **Makes** 4 to 6 servings.

*Substitute 1½ pounds frozen shrimp, thawed, if desired.

SUSAN MARTIN
BIRMINGHAM, ALABAMA

LINGUINE WITH WHITE CLAM SAUCE

family favorite • fast fixin's

Prep: 10 min., Cook: 10 min.

- 8 ounces uncooked linguine
- 3 garlic cloves, minced
- 2 tablespoons olive oil
- 1 (8-ounce) bottle clam juice
- ½ teaspoon dried crushed red pepper
- 3 (6.5-ounce) cans chopped clams, drained
- ½ cup dry white wine
- ½ cup chopped fresh parsley
- ¼ cup chopped fresh basil
- 2 teaspoons fresh lemon juice
- 1 tablespoon butter (optional)

Prepare linguine according to package directions; drain. Keep warm.
Sauté garlic in hot oil in a large skillet over medium-high heat 1 to 2 minutes. Add clam juice and crushed red pepper; bring to a boil, reduce heat, and simmer 5 minutes. Stir in clams and next 4 ingredients; simmer 3 minutes. Toss with pasta and, if desired, 1 tablespoon butter. Serve immediately. **Makes** 4 servings.

MARTHA ANN RICHARDS
NEWPORT NEWS, VIRGINIA

Successful Substitutions

- Uncooked dried pasta of similar shapes can be interchanged in recipes if it's measured by weight, not by volume. Check packages for weight, or use a kitchen scale.
- Cooked pasta can be substituted cup for cup. One (8-ounce) package dry pasta yields about 4 cups cooked pasta.

from our kitchen

Dinner on the Double

For speedy suppers that are big on flavor and low on prep time, plan ahead for leftovers. Roast an extra chicken for a quick casserole later in the week, or sauté a second helping of vegetables to toss with tomorrow night's pasta.

Fried rice is the perfect one-dish meal when time is at a premium. Use a combination of chopped cooked chicken and ham, or substitute leftover beef, pork, or shrimp; simply adjust the ingredients according to what's on hand. If you prefer a spicier version, bump up the heat with another teaspoon of chili-garlic sauce. Available in the Asian section of most supermarkets, it's a fiery-hot blend of ground chili peppers and garlic that also adds fast flavor to marinades and pasta sauce.

Fried Rice 101: Heat 1 tablespoon oil in a large skillet over medium-high heat; add 2 lightly beaten large eggs, and gently stir 1 minute or until softly scrambled. Remove eggs from skillet; chop and set aside. Heat 2 tablespoons oil in skillet; add ½ cup each of diced onion and diced bell pepper, and stir-fry 3 minutes. Add 1 cup chopped cooked meat, poultry, or shrimp and ½ cup frozen sweet peas; stir-fry 2 minutes. Add 3 cups cooked rice, ¼ cup soy sauce, and 1 teaspoon chili-garlic sauce; stir-fry 3 to 4 minutes or until thoroughly heated. Stir in scrambled eggs; sprinkle with sliced green onions and chopped almonds, if desired. Prep: 10 min., Cook: 10 min. **Makes** 4 servings.

Tips and Tidbits

Bagging the Big Bargains

Cutting the cost of a great-tasting meal is easier than you think—even if you don't have time to clip coupons. We trimmed the tab for "5 Money-Saving Menus" beginning on page 42 just by taking advantage of the advertised specials in supermarket circulars.

The best deals are always on the front page of the circular, and the savings can be huge. We found assorted pork chops for $1.19 a pound, whole chickens for 59 cents a pound, and ground chuck for $1.88 a pound. Three-pound bags of apples and onions and 2-pound bags of carrots were all on sale for $1 each. A 5-pound bag of russet potatoes yielded two deliciously different side dishes for less than 15 cents a serving.

Known as loss leaders, these are the weekly specials the store advertises at rock-bottom prices to attract customers. Once inside the store, they hope you'll buy higher priced items as well—but head for a discount store or shopping club to stock up on staples.

Wrap and Roll

All sorts of delicious tidbits can be tucked inside an egg roll wrapper, and they're a cinch to assemble. This recipe offers a crisp, mildly seasoned cabbage filling, but like fried rice, the variations are almost endless. Look for egg roll wrappers in the produce section of the supermarket. One (16-ounce) package yields about 16 egg roll wrappers.

Egg Rolls: Stir together 1 (16-ounce) package coleslaw mix; 1 cup finely chopped cooked meat, poultry, or shrimp; 1½ tablespoons minced fresh ginger; 2 garlic cloves, pressed; 1 teaspoon seasoned pepper; and ½ teaspoon salt. Brush water around outer edge of each egg roll wrapper. Spoon ⅓ cup filling mixture in center of each wrapper. Fold bottom corner over filling, tucking tip of corner under filling; fold left and right corners of wrapper over filling. Tightly roll filled end toward remaining corner; gently press to seal. Pour oil to a depth of 3 inches in a Dutch oven; heat to 375°. Fry egg rolls, in batches, 3 to 4 minutes or until golden brown; drain on paper towels. Serve immediately with desired condiments. Prep: 20 min., Fry: 4 min. per batch. **Makes** 16 egg rolls.

march

52   Healthy & Light Season's First Grilling *Fire up the flavor with these family-pleasing favorites*

54   Laid-back Sunday Dinner *Make-ahead dishes that allow you to relax with family and friends*

55   Hooked on Catfish *Delicious ways to cook this Southern specialty*

56   Good for the Soul *Whip up these freezer meals for those in need*

58   What's for Supper? Tex-Mex Tonight *Cook up a spicy supper*

58   Family-Favorite Casseroles *Mexican dishes made easy*

59   Add Zest With Lemon *A delightful tea bread with a citrus zing*

60   Food and Hospitality Entertaining That's Simple *Get the lowdown on throwing a spectacular wine and cheese party*

61   Fruity Thirst Quenchers *Welcome spring with an ice-cold beverage*

62   Irresistible Ice-Cream Sandwiches *Rich and creamy goodies from the freezer*

62   Lollipop Cookies *Kid-friendly treats that double as the perfect party snacks or centerpiece*

63   You'll Love This Easy-Does-It Cake *Try this delicious—and easy-to-make—Pig Pickin' Cake*

64   Top-Rated Menu March Madness *Enjoy basketball championships with these winning recipes*

64   Ready, Set, Serve *Congealed salads are back in style*

66   Bake These Southern Sides *Comforting vegetable-based casseroles*

67   Quick & Easy Speedy Steaks Fried Right *Crisp, mouthwatering favorites make a marvelous meal*

68   Freshen a Menu With Herbs *Fresh herbs pack in the flavor for this easy meal*

69   Taste of the South Rémoulade Sauce *Stir up this French classic in 10 minutes flat*

70   From Our Kitchen *Cheddar Crescents, Lemon-Orange Rolls, and more*

Season's First Grilling

Warmer days call for firing up the grill—and the flavor.

Hardly anyone can resist the aroma of dinner sizzling outdoors. A beefy portobello mushroom is a divine substitute for a burger, especially when topped with calcium-rich blue cheese. A vitamin C-rich salsa perks up lamb chops, and lean pork is accented by peanuts, which boast a heart-healthy fat. So crank up the flames, and treat yourself to something good—and good for you.

TEA-THYME GRILLED CHICKEN

family favorite

Prep: 20 min., Chill: 1 hr., Grill: 8 min.

Pounding the chicken breasts makes them even and thinner, reducing the grilling time.

**6 skinned and boned chicken
   breasts
1 cup orange juice
3 tablespoons unsweetened
   instant iced tea mix *
2 teaspoons sugar
⅛ teaspoon salt
2 tablespoons chopped fresh
   or 2 teaspoons dried thyme
1 teaspoon minced fresh
   garlic
1 teaspoon finely grated
   lemon rind
1 tablespoon vegetable oil
1 teaspoon pepper
½ teaspoon salt
Vegetable cooking spray**

Place chicken between 2 sheets of heavy-duty plastic wrap, and flatten to a ½-inch thickness, using a mallet or rolling pin. Place chicken in a shallow dish or large zip-top plastic freezer bag.
Stir together orange juice and next 7 ingredients. Reserve ½ cup orange juice mixture; set aside. Pour remaining mixture over chicken. Cover or seal and chill 1 hour, turning occasionally. Remove chicken from marinade, discarding marinade. Sprinkle chicken evenly with pepper and ½ teaspoon salt.
Coat cold grill rack with cooking spray, and place on grill. Grill chicken over medium-high heat (350° to 400°) 4 minutes on each side or until done. (Do not overcook.)
Place reserved orange juice mixture in a microwave-safe glass measuring cup; cover loosely with plastic wrap. Microwave at HIGH 1 to 2 minutes or until bubbly. Serve with chicken.
Makes 6 servings.

Note: For testing purposes only, we used Nestea Unsweetened instant iced tea mix.

* Substitute 1 family-size tea bag or 4 single-serve tea bags for unsweetened tea mix, if desired. Microwave orange juice at HIGH for 1 minute. Steep tea bag in hot orange juice 10 minutes. Remove tea bag. Chill orange juice mixture while preparing chicken. Proceed with recipe as directed.

Calories: 155 (14% from fat); Fat 2.5g (sat 0.5g, mono 0.8g, poly 0.6g); Protein 28g; Carb 3.9g; Fiber 0.2g; Chol 68mg; Iron 0.9mg; Sodium 271mg; Calc 21mg

GRILLED LAMB CHOPS WITH PINEAPPLE-MINT SALSA

Prep: 20 min., Chill: 30 min., Grill: 14 min.

If you can't find lamb chops, feel free to substitute with equal-size pork loin chops. The fresh mint in the salsa adds a crisp fragrance, so don't be tempted to use dried. If you can't find fresh mint, use fresh basil. And be sure to grate the lemon rind before squeezing the fresh juice.

**4 (6- to 7-ounce) bone-in lamb loin
   chops (about 1½ inches thick),
   trimmed
1 tablespoon olive oil
2 tablespoons fresh lemon juice,
   divided
½ teaspoon salt
½ teaspoon pepper
1 teaspoon minced fresh garlic
1 teaspoon grated lemon rind
1 plum tomato, seeded and
   chopped
½ small cucumber, peeled, seeded,
   and chopped (about ½ cup)
¼ cup finely chopped fresh
   pineapple *
2 tablespoons crumbled feta
   cheese
2 green onions, sliced
2 tablespoons chopped fresh mint
¼ teaspoon sugar
⅛ teaspoon salt
Hot cooked couscous**

Rub chops with oil and 1 tablespoon lemon juice; sprinkle evenly with ½ teaspoon salt and pepper. Rub chops with garlic and lemon rind. Cover and chill 30 minutes.
Combine chopped tomato, next 7 ingredients, and remaining 1 tablespoon lemon juice.
Grill lamb, covered with grill lid, over medium-high heat (350° to 400°) 5 to 7 minutes on each side or to desired degree of doneness. Serve chops with salsa over hot cooked couscous. **Makes** 4 servings.

* Substitute ¼ cup drained canned crushed pineapple in juice, if desired.

Calories (with 1 cup cooked couscous): 395 (27% from fat); Fat 11.8g (sat 3.7g, mono 5.8g, poly 1g); Protein 29g; Carb 42g; Fiber 3.2g; Chol 72mg; Iron 2.5mg; Sodium 488mg; Calc 69mg

Pork Saté

family favorite

Prep: 30 min., Cook: 25 min., Cool: 10 min.,
Chill: 1 hr., Soak: 30 min, Grill: 6 min.

Look for dark sesame oil (or you can use
lighter sesame oil), lite coconut milk, and
hot chili sauce on the ethnic food aisle of
your supermarket.

> 1 pound pork loin or boneless
>   chops, trimmed
> 1 small onion, chopped (about
>   ½ cup)
> 2 teaspoons dark sesame oil
> ½ cup lite coconut milk
> ⅓ cup water
> ¼ cup fresh lime juice
> 2 tablespoons sugar
> 3 tablespoons crunchy peanut
>   butter
> 2 tablespoons lite soy sauce
> 1½ tablespoons hot chili sauce
> 1 garlic clove, minced
> 10-inch wooden skewers
>   (about 30)
> 2 (8.8-ounce) packages precooked
>   brown rice
> 2 tablespoons chopped dry-
>   roasted peanuts
> 3 green onions, sliced
> Lime wedges (optional)

Place pork between 2 sheets of heavy-
duty plastic wrap, and flatten to an
⅛-inch thickness, using a mallet or
rolling pin; cut into 1-inch-wide strips.
Set aside.

Sauté onion in hot sesame oil in a
medium saucepan over medium heat 7
to 8 minutes or until onion is tender.
Add coconut milk and next
7 ingredients; bring to a boil. Reduce
heat to medium low, and simmer, stirring often, 15 minutes or until thickened. Cool 10 minutes. Reserve ⅓ cup
coconut milk mixture, and set aside.

Combine pork strips and remaining
coconut milk mixture in a shallow dish
or large zip-top plastic freezer bag.
Cover or seal, and chill 1 hour.

Soak wooden skewers in water for
30 minutes to prevent burning.

Remove pork from marinade, discarding marinade.

Thread pork strips onto skewers.

Grill, covered with grill lid, over
medium heat (300° to 350°) 2 to
3 minutes on each side or until done.
Brush reserved ⅓ cup coconut milk
mixture over grilled pork on skewers.

Heat rice in microwave according to
package directions.

Spoon rice onto serving platter; top
with pork skewers. Sprinkle with
peanuts and green onions. Serve pork
with lime wedges, if desired. **Makes**
6 servings.

Note: For testing purposes only, we
used Uncle Ben's Ready Rice Whole
Grain Brown.

Calories: 320 (35% from fat); Fat 12.3g (sat 3.7g, mono 4.2g,
poly 2.4g); Protein 22g; Carb 31g; Fiber 2.9g; Chol 48mg;
Iron 1.6mg; Sodium 307mg; Calc 37mg

Balsamic-Blue Cheese Portobello Burgers

Prep: 15 min., Chill: 1 hr., Grill: 8 min.

If you don't love blue cheese, use goat
cheese (chèvre) or feta cheese for an
equally delicious, tangy flavor. The gills are
the brownish-black walls on the underside
of mushroom caps. Scrape them off gently
using a spoon. Removing gills keeps other
ingredients from turning a grayish brown.

> 2 large portobello mushroom
>   caps, stemmed
> 3 tablespoons balsamic vinegar
> 1 tablespoon olive oil
> 1 teaspoon minced fresh garlic
> ½ teaspoon pepper
> ¼ teaspoon salt
> ¼ cup crumbled blue cheese or
>   Gorgonzola cheese
> 2 tablespoons light
>   mayonnaise
> 1 teaspoon balsamic vinegar
> 2 whole wheat hamburger buns,
>   split
> Romaine lettuce leaves
> 2 tomato slices

Scrape gills from mushroom caps,
if desired.

Combine 3 tablespoons vinegar, oil,
and next 3 ingredients in a shallow
dish or large zip-top plastic freezer bag;
add mushrooms, turning to coat. Cover
or seal, and chill 1 hour, turning
occasionally. Remove mushrooms from
marinade, discarding marinade.

Grill mushrooms, covered with grill lid,
over medium-high heat (350° to 400°)
3 to 4 minutes on each side or until tender. Remove mushrooms from grill, and
immediately sprinkle undersides evenly
with blue cheese.

Stir together mayonnaise and 1 teaspoon vinegar. Spread mixture evenly
on cut sides of buns; place lettuce,
mushrooms, and tomato slices on
bottom halves of buns, and cover
with tops. Serve burgers immediately.
Makes 2 servings.

Calories: 321 (43% from fat)*; Fat 15.3g (sat 4.7g, mono 5.5g,
poly 4.3g); Protein 9.2g; Carb 34g; Fiber 5.2g; Chol 13mg;
Iron 1.4mg; Sodium 705mg; Calc 143mg

*Fat percentage seems high because mushrooms are very low in
calories. Many of the calories come from small amounts of light
mayonnaise, blue cheese, and olive oil.

Test Kitchen Notebook

These sizzling meats and vegetables allow you to enjoy the
relaxed pace and quick cleanup of
outdoor cooking. And all of these
dishes get a flavor boost from
rubs or marinades. The versatile
Pork Saté can be served as a pick-
up appetizer or a Thai-inspired
main dish over fluffy brown rice.

Joy Zacharia

ASSOCIATE FOODS EDITOR

Laid-back Sunday Dinner

Make-ahead dishes and easy recipes give you time to relax with family and friends.

Warmer weather ushers in a season of carefree celebrations, so dust off those patio chairs and set the table for some backyard fun. Our easy-to-fix menu brings together familiar ingredients in fresh new ways, from a sweet-and-tangy twist on traditional poppy seed dressing to a sophisticated version of lemon icebox pie.

All of the recipes have components that can be prepared ahead on Saturday, reducing the chaos that comes from trying to get everything ready at the last minute. Once home from church, place the chicken on the grill and put the pasta in the oven. Pencil-thin spears of asparagus roast in 10 minutes, tops, and can scoot in the oven when the pasta comes out. Put the finishing touches on the tart, toss the salad, and pour the tea. It's Sunday, and the living is easy.

THREE-CHEESE PASTA BAKE

family favorite • make ahead

Prep: 20 min., Bake: 30 min.

Ziti pasta is long, thin tubes; penne or rigatoni pasta can be substituted, if desired. *(pictured on page 78)*

- 1 (16-ounce) package ziti
- 2 (10-ounce) containers refrigerated Alfredo sauce
- 1 (8-ounce) container sour cream
- 1 (15-ounce) container ricotta cheese
- 2 large eggs, lightly beaten
- ¼ cup grated Parmesan cheese
- ¼ cup chopped fresh parsley
- 1½ cups mozzarella cheese

Prepare ziti according to package directions; drain and return to pot.

Stir together Alfredo sauce and sour cream; toss with ziti until evenly coated. Spoon half of mixture into a lightly greased 13- x 9-inch baking dish.

Stir together ricotta cheese and next 3 ingredients; spread evenly over pasta mixture in baking dish. Spoon remaining pasta mixture evenly over ricotta cheese layer; sprinkle evenly with mozzarella cheese.

Bake at 350° for 30 minutes or until bubbly. **Makes** 8 to 10 servings.

Note: For testing purposes only, we used Buitoni Refrigerated Alfredo Sauce.

AMY FAGGART
CONCORD, NORTH CAROLINA

LEXINGTON-STYLE GRILLED CHICKEN

family favorite • make ahead

Prep: 15 min., Chill: 2 hrs., Grill: 40 min.

Larry Elder says Lexington, North Carolina, pork barbecue inspired him to create this spicy-hot vinegar marinade for chicken. *(pictured on page 78)*

- 2 cups cider vinegar
- ¼ cup firmly packed dark brown sugar
- ¼ cup vegetable oil
- 3 tablespoons dried crushed red pepper
- 4 teaspoons salt
- 2 teaspoons pepper
- 2 (2½- to 3-pound) cut-up whole chickens*

Stir together first 6 ingredients until blended.

Place half each of vinegar mixture and chicken in a large zip-top plastic freezer bag; seal. Repeat procedure with remaining vinegar mixture and chicken, placing in a separate zip-top plastic freezer bag. Chill chicken at least 2 hours or up to 8 hours, turning occasionally.

Remove chicken from marinade, discarding marinade.

Grill chicken, covered with grill lid, over medium-high heat (350° to 400°) 35 to 40 minutes or until done, turning occasionally. **Makes** 8 to 10 servings.

*Substitute 8 skinned and boned chicken breasts and 8 skinned and boned chicken thighs for whole chickens, if desired. Chill in marinade at least 1 to 2 hours, turning occasionally. Grill chicken, covered with grill lid, over medium-high heat (350° to 400°) 4 to 5 minutes on each side or until done.

LARRY ELDER
CHARLOTTE, NORTH CAROLINA

Spinach-and-Strawberry Salad

family favorite • fast fixin's

Prep: 10 min. *(pictured on pages 78 and 79)*

2 (6-ounce) packages fresh baby
    spinach
2 pints fresh strawberries, sliced
Sesame-Poppy Seed Dressing
Toppings: chopped cooked bacon,
    chopped fresh broccoli,
    blanched sugar snap peas,
    sliced red onion

Combine baby spinach and strawberries in a large bowl; toss with ½ cup Sesame-Poppy Seed Dressing just before serving. Serve with remaining dressing and desired toppings. **Makes** 8 to 10 servings.

Sesame-Poppy Seed Dressing:

make ahead

Prep: 5 min., Chill: 24 hrs.

1 cup sugar
½ cup cider vinegar
1 tablespoon minced onion
½ teaspoon Worcestershire sauce
¼ teaspoon salt
1 cup vegetable oil
¼ cup sesame seeds, toasted
2 tablespoons poppy seeds

Pulse first 5 ingredients in a blender 2 or 3 times or until smooth. With blender running, add oil in a slow, steady stream; process until smooth. Stir in seeds; chill 24 hours. **Makes** about 2½ cups.

SHIRLEY DELCOUR
KNOXVILLE, TENNESSEE

Oven-Roasted Asparagus

family favorite • fast fixin's

Prep: 10 min., Bake: 10 min. *(pictured on page 78)*

3 pounds fresh asparagus
2 tablespoons olive oil
3 garlic cloves, minced
¾ teaspoon salt
½ teaspoon freshly ground black
    pepper
½ cup slivered almonds, toasted

Snap off and discard tough ends of asparagus; place asparagus on a lightly greased baking sheet. Drizzle with olive oil; sprinkle with garlic, salt, and pepper. **Bake** at 350° for 10 minutes or to desired degree of tenderness. Transfer asparagus to a serving dish; sprinkle with almonds. **Makes** 8 to 10 servings.

MELANIE REID
PENSACOLA, FLORIDA

Double Citrus Tart

family favorite • make ahead

Prep: 30 min., Bake: 25 min., Chill: 4 hrs. *(pictured on page 79)*

1½ cups crushed gingersnap
    cookies
5 tablespoons butter, melted
2 tablespoons brown sugar
¼ teaspoon ground cinnamon
1 (14-ounce) can sweetened
    condensed milk
⅓ cup frozen orange juice
    concentrate, thawed
¼ cup fresh lemon juice
2 large eggs, separated
1 cup heavy whipping cream
3 tablespoons granulated sugar
Garnishes: fresh mint leaves,
    lemon and orange slices

Stir together first 4 ingredients. Press mixture evenly into a 9-inch tart pan with removable bottom; set aside.
Whisk together sweetened condensed milk, orange juice concentrate, lemon juice, and egg yolks until blended.
Beat egg whites at medium speed with an electric mixer until stiff peaks form; fold into condensed milk mixture. Pour into prepared crust.
Bake at 325° for 20 to 25 minutes or just until filling is set. Remove to a wire rack, and let cool completely. Cover and chill at least 4 hours. Remove tart from pan, and place on a serving dish.
Beat whipping cream and granulated sugar at medium speed with an electric mixer until stiff peaks form. Dollop around edges of tart; garnish, if desired. **Makes** 8 to 10 servings.

MARY ANN LEE
MARCO ISLAND, FLORIDA

Hooked on Catfish

The clean, slightly sweet flavor of catfish makes it perfect with just about anything. Farmed in the South, it's widely available and affordable. Serve it as an entrée with a tangy lemon sauce or in a creamy-spicy appetizer—both dishes are sure to make you a catfish fan.

Layered Catfish Dip

fast fixin's

Prep: 15 min., Cook: 5 min.

3 cups water
2 (8-ounce) catfish fillets
1 (8-ounce) package cream cheese,
    softened
1 (3-ounce) package cream cheese,
    softened
2 tablespoons Worcestershire
    sauce
2 tablespoons mayonnaise
1 tablespoon lemon juice
⅛ teaspoon garlic salt
⅓ cup chopped onion
1 cup chili sauce
Garnish: fresh lemon slice
Assorted crackers

Bring 3 cups water to a boil in a large skillet; add catfish, and return to a boil. Cover, reduce heat, and simmer 5 minutes or until fish flakes with a fork. Remove from skillet; drain well, and cool slightly. Flake fish with a fork.
Stir together both packages cream cheese and next 4 ingredients until blended. Stir in onion. Spread cream cheese mixture in a shallow dish. Add chili sauce, and top with pieces of fish. Garnish, if desired. Serve with crackers. **Makes** 12 appetizer servings.

THE CATFISH INSTITUTE
INDIANOLA, MISSISSIPPI

PECAN CATFISH WITH LEMON SAUCE

Prep: 20 min., Chill: 8 hrs., Cook: 16 min.

3 cups milk
⅛ teaspoon hot sauce
4 (6-ounce) catfish fillets
1 large egg, lightly beaten
¾ cup all-purpose flour
2 teaspoons salt
1 teaspoon ground red pepper
1 teaspoon ground black pepper
1 cup pecans, finely chopped
Vegetable oil
½ cup dry white wine or chicken broth
½ cup whipping cream
¼ cup lemon juice
1 tablespoon all-purpose flour
¼ teaspoon garlic powder
2 tablespoons butter or margarine, cut into pieces

Combine milk and hot sauce in a shallow dish; add catfish. Cover and chill 8 hours, turning occasionally.

Remove catfish from milk mixture. Whisk egg into milk mixture until blended.

Combine ¾ cup flour and next 3 ingredients; dredge catfish in flour mixture, shaking off excess. Dip catfish in egg mixture; coat with pecans.

Pour oil to a depth of 2 inches into a Dutch oven; heat to 360°. Fry catfish 3 minutes on each side or until it flakes with a fork. Drain fish on paper towels.

Bring wine, whipping cream, and lemon juice to a boil, stirring constantly. Whisk in 1 tablespoon flour and garlic powder, and simmer, stirring often, 8 to 10 minutes or until thickened. Remove from heat; whisk in butter. Serve over fish. **Makes** 4 servings.

MARY PAPPAS
RICHMOND, VIRGINIA

Good for the Soul

These freezeable recipes are meant for sharing.

Congregation members of Church of the Highlands in Birmingham know they can count on each other. Led by Duane Donner, a handful of worshippers formed a group called Cooking for the King, which convenes monthly to cook and freeze meals. If congregants or anyone they know experience sickness, loss, or the birth of a new child, the group is there to provide home-cooked meals. Duane's background as a food entrepreneur and founder of Creoles' Market, a frozen packaged food business, makes him an ideal leader for the cooking group. Create your own cooking community, and reach out to those around you.

TRADITIONAL CRAWFISH ÉTOUFFÉE

freezeable • make ahead

Prep: 25 min., Cook: 50 min.

1 cup uncooked long-grain rice
10 tablespoons butter, divided
1 pound frozen cooked peeled crawfish tails, thawed and drained
1 medium onion, chopped
1 green bell pepper, chopped
3 celery ribs, chopped
4 garlic cloves, minced
6 tablespoons all-purpose flour
2¾ cups chicken broth
¼ cup chopped green onions
2 tablespoons chopped fresh parsley
1 tablespoon salt-free Cajun seasoning
¼ teaspoon salt
¼ teaspoon ground red pepper

Prepare rice according to package directions.

Melt 4 tablespoons butter in a large Dutch oven over medium-high heat; add crawfish, and cook 5 minutes or until thoroughly heated. Remove crawfish, and keep warm.

Add onion, bell pepper, and celery to Dutch oven. Cook over medium-high heat 8 minutes or until tender. Add garlic, and cook 1 minute. Remove vegetables, and keep warm.

Melt remaining 6 tablespoons butter in Dutch oven over medium heat. Add flour, and cook, stirring constantly, 20 minutes or until caramel colored. Reduce heat to low, and gradually stir in chicken broth and next 5 ingredients. Cook over medium heat 10 minutes or until slightly thickened. Stir in vegetables and crawfish; cook 5 minutes. Serve with rice. **Makes** 6 servings.

Note: To freeze, divide étouffée evenly into 3 (1-quart) zip-top freezer bags. Freeze up to 1 month. Thaw in refrigerator overnight. Remove from freezer bag, and warm in saucepan, stirring until thoroughly heated. Each bag contains about 2 servings.

Cajun Shrimp and Andouille Alfredo Sauce Over Pasta

freezeable • make ahead

Prep: 45 min., Cook: 40 min.

Duane also makes this dish with chicken. Substitute 3 cups chopped cooked chicken for shrimp. While the fettuccine cooks, start the sausage.

- 1 pound unpeeled, medium-size fresh shrimp
- 1 (12-ounce) package fettuccine
- ½ pound andouille sausage, chopped
- ½ cup butter
- 1 medium onion, chopped
- 1 small green bell pepper, chopped
- 4 celery ribs, chopped (about 1 cup)
- 4 garlic cloves, minced
- 3 tablespoons all-purpose flour
- 1½ tablespoons salt-free Cajun seasoning
- 2 cups chicken broth
- 1½ cups heavy cream
- 6 ounces pasteurized prepared cheese product, cubed
- ¾ cup chopped green onions
- ⅓ cup grated Parmesan cheese
- 3 tablespoons chopped fresh parsley

Peel shrimp, and devein, if desired. Set aside.

Prepare fettuccine according to package directions; drain pasta, and set aside.

Cook sausage in a large Dutch oven over medium heat 10 minutes or until browned; remove sausage, and drain, reserving 1 tablespoon drippings in Dutch oven. Set sausage aside.

Melt butter in drippings in Dutch oven over medium heat. Add shrimp, and cook 5 minutes or just until shrimp turn pink. Remove shrimp, and keep warm.

Add onion and next 3 ingredients; cook, stirring constantly, over medium heat 10 minutes. Stir in flour and Cajun seasoning. Cook over medium heat, 1 minute, stirring constantly. Gradually stir in chicken broth. Bring to a boil over medium-high heat, stirring occasionally. Boil 1 minute. Reduce heat to medium-low, and stir in heavy cream; cook over medium-low heat 8 minutes or until mixture simmers. Add pasteurized cheese cubes, sausage, and shrimp, stirring until cheese melts.

Stir in chopped green onions, Parmesan cheese, and chopped fresh parsley. Serve over hot cooked fettuccine. **Makes** 6 servings.

Note: For testing purposes only, we used Velveeta for pasteurized prepared cheese product. Freeze shrimp and andouille pasta in 3 (8¼- x 5¼- x 1-inch) disposable foil pans covered with aluminum foil. Place in zip-top plastic freezer bags. Freeze up to 1 month, if desired. Remove from freezer bag, and bake, covered, at 350° for 1 hour and 15 minutes. Or thaw in refrigerator overnight, and bake, covered, at 350° for 45 minutes. Each pan contains about 2 servings.

Garlic French Bread

fast fixin's • freezeable

Prep: 10 min., Bake: 20 min.

- ½ cup butter, melted
- 6 garlic cloves, pressed
- 1 teaspoon dried oregano
- ½ teaspoon dried parsley flakes
- 1 (16-ounce) loaf French bread

Combine first 4 ingredients.

Cut bread loaves in half horizontally. Brush cut sides evenly with garlic mixture. Wrap loaves in aluminum foil, and place on a baking sheet.

Bake at 350° for 10 minutes. Remove foil, and bake 10 more minutes or until lightly brown and crisp. Serve immediately. **Makes** 8 to 10 servings.

Note: For testing purposes only, we used Pepperidge Farm Twin French Bread Loaves. Freeze unbaked garlic bread, wrapped in aluminum foil and in a zip-top freezer bag, up to 1 month, if desired. Remove bread from freezer bag, place on a baking sheet, and bake at 375° for 20 minutes. Unwrap foil; bake 5 more minutes or until lightly brown.

Quick Crawfish Étouffée

freezeable • make ahead

Prep: 20 min., Cook: 21 min.

You can purchase frozen, cooked, peeled crawfish tails in the freezer section of your grocery store. Duane prefers Louisiana crawfish tails rather than Chinese ones. Visit **www.cajuncrawfish.com** to mail order.

- 1 cup uncooked long-grain rice
- ¼ cup butter or margarine
- 1 large onion, chopped
- 1 green bell pepper, chopped
- 4 celery ribs, chopped (about 1 cup)
- 4 garlic cloves, minced
- 1 (14.5-ounce) can chicken broth
- 1 (10¾-ounce) can cream of mushroom soup
- 1 tablespoon salt-free Cajun seasoning
- ⅛ to ¼ teaspoon ground red pepper
- 1 pound frozen cooked peeled crawfish tails, thawed and drained
- ¼ cup chopped green onions
- 3 tablespoons chopped fresh parsley

Prepare rice according to package directions.

Melt butter in a large cast-iron skillet or Dutch oven over medium heat. Add onion and next 3 ingredients; cook, stirring constantly, 8 minutes.

Stir together chicken broth and soup. Add to vegetable mixture. Stir in Cajun seasoning and ground red pepper.

Cook over medium-low heat 10 minutes, stirring occasionally. Stir in crawfish, green onions, and parsley; cook 3 minutes or until hot. Serve over rice. **Makes** 6 servings.

Note: To freeze, divide étouffée evenly into 3 (1-quart) zip-top freezer bags. Freeze up to 1 month. Thaw in refrigerator overnight. Remove from freezer bag, and warm in a saucepan, stirring until thoroughly heated. Each bag contains about 2 servings.

Tex-Mex Tonight

Put some spice back into dinner.

FIESTA SALAD

family favorite

Prep: 20 min., Cook: 20 min.

Simply for fun, layer the Fiesta Salad in a large sundae dish or even a banana split boat. Hang a tomato wedge on the rim for garnish, if desired. *(pictured on page 75)*

- **1 pound lean ground beef**
- **1 pound ground pork**
- **¾ cup water**
- **½ (2-ounce) package onion soup-and-dip mix**
- **1 tablespoon chili powder**
- **2 large ripe avocados**
- **1 (8-ounce) container French onion dip**
- **1½ teaspoons lemon juice**
- **1 (9-ounce) bag tortilla chips, divided**
- **2 (5-ounce) packages mixed salad greens**
- **1 (12-ounce) jar pico de gallo or chunky salsa**
- **1 cup (4 ounces) shredded Cheddar cheese**
- **1 (2¼-ounce) can sliced ripe black olives, drained**
- **Garnish: tomato wedges**

Cook ground beef and pork in a large skillet over medium-high heat, stirring until meat crumbles and is no longer pink; drain and return to skillet. Stir in ¾ cup water, onion soup-and-dip mix, and chili powder; reduce heat, and simmer 6 to 7 minutes or until liquid evaporates. Remove from heat, and set aside.

Cut avocados in half. Scoop pulp into a bowl; mash with a fork just until slightly chunky. Stir in onion dip and lemon juice. Coarsely crush half of tortilla chips.

Spread crushed chips evenly in 8 serving dishes; top with salad greens, meat mixture, and avocado mixture. Spoon ¼ cup pico de gallo onto each salad, and sprinkle evenly with cheese and olives. Garnish, if desired. Serve immediately with remaining half of chips. **Makes** 8 servings.

Note: For testing purposes only, we used Lipton Recipe Secrets Onion Recipe Soup & Dip Mix for onion soup-and-dip mix.

JUDIE MOORE
GERMANTOWN, TENNESSEE

MINI-DOUGHNUT STACKS

family favorite • fast fixin's

Prep: 10 min., Broil: 4 min.

- **16 miniature powdered sugar doughnuts**
- **2 tablespoons butter, softened**
- **1 pint chocolate-cherry ice cream**
- **Toppings: hot fudge sauce, whipped cream, maraschino cherries with stems**

Cut doughnuts in half horizontally; spread cut sides evenly with butter. Place buttered sides up on a lightly greased baking sheet.

Broil doughnut halves 3 inches from heat 3 to 4 minutes or until golden brown.

Place 1 to 4 doughnut halves on each serving plate. Top with a small scoop of ice cream. Serve with desired toppings. **Makes** 8 servings.

Note: For testing purposes only, we used Ben & Jerry's Cherry Garcia Ice Cream.

LINDA SCHEND
KENOSHA, WISCONSIN

Family-Favorite Casseroles

You can find what you need for a Mexican feast at almost any supermarket.

TEX-MEX LASAGNA

family favorite • make ahead

Prep: 20 min., Cook: 8 min., Bake: 50 min., Stand: 10 min.

To make ahead, cover and chill unbaked lasagna overnight. Let stand at room temperature 30 minutes. Bake, uncovered, as directed. Serve with sour cream and salsa, if desired.

- **1 pound ground beef**
- **1 (15-ounce) container ricotta cheese**
- **1¾ cups (7 ounces) shredded Monterey Jack cheese, divided**
- **12 egg roll wrappers**
- **1 (16-ounce) can fat-free refried beans**
- **3½ cups chunky salsa**
- **1 large avocado, thinly sliced**

Cook ground beef in a skillet over medium-high heat, stirring until it crumbles and is no longer pink. Drain and set aside.

Stir together ricotta cheese and 1 cup shredded Monterey Jack cheese.

Layer a lightly greased 13- x 9-inch baking dish with 3 egg roll wrappers and one-third each of ground beef, ricotta mixture, and beans; top with ½ cup salsa. Repeat layers twice with egg roll wrappers, beef, ricotta mixture, beans, and salsa. Top with remaining 3 egg roll wrappers and 2 cups salsa.

Bake at 350° for 40 minutes. Sprinkle with remaining ¾ cup Monterey Jack cheese, and bake 10 more minutes or until cheese melts. Let stand 10 minutes before serving. Arrange avocado slices over lasagna. **Makes** 10 to 12 servings.

JENNI DISE
PHOENIX, ARIZONA

CHICKEN-AND-ARTICHOKE OLÉ

family favorite

Prep: 10 min., Cook: 2 min., Bake: 30 min.

- **4 skinned and boned chicken breasts**
- **½ teaspoon salt**
- **½ teaspoon pepper**
- **1 tablespoon canola oil**
- **1 (14-ounce) can quartered artichoke hearts, rinsed and drained**
- **1 (10¾-ounce) can cream of chicken soup**
- **¾ cup Homemade Salsa**
- **1 teaspoon ground cumin**
- **½ teaspoon ground chipotle pepper seasoning (optional)**
- **¼ cup diced red bell pepper (optional)**
- **1 (2¼-ounce) can sliced ripe black olives, drained**
- **¼ cup chopped fresh cilantro**

Sprinkle chicken with salt and pepper.

Brown chicken in hot oil in a large skillet over medium-high heat. Remove from skillet, and place chicken in an 11- x 7-inch baking dish. Top with artichoke hearts.

Stir together soup, Homemade Salsa, cumin, and, if desired, ground chipotle seasoning and bell pepper. Pour sauce

over chicken mixture; sprinkle with sliced olives.

Bake at 350° for 30 minutes. Sprinkle with cilantro. **Makes** 4 servings.

HOMEMADE SALSA:
fast fixin's

Prep: 5 min.

Store leftover salsa in the refrigerator for a quick snack with chips.

- **1 (10-ounce) can diced tomatoes and green chiles**
- **½ small red onion, finely chopped**
- **¼ cup chopped fresh cilantro**
- **1 teaspoon ground cumin**
- **1 teaspoon lemon juice**

Combine all ingredients. Cover and chill until ready to serve. **Makes** 1½ cups.

TERRI FURRIE
LEXINGTON, KENTUCKY

SMOTHERED ENCHILADAS

family favorite

Prep: 10 min., Bake: 25 min.

- **2 pounds ground beef**
- **1 (1¼-ounce) package mild taco seasoning mix**
- **1 (4.5-ounce) can chopped green chiles, divided**
- **2 (10¾-ounce) cans cream of chicken soup**
- **1 (16-ounce) container sour cream**
- **8 (8-inch) flour tortillas**
- **2 cups (8 ounces) shredded Cheddar cheese**
- **Garnishes: Homemade Salsa (recipe above), sour cream, green onion curls, chopped fresh cilantro**

Cook ground beef in a large skillet, stirring until it crumbles and is no longer pink; drain. Stir in taco seasoning and half of green chiles; set aside.

Stir together remaining green chiles, soup, and sour cream. Pour half of mixture into a lightly greased 13- x 9-inch baking dish.

Spoon beef mixture evenly down centers of tortillas; roll up. Place seam sides

down over soup mixture in baking dish; top evenly with remaining soup mixture and cheese.

Bake at 350° for 25 minutes or until thoroughly heated. Garnish, if desired. **Makes** 8 servings.

SHARON MACHACEK
CEDAR RAPIDS, IOWA

Add Zest With Lemon

The delightful zing of fresh citrus transforms an ordinary recipe into an irresistible, gotta-have-it dish.

LEMON-WALNUT TEA BREAD

Prep: 15 min., Bake: 55 min., Stand: 15 min.

- **½ cup butter, softened**
- **1 cup sugar**
- **2 large eggs**
- **1½ cups all-purpose flour**
- **1½ teaspoons baking powder**
- **¼ teaspoon salt**
- **½ cup milk**
- **¾ cup chopped walnuts**
- **2 tablespoons grated lemon rind**
- **2 tablespoons fresh lemon juice**

Beat butter at medium speed with an electric mixer until fluffy; gradually add sugar, beating well. Add eggs, 1 at a time, beating until blended after each addition.

Combine flour, baking powder, and salt; add to butter mixture alternately with milk, beginning and ending with flour mixture. Beat at low speed until blended after each addition. Stir in walnuts, lemon rind, and lemon juice. Pour batter into a greased and floured 9- x 5-inch loafpan.

Bake at 350° for 50 to 55 minutes or until a wooden pick inserted in center comes out clean. Cool in pan on a wire rack 10 to 15 minutes; remove from pan, and cool completely on wire rack. **Makes** 8 to 10 servings.

Entertaining That's Simple

If you're looking for a quick, creative way to entertain, serve a few good cheeses along with complementary wine, fruit, olives, and nuts. These flavorful ingredients create a welcoming party with almost no preparation. Laura Werlin, author of *The All American Cheese and Wine Book* (Stewart, Tabori & Chang, 2003) and *The New American Cheese* (Stewart, Tabori & Chang, 2000) says, "The most basic supermarkets are stocking better cheeses. There's no reason to fall back on bricks of cheese without a whole lot of flavor." She suggests these tips for entertaining with cheese.

■ Try some you've never tasted before. We were impressed with the cheese selection, ready-made trays, prices, and fun cheese-of-the-month club at **www.artisanalcheese.com.**

■ Love Cheddar? Buy the best you can find, says Laura. She suggests going to a nearby farmers market or a local cheesemaker and buying their specialty. The best Cheddars are sold in wedges with a rind versus vacuum-sealed and shaped like a brick.

■ Serve cheese with bread instead of crackers. "Crackers have a flavor all their own and keep the flavor away from cheese," says Laura.

■ Use a different knife to serve each cheese. You don't want delicate cheeses such as a mild fresh goat cheese tasting like a bold blue cheese.

■ Choose a few of these accompaniments: nuts (seasoned or plain); dried fruit such as apricots, dates, and figs; and sliced fresh fruit such as Bosc pears or Gala apples. Chutneys and fruit butters also pair nicely with cheese. If you don't have time to prepare them from scratch, purchase jars from the gourmet section of your supermarket or a specialty shop.

Some of Laura's favorite cheesemakers include Chef John Folse's Bittersweet Plantation Dairy in Gonzales, Louisiana, (**www.jfolse.com**) and Sweet Grass Dairy in Thomasville, Georgia,

(**www.sweetgrassdairy.com**). We love John's Fleur-de-Lis Fromage Triple Cream Cheese; it's irresistibly creamy and buttery. Also try Pure Luck cheeses from Texas. They produce chèvre (in various flavors), feta, and Claire de Lune, a semifirm ripened cheese they say tastes like Brie, slices like Cheddar, and can be grated like Parmesan (**www.purelucktexas.com**).

CANDIED WALNUTS

freezeable • make ahead

Prep: 10 min., Cook: 5 min., Bake: 22 min.

These sweet and crunchy nuts are scrumptious when paired with a creamy Brie or Camembert or sprinkled over salad. They freeze beautifully in a zip-top plastic freezer bag for up to 3 months.

  ½ **cup powdered sugar**
  ¼ **teaspoon salt**
  ¼ **teaspoon ground red pepper**
  4 cups water
  2¼ **cups (8 ounces) walnut halves**

Combine first 3 ingredients in a medium bowl.

Bring 4 cups water to a boil in a medium saucepan. Add walnuts, and cook 3 minutes; drain. Immediately place walnuts in bowl with sugar mixture, tossing to coat. Place walnuts in a single layer on a lightly greased jelly-roll pan.

Bake at 350° for 20 to 22 minutes or until deep golden brown. Cool completely in pan. Store in an airtight container. **Makes** about 2 cups.

LAURA WERLIN
THE NEW AMERICAN CHEESE

Serving Secret

Ice down sparkling or white wine in a large clear glass bowl, and float a few rosebuds or other fresh edible flowers to dress it up. Tie a napkin around the bottle's neck to catch drips.

Serving Savvy

■ Got friends coming over for wine and cheese? Limit cheese choices to three or four for a smaller group and five or six for a larger crowd.

■ Not sure which cheeses to have? Serve a mild, a sharp, and a pungent cheese (or two of each). For example, offer a fresh goat cheese or Brie, an aged Cheddar or Spanish Manchego, and a blue cheese such as Maytag Blue or Roquefort. Alternately, you could serve a cheese (or two) made from each milk type: cow, goat, and sheep. Goat and sheep's milk cheeses tend to be tangy. Roquefort and Pecorino Romano are sheep's milk cheeses. Or serve four or five types of same variety cheeses. You may feature all blue cheeses or all soft-ripened cheeses such as Brie or Camembert.

■ A good rule of thumb is to buy 4 to 5 ounces of cheese per person. A 750-ml bottle of wine will yield about 6 glasses; you can plan on 1 or 2 glasses of wine per person.

■ Steve Jenkins, author of *Cheese Primer* (Workman Publishing, 1996), suggests serving each cheese on an individual wooden cutting board, plate, or piece of marble instead of placing them all on one platter. If you do use one serving tray, separate the cheeses as much as possible so the mild cheeses such as Brie won't taste like a pungent cheese such as Asiago or Taleggio.

■ Always serve cheeses at room temperature (around 70°) to taste their full flavor. Remove from the refrigerator an hour before the gathering. If you have any left, wrap them individually in fresh plastic wrap to get a good seal.

■ Is there an order to cutting and enjoying cheese? Cheese experts recommend starting from the hardest to the softest and saving the blues for last.

Fruity Thirst Quenchers

Although summertime is not yet upon us, it'll soon come rushing in like shoppers stampeding a moonlight madness sale. Not to worry. We're poised and ready—knowing that an ice-cold beverage is a perfect way to rejuvenate. These recipes are great candidates for the job. Freeze some in ice-cube trays, and use the cubes to chill your drinks. They'll help keep the temperature and flavor just right from the first sip to the last. These drinks also make a great nonalcoholic option for your guests at our easy wine-and-cheese party on the facing page.

WHITE GRAPE-AND-ORANGE COOLER

fast fixin's

Prep: 5 min., Cook: 3 min., Chill: 2 hrs.

1 cup water
⅓ cup sugar
1 cup white grape juice
½ cup orange juice
1 (1-liter) bottle ginger ale, chilled
Garnish: orange slices

Bring 1 cup water and sugar to a boil over medium-high heat, and cook, stirring often, 3 minutes or until sugar dissolves. Remove from heat, and cool.
Stir in juices, and chill 2 hours. Stir in ginger ale just before serving. Serve over ice. Garnish, if desired. **Makes** about 6½ cups.

ROSEMARY JOHNSON
IRONDALE, ALABAMA

FIZZY RASPBERRY LEMONADE

fast fixin's

Prep: 10 min.

1 (12-ounce) can frozen lemonade concentrate, thawed and undiluted
1 (10-ounce) package frozen raspberries, partially thawed
3 tablespoons sugar
1 (1-liter) bottle club soda, chilled

Process first 3 ingredients in a blender until smooth, stopping to scrape down sides.
Pour raspberry mixture through a wire-mesh strainer into a large pitcher, discarding seeds; stir in club soda. Serve over ice. **Makes** about 7 cups.

Fizzy Strawberry Lemonade: Substitute 1 (10-ounce) package frozen strawberries, partially thawed, for frozen raspberries. Prepare recipe as directed. Prep: 10 min.

BARBARA SHERRER
BAY CITY, TEXAS

PINEAPPLE-ORANGE HERB TEA

make ahead

Prep: 10 min., Steep: 20 min., Chill: 1 hr.

This fruity drink is as pretty as it is tasty.

2 cups boiling water
12 regular-size herb tea bags
1 (11.5-ounce) can frozen pineapple-orange juice concentrate, thawed and undiluted
2 cups lemon-lime soft drink, chilled

Pour 2 cups boiling water over tea bags, and steep 20 minutes. Remove tea bags; discard. Chill tea 1 hour.
Stir in juice concentrate and soft drink; serve over ice. **Makes** about 6 cups.

Cranberry-Raspberry Herb Tea: Substitute 1 (11.5-ounce) can frozen cranberry-raspberry juice cocktail concentrate, thawed and undiluted, for pineapple-orange juice concentrate.

Note: For testing purposes only, we used Celestial Seasonings Red Zinger Natural Herb Tea.

CRANBERRY-APPLE SPARKLER

fast fixin's • make ahead

Prep: 5 min.

Sparkling apple juice can be found on the juice aisle of your grocery store.

1 (12-ounce) can frozen cranberry juice concentrate, thawed
½ (12-ounce) can frozen apple juice concentrate, thawed and undiluted
5 (10-ounce) bottles 100% sparkling apple juice, chilled
Garnish: Granny Smith apple slices

Stir together first 3 ingredients. Serve over ice; garnish, if desired. **Makes** about 8½ cups.

Irresistible Ice-Cream Sandwiches

If you can't resist the jingle of the ice-cream truck coming down the street, you'll love these easy, creamy goodies from our readers. Soften them at room temperature 15 minutes before serving.

EASY CHOCOLATE-MINT ICE-CREAM SANDWICHES

make ahead

Prep: 15 min.; Freeze: 1 hr., 30 min.

This recipe uses packaged chewy cookies, but check your local bakery for freshly baked ones if you prefer.

- **2 pints vanilla ice cream, softened**
- **15 mint-and-cream-filled chocolate sandwich cookies, chopped**
- **1 (8.5-ounce) package large chewy chocolate cookies**

Stir together ice cream and cookie pieces. Freeze 30 minutes. Spread ice cream evenly on 1 side of 5 large chewy cookies; top with remaining large chewy cookies. Place in plastic or wax paper sandwich bags, and freeze at least 1 hour. **Makes** 5 servings.

Note: For testing purposes only, we used Oreo Double Delight Mint 'n Creme chocolate sandwich cookies and Archway Original Dutch Cocoa chocolate cookies.

Butter Pecan Ice-Cream Sandwiches: Omit mint-and-cream-filled sandwich cookies. Substitute 2 pints butter pecan ice cream for vanilla ice cream and 1 (8.75-ounce) package large chewy sugar cookies for chewy chocolate cookies. Proceed as directed.

Mocha-Almond-Fudge Ice-Cream Sandwiches: Omit mint-and-cream-filled chocolate sandwich cookies. Substitute 2 pints mocha-flavored ice cream with chocolate-covered almonds for vanilla ice cream. Proceed as directed. **Note:** For testing purposes only, we used Starbucks Coffee Almond Fudge Ice Cream.

Oatmeal-Rum-Raisin Ice-Cream Sandwiches: Omit mint-and-cream-filled sandwich cookies. Substitute 1 (8.75-ounce) package large chewy oatmeal cookies for chewy chocolate cookies. Pour $\frac{1}{4}$ cup dark rum over $\frac{1}{2}$ cup golden raisins; let stand 2 hours. Drain and discard rum. Stir rum-soaked raisins into softened ice cream, and proceed as directed.

LESLIE MEADOWS
MONTGOMERY, ALABAMA

PEANUTTY ICE-CREAM SANDWICHES

make ahead

Prep: 20 min.; Cook: 5 min.; Bake: 11 min.;
Freeze: 1 hr., 30 min.

- **$\frac{2}{3}$ cup butter or margarine**
- **2 cups quick-cooking oats, uncooked**
- **$\frac{3}{4}$ cup firmly packed dark brown sugar**
- **$\frac{1}{2}$ cup finely chopped dry-roasted peanuts**
- **1 large egg, lightly beaten**
- **$\frac{1}{4}$ cup all-purpose flour**
- **1 teaspoon vanilla extract**
- **$\frac{1}{4}$ teaspoon baking powder**
- **$\frac{1}{4}$ teaspoon salt**
- **$\frac{1}{2}$ cup chunky peanut butter**
- **3 cups vanilla ice cream, softened**
- **1 cup coarsely chopped dry-roasted peanuts**

Melt butter in a Dutch oven over medium heat. Remove from heat, and stir in oats and next 7 ingredients.
Drop oat mixture by tablespoonfuls 3 inches apart onto a parchment paper-lined baking sheet. Spread each dollop of cookie batter to form a 3-inch circle. Bake at 350° for 9 to 11 minutes or until edges are golden. Remove from pan, and cool completely on a wire rack.

Swirl peanut butter into softened ice cream. Freeze 30 minutes. Scoop ice cream evenly on flat sides of half of cookies; top with remaining cookies, flat sides down. Roll sides of sandwiches in coarsely chopped peanuts. Place in plastic or wax paper sandwich bags, and freeze at least 1 hour. **Makes** 9 servings.

Note: Do not substitute a greased baking sheet for parchment paper. Cookies will slide and tear.

DIANE SPARROW
OSAGE, IOWA

WAFFLE TACO SUNDAES

make ahead

Prep: 15 min.; Freeze: 1 hr., 30 min.

Microwave 8 round frozen waffles, in 2 batches, in a single layer at HIGH 1 to 2 minutes or just until warm. Gently fold each waffle in half to form a taco; place in an 11- x 7-inch baking dish, pressing waffles together to hold shape. Stir together 1 quart chocolate ice cream, softened, and $\frac{1}{2}$ cup miniature marshmallows. Freeze 30 minutes. Spoon ice cream evenly into waffles; cover and freeze 1 hour or until firm. Drizzle with fudge sauce, and top with maraschino cherries and candy sprinkles. **Makes** 8 servings.

MILDRED BICKLEY
BRISTOL, VIRGINIA

Lollipop Cookies

Just three essentials—a simple sugar cookie dough, wooden craft sticks, and edible decorations—are all you need to create these fun-to-eat favors. You can make them a few days in advance and store in a cool, dry place.

It's best to serve these cookies in the milder seasons; a hot Southern summer may cause them to melt and fall apart.

COOKIES ON A STICK

make ahead

Prep: 1 hr., Freeze: 30 min., Bake: 16 min. per batch, Other: 5 min.

Yields will vary depending on the sizes and shapes of your cookie cutters.

   1 cup butter, softened
   ¾ cup sugar
   2 egg yolks
   1 teaspoon vanilla extract
   2¼ cups all-purpose flour
   ¼ teaspoon salt
   Wooden craft sticks or lollipop
      sticks
   Easy Microwave Frosting
   Decorations: colored sugar, pastel
      nonpareils, pastel confetti,
      pastel eggs, pastel jimmies

Beat butter and sugar at medium speed with an electric mixer about 5 minutes or until creamy. Add egg yolks and vanilla, beating until blended. Combine flour and salt; gradually add to butter mixture, beating until blended after each addition. Cover and freeze 30 minutes.

Roll dough to a ⅜-inch thickness on a lightly floured surface. Cut desired shapes using favorite seasonal cutters; place on lightly greased baking sheets, allowing space for craft sticks. Insert 1 craft stick into bottom of each cookie. **Bake** at 350° for 10 to 16 minutes or until edges are golden. (Baking times may vary with different cookie shapes and sizes.) Cool 5 minutes on baking sheets. Slip a metal spatula under cookies to loosen; cool completely on baking sheets.

Spread a generous amount of Easy Microwave Frosting where each stick and cookie are joined to ensure stability. Let dry about 30 minutes. Spread a thin layer of Easy Microwave Frosting on front side of each cookie, and sprinkle with desired decorations before frosting dries; then dry completely. Store in a cool, dry place. **Makes** 7 to 8 dozen.

Chocolate Cookies on a Stick: Reduce all-purpose flour to 1¾ cups, and add ½ cup unsweetened cocoa. Proceed with recipe as directed.

Note: Do not substitute refrigerated cookie dough for this recipe. It contains leavening and tends to spread as it bakes, distorting cookie shapes.

EASY MICROWAVE FROSTING:

fast fixin's

Prep: 10 min.
Decorate cookies however you wish. Use this recipe for a quick colored coating, and embellish with candies and sprinkles.

Microwave 1 (24-ounce) package vanilla candy coating in a glass bowl at HIGH for 2 minutes, stirring every 30 seconds until melted. Divide melted candy coating among individual bowls. (The number of bowls will depend on how many colors you wish to make.) Stir liquid food coloring in desired colors into each bowl. Reheat colored coating as needed. **Makes** 4 cups.

Decorating Fun

■ For a clever centerpiece, put cookies in bud vases filled with small candies.
■ Color your cookies with food-safe markers. Wilton offers FoodWriter Edible Color Markers, available at **www.wilton.com.**
■ Visit the baking aisle of your grocery store, and you'll find a variety of decorating options—from prepackaged colored frostings to self-adhesive edible adornments.
■ Create festive party favors for other holiday events by simply changing your color palette and cookie shape. Make pumpkins and leaves for a fall festival, or decorate edible ornaments and trees for a yuletide celebration.
■ Wrap each finished cookie with cellophane, and tie with colorful ribbon.

You'll Love This Easy-Does-It Cake

This dessert is called a Pig Pickin' Cake because its citrus lift is the perfect ending to a barbecue or pig pickin'. This version from Test Kitchens professional Pam Lolley's mother-in-law captured our taste buds. You'll find it easy to make and delicious.

PIG PICKIN' CAKE

Prep: 15 min., Bake: 30 min., Chill: 4 hrs.

   1 (18.25-ounce) package yellow
      cake mix
   ⅓ cup water
   ⅓ cup vegetable oil
   3 large eggs
   1 (11-ounce) can mandarin
      oranges, drained
   1 (15-ounce) can crushed
      pineapple, undrained
   1 (3.4-ounce) package vanilla
      instant pudding mix
   1 (12-ounce) container frozen
      whipped topping, thawed
   ½ cup chopped pecans
   Garnish: chopped pecans

Beat first 4 ingredients in a large bowl at medium speed with an electric mixer until blended. Stir in oranges. Pour batter into 3 greased and floured 8-inch round cakepans. (Layers will be thin.) **Bake** at 350° for 25 to 30 minutes or until a wooden pick inserted in center comes out clean. Cool layers in pans on wire racks 10 minutes; remove layers from pans, and let cool completely on wire racks.

Stir together crushed pineapple and next 3 ingredients. Spread pineapple mixture evenly between layers and on top of cake. Chill cake 3 to 4 hours. Garnish, if desired. Store cake in refrigerator. **Makes** 12 servings.

RUTH LOLLEY
WINNSBORO, LOUISIANA

March Madness

As the NCAA basketball tournaments heat up, score points with these winning, easy-does-it recipes.

To start the championship season of round ball, look no further than these recipes to feed your family and friends.

SLOW-COOKER BARBECUE BEEF SANDWICHES

freezeable • make ahead

Prep: 15 min., Cook: 7 hrs.

Make your favorite creamy coleslaw to serve with or on this barbecue sandwich. Freeze any leftover meat for up to 1 month.

1 (3½-pound) eye-of-round roast, cut in half vertically
2 teaspoons salt, divided
2 garlic cloves, pressed
1 (10-ounce) can condensed beef broth
1 cup ketchup
½ cup firmly packed brown sugar
½ cup lemon juice
3 tablespoons steak sauce
1 teaspoon coarse ground pepper
1 teaspoon Worcestershire sauce
12 kaiser rolls or sandwich buns
Dill pickle slices

Sprinkle beef with 1 teaspoon salt.
Stir together remaining 1 teaspoon salt, garlic, and next 7 ingredients. Pour half of mixture into a 5½-quart slow cooker. Place beef in slow cooker, and pour remaining mixture over beef.
Cover and cook on HIGH 7 hours.
Shred beef in slow cooker with two forks. Serve in rolls or buns with dill pickle slices. **Makes** 12 servings.

BUFFALO WINGS

make ahead

Prep: 35 min.; Bake: 1 hr., 5 min.

You can bake both pans of wings at the same time. Just switch rack levels and turn pans halfway through the baking times. To make the wings spicier, add more hot sauce to the recipe or at the table. Serve assorted raw veggies alongside the wings and Ranch dressing.

6 pounds chicken wings *
4 (0.7-ounce) envelopes Italian dressing mix, divided
1 cup butter, melted
1 to 1½ cups hot sauce
¼ cup lemon juice
1 teaspoon dried basil
Ranch dressing

Cut off wing tips, and discard; cut chicken wings in half at joint, if desired. Place 1 package Italian dressing mix in a large zip-top plastic bag; add half of wings, and shake to coat. Arrange coated wings in a single layer on a lightly greased rack in an aluminum foil-lined 15- x 10-inch jelly-roll pan. Repeat procedure with 1 package Italian dressing mix, remaining half of wings, and another jelly-roll pan.
Bake at 425° for 35 minutes or until browned. Remove pans from oven, and reduce heat to 350°.
Stir together remaining 2 packages Italian dressing mix, butter, and next 3 ingredients in a large bowl; add wings, and toss until evenly coated. Return wings to racks in pans, and bake at 350° for 30 more minutes. Serve with Ranch dressing. **Makes** 10 to 12 appetizer servings.

*** Substitute 2 (3-pound) packages frozen party-style chicken wings, thawed, if desired.

AMY STRAUTMAN
TUCSON, ARIZONA

CHILE-CHEESE LOGS

make ahead

Prep: 25 min., Chill: 2 hrs.

Make this zesty appetizer up to 3 days ahead.

2 (8-ounce) packages light cream cheese, softened
1 cup (4 ounces) shredded Cheddar cheese
3 green onions, finely chopped
3 canned chipotle peppers in adobo sauce
1 teaspoon adobo sauce from can
½ teaspoon Creole seasoning
½ teaspoon ground cumin
½ teaspoon chili powder
¼ teaspoon Worcestershire sauce
⅛ teaspoon hot sauce
½ cup chopped pecans, toasted
⅓ cup chopped fresh cilantro
Assorted crackers

Process first 10 ingredients in a food processor until smooth, stopping to scrape down sides. Divide cheese mixture into 2 equal portions; shape each portion into an 8-inch log.
Combine pecans and cilantro. Roll cheese logs evenly in pecan mixture; wrap in plastic wrap. Cover and chill at least 2 hours. Serve with assorted crackers. **Makes** 12 appetizer servings.

RUDIE SLAUGHTER
VIENNA, VIRGINIA

Ready, Set, Serve

Fresh, fun, and easy to make, congealed salads are back in style and better than ever. Longtime luncheon favorites, these do-ahead side dishes are also terrific for casual suppers.

RASPBERRY-TOMATO ASPIC

make ahead

Prep: 15 min., Cook: 5 min., Chill: 8 hrs.

- 1⅔ cups tomato juice
- 2 tablespoons sugar
- 2 tablespoons finely chopped fresh mint
- 2 tablespoons red wine vinegar
- 2 tablespoons fresh lemon juice
- ½ bay leaf
- ⅛ teaspoon crushed dried rosemary
- 1 envelope unflavored gelatin
- ½ cup cold water
- 1 (3-ounce) package raspberry-flavored gelatin
- Garnishes: fresh mint sprigs, lemon slices
- Chicken or Shrimp Salad

Bring first 7 ingredients to a boil in a large saucepan; reduce heat, and simmer 5 minutes. Pour tomato juice mixture through a wire-mesh strainer into a large bowl, discarding solids.

Sprinkle unflavored gelatin over ½ cup cold water; let stand 1 minute. Stir softened gelatin mixture into tomato juice mixture, stirring until gelatin dissolves.

Prepare raspberry-flavored gelatin according to package directions; do not chill. Add to tomato juice mixture, stirring until combined. Pour mixture into 10 (6-ounce) punch cups; chill 8 hours or until firm. Garnish, if desired. Serve with Chicken or Shrimp Salad. **Makes** 10 servings.

Chicken Salad: Stir together 6 cups chopped cooked chicken; 1¼ cups mayonnaise; 6 thinly sliced green onions; 3 celery ribs, diced; and salt and pepper to taste. Sprinkle with chopped pecans, if desired. **Makes** 10 servings. Prep: 15 min.

Shrimp Salad: Stir together 6 cups chopped cooked shrimp; 1¼ cups mayonnaise; 6 thinly sliced green onions; 3 celery ribs, diced; 3 teaspoons grated lemon rind; ½ teaspoon ground red pepper; and salt and black pepper to taste. **Makes** 10 servings. Prep: 15 min.

LA JUAN COWARD
JASPER, TEXAS

A Sure Thing

A few insider tips from our Test Kitchen professionals guarantee success with gelatin.

■ Envelopes of unflavored gelatin are as easy to use as the familiar fruit-flavored varieties, with one quick difference. Rather than dissolving directly in boiling water, unflavored gelatin is first sprinkled over a small amount of cold water and allowed to stand for a minute until softened. It's an oh-so-simple procedure, similar to dissolving cornstarch in cold water before adding to hot liquids.

■ Cool gelatin mixtures to room temperature before folding in cold ingredients such as whipped topping.

■ One envelope of plain gelatin is all that's needed to set 2 cups of liquid. Just follow the package directions, and you can turn natural fruit juices into refreshingly light congealed salads.

■ An enzyme in fresh pineapple prevents gelatin from setting, so always use canned instead.

■ Acids such as lemon juice and vinegar interact with gelatin, producing a more fragile texture. Acids are fine to use in small amounts, but don't add more than 1 to 2 tablespoons per cup of liquid.

■ Congealed salads can be chilled in decorative molds or divvied up into individual serving portions. A recipe calling for a 2-quart mold will yield about 8 cups of salad.

CRANBERRY-APPLE SALAD

make ahead

Prep: 15 min., Cook: 5 min., Chill: 8 hrs.

- 2 envelopes unflavored gelatin
- ¼ cup cold water
- 2 (16-ounce) cans whole-berry cranberry sauce
- ½ cup sugar
- 1 large apple, peeled and diced
- 1 celery rib, diced
- 1 cup chopped pecans, toasted

Sprinkle unflavored gelatin over ¼ cup cold water; let stand 1 minute. Stir together softened gelatin mixture, cranberry sauce, and sugar in a large saucepan, and cook over medium heat, stirring constantly, 5 minutes. Remove from heat, and stir in apple, celery, and pecans. Spoon mixture into a lightly greased 5-cup mold. Cover and chill 8 hours or until firm. **Makes** 6 to 8 servings.

GABRIELLE CHAMPAGNE
NEW ORLEANS, LOUISIANA

LEMON-PINEAPPLE SALAD

make ahead

Prep: 15 min., Chill: 9 hrs.

- 2 (3-ounce) packages lemon-flavored gelatin
- 2 cups boiling water
- 1 (21-ounce) can lemon pie filling
- 1 (8-ounce) container frozen whipped topping, thawed
- 1 (15-ounce) can crushed pineapple, undrained
- 2 teaspoons grated lemon rind

Stir together gelatin and 2 cups boiling water in a large bowl until dissolved. Chill 1 hour or until consistency of unbeaten egg whites. Whisk in pie filling and whipped topping until smooth. Fold in pineapple and lemon rind; spoon mixture into a lightly greased 2-quart mold or serving dish. Cover and chill 8 hours or until firm. **Makes** 8 to 10 servings.

JEAN STEPHENS
SHERMAN, WEST VIRGINIA

Bake These Southern Sides

If you can whisk an egg, then you can make these comforting vegetable-based casseroles.

Enjoy the light texture and rich flavors of these can't-miss dishes made with vegetables such as carrots and frozen spinach. Often referred to as Southern soufflés, these tasty sides combine cooked vegetables with a custardlike base of eggs and milk or cream. You won't have to fold in egg whites as in traditional soufflés—all you do is whisk in a few eggs and stir it all together.

Sweet Corn Pudding and Spinach Soufflé start with vegetables from the freezer section, and Carrot Soufflé uses a package of baby carrots, so you can enjoy all of these recipes year-round.

CARROT SOUFFLÉ

family favorite

Prep: 5 min., Cook: 24 min., Bake: 1 hr.

- **1 (16-ounce) package baby carrots***
- **3 large eggs**
- **1¼ cups sugar**
- **½ cup light sour cream**
- **¼ cup butter, softened**
- **¼ cup all-purpose flour**
- **1½ teaspoons baking powder**
- **¼ teaspoon ground cinnamon**

Cook carrots in boiling water to cover in a large saucepan 20 to 24 minutes or until tender. Drain well; cool.
Process carrots and eggs in a food processor until smooth, stopping to scrape down sides. Add sugar and remaining ingredients; process 30 seconds or until smooth. Pour mixture into a lightly greased 8-inch square baking dish.
Bake at 350° for 55 to 60 minutes or until set. **Makes** 6 servings.

*Substitute 1½ pounds carrots, sliced, if desired.

ANN OSTER
OCEAN PINES, MARYLAND

SPINACH SOUFFLÉ

family favorite

Prep: 15 min., Cook: 5 min., Bake: 35 min., Stand: 5 min.

Using fresh Parmesan makes a big difference in flavor and texture in this rich and cheesy soufflé.

- **1 (10-ounce) package frozen chopped spinach, thawed**
- **2 tablespoons butter**
- **1 medium onion, chopped (about ¾ cup)**
- **2 garlic cloves, minced**
- **3 large eggs**
- **2 tablespoons all-purpose flour**
- **½ teaspoon salt**
- **¼ teaspoon ground nutmeg**
- **¼ teaspoon pepper**
- **1 cup milk**
- **1 cup freshly grated Parmesan or Romano cheese**

Drain spinach well, pressing between paper towels to remove all excess liquid.
Melt butter in a large skillet over medium heat; add onion and garlic, and sauté 5 minutes or until garlic is lightly browned and onions are tender. Remove from heat, and stir in spinach until well blended; cool.
Whisk together eggs and next 4 ingredients in a large bowl. Whisk in milk and freshly grated Parmesan cheese; stir in spinach mixture, and pour into a lightly greased 8-inch square baking dish.
Bake at 350° for 33 to 35 minutes or until set. Let stand 5 minutes before serving. **Makes** 4 to 6 servings.

MRS. STAN LIVENGOOD
BARBOURSVILLE, VIRGINIA

SWEET CORN PUDDING

family favorite

Prep: 10 min.; Bake: 1 hr., 5 min.; Stand: 10 min.

The secret ingredient of this melt-in-your-mouth side is frozen cream-style corn.

- **1 cup fresh breadcrumbs**
- **6 tablespoons self-rising white cornmeal mix**
- **1½ tablespoons sugar**
- **½ teaspoon salt**
- **3 large eggs**
- **1¼ cups milk**
- **½ cup half-and-half**
- **2 tablespoons butter, melted**
- **1 (20-ounce) package frozen cream-style corn, thawed**
- **Garnish: green onions**

Combine first 4 ingredients in a large bowl.
Whisk eggs in a large bowl until pale and foamy; whisk in milk, half-and-half, and butter. Whisk egg mixture into breadcrumb mixture; stir in corn. Pour into a lightly greased 9-inch square baking dish.
Bake at 325° for 1 hour to 1 hour and 5 minutes or until set. Let stand 10 minutes before serving. Garnish, if desired. **Makes** 6 servings.

SUSAN FUTCH
VALDOSTA, GEORGIA

Speedy Steaks Fried Right

Whatever you call it—country-fried, chicken-fried, or minute steak—you're gonna love these affordable recipes.

We prefer the tenderness of cubed sirloin and round steaks. In our recipe testing, cubed chuck tenders tended to be too tough. If round or sirloin is not your butcher's choice for cubing, grab a package of either cut and have the steaks run through the store's meat-tenderizing machine twice. The results will be obvious with your first bite.

COUNTRY-FRIED STEAK WITH CREAMY SALSA GRAVY

family favorite

Prep: 15 min., Cook: 19 min.

- 1 cup milk
- 1 large egg
- 1 cup all-purpose flour
- 1 (1.25-ounce) packet chili seasoning mix
- 1 to 1½ pounds cubed sirloin steaks
- ⅓ cup vegetable oil
- 2 (10-ounce) cans diced tomatoes and green chiles, 1 can drained and 1 can undrained
- ⅔ cup whipping cream

Whisk together milk and egg in a medium bowl. Stir together flour and chili seasoning packet in a shallow bowl. Dip steaks in egg mixture; dredge in flour mixture, shaking off any excess.

Fry steaks in hot oil over medium-high heat in a large skillet 4 to 6 minutes on each side or until golden brown. Drain on a wire rack in a jelly-roll pan. Keep steaks warm in a 225° oven.

Stir in drained and undrained tomatoes and green chiles, and cook 1 to 2 minutes, stirring to loosen particles from bottom of skillet. Whisk in cream. Bring to a boil, whisking constantly; reduce heat, and simmer 5 minutes. Serve with steaks. **Makes** 4 to 6 servings.

JENNIFER MILLER
BROOKFIELD, CONNECTICUT

CHICKEN-FRIED STEAK

family favorite

Prep: 10 min., Cook: 14 min.
(pictured on page 73)

- 1½ teaspoons salt, divided
- 2 teaspoons pepper, divided
- 1 to 1½ pounds cubed round steaks
- 1¾ cups all-purpose flour, divided
- ⅛ teaspoon baking soda
- 1 cup water
- Vegetable oil
- 1 (14.5-ounce) can chicken broth

Sprinkle ½ teaspoon each of salt and pepper evenly over steaks. Set aside.

Stir together remaining 1 teaspoon salt, 1 teaspoon pepper, and 1½ cups flour in a shallow dish. Stir baking soda into 1 cup water in a bowl.

Dip each steak in water mixture, and dredge in flour mixture.

Pour oil to a depth of ½ inch in a large heavy skillet; heat to 360°. Fry steaks 3 to 4 minutes on each side or until golden. Drain on a wire rack in a jelly-roll pan. Keep steaks warm in a 225° oven. Drain hot oil, reserving cooked bits and 2 tablespoons drippings in skillet.

Whisk remaining ½ teaspoon pepper and remaining ¼ cup flour into drippings in skillet; cook, whisking constantly, over medium-high heat 1 minute. Whisk in broth; cook, whisking constantly, 5 minutes or until thickened. Serve with steaks. **Makes** 4 to 6 servings.

CANDACE GRANTHAM
DALLAS, TEXAS

MINUTE STEAK WITH MUSHROOM GRAVY

family favorite

Prep: 10 min., Cook: 29 min.

- 1 (10¾-ounce) can reduced-fat cream of mushroom soup
- ½ cup buttermilk
- ¼ cup water
- ¼ teaspoon ground red pepper
- 1½ teaspoons salt
- 1½ teaspoons black pepper
- 1 to 1½ pounds cubed sirloin steaks
- ½ cup all-purpose flour
- 2 tablespoons canola oil
- 1 (8-ounce) package sliced fresh mushrooms
- ½ teaspoon dried thyme

Whisk together first 4 ingredients until smooth; set aside.

Sprinkle 1 teaspoon salt and 1 teaspoon pepper evenly over steaks. Stir together remaining ½ teaspoon salt, ½ teaspoon pepper, and flour in a shallow dish. Dredge steaks in flour mixture.

Fry steaks in hot oil in a large skillet over medium-high heat 2 minutes on each side. Remove steaks, reserving drippings in skillet. Add mushrooms and thyme, and sauté 3 to 4 minutes or until lightly browned.

Stir reserved soup mixture into mushroom mixture in skillet; cook 1 minute, stirring to loosen particles from bottom of skillet. Bring to a boil, and return steaks to skillet. Cover, reduce heat, and simmer 15 to 20 minutes or until done. **Makes** 4 to 6 servings.

REGINA WASHBURN
JACKSON, TENNESSEE

Freshen a Menu With Herbs

Bright flavors enliven these satisfying recipes.

Flavor-Packed Supper

Serves 6

Salmon With Almonds
and Parsley

Rice With Fresh Herbs

Tomato-and-Cucumber Salad

Accompaniments (optional): plain
low-fat yogurt, pickled peaches,
fresh radishes, green onions

On the first day of spring, Susan and Hossein Nilipour celebrate *Norooz* (noh-RHOOZ), the Persian New Year, by treating family and friends to a fabulous menu of cherished home-style dishes. We enjoyed all of their recipes at our tasting table and knew we needed to share them.

We especially loved Salmon With Almonds and Parsley. The Nilipours serve this over Rice With Fresh Herbs, but it's so tasty that you can serve it alone, over salad greens or buttered pasta, or with steamed fresh veggies.

SALMON WITH ALMONDS AND PARSLEY

Prep: 20 min., Cook: 15 min., Broil: 10 min.

This quick-cooking entrée is perfect for rushed weeknights and company too.

8 (6-ounce) salmon fillets
¼ to ½ teaspoon salt
¼ teaspoon pepper
2 tablespoons butter
1 small onion, chopped
2 garlic cloves, minced
3 tablespoons fresh lime juice
¼ cup slivered almonds, toasted
2 tablespoons chopped fresh
  parsley
Garnish: lime slices

Sprinkle fish evenly with salt and pepper. Set aside.
Melt butter in a large heavy skillet over medium-high heat. Add onion, and sauté 8 minutes or until onion is tender. Add garlic, and sauté 2 minutes. Stir in lime juice. Remove from heat.
Arrange fish, skin side down, on a lightly greased rack in an aluminum foil-lined broiler pan. Broil 5 inches from heat 7 to 10 minutes or until fish flakes with a fork. Using a wide metal spatula, lift fish from skin, leaving skin on rack. Transfer to a serving dish. Top fish with onion mixture; sprinkle evenly with toasted almonds and parsley. Garnish, if desired. **Makes** 8 servings.

RICE WITH FRESH HERBS

Prep: 25 min.; Soak: 2 hrs.;
Cook: 1 hr., 10 min.; Cool: 5 min.

While this side dish is somewhat time-consuming, the end result is fragrant, fluffy rice with a surprise buttery, crunchy bottom—which is the best part. We don't recommend substituting dry herbs for fresh in this recipe.

3 cups uncooked basmati rice
8 cups water
2 tablespoons salt
½ teaspoon ground saffron
4 tablespoons hot water, divided
4 green onions, chopped
1 cup chopped fresh dill (about 3
  [1-ounce] packages)
1 cup chopped fresh parsley
  (2 bunches)
1 cup chopped fresh cilantro
  (2 bunches)
⅔ cup butter, melted
3 garlic cloves
½ teaspoon ground cinnamon

Place rice in a large colander, and rinse until water runs clear. Combine rice, 8 cups water, and salt, and soak 2 hours. Drain, pouring salted water into a large nonstick Dutch oven. Bring to a boil, and add rice. Return to a boil, and cook 6 minutes, gently stirring twice to keep rice from sticking to bottom of Dutch oven. Drain rice; rinse with warm water.
Dissolve saffron in 2 tablespoons hot water. Set aside.
Combine green onions and next 3 ingredients in a bowl.
Add half of melted butter to nonstick Dutch oven. Drizzle with 1 tablespoon saffron mixture. Spoon about 1 cup rice over butter; top with about ½ cup green onion mixture, and top with garlic cloves. Repeat layers with remaining rice and green onion mixture, forming a cone shape. Sprinkle with cinnamon, and drizzle with remaining half of butter, remaining 1 tablespoon saffron mixture, and remaining 2 tablespoons hot water.
Place a clean cotton dish towel over Dutch oven (make sure it doesn't touch the burner), and cover firmly with lid to prevent steam from escaping. Cook

over medium heat 10 minutes; reduce heat to low, and cook 50 minutes. Remove from heat; cool 5 minutes. **Scoop** rice, using a spatula, onto the center of an oval serving platter, leaving the crisp bottom intact. Gently lift crisp bottom layer with spatula, and serve on a separate plate, or crumble over rice on serving platter. **Makes** 6 servings.

Quick-Cook Rice With Fresh Herbs: Rinse and soak rice as directed. Boil rice in salted water 12 minutes. Layer rice and herbs in cone shape in Dutch oven as directed. Cover with a cotton dish towel and lid. Cook over high heat 2 minutes. Reduce heat to low, and cook 12 minutes. Remove from heat, and proceed as directed. (The bottom will not be as crusty as it is using the original method.)

TOMATO-AND-CUCUMBER SALAD

fast fixin's

Prep: 25 min.

This light and zesty dish is a refreshing accompaniment with the menu.

- 2 tablespoons fresh lemon juice
- 2 tablespoons olive oil
- 1 garlic clove, minced
- ½ teaspoon salt
- ¼ teaspoon pepper
- 2 large tomatoes, quartered
- 2 small cucumbers, peeled, seeded, and cut into 1-inch cubes
- 2 green onions, sliced
- 4 radishes, sliced
- ¼ cup chopped fresh parsley
- ¼ cup chopped fresh dill

Whisk together first 5 ingredients in a bowl; add tomatoes and remaining ingredients, tossing to coat. **Makes** 4 to 6 servings.

taste of the south
Rémoulade Sauce

Southerners have adopted this French classic as their very own; you might even call it gussied-up tartar sauce. The two share some common ingredients—mayonnaise, sweet pickles, and Worcestershire sauce. But the original rémoulade (ray-muh-LAHD) sauce includes capers, anchovy paste, and often fresh herbs, just as it has been prepared in France for hundreds of years.

At Criolla's Restaurant in Santa Rosa Beach, Florida, chef and co-owner Johnny Earles has been a fan of the original rémoulade for years. "We use all sorts of variations of it," he says. "In warmer months, we lighten it up with a little citrus. The traditional base is just a great concoction. It's one of those sauces that's endured through the ages." Johnny serves it with crab cakes, among other things.

CRIOLLA RÉMOULADE

chef recipe • make ahead

Prep: 10 min., Chill: 1 hr.

This is the classic mayonnaise-based rémoulade, sparked with a touch of seafood seasoning.

- 1 cup mayonnaise
- ¼ cup Creole mustard
- ¼ cup chopped sweet pickles
- 2 tablespoons capers, drained
- 1 tablespoon minced fresh parsley
- 2 teaspoons Worcestershire sauce
- 2 teaspoons prepared horseradish
- 2 teaspoons anchovy paste
- 1 teaspoon Old Bay seasoning
- 1 teaspoon paprika

Stir together all ingredients; cover and chill at least 1 hour or up to 1 week. **Makes** 1½ cups.

Citrus Rémoulade: Prepare Criolla Rémoulade as directed, omitting capers and parsley. Stir in 1 tablespoon chopped cilantro, ½ teaspoon grated lemon rind, 1 tablespoon lemon juice, and 1 teaspoon grated orange rind. Cover and chill as directed. **Makes** 1½ cups.

CHEF JOHNNY EARLES
CRIOLLA'S RESTAURANT
SANTA ROSA BEACH, FLORIDA

CREOLE RÉMOULADE SAUCE

Prep: 15 min., Chill: 1 hr.

Deborah Blouin of the Junior League of Baton Rouge says this sauce's spiciness is due to its Creole heritage. "It's the 'oomph' that gives the sauce a difference," she says with a laugh.

- ¼ cup lemon juice
- ¼ cup cider vinegar
- ¼ cup prepared mustard
- ¼ cup prepared horseradish
- 2 teaspoons paprika
- 1 teaspoon salt
- ½ teaspoon black pepper
- Dash ground red pepper
- 2 tablespoons ketchup (optional)
- 1 cup vegetable oil
- ½ cup finely chopped celery
- ½ cup finely chopped green onions

Whisk together first 8 ingredients, and, if desired, ketchup in a bowl; gradually whisk in oil until thickened. Stir in celery and green onions. Cover and chill at least 1 hour or up to 1 week. **Makes** 2 cups.

RIVER ROAD RECIPES
(FAVORITE RECIPES PRESS, 1959)
JUNIOR LEAGUE OF BATON ROUGE

from our kitchen

Rising to the Occasion

One warm-from-the-oven bite will tell you why these little rolls are some of our favorites. Best of all, each recipe offers a clever shortcut, so if you've never worked with yeast before, this is a great way to get started.

Tiny spirals of Lemon-Orange Rolls dough begin with a box of hot roll mix, which comes with a packet of yeast. Rather than combining the yeast with warm water, just add it directly to the dry ingredients. All-purpose baking mix is the secret to buttery little Cheddar Crescents, and they rise in only 20 minutes.

The quickest shortcut of all comes straight from the frozen bread section in the supermarket. Several different brands of roll dough are available, including a new one from White Lily. Irresistibly light and tender with a hint of sweetness, these melt-in-your-mouth rolls received top ratings in the Test Kitchens. Once thawed, they can be shaped in dozens of different ways. To make miniature Cloverleaf Rolls, use scissors to cut thawed balls of dough into thirds; then quarter each small piece, and place the four pieces in a lightly greased miniature muffin cup. Bake at 375° for 8 to 10 minutes or until golden.

All of these rolls can be baked up to 1 month ahead and frozen in zip-top plastic freezer bags. Thaw at room temperature, and reheat, uncovered, at 350° for 3 to 5 minutes.

CHEDDAR CRESCENTS

freezeable • make ahead

Prep: 20 min., Rise: 20 min., Bake: 12 min.

- 1 (¼-ounce) envelope active dry yeast
- ½ cup warm water (100° to 110°)
- 2½ cups all-purpose baking mix
- 1¼ cups (5 ounces) shredded Cheddar cheese
- 1 large egg, beaten

Stir together yeast and ½ cup warm water in a large bowl; let stand 5 minutes. Stir in baking mix, cheese, and egg, stirring until a soft dough forms. Turn out onto a well-floured surface, and knead 20 times. Place dough in a bowl coated with cooking spray, turning to grease top. Cover and let rise 20 minutes.

Divide dough into 4 equal portions. Roll 1 portion of dough at a time into an 8-inch circle on a lightly floured surface. Cut circle into 8 wedges; roll up wedges, starting at wide end, to form a crescent shape. Place, point side down on a lightly greased baking sheet. Repeat procedure with remaining dough.

Bake at 350° for 10 to 12 minutes or until golden brown. **Makes** 32 rolls.

Note: For testing purposes only, we used Bisquick for the all-purpose baking mix.

LEMON-ORANGE ROLLS

freezeable • make ahead

Prep: 20 min., Rise: 20 min., Bake: 10 min.

If you don't have four miniature muffin pans, you can let these little rolls rise and bake them in batches; just be sure to keep the extra portions of dough in the refrigerator until you're ready to fill the pans again.

- 1 (16-ounce) package hot roll mix
- ¼ cup butter, softened and divided
- ⅔ cup granulated sugar
- 2 tablespoons grated orange rind
- 1 tablespoon grated lemon rind
- 2 cups powdered sugar
- ¼ cup orange juice

Prepare hot roll dough according to package directions.

Divide dough into 2 equal portions. Roll 1 portion of dough into a 12- x 8-inch rectangle on a lightly floured surface. Spread with 2 tablespoons butter.

Stir together granulated sugar and grated rinds; sprinkle half of sugar mixture evenly over butter on rectangle. Roll up rectangle, jelly-roll fashion, starting at a long edge. Repeat procedure with remaining half of dough, 2 tablespoons butter, and remaining half of sugar mixture.

Cut each roll into ½-inch-thick slices, and place in lightly greased miniature muffin pans.

Cover and let rise in a warm place (85°), free from drafts, 20 minutes.

Bake at 375° for 8 to 10 minutes or until golden. Remove from pans, and place on wire racks.

Stir together powdered sugar and orange juice until smooth; spoon evenly over tops of rolls. **Makes** 4 dozen miniature rolls.

Note: For testing purposes only, we used Pillsbury Hot Roll Mix. Look for it in the cake mix section of your grocery store.

april

72   Easy Menu for Passover *A perfect meal for spring celebrations*

82   Flavor Lamb With Fresh Herbs *Great recipes for graceful entertaining*

83   Make Bread in the Mixer *Here's how to skip the step of kneading the dough*

84   Food and Hospitality Grilling Smarter *Keep down the cost while you kick up the flavor*

85   Stir Up Some Veggies *Give supper a fresh spin with easy, flavorful sides*

86   Cut Up a Pineapple With Ease *Simple steps for perfectly chopped chunks*

87   Milk and Cookies Anytime *Discover the Ultimate Chocolate Chip Cookies*

88   Quick & Easy Family Weekend Breakfast *Great dishes you can serve anytime*

89   Good to the Last Bite *Savor every bit of these delicious ice cream sandwiches*

90   Savor Easy Pork Roast *Moist, tender recipes that your whole family will love*

91   Start With Slaw Mix *Salad-making just got easier with these shortcut recipes*

92   What's for Supper? Have a Deli-Style Dinner *Quick sandwiches make mealtime a snap*

93   Stuff a Dozen (or Two) *Deviled eggs don't get any dandier*

94   To Market, To Market *Sample some delicious food from a Shreveport, Louisiana, grocery*

96   Top-Rated Menu New-Fashioned Luncheon Party *Host a great gathering with these make-ahead favorites*

97   Speedy Appetizers *These flavorful nibbles all have hands-on prep times of 10 minutes*

98   Lunch in the Lowcountry *Charleston's tearooms offer some fine fare*

99   Taste of the South Hush Puppies *These addictive bites of fried cornbread are easy to make*

100   Healthy & Light Italian Made Fresh *Savor the irresistible flavors of these enticing dishes*

102   From Our Kitchen *Party pizzazz, shelf magic, and more*

Easy Menu for Passover

Host this dinner for any spring celebration.

Spring Holiday Menu

Serves 6

Roasted Red Pepper Soup

Peppered Tuna With
Mushroom Sauce

Dill-and-Almond Green Beans

Flourless Chocolate Torte
or
Matzoh-and-Honey Fritters

Here's a menu to please all your guests. While it's a perfect meal to celebrate Passover, the dishes also work well within the guidelines of many popular diet plans. If you adhere to Passover dietary guidelines, look for pareve butter and ingredients that have been labeled Kosher for Passover. The recipes are simple with none having more than 15 minutes prep time. No matter who's coming to dinner, this meal fills the bill.

ROASTED RED PEPPER SOUP

Prep: 15 min., Bake: 45 min., Stand: 35 min., Cook: 55 min.

- **4 pounds red bell peppers (about 8 large), halved**
- **3 tablespoons olive oil, divided**
- **2 medium onions, chopped (about 2 cups)**
- **5 garlic cloves, chopped**
- **3½ cups vegetable broth**
- **¾ cup whipping cream**
- **¼ cup fresh basil, finely chopped**
- **2½ teaspoons salt**
- **1 teaspoon freshly ground pepper**
- **1 tablespoon lemon juice**
- **Sour cream**

Brush skin side of peppers with 1 tablespoon oil. Bake peppers, skin side up, on lightly greased aluminum foil-lined baking sheets at 400° for 45 minutes or until peppers look blistered.

Place peppers in a large zip-top freezer bag; seal and let stand 20 minutes. Peel peppers; remove and discard seeds.

Sauté onions in remaining 2 tablespoons hot oil in a Dutch oven over medium-high heat 10 minutes or until tender; add garlic, and cook 1 more minute. Add vegetable broth and peppers, and bring to a boil; reduce heat to medium, cover, and simmer, stirring occasionally, 30 minutes.

Remove from heat; let stand 15 minutes. Process red pepper mixture, in batches, in a food processor or blender until smooth.

Return pureed mixture to Dutch oven; cook over medium heat 5 minutes. Stir in cream and next 3 ingredients, and cook 5 more minutes or until thoroughly heated. Stir in lemon juice. Serve with sour cream. **Makes** 6 servings.

JAMIE ESTES
LOUISVILLE, KENTUCKY

PEPPERED TUNA WITH MUSHROOM SAUCE

Prep: 15 min., Cook: 20 min.

If you can't find fresh tuna, frozen tuna steaks will work just fine; just be sure to thaw the frozen tuna steaks before using them.

- **3 tablespoons butter**
- **1 cup sliced fresh mushrooms**
- **¾ cup plum sauce**
- **¼ cup lite soy sauce**
- **1 teaspoon ground ginger**
- **2 tablespoons vegetable oil**
- **6 (6-ounce) tuna steaks (about 1½ inches thick)**
- **1 tablespoon freshly ground multicolored peppercorns ✱**

Melt butter in a large skillet over medium-high heat until lightly browned. Add sliced mushrooms, and sauté 4 to 7 minutes or until lightly browned and tender. Stir in plum sauce, soy sauce, and ground ginger. Bring to a boil, reduce heat, and simmer, stirring often, 3 to 4 minutes. Keep mixture warm.

Heat oil in a large nonstick skillet over medium-high heat. Sprinkle tuna steaks evenly with pepper, and cook 4 minutes on each side (rare) or to

Grilled Steaks Balsamico, page 84

Strawberry-Citrus Chicken Salad, page 84

74

Fiesta Salad, page 58

White Bean-and-Asparagus Salad, page 100

Chive-Tarragon Deviled Eggs, page 93

Turkey, Bacon, and Havarti Sandwich, page 92

77

Oven-Roasted Asparagus, page 55;
Lexington-Style Grilled Chicken, page 54;
Spinach-and-Strawberry Salad, page 55;
Three-Cheese Pasta Bake, page 54

Double Citrus Tart, page 55

Spinach-and-Strawberry Salad, page 55

Strawberry Smoothie Ice-Cream Pie, page 89

desired degree of doneness. Serve tuna with warm mushroom sauce. **Makes** 6 servings.

Note: For testing purposes only, we used Honan Plum Sauce. Look for plum sauce in the ethnic foods aisle of the supermarket.

✱ Substitute freshly ground black pepper, if desired.

DILL-AND-ALMOND GREEN BEANS

fast fixin's

Prep: 10 min., Cook: 15 min.

Not a huge dill lover? Substitute fresh basil or flat-leaf parsley.

- **1 pound fresh green beans, trimmed**
- **¼ cup slivered almonds**
- **1 tablespoon olive oil**
- **1 garlic clove, minced**
- **1 tablespoon chopped fresh dill**
- **½ teaspoon salt**
- **½ teaspoon pepper**

Cook green beans in boiling water to cover in a Dutch oven over medium-high heat 10 minutes. Plunge beans into ice water to stop the cooking process; drain.
Sauté almonds in hot oil in a large skillet over medium heat 3 minutes or until lightly browned. Add garlic; sauté 30 seconds. Stir in green beans, dill, salt, and pepper; cook 2 minutes or until thoroughly heated. Serve immediately. **Makes** 6 servings.

MARIAN LOVENE GRIFFEY
GAINESVILLE, FLORIDA

FLOURLESS CHOCOLATE TORTE

family favorite

Prep: 15 min., Cook: 7 min., Bake: 25 min., Stand: 10 min.

- **Unsweetened cocoa**
- **2 (8-ounce) packages semisweet chocolate squares, coarsely chopped**
- **½ cup butter**
- **5 large eggs, separated**
- **1 tablespoon vanilla extract**
- **¼ cup sugar**

Grease a 9-inch springform pan, and dust with unsweetened cocoa; set aside.
Melt chopped chocolate and butter in a heavy saucepan over low heat, stirring until smooth.
Whisk together egg yolks and vanilla in a large bowl. Gradually stir in chocolate mixture, whisking until well blended.
Beat egg whites at high speed with an electric mixer until soft peaks form. Gradually add sugar, beating until sugar dissolves and stiff peaks form. Fold one-third beaten egg white mixture into chocolate mixture; gently fold in remaining egg white mixture just until blended. Spoon batter into prepared pan, spreading evenly.
Bake at 375° for 25 minutes. (Do not overbake.) Let stand in pan on a wire rack 10 minutes before removing sides of pan. **Makes** 8 servings.

RONNIE MAND
DANVILLE, VIRGINIA

MATZOH-AND-HONEY FRITTERS

Prep: 15 min., Stand: 5 min., Fry: 4 min. per batch

- **1 (10-ounce) package plain matzoh**
- **2¼ cups water**
- **5 large eggs, lightly beaten**
- **½ cup golden raisins or chopped dried plums**
- **½ cup sugar**
- **1 teaspoon vanilla extract**
- **½ to 1 teaspoon ground cinnamon**
- **Vegetable oil**
- **½ cup honey**
- **1 cup chopped walnuts, toasted**

Break matzoh into pieces, and place in a large bowl. Cover with 2¼ cups water; let stand 5 minutes or until matzoh is softened. Add lightly beaten eggs and next 4 ingredients, stirring until blended.
Pour oil to a depth of 2 inches into a large skillet, and heat to 375°. Drop batter by ¼ cupfuls into hot oil; fry, in batches, 2 minutes on each side or until golden and done in center. Drain on paper towels.
Arrange fritters on a serving platter. Drizzle evenly with honey, and sprinkle with chopped toasted walnuts. Serve fritters immediately. **Makes** 16 fritters.

Test Kitchen Notebook

History, tradition, and culture merge with the eight-day Jewish observance called Passover that marks the Exodus and freedom of the Israelites from Egypt.

Passover is a time of family gatherings and ceremonial dinners. Matzoh, a flat, brittle bread baked without any leavening, is a signature food. The bread of slavery and freedom, Matzoh came about when the Israelites were forced to flee Egypt. There was no time to let the dough rise. The raw dough that they took with them quickly baked in the hot sun, forming matzoh crackers.

Greens, such as Dill-and-Almond Green Beans, represent rebirth and spring, while strong herbs in the meal indicate the bitterness of slavery.

Any baked goods consumed during the holiday need to be made without flour, which makes the Flourless Chocolate Torte a nice ending to the meal.

Andria Scott Hurst
SENIOR WRITER

Flavor Lamb With Fresh Herbs

Try these recipes for graceful entertaining.

Lamb, roasted to perfection, is delicious for any springtime feast and is best served medium-rare (150°) to medium (160°) for full, tender flavor. If you like the meat cooked through, slow cook the shoulder and shank cuts for maximum taste. Both these recipes use fresh herbs to enhance the lamb. If you're looking for something really easy, try Creamy Dijon Lamb Chops or simply grill chops seasoned with salt, pepper, olive oil, and your favorite fresh herb.

CREAMY DIJON LAMB CHOPS

family favorite

Prep: 15 min., Cook: 13 min., Bake: 15 min., Stand: 5 min.

- 8 (2-inch-thick) lamb chops, trimmed
- ½ teaspoon salt
- ¼ teaspoon freshly ground pepper
- 1 tablespoon olive oil
- 2 garlic cloves, pressed
- ½ cup whipping cream
- ⅓ cup Dijon mustard
- 2 tablespoons chopped fresh thyme
- 1 to 2 tablespoons chopped fresh rosemary

Sprinkle lamb chops evenly with salt and pepper.

Brown chops in hot oil in a heavy skillet over medium-high heat 2 minutes on each side; place chops in a 13- x 9-inch baking dish, reserving drippings in skillet.

Bake at 400° for 15 minutes or until a meat thermometer inserted into thickest portion registers 150° (medium-rare). Let lamb chops stand 5 minutes before serving.

Sauté garlic in reserved drippings over medium heat 3 minutes or until lightly browned.

Stir together cream and next 3 ingredients in a small bowl. Add mixture to skillet, and bring to a boil over medium heat, stirring occasionally. Reduce heat, and simmer 5 minutes. Serve sauce with chops. **Makes** 4 servings.

ROSEMARY-CRUSTED LAMB WITH TZATZIKI SAUCE

family favorite

Prep: 10 min., Bake: 45 min., Stand: 10 min.

Grate the lemon rind for the Tzatziki Sauce before squeezing the juice for the lamb. You'll find this dish to be easy and delicious.

- ¼ cup chopped fresh rosemary
- 3 garlic cloves
- 3 tablespoons fresh lemon juice
- 3 tablespoons olive oil
- 1 teaspoon salt
- 1 teaspoon pepper
- 1 (6-pound) leg of lamb, boned and trimmed
- Tzatziki Sauce
- Garnish: fresh rosemary sprigs

Process first 6 ingredients in a food processor until smooth. Spread rosemary mixture evenly on lamb. Place lamb on a lightly greased rack in a roasting pan.

Bake at 450° for 45 minutes or until a meat thermometer inserted into thickest portion registers 160° (medium). **Let** stand 10 minutes before slicing. Serve with Tzatziki Sauce. Garnish, if desired. **Makes** 4 servings.

TZATZIKI SAUCE:
fast fixin's

Prep: 20 min.

This is a Greek sauce made with thick, creamy yogurt. It can also be served as a dip with pita bread rounds, a spread for sandwiches, or thinned out with good olive oil for a refreshing salad dressing.

- 1 (16-ounce) container plain yogurt
- 1 large cucumber, peeled, seeded, and diced
- 1 tablespoon chopped fresh dill
- 1 tablespoon chopped fresh mint
- 1 teaspoon salt
- 1 teaspoon grated lemon rind
- 1 garlic clove, pressed

Stir together all ingredients in a large bowl. Cover and chill until ready to serve. **Makes** 2½ cups.

MATTHEW THOMAS ROCCHIO
HOUSTON, TEXAS

Lamb Tips

When selecting lamb, look for a bright pink color, pink bones, and white fat. If the meat and bones are dark red, it usually means the meat is older.

Ground lamb can be refrigerated 1 day or frozen up to 4 months, while all other lamb cuts can be refrigerated 2 days or frozen up to 9 months. Cooked lamb can be refrigerated 4 days; freezing is not recommended.

Make Bread in the Mixer

If you love homemade bread but hate the chore of kneading, then try these recipes.

This great recipe offers a version for any taste; the one with dried tomatoes and black olives is perfect to slice for turkey sandwiches. A heavy-duty stand mixer equipped with a dough hook replaces your manual labor. A word of caution: Bread dough is heavy, so you'll need a mixer with a strong motor (we used a 325-watt KitchenAid) and a dough hook or paddle attachment. Regular beaters are likely to bend under the pressure.

CHEESY GRITS BREAD

family favorite

Prep: 15 min.; Cook: 10 min.; Stand: 30 min.; Rise: 1 hr., 45 min.; Bake: 40 min.

We added some of our own twists to reader Catherine Boettner's flavorful recipe.

2 cups milk
¾ cup quick-cooking grits, uncooked
2 teaspoons salt
1 (10-ounce) block white Cheddar cheese, shredded
1 cup warm water (100° to 110°)
¼ cup sugar
2 (¼-ounce) envelopes rapid-rise yeast
5 to 6 cups bread flour

Bring milk to a boil in a large saucepan over medium heat; stir in grits, and cook, stirring often, 5 minutes (mixture will be very thick.) Remove from heat; add salt and cheese, stirring until cheese is melted. Let stand 25 minutes, stirring occasionally.

Combine 1 cup warm water, sugar, and yeast in the mixing bowl of a heavy-duty stand mixer; let stand 5 minutes. Add grits mixture, beating at medium-low speed with the dough hook attachment until well blended.
Add 4 cups flour, 1 cup at a time, beating until blended after each addition and stopping to scrape down sides as necessary. Gradually add enough flour to make a stiff but slightly sticky dough. Dough will form a ball around mixer attachment.
Shape dough into a ball with well-floured hands; place in a well-greased bowl, turning to coat top. Cover and let rise in a warm place (85°), free from drafts, 1 hour or until doubled in bulk.
Punch dough down, and divide into thirds; shape each portion into a loaf. Place into lightly greased 9- x 5-inch loafpans; cover and let rise in a warm place (85°), free from drafts, 45 minutes or until doubled in bulk.
Bake at 350° for 35 to 40 minutes or until golden. Let bread cool in pans on wire racks 10 minutes. Remove from pans, and cool completely on wire racks. **Makes** 3 loaves.

Note: For testing purposes only, we used Cracker Barrel Vermont Sharp White Cheddar.

CATHERINE BOETTNER
CHARLESTON, TENNESSEE

Bacon-Cheddar Grits Bread: Prepare dough as directed. After dividing dough, roll each third into a 14- x 9-inch rectangle on a lightly floured surface. Sprinkle each dough rectangle evenly with ½ cup cooked, crumbled bacon and ¾ cup shredded sharp Cheddar cheese. Roll up, jelly-roll fashion, starting with each short side and ending at middle of dough. You will form 2 rolls per loaf. Place into prepared loafpans; let rise, and bake as directed.

Tomato-Black Olive Grits Bread: Prepare dough as directed. After dividing dough, roll each third into a 14- x 9-inch rectangle on a lightly floured surface. Sprinkle each dough rectangle evenly with ½ cup julienne-cut dried tomatoes with herbs in oil (drained and patted dry with paper towels) and ½ cup sliced black olives (drained and patted dry with paper towels). Roll up, jelly-roll fashion, starting with each short side and ending at middle of dough. You will form 2 rolls per loaf. Place into prepared loafpans; let rise, and bake as directed.

Note: For testing purposes only, we used California Sun-Dry sun-dried julienne cut tomatoes with herbs.

Basil Pesto-Cheese Grits Bread: Prepare dough as directed. After dividing dough, roll each third into a 14- x 9-inch rectangle on a lightly floured surface. Spread ¼ cup prepared basil pesto evenly over each dough rectangle; sprinkle each with ¾ cup shredded mozzarella or crumbled goat cheese. Roll up, jelly-roll fashion, starting with each short side and ending at middle of dough. You will form 2 rolls per loaf. Place into prepared loafpans; let rise, and bake as directed.

Easy Rising

Letting the dough rise in a place that's warm enough but not too warm will ensure the best results. Try this tip from Test Kitchens professional **Alyssa Porubcan**. Place a cakepan filled with water on the bottom rack of the oven. Preheat oven to 200°. Turn off oven, and partially open door. Let cool 20 minutes. Place loaves in oven on middle rack, and let rise as directed with oven door closed.

Grilling Smarter

Kick up the flavor, and keep down the costs with tender and juicy cuts of beef, pork, and chicken.

Even with today's high meat prices, grilling is an affordable luxury. If you haven't discovered the new cuts of bargain steaks, start with Grilled Steaks Balsamico. We used boneless beef chuck-eye steaks, a distant cousin of the rib-eye.

Marinated London Broil, an extra-thick cut of boneless top round steak, serves six to eight people for just under $12. Keep a close watch for buy-one-get-one-free sales, and you'll slice that price in half.

MARINATED LONDON BROIL

family favorite

Prep: 5 min., Chill: 24 hrs., Grill: 30 min., Stand: 10 min.

For the juiciest flavor, remove this hearty cut of beef from the grill before it reaches medium (155°). It will continue to cook as it stands.

1 (12-ounce) can cola soft drink
1 (10-ounce) bottle teriyaki sauce
1 (2½- to 3-pound) London broil

Combine cola and teriyaki sauce in a shallow dish or large zip-top freezer bag; add London broil. Cover or seal, and chill 24 hours, turning occasionally. Remove London broil from marinade, discarding marinade.
Grill, covered with grill lid, over medium heat (300° to 350°) 12 to 15 minutes on each side or to desired degree of doneness. Let stand 10 minutes; cut diagonally into thin slices across the grain. **Makes** 6 to 8 servings.

ANNETTE PACETTI
BRENTWOOD, TENNESSEE

GRILLED STEAKS BALSAMICO

Prep: 15 min., Chill: 2 hrs., Grill: 14 min., Cook: 4 min.

These delicious steaks won top honors at the National Beef Cook-Off. We served the cheese sauce in hollowed-out lemon halves. (pictured on page 73)

⅔ cup balsamic vinaigrette
¼ cup fig preserves
4 (6- to 8-ounce) boneless beef chuck-eye steaks
1 teaspoon salt
1 teaspoon freshly ground pepper
1 (6.5-ounce) container buttery garlic-and-herb spreadable cheese

Process vinaigrette and preserves in a blender until smooth. Place steaks and vinaigrette mixture in a shallow dish or a large zip-top freezer bag. Cover or seal, and chill at least 2 hours. Remove steaks from marinade, discarding marinade.
Grill, covered with grill lid, over medium-high heat (350° to 400°) 5 to 7 minutes on each side or until desired degree of doneness. Remove to a serving platter, and sprinkle evenly with salt and pepper; keep warm.
Heat cheese in a small saucepan over low heat, stirring often, 2 to 4 minutes or until melted. Serve cheese sauce with steaks. **Makes** 4 servings.

Note: For testing purposes only, we used Alouette Garlic + Herbs Spreadable Cheese.

LORI WELANDER
RICHMOND, VIRGINIA

Strawberry-Citrus Chicken Salad
(pictured on page 74)

Often on sale, boneless chicken breasts are the perfect quick and easy weeknight entrée.

Test Kitchens Specialist/Food Stylist Vanessa McNeil likes to use them in her Strawberry-Citrus Chicken Salad. Just sprinkle the chicken evenly with salt and pepper, and grill, covered with grill lid, over medium-high heat (350° to 400°) 5 to 7 minutes on each side or until done. Let stand 10 minutes, and cut into ½-inch-thick slices.

Fill individual containers or serving dishes evenly with lettuce; top with grilled chicken, sliced strawberries, navel orange segments, and sliced red onion. Serve salad with Strawberry-Balsamic Vinaigrette.

STRAWBERRY-BALSAMIC VINAIGRETTE:
fast fixin's
Prep: 5 min.

If you're cutting back on sugar, substitute an equal amount of strawberry fruit spread for the preserves. We used white balsamic vinegar to retain the bright color of the strawberries, but a dark balsamic will taste just as good.

1½ cups strawberry preserves
¼ cup white balsamic vinegar
¼ cup olive oil
¼ teaspoon crushed rosemary
¼ teaspoon salt
¼ teaspoon pepper

Pulse all ingredients in a blender 5 or 6 times or until smooth. **Makes** about 2 cups.

MOLASSES-GLAZED CHICKEN THIGHS

family favorite

Prep: 15 min., Chill: 8 hrs., Grill: 12 min.

Skinned and boned chicken thighs are available in the fresh poultry section of most supermarkets.

- ¾ cup molasses
- ⅓ cup soy sauce
- ¼ cup fresh lemon juice
- ¼ cup olive oil
- 3 garlic cloves, minced
- 1 teaspoon pepper
- 12 skinned and boned chicken thighs

Combine first 6 ingredients in a shallow dish or large zip-top freezer bag; add chicken thighs. Cover or seal, and chill 8 hours, turning occasionally.
Remove chicken from marinade, discarding marinade.
Grill chicken thighs, covered with grill lid, over medium heat (300° to 350°) 5 to 6 minutes on each side or until done. **Makes** 6 to 8 servings.

THAI PORK CHOPS WITH CARAMELIZED ONIONS

family favorite

Prep: 15 min., Cook: 17 min., Grill: 10 min.

Thick-cut boneless pork chops can be pricey, but not if you slice them yourself from a boneless pork loin. Frequently on sale for $1.99 a pound, this lean and tender cut of pork is easily sliced into thick or thin chops that can be frozen in zip-top freezer bags for up to 3 months.

- 3 tablespoons brown sugar
- 3 tablespoons peanut butter
- 2 tablespoons soy sauce
- 2 teaspoons grated fresh ginger
- 1 garlic clove, minced
- ¼ to ½ teaspoon dried crushed red pepper
- 1 large sweet onion, sliced
- ⅓ cup orange juice
- 4 (1-inch-thick) boneless pork chops
- ½ teaspoon salt

Cook first 6 ingredients in a small saucepan over medium-high heat, stirring constantly, 1 to 2 minutes or until thoroughly heated. Add sliced onion, and sauté 15 minutes or until onion is caramelized. Remove onion with a slotted spoon, reserving liquid and onion. Stir orange juice into reserved liquid in pan. Brush mixture evenly over pork chops, and sprinkle evenly with salt.
Grill pork, covered with grill lid, over medium-high heat (350° to 400°) 4 to 5 minutes on each side or until done. Remove to a serving platter; top with caramelized onion. **Makes** 4 servings.

JONI HILTON
ROCKLIN, CALIFORNIA

MARGARITA PORK TENDERLOIN

family favorite

Prep: 15 min., Chill: 1 hr., Grill: 8 min.

- 3 garlic cloves, minced
- 1 green onion, minced
- ½ jalapeño pepper, minced
- 3 tablespoons chopped fresh cilantro
- 2 tablespoons fresh lime juice
- 1½ tablespoons tequila
- 1 tablespoon fresh orange juice
- 1 teaspoon salt
- 1 teaspoon ground cumin
- ½ teaspoon chili powder
- 2 (1-pound) pork tenderloins

Combine first 10 ingredients in a shallow dish or large zip-top plastic freezer bag. Cut pork diagonally into 1-inch-thick slices, and add to tequila mixture. Cover or seal, and chill 1 hour, turning occasionally.
Remove pork from marinade, discarding marinade.
Grill, covered with grill lid, over high heat (400° to 500°) 3 to 4 minutes on each side or until done. **Makes** 6 servings.

ANNE HOLLENBECK
AZLE, TEXAS

Stir Up Some Veggies

Round out tonight's menu with one of these great vegetable dishes. All have short ingredient lists and require little hands-on time once they're in the pan. You can speed the process even more with precut bell pepper and onion from the supermarket produce section.

HOT PECAN PEAS

family favorite

Prep: 15 min., Cook: 35 min.

Use turkey bacon (which yields less drippings) and a nonstick skillet to make this dish more healthful.

- 4 bacon slices, chopped
- ½ cup chopped onion
- 2 (16-ounce) packages frozen baby sweet peas (do not thaw)
- ½ cup water
- 1 teaspoon Creole seasoning
- 1 cup chopped pecans, toasted

Cook bacon in a large skillet over medium heat until crisp; remove bacon, and drain on paper towels, reserving 1 tablespoon drippings in skillet.
Stir onion into hot drippings in skillet. Reduce heat to medium-low; cook 15 minutes or until lightly browned. Add peas, ½ cup water, and Creole seasoning; cook 10 minutes, stirring occasionally, or until peas are tender. Stir in bacon and pecans. **Makes** 8 to 10 servings.

Note: To toast pecans, bake in a shallow pan at 350°, stirring occasionally, 8 to 10 minutes.

VANESSA BROUSSARD
BATON ROUGE, LOUISIANA

STIR-FRIED CABBAGE

fast fixin's

Prep: 15 min., Cook: 18 min.

- 5 bacon slices
- 1 small head cabbage, cut into ½-inch-thick slices (about 12 cups)
- 1 medium onion, chopped
- 1 small green bell pepper, chopped
- 1 tablespoon lite soy sauce
- 1 teaspoon Worcestershire sauce
- ½ teaspoon salt
- ½ teaspoon pepper

Cook bacon in a large skillet over medium heat until crisp; remove bacon, and drain on paper towels, reserving 3 tablespoons drippings in skillet. Crumble bacon.

Sauté cabbage, onion, and bell pepper in hot drippings over medium-high heat, 5 to 6 minutes or until cabbage is crisp-tender. Stir in soy sauce and next 3 ingredients; cook 2 minutes. Top with crumbled bacon. **Makes** 4 servings.

SHELA GOBER
ELECTRA, TEXAS

STIR-FRIED ASPARAGUS WITH GARLIC

family favorite • fast fixin's

Prep: 10 min., Cook: 10 min.

Use lite soy sauce for a lower sodium option. If your skillet doesn't have a lid, cover it with a baking sheet.

- 2 pounds asparagus
- 8 garlic cloves, finely chopped
- 2 tablespoons canola oil
- 3 tablespoons soy sauce

Snap off tough ends of asparagus. Cut asparagus in half.

Sauté asparagus and garlic in hot oil in a large skillet over medium-high heat 3 to 5 minutes or until asparagus is crisp-tender. Add soy sauce; reduce heat to medium-low, and cover. Cook 5 minutes or until asparagus is tender. **Makes** 6 to 8 servings.

KATHLEEN A. KENNEDY-HANSON
VALRICO, FLORIDA

QUICK BROCCOLI SKILLET

family favorite • fast fixin's

Prep: 20 min., Cook: 10 min.

- ½ (16-ounce) container grape tomatoes
- 1 pound fresh broccoli, cut into florets
- 2 tablespoons butter
- 3 garlic cloves, minced
- 2 tablespoons lemon juice
- ½ red bell pepper, chopped
- ½ teaspoon salt
- ½ teaspoon pepper

Cut grape tomatoes in half; set aside.

Cook broccoli in boiling water to cover 3 to 5 minutes or until crisp-tender; plunge into ice water to stop the cooking process. Drain.

Melt butter in a large nonstick skillet over medium-high heat; stir in garlic and lemon juice, and sauté 2 minutes. Stir in broccoli; sauté 2 minutes. Stir in tomatoes, bell pepper, salt, and pepper; sauté 1 minute. Serve immediately. **Makes** 4 to 6 servings.

CINDY PIESTER
LINCOLN, NEBRASKA

Cutting a Pineapple

1. Using a sharp nonserrated knife, cut off a thin slice from the top and bottom of the pineapple, removing the leaves and creating a flat surface on each end.

2. Position pineapple upright on cutting board. Thinly slice downward around pineapple to remove rough skin, being careful not to waste fruit.

3. Cut pineapple lengthwise into eighths.

4. Cut core away from each slice; discard core.

5. Chop each slice into chunks. Refrigerate in an airtight container up to 3 days.

Cut Up a Pineapple With Ease

There's more than one way to cut up a pineapple, but if the mere thought seems a bit burdensome, you're not alone. Many are hesitant when it comes to this tropical beauty with its pointed leaves and pineconelike skin. It's easier than you think, and you can save money by doing it yourself. Small amounts of precut pineapple in the produce section can sometimes cost more per pound than a whole one (available year-round). Look for a slightly soft skin with strong, consistent color, and avoid brown tips on the green leaves.

Just follow these simple steps, and snack on the juicy chunks, or reserve them for grilled kabobs, fresh salads, and savory stir-fries. Chop the chunks into smaller pieces for our Pineapple Salsa. It's great with tortilla chips, stirred into hot cooked rice, or with grilled chicken or pork. Try it with our Margarita Pork Tenderloin on page 85.

PINEAPPLE SALSA

make ahead

Prep: 20 min., Chill: 1 hr.

- 1 fresh pineapple, cored and diced
- 3 green onions, chopped
- 2 jalapeño peppers, seeded and diced
- 2 tablespoons chopped fresh cilantro
- 2 tablespoons lime juice
- 1 teaspoon salt
- ½ teaspoon ground cumin

Combine all ingredients in a bowl. Cover and chill 1 hour. **Makes** 6 servings.

Milk and Cookies Anytime

Warm or cold, soft or crisp, this cookie recipe delivers in flavor, texture, and appearance, as a good one should.

After testing dozens of chocolate chip cookie recipes over the last year and a half, our staff agrees that this one and its variations are tops. Reader Susan Hefilfinger improved the look and texture by reducing the amount of butter and sugar often called for in other recipes. You'll want to reach for these the next time you crave homemade cookies.

ULTIMATE CHOCOLATE CHIP COOKIES

family favorite • make ahead

Prep: 30 min., Bake: 14 min. per batch

Bake a batch of cookies 8 minutes for soft and gooey cookies or up to 14 minutes for crispy cookies.

- ¾ **cup butter, softened**
- ¾ **cup granulated sugar**
- ¾ **cup firmly packed dark brown sugar**
- 2 **large eggs**
- 1½ **teaspoons vanilla extract**
- 2¼ **cups plus 2 tablespoons all-purpose flour**
- 1 **teaspoon baking soda**
- ¾ **teaspoon salt**
- 1 **(12-ounce) package semisweet chocolate morsels**

Beat butter and sugars at medium speed with an electric mixer until creamy. Add eggs and vanilla, beating until blended.

Combine flour, soda, and salt in a small bowl; gradually add to butter mixture, beating well. Stir in morsels. Drop by tablespoonfuls onto lightly greased baking sheets.
Bake at 350° for 8 to 14 minutes or until desired degree of doneness. Remove to wire racks to cool completely. **Makes** about 5 dozen.

Peanut Butter-Chocolate Chip Cookies: Decrease salt to ½ teaspoon. Add 1 cup creamy peanut butter with butter and sugars. Increase flour to 2½ cups plus 2 tablespoons. Proceed as directed. (Dough will look a little moist.)

Oatmeal-Raisin Chocolate Chip Cookies: Reduce flour to 2 cups. Add 1 cup uncooked quick-cooking oats to dry ingredients and 1 cup raisins with morsels. Proceed as directed.

Pecan-Chocolate Chip Cookies: Add 1½ cups chopped, toasted pecans with morsels. Proceed as directed.

Almond-Toffee Chocolate Chip Cookies: Reduce morsels to 1 cup. Add ½ cup slivered toasted almonds and 1 cup toffee bits. Proceed as directed.
Note: For testing purposes only, we used Hershey's Heath Bits O'Brickle Toffee Bits.

Dark Chocolate Chip Cookies: Substitute 1 (12-ounce) package dark chocolate morsels for semisweet chocolate morsels. Proceed as directed.
Note: For testing purposes only, we used Hershey's Special Dark Chips.

Chunky Cherry-Double Chip Cookies: Microwave 1 tablespoon water and ½ cup dried cherries in a glass bowl at HIGH 30 seconds, stirring once. Let stand 10 minutes. Substitute 1 (12-ounce) package semisweet chocolate chunks for morsels. Add 1 cup white chocolate morsels, ⅓ cup slivered toasted almonds, and cherries with chocolate chunks. Proceed as directed.

Coconut-Macadamia Chunk Cookies: Substitute 1 (12-ounce) package semisweet chocolate chunks for morsels. Add 1 cup white chocolate morsels, ½ cup sweetened flaked coconut, and ½ cup macadamia nuts with chocolate chunks. Proceed as directed.

SUSAN HEFILFINGER
MANDEVILLE, LOUISIANA

Cook's Notes

Quality ingredients yield the best results. Here's what we discovered.
- The molasses in dark brown sugar produces cookie dough rich in flavor.
- Don't skimp with store-brand chocolate chips that are generally made with fat substitutes and little, if any, cocoa butter. Brand-name chocolate is best.
- We used salted butter in these recipes for a melt-in-your-mouth flavor.

Family Weekend Breakfast

Serve a meal anytime with these sure-to-please recipes that use ingredients you have on hand.

Bacon or sausage, scrambled eggs, and toast have always been sure winners to get food to the table fast—for breakfast or for supper. Take this idea to a new level with these dishes, which include other already-familiar foods. They'll be ready to serve in no time.

SAUSAGE-AND-SCRAMBLED EGG PIZZA

family favorite

Prep: 5 min., Bake: 20 min., Cook: 16 min.

- 1 (13.8-ounce) can refrigerated pizza crust
- 1 pound hot ground pork sausage
- 6 large eggs, lightly beaten
- ½ teaspoon seasoned pepper
- 1 (16-ounce) jar salsa
- 1 (8-ounce) package shredded Mexican four-cheese blend
- Sour cream (optional)

Unroll refrigerated pizza crust, and press into a lightly greased 15- x 10-inch jelly-roll pan.

Bake at 425° for 6 to 8 minutes. Remove from oven, and set aside.

Brown ground sausage in a large non-stick skillet, stirring until it crumbles and is no longer pink. Drain and pat dry with paper towels; set aside. Wipe skillet clean.

Whisk together eggs and seasoned pepper. Cook in a lightly greased skillet over medium heat, without stirring, until eggs begin to set on bottom. Draw a spatula across bottom of skillet to form large curds. Continue cooking until eggs are thickened but still moist. (Do not stir constantly.) Remove skillet from heat.

Spoon and spread salsa evenly over partially baked crust; top evenly with sausage, scrambled eggs, and cheese.

Bake at 425° for 12 minutes or until crust is deep golden brown. Serve with sour cream, if desired. **Makes** 8 servings.

Note: To lighten the pizza, substitute 1 (12-ounce) package reduced-fat ground pork sausage, and prepare as directed. Substitute 1½ cups egg substitute for eggs, and whisk together with seasoned pepper, ¼ teaspoon hot sauce, and, if desired, ⅛ teaspoon salt. Cook as directed. Substitute 1 (8-ounce) package reduced-fat Mexican four-cheese blend. Assemble and bake as directed. Serve with reduced-fat sour cream, if desired.

DONNA LEWIS
HANCEVILLE, ALABAMA

BACON-AND-EGG QUESADILLAS

family favorite

Prep: 20 min., Cook: 23 min.

- 6 large eggs
- 2 tablespoons minced onion
- 2 tablespoons finely chopped green bell pepper
- 6 pickled jalapeño pepper slices, finely chopped
- ½ teaspoon seasoned salt
- ½ teaspoon seasoned pepper
- ½ cup Ranch dressing
- ½ cup salsa
- 1 (8-ounce) package shredded Mexican four-cheese blend
- 4 (10-inch) flour tortillas
- 4 bacon slices, cooked and crumbled
- ½ cup diced ham

Whisk together first 6 ingredients. Cook in a lightly greased large skillet over medium heat, without stirring, until eggs begin to set on bottom. Draw a spatula across bottom of skillet to form large curds. Continue cooking until eggs are thickened but still moist. (Do not stir constantly.) Remove egg mixture from skillet, and set aside. Wipe skillet clean.

Stir together Ranch dressing and salsa; set aside.

Sprinkle ¼ cup cheese evenly onto half of each tortilla; top evenly with one-fourth each of egg mixture, bacon, and ham. Top each half with ¼ cup more cheese. Fold tortilla in half over filling, pressing gently to seal.

Heat skillet coated with cooking spray over medium-high heat. Add quesadillas in 2 batches, and cook 3 to 4 minutes on each side or until golden brown. Serve with salsa mixture. **Makes** 4 servings.

KELLY TOWNSEND
LINCOLN, NEBRASKA

Good to the Last Bite

Enjoying a piece of these do-ahead ice-cream pies is a dreamy experience—from the clever crusts up. Test Kitchens professional Angela Sellers came up with two juicy fresh strawberry-and-ice-cream concoctions to partner with either a pretzel or waffle-cone crust. We think they're perfect for spring entertaining and are scrumptious to the last crumb.

SPIKED STRAWBERRY-LIME ICE-CREAM PIE

freezeable • make ahead

Prep: 30 min., Bake: 10 min., Stand: 30 min., Freeze: 3 hrs.

This pie will soften quickly due to the alcohol content, which lowers the freezing temperature of the ice cream.

- **4 cups pretzel twists**
- **½ cup butter, melted**
- **2 tablespoons granulated sugar**
- **1 (½-gallon) container premium strawberry ice cream**
- **1 (16-ounce) container fresh strawberries (1 quart), stemmed**
- **½ cup powdered sugar**
- **1 (6-ounce) can frozen limeade concentrate, partially thawed**
- **½ cup tequila**
- **¼ cup orange liqueur**
- **Garnishes: lime rind curls, fresh whole strawberries, pretzels**

Process first 3 ingredients in a food processor until pretzels are finely crushed. Firmly press mixture onto bottom of a lightly greased 10-inch springform pan.

Bake at 350° for 10 minutes. Cool completely in pan on a wire rack.

Let strawberry ice cream stand at room temperature 20 minutes or until slightly softened.

Process strawberries and powdered sugar in food processor until pureed, stopping to scrape down sides.

Place ice cream in a large bowl; cut into large (3-inch) pieces. Fold strawberry mixture, limeade concentrate, tequila, and orange liqueur into ice cream until mixture is well blended. Spoon mixture into prepared crust in springform pan. Freeze 3 hours or until firm. Let stand 10 minutes at room temperature before serving. Garnish pie, if desired. **Makes** 10 to 12 servings.

Note: For testing purposes only, we used Blue Bell ice cream and Triple Sec orange liqueur.

Strawberry-Lime Ice-Cream Pie: Omit tequila and orange liqueur, and add 1 (6-ounce) can frozen orange juice concentrate, partially thawed. Proceed with recipe as directed. Let stand 15 minutes at room temperature before serving. Garnish, if desired.

STRAWBERRY SMOOTHIE ICE-CREAM PIE

freezeable • make ahead

Prep: 50 min.; Bake: 10 min.; Stand: 35 min.; Freeze: 4 hrs., 30 min.

The waffle-cone crust idea came from Cheryl F. Rogers of Kenner, Louisiana. *(pictured on page 80)*

- **1 (7-ounce) package waffle cones, broken into pieces**
- **6 tablespoons butter, melted**
- **1 tablespoon granulated sugar**
- **2 (1-quart) containers premium vanilla ice cream, divided**
- **1 (16-ounce) container fresh strawberries (1 quart), stemmed**
- **¼ cup powdered sugar, divided**
- **1 pint fresh blueberries**
- **2 ripe bananas**
- **Garnishes: waffle cone pieces, fresh whole strawberries, fresh blueberries**

Process first 3 ingredients in a food processor until finely crushed. Firmly press mixture onto bottom of a lightly greased 10-inch springform pan.

Bake at 350° for 10 minutes. Cool completely in pan on a wire rack.

Let vanilla ice cream stand at room temperature 20 minutes or until slightly softened.

Process strawberries and 2 tablespoons powdered sugar in a food processor until pureed, stopping to scrape down sides; remove strawberry mixture, and set aside.

Process blueberries and 1 tablespoon powdered sugar in food processor until pureed, stopping to scrape down sides; set aside.

Mash bananas with a fork in a large bowl; stir in remaining 1 tablespoon powdered sugar. Set aside.

Place 1 quart of ice cream in a large bowl; cut into large (3-inch) pieces. Fold strawberry mixture into ice cream until blended. Place in freezer until slightly firm.

Divide remaining quart of ice cream in half, placing halves in separate bowls. Stir blueberry mixture into half and mashed banana mixture into remaining half. Place bowls in freezer.

Spread half of strawberry mixture evenly into prepared crust in springform pan. Place pan and remaining strawberry mixture in freezer. Freeze 30 minutes or until strawberry layer in pan is slightly firm. Spread banana mixture evenly over strawberry layer in pan; return pan to freezer, and freeze 30 minutes or until banana layer is slightly firm. Repeat procedure with blueberry mixture. Spread remaining strawberry mixture over blueberry layer in pan, and freeze 3 hours or until all layers are firm. Let pie stand at room temperature 15 minutes before serving. Garnish, if desired. **Makes** 10 to 12 servings.

Note: For testing purposes only, we used Häagen-Dazs ice cream.

Savor Easy Pork Roast

This budget-friendly cut stars in these moist, tender recipes.

When you crave the fall-apart goodness of a perfectly cooked pork roast, nothing else will do. If you think you're too busy to cook one yourself, consider these options.

BOSTON BUTT ROAST WITH GRAVY

family favorite

Prep: 20 min.; Bake: 3 hrs., 30 min.; Stand: 10 min.; Cook: 15 min.

For the ultimate in comfort food, serve with roasted potatoes, carrots, and onions.

- **1 (5- to 6-pound) Boston butt pork roast, trimmed**
- **1½ tablespoons salt**
- **½ tablespoon Italian seasoning**
- **1 teaspoon garlic powder**
- **1 teaspoon pepper**
- **6 tablespoons all-purpose flour, divided**
- **2 cups water**
- **¼ cup white vinegar**
- **1 onion, chopped**
- **4 garlic cloves**
- **¼ cup hot sauce**
- **2 tablespoons butter or margarine**
- **1 cup low-sodium beef broth**
- **¼ cup red wine**
- **½ teaspoon Italian seasoning**
- **Salt and pepper to taste**

Place roast in an aluminum foil-lined roasting pan. Sprinkle pork evenly with 1½ tablespoons salt and next 3 ingredients. Sprinkle evenly with 4 tablespoons flour. Pour 2 cups water and vinegar into roasting pan. Add onion and garlic cloves. Drizzle pork evenly with hot sauce.

Bake at 375° for 3½ hours or until tender. Remove pork from roasting pan, and wrap in aluminum foil. Pour about 1 cup pan drippings into a 2-cup glass measuring cup. Let stand 10 minutes, and skim fat from drippings.

Melt butter in a large skillet over medium-high heat; whisk in remaining 2 tablespoons flour, pan drippings, broth, wine, and ½ teaspoon Italian seasoning. Bring to a boil, whisking constantly; reduce heat to medium, and simmer 10 minutes. Season with salt and pepper to taste. Serve gravy over sliced pork. **Makes** 6 to 8 servings.

ZESTY FRIED PORK BITES

family favorite

Prep: 10 min.; Cook: 1 hr., 30 min.

This unconventional method of cooking meat in water until it evaporates and then browning in its drippings makes the meat juicy on the inside and crispy and golden on the outside.

- **⅓ cup fresh lime juice**
- **2 garlic cloves, pressed**
- **¼ teaspoon salt**
- **½ teaspoon pepper**
- **2 cups water**
- **1 tablespoon salt**
- **2½ pounds Boston butt roast, untrimmed and cut into 1-inch cubes**
- **Lime wedges**

Stir together first 4 ingredients. Cover and chill until ready to serve.

Bring 2 cups water and 1 tablespoon salt to a boil in a Dutch oven over medium-high heat. Add pork; reduce heat to medium-low, and cook 1 hour and 15 minutes or until water evaporates. (Meat will look pale.) Cook, stirring occasionally, 10 more minutes or until pork cubes are golden brown. Drain on layers of paper towels. Serve with garlic mixture and lime wedges. **Makes** 4 to 6 servings.

SUZY ESPINOSA
ATLANTA, GEORGIA

POLYNESIAN PORK

family favorite

Prep: 10 min., Chill: 30 min., Bake: 4 hrs.

- **1 tablespoon all-purpose flour**
- **1 large oven bag**
- **1 tablespoon salt**
- **1 teaspoon curry powder**
- **1 (4- to 5-pound) Boston butt pork roast, untrimmed**
- **1 garlic clove, minced**
- **¼ cup mango chutney**
- **1 (6-ounce) can pineapple juice**
- **Toppings: toasted sesame seeds, sweetened flaked coconut, chopped fresh parsley or cilantro**

Add flour to oven bag; twist end, and shake to coat.

Sprinkle salt and curry powder evenly over pork; rub evenly with garlic. Cover and chill 30 minutes.

Spread chutney evenly over roast. Place roast inside oven bag; pour pineapple juice over roast, and twist end of bag. Close bag with tie; cut 6 (½-inch) slits in top of bag. Place bag in a roasting pan, tucking ends of bag in the pan.

Bake at 350° for 3½ to 4 hours or until tender. Serve with desired toppings. **Makes** 6 to 8 servings.

Note: For testing purposes only, we used Reynolds Large Size Oven Bags.

KAREN WHITEHEAD
ENTERPRISE, ALABAMA

Start With Slaw Mix

Hail to the best-kept secret in supermarket produce—prepackaged slaw mix, a convenient and versatile ingredient. Choose from finely shredded cabbage, regular coleslaw mix, and broccoli slaw for a quick toss in any of these time-friendly favorites. Rinse your mix with cold water to keep the shreds cool and crisp. Drain well (or spin dry) before tossing.

CABBAGE-APPLE SALAD WITH SUGARED PECANS

fast fixin's

Prep: 15 min., Cook: 5 min.

- 1 (16-ounce) bag shredded coleslaw mix
- 1 Granny Smith apple, cut into ½-inch cubes
- 2 tablespoons fresh lemon juice
- ½ teaspoon salt
- 2 tablespoons butter
- ½ cup pecan halves, chopped
- 4 teaspoons sugar
- 2 tablespoons chopped fresh chives

Rinse slaw mix with cold water; drain well. Toss together slaw and next 3 ingredients, and set aside.

Melt butter in a small skillet over medium heat. Add chopped pecans, and cook, stirring often, 3 minutes or until toasted. Sprinkle sugar over pecans, and cook, stirring constantly, 1 minute or until sugar dissolves and pecans are coated. Remove from heat, and cool slightly.

Add pecan mixture and chives to slaw mixture, tossing to combine. **Makes** 6 servings.

BETTY RABE
PLANO, TEXAS

SWEET BROCCOLI SLAW SALAD

make ahead

Prep: 15 min., Chill: 8 hrs.

This is adapted from a favorite cookbook, *Southern Scrumptious: How to Cater Your Own Party* (Favorite Recipes Press, 2002), by Betty Sims.

- 2 (12-ounce) packages broccoli slaw mix
- 1 cup light or regular mayonnaise
- ½ cup sugar
- 2 tablespoons cider vinegar
- 1 small red onion, chopped
- ½ cup sweetened dried cranberries
- 4 bacon slices, cooked and crumbled
- ½ cup toasted chopped pecans (optional)

Rinse broccoli slaw mix with cold water; drain well.

Stir together mayonnaise, sugar, and vinegar in a large bowl; add slaw, onion, and dried cranberries, tossing gently to coat. Cover and chill 8 hours. Sprinkle with bacon and, if desired, pecans just before serving. **Makes** 6 to 8 servings.

Note: For testing purposes only, we used Craisins for sweetened dried cranberries.

BETTY SIMS
DECATUR, ALABAMA

BLUE CHEESE-BACON SLAW

fast fixin's

Prep: 15 min.

- 1 (16-ounce) bottle Ranch dressing
- 1 cup crumbled blue cheese
- 2 (12-ounce) packages broccoli slaw mix
- 1 small onion, chopped
- 6 bacon slices, cooked and crumbled

Stir together Ranch dressing and blue cheese in a large bowl. Rinse slaw mix with cold water; drain well. Combine slaw mix, onion, and bacon; toss. Top with dressing just before serving. **Makes** 8 servings.

SPRING SALAD WITH RASPBERRY VINAIGRETTE

fast fixin's

Prep: 20 min.

Finely shredded cabbage or coleslaw mix is also known as angel hair slaw.

- 1 (10-ounce) package finely shredded coleslaw mix
- 2 cups chopped cooked chicken
- ½ cup fresh raspberries
- 1 small red bell pepper, cut into thin strips
- ¼ red onion, thinly sliced
- ⅓ cup chopped fresh mint
- Raspberry Vinaigrette
- 1 small head Red Leaf lettuce, torn
- ⅓ cup sunflower kernels

Rinse slaw mix with cold water; drain well. Toss together slaw, next 5 ingredients, and half of Raspberry Vinaigrette. Serve slaw mixture over lettuce, and sprinkle with sunflower kernels. Serve with remaining vinaigrette. **Makes** 6 servings.

RASPBERRY VINAIGRETTE:
fast fixin's

Prep: 10 min.

- ⅓ cup raspberry vinegar
- 1 tablespoon Dijon mustard
- ½ teaspoon sugar
- ½ teaspoon salt
- ½ teaspoon pepper
- ½ cup olive oil

Whisk together first 5 ingredients; gradually whisk in oil until blended. **Makes** about 1 cup.

RONDA CARMAN
HOUSTON, TEXAS

Have a Deli-Style Dinner

These sandwiches are a fast dash from prep to table.

Serve a sandwich with chips, fries, or veggie sticks and cut-up fruit, and you have a real meal that's ready in no time. At your grocery store's deli counter, ask for meats to be thinly sliced, not shaved. This will bring out the flavor, and it will be easier to separate the slices. Plan to repackage the meat in zip-top plastic bags once you're home, and use it within five days. Sandwich suppers are so easy and so good.

Crunchy Sides

Our favorite chips are Zapp's Potato Chips (**www.zapps.com**) in any flavor and Terra Chips (**www.terrachips.com**), but we really love Ranch-Seasoned French Fries (recipe on opposite page).

TANGY-AND-SWEET ROAST BEEF WRAPS

family favorite

Prep: 15 min.

Find wheat wraps on the bread aisle of the supermarket. They are thinner than tortillas and soft enough to wrap around the fixings without tearing easily. If you can't find them, use large flour tortillas. Serve this with red grapes, pear slices, or pineapple chunks (see "Cut Up a Pineapple With Ease" on page 86).

- ¼ cup Dijon mustard
- ¼ cup pineapple preserves
- 2 tablespoons horseradish sauce
- 4 (9-inch) wheat wraps
- ½ pound thinly sliced deli roast beef
- 4 green leaf lettuce leaves
- 1 (8-ounce) package Cheddar cheese slices
- ¼ cup chopped walnuts, toasted
- 2 tablespoons sliced green onions

Stir together first 3 ingredients. Spread mixture evenly on wraps. Layer each wrap evenly with roast beef, lettuce, and cheese slices; sprinkle each wrap with nuts and green onions. Roll up tightly. Cut in half diagonally. **Makes** 4 servings.

Note: For testing purposes only, we used Boar's Head Brand Pub Style Horseradish Sauce and Toufayan Bakeries Wheat Wraps.

TURKEY, BACON, AND HAVARTI SANDWICH

family favorite • make ahead

Prep: 20 min., Chill: 1 hr.

Use precooked bacon to save time. Microwave according to package directions to crisp before you assemble the sandwich. Havarti is a Danish cheese that's semisoft with small irregular holes and a mild flavor; substitute Muenster if you can't find it. Strawberries, apple slices, or cantaloupe will pair nicely with these flavors. *(pictured on page 77)*

- 1 (7-inch) round sourdough bread loaf
- ¼ cup balsamic vinaigrette
- ½ pound thinly sliced smoked deli turkey
- 1 (12-ounce) jar roasted red bell peppers, drained and sliced
- 6 (1-ounce) slices Havarti cheese
- 4 fully cooked bacon slices
- Garnish: dill pickle spears

Cut top 2 inches off sourdough loaf, reserving top; hollow out loaf, leaving a 1-inch-thick shell. (Reserve soft center of bread loaf for other uses, if desired.)

Drizzle 2 tablespoons vinaigrette evenly in bottom bread shell; layer with half each of turkey, peppers, and cheese. Repeat layers, and top with bacon. Drizzle evenly with remaining 2 tablespoons vinaigrette, and cover with reserved bread top; press down firmly. Wrap in plastic wrap, and chill at least 1 hour or up to 8 hours before serving. Cut into 4 wedges. Garnish, if desired. **Makes** 4 servings.

Note: For testing purposes only, we used Newman's Own Balsamic Vinaigrette salad dressing.

ELIZABETH M. DELL
FAIRPORT, NEW YORK

RANCH-SEASONED FRENCH FRIES

family favorite

Prep: 5 min., Bake: 45 min.

Our directions call for cooking the fries at a lower temperature and a little longer than the directions on the package.

1 (26-ounce) bag frozen extra-crispy French fried potatoes
Vegetable cooking spray
1 (1-ounce) package Ranch dressing mix

Spray potatoes evenly with cooking spray, and place in a large zip-top plastic bag. Add dressing mix; seal bag, and shake to coat fries. Place in a single layer on a 15- x 10-inch jelly-roll pan. **Bake** at 425° for 30 to 35 minutes; stir and bake 5 to 10 more minutes or until golden. **Makes** 6 servings.

Note: For testing purposes only, we used Ore-Ida Extra Crispy Golden Crinkles French Fried Potatoes.

Stuff a Dozen (or Two)

A friendly contest among the food professionals of the Southern Foodways Alliance (SFA) to find the best deviled egg ended with these recipes reaching the finals. The alliance is dedicated to the celebration and preservation of our region's food heritage, and dozens of its members entered recipes.

Everyone at the 2004 conference in Oxford, Mississippi, loved these, so we knew you would too. Enjoy!

BUTTERY DIJON DEVILED EGGS

make ahead

Prep: 15 min., Chill: 1 hr.

1 dozen large eggs, hard-cooked and peeled
¼ cup butter, softened
¼ cup mayonnaise
1 tablespoon Dijon mustard
1 teaspoon fresh lemon juice
¼ teaspoon ground red pepper
Salt to taste
Ground white pepper to taste
Paprika (optional)

Cut eggs in half lengthwise; carefully remove yolks. Mash yolks; stir in butter and next 4 ingredients. Stir in salt and white pepper to taste. Spoon or pipe yolk mixture evenly into egg white halves. Sprinkle eggs with paprika, if desired. Cover and chill at least 1 hour or until ready to serve. **Makes** 2 dozen.

RICK ELLIS
NEW YORK, NEW YORK

DEVILED EGGS WITH CAPERS

make ahead

Prep: 15 min., Chill: 1 hr.

6 large eggs, hard-cooked and peeled
2 tablespoons mayonnaise
1 tablespoon butter, softened
2 teaspoons drained capers
1 teaspoon chopped fresh chives
⅛ teaspoon dry mustard
Salt and pepper to taste
Paprika (optional)
Fresh parsley sprigs (optional)

Cut eggs in half lengthwise; carefully remove yolks. Mash yolks; stir in mayonnaise and next 4 ingredients. Stir in salt and pepper to taste. Spoon or pipe egg yolk mixture evenly into egg white halves. Cover and chill at least 1 hour or until ready to serve. Sprinkle with paprika and top with parsley sprigs, if desired. **Makes** 1 dozen.

MARGARET ANNE MITCHELL
JACKSON, MISSISSIPPI

How to Make Hard-Cooked Eggs

Place eggs in a single layer in a saucepan; add water to a depth of 3 inches. Bring to a boil; cover, remove from heat, and let stand 15 minutes. Drain and fill the pan with cold water and ice. Cover the pot, and shake so the eggs crack all over. Peel under cold running water, starting at the large end.

CHIVE-TARRAGON DEVILED EGGS

make ahead

Prep: 15 min., Chill: 1 hr. *(pictured on page 77)*

1 dozen large eggs, hard-cooked and peeled
½ cup mayonnaise
1 tablespoon lemon juice
⅛ teaspoon hot sauce
2 tablespoons finely chopped fresh chives
2 teaspoons finely chopped fresh tarragon
½ teaspoon salt
½ teaspoon dry mustard
Garnishes: chopped fresh chives, fresh flat-leaf parsley sprigs

Cut eggs in half lengthwise; carefully remove yolks. Mash egg yolks; stir in mayonnaise, lemon juice, hot sauce, and next 4 ingredients. Spoon or pipe egg yolk mixture evenly into egg white halves. Cover and chill at least 1 hour or until ready to serve. Garnish, if desired. **Makes** 2 dozen.

ELIZABETH H. HOWARD
NEW ORLEANS, LOUISIANA

To Market, To Market

Fairfield Grocery & Market is a blast. Step inside, sample delicious food, and meet some friendly folks.

Fairfield Grocery & Market, a refreshing testament to the bygone days of the small grocery store, stands smack-dab in the middle of the rapidly growing city of Shreveport, Louisiana. Fairfield, as it is called by its local following, has survived in the midst of all the fancy grocery stores that have grown up around it.

Current owners Syndy and John Johnson continue to offer personal service. "I dreamed of owning and running a place like Fairfield," Syndy says, "maybe even adding homemade meals for delivery as well as groceries." The idea was a hit. Today, when life gets too busy, Shreveport families can rely on home-cooked comfort from Fairfield.

It's nice to know there is still a grocery store where you can park near the front door, stock up on necessities and goodies, and catch up on the latest with friends.

MILLIONAIRE SHORTBREAD

Prep: 15 min., Bake: 20 min., Cook: 34 min., Chill: 45 min.

This recipe came from Fairfield Grocery employee Jane and her husband's good friend, Dr. Anne Peters of Edinburgh, Scotland. It uses white rice flour, which gives the shortbread a crispy texture. You can substitute all-purpose flour for the rice flour.

- 1½ cups butter, softened and divided
- 2 cups all-purpose flour
- ¾ cup white rice flour *
- ½ cup granulated sugar
- Cooking spray for baking
- 1 (14-ounce) can sweetened condensed milk
- ¼ cup light corn syrup
- 1 cup firmly packed light brown sugar
- 1½ cups semisweet chocolate morsels

Pulse 1 cup butter, flours, and granulated sugar in a food processor 10 to 15 times or until crumbly. Press mixture evenly into a 15- x 10-inch jelly-roll pan coated with cooking spray for baking.

Bake at 350° for 18 to 20 minutes or until light golden brown.

Stir together remaining ½ cup butter, condensed milk, and corn syrup in a 2-quart heavy saucepan over low heat 4 minutes or until butter is melted and mixture is blended. Add brown sugar, and cook, stirring constantly, 25 to 30 minutes or until caramel colored and thickened. Pour evenly over baked cookie in pan, and spread into an even layer. Chill 30 minutes or until caramel is set.

Microwave morsels in a small glass bowl at HIGH 1 minute or until almost melted. Stir until smooth. Spread over caramel layer in pan. (The chocolate layer will be thin.) Chill 15 minutes or until chocolate is firm. Cut into 2-inch squares; if desired, cut each square into 2 triangles. **Makes** about 3 dozen squares or 6 dozen triangles.

*Substitute ¾ cup all-purpose flour, if desired.

JANE BICKNELL
FAIRFIELD GROCERY & MARKET
SHREVEPORT, LOUISIANA

CHICKEN SALAD

make ahead

Prep: 30 min., Cook: 40 min., Stand: 15 min., Chill: 4 hrs.

This is Fairfield Grocery's signature dish. They shred rather than chop the chicken; the tines of two forks make shredding a snap. This versatile salad tastes great as a spreadable appetizer.

- 3 pounds skinned and boned chicken breasts
- 1 (49½-ounce) can chicken broth
- 1 cup finely chopped celery
- ½ cup finely chopped water chestnuts, rinsed and drained
- ½ cup finely chopped red bell pepper
- ½ cup finely chopped yellow bell pepper
- ½ cup finely chopped red onion
- 3 cups mayonnaise
- 1 teaspoon ground red pepper
- ½ teaspoon salt
- ½ teaspoon ground white pepper

Place chicken breasts in a large skillet; add chicken broth. Cover and bring to a boil over high heat. Reduce heat to medium-low, and simmer, covered, 30 minutes or until chicken is done. Remove chicken from skillet, and let stand 15 minutes or until cool to touch. Shred chicken.

Combine shredded chicken, celery, water chestnuts, and next 3 ingredients in a large bowl.

Stir together mayonnaise, ground red pepper, salt, and white pepper until well blended; spoon over shredded chicken mixture, stirring to coat. Cover and chill at least 4 hours. **Makes** about 8 (1-cup) servings.

Shrimp Salad: Substitute 3 pounds chopped cooked shrimp for chicken breasts and broth. Do not cook. Reduce mayonnaise to 2 cups and salt to ¼ teaspoon. Proceed with recipe as directed.

GINA JESTER
FAIRFIELD GROCERY & MARKET
SHREVEPORT, LOUISIANA

SPINACH MADELEINE

fast fixin's

Prep: 15 min., Cook: 10 min.

> 2 (10-ounce) packages frozen chopped spinach
> ¼ cup butter
> ½ teaspoon minced fresh garlic
> 2 tablespoons all-purpose flour
> 1 cup milk
> 1 (8-ounce) package pasteurized prepared cheese product, cubed
> 1 teaspoon hot sauce
> ½ teaspoon Creole seasoning

Cook spinach according to package directions; drain and set aside.

Melt butter in a medium saucepan over medium heat; add garlic, and sauté 1 minute. Whisk in flour until smooth, and cook mixture, whisking constantly, 1 minute. Gradually whisk in milk, and cook, whisking constantly, 2 minutes or until mixture is thickened and bubbly.

Add cheese, hot sauce, and Creole seasoning; whisk until cheese is melted. Stir in spinach, and cook until thoroughly heated. Serve immediately. **Makes** about 8 servings.

SYNDY JOHNSON
FAIRFIELD GROCERY & MARKET
SHREVEPORT, LOUISIANA

OLD-FASHIONED MEAT LOAF

family favorite

Prep: 20 min., Cook: 7 min., Bake: 1 hr., Stand: 10 min.

> 1 tablespoon butter
> 3 celery ribs, finely chopped
> ½ large onion, finely chopped
> 2 pounds lean ground beef
> 2 tablespoons Worcestershire sauce, divided
> ½ cup Italian-seasoned breadcrumbs
> ⅓ cup ketchup
> 2 teaspoons Creole seasoning
> 1 teaspoon Greek seasoning
> 1 teaspoon garlic powder
> 2 large eggs, lightly beaten
> 1 (8-ounce) can tomato sauce
> 3 tablespoons tomato paste
> 1 tablespoon ketchup
> Garnish: chopped fresh flat-leaf parsley

Melt butter in a medium-size nonstick skillet over medium heat; add celery and onion, and sauté 7 minutes or just until tender.

Stir together celery mixture, ground beef, 1 tablespoon Worcestershire sauce, breadcrumbs, and next 5 ingredients in a large bowl. Shape into a 10- x 5-inch loaf; place on a lightly greased broiler rack. Place rack in an aluminum foil-lined broiler pan.

Bake at 350° for 45 minutes. Stir together remaining 1 tablespoon Worcestershire sauce, tomato sauce, tomato paste, and 1 tablespoon ketchup until blended; pour evenly over meatloaf, and bake 10 to 15 more minutes or until no longer pink in center. Let stand 10 minutes before serving. **Makes** 6 to 8 servings.

Note: For testing purposes only, we used Tony Chachere's Original Creole Seasoning and Cavender's All Purpose Greek Seasoning.

GINA JESTER
FAIRFIELD GROCERY & MARKET
SHREVEPORT, LOUISIANA

BLACK BEAN 'N' SPINACH ENCHILADAS

family favorite

Prep: 25 min., Bake: 35 min.

> 2 (15-ounce) cans black beans, rinsed and drained
> 2 tablespoons fresh lime juice
> 1 teaspoon Creole seasoning
> 1 teaspoon chili powder
> ½ teaspoon ground cumin
> ½ teaspoon garlic powder
> ½ teaspoon onion powder
> ½ recipe Spinach Madeleine (2 cups) (recipe on this page)
> 1 (8-ounce) container sour cream
> 8 (8-inch) flour tortillas
> 1 (12-ounce) block Monterey Jack cheese, shredded and divided

Combine first 7 ingredients in a medium bowl; set aside.

Stir together Spinach Madeleine and sour cream until blended.

Spoon about ½ cup black bean mixture down center of each tortilla. Top each with ⅓ cup Spinach Madeleine mixture, and sprinkle with 3 tablespoons cheese. Roll up tortillas, and place, seam sides down, in 2 lightly greased 11- x 7-inch baking dishes. Sprinkle remaining cheese evenly over tops.

Bake, covered, at 350° for 25 minutes. Uncover and bake 5 to 10 more minutes or until cheese is melted. **Makes** 8 servings.

Black Bean-Chicken-Spinach Enchiladas: Substitute 1 cup chopped, cooked chicken for 1 can black beans. Proceed as directed.

SYNDY JOHNSON
FAIRFIELD GROCERY & MARKET
SHREVEPORT, LOUISIANA

New-Fashioned Luncheon Party

Throw a make-ahead get-together for your friends
with these spiffed-up recipes.

Party Menu

Serves 8

Apricot Bellinis

Cheese Wafers (facing page)

Cucumber-Dill Rounds

Smoked Turkey Tetrazzini

assorted fresh fruit

bakery rolls

I t's a perfect time to entertain the girls or couples. We've updated a favorite casserole along with other recipes that garnered rave reviews. Begin with Cucumber-Dill Rounds—they're fun to eat and a snap to prepare. The tetrazzini has just a hint of smoky flavor and uses colored fettuccine instead of spaghetti. Finally, the very popular Bellini—a fruit and sparkling wine beverage—goes from peach to apricot.

APRICOT BELLINIS

fast fixin's

Prep: 15 min.

You can use 12 fresh apricots, halved, in place of the canned ones. Fresh ones are in season in June.

  2 (15-ounce) cans apricot halves,
     drained
  2 (11.5-ounce) cans apricot nectar
  ½ cup sugar
  Crushed ice
  1 (750-milliliter) bottle sparkling
     wine or Champagne, chilled*
  Garnish: fresh mint sprigs

Process half each of first 3 ingredients in a blender until smooth, stopping to scrape down sides. Repeat with remaining apricot halves, nectar, and sugar. Serve over crushed ice with sparkling wine. Garnish, if desired. **Makes** 8 (1-cup) servings.

*Substitute 2 (12-ounce) cans ginger ale or lemon-lime soda, if desired.

Note: You can stir together the apricot mixture and the sparkling wine in a pitcher. Be sure and do this just before serving.

CUCUMBER-DILL ROUNDS

fast fixin's

Prep: 20 min.

Stir together 1 (8-ounce) package softened cream cheese, 1 tablespoon chopped fresh dill, and 1 teaspoon garlic salt. Dollop or pipe mixture onto 24 cucumber slices. Garnish each with a fresh dill sprig, if desired. **Makes** 8 appetizer servings.

SMOKED TURKEY TETRAZZINI

family favorite • make ahead

Prep: 10 min., Cook: 15 min., Bake: 25 min.

Assemble this delicious casserole the night before, if desired, and chill. Let stand at room temperature 30 minutes before baking.

  1 (12-ounce) package amber-and-
     spinach-colored fettuccine *
  ¼ cup butter or margarine
  1 medium-size yellow onion,
     coarsely chopped
  3 tablespoons all-purpose flour
  1 teaspoon salt
  1 teaspoon freshly ground pepper
  ¼ teaspoon hot sauce
  3 cups milk
  3 cups chopped smoked turkey
  1 (6-ounce) jar sliced mushrooms,
     drained
  1 cup white wine
  1 cup freshly shredded Parmesan
     cheese, divided
  1 cup sliced almonds
  3 tablespoons chopped fresh
     parsley

Cook pasta according to package directions; drain and set aside.
Melt ¼ cup butter in a large skillet over medium-high heat; add onion, and sauté 7 to 10 minutes or until tender. Gradually stir in flour and next 3 ingredients until smooth; add milk, and cook, stirring constantly, 5 minutes or until thickened. Remove from heat, and stir in turkey, mushrooms, and wine.
Layer a lightly greased 13- x 9-inch baking dish with half each of pasta,

turkey mixture, and Parmesan cheese. Repeat layers with remaining pasta and turkey mixture.

Combine remaining 1/2 cup Parmesan cheese, almonds, and parsley. Sprinkle evenly over casserole.

Bake at 400° for 20 to 25 minutes or until bubbly and almonds are lightly toasted. **Makes** 8 servings.

Note: For testing purposes only, we used Ronzoni Fettuccine Florentine.

*****Substitute 1(12-ounce) package regular fettuccine, if desired.

MAGGIE ELLWOOD
GRAND RAPIDS, MICHIGAN

Smoked Turkey Tetrazzini With Artichokes and Red Bell Peppers:
Prepare recipe as directed, adding 1 (14-ounce) can artichoke hearts, drained and chopped, and 1 (7-ounce) jar roasted red bell peppers, drained and chopped, with turkey, mushrooms, and wine. Proceed as directed.

Speedy Appetizers

Fix these tasty appetizers for your next get-together or anytime you're in need of a quick snack. Red Pepper Hummus is not only packed with zesty ingredients, but it's also good for you. Pair it with Benne Seed Pita Triangles for an unbeatable chip-and-dip combination.

RED PEPPER HUMMUS

fast fixin's •make ahead

Prep: 10 min.

You can easily double this recipe. Stir the tahini thoroughly before measuring it.

> 2 (15-ounce) cans chickpeas, rinsed and drained
> 3 garlic cloves
> 1/2 cup jarred roasted red bell peppers, drained
> 1/2 cup tahini
> 1/4 cup water
> 2 tablespoons olive oil
> 1 1/2 teaspoons salt
> 1/2 teaspoon ground cumin
> 1/4 teaspoon ground red pepper
> 1/3 to 1/2 cup fresh lime juice
> Garnish: fresh flat-leaf parsley sprigs

Process first 9 ingredients and 1/3 cup lime juice in a food processor or blender until smooth, stopping to scrape down sides; add additional lime juice, if necessary, until desired consistency. Cover and chill until ready to serve. Garnish, if desired. **Makes** 3 1/4 cups.

BENNE SEED PITA TRIANGLES

fast fixin's • make ahead

Prep: 10 min., Bake: 13 min.

We used a thicker-style pita bread for this recipe, which makes sturdy chips that are easy to dip.

> 1 (18-ounce) package large pita bread rounds
> 6 tablespoons butter, melted
> 1/2 teaspoon freshly ground pepper
> 2 tablespoons benne or sesame seeds
> 1/4 teaspoon salt

Split each pita round horizontally into 2 rounds; stack rounds, and cut into 6 wedges to make 72 triangles. Arrange triangles on baking sheets.

Stir together butter and pepper. Brush mixture evenly over split sides of pita triangles. Sprinkle evenly with benne seeds and salt.

Bake at 375° for 10 to 13 minutes or until golden. **Makes** 12 servings.

Note: For testing purposes only, we used Toufayan Pita Bread. Triangles may be made up to a day ahead. Store in zip-top freezer bags until ready to serve.

CHEESE WAFERS

fast fixin's • make ahead

Prep: 10 min., Bake: 15 min.

For the best results, shred the Cheddar cheese from a block or round. Preshredded, bagged cheese doesn't work well in this recipe. The sharp Cheddar gives extra flavor—don't substitute regular Cheddar.

> 1 1/2 cups (6 ounces) shredded sharp Cheddar cheese
> 1/2 cup butter, softened
> 1 cup all-purpose flour
> Dash of salt
> Dash of paprika
> 1 1/2 cups cornflakes cereal, crushed
> 1/2 cup finely chopped almonds

Process cheese and butter in a food processor until blended. Add flour, salt, and paprika; process until mixture forms a ball, stopping once to scrape down sides. Add cereal and almonds; process until blended, stopping twice to scrape down sides.

Shape dough into 1-inch balls. Place balls 2 inches apart on ungreased baking sheets. Flatten each dough ball in a crisscross pattern with a fork dipped in flour.

Bake at 350°, in batches, for 14 to 15 minutes or until lightly browned. Remove to wire racks to cool. Store in an airtight container up to 1 week. **Makes** 4 dozen.

LIZ CHIZ
LOS ANGELES, CALIFORNIA

Lunch in the Lowcountry

Enjoy these dishes from Charleston's tearooms.

Congregations of several area churches operate annual tearooms in the spring to help fund parish activities or charities. Visitors dine on specialties such as Okra Soup and Huguenot Torte, both long-standing staples of the region's home cooking. We're happy to share some of their recipes here.

SHRIMP PASTE

fast fixin's

Prep: 15 min.

Use as a sandwich filling or appetizer spread. Boost the flavor with 2 tablespoons chopped green onions or fresh herbs, if desired.

- 1 pound peeled and cooked shrimp
- 1 (8-ounce) package cream cheese, softened
- 3 tablespoons lemon juice
- 1 garlic clove, pressed
- ½ teaspoon hot sauce
- ¼ to ½ teaspoon salt
- ⅛ teaspoon pepper

Process shrimp in a food processor until coarsely ground. Add remaining ingredients, processing until smooth. **Makes** 3½ cups.

CHARLESTON FAMILY AND YOUTH
CHARLESTON, SOUTH CAROLINA

OKRA SOUP

family favorite

Prep: 25 min., Cook: 4 hrs., Cool: 15 min.

- 1 (2½- to 3-pound) boneless chuck roast, trimmed
- 1 teaspoon salt
- 1 teaspoon pepper
- 2 tablespoons vegetable oil
- 12 cups water
- 2 medium onions, chopped
- 2 celery ribs, chopped
- 2 (16-ounce) bags frozen sliced okra
- 2 (14.5-ounce) cans diced tomatoes
- ¼ cup sugar
- 2½ to 3 teaspoons salt
- 1 teaspoon pepper
- 2½ teaspoons hot sauce
- ½ teaspoon Worcestershire sauce
- 3 beef bouillon cubes

Sprinkle roast with 1 teaspoon salt and 1 teaspoon pepper.
Brown roast on all sides in hot oil in a Dutch oven over medium-high heat. Add 12 cups water, and bring to a boil; cover, reduce heat to low, and simmer 2 hours.
Remove roast from broth, reserving broth; cool 15 minutes. Shred roast, and return to broth.
Add onions and remaining ingredients to broth; cover and cook over low heat, stirring occasionally, 2 hours. **Makes** 18 cups.

CHRIST EPISCOPAL CHURCH
MOUNT PLEASANT, SOUTH CAROLINA

SHE-CRAB SOUP

family favorite

Prep: 20 min., Cook: 30 min.

You can halve this recipe for smaller families.

- ½ cup butter
- 2 celery ribs, chopped
- 1 medium onion, diced (1 cup)
- 2 pounds fresh crabmeat, drained and picked
- 1 quart whipping cream
- 1 quart half-and-half
- 2 cups milk
- 2 teaspoons Old Bay seasoning
- ¼ cup cornstarch
- ¼ cup water
- 2 teaspoons salt
- Dry sherry (optional)

Melt butter in a Dutch oven over medium heat; add celery and onion, and sauté 5 minutes or until tender. Add crabmeat and next 4 ingredients; cook over medium heat, stirring often, until thoroughly heated.
Stir together cornstarch and ¼ cup water; stir in 2 tablespoons hot soup. Stir cornstarch mixture and salt into soup; cook 5 to 7 minutes until thickened, stirring often. Top each serving with 1 teaspoon sherry, if desired. **Makes** 15 cups.

GRACE EPISCOPAL CHURCH
CHARLESTON, SOUTH CAROLINA

HUGUENOT TORTE

family favorite

Prep: 15 min., Bake: 45 min.

- 2 large eggs
- 1½ cups sugar
- ¼ cup all-purpose flour
- 1 tablespoon baking powder
- ¼ teaspoon salt
- 1 Granny Smith apple, chopped (1 cup)
- 1 cup chopped pecans
- 1 teaspoon vanilla extract
- Whipped cream

Beat eggs at high speed with an electric mixer 5 minutes or until doubled in volume and lemon colored. Gradually add sugar, beating at medium speed until tripled in volume. Stir in flour and next 5 ingredients just until blended.

Spoon into a greased or aluminum foil-lined 13- x 9-inch pan. (A light-colored metal pan works best.)

Bake at 325° for 45 minutes or until golden. (Torte will puff up and then fall.) Run a knife around edge of pan while still warm. Cut into 3-inch squares. Serve with whipped cream. **Makes** 12 servings.

Note: We lined the pan with Reynold's Wrap Release Non-Stick Aluminum Foil for easier cleanup.

OLD ST. ANDREW'S PARISH CHURCH
CHARLESTON, SOUTH CAROLINA

taste of the south
Hush Puppies

Both a fish fry and barbecue staple, hush puppies are made from a six-ingredient batter, which is dropped by spoonfuls into hot oil to cook. You can make them yourself—we walk you through the steps with our tips. So, how did they get their name? They were perhaps the original treat (aka bribe) for Fido. Legends tell how Southern fishermen and Civil War soldiers first made the golden nuggets from scraps just to toss to barking and begging dogs with the command to "Hush, puppy."

HUSH PUPPIES

family favorite

Prep: 10 min., Stand: 10 min.,
Cook: 6 min. per batch

This recipe was adapted from a favorite of The Catfish Institute in Belzoni, Mississippi. Substituting beer for milk makes these lighter and tangier.

> **1 cup self-rising white cornmeal mix**
> **½ cup self-rising flour**
> **½ cup diced onion**
> **1 tablespoon sugar**
> **1 large egg, lightly beaten**
> **½ cup milk or beer**
> **Vegetable oil**

Combine first 4 ingredients in a large bowl.

Add egg and milk to dry ingredients, stirring just until moistened. Let stand 10 minutes.

Pour oil to a depth of 2 inches into a Dutch oven; heat to 375°.

Drop batter by rounded tablespoonfuls into hot oil, and fry, in batches, 2 to 3 minutes on each side or until golden brown. Drain on a wire rack over paper towels; serve immediately. **Makes** 1½ dozen.

Note: Keep fried hush puppies warm in oven at 225° for up to 15 minutes. For testing purposes only, we used White Lily Self-Rising White Cornmeal Mix.

Jalapeño Hush Puppies: Add 1 seeded, diced jalapeño to batter. Proceed with recipe as directed.

Cook's Notes

1. The Batter: Stir 10 times around the bowl—just until dry and liquid ingredients are barely combined. Overmixing causes a tough texture.

2. The Pot: Use a pot that's at least 6 inches deep and fits the largest element on your cooktop. Our Test Kitchens had excellent results frying this recipe in both a 6-quart Dutch oven and in a deep cast-iron skillet. We also tried an electric deep-fat fryer with a temperature control dial and found the batter stuck to the basket and the temperature did not get hot enough to properly fry the hush puppies. So, stick with the old-fashioned pot-on-a-stove method.

3. The Oil: A clean ruler placed in the pot can help you determine the line for a 2-inch depth of oil. (Don't skimp; the batter needs to submerge in the oil.) For great results, the oil needs to maintain 375°. Too low and the hush puppies absorb oil, too high and the outside burns before the inside is done. Plan to adjust the temperature dial on your range slightly up or down throughout the frying to keep the temperature at 375°. A candy/deep-fat fry thermometer (now sold in many grocery stores for about $5) is a must.

4. The Drop: You can drop the batter using two soup-size spoons sprayed with vegetable cooking spray or a 1 tablespoon-measure ice-cream scoop.

5. The Flip: Sometimes hush puppies will flip themselves over. Use a slotted spoon or frying utensil to turn the rest.

6. The Finish: Hush puppies are usually done at the point you think they might need to cook longer—when the rough bumps or high spots are rich golden brown. Oil may be used for one more fry job if stored properly. After all the hush puppies are cooked, let the oil cool thoroughly. To remove cooked particles, strain the oil through a fine wire-mesh strainer lined with cheesecloth or a coffee filter. Use a funnel to pour the cooled oil into an empty vegetable oil bottle or a disposable plastic container with a lid. Label, date, and store in the fridge; use within one month.

Italian Made Fresh

The scent of wholesome, fragrant ingredients will entice you to the kitchen.

The smell of fresh garlic sizzling on your cooktop, the scent of fresh sage, and a simple tomato sauce seasoned with mint are sure to make your mouth water. These recipes are guaranteed to reinvigorate your cooking regimen. Built around fresh and healthy ingredients, their flavors are irresistible—and you'll reap plenty of health benefits too. Boot the idea of oily restaurant pasta swimming with butter. The best Italian in town is at your house tonight.

SPAGHETTI WITH MINT-AND-GARLIC TOMATO SAUCE

family favorite

Prep: 25 min., Cook: 20 min.

12 ounces uncooked spaghetti
4 garlic cloves, minced
1 tablespoon olive oil
3 pounds plum tomatoes, seeded and chopped
2 teaspoons sugar
½ teaspoon salt
½ teaspoon freshly ground pepper
1 tablespoon chopped fresh mint leaves
¼ cup grated Parmesan or Romano cheese

Cook spaghetti according to package directions, omitting salt and oil. Drain and set aside.
Sauté garlic in hot oil in a large skillet over medium-high heat 1 minute. Add tomatoes, and cook, stirring occasionally, 12 to 15 minutes or until sauce is thickened and chunky. Remove from heat, and stir in sugar, salt, and pepper.
Add cooked spaghetti and mint to sauce in skillet, tossing to coat. Sprinkle with cheese. **Makes** 4 servings.

PATSY BELL HOBSON
LIBERTY, MISSOURI

Per serving: Calories 429 (15% from fat); Fat 7.3g (sat 1.7g, mono 3.3g, poly 1.4g); Protein 15g; Carb 78g; Fiber 7.4g; Chol 4.4mg; Iron 4.6mg; Sodium 401mg; Calc 95mg

WHITE BEAN-AND-ASPARAGUS SALAD

family favorite

Prep: 20 min., Cook: 4 min., Chill: 1 hr.

After cooking the asparagus, this is practically a dump-and-stir recipe. *(pictured on page 76)*

½ pound fresh asparagus, trimmed
7 dried tomatoes
1 garlic clove, minced
1 tablespoon brown sugar
2 tablespoons extra-virgin olive oil
2 tablespoons white wine vinegar
1 tablespoon water
1 teaspoon spicy brown mustard
¼ teaspoon dried rubbed sage
¼ teaspoon salt
¼ teaspoon pepper
1 (19-ounce) can cannellini beans, rinsed and drained
¼ cup chopped red onion
2 teaspoons drained capers
1 (5-ounce) bag gourmet mixed salad greens
1 tablespoon shredded Parmesan cheese

Snap off tough ends of asparagus; arrange asparagus and dried tomatoes in a steamer basket over boiling water. Cover and steam 2 to 4 minutes or until asparagus is crisp-tender. Set tomatoes aside. Plunge asparagus into ice water to stop the cooking process; drain. Cut asparagus into 1-inch pieces, and chill until ready to use. Chop tomatoes.
Whisk together garlic and next 8 ingredients in a medium bowl; add asparagus, tomatoes, beans, onion, and capers, tossing to coat. Cover and chill 1 hour. Serve asparagus mixture over salad greens; sprinkle with cheese. **Makes** 6 servings.

PATRICIA A. HARMON
BADEN, PENNSYLVANIA

Per serving: Calories 127 (39% from fat); Fat 5.5g (sat 1g, mono 3.6g, poly 0.8g); Protein 4.8g; Carb 15.3g; Fiber 4.4g; Chol 1.3mg; Iron 2mg; Sodium 351mg; Calc 61mg

ITALIAN CARAMELIZED ORANGES

family favorite

Prep: 20 min., Cook: 15 min., Chill: 8 hrs.

This recipe comes from Crescent Dragonwagon's book, *Passionate Vegetarian* (Workman Publishing, 2002). Serve over low-fat ice cream with chocolate biscotti for a refreshing finale.

> 6 small oranges
> 1 cup sugar
> ¼ cup water
> 1 tablespoon corn syrup
> ¼ cup fresh orange juice
> 1 teaspoon fresh lemon juice
> 1 tablespoon orange liqueur

Grate oranges to equal 2 teaspoons grated rind; set rind aside.

Peel oranges. Remove and discard white pith; separate into sections. Place orange sections in a heatproof serving bowl; set aside.

Cook sugar, ¼ cup water, and corn syrup in a heavy saucepan over medium heat, stirring often until sugar dissolves.

Increase heat to medium high, and bring mixture to a boil. Boil, without stirring, 8 to 12 minutes or until syrup is a pale golden-amber color. Carefully stir in orange juice, lemon juice, and reserved orange rind. (Mixture will harden.) Cook, stirring constantly, 3 minutes or until mixture returns to liquid consistency.

Remove from heat, and immediately pour hot syrup over orange sections. Let cool to room temperature. Stir in liqueur. Cover and chill 8 hours. Gently stir oranges before serving. **Makes** 6 servings.

CRESCENT DRAGONWAGON
EUREKA SPRINGS, ARKANSAS

Per serving: Calories 212 (1% from fat); Fat 0.4g (sat 0.1g, mono 0.1g, poly 0.1g); Protein 1.4g; Carb 53g; Fiber 3.1g; Chol 0mg; Iron 0.2mg; Sodium 5mg; Calc 51mg

FRESH VEGETABLE PENNE

vegetarian

Prep: 25 min., Bake: 30 min., Cook: 25 min.

Even though butternut squash is a winter squash, you can find it in larger supermarkets this time of year. It's packed with vitamins A and D. To lower the amount of sodium in the recipe, use a low-sodium broth and reduce the amount of salt.

> 1 (2-pound) butternut squash, peeled and cut into 1½-inch cubes
> Vegetable cooking spray
> 1 tablespoon olive oil, divided
> ¾ teaspoon salt, divided
> ½ teaspoon freshly ground black pepper, divided
> 1 cup chopped leek (about 1 medium)
> ½ teaspoon minced fresh garlic
> 1½ cups vegetable or chicken broth
> ½ cup fat-free half-and-half
> 16 ounces uncooked penne pasta
> ½ cup frozen baby sweet peas
> 1 tablespoon chopped fresh sage leaves
> ⅛ to ¼ teaspoon dried crushed red pepper
> ¼ cup shredded Italian three-cheese blend
> Garnish: fresh sage leaves

Place squash cubes on a large aluminum foil-lined jelly-roll pan coated with cooking spray. Drizzle squash with 1 teaspoon oil, and sprinkle with ¼ teaspoon salt and ¼ teaspoon black pepper. Toss to coat.

Bake at 425° for 25 to 30 minutes or until squash is tender and golden, stirring occasionally.

Heat remaining 2 teaspoons oil in a large nonstick skillet over medium-high heat; add leek, and sauté 5 minutes or until tender and lightly browned. Add garlic; sauté 1 minute. Remove from heat, and set aside.

Process butternut squash, vegetable broth, and half-and-half in a food processor until smooth.

Cook pasta according to package directions, omitting salt and oil. Add peas to boiling water during last 2 minutes of cooking time; drain. Return pasta and peas to pan. Stir in leek mixture, remaining ½ teaspoon salt, remaining ¼ teaspoon black pepper, 1 tablespoon chopped sage, and crushed red pepper. Add processed squash mixture, tossing to coat. Sprinkle with Italian three-cheese blend. Garnish, if desired, and serve immediately. **Makes** 6 servings.

ELLEN WADE
ROANOKE, VIRGINIA

Per serving: Calories 386 (11% from fat); Fat 4.8g (sat 1.3g, mono 1.7g, poly 0.3g); Protein 14g; Carb 73g; Fiber 6.1g; Chol 3.3mg; Iron 3.6mg; Sodium 1,149mg; Calc 132mg

Making Smart Choices

Follow these tips for great flavor and good nutrition.

■ Whole wheat pasta offers more fiber than white durum pasta. Fiber helps lower cholesterol and increases satiety, reducing the tendency to overeat.

■ Tomatoes, whether canned or fresh, are packed with cancer-fighting lycopene and vitamin C. Because of innovations at the packing plants, canned tomatoes sometimes retain even more lycopene than fresh.

■ Asparagus serves up crisp color, fiber, vitamins C and A, and folic acid. Cooking it activates the vitamins and minerals, making it more nutritious than eating it raw.

from our kitchen

Cash in on Flavor

For our budget grilling story on page 84, we passed by the premium meat counter and headed straight for the big bargains. London broil, an extra-thick cut of boneless top-round steak, is frequently on sale and is an economical way to serve a crowd.

At around $3.98 a pound, chuck-eye steaks—not chuck steaks—are one of the trendy new cuts of beef. Cut from the chuck section traditionally sold as pot roast, these tender and flavorful steaks are an ideal choice for grilling. Top blade or flat-iron steaks also come from the chuck section and are equally inexpensive.

For maximum tenderness, these budget cuts of beef need to marinate before grilling. Be careful not to overcook them; they're best when pulled off the grill between 145° and 155°, before they reach a medium degree of doneness.

Party Pizzazz

Looking for an easy but impressive way to entertain? Grab a decorative planter box from the garden shop or flea market, and set up a salad bar. Few things are simpler to make than salads, and if you're really short on time, you can always purchase a great-tasting assortment from a cafe or delicatessen.

We filled our planter box with colorful bowls of Chicken Salad (page 94), fresh-cut fruit, and a favorite pasta salad made with refrigerated tortellini. (Prepare cheese tortellini according to package directions; toss with Ranch dressing, a handful of sliced green onions, and thawed frozen peas.) Store-bought crunchy breadsticks and a quick mixture of toppings (toasted sliced almonds and crumbled ramen noodles) add the finishing touches.

Planter boxes, lined with plastic and filled with ice, are also a terrific way to keep boiled shrimp or beverages chilled for a cocktail supper.

Shelf Magic

Spicy black bean dip, a versatile south-of-the-border specialty, is delicious with tortilla chips but is even better when used as a time-saving ingredient in recipes. It delivers a bold and spirited surge of Tex-Mex flavor without adding a lot of extra spices, seasonings, and fat.

We like to use it in everything from casseroles to quesadillas, replacing refried beans with an equal amount of spicy black bean dip. Try it in Mexican lasagna or on a pizza topped with salsa and shredded cheese. It's also a healthy and nutritious way to thicken and season homemade chili or vegetable soup. Several brands of black bean dip are available, each with a slightly different flavor profile. One of our favorite black bean dips for cooking with is a fat-free version made by Guiltless Gourmet (**www.guiltlessgourmet.com**), which comes in spicy or mild. Top-rated Chicken-and-Black Bean Soup (recipe below) tastes as if it's simmered for hours, but is ready for the table in only 20 minutes. Serve with a skillet of hot cornbread.

Chicken-and-Black Bean Soup: Dice 1 small onion and $1/2$ green bell pepper; sauté in 1 teaspoon hot canola oil in a Dutch oven over medium-high heat 3 minutes. Whisk in 4 cups chicken broth and 1 (16-ounce) jar spicy black bean dip until smooth. Bring to a boil, and stir in 2 (16-ounce) cans black beans, rinsed and drained, and 2 cups chopped cooked chicken. Cook 5 minutes or until thoroughly heated. Top individual bowls of soup with low-fat sour cream, shredded Cheddar cheese, baked tortilla strips, diced tomatoes, and avocado slices. **Makes** about 2 quarts. Prep: 10 min., Cook: 10 min.

favorites

104   Mid-Atlantic Flavors *Enjoy a taste of dishes from Maryland and Virginia*

106   Shortcuts to Top-Rated Cakes *Desserts so tasty that no one will ever guess they weren't made from scratch*

108   Mountain Country Recipes *Sublime food traditions from the Appalachian region*

110   A Southern Sampler *Comfort food from the Deep South*

111   Lowcountry Cuisine *Re-create the flavors of this coastal region at home*

112   Comfort Food, Delta Style *The fertile river basin is home to some of the most diverse cuisine in the South*

117   Food You'll Yee-Haw Over *If a dish is considered Southern, you'll find it in the Lone Star State*

118   Bayou Cooking *The mix of cultures built a world-renowned cuisine*

120   A Taste of Sunshine *Sample some of the mouthwatering delicacies that Florida has to offer*

Mid-Atlantic Flavors

Timeless recipes celebrate the rich soil and bountiful waters of Maryland and Virginia.

Dinner on the Chesapeake

Serves 4

Sweet Potato-Peanut Soup

Currant-Glazed Ham

Maryland Crab Cakes

Marinated Asparagus

Memmie's Spoonbread

Maryland Black Walnut Cake

Coastal cooking along the shores of the Chesapeake Bay conjures up images of freshly shucked oysters and juicy soft-shell crabs. Travel inland, and you'll find crusty golden brown chicken pan-fried in cast-iron skillets and smoky Smithfield hams. Local produce yields a culinary roll call of Southern side dishes, from baked apples and black-eyed peas to speckled butter beans and frost-kissed collards.

SWEET POTATO-PEANUT SOUP

Prep: 20 min., Cook: 50 min.

Peanut soup is a signature Virginia specialty. Here, it's made even better with the addition of sweet potatoes.

> 1 tablespoon butter
> ½ large sweet onion, chopped
> 1 small celery rib, diced
> 2 carrots, sliced
> ¼ teaspoon ground red pepper
> 1½ pounds sweet potatoes, peeled and cubed
> 3¼ cups chicken broth
> 1 cup half-and-half
> ½ cup creamy peanut butter
> Nutmeg-Molasses Cream
> Chopped toasted peanuts

Melt butter in a large Dutch oven; add onion and next 3 ingredients, and sauté over medium heat 3 minutes. Add sweet potato cubes and chicken broth;

cook over medium heat, stirring occasionally, 30 minutes.

Process mixture, in batches, in a blender or food processor until smooth.

Return mixture to Dutch oven; whisk in half-and-half and peanut butter. Reduce heat to low, and simmer, stirring often, 15 minutes. Serve with Nutmeg-Molasses Cream and peanuts. **Makes** 8 servings.

NUTMEG-MOLASSES CREAM:
fast fixin's
Prep: 5 min.

> 1 cup whipping cream
> 3 tablespoons molasses
> ¼ teaspoon ground nutmeg

Beat whipping cream at medium speed with an electric mixer until soft peaks form; gradually beat in molasses and nutmeg. Cover and chill until ready to serve. **Makes** about 2 cups.

CURRANT-GLAZED HAM

family favorite
Prep: 20 min.; Cook: 5 min.;
Bake: 2 hrs., 30 min.; Stand: 20 min.

> 1 (10-ounce) jar red currant jelly
> 1 cup firmly packed brown sugar
> 1 cup orange juice
> ½ cup dry sherry
> 3 tablespoons spicy brown mustard
> 1 (8- to 10-pound) smoked, fully cooked bone-in ham half
> 36 whole cloves

Combine first 5 ingredients in a medium saucepan over medium heat; cook, stirring constantly, until jelly melts and mixture is smooth. Set mixture aside.

Remove skin from ham, trimming fat to ¼-inch thickness. Make shallow cuts in fat 1 inch apart in a diamond pattern. Push clove stems into center of each diamond.

Place ham in a lightly greased roasting pan, and pour jelly mixture over ham. **Bake** on lower oven rack at 350° for 2 hours and 30 minutes, basting with pan juices every 15 to 20 minutes. Remove ham from oven; let stand 20 minutes before carving. **Makes** 12 servings.

MARYLAND CRAB CAKES

Prep: 20 min., Cook: 10 min. per batch

Gentle mixing is the secret to these succulent crab cakes. Use only enough crackers to hold the mixture together. Old Bay seasoning is a favored Chesapeake crab boil seasoning, and available on the supermarket spice aisle.

- 1 pound fresh crabmeat
- 6 to 8 saltine crackers, finely crushed
- ½ cup mayonnaise
- 1 large egg, lightly beaten
- 1 tablespoon minced fresh parsley
- 1½ teaspoons Old Bay seasoning
- ½ teaspoon dry mustard
- ½ teaspoon pepper
- ½ teaspoon Worcestershire sauce
- 2 tablespoons butter or margarine
- Garnishes: fresh watercress, lemon slices
- Caper Sauce

Drain crabmeat, removing any bits of shell.
Combine crushed crackers and next 7 ingredients; gently fold crabmeat into mixture. Shape into 8 thin patties.
Melt butter in a skillet over medium heat. Add crab cakes; cook, in batches, 4 to 5 minutes on each side or until golden. Drain on paper towels. Garnish, if desired. Serve crab cakes with Caper Sauce. **Makes** 4 servings.

CAPER SAUCE:
fast fixin's • make ahead
Prep: 10 min.

- 1 cup mayonnaise
- 3 shallots, minced
- 2 teaspoons grated lemon rind
- 1½ tablespoons fresh lemon juice
- 1½ tablespoons drained capers
- ¼ teaspoon salt
- ¼ teaspoon seasoned pepper

Whisk together all ingredients in a small bowl. Cover and chill until ready to serve. **Makes** about 1¼ cups.

MARINATED ASPARAGUS

family favorite • make ahead
Prep: 15 min., Cook: 3 min., Chill: 8 hrs.

Fresh asparagus is harvested along the Eastern Shore of the Chesapeake.

- 2 pounds fresh asparagus
- ¾ cup olive oil
- ½ cup white balsamic vinegar
- 4 garlic cloves, minced
- 1 tablespoon sugar
- 1 teaspoon dried crushed red pepper

Snap off and discard tough ends of asparagus. Cook asparagus in boiling water to cover 3 minutes or until crisp-tender; drain.
Plunge asparagus into ice water to stop the cooking process; drain. Arrange asparagus in a 13- x 9-inch dish.
Whisk together olive oil and next 4 ingredients until well blended; pour over asparagus. Cover and chill 8 hours. Drain before serving. **Makes** 6 to 8 servings.

MEMMIE'S SPOONBREAD

family favorite

Prep: 15 min., Stand: 10 min., Bake: 50 min.

- 3 cups boiling water
- 2 cups cornmeal
- ½ cup butter, cut up
- 2 teaspoons salt
- 2 cups milk
- 4 large eggs, lightly beaten
- 1 tablespoon baking powder

Pour 3 cups boiling water gradually over cornmeal, stirring until smooth. Add butter and salt, stirring until smooth; let stand 10 minutes. Gradually stir in milk and lightly beaten eggs. Stir in baking powder. Pour mixture into a lightly greased 13- x 9-inch baking dish.
Bake at 375° for 45 to 50 minutes or until lightly browned and set. **Makes** 10 to 12 servings.

Test Kitchen *Notebook*

The Southern soufflé, spoonbread, may take its name from suppon or suppawn, an Indian porridge, and perhaps the name stuck because this comfort food is best eaten with a spoon. Spoonbread is an any-meal kind of food; Thomas Jefferson, for instance, ate it for breakfast, lunch, and dinner.

Mary Allen Perry
ASSOCIATE FOODS EDITOR

Shortcuts to Top-Rated Cakes

Now you don't have to bake from scratch to make some of our most-requested recipes. We won't tell if you don't.

MARYLAND BLACK WALNUT CAKE

Prep: 20 min., Bake: 50 min.

- **1½ cups chopped black walnuts**
- **1 cup butter, softened**
- **1½ cups granulated sugar**
- **3 large eggs, separated**
- **1 teaspoon vanilla extract**
- **2 cups all-purpose flour**
- **1 tablespoon baking powder**
- **¼ teaspoon salt**
- **¾ cup milk**
- **¼ cup powdered sugar**
- **Vanilla ice cream (optional)**
- **Sliced fresh strawberries (optional)**

Pulse black walnuts in a food processor 8 to 10 times or until finely ground; set aside.

Beat butter at medium speed with an electric mixer until creamy; gradually add granulated sugar, beating until light and fluffy. Add egg yolks and vanilla, beating just until blended.

Sift together flour, baking powder, and salt; add to butter mixture alternately with milk, beginning and ending with flour mixture. Beat batter at low speed just until blended after each addition.

Beat egg whites at medium speed with an electric mixer until stiff peaks form; fold into batter. Fold ground walnuts into batter. Spoon batter evenly into a greased and floured 10-inch Bundt pan.

Bake at 350° for 50 minutes or until a wooden pick inserted in center comes out clean. Cool in pan on a wire rack 10 minutes; remove from pan, and cool completely on wire rack. Sprinkle evenly with powdered sugar. Serve with vanilla ice cream and sliced fresh strawberries, if desired. **Makes** 12 servings.

JOHN SHIELDS
CHESAPEAKE BAY COOKING
BROADWAY BOOKS, 1998
BALTIMORE, MARYLAND

These streamlined recipes for time-honored cakes are sure to become your new standbys. Quick Coconut-Pineapple Cake is a two-layer interpretation of a *Southern Living* Holiday Recipe Contest winner, Nanny's Famous Coconut-Pineapple Cake from Erma Jean Reese of Warrenton, Georgia. Pineapple preserves and lemon curd from the supermarket replace the cooked filling, while buttermilk lends homemade taste to the white cake mix.

Homemade Coconut-Pecan Filling covers an easy 13- x 9-inch German Chocolate Cake that's dressed up with a stir-in of tangy sour cream. This topping is so much tastier than all of the convenience products we tested; we didn't need to change a thing. You will save time, though, with the cake mix.

Purchase ice cream and an angel food cake to create the make-ahead No-Bake Ice-Cream Angel Food Cake adapted from *The Southern Living Cookbook* (Oxmoor House, 1995). We like chocolate, vanilla, and strawberry ice cream in ours, but choose flavors to suit your family's tastes.

QUICK COCONUT-PINEAPPLE CAKE

family favorite

Prep: 10 min., Bake: 25 min.

Look for lemon curd on the jam and jelly aisle of your supermarket. This cake delivers such a great made-from-scratch taste that no one will guess that it begins with a mix.

- **1 (18.25-ounce) package white cake mix**
- **3 egg whites**
- **1¼ cups buttermilk**
- **2 tablespoons vegetable oil**
- **1 teaspoon lemon extract**
- **1 (16-ounce) jar pineapple preserves**
- **½ cup lemon curd**
- **1 (16-ounce) container cream cheese frosting**
- **1 (6-ounce) package frozen flaked coconut, thawed**
- **Garnish: fresh mint sprig**

Beat first 5 ingredients at low speed with an electric mixer 30 seconds or just until moistened; beat at medium speed 2 minutes. Pour batter evenly into 2 greased and floured 9-inch round cakepans.

Bake at 350° for 20 to 25 minutes or until a wooden pick inserted in center comes out clean. Remove from pans immediately; cool layers completely on wire racks.

Combine preserves and lemon curd. Spread ¾ cup filling between cake layers; spread remaining filling on top of cake. Spread frosting on sides of cake; gently press coconut evenly onto sides of cake. Garnish, if desired. **Makes** 12 servings.

No-Bake Ice-Cream Angel Food Cake

freezeable • make ahead

Prep: 20 min.; Freeze: 8 hrs., 30 min.

1 (10-inch) angel food cake
1 pint chocolate ice cream
1 pint vanilla ice cream
1 pint strawberry ice cream
Whipped Cream Frosting
¼ cup slivered almonds, toasted

Wrap cake in plastic wrap, and freeze 30 minutes. (Freezing makes it easier to cut into layers.)

Let ice cream stand at room temperature 20 minutes to soften.

Slice cake horizontally into 4 equal layers using a serrated knife. Place bottom cake layer on a serving plate; spread top of layer with chocolate ice cream, leaving a ½-inch border around edge. Top with second cake layer, and repeat layers with vanilla ice cream, a cake layer, strawberry ice cream, and remaining cake layer. Wrap cake in plastic wrap; freeze at least 8 hours or overnight.

Spread Whipped Cream Frosting on top and sides of cake. Sprinkle top evenly with toasted almonds. **Makes** 12 servings.

Whipped Cream Frosting:
fast fixin's

Prep: 5 min.

Beat 2 cups whipping cream at high speed with an electric mixer until cream is foamy; gradually add 2 tablespoons powdered sugar and 1 teaspoon vanilla extract, beating until stiff peaks form. **Makes** 4 cups.

No Bake Angel Food Cake

Fill Cake layers with different flavors of store-bought ice cream.

German Chocolate Cake

family favorite

Prep: 15 min., Bake: 35 min.

You can substitute light sour cream in this recipe, but don't use nonfat sour cream.

1 (18.25-ounce) package German chocolate cake mix
3 large eggs
1 (8-ounce) container sour cream
⅓ cup vegetable oil
Coconut-Pecan Filling

Beat first 4 ingredients at low speed with an electric mixer 30 seconds or just until moistened; beat mixture at medium speed 2 minutes. Pour batter evenly into a greased and floured 13- x 9-inch pan.

Bake at 350° for 32 to 35 minutes or until a wooden pick inserted in center comes out clean. Cool cake completely in pan on a wire rack.

Spread Coconut-Pecan Filling evenly on top of cake. **Makes** 12 servings.

Note: For testing purposes only, we used Betty Crocker Super Moist German Chocolate Cake Mix.

Coconut-Pecan Filling:
fast fixin's

Prep: 10 min., Cook: 10 min.

1 cup sugar
1 cup whipping cream
3 egg yolks
½ cup butter
1 teaspoon vanilla extract
1⅓ cups sweetened flaked coconut
1 cup chopped pecans, toasted

Combine first 4 ingredients in a medium saucepan; cook over medium heat, stirring constantly, 8 to 10 minutes or until thickened. Remove from heat, and stir in vanilla. Stir in coconut and pecans, and let cool completely. **Makes** about 3 cups.

Test Kitchen *Notebook*

Use these problem-solving tips from our Test Kitchen Staff to help correct problems:

• Overmixing the batter can cause the batter to overflow, peaks in the center of the cake, a dry texture, and a heavy texture. Undermixing the batter can cause the cake to fall and a coarse texture.

• Too low oven temperature can cause a sticky crust, a heavy texture, a coarse texture, or a cake to fall. And Too high oven temperature can cause dry texture and peaks in center.

Vicki Poellnitz
ASSISTANT FOODS EDITOR

Mountain Country Recipes

The Appalachian region offers sublime food traditions from sweet, crunchy apples to salty country ham.

The people who settled the Appalachian mountains embraced simplicity and common sense. Home to windy, snowy winters and moderate summers, the region's food adapted to its weather. Most of the flavors synonymous with this area are the result of the determination of its people to preserve the fall and summer bounty for those hard winters.

Traditional foods still show up on mountain dinner tables today, although they've been updated for our busy lifestyles. We think those early settlers would be proud of what we've done with these new takes on classic recipes. See what you think.

BAKED WHOLE SWEET POTATOES

family favorite

Prep: 5 min., Bake: 1 hr, 30 min.

Wash 6 sweet potatoes, and remove any blemishes or dark spots; wrap each potato in aluminum foil. Bake, folded side of foil up, at 350° for 1 to 1½ hours or until a fork easily presses into the center. If desired, serve with butter, pepper, and salt. **Makes** 6 servings.

MARK SOHN
PIKEVILLE, KENTUCKY
ADAPTED FROM *MOUNTAIN COUNTRY COOKING*
ST. MARTIN'S PRESS, 1996

APPLE STACK CAKE

freezeable • make ahead

Prep: 25 min., Bake: 10 min. per batch,
Stand: 2 days

Jill Sauceman's grandmother used a less spicy filling during the Depression because spices were hard to come by. We combined her cake recipe with a spicier filling version. Don't be tempted to eat the cake until it has stood for two days. This seasoning allows the moisture from the filling to soften the cake layers. This cake also freezes well.

⅓ cup vegetable shortening
½ cup sugar
1 large egg
4 cups all-purpose flour
1 teaspoon baking powder
1 teaspoon baking soda
½ teaspoon salt
½ cup buttermilk
½ cup molasses
2½ teaspoons sugar
Dried Apple Filling

Beat shortening at medium speed with an electric mixer 2 minutes or until creamy. Gradually add ½ cup sugar, beating 5 to 7 minutes. Add egg, beating until yellow disappears.
Combine flour and next 3 ingredients. Stir together buttermilk and molasses in a large measuring cup. Gradually add flour mixture to shortening mixture alternately with buttermilk mixture, beginning and ending with flour mixture; beat until blended.

Divide dough into 5 equal portions; place each portion in a 9-inch greased and floured cakepan or cast-iron skillet, and firmly press with floured fingers into pan. Prick dough several times with a fork. Sprinkle each layer evenly with ½ teaspoon sugar.
Bake at 400° for 10 minutes or until golden brown. (Only bake layers on one rack at a time.) Repeat procedure as needed to bake in pans. Remove layers from pans; cool completely on wire racks.
Spread 1½ cups Dried Apple Filling between each layer to within ½ inch of edge, beginning and ending with a cake layer. (Save your prettiest cake layer for the top.) Loosely cover cake, and let stand 2 days at room temperature.
Makes 12 to 16 servings.

JILL SAUCEMAN
JOHNSON CITY, TENNESSEE

DRIED APPLE FILLING:
Prep: 5 min., Cook: 45 min.

3 (6-ounce) packages dried sliced
    apples
6 cups water
1 cup firmly packed brown sugar
1 teaspoon ground ginger
    (optional)
1 teaspoon ground cinnamon
    (optional)
½ teaspoon ground allspice
    (optional)
½ teaspoon ground nutmeg
    (optional)

Stir together apples and 6 cups water in a large saucepan or Dutch oven. Bring to a boil; reduce heat, and simmer 30 minutes or until tender. Stir in sugar, and, if desired, spices. Return mixture to a boil; reduce heat, and simmer, stirring occasionally, 10 to 15 minutes or until most of liquid has evaporated. Cool completely. **Makes** 6 cups.

COUNTRY HAM SAUCE

Prep: 20 min., Cook: 25 min.

Serve this versatile sauce over hot cooked pasta or grilled chicken breasts, or offer it as a dip with chips.

- **1 (10-ounce) package frozen chopped spinach, thawed**
- **3 tablespoons butter or margarine**
- **3 tablespoons all-purpose flour**
- **2 cups chicken broth**
- **1½ cups whipping cream**
- **1 cup chopped country ham**
- **½ cup freshly grated Parmesan cheese**
- **1 teaspoon freshly ground pepper**
- **⅛ teaspoon ground nutmeg**

Drain spinach well, pressing between paper towels; set aside.

Melt butter in a heavy saucepan over low heat; add flour, stirring until smooth. Cook, stirring constantly, 2 to 3 minutes or until lightly browned.

Whisk in broth and whipping cream gradually; cook over medium heat, whisking constantly, until mixture begins to boil. Reduce heat, and simmer 10 to 15 minutes or until slightly thickened. Stir in spinach, ham, and remaining ingredients; cook until thoroughly heated. **Makes** about 6 cups.

FRIED APPLES

family favorite

Prep: 25 min., Cook: 22 min.

Melt ¼ cup butter in a large skillet over medium-high heat. Add 5 large peeled, cored, and sliced Granny Smith apples; 1 cup sugar; 1 teaspoon ground cinnamon; and ¼ teaspoon ground nutmeg. Sauté 15 to 20 minutes or until apples are tender. **Makes** 4 to 6 servings.

SHUCK BEANS

Prep: 45 min., Soak: 24 hrs., Cook: 1 hr.

Shuck beans are easy to cook but hard to find. The younger members of our Test Kitchens said the shuck beans had an "earthy, fresh bean taste."

- **½ pound shuck beans**
- **6 ounces salt pork**
- **½ teaspoon salt (optional)**

Wash shuck beans; discard any dark or discolored beans. Break shuck beans in half; place in a 6-quart pressure cooker with water to cover (about 6 cups). Cover and chill. Soak beans for 24 hours; do not drain. Bring to a boil, uncovered; reduce heat to medium, and cook 30 minutes. Drain and rinse beans.

Return beans to pressure cooker; add salt pork and, if desired, salt. Add 1 inch cold water to cover (about 4 cups) to pressure cooker.

Cover cooker with lid, and seal securely; place pressure control over vent and tube. Cook over medium-high heat 12 minutes or until pressure control rocks quickly back and forth. Reduce heat to medium low; cook 15 more minutes. (Pressure control will rock occasionally.)

Remove pressure cooker from heat; run cold water over cooker to reduce pressure. Carefully remove lid so that steam escapes away from you. **Makes** 6 to 8 servings.

Note: For testing purposes only, we used a Mirro 6-quart rocker top pressure cooker. If you have another model, cook according to manufacturer's instructions.

LORENE POTTER
ASHCAMP, KENTUCKY

Shuck Beans

The shuck bean might be the most symbolic Appalachian food. Early mountain settlers strung fresh green beans on threads and hung them up to dry. The beans were spaced far enough apart on the string to allow air to circulate, so none of them would spoil. Today's drying process can take up to one day in a commercial vegetable dryer or two to three months in a toasty attic. (Be careful to keep them out of direct sunlight.)

Also known as shucky beans and leather britches, the dried beans are easy to cook. Simply remove them from the string, soak them (refrigerate them to soak, or they'll mold), and then use a pressure cooker, or boil. We enjoyed reading the recipe in *The Foxfire Book* (Anchor Books, 1972), a collection of Appalachian lore and traditions: "Sometime during the winter take a string of dried green beans down, remove the thread, and drop them in a pot of scalding water. Then add 'a good hunk 'a meat' (ham, pork, or the like, depending on your taste) and cook all morning."

Shuck beans are getting harder to find as the tradition ebbs in the face of fast food and convenience. We tracked some down at an Asheville farmers market. You can also find them at roadside stands and farmers markets throughout eastern Kentucky and Tennessee and in western North Carolina. They're available in late summer and early fall.

A Southern Sampler

Wherever you travel in the South, you're bound to find one of these dishes on the table.

Food in the Deep South is comfort, heritage, and hospitality, with home-style dishes favored by all. You'd be hard-pressed to find a meat-and-three restaurant that didn't serve macaroni and cheese, greens, black-eyed peas, sweet potatoes, squash casserole, cornbread, fried chicken, pork chops, and potato salad. This food is the soul of the South, and you'll find it in every state in the region. Wherever you're from, there's a dish here that's sure to please.

SAWMILL GRAVY

family favorite • fast fixin's

Prep: 5 min., Cook: 20 min.

- ½ pound ground pork sausage
- ¼ cup butter
- ⅓ cup all-purpose flour
- 3¼ cups milk
- ½ teaspoon salt
- ¾ teaspoon pepper
- ⅛ teaspoon dried Italian seasoning (optional)

Cook sausage in a large skillet over medium heat, stirring until it crumbles and is no longer pink. Remove sausage, and drain on paper towels. Wipe skillet clean.

Melt butter in skillet over low heat. Whisk in flour until smooth. Cook, whisking constantly, 1 minute. Gradually whisk in milk, and cook, whisking constantly, over medium heat about 10 to 12 minutes or until thickened and bubbly. Stir in sausage, salt, pepper, and, if desired, Italian seasoning. **Makes** 3¾ cups.

SWEET POTATO SOUFFLÉ

chef recipe • family favorite

Prep: 20 min., Cook: 20 min., Bake: 45 min.

Martha Hawkins serves this specialty at her restaurant, Martha's Place, in Montgomery, Alabama.

- 3½ pounds sweet potatoes, peeled and sliced (about 3 large potatoes)
- 1 cup sugar
- 1 large egg
- ¼ cup butter
- 1 teaspoon vanilla extract
- ½ cup evaporated milk
- ½ teaspoon ground nutmeg
- ¼ teaspoon salt
- ½ cup raisins (optional)
- 2 cups miniature marshmallows

Bring sweet potatoes and water to cover to a boil, and cook 20 minutes or until tender; drain.

Beat sweet potatoes, sugar, and next 6 ingredients at medium speed with an electric mixer until smooth. Stir in raisins, if desired. Pour mixture into a lightly greased 13- x 9-inch baking dish.

Bake at 350°, uncovered, for 30 minutes or until bubbly; top evenly with marshmallows. Bake, uncovered, for 15 more minutes or until lightly browned. **Makes** 6 servings.

CHEF MARTHA HAWKINS
MARTHA'S PLACE
MONTGOMERY, ALABAMA

COCONUT CREAM PIE

family favorite • make ahead

Prep: 10 min., Cook: 10 min., Stand: 30 min., Chill: 30 min.

This rich, fluffy pie would be the glory of any dessert table. It received our highest rating.

- ½ (15-ounce) package refrigerated piecrusts
- ½ cup sugar
- ¼ cup cornstarch
- 2 cups half-and-half
- 4 egg yolks
- 3 tablespoons butter
- 1 cup sweetened flaked coconut
- 2½ teaspoons vanilla extract, divided
- 2 cups whipping cream
- ⅓ cup sugar
- Garnish: toasted coconut

Fit 1 piecrust into a 9-inch pieplate according to package directions; fold edges under, and crimp. Prick bottom and sides of piecrust with a fork. Bake according to package directions for a one-crust pie.

Combine ½ cup sugar and cornstarch in a heavy saucepan. Whisk together half-and-half and egg yolks. Gradually whisk egg mixture into sugar mixture; bring to a boil over medium heat, whisking constantly. Boil 1 minute; remove from heat.

Stir in butter, 1 cup coconut, and 1 teaspoon vanilla. Cover with plastic wrap, placing plastic wrap directly on filling in pan; let stand 30 minutes. Spoon custard mixture into prepared crust, cover and chill 30 minutes or until set.

Beat whipping cream at high speed with an electric mixer until foamy;

gradually add ⅓ cup sugar and remaining 1½ teaspoons vanilla, beating until soft peaks form. Spread or pipe whipped cream over pie filling. Garnish, if desired. **Makes** 6 to 8 servings.

Lowcountry Cuisine

Chances are you already have some of the makings for these luscious recipes. Benne Seed Wafers, a traditional Carolina cookie recipe, uses pantry items—all you'll need are the sesame (benne) seeds. Frogmore Stew includes smoked sausage for down-home flavor.

BENNE SEED WAFERS

family favorite

Prep: 15 min., Cook: 5 min., Chill: 1 hr., Bake: 10 min. per batch

These are thin sesame cookies with a crispy texture. Buy sesame seeds at the health food store, where they're more reasonably priced.

- ½ cup sesame (benne) seeds
- ½ cup butter or margarine, softened
- 1 cup sugar
- 1 large egg
- ½ teaspoon vanilla extract
- 1¾ cups all-purpose flour
- 2 teaspoons baking powder
- ½ teaspoon baking soda
- ½ teaspoon salt

Cook sesame seeds in a heavy skillet over medium heat, stirring often, 5 minutes or until toasted.
Beat butter at medium speed with an electric mixer until creamy; gradually add sugar, beating well. Stir in sesame seeds, egg, and vanilla.

Combine flour and next 3 ingredients; stir into butter mixture. Cover dough, and chill at least 1 hour.
Shape dough into ½-inch balls; place on a lightly greased baking sheet. Flatten to a ¹⁄₁₆-inch thickness with floured fingers or a flat-bottomed glass.
Bake at 325° for 8 to 10 minutes or until lightly browned. Transfer to wire racks to cool. **Makes** 10 dozen.

Tip: Pressing dough into a teaspoon measuring spoon creates about a ½-inch ball.

CLEMENTA FLORIO
WADMALAW ISLAND, SOUTH CAROLINA

GARLIC SHRIMP AND GRITS

family favorite

Prep: 20 min., Cook: 15 min.

This classic combo has become a flagship recipe of the area. It was born out of the Lowcountry's abundance of seafood paired with grits, a humble breakfast dish for fishermen. Leave the tails on the shrimp you use as a garnish for an attractive presentation.

- 1 pound unpeeled, medium-size fresh shrimp, cooked
- 3 cups water
- 1 cup whipping cream
- ¼ cup butter or margarine
- 1 teaspoon salt
- 1 cup quick-cooking grits, uncooked
- 1 cup (4 ounces) shredded extra-sharp Cheddar cheese
- 2 garlic cloves, minced
- Garnishes: chopped fresh chives, peeled and cooked shrimp, freshly ground black pepper

Peel shrimp, and devein, if desired.
Bring 3 cups water, whipping cream, butter, and salt to a boil in a large saucepan over medium-high heat. Reduce heat to medium, and whisk in grits. Cook, whisking constantly, 7 to 8 minutes or until mixture is smooth. Stir in shrimp, cheese, and garlic, and cook

1 to 2 minutes or until thoroughly heated. Garnish, if desired. **Makes** 4 servings.

IRENE SMITH
COVINGTON, GEORGIA

FROGMORE STEW

Prep: 10 min., Cook: 30 min.

The name "Frogmore" is the namesake of an old fishing community on St. Harbor Island, South Carolina. According to legend, a fisherman developed the recipe when he couldn't find fish for sale. He scavenged for leftovers, cooked what shrimp and crab he did catch, and the rest is history.

- 5 quarts water
- ¼ cup Old Bay seasoning
- 4 pounds small red potatoes
- 2 pounds kielbasa or hot smoked link sausage, cut into 1½-inch pieces
- 6 ears fresh corn, halved
- 4 pounds unpeeled, large fresh shrimp
- Old Bay seasoning
- Cocktail sauce

Bring 5 quarts water and ¼ cup Old Bay seasoning to a rolling boil in a large covered stockpot.
Add potatoes; return to a boil, and cook, uncovered, 10 minutes.
Add sausage and corn, and return to a boil. Cook 10 minutes or until potatoes are tender.
Add shrimp to stockpot; cook 3 to 4 minutes or until shrimp turn pink. Drain. Serve with Old Bay seasoning and cocktail sauce. **Makes** 12 servings.

Note: For testing purposes only, we used Hillshire Farm Polska Kielbasa.

Comfort Food, Delta Style

The food of this diverse region resonates with a down-home and simple quality, but the flavors are nothing short of spectacular.

For a truly singular taste of The Delta, don't miss Helena Tamales. Unlike their Tex-Mex cousins, which are traditionally steamed, these gently simmer in a tomato broth.

HELENA TAMALES

Prep: 40 min.; Soak: 1 hr.;
Cook: 3 hrs., 15 min.

We call for using an entire package of corn husks in this recipe because some of them will be torn or split.

1 (6-ounce) package dried corn husks
Cornmeal Dough
Chicken Filling
1 (15-ounce) can tomato sauce
1 teaspoon chili powder
1 teaspoon ground cumin
2½ quarts water

Soak corn husks in hot water to cover 1 hour or until softened. Drain husks, and pat dry.
Spread 2 tablespoons Cornmeal Dough into a 3- x 5-inch rectangle on 1 side of 1 husk, leaving a 2-inch border at bottom narrow edge and a ½-inch border at 1 long side.
Spoon 2 heaping tablespoons Chicken Filling down center of cornmeal dough rectangle, creating a 1-inch-wide strip. Roll up husk, starting at the long side

with ½-inch border, enclosing meat filling with the first turn. Fold bottom end with 2-inch border over, and secure with kitchen string or narrow strip of softened corn husk. Repeat procedure using remaining Cornmeal Dough and Chicken Filling.
Bundle together 6 filled corn husks, seam sides inward and open ends facing same direction, and secure with kitchen string. Repeat procedure with remaining filled corn husks, making 2 more bundles of 6 filled corn husks each.
Stand all 3 corn husk bundles, open ends up, in a large 12-quart stockpot. (If the bundles won't stand upright in the stockpot, place a 2-cup glass measuring cup upside down in the stockpot for the corn husk bundles to rest upon.)
Stir together tomato sauce, chili powder, and cumin. Pour tomato sauce mixture and 2½ quarts water around corn husk bundles in stockpot. (Do not pour directly over corn husks.) Cover and bring to a boil over medium-high heat. Reduce heat to low, and simmer, covered, 3 hours. Remove tamales, discarding tomato sauce mixture. **Makes** 18 tamales.

CORNMEAL DOUGH:
fast fixin's
Prep: 10 min.

⅔ cup vegetable shortening
1½ cups yellow cornmeal
1 cup warm chicken broth
2 teaspoons salt
1 teaspoon paprika

Beat shortening at medium speed with an electric mixer 5 minutes or until light and fluffy.
Stir together cornmeal and warm chicken broth in a medium bowl until well blended. Gradually add cornmeal mixture to shortening, beating at medium speed just until blended after each addition. Add salt and paprika, beating just until blended. Cover dough with plastic wrap, and set aside until ready to use. **Makes** enough for 18 tamales.

1. After soaking corn husks in hot water, spread Cornmeal Dough over the moistened husks.
2. Spoon Chicken Filling onto Cornmeal Dough in the husk.
3. Bring ends of the corn husk around to seal, and secure with kitchen string or a strip of sofened corn husk.

Grilled New York Steaks over Coffee-Onion Jam,
page 123; Easy Spicy Caesar Salad, page 122;
Potato-Stuffed Grilled Bell Peppers, page 123

Marinated Vegetable Salad
and Marinated Dill Green Beans, page 129

114

Pesto Focaccia Sandwich, page 131

Quick Coconut-Pineapple Cake,
page 106

CHICKEN FILLING:
fast fixin's
Prep: 10 min.

- **3 cups finely chopped cooked chicken**
- **1 (4.5-ounce) can chopped green chiles**
- **2 teaspoons garlic powder**
- **2 teaspoons onion powder**
- **1 teaspoon chili powder**
- **1 teaspoon salt**
- **½ teaspoon ground red pepper**

Stir together all ingredients. **Makes** enough for 18 tamales.

JOYCE ST. COLUMBIA
HELENA, ARKANSAS

Food You'll Yee-Haw Over

Driving down a Texas highway, you're likely to see bumper stickers on cars touting "I wasn't born in Texas but got here as soon as I could." One reason—the food. The state of Texas is always adding new dishes to the menu of tradition. It's been that way since the settlers spilled in, bringing with them the recipes of the Deep South. It's been that way since the Mexican cooks added heat to the palate. It's been that way since the Germans and Czechs began to flavor the Hill Country with their homeland favorites. Nowadays, those—and more— are all Texas. The recipes here represent two different cuisines from the state.

VIETNAMESE FAJITAS (*BO NUONG XA*)

chef recipe

Prep: 30 min., Chill: 30 min., Grill: 4 min.

Houston is home to a large Vietnamese population and the Kim Son Restaurant. Adapted from their house specialty, this top-rated recipe is a meal in itself—so don't let the long ingredient list stop you from trying it. The grilled, marinated flank steak also makes a great main dish on its own.

- **1 pound flank steak**
- **2 tablespoons sugar**
- **1 tablespoon chopped lemon grass**
- **1 tablespoon minced garlic**
- **1 tablespoon soy sauce**
- **1 tablespoon vegetable oil**
- **¾ teaspoon cornstarch**
- **1 teaspoon salt**
- **½ teaspoon pepper**
- **1¼ cups hot water**
- **½ cup fish sauce**
- **⅓ cup sugar**
- **2 teaspoons rice wine vinegar**
- **1 cup grated carrot, divided**
- **Hot water**
- **16 (6-inch) rice paper spring roll wrappers (bánh tráng)**
- **½ cup bean sprouts**
- **½ cucumber, peeled, seeded and cut into 2- x ⅛-inch matchsticks**
- **½ cup fresh pineapple slices, cut into 2- x ⅛-inch matchsticks**
- **¼ cup chopped fresh mint**
- **¼ cup chopped fresh cilantro**
- **½ head iceberg lettuce or green leaf lettuce, shredded**

Cut steak diagonally across the grain into 16 (⅛- to ¼-inch-thick) slices.
Stir together 2 tablespoons sugar and next 5 ingredients in a large bowl. Add meat, stirring to coat. Cover and chill 30 minutes. Remove meat from marinade, discarding marinade. Sprinkle steak evenly with salt and pepper.
Grill flank steak slices over medium-high heat (350° to 400°), uncovered, 2 minutes on each side or until done. Cover with aluminum foil to keep warm.

Stir together 1¼ cups hot water, fish sauce, ⅓ cup sugar, and vinegar until sugar dissolves. Stir in ⅓ cup carrot. Set aside.
Pour hot water to a depth of 1 inch in a large shallow dish. Dip 1 spring roll wrapper in hot water briefly to soften; pat dry with paper towels.
Combine remaining ⅔ cup carrot, bean sprouts, and next 4 ingredients. Place 1 slice of beef on 1 side of wrapper; top with ⅓ cup lettuce. Place about ⅓ cup bean sprout mixture on lettuce on wrapper. Fold sides of wrapper over filling, and roll up, jelly-roll style. Serve with fish sauce mixture for dipping. **Makes** 4 to 6 servings.

Note: Prepare fresh lemon grass as you would a green onion—peel off the outer layer, remove the root end, and use the white portion. Fish sauce and rice paper wrappers can be found on the ethnic foods aisle of most grocery stores.

TRI LA
KIM SON RESTAURANT
HOUSTON, TEXAS

Test Kitchen *Notebook*

I am just in the learning stages of Vietnamese cooking myself, and the Vietnamese Fajitas recipe can look overwhelming. Basically you marinate a sliced steak and grilling it, bundle steak and vegetables and fruits in spring roll wrappers, and make a thin dipping sauce for the bundles. At the restaurant all the fixings for the Fajitas are served family-style and everyone at the table assembles their own. Sounds good for at home, too!

Shirley Harrington
ASSOCIATE FOODS EDITOR

GRILLED CORN ON THE COB WITH RED CHILE PASTE

family favorite • fast fixin's

Prep: 10 min., Grill: 22 min.

**6 ears fresh corn, husks removed
Red Chile Paste**

Grill corn, covered with grill lid, over medium-high heat (350° to 400°) 20 to 22 minutes, turning one quarter of a turn every 3 to 4 minutes. (Corn will brown in spots.)
Spread 1 to 2 tablespoons Red Chile Paste evenly over each ear of cooked corn, and serve immediately. **Makes** 6 servings.

RED CHILE PASTE:

Prep: 15 min., Cook: 20 min., Cool: 10 min.

**6 dried New Mexico, ancho, or red
  chile peppers
4 cups water
1 red bell pepper, chopped
2 garlic cloves, pressed
1 teaspoon dried oregano leaves
1 teaspoon paprika
1 teaspoon ground cumin
1 teaspoon salt
2 tablespoons cider vinegar
1 tablespoon olive oil
2 cups torn sourdough bread
  pieces**

Bring chile peppers and 4 cups water to a boil in a medium saucepan; boil 15 minutes. Drain chile peppers, discarding liquid, and let cool 10 minutes. Remove and discard stems and, if desired, seeds. Chop peppers.
Pulse chile peppers, red bell pepper, and next 5 ingredients 8 times or until finely chopped. Add vinegar, olive oil, and bread; process until smooth (about 30 seconds). **Makes** 1 cup.

BILL CAUBLE AND CLIFF TEINERT
BARBECUE, BISCUITS & BEANS:
CHUCK WAGON COOKING
BRIGHT SKY PRESS, 2002

Bayou Cooking

Enjoy some authentic Louisiana flavors
for dinner tonight.

Cajun Supper

Serves 6

Crawfish Jambalaya

Blackened Fish

mixed salad greens

crusty French bread

Pineapple-Apple Bread Pudding
With Bourbon Sauce

Cajun and Creole cooks seem to know how to put full flavor and pizzazz into every dish, creating comfort food that doesn't use complicated ingredients. The mix of cultures––French, Acadian, Spanish, African, and Italian––built a world-renowed cuisine. This amazing mix of cultures is like a gumbo; rich, spicy, and layered with flavor. Many hands seasoned this pot, fashioning a unique and vibrant cuisine that borrowed from one another's dishes and used local ingredients.

Typically, many Cajun entrées are one-pot dishes, cooked a long time. Most of these dishes start with a roux—flour browned in fat. Whether light or dark in color, roux lends a dusky richness to a variety of dishes.

CRAWFISH JAMBALAYA

family favorite

Prep: 15 min., Cook: 55 min.

This jambalaya showcases two plentiful Louisiana ingredients: crawfish and rice.

**1 cup uncooked long-grain rice
2 cups chicken broth
¼ cup butter
1 medium onion, chopped
½ cup chopped green bell pepper
½ cup chopped celery
4 garlic cloves, minced
1 (14.5-ounce) can stewed
  tomatoes, undrained
1 teaspoon Cajun seasoning
1 pound frozen crawfish tails,
  thawed, rinsed, and drained
1 cup chopped green onions
⅛ teaspoon pepper
Garnish: chopped green onions**

Cook rice according to package directions, substituting 2 cups chicken broth for water; set aside.

Melt butter in a Dutch oven over medium-high heat; sauté onion, bell pepper, and celery 8 minutes or until vegetables are tender. Add garlic; sauté 1 minute.

Stir in stewed tomatoes and Cajun seasoning; reduce heat to low, and simmer, uncovered, 15 to 20 minutes. Add crawfish tails, and cook 5 minutes. Stir in 1 cup chopped green onions, cooked rice, and pepper. Garnish, if desired. **Makes** 4 to 6 servings.

BLACKENED FISH

Prep: 5 min., Cook: 36 min.

Chef Paul Prudhomme created this dish in the 1980s. This makes a lot of spicy smoke, so it's best to cook it outside over a burner or on a stove with a strong exhaust fan.

- 6 (6- to 8-ounce) redfish, grouper, or catfish fillets (about ½ inch thick)
- 1 cup unsalted butter, melted
- 2 tablespoons blackened fish seasoning
- Lemon wedges

Dip fillets in melted butter. Sprinkle 1 teaspoon seasoning evenly over both sides of each fillet. Press seasoning into fish, and place on wax paper.

Heat a large cast-iron skillet over medium-high heat 10 minutes or until smoking. Place 2 fillets in the skillet, and cook 4 minutes on each side or until lightly charred. Transfer fillets to a serving dish; cover and keep warm. Drain butter from skillet, and carefully wipe clean with paper towels.

Heat skillet 5 minutes or until smoking. Place 2 fillets in skillet, and repeat cooking procedure. Repeat with remaining 2 fillets. Serve with lemon wedges. **Makes** 6 servings.

Note: For testing purposes only, we used Chef Paul Prudhomme's Magic Seasoning Blends Blackened Redfish Magic for seasoning.

PINEAPPLE-APPLE BREAD PUDDING WITH BOURBON SAUCE

chef recipe

Prep: 35 min., Cook: 45 min., Stand: 2 min.

This bread pudding from New Orleans chef Leah Chase, the queen of Creole cuisine, is our hands-down favorite.

- 1 (16-ounce) day-old French bread loaf, cubed
- 2 (12-ounce) cans evaporated milk
- 1 cup water
- 6 large eggs, lightly beaten
- 1 (8-ounce) can crushed pineapple, drained
- 1 large Red Delicious apple, grated
- 1 cup raisins
- 1½ cups sugar
- 5 tablespoons vanilla extract
- ¼ cup butter or margarine, cut up and softened
- Bourbon Sauce

Combine first 3 ingredients, and stir in eggs, blending well. Stir in crushed pineapple and next 4 ingredients. Stir in butter, blending well. Pour mixture into a greased 13- x 9-inch baking dish.

Bake, uncovered, at 350° for 35 to 45 minutes or until set and crust is golden. Remove from oven, and let stand 2 minutes. Serve with Bourbon Sauce. **Makes** 8 servings.

BOURBON SAUCE:
fast fixin's

Prep: 5 min., Cook: 14 min.

- 3 tablespoons butter
- 1 tablespoon all-purpose flour
- ½ cup sugar
- 1 cup whipping cream
- 2 tablespoons bourbon or whiskey
- 1 tablespoon vanilla extract
- 1 teaspoon ground nutmeg

Melt butter in a small saucepan over medium-low heat; whisk in flour, and cook, whisking constantly, 5 minutes. Stir in sugar and cream; cook, whisking constantly, 3 minutes or until thickened. Stir in bourbon, vanilla, and nutmeg; simmer 5 minutes. **Makes** 1½ cups.

CHEF LEAH CHASE
DOOKY CHASE RESTAURANT
NEW ORLEANS, LOUISIANA

Test Kitchen *Notebook*

Ever wonder why nearly every New Orleans restaurant offers bread pudding on its menu? Rather than waste stale bread, the Acadians (Cajuns) used it in bread pudding, hence its French name pain perdu or "lost bread." Its long tradition has made bread pudding a Louisiana favorite—especially when served with a sumptuous sauce—and it's still a great use for leftover French bread. Because it requires only basic ingredients—bread, eggs, milk or cream, and sugar, it's also an affordable way to satisfy family and friends.

Donna Florio
SENIOR WRITER

A Taste of Sunshine

Two important components of Florida cuisine are mangoes and Cuban cooking. These recipes bring the real thing right into your kitchen.

MANGO UPSIDE-DOWN CAKE

family favorite

Prep: 30 min., Cook: 8 min., Bake: 35 min., Cool: 30 min.

2 ripe mangoes, peeled
½ cup unsalted butter
¾ cup firmly packed brown sugar
2 tablespoons dark rum
⅓ cup unsalted butter, softened
¾ cup granulated sugar
2 large eggs
1 teaspoon vanilla extract
1 teaspoon dark rum
1⅔ cups all-purpose flour
2 teaspoons baking powder
¼ teaspoon salt
¾ cup milk

Cut mangoes into 3- to 4-inch-long, 1-inch-wide strips.

Melt ½ cup butter in a medium saucepan over medium heat. Add mangoes and brown sugar. Cook, stirring occasionally, 5 minutes or just until mangoes are tender and sugar is melted.

Remove mangoes from saucepan using a slotted spoon. Cook sugar mixture, stirring constantly, 3 more minutes or until reduced to a thick syrup. Remove saucepan from heat, and stir in 2 tablespoons rum.

Arrange mango slices in a spoke design in a single layer in a lightly greased 9-inch round cakepan. Add ½ cup sugar syrup to cover mango slices, reserving remaining syrup.

Beat ⅓ cup softened butter at medium speed with an electric mixer until creamy. Gradually add granulated sugar, beating until fluffy. Add eggs, vanilla, and 1 teaspoon rum, beating until blended. Combine flour, baking powder, and salt; add to butter mixture alternately with milk, beginning and ending with flour mixture, beating on low speed until smooth. Carefully spread batter over fruit. (Batter will be very thick.)

Bake at 350° for 30 to 35 minutes or until golden and a long wooden pick inserted into center comes out clean. Cool in pan on a wire rack 30 minutes. Invert onto a cake plate; remove pan. Pour reserved sugar syrup evenly over cake. **Makes** 8 servings.

ERIN ALLEN
LAKE WORTH, FLORIDA

COLUMBIA'S FLAN

chef recipe • make ahead

Prep: 10 min., Cook: 2 min., Bake: 1 hr., Chill: 8 hrs.

⅔ cup sugar
1 (14-ounce) can sweetened condensed milk
3 large eggs
1 cup evaporated milk
½ cup milk
1¼ teaspoons vanilla extract

Cook sugar in a medium skillet over medium heat 2 minutes, gently shaking skillet until sugar melts and turns a light golden brown. Quickly pour caramelized sugar into 6 (6-ounce) custard cups.

Whisk together condensed milk and next 4 ingredients in a medium bowl until blended. Pour milk mixture evenly into prepared custard cups. Place cups in a 13- x 9-inch pan; add hot tap water to pan to a depth of ½ inch. Cover all custard cups with 1 large piece of aluminum foil.

Bake at 350° for 1 hour or until set and knife inserted comes out clean. (Do not let water boil.)

Remove cups from pan to a wire rack, and let cool completely. Cover and chill 8 hours or until cold.

Unmold custard cups by lightly pressing edges of custard with a spoon to break away from sides of cup; invert onto serving plates. Drizzle caramelized sugar from bottom of cups over top of each custard. **Makes** 6 servings.

COLUMBIA RESTAURANT
TAMPA, FLORIDA

BLACK BEAN SOUP

chef recipe

Prep: 20 min.; Soak: 8 hrs.; Cook: 5 hrs., 5 min.

1 (16-ounce) package dried black beans
3 quarts water
3 chicken bouillon cubes
½ small onion
¼ small green bell pepper
6 garlic cloves, minced
2 tablespoons olive oil
1 teaspoon dried oregano
1 teaspoon ground cumin
1½ teaspoons sugar
1 teaspoon salt
½ teaspoon pepper
Garnish: minced onion

Wash beans, and remove any foreign particles and debris.

Soak beans in water to cover in a 6-quart stockpot 8 hours. Rinse and drain beans.

Bring beans, 3 quarts water, and bouillon to a boil. Cover, reduce heat to low, and simmer 3 hours. Do not drain.

Process ½ small onion and bell pepper in a blender or food processor until smooth, stopping to scrape down sides.

Sauté garlic in hot oil in a large skillet over medium-high heat 1 minute. Add onion mixture, and cook, stirring constantly, 4 minutes.

Stir onion-and-garlic mixture into beans. Add oregano and next 4 ingredients. Simmer, uncovered, 1½ to 2 hours or until beans are tender and soup is thick. Garnish, if desired. **Makes** 8 servings.

COLUMBIA RESTAURANT
TAMPA, FLORIDA

may

122   Start the Party in the Kitchen *An easy menu to help you host a "let's-cook-together" evening*

124   Secrets to Great Seafood *Chesapeake Bay restaurant owners share their tried-and-true recipes*

124   Keep That Knife Sharp *A fine-tuned blade makes life in the kitchen easier*

125   Coleslaw Three Ways *Toss together one of these sides for your next barbecue or covered-dish supper*

126   Healthy & Light Taste the Goodness of Grains *Simple substitutions for better health*

127   Exceptional Eggplant *Savor this fruit's uniqueness in two tasty recipes*

128   Dill-icious Ideas *This wispy herb isn't just for pickles*

129   Make Ahead and Marinate *Add flavor to fresh vegetables with simple vinaigrettes*

130   Easy Beach Menu *Get ready for summer with these refreshing dishes*

131   Quick & Easy Ready-to-Assemble Meals *Speed up supper with time-saving ingredients and quick-fix recipes*

132   Enjoy Fresh Strawberries *It's prime season for this plump and juicy fruit*

133   Chillin' Out With Sherbets *These frosty recipes boast short ingredient lists and easy preparation*

134   Taste of the South Chocolate-Nut Pies *Celebrate a Kentucky tradition by serving these easy-to-make desserts*

134   Tea Is the Key *This unexpected flavor enhances cakes and more*

136   Pamper Mom With Breakfast *Rich morning favorites to honor her special day*

137   A Taste of Honey *Sweeten your cooking with this old-fashioned favorite*

138   Top-Rated Menu Southwestern Starters *Celebrate Cinco de Mayo with a fiesta*

139   Skillet Suppers *What could be better than a hearty one-dish meal?*

140   What's for Supper? Dish Up Pasta *Comforting dinners that'll bring your family back for seconds*

141   Savor Sweet Onion Sides *Enjoy the mellow flavor of Vidalias*

142   Lunch on the Go *Foods that are a snap to make and even easier to pack up*

143   Cheesy Bites *Focus on fun with these easy, make-ahead appetizers*

144   From Our Kitchen *Cool meals, great mayonnaise, and more*

Start the Party in the Kitchen

Cooking together is half the fun with this easy menu.

A Cooking Party Menu

Serves 8

Sunset Vodka-Orange Sipper

Easy Spicy Caesar Salad

Grilled New York Steaks

Coffee-Onion Jam

Potato-Stuffed
Grilled Bell Peppers

Mint Nectarines With
Pineapple-Coconut Ice Cream

You'll wow your dinner group with this let's-cook-together evening. Part of the entertainment is the preparation of the meal itself. Each recipe offers a variation on a dish you might order at a steak house restaurant. We promise they're impressive and easy.

This menu serves eight. As host, plan to shop for groceries, set the table, and organize each recipe's workstation in the kitchen. Don't worry about tight space—cooking elbow-to-elbow makes it fun. Ask your spouse or call on one guest to come early to tend bar, set out nibbles, and bake the potatoes ahead. When the other guests arrive, break them into pairs and give each team a copy of a recipe. Each pair will make one dish, and everyone will pitch in on dessert. Have a great time.

SUNSET VODKA-ORANGE SIPPER

fast fixin's

Prep: 5 min.

Buy a carton or bottle of orange juice labeled "not from concentrate" for the best flavor.

- 2 to 3 cups vodka
- 3 cups orange juice
- 2 (12-ounce) cans lemon-lime soft drink
- Ice cubes
- ⅓ cup maraschino cherry juice
- Garnishes: lime slices, maraschino cherries

Stir together first 3 ingredients in a pitcher. Fill 8 glasses with ice cubes, filling three-quarters full. Pour vodka mixture evenly over ice. Spoon 2 teaspoons cherry juice into each glass (do not stir). Garnish, if desired, and serve immediately. **Makes** about 10 cups.

EASY SPICY CAESAR SALAD

fast fixin's

Prep: 20 min.

Cut rather than tear the romaine into strips; it's a technique called chiffonade. Use a vegetable peeler to cut or shave thin slices from a wedge of Parmesan cheese. *(pictured on page 113)*

- 1 head romaine lettuce, cored
- 1¼ cups creamy-style Caesar dressing
- 1 jalapeño pepper, quartered and unseeded
- 1 tablespoon fresh lime or lemon juice
- ⅔ cup shredded Parmesan cheese
- 1 (5.5-ounce) package gourmet Caesar croutons
- Garnish: Parmesan cheese shavings

Separate lettuce into leaves; wash and pat leaves dry with paper towels. Stack 5 leaves, and roll up tightly, beginning at 1 long end; cut crosswise into 1-inch pieces, making strips.

Process Caesar dressing, jalapeño pepper with seeds, and lime juice in a blender until smooth, stopping to scrape down sides. Cover and chill until ready to serve.

Place romaine strips and ⅔ cup shredded cheese in a large bowl; drizzle with dressing mixture, and gently toss until coated. Sprinkle with croutons, and serve immediately. Garnish, if desired. **Makes** 8 servings.

Note: For testing purposes only, we used Wishbone Creamy Caesar dressing for a sweeter flavor and Ken's Steak House Creamy Caesar dressing for a tangier flavor. For the gourmet croutons, we used Cardini's Gourmet Cut Caesar Croutons.

JULIA MITCHELL
LEXINGTON, KENTUCKY

Grilled New York Steaks

fast fixin's

Prep: 5 min., Grill: 20 min.

To keep costs down, we bought thick-cut New York strip steaks and cut them in half to mimic more expensive filet mignons (about $17 per pound). Expect to pay about $10 per pound for the strip steaks, or about $40 for 8 (8-ounce) servings. *(pictured on page 113)*

- 4 (1½-inch-thick) New York strip steaks, cut in half
- 1 tablespoon kosher salt
- 2½ teaspoons freshly ground pepper
- Garnish: fresh flat-leaf parsley sprigs

Sprinkle steaks evenly on both sides with salt and pepper.

Grill steaks, covered with grill lid, over medium-high heat (350° to 400°) 8 to 10 minutes on each side or to desired degree of doneness. Garnish, if desired. **Makes** 8 servings.

Coffee-Onion Jam

chef recipe

Prep: 10 min., Cook: 30 min.

Serve this glistening jam with a juicy grilled steak. *(pictured on page 113)*

- 3 large yellow onions, sliced ¼ inch thick
- 6 tablespoons vegetable oil
- ½ cup hot strong brewed coffee
- ¼ cup sugar
- ½ teaspoon salt
- ¼ teaspoon freshly ground pepper

Cook onions in hot oil in a large skillet over medium-high heat, stirring often, 15 to 20 minutes or until onions are caramel colored. Stir in coffee and remaining ingredients, and cook, stirring occasionally, 5 to 10 more minutes or until liquid has evaporated. **Makes** 2¼ cups.

MARC COLLINS
CHEF, CIRCA 1886
WENTWORTH MANSION
CHARLESTON, SOUTH CAROLINA

Potato-Stuffed Grilled Bell Peppers

family favorite

Prep: 25 min.; Bake: 1 hr., 30 min.;
Cool: 15 min.; Grill: 18 min.

Think twice-baked potato, except the potato mixture is stuffed into a bell pepper half. The peppers roast and char on the bottom, imparting a wonderful sweet flavor, while the upper edges stay crisp-tender. Don't forget to bake the potatoes before the guests arrive. *(pictured on page 113)*

- 4 large baking potatoes (about 3½ to 4 pounds)
- 4 large red bell peppers
- 1 (16-ounce) container sour cream
- ½ cup shredded Gouda cheese
- ¼ cup sliced green onions
- 3 tablespoons butter
- 3 tablespoons chopped fresh flat-leaf parsley
- ¾ teaspoon salt
- ½ teaspoon ground pepper
- ¼ teaspoon paprika

Pierce each potato 3 or 4 times with a fork, and place directly on oven rack.
Bake potatoes at 450° for 1 hour and 30 minutes. Let cool slightly, about 15 minutes.
Cut bell peppers in half lengthwise, cutting through stems and keeping intact. Remove and discard seeds and membranes; rinse and pat dry. Set aside. Cut baked potatoes in half. Scoop out pulp into a large bowl, discarding shells. Add sour cream and next 6 ingredients to pulp, blending well with a fork or potato masher.
Spoon potato mixture evenly into bell pepper halves. Sprinkle with paprika.
Grill peppers, covered with grill lid, over medium-high heat (350° to 400°) 18 minutes or until peppers are blistered and potato mixture bubbles around edges. Serve immediately. **Makes** 8 servings.

Note: We tried microwaving the potatoes, but the texture is mealy; baking is the best choice.

Grilled Stuffed Potatoes: Omit red bell peppers. Proceed with recipe as directed, reserving potato shells and spooning potato mixture into reserved potato shells. Grill as directed, or bake at 350° for 20 minutes or until thoroughly heated.

Mint Nectarines With Pineapple-Coconut Ice Cream

fast fixin's

Prep: 25 min., Cook: 5 min.

Cap off the evening with this summery sundae bursting with the flavors of fruit and mint.

- 12 ripe nectarines
- 2 tablespoons butter
- ¼ cup firmly packed brown sugar
- 1 tablespoon fresh lemon juice (about 1 small lemon)
- 2 tablespoons chopped fresh mint
- 3 pints pineapple-coconut ice cream
- Garnishes: fresh mint sprigs, toasted flaked coconut

Peel nectarines, and cut each into 8 wedges, discarding pits.
Melt butter in a large nonstick skillet over medium-high heat. Add nectarines; sprinkle brown sugar and lemon juice over nectarines, and gently fold until blended. Cook, stirring occasionally, 2 to 4 minutes or until nectarines start to release their juice. Remove from heat; stir in mint.
Divide and scoop ice cream into 8 individual serving dishes. Top evenly with warm nectarine sections, and serve immediately. Garnish, if desired. **Makes** 8 servings.

Note: For testing purposes only, we used Häagen-Dazs Pineapple Coconut Ice Cream.

Mint Peaches With Pineapple-Coconut Ice Cream: Substitute 2 (16-ounce) packages frozen sliced peaches, thawed, for nectarines. Proceed with recipe as directed. Prep: 5 min., Cook: 5 min.

Secrets to Great Seafood

On tiny Tangier Island, Virginia, seafood rules—and with good reason. Fishing has been a way of life for generations on this remote island, providing sustenance as well as income. Entrepreneurs and best friends Irene Eskridge, Stuart Parks, and Noel Marshall parlayed that seafood heritage into success at their restaurant, The Fisherman's Corner.

HOT CRAB DIP

chef recipe

Prep: 15 min., Bake: 35 min.

For a lighter version, substitute reduced-fat cream cheese, light sour cream, 2% reduced-fat Cheddar cheese, and light mayonnaise.

- 2 (8-ounce) packages cream cheese, softened
- 1 (8-ounce) container sour cream
- ¼ cup mayonnaise
- 1 tablespoon Worcestershire sauce
- 1 tablespoon lemon juice
- 1 teaspoon dry mustard
- ¼ teaspoon garlic salt
- 1 pound fresh crabmeat, drained and picked
- 1 cup (4 ounces) shredded Cheddar cheese
- Garnish: chopped fresh parsley
- Crackers or toasted French bread rounds

Combine first 7 ingredients, stirring until blended. Fold in crabmeat.
Spoon mixture into an 11- x 7-inch baking dish; sprinkle with Cheddar cheese.
Bake at 350° for 35 minutes or until bubbly. Garnish, if desired. Serve immediately with crackers or toasted French bread rounds. **Makes** 6 servings.

THE FISHERMAN'S CORNER
TANGIER ISLAND, VIRGINIA

UNCLE FRANK'S CRAB CAKES

chef recipe

Prep: 20 min., Chill: 1 hr., Cook: 8 min. per batch

If you plan to make Stuffed Jumbo Shrimp, leave 2 or more of these crab cakes uncooked to use for the shrimp recipe. Add an additional teaspoon of Old Bay seasoning for more flavor.

- 3 white bread slices
- ¼ cup mayonnaise
- 1 large egg
- 1 teaspoon baking powder
- 1 teaspoon Old Bay seasoning
- 1 teaspoon Worcestershire sauce
- 1 teaspoon prepared mustard
- ¼ teaspoon salt
- ¼ teaspoon dried parsley flakes
- Pinch of pepper
- Dash of hot sauce
- 1 pound fresh jumbo lump crabmeat, drained and picked
- ½ cup vegetable oil

Pulse bread in food processor 6 times or until coarsely crumbled.
Whisk together mayonnaise and next 9 ingredients in a large bowl; gently fold in breadcrumbs and crabmeat (being careful not to break up crab). Shape mixture into 6 patties; place on a baking sheet. Cover and chill at least 1 hour.
Cook crab cakes, in batches, in hot oil in a medium skillet over medium-high heat 3 to 4 minutes on each side or until golden. **Makes** 6 cakes.

THE FISHERMAN'S CORNER
TANGIER ISLAND, VIRGINIA

STUFFED JUMBO SHRIMP

chef recipe • fast fixin's

Prep: 10 min., Bake: 15 min.

This recipe can be easily tripled to feed 6.

- 8 unpeeled, jumbo fresh shrimp
- 2 Uncle Frank's Crab Cakes, uncooked (recipe above)
- ½ to ⅔ cup fine, dry breadcrumbs
- ¼ cup Butter Sauce
- Garnish: lemon wedges

Peel shrimp, leaving tails on; devein shrimp, if desired. Butterfly shrimp by making a deep slit down the back of each from the large end to the tail, cutting to, but not through, the inside curve.
Divide each crab cake evenly into 4 portions. Shape 1 portion around each shrimp, forming a ball (leave tail exposed). Repeat with remaining crab cake portions and shrimp. Divide shrimp between 2 large ramekins. Sprinkle with breadcrumbs; spoon Butter Sauce over shrimp.
Bake at 400° for 15 minutes or until golden. Garnish, if desired. **Makes** 2 servings.

THE FISHERMAN'S CORNER
TANGIER ISLAND, VIRGINIA

BUTTER SAUCE

chef recipe • fast fixin's

Prep: 5 min.

Irene, Stuart, and Noel use this sauce in many of their seafood dishes. Use some of it in the Stuffed Jumbo Shrimp recipe. It's also a great dip for any fresh seafood or French bread.

Stir together 1 cup butter, melted; 1 teaspoon Old Bay seasoning; and 1 teaspoon lemon pepper. **Makes** 1 cup.

THE FISHERMAN'S CORNER
TANGIER ISLAND, VIRGINIA

Keep That Knife Sharp

Dull knives are the culprit of more cuts and kitchen accidents than almost anything else. A sharp knife actually *reduces* the risk of cutting yourself. It will cut food easily without tearing; you don't have to saw back and forth. Most knives need to be sharpened once every 6 to 12 months. In the meantime use a steel to keep the edge in alignment. To get that razor-sharp edge, take the knife through a couple of quick passes over the steel. (See box on the opposite page.) You'll be glad to have a sharp knife when making Red Beans and Rice With Sausage.

RED BEANS AND RICE WITH SAUSAGE

Prep: 15 min., Cook: 38 min., Stand: 10 min.

- 1 pound spicy smoked sausage
- 1 large onion, diced
- 2 celery ribs, diced
- 3 garlic cloves, minced
- 2 teaspoons Cajun seasoning, divided
- 2 cups uncooked long-grain rice
- 2 (14-ounce) cans chicken broth
- 2 (15-ounce) cans kidney beans, rinsed and drained
- 1 (15-ounce) can diced tomatoes
- 2 bay leaves
- ½ cup chopped fresh parsley
- Hot sauce (optional)

Cut smoked sausage into ¼-inch-thick slices. Cook in a large Dutch oven over medium-high heat 8 to 10 minutes or until slices are browned. Remove sausage, and drain on paper towels, reserving 1 teaspoon drippings in pan.
Sauté onion and celery in hot drippings in Dutch oven over medium-high heat 4 to 5 minutes. Stir in garlic, ½ teaspoon Cajun seasoning, and rice; sauté 3 minutes. Stir in broth, next 3 ingredients, and remaining 1½ teaspoons Cajun seasoning. Bring to a boil; cover, reduce heat, and simmer 15 to 20 minutes. Remove from heat; stir in sausage and parsley; let stand, covered, 10 minutes or until rice is tender. Discard bay leaves. Serve with hot sauce, if desired. **Makes** 6 servings.

JANICE WALCZAK
BOLINGBROOK, ILLINOIS

How to Use a Steel

Hold steel perpendicular to the counter with the tip firmly positioned against a cutting board or towel. Place knife edge against steel at a 20-degree angle, blade side down. Starting at the back of the knife, pull slowly toward you while using moderate pressure to press down on the knife. Repeat two times before switching to the other side of the knife.

Coleslaw Three Ways

Coleslaw, or slaw, as it's often called, has many variations. From creamy, mayonnaise-dressed versions to sweet-and-tart, vinegar-based ones, no two are alike. Cabbage being the main ingredient, these recipes are easy to toss together. Most varieties of slaw get better with time as their flavors blend and mellow, so they're tastier the next day. You'll find this trio of recipes colorful and refreshing. All take 20 minutes or less to prepare, but be sure to add chilling time to your schedule.

ZESTY VINEGAR COLESLAW

make ahead

Prep: 20 min., Chill: 8 hrs.

Turmeric adds a pungent flavor and a deep yellow color. Find it in the spice section of your grocery store.

- ½ cup sugar
- ½ cup cider vinegar
- ½ cup vegetable oil
- 1 teaspoon mustard seeds
- 1 teaspoon celery seeds
- ½ teaspoon salt
- ¼ teaspoon ground turmeric
- 1 large green cabbage, chopped
- 1 medium-size green bell pepper, chopped
- 1 (4-ounce) jar diced pimiento, drained
- 1 medium onion, chopped (optional)

Microwave first 7 ingredients in a 1-quart glass bowl at HIGH 3 to 4 minutes or until thoroughly heated, stirring once. Let cool.
Combine cabbage, bell pepper, pimiento, and, if desired, onion in a bowl. Drizzle with dressing, tossing to coat. Cover and chill at least 8 hours or up to 3 days. **Makes** 7 cups.

LINDA EUDY
MOUNT PLEASANT, NORTH CAROLINA

SWEET-AND-TART RED CABBAGE COLESLAW

make ahead

Prep: 20 min., Chill: 1 hr.

- ⅓ cup pineapple juice
- ¼ cup sugar
- ¼ cup olive oil
- ¼ cup lemon or lime juice
- ¼ cup rice wine vinegar
- ½ teaspoon salt
- ½ teaspoon pepper
- ⅛ teaspoon hot sauce
- 1 large red cabbage, finely shredded
- 1 small Granny Smith apple, chopped
- 1 large carrot, shredded
- 1 small sweet onion, minced
- 5 to 6 bacon slices, cooked and crumbled

Whisk together first 8 ingredients in a large bowl until sugar dissolves.
Add cabbage and next 3 ingredients, tossing to coat. Cover and chill at least 1 hour. Sprinkle with bacon before serving. **Makes** 8 cups.

AMY HALL
KNOXVILLE, TENNESSEE

CREAMY-AND-SWEET COLESLAW

make ahead

Prep: 15 min., Chill: 8 hrs.

- ½ cup mayonnaise
- 2 tablespoons sugar
- 2 tablespoons lemon juice
- 2 tablespoons buttermilk
- 1 medium-size green cabbage, shredded
- 1 large carrot, finely shredded
- 1 small green bell pepper, finely chopped
- ¼ teaspoon salt
- ¼ cup chopped sweet salad cube pickles (optional)

Stir together first 4 ingredients in a large bowl. Add cabbage, next 3 ingredients, and, if desired, pickles, tossing to coat. Cover and chill 8 hours. Serve with a slotted spoon. **Makes** 4½ cups.

JOYCE ANTHONY MARSH
TAMPA, FLORIDA

Taste the Goodness of Grains

Dish up new recipes with hearty flavor and great nutrition at your next meal.

Improve your diet painlessly by adding some whole grains. Instead of white rice, try brown rice, or choose stone-ground grits instead of regular grits.

Research shows that eating whole grain foods reduces the risk of heart disease, stroke, cancer, diabetes, and obesity. That's because the outer layers of grains removed in processed foods contain antioxidants, B vitamins, protein, fiber, minerals, and healthy fats. Try these fresh ideas to help get more of these important nutrients into meals throughout the day.

Get More Grains

- Stir whole grain, ready-to-eat cereal into yogurt, or sprinkle it over fruit.
- Top a salad with granola cereal or a crumbled granola bar.
- Make sandwiches with whole grain breads.
- Substitute whole grain pasta for regular semolina pasta.
- Add ½ cup cooked brown rice to a cup of soup.
- Use stone-ground cornmeal for cornbread.
- Add 1 cup cooked wild rice or barley to bread stuffing.

DRIED CHERRY-AND-PECAN OATMEAL

fast fixin's

Prep: 10 min., Cook: 20 min.

Whole oats take a little longer to cook than instant, but they're higher in fiber, have a chewier texture, and stick to your ribs longer.

- 3 cups water
- 3 cups fat-free milk
- 2 cups whole oats (not instant)
- ½ cup dried cherries, coarsely chopped
- ½ teaspoon salt
- 5 tablespoons brown sugar
- 1 tablespoon butter
- ¼ teaspoon ground cinnamon
- ¼ teaspoon vanilla extract
- 2 tablespoons chopped pecans, toasted

Bring first 5 ingredients to a boil; reduce heat, and simmer, stirring occasionally, 20 minutes or until thickened. Remove from heat. Stir in 4 tablespoons brown sugar and next 3 ingredients. Spoon 1 cup oatmeal in each of 6 bowls. Sprinkle evenly with pecans and remaining 1 tablespoon brown sugar. Serve oatmeal immediately. **Makes** 6 (1-cup) servings.

Per serving: Calories 394 (18% from fat); Fat 8g (sat 2.3g, mono 2.9g, poly 2.1g); Protein 13.3g; Carb 66g; Fiber 7.7g; Chol 7.5mg; Iron 3.2mg; Sodium 280mg; Calc 197mg

BARLEY-PINE NUT SALAD

Prep: 25 min., Cook: 10 min., Stand: 5 min.

This recipe or the brown rice version following it makes a chewy, nutty light meal. Extra-virgin olive oil and toasted pine nuts give this dish rich flavor.

- 2 cups low-sodium fat-free chicken broth
- 1 cup uncooked quick-cooking barley
- ¾ cup chopped jarred roasted red bell peppers
- 1 small cucumber, diced
- 1 tablespoon chopped fresh dill
- 1 tablespoon chopped fresh parsley
- 3 tablespoons fresh lemon juice
- 2 tablespoons extra-virgin olive oil
- ¾ teaspoon sugar
- ½ teaspoon salt
- ½ teaspoon pepper
- 2 tablespoons pine nuts, toasted
- 2 tablespoons crumbled feta cheese

Bring 2 cups chicken broth to a boil in a 2-quart saucepan; stir in barley. Cover, reduce heat, and simmer 10 minutes or until barley is tender. Remove from heat; let stand, covered, 5 minutes. Drain well.

Combine cooked barley, roasted red bell peppers, and next 3 ingredients in a large bowl.

Whisk together lemon juice and next 4 ingredients. Drizzle over barley mixture, tossing to coat. Sprinkle evenly with toasted pine nuts and crumbled feta cheese; serve immediately. **Makes** 6 (¾ cup) servings.

LOUISE BODZIONY
GLADSTONE, MISSOURI

Per serving: Calories 202 (35% from fat); Fat 8g (sat 1.4g, mono 4.4g, poly 1.8g); Protein 6.5g; Carb 28g; Fiber 6.3g; Chol 2.8mg; Iron 1.6mg; Sodium 494mg; Calc 41mg

Brown Rice-Pine Nut Salad: Substitute 1 cup brown rice for barley. Increase broth to 2¼ cups, and increase cooking time to 45 minutes. Proceed as directed.

Per serving: Calories 208 (35% from fat); Fat 8.3g (sat 1.5g, mono 4.6g, poly 1.8g); Protein 5.4g; Carb 29g; Fiber 2.8g; Chol 2.8mg; Iron 1mg; Sodium 522mg; Calc 41mg

BARLEY, VEGETABLE, AND FRUIT MEDLEY

Prep: 10 min., Cook: 22 min.

We've used quick-cooking barley for extra convenience. For maximum benefits of whole grain, hulled barley and Scotch barley are the best choices. Look for these grains at a health food store or in the health food aisle of your supermarket.

- 2¼ cups low-sodium fat-free chicken or vegetable broth, divided
- ½ teaspoon pepper
- ¼ teaspoon salt
- ¼ teaspoon dried thyme
- ¼ teaspoon dried rosemary
- 1 cup uncooked quick-cooking barley
- 1 (16-ounce) package frozen vegetable seasoning blend, thawed *
- 2 teaspoons vegetable oil
- ¾ cup diced dried mixed fruit
- 3 tablespoons chopped pecans, toasted

Bring 2 cups chicken broth, pepper, and next 3 ingredients to a boil in a large saucepan; stir in barley, and simmer 10 to 12 minutes or until barley is tender and liquid is absorbed. Remove pan from heat.

Sauté vegetable blend in hot oil in a large skillet over medium-high heat 10 minutes or until vegetables are lightly browned. Stir in cooked barley, dried mixed fruit, and remaining ¼ cup chicken broth. Sprinkle evenly with chopped toasted pecans, and serve immediately. **Makes** 8 (½-cup) servings.

Note: Vegetable seasoning blend contains chopped red and green bell peppers, onions, and celery and is found in the frozen foods section. For testing purposes only, we used SunMaid Fruit-Bits for dried mixed fruit.

*Substitute 1 onion, chopped; half each of a green and red bell pepper, chopped; and 1 celery rib, chopped, if desired.

Per serving: Calories 199 (19% from fat); Fat 4.6g (sat 0.7g; mono 1.7g; poly 1.5g); Protein 6.1g; Carb 36.4g; Fiber 8g; Chol 1.1mg; Iron 1.7; Sodium 133mg; Calc 34mg

WILD RICE-AND-CHICKEN BOWL

family favorite

Prep: 20 min., Cook: 55 min.

If you're pressed for time, buy quick-cooking wild rice or precooked brown rice in microwaveable pouches to equal 8 cups cooked rice.

- 2 cups uncooked wild rice
- 2 cups shredded, cooked chicken breasts
- ½ cup golden raisins
- ½ cup chopped red bell pepper
- ¼ cup chopped red onion
- 2 tablespoons fresh lemon juice
- 1 tablespoon extra-virgin olive oil
- 1 tablespoon Dijon mustard
- 1 tablespoon honey
- 1 teaspoon white wine vinegar
- ¼ teaspoon salt
- 1 tablespoon chopped fresh mint
- 2 tablespoons chopped fresh parsley
- 2 tablespoons sliced almonds, toasted
- Garnishes: apple slices, fresh flat-leaf parsley sprigs

Cook wild rice according to package directions.

Combine cooked rice, chicken, and next 3 ingredients in a large bowl.

Whisk together lemon juice and next 5 ingredients. Drizzle over rice mixture, tossing to coat. Stir in mint and parsley. Sprinkle with almonds. Garnish, if desired. **Makes** 8 servings.

Note: For testing purposes only, we used Gourmet House Quick Cooking Wild Rice.

Per serving: Calories 298 (18% from fat); Fat 6g (sat 1.2g, mono 3g, poly 1.3g); Protein 18g; Carb 45g; Fiber 3.7g; Chol 29mg; Iron 1.7mg; Sodium 152mg; Calc 25mg

---

What's New?

Watch for more whole grain products in the supermarket bearing the new symbol from the Whole Grains Council. The symbol will help identify how much whole grain the product contains. For more information visit **www.wholegrainscouncil.org.**

Exceptional Eggplant

Eggplant is full of surprises. Not only is it a fruit, but more specifically, it's a berry. And it can be used in a variety of ways. Garden Eggplant Pizza is just right for a vegetarian meal, and for an inventive side dish, try Eggplant Fritters (recipe on following page).

GARDEN EGGPLANT PIZZA

family favorite

Prep: 30 min., Cook: 10 min., Bake: 10 min.

To substitute fresh herbs, use three times more than dried.

- 1 large eggplant, peeled
- 1 medium tomato
- 1 red bell pepper
- 1 onion
- 1 small zucchini
- 3 tablespoons olive oil, divided
- 1 (14-ounce) package prebaked Italian pizza crust
- 2 cups (8 ounces) shredded mozzarella cheese
- ½ teaspoon dried basil
- ½ teaspoon dried oregano
- ½ teaspoon dried thyme
- ¼ teaspoon garlic powder
- ½ teaspoon salt
- ¼ teaspoon freshly ground pepper

Chop first 5 ingredients coarsely; sauté in 1 tablespoon oil in a large skillet over medium-high heat 10 minutes or until tender.

Layer pizza crust evenly with cheese and eggplant mixture; sprinkle with basil and next 5 ingredients. Drizzle with remaining 2 tablespoons oil.

Bake at 425° for 10 minutes or until golden. **Makes** 6 servings.

Note: For testing purposes only, we used a Boboli pizza crust.

LINDA KIRKPATRICK
WESTMINSTER, MARYLAND

EGGPLANT FRITTERS

family favorite

Prep: 15 min., Cook: 20 min., Chill: 30 min.,
Fry: 4 min. per batch

> 1 medium eggplant, peeled
> 2 green onions, chopped
> ⅓ cup minced bell pepper
> 2 teaspoons vegetable oil
> 2 white bread slices, toasted and
>   cubed
> ½ teaspoon salt
> ¼ teaspoon garlic powder
> ¼ teaspoon freshly ground black
>   pepper
> 2 large eggs, lightly beaten
> Vegetable oil

Chop eggplant into bite-size pieces.
Drop eggplant into a large pot of water
as you chop to keep it from discoloring.
Add extra water to cover, if necessary.
Bring to a boil, and cook 10 minutes or
until tender; drain and cool.

Sauté onions and bell pepper in 2 teaspoons hot vegetable oil in a skillet over
medium-high heat 5 minutes or until
tender; set aside.

Pulse bread in a food processor 3 or
4 times or until finely crumbled to
equal ¾ cup; remove and set aside.

Pulse eggplant, salt, garlic powder, and
ground pepper in food processor
3 times or until blended.

Stir together eggplant puree, breadcrumbs, vegetables, and egg until combined; chill 30 minutes.

Pour oil to a depth of 1 inch into a large
skillet; heat to 350°. Drop eggplant
mixture by heaping tablespoonfuls, in
batches, into hot oil; fry 2 minutes on
each side or until browned. Drain on
paper towels. **Makes** 2 dozen.

JULIE ABSHIRE
GROVES, TEXAS

Dill-icious Ideas

Fresh dill takes simple care. Rinse, pat
dry with paper towels (moisture rapidly wilts and discolors the leaves), and
seal in a zip-top plastic bag. To prep, use
fingers to strip the leaves from the top of
the stem downward, and gather into a
bunch. Coarsely chop to keep the wispy
quality of the leaves. Switch to dried dill
when fresh is not available; just use one-
third the amount of dried for fresh.

GREEK CHICKEN ROLLUPS

family favorite

Prep: 20 min., Grill: 16 min., Stand: 10 min.

> 3 to 4 skinned and boned chicken
>   breasts
> 1 tablespoon olive oil
> 1 to 2 teaspoons Greek seasoning
> 4 to 6 slices Italian herb
>   flatbread *
> 1 cup Low-Cal Dilled Yogurt
>   Dressing (see recipe)
> 1 cucumber, thinly sliced
> 4 plum tomatoes, thinly sliced
> 6 green leaf lettuce leaves

Brush chicken breasts with oil, and
sprinkle evenly with Greek seasoning.

Grill chicken breasts, covered with grill
lid, over medium-high heat (350° to
400°) 6 to 8 minutes on each side
or until chicken is done. Let chicken
stand 10 minutes; cut into ¼-inch-
thick slices.

Place sliced chicken down center
of warmed flatbread slices. Top with
Low-Cal Dilled Yogurt Dressing,
cucumber slices, tomato slices, and lettuce; roll up. Serve immediately. **Makes**
4 to 6 servings.

*Substitute pita bread rounds for flat-
bread, if desired. Line warmed pita
rounds with Low-Cal Dilled Yogurt
Dressing, lettuce, tomato slices, and
cucumber slices. Fill with sliced
chicken, and serve immediately.

LOW-CAL DILLED YOGURT DRESSING

make ahead

Prep: 10 min., Chill: 1 hr.

This tangy, creamy dressing is great as a dip
with vegetables or as a sauce for grilled
chicken, lamb, or seafood.

> 1 cup plain nonfat yogurt
> ½ small onion, chopped
> 2 tablespoons chopped fresh or
>   2 teaspoons dried dill
> ¼ teaspoon dried mustard
> ¼ teaspoon minced garlic
> ¼ cup fat-free mayonnaise

Process first 5 ingredients in a blender or
food processor until smooth, stopping to
scrape down sides. Whisk in mayonnaise.
Cover and chill 1 hour. **Makes** 1½ cups.

SUZAN L. WIENER
SPRING HILL, FLORIDA

DILLED POTATO SALAD WITH FETA

make ahead

Prep: 15 min., Cook: 35 min., Chill: 2 hrs.

> 2 pounds small red potatoes,
>   unpeeled
> ⅓ cup red wine vinegar
> ⅓ cup vegetable oil
> 3 tablespoons chopped fresh or
>   1 tablespoon dried dill
> ½ to 1 teaspoon salt
> ½ teaspoon pepper
> 1 large red bell pepper,
>   chopped
> 1 cucumber, cut in half lengthwise
>   and sliced
> ½ cup sliced green onions
> 1 (4-ounce) package crumbled feta
>   cheese

Bring potatoes and water to cover to a
boil. Cook 25 to 30 minutes or just
until tender; drain and cool. Cut potatoes into quarters.

Whisk together vinegar, oil, dill, salt,
and pepper. Pour over warm potatoes.

Stir in chopped bell pepper, cucumber,
and green onions; add cheese, and toss
to combine. Cover and chill at least
2 hours. **Makes** 6 to 8 servings.

Make Ahead and Marinate

If you've grown bored with the traditional tossed salad, a marinated mixture makes a great change of pace. Fresh vegetables yield spectacular taste when tossed with olive oil, vinegar, and herbs.

Marinate food in a glass or ceramic container—acidic ingredients, such as vinegar or lemon juice, react with metal, which affects the flavor. Sturdy vegetables, such as cauliflower, broccoli, carrots, and celery, stand up well to marinades. Mix things early in the day for best results.

MARINATED DILL GREEN BEANS

make ahead

Prep: 10 min., Cook: 8 min., Chill: 3 hrs.

Choose beans that are crisp and blemish free. *(pictured on page 114)*

- ½ pound small fresh green beans
- ¼ cup olive oil
- 2 tablespoons rice or white wine vinegar
- 1 teaspoon grated lemon rind
- 1 teaspoon chopped fresh dill
- ½ teaspoon salt
- ¼ teaspoon pepper
- ½ medium onion, thinly sliced
- 1 garlic clove

Cook beans in boiling water to cover 3 to 5 minutes or until crisp-tender; drain. Plunge into ice water to stop the cooking process; drain and set aside.
Heat oil and next 5 ingredients in a saucepan over medium heat.
Combine beans, onion, and garlic; drizzle with warm vinaigrette, tossing to coat. Cover and chill at least 3 hours. Discard garlic clove before serving. **Makes** 2 cups.

MARINATED VEGETABLE SALAD

family favorite • make ahead

Prep: 20 min., Chill: 5 hrs. *(pictured on page 114)*

- 1 (16-ounce) package fresh broccoli and cauliflower florets
- 1 (16-ounce) package cherry tomatoes
- 1 (15-ounce) can chickpeas, rinsed and drained
- 1 (6-ounce) can ripe black olives, drained and sliced
- 1 cup slivered snow peas
- 3 green onions, chopped
- 1 medium carrot, cut into thin strips
- 1 small red bell pepper, chopped
- ½ cup olive oil
- ⅓ cup red wine vinegar
- 2 garlic cloves, chopped
- ½ teaspoon salt
- ½ teaspoon sugar
- 1½ teaspoons chopped fresh or ½ teaspoon dried basil
- ¼ teaspoon pepper
- Garnish: fresh parsley sprig

Combine first 8 ingredients in a large bowl.
Process oil and next 6 ingredients in a blender until smooth; add to vegetables, tossing to coat. Cover and chill 5 hours. Garnish, if desired. **Makes** 10 cups.

STEPHANIE SEARLE
BRENTWOOD, TENNESSEE

MARINATED SQUASH

family favorite • make ahead

Prep: 15 min., Chill: 3 hrs.

- 3 medium-size yellow squash
- 3 celery ribs
- 3 carrots
- 3 green onions
- ¾ cup olive oil-and-vinegar dressing
- 1 teaspoon sugar
- 1 teaspoon chopped fresh rosemary

Chop first 4 ingredients. Stir together olive oil-and-vinegar dressing, sugar, and rosemary in a large bowl; add vegetables, tossing to coat. Cover and chill 3 hours. **Makes** 2 cups.

Note: For testing purposes only, we used Newman's Own Oil & Vinegar Dressing.

HOT TOMATO SALAD

make ahead

Prep: 15 min., Chill: 4 hrs.

- 4 yellow banana peppers
- 2 green banana peppers
- 2 jalapeño peppers
- 4 to 5 large tomatoes
- 2 garlic cloves, minced
- 1 tablespoon chopped fresh basil
- 1 tablespoon chopped fresh parsley
- 1 teaspoon chopped fresh rosemary
- 1 teaspoon chopped fresh oregano
- 2 ounces smoked Cheddar cheese, cubed (optional)
- ½ cup olive oil
- 1 tablespoon lemon juice
- 1 teaspoon salt
- ½ teaspoon pepper
- 2 teaspoons sugar (optional)
- Garnish: fresh basil sprig

Remove and discard seeds from peppers and tomatoes. Dice peppers and tomatoes; place in a large bowl. Toss in garlic, herbs, and, if desired, cheese.
Stir together oil, next 3 ingredients, and, if desired, sugar; add to tomato mixture, tossing to coat. Cover and chill 2 to 4 hours. Serve with a slotted spoon. Garnish, if desired. **Makes** 5 cups.

DIANA COX
CLYDE, TEXAS

Easy Beach Menu

Anticipate the beginning of summer
with these make-ahead dishes.

Seaside Menu

Serves 6

Broiled Mahi-Mahi With Parsleyed
Tomatoes

Greek Pasta Salad

French bread slices

Almond Sand Dollar Cookies

ice cream

Memorial Day weekend is the first chance at beach fun for the summer. This menu can be easily made at a rented condo or beach house because it doesn't need any special equipment. And after dinner, you'll have time to wiggle your toes in the sand.

BROILED MAHI-MAHI WITH PARSLEYED TOMATOES

Prep: 15 min., Cook: 13 min., Broil: 8 min.

- 2 medium onions, sliced
- 2 tablespoons olive oil
- 2 tomatoes, seeded and chopped
- 2 tablespoons chopped fresh parsley
- ¼ cup white wine
- 1 tablespoon tomato paste
- 2 garlic cloves, chopped
- ½ teaspoon salt, divided
- ½ teaspoon pepper, divided
- 6 (6- to 8-ounce) mahi-mahi fillets
- 1 (4-ounce) package crumbled feta cheese
- Garnish: lemon slices

Sauté sliced onions in hot olive oil over medium-high heat 8 minutes or until tender. Add chopped tomatoes, next 4 ingredients, and ¼ teaspoon each of salt and pepper. Simmer, stirring occasionally, 5 minutes. Set onion-and-tomato mixture aside.

Place fish in a single layer on a lightly greased rack in an aluminum foil-lined broiler pan; sprinkle with remaining ¼ teaspoon each of salt and pepper.

Broil 5 inches from heat 8 minutes or until fish flakes with a fork.

Spoon onion-and-tomato mixture evenly onto a platter; top with fish fillets. Sprinkle evenly with crumbled feta cheese, and garnish, if desired. **Makes** 6 servings.

MARY PAPPAS
RICHMOND, VIRGINIA

GREEK PASTA SALAD

family favorite

Prep: 30 min., Cook: 8 min.

- 1 (8-ounce) package sliced fresh mushrooms
- 4 to 5 shallots, chopped (about ½ cup)
- 6 tablespoons olive oil, divided
- 2 tablespoons lemon juice
- 3 tablespoons mayonnaise
- 1 tablespoon Greek seasoning
- 1 (8-ounce) package penne pasta, cooked
- 2 (2.5-ounce) cans sliced ripe black olives, drained
- 1 (4-ounce) jar diced pimiento, drained

Sauté sliced mushrooms and chopped shallots in 2 tablespoons hot olive oil in a large skillet over medium-high heat 7 to 8 minutes or until tender. Remove from heat.

Whisk together remaining 4 tablespoons oil, juice, mayonnaise, and seasoning in a large bowl, blending well. Add cooked pasta, mushroom mixture, olives, and pimiento, tossing to coat. Cover and chill 8 hours, if desired. **Makes** 4 to 6 servings.

BETTY M. CARTER
NEW MARKET, VIRGINIA

ALMOND SAND DOLLAR COOKIES

family favorite

Prep: 25 min., Chill: 1 hr.,
Bake: 8 min. per batch

- 1 cup butter, softened
- 2 cups sifted powdered sugar
- 2 large eggs
- 1 large egg, separated
- 3⅓ cups all-purpose flour
- ½ teaspoon baking powder
- ¼ cup granulated sugar
- 1 teaspoon ground cinnamon
- Sliced almonds

Beat 1 cup softened butter at medium speed with an electric mixer until creamy; gradually add 2 cups sifted powdered sugar, beating until well blended. Add 2 eggs and 1 egg yolk, beating until blended.

Combine flour and baking powder. Add to butter mixture, beating at low speed until blended. Shape dough into a ball, and wrap in plastic wrap. Chill 1 hour.

Roll dough to an ⅛-inch thickness on a lightly floured surface; cut with a 3-inch round cutter. Place on lightly greased, parchment paper-lined baking sheets; brush with lightly beaten egg white.

Stir together granulated sugar and ground cinnamon, and sprinkle evenly over cookies. Gently press 5 almond slices in a spoke design around center of each cookie.

Bake at 350° for 4 minutes; remove pan from oven, and gently press almonds into cookies again. Bake 4 more minutes or until edges are lightly browned. Remove cookies to wire racks to cool. **Makes** 4 dozen.

BETTY GARRISON
ELMER, NEW JERSEY

quick & easy
Ready-to-Assemble Meals

A focaccia loaf, tortillas, and pizza dough team up effortlessly with deli-sliced meats, cheeses, prepared dressings, and sauces to create filling main courses. Serve them for family meals or casual get-togethers.

REUBEN QUESADILLAS

family favorite

Prep: 15 min., Cook: 6 min. per batch

- ½ cup Thousand Island dressing
- 4 (10-inch) flour tortillas
- 1 pound thinly sliced corned beef
- 2 cups shredded sauerkraut, well drained
- 8 Swiss cheese slices
- Vegetable cooking spray

Spread 2 tablespoons dressing on 1 side of each tortilla. Layer one-fourth of corned beef, ½ cup sauerkraut, and 2 cheese slices evenly onto half of each tortilla. Fold tortillas in half over filling, pressing gently to seal.

Heat a large nonstick skillet coated with cooking spray over medium heat. Add quesadillas, in batches, and cook 2 to 3 minutes on each side or until golden brown and cheese is melted. Cut quesadillas into wedges, and serve immediately. **Makes** 4 servings.

PESTO FOCACCIA SANDWICH

fast fixin's

Prep: 10 min., Bake: 10 min.

Serve with fresh fruit and oven-baked fries. *(pictured on page 115)*

- 1 large deli-loaf focaccia or ciabatta bread
- 1 (3.5-ounce) jar prepared pesto sauce
- ½ pound thinly sliced Black Forest ham
- ½ pound thinly sliced roasted turkey breast
- 6 provolone cheese slices
- ½ small red onion, thinly sliced

Cut bread in half horizontally using a serrated knife. Spread pesto evenly over cut sides. Layer ham and next 3 ingredients over bottom half. Top with remaining bread half. Wrap in aluminum foil. **Bake** at 450° for 10 minutes. Cut into 6 wedges. **Makes** 6 servings.

CLAUDETTE CLEMENTS
GRANITE BAY, CALIFORNIA

BISTRO GRILLED CHICKEN PIZZA

family favorite • fast fixin's

Prep: 15 min., Grill: 10 min.

Use long-handled grilling tongs and a spatula to turn the dough with ease.

- 1 (13.8-ounce) can refrigerated pizza crust dough
- 1 teaspoon olive oil
- ¾ cup pizza sauce
- 4 plum tomatoes, sliced
- 2 cups chopped cooked chicken
- 1 (4-ounce) package tomato-and-basil feta cheese
- 1 cup (4 ounces) shredded mozzarella cheese
- 2 tablespoons chopped fresh basil

Unroll dough, and place on a lightly greased 18- x 12-inch sheet of heavy-duty aluminum foil. Starting at center, press out dough with hands to form a 13- x 9-inch rectangle. Brush dough evenly with olive oil.

Invert dough onto grill cooking grate; peel off foil. Grill, covered with grill lid, over medium heat (300° to 350°) 2 to 3 minutes or until bottom of dough is golden brown. Turn dough over, and grill, covered with grill lid, 1 to 2 minutes or until bottom is set. Carefully remove crust from grill to an aluminum foil-lined baking sheet.

Microwave pizza sauce in a small glass bowl at HIGH 30 seconds or until warm, stirring once. Spread sauce evenly over crust; top with tomatoes and chicken. Sprinkle evenly with cheeses and basil. Return pizza to cooking grate (pizza should slide easily). Grill, covered with grill lid, 3 to 5 more minutes or until crust is done and cheese is melted. **Makes** 6 servings.

JOHN PACANOVSKY
MORRISVILLE, NORTH CAROLINA

Enjoy Fresh Strawberries

These sweet red treats perk up everything.

May is the prime time for fresh strawberries. Although they're available almost year-round, they taste best right now. The bright red fruit is so versatile, it's equally at home on the breakfast table, in main-dish salads, and in desserts.

CHICKEN-AND-STRAWBERRY SALAD

family favorite • make ahead

Prep: 20 min., Chill: 30 min.

- ½ cup poppy seed dressing
- ¼ cup mayonnaise
- 1½ pounds chopped cooked chicken (about 3½ cups)
- 2 celery ribs, sliced
- 1 pint fresh strawberries, halved
- 1 avocado, cut into 1-inch cubes
- ½ small red onion, thinly sliced
- ½ cup slivered almonds, toasted
- 1 (10-ounce) package mixed salad greens
- Garnishes: avocado slices, whole strawberries

Whisk together dressing and mayonnaise in a large bowl; cover and chill 30 minutes.
Add chicken and next 5 ingredients to dressing mixture, gently tossing to coat. Serve over mixed salad greens. Garnish, if desired. **Makes** 6 servings.

RAE MCMANUS
CHENEYVILLE, LOUISIANA

CROISSANT FRENCH TOAST WITH FRESH STRAWBERRY SYRUP

family favorite • fast fixin's

Prep: 15 min., Cook: 4 min. per batch

- 4 large day-old croissants
- ¾ cup milk
- 2 large eggs
- 1 teaspoon vanilla extract
- 2 tablespoons butter
- 3 tablespoons powdered sugar
- Sweetened Whipped Cream (optional)
- Fresh Strawberry Syrup

Slice croissants in half lengthwise.
Whisk together milk, eggs, and vanilla. Pour into a shallow dish. Dip croissant halves into egg mixture, coating well.
Melt 1 tablespoon butter in a large nonstick skillet over medium heat. Add 4 croissant halves, and cook about 2 minutes on each side or until golden brown. Repeat procedure with remaining butter and croissant halves. Sprinkle with powdered sugar; top with Sweetened Whipped Cream, if desired, and Fresh Strawberry Syrup. **Makes** 4 servings.

FRESH STRAWBERRY SYRUP:

Prep: 10 min., Stand: 30 min., Cook: 5 min.

- 1 quart fresh strawberries, sliced
- ½ cup sugar
- ¼ cup orange liqueur or orange juice
- 1 teaspoon grated orange rind

Combine all ingredients in a saucepan, and let stand 30 minutes or until sugar dissolves. Cook over low heat, stirring occasionally, 5 minutes or until warm. **Makes** about 2 cups.

MARTHA JORDAN NEWBERRY
PALM BAY, FLORIDA

SWEETENED WHIPPED CREAM:

fast fixin's

Prep: 5 min.

- ½ cup whipping cream
- 1½ tablespoons powdered sugar

Beat cream at medium speed with an electric mixer until soft peaks form. Add powdered sugar, beating until stiff peaks form. **Makes** about 1 cup.

STRAWBERRY-RHUBARB PIE

family favorite

Prep: 30 min., Stand: 20 min., Chill: 10 min., Bake: 45 min.

- 1 cup sugar
- ¼ cup cornstarch
- 1 teaspoon grated lemon rind
- ⅛ teaspoon ground nutmeg
- 2½ cups sliced fresh strawberries
- 2½ cups fresh (⅛-inch-thick) rhubarb slices
- 2 tablespoons fresh lemon juice
- 1 (15-ounce) package refrigerated piecrusts, divided
- 2 tablespoons butter or margarine, cut into pieces
- 2 teaspoons sugar

Combine first 4 ingredients; stir in strawberries, rhubarb, and lemon juice. Let stand 20 minutes.
Roll 1 piecrust to an ⅛-inch thickness on a lightly floured surface. Fit piecrust into a 9-inch pieplate according to package directions; fold edges under, and crimp. Chill 10 minutes.
Spoon strawberry mixture into piecrust; dot with butter.
Roll remaining piecrust to an ⅛-inch thickness; cut into ½-inch strips. Arrange in a lattice design over filling. Sprinkle with 2 teaspoons sugar.
Bake at 425° for 15 minutes; reduce heat to 350°, and bake 30 more minutes or until crust browns. **Makes** 6 to 8 servings.

Strawberry Salad With Cinnamon Vinaigrette

fast fixin's

Prep: 20 min.

This salad's dressing offers a wonderful balance of tastes. It's so delicious, we gave it our highest rating.

- 1 (11-ounce) can mandarin oranges, drained
- 1 pint fresh strawberries, stemmed and quartered
- 1 small red onion, thinly sliced
- ½ cup coarsely chopped pecans, toasted
- 1 avocado, sliced
- 1 (10-ounce) package romaine lettuce
- Cinnamon Vinaigrette

Combine first 6 ingredients in a large bowl. Drizzle with half of Cinnamon Vinaigrette, tossing to coat. Serve remaining vinaigrette with salad. **Makes** 6 to 8 servings.

Cinnamon Vinaigrette:
make ahead

Prep: 5 min., Chill: 2 hrs.

- ⅓ cup olive oil
- ⅓ cup raspberry vinegar
- 1 tablespoon sugar
- ½ teaspoon salt
- ½ teaspoon ground cinnamon
- ¼ teaspoon pepper
- ½ teaspoon hot sauce

Combine all ingredients in a jar; cover tightly, and shake vigorously. Chill at least 2 hours. Shake well before serving. **Makes** ⅔ cup.

RUTH HUEBNER
LAKEWOOD, COLORADO

Chillin' Out With Sherbets

To know Associate Foods Editor Kate Nicholson is to know a die-hard chocolate ice-cream fan—one who consumes untold amounts of this frozen confection. What folks don't know, however, is that she's equally passionate about full-flavored fruit sherbets. Often confused with sorbets, sherbets frequently include milk as an ingredient, while sorbets never contain milk. Right now is the perfect time to enjoy the season's bounty in cool, refreshing sherbets. So dust off your ice-cream maker, and get ready to enjoy a bit of heaven.

Raspberry-Buttermilk Sherbet

family favorite • freezeable

Prep: 20 min., Freeze: about 30 min.

- 2 cups fresh raspberries *
- 1 cup sugar
- 2 cups buttermilk
- 1 teaspoon vanilla extract
- Garnishes: fresh mint sprigs, fresh raspberries

Process raspberries in a food processor or blender until smooth, stopping to scrape down sides. Press raspberry puree through a fine wire-mesh strainer into a large bowl, discarding solids. Add sugar, buttermilk, and vanilla to bowl, and stir until well blended.
Pour raspberry mixture into freezer container of a 4-quart ice-cream maker, and freeze according to manufacturer's instructions. Garnish each serving, if desired. **Makes** about 4 cups.

*Substitute 1 (14-ounce) package frozen raspberries, thawed, for fresh, if desired.

HEIDI CUMMINGS
BIRMINGHAM, ALABAMA

Blueberry-Buttermilk Sherbet: Substitute an equal amount of fresh or frozen blueberries for raspberries. Proceed with recipe as directed. Garnish with fresh blueberries and lemon rind strips, if desired.

Blackberry-Buttermilk Sherbet: Substitute an equal amount of fresh or frozen blackberries for raspberries. Proceed with recipe as directed. Garnish with fresh blackberries and lemon rind strips, if desired.

Refreshing Lime Sherbet

family favorite • freezeable

Prep: 15 min., Freeze: about 35 min.

Be careful not to remove any of the white pith underneath when grating the rind, or your sherbet will taste bitter.

- 4 teaspoons finely grated lime rind (about 1 large lime)
- 1 cup sugar
- 3 cups half-and-half
- ½ cup fresh lime juice (about 4 limes)
- ½ cup water
- ⅛ teaspoon salt
- Garnishes: fresh mint sprigs, thinly sliced lime wedges, lime rind strips

Stir together first 6 ingredients in a large bowl, stirring until well blended. **Pour** lime mixture into freezer container of a 4-quart ice-cream maker; freeze according to manufacturer's instructions. Garnish each serving, if desired. **Makes** 5 cups.

Refreshing Lemon Sherbet: Substitute a large lemon for the lime and fresh lemon juice for lime juice. Proceed as directed. Garnish with fresh mint sprigs, thinly sliced lemon wedges, and lemon rind strips, if desired.

Chocolate-Nut Pies

This time of year, the spotlight falls on chocolate-nut pie. Along with the muddling of fresh mint in julep cups, this springtime favorite cues the arrival of the Kentucky Derby. Whether baked up in the suburbs of Louisville (home of Churchill Downs) or the Louisiana bayou, the chocolaty concoction is enjoyed throughout our region.

The variations and interpretations of this well-known dessert are diverse. When the forks finally hit our testing table, two recipes—both using refrigerated piecrusts and semisweet chocolate morsels—rose to the top, providing very different yet equally satisfying results.

Whether you serve the pies warm or chilled, and whether you like it topped with bourbon whipped cream or plain, you can't go wrong with either recipe.

CHOCOLATE-BOURBON PECAN PIE

Prep: 10 min., Cook: 5 min., Bake: 55 min.

This recipe came from former staff member Cynthia Ann Briscoe, a Louisville native and ardent Derby fan.

- ½ (15-ounce) package refrigerated piecrusts
- 1½ cups chopped pecans
- 1 cup (6 ounces) semisweet chocolate morsels
- 1 cup dark corn syrup
- ½ cup granulated sugar
- ½ cup firmly packed brown sugar
- ¼ cup bourbon or water
- 4 large eggs
- ¼ cup butter or margarine, melted
- 2 teaspoons cornmeal
- 2 teaspoons vanilla extract
- ½ teaspoon salt

Fit piecrust into a 9-inch deep-dish pieplate according to package directions; fold edges under, and crimp.

Sprinkle pecans and chocolate evenly onto bottom of piecrust; set aside.

Combine corn syrup and next 3 ingredients in a large saucepan, and bring to a boil over medium heat. Cook, stirring constantly, 3 minutes. Remove from heat.

Whisk together eggs and next 4 ingredients. Gradually whisk one-fourth of hot mixture into egg mixture; add to remaining hot mixture, whisking constantly. Pour filling into prepared piecrust.

Bake at 325° for 55 minutes or until set; cool on a wire rack. **Makes** 8 servings.

CYNTHIA ANN BRISCOE
BIRMINGHAM, ALABAMA

CHOCOLATE-WALNUT PIE

family favorite

Prep: 10 min., Bake: 30 min.

We recommend using a standard 1½-inch-deep 9-inch pieplate for this easy-to-make Kentucky favorite. It tastes great warm, chilled, or at room temperature.

- ½ (15-ounce) package refrigerated piecrusts
- 1 cup sugar
- ½ cup all-purpose flour
- ½ cup margarine, melted
- 2 eggs, lightly beaten
- 1 teaspoon vanilla extract
- ¾ cup chopped walnuts
- ¾ cup semisweet chocolate morsels

Fit piecrust into a 9-inch pieplate according to package directions; fold edges under, and crimp.

Stir together sugar and next 4 ingredients until well blended; stir in walnuts and chocolate. Pour filling into piecrust.

Bake at 350° on lowest oven rack for 30 minutes or until pie is set; cool on a wire rack. **Makes** 8 servings.

RECIPE FROM *MY OLD KENTUCKY HOMES COOKBOOK* AS CONTRIBUTED TO *BEST OF THE BEST FROM KENTUCKY* COOKBOOK (QUAIL RIDGE PRESS, 2000)

The Power of Pie

The *Derby-Pie*® was created 50 years ago at the Melrose Inn in Prospect, Kentucky, by George, Walter, and Leaudra Kern. Today, the dessert is a registered trademark of Kern's Kitchen in Louisville. Although the recipe is a tightly held family secret, Alan Rupp, Kern's Kitchen president and Walter and Leaudra's grandson, confirms a few facts: Among other ingredients, the pie contains English walnuts, chocolate chips, and vanilla. It does not contain corn syrup or bourbon.

Derby fever kicks in around the first of April and continues through race day in May. Between that time, Alan says more than 50,000 *Derby-Pies* are sold. If you'd like one delivered to your front door, visit **www.derbypie.com.**

Tea Is the Key

Some of our best inspirations for stories come from our fellow *Southern Living* staffers. Associate Travel Editor Cassandra M. Vanhooser suggested we look into the delicious offerings from The Tea Room in Savannah, Georgia. We've included two of their recipes here, Lapsang-Poached Chicken Salad and Vanilla-Jasmine-Sour Cream Tea Cake. You can purchase the teas used for the recipes from The Tea Room ([912] 239-9690 or **www.savannahtearoom.com**), or check your local supermarket.

At the same time, Editor John Floyd challenged us to find good iced tea made with no-calorie sweeteners. We hit pay dirt rather quickly—Marian Cooper, Assistant to the Editor in Chief, happily shared her recipe for iced tea.

MARIAN'S ICED TEA

family favorite

Prep: 10 min., Cook: 5 min., Steep: 30 min.

- 4 regular-size tea bags
- 5 cups water, divided
- 14 (0.035-ounce) packets no-calorie sweetener*
- Garnishes: lemon slices, fresh mint sprigs

Bring tea bags and 2 cups water to a boil in a saucepan; turn off heat.

Cover and steep 30 minutes. Remove and discard tea bags.

Pour into a 1/2-gallon pitcher, and add 3 cups water and sweetener, stirring well. Serve over ice. Garnish, if desired. **Makes** 5 cups.

Note: For testing purposes only, we used Luzianne Tea and Splenda.

*Substitute 1/2 cup sugar, 13 (0.035-ounce) packets Equal, or 1/2 cup Equal Sugar Lite, if desired.

MARIAN COOPER
MCCALLA, ALABAMA

LAPSANG-POACHED CHICKEN SALAD

chef recipe • make ahead

Prep: 25 min., Cook: 25 min., Stand: 30 min.

Lapsang Souchong tea gives this chicken salad a distinct smoky flavor. One ounce is enough for the recipe.

- 4 large bone-in chicken breasts
- 11 tablespoons soy sauce, divided
- 2 tablespoons Lapsang loose tea leaves
- 3/4 cup light mayonnaise
- 1/3 cup diced red bell pepper
- 1/3 cup diced yellow bell pepper
- 1 small Granny Smith apple, diced
- 1 garlic clove, minced
- 1 1/4 teaspoons grated fresh ginger
- 1/4 teaspoon freshly ground pepper

Place chicken and cold water to cover in a Dutch oven; add 9 tablespoons soy sauce and tea leaves. Bring to a boil over medium-high heat; reduce heat, and simmer 20 minutes. Remove chicken, and let stand 30 minutes to cool; roughly chop chicken.
Stir together chicken, mayonnaise, and next 6 ingredients in a large bowl; stir in remaining 2 tablespoons soy sauce. Cover and chill until ready to serve. **Makes** 4 to 6 servings.

ANDRÉ BAXTER AND GLORIA HORTSMAN
THE TEA ROOM
SAVANNAH, GEORGIA

VANILLA-JASMINE-SOUR CREAM TEA CAKE

chef recipe • family favorite

Prep: 25 min., Bake: 40 min.

- 1/2 cup firmly packed brown sugar
- 1/4 cup chopped pecans
- 1 1/2 tablespoons vanilla-jasmine loose tea leaves *
- 1 1/2 tablespoons all-purpose flour
- 1 tablespoon ground cinnamon
- 1/2 teaspoon ground allspice
- 1/2 cup unsalted butter, melted
- 1 cup granulated sugar
- 2 large eggs
- 1 cup sour cream
- 1 1/4 cups all-purpose flour
- 1 teaspoon salt
- 1 teaspoon baking powder
- 1 teaspoon baking soda
- 1 teaspoon vanilla extract
- Garnishes: sweetened whipped cream, fresh mint sprig

Stir together first 6 ingredients in a small bowl. Set aside.
Beat butter and granulated sugar at medium speed with an electric mixer until well blended. Add eggs, 1 at a time, beating well after each addition. Add sour cream, beating until well blended.
Sift together 1 1/4 cups flour and next 3 ingredients. Add to butter mixture, beating until well blended. Stir in vanilla. Spoon half of batter into a greased and floured 9-inch cakepan. Sprinkle evenly with 2/3 cup brown sugar mixture; spoon remaining half of batter evenly over brown sugar mixture in pan; sprinkle evenly with remaining brown sugar mixture.
Bake at 350° for 35 to 40 minutes or until a wooden pick inserted in center comes out clean. Let cool in pan on a wire rack; garnish, if desired. **Makes** 8 servings.

Note: For testing purposes only, we used The Tea Room's Vanilla Jasmine Tea for the cake.

*Substitute 1 tablespoon Bigelow French Vanilla tea leaves, if desired.

ANDRÉ BAXTER AND GLORIA HORTSMAN
THE TEA ROOM
SAVANNAH, GEORGIA

Pamper Mom With Breakfast

These rich morning favorites are perfect for honoring her special day.

Treat Mom to a home-cooked breakfast on Mother's Day. This menu is so divine she'll forget about the kids' undone chores and dad's lingering "honey-do" list. Rich ingredients and indulgent flavors lend an irresistible twist to these scrumptious recipes. Sip on Coffee-Ice Cream Punch for a luscious start while cheesy Southwest Breakfast Strata bakes to a bubbly finish; both make great brunch items for company, too.

SOUTHWEST BREAKFAST STRATA

family favorite • make ahead

Prep: 15 min., Cook: 25 min., Bake: 30 min.

This recipe received our highest rating. You can prepare it the night before and pop it in the oven just before breakfast. Let the strata stand at room temperature 30 minutes before baking.

- 1 pound mild ground pork sausage
- 1 small onion, chopped
- ½ green bell pepper, chopped
- 2 (10-ounce) cans diced tomatoes and green chiles
- 8 (10-inch) flour tortillas, torn into bite-size pieces
- 3 cups (12 ounces) shredded colby-Jack cheese blend
- 6 large eggs
- 2 cups milk
- 1 teaspoon salt
- ½ teaspoon pepper

Cook sausage in a large skillet over medium-high heat, stirring until it crumbles and is no longer pink. Drain and return to skillet.

Add chopped onion and bell pepper to sausage in skillet, and sauté over medium-high heat 5 minutes or until vegetables are tender. Stir in tomatoes and green chiles; reduce heat, and simmer 10 minutes.

Layer half each of tortilla pieces, sausage mixture, and cheese in a lightly greased 13- x 9-inch baking dish. Repeat layers.

Whisk together eggs, milk, salt, and pepper; pour over layers in baking dish.

Cover and chill up to 8 hours, if desired.

Bake, lightly covered with aluminum foil, at 350° for 30 minutes or until golden and bubbly. **Makes** 6 to 8 servings.

LINDSAY POWELL FOOSHEE
JOHNSON CITY, TENNESSEE

COFFEE-ICE CREAM PUNCH

fast fixin's

Prep: 20 min.

You'll quickly discover that you can't drink just one cup of this creamy concoction. Go ahead and indulge.

- 1 quart chilled Coffee Concentrate✱
- 1 cup whipping cream
- ½ teaspoon almond extract
- Dash of salt
- 1 quart vanilla ice cream
- 1 quart chocolate ice cream
- Garnishes: whipped cream, freshly grated nutmeg

Whisk together first 4 ingredients in a large bowl.

Scoop vanilla and chocolate ice creams into a punch bowl; add Coffee Concentrate mixture, gently stirring until ice cream slightly melts. Serve punch in glass mugs. Garnish, if desired. **Makes** about 13 cups.

✱Substitute strong brewed coffee for Coffee Concentrate, if desired.

JOAN HARTSON
NEW ORLEANS, LOUISIANA

COFFEE CONCENTRATE:

make ahead

Prep: 30 min., Stand: 12 hrs.

Use this recipe, adapted from a recipe in *Commander's Kitchen* cookbook (Broadway, 2000), to make a big batch to last up to a month in the refrigerator.

- 1 pound ground coffee with chicory or dark roast ground coffee
- 3½ quarts cold water

Stir together coffee and 3½ quarts cold water in a 1 gallon pitcher until all ground coffee is wet; let stand 12 hours at room temperature.

Pour coffee mixture through a large, fine wire-mesh strainer, discarding grounds. Clean strainer; place a coffee filter or double layer of cheesecloth in strainer, and pour coffee mixture through lined strainer. Return coffee concentrate mixture to pitcher; cover and chill up to 1 month. **Makes** about 3 quarts.

Note: To make iced coffee, stir together ¼ cup each of Coffee Concentrate and water. If desired, stir in milk and sugar. Serve over ice.

A Taste of Honey

Texas is one of the South's largest honey producers, and Walker Honey Company in Rogers has been working with the sweet stuff for more than 70 years. This family of beekeepers gave us a couple of their best honey recipes, and B. Weaver Apiaries in Navasota shared a favorite as well.

To order Texas honey, call Walker Honey Company at (254) 983-2337 or visit **www.walkerhoney.com.** You can also contact B. Weaver Apiaries at (936) 825-7312.

FRUIT SALAD WITH HONEY DRESSING

family favorite • fast fixin's

Prep: 20 min.

Dressing will become thin if it sits overnight.

- ½ cup sour cream
- 2 tablespoons huajillo or other wildflower honey
- 2 teaspoons fresh lemon juice
- 2 Pink Lady or Red Delicious apples, thinly sliced
- 1 Bartlett pear, cored and thinly sliced
- Mixed baby greens
- ¼ cup coarsely chopped pecans, toasted

Stir together first 3 ingredients until well blended.

Toss apple and pear slices with half of dressing.

Arrange greens on a serving plate; top with apple and pear slices. Sprinkle with pecans. Drizzle with additional dressing, if desired. **Makes** 4 to 6 servings.

BETH WALKER
ROGERS, TEXAS

BUTTERMILK 'N' HONEY PANCAKES

family favorite • fast fixin's

Prep: 10 min., Cook: 3 min. per batch

Laura Weaver of B. Weaver Apiaries adds sweetness, flavor, and moisture to these pancakes with honey.

- 1 cup all-purpose flour
- 1 teaspoon baking powder
- ½ teaspoon baking soda
- ¼ teaspoon salt
- 1 large egg, lightly beaten
- 1 cup buttermilk
- 2 tablespoons dark honey
- Pecan-Honey Butter (optional)

Stir together first 4 ingredients in a medium bowl. Add egg, buttermilk, and honey, stirring until well blended.

Pour ¼ cup batter onto a hot, lightly greased griddle or skillet. Cook 1 to 2 minutes or until top is covered with

bubbles and edges look cooked. Turn and cook 1 more minute. Repeat with remaining batter. Top pancakes with Pecan-Honey Butter, if desired. **Makes** about 13 (3-inch) pancakes.

PECAN-HONEY BUTTER:

family favorite • fast fixin's

Prep: 5 min.

- ½ cup butter, softened
- ⅓ cup finely chopped pecans, toasted
- 2 tablespoons wildflower honey
- ⅛ to ¼ teaspoon ground cinnamon

Stir together all ingredients until blended. Cover and chill until ready to serve. **Makes** about ¾ cup.

LAURA WEAVER
NAVASOTA, TEXAS

HONEY-SWEET CORNBREAD

family favorite • fast fixin's

Prep: 15 min., Bake: 12 min.

This is a thin, crisp cornbread.

- ¾ cup plus 2 tablespoons stone-ground cornmeal
- 6 tablespoons all-purpose flour
- ¼ teaspoon baking soda
- 2 teaspoons baking powder
- ½ teaspoon salt
- ¾ cup buttermilk
- ¼ cup canola oil
- 2 tablespoons yaupon or other wildflower honey
- 1 large egg
- 1 teaspoon canola oil

Combine first 5 ingredients in a bowl. Stir in buttermilk and next 3 ingredients until well blended.

Heat 1 teaspoon oil in a 9-inch cast-iron skillet over medium-high heat. Pour batter into skillet.

Bake at 450° for 10 to 12 minutes or until golden brown. **Makes** 4 to 6 servings.

BETH WALKER
ROGERS, TEXAS

Southwestern Starters

Celebrate Cinco de Mayo with these flavorful nibbles.

Serving appetizers with a Southwest flair is a hit at any gathering. However, when preparing for a get-together, you want to limit the amount of time you spend in the kitchen. Taking this into consideration, we've assembled reader recipes with bold, tried-and-true flavors, as well as make-ahead ease. With extra time to spare, you, too, can relax and enjoy these delicious treats.

Fiesta With Flair

Serves 6

Meaty Empanadas
Cinco de Mayo Shrimp Cocktail
Armadillo Eggs
chips and salsa
margaritas and Mexican beer

MEATY EMPANADAS

Prep: 30 min., Cook: 35 min., Chill: 1 hr.

- ¾ pound ground beef
- ¼ pound sweet Italian sausage
- 1 large sweet onion, diced
- 1½ cups sliced fresh mushrooms
- 1 (8-ounce) can tomato sauce
- 1½ tablespoons Cajun seasoning
- ½ cup (2 ounces) shredded Monterey Jack cheese
- 3 (7.5-ounce) cans refrigerated biscuits
- 1 large egg, lightly beaten
- Vegetable oil
- Toppings: salsa, sour cream

Cook ground beef and sausage in a large skillet over medium heat, stirring until mixture crumbles and is no longer pink. Drain and set aside, reserving 2 tablespoons drippings in skillet.

Sauté onion in hot drippings 5 minutes or until tender. Add mushrooms; sauté 2 minutes.

Return beef mixture to skillet; stir in tomato sauce and Cajun seasoning. Simmer, stirring occasionally, 8 minutes or until liquid evaporates. Cool completely. Stir in cheese. Cover and chill thoroughly.

Roll biscuits into 4-inch circles on a lightly floured surface. Spoon 1 tablespoon beef mixture in center of each circle; brush edges with egg. Fold edges over, pressing with a fork to seal. Place on baking sheets, and cover with a damp cloth. Chill up to 2 hours, if desired.

Pour oil to a depth of ½ inch into a Dutch oven. Fry empanadas in hot oil, in batches, 30 seconds on each side or until golden. Drain on paper towels; serve with desired toppings. **Makes** 12 appetizer servings.

VIVIAN WATERS
THOMASVILLE, GEORGIA

CINCO DE MAYO SHRIMP COCKTAIL

make ahead

Prep: 35 min., Cook: 5 min.

- 4 plum tomatoes, coarsely chopped
- ½ red onion, sliced
- ¼ cup chopped fresh cilantro
- 1 jalapeño pepper, seeded
- 2 garlic cloves
- ¼ cup fresh lime juice
- 2 teaspoons sugar
- ½ teaspoon salt (optional)
- ¼ teaspoon chili powder
- ¼ teaspoon pepper
- 6 cups water
- 30 unpeeled, large fresh shrimp
- 1 large avocado, diced
- Garnish: lime slices
- Lime-flavored tortilla chips

Process first 10 ingredients in a blender or food processor until smooth, stopping to scrape down sides. Cover and chill sauce up to 1 week.

Bring 6 cups water to a boil; add shrimp, and cook 2 to 3 minutes or just until shrimp turn pink. Drain and rinse with cold water. Chill up to 24 hours, if desired.

Peel shrimp, leaving tails on; devein, if desired.

Stir avocado into sauce; spoon sauce evenly into 6 chilled martini glasses or small bowls. Arrange 5 shrimp around edge of each glass; garnish, if desired. Serve with lime-flavored tortilla chips. **Makes** 6 servings.

SUSAN GEORGIADIS
ORLANDO, FLORIDA

Armadillo Eggs

freezeable • make ahead

Prep: 45 min., Bake: 30 min.

Unbaked Armadillo Eggs can be frozen up to 1 month. Remove from freezer, and bake at 375° for 30 to 35 minutes or until golden.

- **20 canned whole jalapeño peppers** *
- **3 cups (12 ounces) shredded sharp Cheddar cheese, divided**
- **2 cups (8 ounces) shredded Monterey Jack cheese**
- **1 pound ground mild pork sausage**
- **2 cups all-purpose baking mix**
- **2 large eggs, lightly beaten**
- **1 (6-ounce) package seasoned coating mix for pork**

Cut a slit lengthwise on 1 side of peppers, leaving other side intact; remove seeds. Stuff each pepper with about 2 teaspoons sharp Cheddar cheese. Pinch edges to close; set aside.

Combine remaining 2 cups sharp Cheddar cheese, Monterey Jack cheese, sausage, and baking mix.

Pinch off about 2 rounded tablespoons of dough; shape into a ¼-inch-thick patty. Place a pepper in center of patty, and wrap dough around pepper. Dip in egg; dredge in seasoned coating mix. Place on a lightly greased 15- x 10-inch jelly-roll pan. Repeat with remaining dough and peppers; cover and chill up to 2 hours, if desired.

Bake at 375° for 30 minutes or until golden. **Makes** 10 appetizer servings.

Note: For testing purposes only, we used Shake 'N Bake Seasoned Coating Mix for Pork for the seasoned coating mix and Bisquick for the all-purpose baking mix.

*Substitute whole pepperoncini peppers for jalapeño peppers, if desired.

MARIE JACKSON
PEARL, MISSISSIPPI

Skillet Suppers

Bold family-friendly flavors conveniently cooked up in one skillet make these delicious recipes ideal for weeknights.

Southwest Pork in Black Bean Sauce

family favorite

Prep: 15 min., Cook: 15 min., Stand: 5 min.

For less spice, substitute a can of regular diced tomatoes for the mild diced tomatoes with green chiles.

- **1 to 1½ pounds boneless pork loin chops**
- **1 tablespoon ground cumin**
- **1 teaspoon ground chipotle chile pepper**
- **1 teaspoon garlic salt**
- **1 teaspoon paprika**
- **2 (10-ounce) cans mild diced tomatoes with green chiles**
- **1 (15-ounce) can black beans, rinsed and drained**
- **1 (8-ounce) can whole kernel corn, drained**
- **1 tablespoon vegetable oil**
- **1 small red onion, diced**
- **1 cup uncooked instant rice**
- **1 cup (4 ounces) grated Cheddar cheese**
- **2 tablespoons chopped fresh cilantro**
- **Flour tortillas**
- **Lime wedges**

Cut pork into ½-inch cubes.

Combine cumin, chipotle chile pepper, garlic salt, and paprika in a large zip-top plastic bag. Remove 2 teaspoons cumin mixture, and reserve. Add pork to zip-top bag. Seal and shake to coat. Set aside.

Stir together reserved 2 teaspoons cumin mixture, diced tomatoes with green chiles, black beans, and corn in a large bowl.

Heat vegetable oil in a large skillet over medium-high heat. Add pork and red onion, and sauté 6 to 8 minutes or until pork is browned. Stir in tomato mixture; bring mixture to a boil, and stir in rice. Cover and remove from heat. Let stand 5 minutes.

Sprinkle evenly with Cheddar cheese and chopped fresh cilantro. Serve with flour tortillas and lime wedges. **Makes** 6 servings.

Note: For testing purposes only, we used McCormick Gourmet Collection Chipotle Chile Pepper.

MARY ANN LEE
NAPLES, FLORIDA

Chicken Breasts With Artichoke-Pepper Sauce

family favorite • fast fixin's

Prep: 10 min., Cook: 20 min.

- **1 (6-ounce) jar marinated artichoke hearts**
- **½ cup roasted red bell peppers, drained and coarsely chopped**
- **4 skinned and boned chicken breasts**
- **½ to 1 teaspoon salt**
- **6 garlic cloves, pressed**
- **½ cup dry white wine**
- **1 teaspoon paprika**
- **¼ teaspoon ground red pepper**

Drain artichoke hearts, reserving marinade. Finely chop artichoke hearts, and toss with roasted peppers; set aside.

Sprinkle chicken evenly with salt.

Heat 2 tablespoons reserved artichoke marinade in a large nonstick skillet over medium-high heat; add chicken, and cook 2 to 3 minutes on each side or until golden. Remove from skillet, and keep warm.

Add garlic to skillet; sauté 30 seconds. Stir in remaining artichoke marinade, roasted pepper mixture, wine, paprika, and ground red pepper, stirring to loosen browned particles from bottom of skillet. Return chicken to skillet; cover and cook 10 minutes or until chicken is done. **Makes** 4 servings.

JULIE DEMATTEO
CLEMENTON, NEW JERSEY

what's for supper?

Dish Up Pasta

So good, your family will go back for seconds.

You'll like the great flavor and comfort appeal of these pasta dishes. Whether you're in the mood for a vegetarian, steak, or seafood entrée, Red Wine-Tomato Pasta and its variations have you covered. Serving a crowd? Opt for Fiesta Taco Lasagna.

RED WINE-TOMATO PASTA

Prep: 20 min., Cook: 25 min.

Opening a bottle of wine for a small amount may seem wasteful unless you plan to serve the rest with dinner. Opt to buy the small bottles, usually sold in four-packs in the wine section of the supermarket. Use a Chianti or Merlot for red wine and Pinot Grigio for white in the White Wine-Tomato-and-Clam Pasta variation.

- **1½ teaspoons minced fresh garlic**
- **2 tablespoons olive oil**
- **½ cup dry red wine**
- **2 (14½-ounce) cans petite diced tomatoes, undrained**
- **2 tablespoons chopped fresh or 1 teaspoon dried basil**
- **1 tablespoon chopped fresh or ½ teaspoon dried oregano**
- **1 teaspoon sugar**
- **¼ teaspoon freshly ground black pepper**
- **12 ounces uncooked thin spaghetti**
- **1 (4-ounce) block mozzarella cheese, shredded**
- **⅓ cup freshly grated Parmesan cheese**
- **Toppings: chopped fresh basil, freshly grated Parmesan cheese**

Sauté garlic in hot oil in a large skillet over medium heat 1 minute or until lightly browned. Carefully stir in wine and next 5 ingredients; bring to a boil. Reduce heat to medium-low, and simmer, stirring occasionally, 20 minutes or until thickened.

Cook pasta according to package directions; drain. Stir together hot pasta, mozzarella cheese, and ⅓ cup Parmesan cheese in a large serving bowl, tossing to coat until cheeses start to melt. Pour tomato sauce over pasta mixture, and toss to combine. Serve immediately with desired toppings. **Makes** 6 servings.

DEBRA MCCORRY
OCALA, FLORIDA

Red Wine-Tomato-and-Steak Pasta: Prepare sauce as directed. Stir 2 cups thinly sliced cooked steak into tomato mixture before simmering. Simmer 20 minutes or until thickened. Substitute 12 ounces penne pasta for thin spaghetti.

White Wine-Tomato-and-Clam Pasta: Prepare sauce as directed, substituting dry white wine for red wine. Stir in 2 drained (6.5-ounce) cans chopped clams to tomato mixture just before tossing with pasta mixture.

Salad in Seconds

To create a tasty side salad, add 2 tablespoons of chopped fresh parsley or basil to a bag of salad mix, and toss with a vinaigrette or creamy Italian dressing.

FIESTA TACO LASAGNA

family favorite

Prep: 15 min., Cook: 15 min., Bake: 45 min., Stand: 5 min.

No-boil lasagna noodles make assembly easy.

- **1 pound lean ground beef**
- **1 (1.25-ounce) package taco seasoning**
- **1 (11-ounce) can yellow corn with red and green peppers, drained**
- **½ cup water**
- **1 (8-ounce) container soft onion-and-chive cream cheese**
- **2 cups (8 ounces) shredded Cheddar-Monterey Jack cheese blend, divided**
- **4½ cups salsa**
- **9 no-boil lasagna noodles**
- **Toppings: sour cream, chopped fresh cilantro**

Cook ground beef in a large skillet over medium-high heat, stirring until it crumbles and is no longer pink; drain and return to skillet. Stir in taco seasoning, corn, and ½ cup water. Cook, uncovered, stirring occasionally, 5 minutes or until thickened. Add cream cheese, stirring until melted. Remove from heat, and stir in 1 cup Cheddar-Monterey Jack cheese.

Spread 1 cup salsa evenly in a lightly greased 13- x 9-inch baking dish. Layer with 3 lasagna noodles (noodles should not touch each other or sides of dish), 2 cups ground beef mixture, and ¾ cup salsa. Repeat layers using 3 lasagna noodles, remaining ground beef mixture, and ¾ cup salsa. Top with remaining 3 noodles and 2 cups salsa, covering noodles completely. Sprinkle evenly with remaining 1 cup Cheddar-Monterey Jack cheese. **Bake,** covered, at 375° for 30 minutes. Uncover and bake 10 to 15 more minutes or until cheese is melted and edges are lightly browned. Let stand 5 minutes. Serve with desired toppings. **Makes** 9 servings.

Note: For testing purposes only, we used Skinner Oven Ready Lasagne and Old El Paso Thick 'n Chunky salsa.

JILL GIBSON
GAHANNA, OHIO

Savor Sweet Onion Sides

At last, Vidalia onion season is here again. If you haven't experienced these sweet, juicy Georgia gems, then get ready for the most delicately sweet onions you've ever tasted. We baked, grilled, and even marinated them for side dishes that deliver a mouthful of flavor. Try Balsamic Onion Stacks layered with melted fresh mozzarella cheese, fragrant basil, and ripe tomato slices. Hurry up and grab a bunch of these sweet bulbs while you can—a typical season lasts only through June. For longer availability, call 1-800-843-2542, or visit www.blandfarms.com.

FLORENTINE STUFFED ONIONS

Prep: 30 min., Cook: 26 min., Bake: 1 hr.

- **4 medium-size sweet onions**
- **1 (5-ounce) package fresh baby spinach**
- **1 garlic clove, minced**
- **1 tablespoon olive oil**
- **1 tablespoon butter or margarine**
- **1 tablespoon all-purpose flour**
- **¼ teaspoon salt**
- **¼ teaspoon pepper**
- **⅛ teaspoon dry mustard**
- **⅓ cup milk**
- **½ (8-ounce) package cream cheese**
- **½ cup freshly shredded Parmesan cheese**

Peel onions, and cut in half crosswise. Cook in a large Dutch oven in boiling salted water to cover 15 minutes or until almost tender. Cut a thin slice from bottom (rounded end) of each half, forming a base for onions to stand. Place in a lightly greased 13- x 9-inch baking dish.
Remove onion centers, leaving 1-inch-thick shells. Chop centers, reserving 1 cup chopped onion for the stuffing. Reserve remaining onion for another use, if desired.

Sauté spinach, garlic, and 1 cup chopped onion in hot oil in a large skillet over medium-high heat about 4 minutes or until spinach is wilted. Remove mixture from pan.
Melt butter in same skillet over medium heat. Stir in flour and next 3 ingredients until smooth. Stir in milk, and cook, stirring constantly, 2 to 3 minutes or until thickened. Reduce heat to low; stir in cream cheese, stirring until melted. Stir in spinach mixture. Spoon hot mixture evenly into onion halves.
Bake at 350° for 45 minutes. Sprinkle evenly with Parmesan cheese, and bake 15 more minutes or until golden and bubbly. **Makes** 8 servings.

SELENE GRAPPEN
PLANTATION, FLORIDA

BALSAMIC ONION STACKS

Prep: 15 min., Chill: 8 hrs., Grill: 7 min.

- **8 (½-inch-thick) sweet onion slices (about 3 onions)**
- **⅓ cup balsamic vinegar**
- **¼ cup olive oil**
- **1½ teaspoons paprika**
- **1 teaspoon salt**
- **½ teaspoon freshly ground pepper**
- **1 (8-ounce) package fresh mozzarella cheese, cut into 4 (½-inch-thick) rounds**
- **8 large fresh basil leaves**
- **4 (½-inch-thick) fresh tomato slices (about 2 tomatoes)**
- **Garnish: fresh basil sprigs**

Arrange onion slices in a single layer in a 13- x 9-inch baking dish.
Stir together vinegar and next 4 ingredients. Pour over onion slices. Cover and chill 8 hours, turning once.
Remove onions from dressing with a slotted spatula, reserving dressing.
Grill onion slices, covered with grill lid, over medium-high heat (350° to 400°) 2 minutes on each side or until crisp-tender and golden.
Layer half of grilled onion slices each with 1 cheese round, 2 basil leaves, and 1 tomato slice; top with remaining half of onion slices.
Grill onion stacks, covered with grill lid, over medium-high heat 3 minutes or until cheese melts. Serve onion stacks with reserved dressing. Garnish, if desired. **Makes** 4 servings.

TOMATO-AND-SWEET ONION SALAD

Prep: 15 min.; Chill: 8 hrs.

- **3 tablespoons red wine vinegar**
- **1 tablespoon olive oil**
- **½ teaspoon sugar**
- **½ teaspoon salt**
- **½ teaspoon prepared mustard**
- **¼ teaspoon pepper**
- **2 sweet onions, thinly sliced**
- **2 large tomatoes, cut into thin wedges**
- **⅓ cup fresh basil leaves, thinly sliced**
- **Salt and pepper to taste**

Whisk together first 6 ingredients in a large bowl; add onions, and toss to coat. Cover and chill at least 8 hours.
Add tomatoes, basil, and salt and pepper to taste to onion mixture, tossing to coat. **Makes** 6 to 8 servings.

CHARLOTTE BRYANT
GREENSBURG, KENTUCKY

Test Kitchen Notebook

Vidalia onions are mild, sweet, and juicy and named for their place of origin, since due to soil and climate, they lose their characteristic sweetness if grown elsewhere. Because they are so sweet, they have a shorter storage life than other dry onions.

Shannon Sliter Satterwhite
ASSOCIATE FOODS EDITOR

Lunch on the Go

These easy-to-transport recipes are just right for a picnic or family road trip.

Take-Out Lunch

Serves 8

Bacon-Pimiento Cheese
with crackers

Chinese Cabbage Salad

Favorite Chocolate Chip Cookies

iced tea

This time of the year, you need foods that are a snap to make and even easier to pack up—and that's just what we offer here. Bacon-Pimiento Cheese is simple to prepare, yet it takes a Southern staple to a new level by adding smoked Cheddar. (For best results, we recommend shredding the cheese yourself instead of using packaged shredded cheese.)

Be sure to try Chinese Cabbage Salad, which begins with ramen noodle soup mix. The mild flavor of Chinese cabbage (also called Napa cabbage) is perfect for this refreshing salad. Store the cabbage mixture, noodle mixture, and dressing in separate containers, and toss together just before serving. And for a sweet bite, you'll want to have plenty of Favorite Chocolate Chip Cookies on hand.

BACON-PIMIENTO CHEESE

family favorite • fast fixin's

Prep: 20 min., Cook: 5 min.

- **8 bacon slices**
- **2 (8-ounce) blocks smoked Cheddar cheese, shredded**
- **2 (8-ounce) blocks Cheddar cheese, shredded**
- **1½ cups mayonnaise**
- **1 (4-ounce) jar diced pimiento, drained**
- **1 tablespoon sugar**
- **¼ teaspoon salt**
- **¼ teaspoon pepper**

Cook bacon in a skillet until crisp; remove bacon, and drain on paper towels. Crumble bacon.
Stir together bacon, cheeses, and remaining ingredients in a bowl. Serve immediately. **Makes** 1 quart.

CHINESE CABBAGE SALAD

family favorite

Prep: 20 min., Chill: 1 hr., Cook: 5 min.

- **2 (3-ounce) packages ramen noodle soup mix**
- **1 Chinese cabbage, shredded**
- **1 bunch green onions, sliced**
- **¼ cup sesame seeds**
- **½ cup vegetable oil**
- **6 tablespoons rice wine vinegar**
- **2 tablespoons sesame oil**
- **2 (2.5-ounce) packages sliced almonds**

Remove flavor packets from soup mix, and reserve. Break up ramen noodles, and set aside.

Toss together cabbage, green onions, and sesame seeds in a bowl.
Whisk together reserved flavor packets, vegetable oil, vinegar, and sesame oil; toss with cabbage mixture. Cover and chill 1 hour.
Sauté noodles and almonds in a skillet over medium heat or until lightly browned; stir into cabbage mixture.
Makes 8 servings.

FAVORITE CHOCOLATE CHIP COOKIES

family favorite

Prep: 20 min., Bake: 10 min. per batch

- **1 cup butter or margarine, softened**
- **¾ cup firmly packed brown sugar**
- **½ cup granulated sugar**
- **2 large eggs**
- **2 teaspoons vanilla extract**
- **2¾ cups all-purpose flour**
- **1 teaspoon baking soda**
- **¼ teaspoon salt**
- **1 cup chopped pecans**
- **1 (12-ounce) package semisweet chocolate morsels**
- **½ (12-ounce) package milk chocolate morsels**

Beat butter and sugars at medium speed with an electric mixer until fluffy; gradually add eggs and vanilla, beating well.
Combine flour, baking soda, and salt; add to butter mixture, beating at low speed until blended. Stir in pecans and chocolate morsels.
Drop by heaping tablespoonfuls onto lightly greased baking sheets.
Bake at 350° for 8 to 10 minutes or until golden; remove to wire racks to cool. **Makes** 4 dozen.

Cheesy Bites

You'll love the fresh herb taste in every buttery mouthful of these cheese spreads. We were so inspired by the look of the Basil-Cheese Roulade and Herb-and-Garlic Goat Cheese Truffles that we tried shaping some of our other favorite cheese ball recipes in similar ways. We found any cheese mixture that sets firmly when chilled can form the base of a roulade or be shaped into bite-size truffles.

BASIL-CHEESE ROULADE

make ahead

Prep: 30 min., Chill: 3 hrs.

1 (8-ounce) package cream cheese, softened
4 ounces Roquefort cheese, softened
1 cup fresh baby spinach leaves
¾ cup fresh flat-leaf parsley
¼ cup fresh basil leaves
1 garlic clove, sliced
3 tablespoons olive oil
1 cup (4 ounces) freshly grated Parmesan cheese
¼ cup finely chopped walnuts
¼ cup finely chopped sun-dried tomatoes
Garnishes: fresh flat-leaf parsley, fresh basil, edible flowers
Assorted crackers

Beat cream cheese and Roquefort cheese at medium speed with an electric mixer until smooth. Line a baking sheet with parchment paper. Spread cheese mixture into an 11- x 8-inch rectangle on parchment paper. Cover and chill 1 hour.

Process spinach and next 4 ingredients in a food processor until smooth. Stir in freshly grated Parmesan cheese, chopped walnuts, and chopped sun-dried tomatoes.

Spread spinach mixture evenly over cheese rectangle. Using the parchment paper as a guide, roll up, jelly-roll fashion. Wrap in parchment paper, sealing at ends, and chill at least 2 hours. Remove paper,

and garnish, if desired. Serve with assorted crackers. **Makes** 12 servings.

FRAN M. BAKER
ROCKLEDGE, FLORIDA

MEDITERRANEAN CHEESE BALL

make ahead

Prep: 20 min., Chill: 3 hrs.

2 (8-ounce) packages cream cheese, softened
1 (8-ounce) package feta cheese, crumbled
⅓ cup finely chopped ripe black olives
3 tablespoons capers
½ small red bell pepper, diced
⅓ cup chopped fresh basil
2 garlic cloves, minced
1 cup pine nuts, toasted
Toasted pita wedges

Beat cheeses at medium speed with an electric mixer until smooth. Stir in olives and next 4 ingredients. Shape mixture into a ball; cover and chill at least 3 hours. Roll in toasted pine nuts just before serving. Serve with toasted pita wedges. **Makes** 12 to 16 servings.

MELINDA BACURIN
MURFREESBORO, TENNESSEE

HERB-AND-GARLIC GOAT CHEESE TRUFFLES

make ahead

Prep: 30 min., Chill. 3 hrs.

These bite-size cheese bites make a fun, easy appetizer.

1 (8-ounce) package cream cheese, softened
1 (6-ounce) log mild, creamy goat cheese
1 teaspoon fresh lemon juice
1 tablespoon minced fresh chives
1 tablespoon minced fresh basil
1 to 2 teaspoons minced roasted garlic
½ teaspoon cracked black pepper
1 cup finely chopped pecans, toasted
Strawberry slices, melon wedges

Beat first 3 ingredients at medium speed with an electric mixer until smooth. Stir in chives and next 3 ingredients. Cover and chill 2 hours or until firm.

Shape mixture into 24 (1½-inch) balls; roll evenly in pecans. Cover and chill at least 1 hour. Serve with fruit. **Makes** 24 truffles.

BOB GADSBY
GREAT FALLS, MONTANA

Roulade Step-by-Step

Step 1: Line a baking sheet with lightly greased parchment paper. Using an offset spatula, spread the cheese mixture into an 11- x 8-inch rectangle on the parchment paper. Cover and chill 1 hour. (The baking sheet is needed to support the layer of cheese as it chills.) Spread the spinach-basil filling evenly over the chilled cheese mixture, leaving a narrow border around edges (photo 1).

Step 2: Using the parchment paper as a guide, roll up the rectangle, jelly-roll fashion (photo 2). Wrap in parchment paper, sealing at ends, and chill. Remove paper before garnishing and serving. To garnish, gently press fresh parsley and edible flowers onto the top of the roulade.

from our kitchen

Frozen Assets

It's not often that we find a convenience product that tastes as good as these buttery slice-and-bake cheese wafers. Studded with crunchy bits of chopped pecans, Mamie's Famous Cheese Wafers are made without preservatives. Sold frozen for around $7.95 a roll (baked according to package directions, one roll yields about 5 dozen wafers), they're terrific to keep on hand for drop-in guests. If your local grocery store doesn't already carry them, ask the manager to place an order for you. For more information visit **www.mamieswafers.com.**

▲ Packed With Pizzazz

Flavored mayonnaises take only minutes to make but yield big dividends in quick and easy recipes for last-minute entertaining. They can be prepared with regular or reduced-fat commercial mayonnaise, and they can be stored in the refrigerator for up to one week. When testing with store-bought mayonnaise, we preferred Hellman's Real Mayonnaise and Hellman's Light Mayonnaise.

Fresh Herb Mayonnaise: Stir together 2 cups mayonnaise, 2 tablespoons of chopped fresh parsley, 2 tablespoons of chopped fresh chives, 1 tablespoon of chopped fresh basil, 1 tablespoon of chopped fresh dill, and 1 tablespoon of chopped fresh oregano. Make a simple salad with boiled new potatoes and sliced green onions, or dollop on grilled chicken and pasta. Add to deviled eggs, or use as a dip for fresh vegetables.

Béarnaise Mayonnaise: Cook ⅓ cup dry white wine, 1 tablespoon white wine vinegar, and 2 minced shallots in a small saucepan over medium-high heat 5 minutes or until liquid is reduced to 1 tablespoon. Remove from heat, and cool. Stir together 1 cup mayonnaise, 1 tablespoon chopped fresh tarragon, 1 teaspoon grated lemon rind, ⅛ teaspoon pepper, and wine reduction liquid. Serve mayonnaise with any type of beef, from grilled burgers to steak sandwiches. Dollop a spoonful over hot, steamed broccoli, or toss with chopped cooked chicken and canned artichoke hearts.

Lemon-Rosemary Mayonnaise: Stir together 2 cups mayonnaise, 2 tablespoons chopped fresh rosemary, 1½ tablespoons grated lemon rind, and 1 pressed garlic clove. Use in place of tartar sauce when serving fresh seafood. Toss with canned tuna, or spread on a smoked turkey sandwich. If you prefer a milder flavor, substitute fresh parsley for rosemary.

june

146   Serve a Pretty Salad *Trendy, make-ahead creations loaded with color*

148   Growing Made Simple *Turn your backyard harvest into these great dishes*

157   Easy Icebox Pies *Enjoy every delicious bite of these cool concoctions that you can make ahead*

158   Great Time Get-together *Healthful recipes for a fun outdoor gathering*

159   Avocados for Any Occasion *Three mouthwatering reasons to try this buttery-smooth green gem*

160   Quick & Easy Take Five for Sides *Five ingredients add up to lots of flavor in these sensations*

161   Guilt-Free Comfort Food *Satisfy your cravings for flavor*

162   What's for Supper? Barbecue Spuds *Leftovers make a hearty weeknight meal*

162   Hot Off the Grill *These sizzling summer entrées will delight one and all*

164   From Our Kitchen *Shortcakes, piecrust tricks, and more*

Serve a Pretty Salad

These layered sensations are easy to prepare, loaded with color, and, best of all, you can make them ahead.

Layered salads are back. "Stacked" might be today's trendy word, but these make-ahead favorites have been around for quite some time. From congealed gelatin salads to options made with cornbread and vegetables, we've included an array of recipes so you can taste and explore the many possibilities. All make great choices for family reunions, cookouts, weeknight dinners, or chic entertaining. Layered Lebanese Salad (on page 148) and Layered Cornbread-and-Turkey Salad (opposite page) can serve as main or side dishes. And they're so lovely to look at, you just may be tempted to use one as a centerpiece.

Colorful Fruit Layers

This is the perfect time to enjoy a variety of fresh fruit, especially when combined in a salad. But rather than the usual mixed version, create layers of color using your favorite seasonal fruits. Garnish with melon wedges or fresh mint sprigs.

LAYERED GREEN BEAN-RED POTATO SALAD

make ahead

Prep: 20 min., Cook: 25 min., Stand: 25 min., Chill: 4 hrs.

- 1½ cups mayonnaise
- ¼ cup white wine vinegar
- 3 tablespoons sugar
- 1 tablespoon finely chopped fresh or 1 teaspoon dried tarragon
- ¼ teaspoon salt
- ¼ teaspoon freshly ground pepper
- 4 pounds small red potatoes
- 1½ pounds fresh green beans, trimmed and cut into 1½-inch pieces*
- 1 teaspoon salt
- 2 large sweet onions, cut into ⅛-inch slices and quartered

Stir together first 6 ingredients in a small bowl until blended; cover and chill.

Bring potatoes and water to cover to a boil over medium-high heat; cook 10 to 15 minutes or until potatoes are fork-tender. Drain potatoes, and let stand 25 minutes at room temperature or until cool. Cut into ¼-inch-thick slices.

Cook green beans in boiling water to cover 3 to 4 minutes or until crisp-tender; drain and plunge into ice water to stop the cooking process. Drain and pat dry.

Layer half of potato slices in a large glass bowl; sprinkle evenly with ½ teaspoon salt. Layer half each of green beans and onions over potatoes; spoon half of dressing evenly over top. Repeat layers, ending with dressing. Cover and chill at least 4 hours or up to 24 hours. **Makes** 8 to 10 servings.

*Substitute 2 (12-ounce) bags fresh ready-to-cook trimmed green beans, if desired.

LAYERED FRUIT CONGEALED SALAD

family favorite • make ahead

Prep: 30 min.; Cook: 50 min.; Chill: 4 hrs., 15 min.

Don't cover bowls or glasses during each chill time (except at very end). This shortens the required time in the refrigerator as you move through the steps. (pictured on page 150)

- 1 small navel orange
- 2 cups water
- 2½ cups sugar, divided
- 2 (3-ounce) packages peach-flavored gelatin
- 4 cups boiling water, divided
- ½ cup half-and-half
- ¼ cup cold water
- 2 teaspoons unflavored gelatin
- ½ (8-ounce) package cream cheese
- ¼ teaspoon vanilla extract
- 2 (3-ounce) packages raspberry-flavored gelatin
- 2 cups fresh raspberries

Cut orange into thin (⅛-inch-thick) slices, discarding ends.

Stir together 2 cups water and 2 cups sugar in a large saucepan over medium-high heat. Bring to a boil, and stir until sugar dissolves. Gently stir in orange slices, and bring to a simmer; reduce heat to low, and simmer, occasionally pressing orange slices into liquid, for 40 minutes. Remove orange slices using a slotted spoon, and place in a single layer on wax paper; cool completely. Discard liquid in pan.

Place 1 orange slice in bottom of each of 6 (1½- to 2-cup) water glasses, discarding or reserving remaining orange slices for another use. (Orange slices will not lay flat against bottoms of glasses.) Set aside.

Remove and discard 2 tablespoons peach-flavored gelatin from 1 package. Stir together remaining flavored gelatin and 2 cups boiling water in a bowl 1 to 2 minutes or until gelatin dissolves. Pour about 1/3 cup flavored gelatin mixture over orange slice in each glass. Chill 1 hour or until firm.

Stir together half-and-half and 1/4 cup cold water in a medium saucepan. Sprinkle with 2 teaspoons unflavored gelatin, and stir. Place pan over medium heat; stir in remaining 1/2 cup sugar, and cook, stirring often, 3 to 5 minutes or until sugar and gelatin dissolve. (Do not boil). Remove pan from heat.

Microwave cream cheese at MEDIUM (50% power) 45 seconds or until very soft; stir until smooth. Whisk cream cheese into half-and-half mixture until smooth; whisk in vanilla, and chill 30 minutes or until slightly cool. Spoon about 3 tablespoons cream cheese mixture in an even layer over firm peach layer in each glass; chill.

Remove and discard 2 tablespoons raspberry-flavored gelatin from 1 package. Stir together raspberry-flavored gelatin and remaining 2 cups boiling water 1 to 2 minutes or until gelatin dissolves. Chill 45 minutes or until consistency of unbeaten egg white. Stir in raspberries, and spoon about 1/2 cup raspberry mixture in an even layer over cream cheese mixture in each glass. Cover and chill at least 2 hours or up to 24 hours. **Makes** 6 servings.

LAYERED CORNBREAD-AND-TURKEY SALAD

family favorite • make ahead

Prep: 45 min., Chill: 3 hrs. *(pictured on page 151)*

- 1 (6-ounce) package buttermilk cornbread mix
- 1 (12-ounce) bottle Parmesan-peppercorn dressing
- 1/2 cup mayonnaise
- 1/4 cup buttermilk
- 1 (9-ounce) package romaine lettuce, shredded
- 2 1/2 cups chopped smoked turkey (about 3/4 pound)
- 2 large yellow bell peppers, chopped
- 2 large tomatoes, seeded and chopped
- 1 red onion, chopped
- 1 cup diced celery (about 3 celery ribs)
- 2 cups (8 ounces) shredded Swiss cheese
- 10 bacon slices, cooked and crumbled
- 2 green onions, sliced

Prepare cornbread according to package directions; cool and crumble. Set aside.

Stir together dressing, mayonnaise, and buttermilk until blended.

Layer crumbled cornbread, shredded lettuce, and next 7 ingredients evenly into 6 (3- to 4-cup) glass containers; spoon half of dressing mixture evenly over tops. Cover and chill at least 3 hours or up to 24 hours. Sprinkle with green onions just before serving. Serve with remaining half of dressing mixture on the side. **Makes** 6 servings.

Note: For testing purposes only, we used Martha White Buttermilk Cornbread Mix and Girard's Parmesan-Peppercorn Dressing. We used 3-cup marquis-shaped canning jars with lid and screw ring. To find a retailer, visit **www.leifheitusa.com**, or call toll-free 1-866-695-3434.

JOANNA L. HAY
ARCADIA, FLORIDA

To make 1 large salad: Layer half each of crumbled cornbread, shredded lettuce, and next 7 ingredients in a large glass bowl; spoon half of dressing mixture evenly over top. Repeat layers ending with dressing mixture. Cover and chill at least 8 hours or up to 24 hours. Sprinkle top of salad evenly with green onions just before serving. Prep: 45 min., Chill: 8 hrs.

Layered Southwest Cornbread-and-Turkey Salad: Substitute 1 (6-ounce) package Mexican cornbread mix for 1 (6-ounce) package buttermilk cornbread mix; 1 (16-ounce) bottle buttermilk-Ranch dressing for Parmesan-peppercorn dressing; 1 (8-ounce) package finely shredded Cheddar and Monterey Jack cheeses with jalapeño peppers for shredded Swiss cheese; and 1 (11-ounce) can sweet whole kernel corn, drained, and 1 (15-ounce) can black beans, rinsed and drained, for yellow bell peppers. Prepare recipe as directed, omitting mayonnaise.

Note: For testing purposes only, we used Gladiola Mexican style cornbread mix and Ken's Steak House Buttermilk Ranch dressing.

For the Love of Layers

■ Use clear glass or acrylic bowls or other see-through containers to show off layers.

■ Think outside the round bowl. Go for a fun and unexpected shape, such as square, rectangular, or scallop-edged bowls. A trifle bowl is also a good option. With so much to choose from, don't forget glassware for some unique individual serving possibilities.

■ Select fresh, crisp vegetables and salad greens. They make sturdy layers and will hold up best.

■ The combinations of vegetables, salad greens, and dressings are endless, so be creative, and design your own version.

LAYERED LEBANESE SALAD

make ahead

Prep: 45 min., Stand: 30 min., Chill: 24 hrs.

This twist on a Middle Eastern favorite, tabbouleh salad, is the ultimate make-ahead choice. It needs a full 24-hour chill time so the bulgur will soften and absorb the dressing. It's definitely worth the wait.

> 1 cup uncooked bulgur wheat
> 1/3 cup fresh lemon juice
> 1/3 cup vegetable or chicken broth
> 1/3 cup extra-virgin olive oil
> 3 garlic cloves, minced
> 1 1/2 teaspoons salt
> 1/4 teaspoon freshly ground pepper
> 2 cups finely chopped red onion
> 5 cups chopped tomato (about 4 large tomatoes)
> 1/2 cup chopped fresh parsley
> 1/2 cup chopped fresh mint
> 1/4 cup chopped fresh dill
> 2 cups peeled, seeded, and chopped cucumber (about 2 medium cucumbers)
> 1 to 2 large red bell peppers, chopped

Place bulgur in a large glass bowl. Stir together lemon juice and next 5 ingredients; drizzle lemon juice mixture evenly over bulgur, and let stand 30 minutes at room temperature.
Layer onion and next 6 ingredients over bulgur mixture. Cover and chill at least 24 hours or up to 48 hours.
Makes 10 to 12 servings.

Growing Made Simple

Last summer Assistant Features Editor Allison Barnes decided to start a vegetable garden. Having never gardened before, and not having much space, she figured that her first go would be a challenge. Initially, she asked seasoned experts around the office and at church for information, shortcuts, and tips that she could use. Allison even searched the Internet to find out other great insider secrets. In doing all this, she discovered the wonderful world of container gardening.

Inside the Box

Growing plants in containers or specially designed structures, such as the EarthBox, yields an excellent harvest of vegetables. Plus, it's virtually effortless. And it provides countless health benefits like stimulating the senses and raising our awareness of the environment around us.

Make sure the container you choose is big enough for the types of vegetables you wish to grow. Some containers will need to be elevated to allow proper drainage. However, with the EarthBox, there's no drainage needed, and the plants water themselves as they grow. Furthermore, container gardening increases the mobility of your plants, so if you don't like your peppers on one side of the deck, move them to the other side.

The Proof Is in the Produce

Container gardening opens up the world of growing to those who have small amounts of space, as well as to those with physical limitations that may restrict their range of movement.

Last summer, the plants grown in the EarthBox and in the pots did great on the back deck, yielding plenty of peppers and tomatoes for all. This year, when the gardening bug bites again, she thinks she'll grab some more containers and try growing lettuce along with her tomatoes and peppers. And maybe she'll try carrots, too, and perhaps some beans. You know, some squash might also be nice....

SWEET PEPPER-MANGO SALSA

fast fixin's • make ahead

Prep: 15 min.

Serve over grilled meats and fish or as an appetizer with toasted pita chips.

Stir together 1 chopped red bell pepper, 1 chopped yellow bell pepper, 1 cup chopped fresh mango, 1 chopped and seeded jalapeño pepper, 1/4 cup chopped cilantro, 2 tablespoons fresh orange juice, 1/2 teaspoon salt, and 1/8 teaspoon ground red pepper. Cover and chill until ready to serve. **Makes** about 3 cups.

Per 1/2-cup serving: Calories 36 (7% from fat); Fat 0.3g (sat 0.05g, mono 0.03g, poly 0.11g); Protein 0.77g; Carb 8.7g; Fiber 0.54g; Chol 0mg; Iron 0.32mg; Sodium 196mg; Calc 8.2mg

FETA-STUFFED TOMATOES

fast fixin's

Prep: 15 min., Bake: 15 min.

Cut 4 large tomatoes in half horizontally. Scoop out pulp from each tomato half, leaving shells intact; discard seeds and coarsely chop pulp. Stir together pulp; 4 ounces crumbled feta cheese; 1/4 cup fine, dry breadcrumbs; 2 tablespoons chopped green onions; 2 tablespoons chopped fresh parsley; and 2 tablespoons olive oil in a medium bowl. Spoon mixture into tomato shells, and place in a 13- x 9-inch baking dish. Bake at 350° for 15 minutes. Garnish with Italian parsley sprigs, if desired. **Makes** 8 servings.

KAREN C. GREENLEE
LAWRENCEVILLE, GEORGIA

Per serving: Calories 101 (58% from fat); Fat 6.8g (sat 2.6g, mono 3.2g, poly 0.6g); Protein 3.4g; Carb 7.6g; Fiber 1.3g; Chol 12.7mg; Iron 0.7mg; Sodium 267mg; Calc 79.4mg

Creative Containers

- Oversize terra-cotta pots, ceramic pots, and metal tubs work great for tomatoes.
- Wooden crates or bushel baskets provide sturdy frames for lettuce plants.
- The EarthBox will grow just about anything, and it has a built-in irrigation system (toll-free 1-877-475-1501 or **www.earthbox.com**).
- Hanging baskets make happy homes for cherry tomatoes and herbs.

Salad With Red Grapefruit-Lemon Vinaigrette,
page 161

Layered Fruit Congealed Salad, page 146

Layered Cornbread-and-Turkey
Salad, page 147

Colorful fruit layers,
pages 146-147

151

Spicy Cheddar-Stuffed Burger, page 163

Bacon Potato Salad, page 171

Tabb's Barbecue Pork, page 166;
Honey–Mustard Barbecue Sauce, page 167

154

Double Chocolate Chunk Cookies, page 181

Chocolate Icebox Pie, page 157

Frozen Hawaiian Pie, page 157

Easy Icebox Pies

There's always room on the menu for one of these luscious concoctions.

CHOCOLATE ICEBOX PIE

family favorite • make ahead

Prep: 20 min., Cook: 8 min., Chill: 8 hrs.
(pictured on page 155)

⅔ cup milk
¾ cup semisweet chocolate
    morsels
¼ cup cold water
2 tablespoons cornstarch
1 (14-ounce) can sweetened
    condensed milk
3 large eggs, beaten
1 teaspoon vanilla extract
3 tablespoons butter or margarine
1 (6-ounce) ready-made chocolate
    crumb piecrust
1 cup whipping cream
¼ cup sugar
½ cup chopped pecans, toasted
1 (1.55-ounce) milk chocolate
    candy bar, chopped

Heat milk over medium heat in a 3-quart saucepan until it just begins to bubble around the edges (do not boil). Remove from heat, and whisk in chocolate morsels until melted. Cool slightly. Stir together cold water and cornstarch until dissolved.
Whisk cornstarch mixture, sweetened condensed milk, eggs, and vanilla into chocolate mixture. Bring to a boil over medium heat, whisking constantly. Boil 1 minute or until mixture thickens and is smooth. (Do not overcook.)
Remove from heat, and whisk in butter. Spoon mixture into piecrust. Cover and chill at least 8 hours.
Beat whipping cream at high speed with an electric mixer until foamy; gradually add sugar, beating until soft peaks form. Spread whipped cream evenly over pie filling, and sprinkle with pecans and candy bar pieces.
Makes 8 servings.

FROZEN HAWAIIAN PIE

freezeable • make ahead

Prep: 30 min., Freeze: 12 hrs., Stand: 10 min.
(pictured on page 156)

1 (14-ounce) can sweetened
    condensed milk
1 (12-ounce) container frozen
    whipped topping, thawed
1 (20-ounce) can crushed
    pineapple, drained
2 tablespoons lemon juice
½ cup mashed ripe banana (about
    1 large banana)
1 large orange, peeled and
    sectioned
½ cup sweetened flaked coconut
½ cup chopped walnuts, toasted
½ cup maraschino cherries
2 (9-inch) ready-made graham
    cracker crusts
Garnishes: chopped pineapple,
    maraschino cherries, chopped
    walnuts, whipped topping,
    toasted coconut, fresh mint sprigs

Stir together condensed milk and whipped topping. Fold in next 7 ingredients. Pour into graham cracker crusts.
Cover and freeze 12 hours or until firm. Remove from freezer, and let stand 10 minutes before serving. Garnish, if desired. **Makes** 16 servings.

JOHNNIE MAE KEMP
KROTZ SPRINGS, LOUISIANA

ZESTY LEMON PIE

family favorite • make ahead

Prep: 20 min., Bake: 15 min., Chill: 4 hrs.

6 egg yolks, lightly beaten
3 (14-ounce) cans sweetened
    condensed milk
1½ cups fresh lemon juice
2 (9-inch) ready-made graham
    cracker crusts
2 cups whipping cream
¼ cup sugar
Fresh lemon slices (optional)
Fresh mint sprig (optional)

Whisk together first 3 ingredients. Pour evenly into crusts.

Bake at 350° for 15 minutes. Remove to a wire rack to cool. Cover and chill 4 hours.
Beat whipping cream at high speed with an electric mixer until foamy; gradually add sugar, beating until soft peaks form. Spread cream mixture evenly over chilled pies. Top pies with fresh lemon slices and a mint sprig before serving, if desired. **Makes** 16 servings.

SHERI LACROIX
NEW ORLEANS, LOUISIANA

RUM-COCONUT KEY LIME PIE

make ahead

Prep: 15 min., Chill: 12 hrs.

1 (8-ounce) package cream cheese,
    softened
1 (14-ounce) can sweetened
    condensed milk
½ cup lime juice
1 teaspoon rum (optional)
Coconut Crust
1 tablespoon sweetened flaked
    coconut, toasted

Beat cream cheese and milk at medium speed with an electric mixer until smooth. Add lime juice and, if desired, rum, stirring to combine. Pour filling into Coconut Crust. Sprinkle evenly with coconut. Cover and chill at least 12 hours or until set. **Makes** 8 servings.

COCONUT CRUST:

make ahead

Prep: 10 min., Chill: 30 min.

12 to 14 cream-filled vanilla
    sandwich cookies, finely
    crushed (about 1½ cups)
1 cup sweetened flaked coconut,
    toasted
6 tablespoons butter or
    margarine, melted

Combine all ingredients. Firmly press on bottom and up sides of a 9-inch pieplate. Cover and chill 30 minutes. **Makes** 1 (9-inch) piecrust.

GAIL SCHROEDER
BOCA RATON, FLORIDA

Great Time Get-together

Of all the seasons, summer offers countless opportunities to get outside for food, fun, and fellowship. To jump-start these gatherings, combine familiar foods with fresh flavor.

Summer Supper

Serves 8

Pickled Shrimp

Shredded Flank Steak Mini-Sandwiches

Tangy Bean Salad with chips

Key Lime-Coconut Mini-Cheesecakes

PICKLED SHRIMP

make ahead

Prep: 20 min., Chill: 12 hrs.

Shrimp ranks second to tuna as America's most popular seafood and is low in fat and calories. With its mild flavor, this shellfish blends well with other ingredients.

- **5 pounds unpeeled, cooked jumbo shrimp**
- **1 (4-ounce) jar capers, drained**
- **2 medium-size white onions, sliced**
- **1 large red bell pepper, sliced**
- **2 teaspoons celery seeds**
- **3 lemons, thinly sliced**
- **2 (0.6-ounce) envelopes Italian dressing mix**
- **½ cup vegetable oil**
- **½ cup cider vinegar**
- **1 tablespoon prepared horseradish**

Peel shrimp, and devein, if desired.
Layer a 13- x 9-inch baking dish with one-third each of shrimp, capers, onion slices, bell pepper slices, celery seed, and lemon slices. Repeat layers twice.
Whisk together dressing mix and next 3 ingredients. Pour evenly over shrimp. Cover and chill at least 12 hours. **Makes** 8 servings.

PAT CLEMENT
PASS CHRISTIAN, MISSISSIPPI

Per serving: Calories 318 (27% from fat); Fat 9.9g (sat 1.5g, mono 3.6g, poly 4.1g); Protein 49g; Carb 10.0g; Fiber 2.7g; Chol 442mg; Iron 8.0mg; Sodium 1,154mg; Calc 134mg

---

SHREDDED FLANK STEAK MINI-SANDWICHES

family favorite

Prep: 30 min.; Cook: 1 hr., 15 min.

- **1¾ pounds flank steak, trimmed**
- **1¼ teaspoons salt, divided**
- **1 large onion, quartered**
- **4 garlic cloves, pressed**
- **1 cup low-sodium fat-free chicken broth**
- **1 large onion, chopped**
- **1 large green bell pepper, chopped**
- **2 teaspoons olive oil**
- **4 garlic cloves, minced**
- **1 (14½-ounce) can diced tomatoes, undrained**
- **2 tablespoons fresh lime juice**
- **1 to 1½ teaspoons hot sauce**
- **½ teaspoon ground cumin**
- **½ teaspoon pepper**
- **16 mini-Hawaiian bread rolls, split ***

Sprinkle steak with ¼ teaspoon salt.
Place steak, quartered onion, pressed garlic, and broth in a 3-quart pressure cooker.
Cover cooker with lid, and seal securely. Set on high-pressure setting, if available. Cook over medium-high heat until pressure cooker steams and full pressure is achieved. Reduce heat to medium, and cook for 45 minutes.
Remove from heat; release pressure. Carefully remove lid so that steam escapes away from you. Remove meat from cooker. Let cool slightly. Strain onion mixture, reserving broth for another use; discard solids.
Sauté chopped onion and bell pepper in hot oil in a Dutch oven over medium-high heat 7 minutes or until tender. Add minced garlic, and sauté 2 minutes. Stir in remaining 1 teaspoon salt, diced tomatoes, and next 4 ingredients; cook, stirring occasionally, 7 minutes or until most of the liquid evaporates.
Shred beef, and coarsely chop; add to tomato mixture. Spoon about ¼ cup meat mixture over bottom half of each roll; cover with tops of rolls. **Makes** 16 mini-sandwiches.

Note: For testing purposes only, we used a Fagor 3-Quart MULTIRAPID Pressure Cooker. If you have another model, cook according to manufacturer's instructions.

***Look for Hawaiian bread rolls in the deli section of your supermarket. Substitute other rolls, if desired.

Per serving: Calories 189 (22% from fat); Fat 5g (sat 1.3g, mono 2g, poly 0.5g); Protein 13g; Carb 23g; Fiber 2g; Chol 14mg; Iron 2mg; Sodium 512mg; Calc 58mg

---

TANGY BEAN SALAD

fast fixin's

Prep: 10 min.

- **1 (15-ounce) can garbanzo beans, rinsed and drained**
- **1 (15-ounce) can dark red kidney beans, rinsed and drained**
- **1 (15-ounce) can pinto beans, rinsed and drained**
- **1 cup frozen whole kernel corn, thawed**
- **1 small red onion, finely chopped**
- **2 (4.5-ounce) cans diced green chiles**
- **1 (4-ounce) jar diced pimientos, drained**
- **1 teaspoon grated lime rind**
- **¼ cup fresh lime juice**
- **1 teaspoon hot sauce**
- **½ teaspoon ground cumin**
- **¼ teaspoon salt**
- **Garnish: lime slices**

Stir together first 12 ingredients. Cover and chill until ready to serve. Garnish, if desired. **Makes** 8 servings.

Per about ⅔ cup serving: Calories 144 (7% from fat); Fat 1g (sat 0.2g, mono 0.2g, poly 0.5g); Protein 7.2g; Carb 28.2g; Fiber 6.3g; Chol 0mg; Iron 1.8mg; Sodium 270mg; Calc 45mg

KEY LIME-COCONUT MINI-CHEESECAKES

make ahead

Prep: 20 min., Bake: 12 min., Cool: 15 min., Chill: 2 hrs.

- Vegetable cooking spray
- 14 vanilla wafers
- 1 (8-ounce) package fat-free cream cheese, softened
- 1 (8-ounce) package ⅓-less-fat cream cheese, softened
- ¾ cup sugar
- ½ cup egg substitute
- 3 tablespoons Key lime juice
- ½ teaspoon vanilla extract
- ¼ teaspoon coconut extract
- ½ cup fat-free sour cream
- 1 tablespoon sugar
- 7 teaspoons sweetened flaked coconut, toasted
- 2 teaspoons grated lime rind

Place 14 paper baking cups in muffin pans, and coat lightly with cooking spray. Place 1 vanilla wafer in each baking cup.

Beat together fat-free and ⅓-less-fat cream cheeses and ¾ cup sugar at medium speed with an electric mixer until smooth. Add egg substitute and next 3 ingredients, beating until smooth. Spoon mixture evenly into baking cups.

Bake at 350° for 10 to 12 minutes or until set. Remove pan from oven. Stir together sour cream and 1 tablespoon sugar. Spread 1 teaspoon sour cream mixture over top of each cheesecake. (Sour cream mixture will not completely cover each top.) Cool on a wire rack 15 minutes. Cover and chill 2 hours. Sprinkle tops evenly with toasted coconut and lime rind. **Makes** 14 servings.

Note: For testing purposes only, we used Nellie & Joe's Famous Key West Lime Juice.

VALERIE HOLT
CARTERSVILLE, GEORGIA

Per serving: Calories 137 (29% from fat); Fat 4.4g (sat 2.5g, mono 1.1g, poly 0.3g); Protein 5.7g; Carb 18.9g; Fiber 0.2g; Chol 11.6mg; Iron 0.7mg; Sodium 174mg; Calc 69.2mg

Avocados for Any Occasion

The rich, tropical flavor and velvety texture of avocados are unmistakable. This time of year their abundance in grocery stores makes them an ideal ingredient in the Southern kitchen. Take full advantage of their availability by trying this tempting collection of recipes.

LOADED TURKEY MELT

family favorite

Prep: 30 min., Cook: 12 min. per batch

- 2 ripe avocados, peeled and mashed
- 2 tablespoons mayonnaise
- 1 teaspoon garlic powder
- 8 bread slices
- 1 pound thinly sliced deli turkey
- 4 tomato slices
- 4 sliced red onion rings
- 8 bacon slices, cooked
- ¼ pound smoked mozzarella cheese slices
- 3 tablespoons butter, softened

Stir together avocado, mayonnaise, and garlic powder. Spread avocado mixture on 1 side of 4 bread slices. Top evenly with turkey, tomato, onion, bacon, cheese, and remaining bread slices.

Spread half of butter on 1 side of each sandwich. Place, buttered sides down, in a large hot nonstick skillet. Cook over medium heat 6 minutes or until golden.

Spread remaining butter on ungrilled sides; turn and cook 6 more minutes or until golden. Repeat procedure, if necessary, for any remaining sandwiches. **Makes** 4 sandwiches.

JACKIE OGLESBY
BOCA RATON, FLORIDA

Oven-Grilled Loaded Turkey Melts: Place buttered sandwiches on a baking sheet. Place a second baking sheet on top of sandwiches. Bake at 400° for 20 minutes or until golden.

AVOCADO SOUP

make ahead

Prep: 25 min., Chill: 1 hr.

- 2 ripe avocados, quartered
- ¼ cup chopped green onions
- 2 tablespoons fresh orange or pineapple juice
- 1 tablespoon chopped fresh cilantro
- ½ to 1 teaspoon salt
- ¼ teaspoon ground red pepper
- ¼ teaspoon ground black pepper
- ⅛ teaspoon ground cumin
- 3 cups chicken broth, chilled
- 1 (8-ounce) container fat-free plain yogurt
- Garnishes: cooked shrimp, avocado slices

Process avocado quarters in a blender or food processor until smooth, stopping to scrape down sides. Remove from blender.

Process green onions and next 7 ingredients until smooth, stopping to scrape down sides. Pour into a large bowl; gradually whisk in avocado and yogurt. Cover and chill 1 hour. Garnish, if desired. **Makes** 4 cups.

CARSON MORRIS
ATLANTA, GEORGIA

AVOCADO BUTTER

make ahead

Prep: 20 min., Chill: 1 hr.

- 2 ripe avocados
- 1 tablespoon fresh lime juice
- ¼ teaspoon salt
- ⅛ teaspoon garlic powder
- ⅛ teaspoon ground red pepper
- ⅛ teaspoon ground black pepper
- ¼ cup extra-virgin olive oil

Cut avocados in half. Scoop pulp into a food processor or blender.

Add lime juice and next 4 ingredients; process until smooth, stopping to scrape down sides. With processor running, pour oil in a slow, steady stream through food chute; process until smooth. Chill 1 hour. **Makes** 1¼ cups.

VANCE BAGLEY
ORLANDO, FLORIDA

Take Five for Sides

Once you calculate the short ingredient lists for these recipes, all the dishes add up to good. You won't find better accompaniments with supper.

SNAPPY FRUIT SALAD DRESSING

make ahead

Prep: 10 min., Chill: 30 min.

Toss ½ cup dressing with 6 cups cubed fresh fruit, or serve as a quick dip with gingersnaps.

- ½ cup light sour cream
- ½ cup light mayonnaise
- ¼ cup powdered sugar
- 1½ teaspoons lemon juice
- ½ teaspoon dried ground ginger*

Stir together all ingredients in a small bowl. Cover and chill at least 30 minutes. Store in refrigerator up to 3 days. **Makes** about 1 cup.

*Substitute ½ teaspoon ground cinnamon, if desired.

CAROL S. NOBLE
BURGAW, NORTH CAROLINA

SAUTÉED GREEN BEANS WITH BACON

family favorite

Prep: 25 min., Cook: 15 min.

- 1¾ pounds fresh green beans, trimmed
- ¼ cup water
- 8 bacon slices, chopped
- 5 green onions (white bottoms and light green parts of tops only), chopped
- ½ teaspoon salt
- ½ teaspoon pepper

Place beans and ¼ cup water in a large microwave-safe bowl. Cover with plastic wrap, and pierce plastic wrap with a fork. Microwave at HIGH 4 to 7 minutes or until crisp-tender. Plunge green beans into ice water to stop the cooking process. Drain well, and set aside.
Cook chopped bacon in a large non-stick skillet over medium heat until crisp; remove bacon, and drain on paper towels, reserving 2 tablespoons drippings in a small bowl. Discard remaining drippings. Wipe skillet clean with a paper towel.
Sauté green onions in skillet in hot reserved drippings over medium-high heat 1 minute. Stir in green beans, salt, and pepper; sauté 2 to 3 minutes or until thoroughly heated. Stir in bacon. **Makes** 4 to 6 servings.

DEBORAH S. WALTHALL
WAKE FOREST, NORTH CAROLINA

Kitchen Express: Substitute 2 (12-ounce) packages ready-to-eat trimmed fresh green beans for the fresh green beans, omitting water. Pierce bags with a fork and microwave at HIGH 4 to 5 minutes or until crisp-tender. Proceed with recipe as directed.

BAKED PINEAPPLE

family favorite

Prep: 15 min., Bake: 30 min.

Serve this favorite dish with ham, pork, chicken, or turkey or at a brunch.

- 2 (20-ounce) cans pineapple chunks in heavy syrup
- 1 tablespoon all-purpose flour
- ½ (8-ounce) block Cheddar cheese, shredded
- 38 round buttery crackers, crushed (1 sleeve)
- ¼ cup butter, melted

Drain pineapple chunks, reserving ½ cup syrup.
Sprinkle flour over pineapple chunks in a medium bowl, and toss to combine. Spread pineapple mixture evenly into a lightly greased 8-inch-square baking dish. Drizzle with reserved ½ cup syrup.

Top with cheese and cracker crumbs; drizzle with butter.
Bake at 350° for 25 to 30 minutes or until browned. Serve immediately. **Makes** 4 to 6 servings.

Note: For testing purposes only, we used Ritz crackers.

BLUE CHEESE ICEBERG WEDGES

fast fixin's

Prep: 15 min.

Add a little bit of chopped tomato to dress up this dish.

- ¾ cup blue cheese dressing
- 1 small head iceberg lettuce, cut into 4 wedges
- ½ cup crumbled blue cheese
- Freshly ground pepper to taste
- 4 bacon slices, cooked and crumbled

Pour dressing evenly over lettuce wedges; sprinkle wedges evenly with cheese, pepper, and bacon. **Makes** 4 servings.

SHIRL CIEUTAT
NEW ORLEANS, LOUISIANA

Greek Iceberg Wedges: Pour ¾ cup Greek dressing evenly over lettuce wedges; sprinkle evenly with ¼ cup crumbled feta cheese, ¼ cup chopped red onion, and ¼ cup chopped ripe black olives. For testing purposes only, we used Athenos Greek With Feta Cheese Mediterranean Dressing.

Caesar Iceberg Wedges: Pour ¾ cup Caesar dressing evenly over lettuce wedges; top evenly with ¼ cup shaved Parmesan cheese. For testing purposes only, we used Ken's Steak House Caesar Dressing.

Guilt-Free Comfort Food

Satisfy your cravings for flavor by using a few simple strategies at mealtime. Plan your menu around fresh vegetables instead of meat. Eat from all food groups, and pay attention while you eat.

HERB-AND-VEGGIE MEAT LOAF

Prep: 20 min., Cook: 7 min., Bake: 1 hr., Stand: 10 min.

For an equally flavorful, lower fat version, try the Herb-and-Veggie Turkey Loaf. Shorten prep time by using jarred minced garlic and preshredded carrots, which you can also use in Salad With Red Grapefruit-Lemon Vinaigrette. Pair meat loaf with your favorite refrigerated or frozen mashed potatoes prepared with reduced-fat milk.

- 1 medium onion, chopped
- 1 teaspoon minced garlic
- 2 teaspoons canola or vegetable oil
- 1 cup shredded carrots
- 1 cup roasted garlic-and-herb pasta sauce, divided
- 1½ pounds extra-lean ground beef
- 8 ounces 50%-less-fat fresh pork sausage
- 1 (10-ounce) package frozen chopped spinach, thawed and drained
- ½ cup uncooked regular oats
- 2 teaspoons dried Italian seasoning
- 1¼ teaspoons salt
- 1 teaspoon pepper
- 1 large egg, lightly beaten
- Vegetable cooking spray
- Additional roasted garlic-and-herb pasta sauce (optional)

Sauté onion and garlic in hot oil in a large nonstick skillet over medium-high heat 3 minutes. Add carrots, and sauté 3 to 4 minutes or until onion is tender; cool slightly.
Combine onion mixture, ½ cup pasta sauce, beef, and next 7 ingredients in a large bowl until blended. Shape mixture into a 10- x 5-inch loaf. Place on a rack coated with cooking spray; place rack in a broiler pan coated with cooking spray.
Bake at 350° for 45 minutes. Spread remaining ½ cup pasta sauce over loaf, and bake 10 to 15 more minutes or until a meat thermometer inserted into thickest portion registers 155°. Cover loosely with aluminum foil; let stand 10 minutes. Serve with additional pasta sauce, if desired. **Makes** 8 servings.

Note: For testing purposes only, we used Prego Roasted Garlic-and-Herb Pasta Sauce.

Per serving: Calories 240 (46% from fat); Fat 12.2g (sat 4.1g, mono 3.5g, poly 0.9g); Protein 21g; Carb 12g; Fiber 3.3g; Chol 65mg; Iron 3.4mg; Sodium 670mg; Calc 88mg

Herb-and-Veggie Turkey Loaf: Substitute 2 pounds lean ground turkey for beef and pork. Proceed with recipe as directed.

Per serving: Calories 203 (25% from fat); Fat 5.6g (sat 1.5g, mono 1g, poly 0.6g); Protein 26g; Carb 12g; Fiber 3.3g; Chol 82mg; Iron 2.4mg; Sodium 884mg; Calc 83mg

SALAD WITH RED GRAPEFRUIT-LEMON VINAIGRETTE

fast fixin's

Prep: 15 min. *(pictured on page 149)*

- ⅓ cup fresh red grapefruit juice
- 1 teaspoon grated lemon rind
- 2 tablespoons fresh lemon juice
- 2 tablespoons vegetable oil
- 2 tablespoons honey
- 1½ tablespoons Dijon mustard
- ¼ teaspoon salt
- ¼ teaspoon freshly ground pepper
- 1 (10-ounce) package chopped romaine lettuce
- 1 cup shredded carrots
- 1 cup red grapefruit segments
- ¼ small red onion, thinly sliced
- ¼ cup dry-roasted sunflower seeds (optional)

Whisk together first 8 ingredients in a small bowl.
Combine romaine lettuce an next 3 ingredients in a large bowl. Sprinkle with sunflower seeds, if desired. Serve with vinaigrette. **Makes** 6 servings.

Note: Store remaining vinaigrette in an airtight container in refrigerator up to 1 week.

Per serving (with seeds): Calories 135 (53% from fat); Fat 7.9g (sat 0.8g, mono 2.6g, poly 4g); Protein 2.4g; Carb 17g; Fiber 2.8g; Chol 0mg; Iron 0.9mg; Sodium 209mg; Calc 38mg

Per serving (without seeds): Calories 104 (45% from fat); Fat 5.3g (sat 0.6g, mono 2.1g, poly 2.2g); Protein 1.3g; Carb 15.4g; Fiber 2.2g; Chol 0mg; Iron 0.7mg; Sodium 209mg; Calc 35mg

LIGHT PIMIENTO CHEESE-STUFFED CELERY

fast fixin's • make ahead

Prep: 15 min.

Don't be tempted to use preshredded cheese. It takes a few more minutes to shred your own, but you'll be much more pleased with the creamy texture.

- 1¼ cups light mayonnaise
- 1 (4-ounce) jar diced pimiento, drained
- 1 teaspoon Worcestershire sauce
- 1 teaspoon finely grated onion
- ¼ teaspoon ground red pepper
- 2 (8-ounce) blocks 2% reduced-fat sharp Cheddar cheese, finely shredded
- 6 celery ribs, cut into 4-inch pieces
- Garnish: paprika

Stir together first 5 ingredients in a medium bowl. Stir in cheese.
Spread 1 tablespoon cheese mixture into each celery rib. Garnish, if desired. **Makes** about 3 cups pimiento cheese.

Note: Store remaining pimiento cheese in an airtight container in refrigerator up to 1 week.

Per 4-inch piece with 1 tablespoon pimiento cheese: Calories 54 (68% from fat); Fat 4.1g (sat 1.8g, mono 0g, poly 0g); Protein 2.5g; Carb 1.5g; Fiber 0.4g; Chol 9mg; Iron 0.1mg; Sodium 147mg; Calc 75mg

Barbecue Spuds

It's hard to beat a creamy twice-baked potato—especially when it's chock-full of tangy, tender chopped barbecue. We call for pork, but you can use chicken, turkey, or brisket—just be sure to begin with 3 cups of chopped meat.

Round out the menu with one of our icebox pies on page 157, which can be made the night before, for a hearty weeknight supper.

Cook's Notes

■ For the potatoes, we recommend high-starch, low-moisture baking potatoes such as russet or Idaho, which produce the fluffiest pulp.

■ For extra-crispy potato skins, place the scooped-out shells in the oven for about 10 minutes while preparing the filling and while the oven is cooling to 375°.

■ For a flavorful twist, try sharp Cheddar, Monterey Jack with peppers, or Swiss cheese in place of regular Cheddar.

■ Don't let leftover pulp go to waste. Reheat it later in the week for a simple but unbeatable version of mashed potatoes—perfect for lunch or an afternoon snack for the kids. To 2 cups potato pulp, stir in ½ cup sour cream, 1 tablespoon melted butter, 1 tablespoon chopped chives, ¼ teaspoon salt, and ⅛ teaspoon pepper.

■ If time is an issue, bake potatoes the night before, and scoop out the pulp. Refrigerate pulp and shells. Heat them in microwave on LOW power until warm, and proceed as directed.

DOUBLE-STUFFED BARBECUE POTATOES

family favorite

Prep: 30 min.; Bake: 1 hr., 10 min.

Each potato yields about 1 cup of pulp. The recipe calls for 8 potatoes, but you'll use the pulp of only 6 (which, when combined with the other ingredients, fills the 8 shells).

- 8 large baking potatoes
- 1 (8-ounce) container softened cream cheese
- ½ cup mayonnaise
- 1 tablespoon white wine vinegar
- 1 teaspoon seasoned pepper
- 2 teaspoons fresh lemon juice
- ¾ teaspoon salt
- 3 cups chopped barbecued pork, warmed
- 1 cup (4 ounces) shredded Cheddar cheese
- ¼ cup chopped fresh chives

Wrap each potato in a piece of aluminum foil; place potatoes on a baking sheet.
Bake potatoes at 425° for 45 minutes or until tender.
Cut a 4- x 2-inch strip from top of each baked potato. Carefully scoop out pulp into a large bowl, leaving 8 shells intact; set aside about 2 cups of pulp for another use. (See "Cook's Notes.")

Mash together remaining potato pulp, cream cheese, and next 5 ingredients; stir in pork. Spoon mixture evenly into shells; top evenly with Cheddar cheese and chives. Place on a lightly greased baking sheet.
Bake at 375° for 20 to 25 minutes or until shells are thoroughly heated.
Makes 8 servings.

CAROLYN WALTHALL
OXFORD, MISSISSIPPI

TANGY CABBAGE SALAD

Prep: 10 min.

Turn this into a lettuce-based salad by substituting 1 (10-ounce) package mixed salad greens for the cabbage. For a Greek version, add ¼ cup feta cheese.

- ½ cup olive oil
- 2 tablespoons lemon juice
- 2 tablespoons red wine vinegar
- 2 garlic cloves, minced
- 1 teaspoon chopped fresh oregano
- ½ teaspoon pepper
- ¼ teaspoon salt
- ⅛ teaspoon dry mustard
- 1 (10-ounce) package finely shredded cabbage
- 1 cup cherry tomatoes, halved

Whisk together first 8 ingredients until blended.
Place cabbage in a large bowl, and drizzle with ½ cup dressing. Add tomatoes, tossing gently to coat. Serve with remaining dressing. **Makes** 6 servings.

LOGAN GEORGIADIS
ORLANDO, FLORIDA

Hot Off the Grill

If you're in the market for a dynamic grill recipe, here are some that we rated tops. Regardless of what kind of grill you have, these great recipes won't disappoint.

Our recipes were tested and timed on the Fiesta Optima grill. Each grill has its own personality so use our recipes as guidelines. Times will vary due to the weather and the technology your grill design embraces. For best results and food safety, use a meat thermometer to check for exact doneness.

Slow-Grilled Pork With Ranch-Barbecue Sauce

family favorite

Prep: 15 min.; Chill: 8 hrs.; Stand: 45 min.; Grill: 4 hrs., 30 min.

This recipe is for a two-burner gas grill. If your grill has one burner, be sure to see directions for indirect cooking in the owner's manual.

- 1 (1-ounce) envelope Ranch dressing mix
- 1 (5-pound) bone-in pork shoulder roast (Boston butt)
- ½ (16-ounce) bottle Creole butter injector sauce (with injector)
- Ranch-Barbecue Sauce
- Garnish: bread-and-butter pickle slices

Rub dressing mix evenly over roast. Inject butter sauce into roast. Wrap tightly with plastic wrap, and place in a shallow dish or large zip-top plastic freezer bag; cover or seal and chill 8 hours. Let stand at room temperature 30 minutes before grilling. Remove plastic wrap.

Light 1 side of grill, heating to high heat (400° to 500°); leave other side unlit. Place roast, fat side up, over unlit side of grill, and grill, covered with grill lid, 3½ to 4½ hours or until a meat thermometer inserted into thickest portion registers 185°. (Meat will easily pull away from bone.) Let stand 15 minutes. Coarsely chop, and serve with Ranch-Barbecue Sauce. Garnish, if desired. **Makes** 6 servings.

Note: For testing purposes only, we used Cajun Injector Creole Butter Injectable Marinade.

Ranch-Barbecue Sauce:
fast fixin's

Prep: 5 min., Cook: 20 min.

- 1 (18-ounce) bottle barbecue sauce
- 1 (1-ounce) envelope Ranch dressing mix
- ¼ cup honey
- ½ teaspoon dry mustard

Stir together all ingredients in a saucepan over medium-high heat; bring to a boil. Reduce heat, and simmer, stirring occasionally, 20 minutes. **Makes** about 1¼ cups.

Note: For testing purposes only, we used Stubb's Original Bar-B-Q Sauce.

Mojo-Marinated Chicken

family favorite

Prep: 10 min., Chill: 8 hrs., Grill: 1 hr.

If your grill has only one burner, you'll want to follow the directions in our note at the end of the recipe for cooking the chicken directly over the heat.

- 1 (24-ounce) bottle mojo criollo Spanish marinating sauce
- 1 (19-ounce) can mild enchilada sauce
- 6 bone-in, skin-on chicken breasts
- Garnishes: fresh parsley sprigs, orange slices

Combine sauces in a large zip-top freezer bag. Add chicken, turning to coat. Seal and chill 8 hours, turning occasionally.

Light 1 side of grill, heating to high heat (400° to 500°); leave other side unlit. Remove chicken from marinade, discarding marinade. Arrange chicken breasts, skin side up, on unlit side of grill, and grill, covered with grill lid, 1 hour or until a meat thermometer inserted into thickest portion registers 170°. Garnish, if desired. **Makes** 6 servings.

Grilled Chicken Thighs: Substitute 6 skin-on, bone-in chicken thighs for chicken breasts. Arrange chicken thighs, skin side up, on unlit side of grill, and grill, covered with grill lid, 1 hour or until a meat thermometer inserted into thickest portion registers 180°.

Direct Heat Cooking Times: To cook chicken breasts directly over heat, reduce heat to medium (350° to 400°), and grill, covered with grill lid, turning chicken breasts every 7 minutes, for

28 minutes or until a meat thermometer inserted into thickest portion registers 170°. To cook chicken thighs directly over heat, reduce heat to medium (350° to 400°), and grill, covered, turning every 8 to 10 minutes, for 20 minutes or until meat thermometer inserted into thickest portion registers 180°.

Note: For testing purposes only, we used Goya Mojo Criollo Marinade.

Spicy Cheddar-Stuffed Burgers

family favorite

Prep: 10 min., Chill: 30 min., Grill: 16 min.
(pictured on page 152)

- 1 (7-ounce) can chipotle peppers in adobo sauce, undrained
- 2 pounds lean ground beef
- 2 teaspoons steak seasoning
- ½ (10-ounce) package Cheddar cheese, cut into 4 thick (1.25-ounce) slices
- 4 sesame seed hamburger buns
- Toppings: tomato slices, red onion slices, romaine lettuce leaves, yellow mustard, mayonnaise

Process chipotle peppers in a blender until smooth. Measure 4 teaspoons puree, reserving remainder for another use, if desired.

Combine 4 teaspoons puree, ground beef, and steak seasoning in a large bowl until blended. (Do not overwork meat mixture.) Shape mixture into 8 (4-inch) patties; place 1 cheese slice on each of 4 patties. Top with remaining 4 patties, pressing edges to seal. Cover and chill at least 30 minutes.

Grill, covered with grill lid, over medium-high heat (350° to 400°) 7 to 8 minutes on each side or until beef is no longer pink. Serve burgers on buns with desired toppings. **Makes** 4 servings.

Note: For testing purposes only, we used McCormick Grill Mates Montreal Steak Seasoning and Cracker Barrel Sharp Cheddar Cheese.

from our kitchen

You'll Love Individual Shortcakes

The new refrigerated piecrusts from Pillsbury are rolled rather than folded, so they're easier than ever to use. The dough is sized to fit 8- to 9-inch pie-plates and 10-inch tart pans, but it can also be cut into dozens of other shapes for quick-and-easy desserts, such as layered fruit pastries. Pretty enough for a party, layered pastries provide a speedy twist on traditional short-cake and pair crisp, flaky rounds of sugared pastry with a medley of sweet and juicy summer fruits.

Just unroll the dough on a lightly floured surface. Cut circular shapes using a 3-inch round cutter (you'll get 9 circles from each round of piecrust dough—a few more if you reroll the scraps). Brush the top of each 3-inch circle with lightly beaten egg, and sprinkle evenly with white sparkling sugar or granulated sugar. Arrange circles on ungreased baking sheets. Bake at 350° for 10 to 12 minutes or until golden brown. Remove from baking sheets, and cool completely on wire racks. Layer with fresh sliced fruits and berries tossed with granulated sugar and a generous dollop of whipped cream.

We used a mixture of sliced nectarines, strawberries, blueberries, and raspberries with a garnish of fresh mint, but almost any combination of sea-sonal fruits will work equally well.

Quick Tricks With Refrigerated Piecrusts

Look for ready-made piecrust dough in the refrigerated dairy case of the supermarket, usually near the butter and margarine. Let piecrust dough stand at room temperature for 15 to 20 minutes before unrolling. To prevent tearing as well as shrinkage when baking, avoid pulling and stretching the dough when fitting it in the pieplate, but do press it firmly against the bottom and sides to eliminate any air pockets that might push the crust out of shape. If the dough should crack or tear before baking, dampen fingertips with cold water and press the torn edges together. See photos and tips at left below for creating a beautiful crust.

Piecrust Pointers

1

Leave the excess dough around the outer edge of the pieplate for fluting, or use it to seal the top crust of a double-crusted fruit pie.

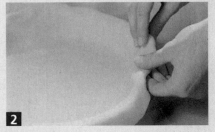

2

When preparing a single crust pie, fold the excess dough underneath itself, even with the pieplate's rim, and crimp.

3

After folding dough under, create a check-ered border by cutting decorative slits at ½-inch intervals. Gently press the tabs in opposite directions.

4

Rather than cutting and weaving strips of dough, use a small canapé cutter to create the look of a lattice-top crust for fruit pies.

Tips and Tidbits

- Use refrigerated and frozen piecrust before the expiration date printed on the package.
- Bake a refrigerated piecrust in a glass pieplate—it absorbs the radiant heat of an oven, unlike shiny metal or aluminum pie pans that reflect heat and can prevent the bottom of the crust from browning. When using a frozen piecrust in a disposable aluminum pan, bake the pie on a preheated baking sheet.
- Brush an unbaked piecrust with lightly beaten egg white before adding the filling. The egg white acts as a seal, keeping the bottom crust crisp. Bake pies on the lowest oven rack, and cool on a wire rack after baking.

july

166 Barbecue Buddies *Friends share some of their award-winning North Carolina 'cue recipes*

168 Cherry Jewels *Sweet juicy cherries are the secret to this culinary delight*

169 Healthy & Light Simple and Fresh Brunch *Treat your friends to good food and good health with this easy-to-prepare menu*

170 What's for Supper? Quick Catfish Tonight *Start a fast dinner on the cooktop*

171 Potato Salad Like You've Never Had *Whether you use white or sweet potatoes, this dish is a summer favorite*

Summer Living®

172 Savor a Sunset Supper *Delicious dinner to go with a beautiful setting*

174 Backyard Smokehouse in Dallas *Neighbors know when the grill master's cooking*

176 Add Flavor With Goat Cheese *Use fresh selections to make these scrumptious recipes*

177 Summer-Fresh Produce *Mouthwatering side dishes start with a trip to the farmers market*

178 Gather for a Blueberry Bash *Host a festive gathering with a menu featuring this summer fruit*

180 Casual Outdoor Get-together *Fast recipes that get you out of the kitchen and let you enjoy the party*

181 Bake Up Some Fun *Welcome the season with a batch of homemade cookies*

182 From Our Kitchen *Herb-infused oils, blackberries, and more*

Barbecue Buddies

Here's a menu that's really smokin'. These guys know how to do barbecue up just right.

Backyard Barbecue Menu

Serves 6 to 8

Tabb's Barbecue Pork

Honey-Mustard Barbecue Sauce

Creamy Carolina Coleslaw

Tomato-and-Onion Salad

Barbecue Deviled Eggs

Peach-Cinnamon Ice Cream

"If that's not a beautiful sight, I don't know what is," crows Jim "Trim" Tabb as a gorgeous plume of hickory-fueled smoke leaves the chimney of his barbecue rig. It's just after breakfast, but Jim, an award-winning barbecue aficionado from Tryon, North Carolina, has already been at his smoker for more than six hours. His good friend, Garrett Oliver, author and brewmaster at Brooklyn Brewery in New York, couldn't agree more. The two men have been hosting barbecue and beer pairings at the brewery for nearly five years.

Today the buddies are in Columbia, South Carolina, preparing for a family reunion at the home of Bill and Madelaine Miller, Garrett's uncle and aunt. Jim's supplying the barbecue. "Low and slow," is Jim's motto when it comes to barbecue. His succulent pork is out of this world when drizzled with Honey-Mustard Barbecue Sauce, a South Carolina specialty. Garrett is pairing beer with the menu, and Madelaine is kind enough to share a few of her favorite recipes.

TABB'S BARBECUE PORK

family favorite

Prep: 30 min.; Chill: 8 hrs.; Stand: 1 hr., 15 min.; Soak: 1 hr.; Smoke: 8 hrs. *(pictured on page 154)*

1 (6-pound) bone-in pork shoulder roast (Boston butt)
1 cup Barbecue Rub
Hickory wood chunks
Apple juice

Trim fat on pork shoulder roast to about ⅛ inch thick.

Sprinkle pork evenly with Barbecue Rub; rub thoroughly into meat. Wrap pork tightly with plastic wrap, and chill 8 hours.

Discard plastic wrap. Let pork stand at room temperature 1 hour.

Soak hickory chunks in water 1 hour. Prepare smoker according to manufacturer's instructions, bringing internal temperature to 225° to 250°; maintain temperature for 15 to 20 minutes.

Drain wood chunks, and place on coals. Place pork on lower cooking grate, fat side up.

Spritz pork with apple juice each time charcoal or wood chunks are added to the smoker.

Smoke pork roast, maintaining the temperature inside smoker between 225° and 250°, for 6 hours or until a meat thermometer inserted horizontally into thickest portion of pork registers 170°. Remove pork from smoker, and place on a sheet of heavy-duty aluminum foil; spritz with apple juice. Wrap tightly, and return to smoker, and smoke 2 hours or until thermometer inserted horizontally into thickest portion of pork registers 190°. Remove pork from smoker, and let stand 15 minutes. Remove bone, and chop pork. **Makes** 8 servings.

BARBECUE RUB:
fast fixin's

Prep: 20 min.

1¼ cups firmly packed dark brown sugar
⅓ cup kosher salt
¼ cup granulated garlic
¼ cup paprika
1 tablespoon chili powder
1 tablespoon ground red pepper
1 tablespoon ground cumin
1 tablespoon lemon pepper
1 tablespoon onion powder
2 teaspoons dry mustard
2 teaspoons ground black pepper
1 teaspoon ground cinnamon

Combine all ingredients. Store in an airtight container. **Makes** about 3 cups.

JIM TABB
TRYON, NORTH CAROLINA

HONEY-MUSTARD BARBECUE SAUCE

make ahead

Prep: 15 min., Cook: 18 min.

This is a thick, hearty sauce. If you prefer a thinner sauce, add ¼ cup water. *(pictured on page 154)*

- **1 bacon slice, diced**
- **1 small onion, diced**
- **1 garlic clove, minced**
- **1 cup cider vinegar**
- **¾ cup prepared mustard**
- **¼ cup firmly packed brown sugar**
- **¼ cup honey**
- **1 teaspoon black pepper**
- **1 teaspoon Worcestershire sauce**
- **¼ teaspoon ground red pepper**

Cook bacon in a medium saucepan until crisp; remove bacon, and drain on paper towels, reserving drippings in saucepan. **Sauté** onion and garlic in hot drippings about 3 minutes or until tender. Stir in bacon, vinegar, and remaining ingredients; bring to a boil. Reduce heat, and simmer, stirring occasionally, 10 minutes. Store in refrigerator for up to 1 week. **Makes** 1½ cups.

MADELAINE MILLER
COLUMBIA, SOUTH CAROLINA

CREAMY CAROLINA COLESLAW

make ahead

Prep: 10 min., Chill: 1 hr.

You may substitute light mayonnaise and light sour cream for regular in this dish.

- **1 cup mayonnaise**
- **1 cup sour cream**
- **2 tablespoons sugar**
- **2 tablespoons cider vinegar**
- **2 tablespoons fresh lemon juice**
- **1 teaspoon dry mustard**
- **½ teaspoon celery seeds**
- **½ teaspoon pepper**
- **¼ teaspoon salt**
- **⅛ teaspoon hot sauce**
- **2 (16-ounce) packages shredded coleslaw mix**

Stir together first 10 ingredients in a large bowl. Add coleslaw, tossing well to coat. Cover and chill 1 hour. Serve with a slotted spoon. **Makes** 8 servings.

MADELAINE MILLER
COLUMBIA, SOUTH CAROLINA

TOMATO-AND-ONION SALAD

make ahead

Prep: 10 min., Stand: 2 hrs.

The flavors of this recipe really shine with sweet Vidalia onions.

- **¼ cup extra-virgin olive oil**
- **1½ tablespoons balsamic vinegar**
- **½ teaspoon salt**
- **¼ teaspoon sugar**
- **¼ teaspoon pepper**
- **4 large tomatoes, thinly sliced**
- **1 medium-size sweet onion, thinly sliced**
- **¼ cup chopped fresh basil**

Whisk together first 5 ingredients in a large bowl. Arrange tomato and onion slices in rows in a serving dish. Sprinkle with chopped basil, and drizzle with marinade. Cover and let stand at room temperature for at least 2 hours. Serve with a slotted spoon. **Makes** 8 servings.

MADELAINE MILLER
COLUMBIA, SOUTH CAROLINA

BARBECUE DEVILED EGGS

Prep: 30 min., Cook: 6 min., Stand: 15 min.

Finely chopped pork is the secret to the filling in these favorites. If you want to omit the chopped pork, Madelaine suggests adding a drop of liquid smoke to provide a barbecue-like flavor.

- **12 large eggs**
- **¼ cup mayonnaise**
- **⅓ cup finely chopped smoked pork**
- **1 tablespoon Dijon mustard**
- **¼ teaspoon salt**
- **½ teaspoon pepper**
- **⅛ teaspoon hot sauce**
- **Garnish: paprika**

Place eggs in a single layer in a large saucepan; add water to a depth of 3 inches. Bring to a boil; cover, remove from heat, and let stand 15 minutes.
Drain and fill pan with cold water and ice. Tap each egg firmly on the counter until cracks form all over the shell. Peel under cold running water.
Cut eggs in half lengthwise, and carefully remove yolks. Mash yolks with mayonnaise. Stir in pork and next 4 ingredients; blend well.
Spoon yolk mixture evenly into egg white halves. Garnish, if desired.
Makes 12 servings.

MADELAINE MILLER
COLUMBIA, SOUTH CAROLINA

Barbecue Like a Pro

Follow Jim's tips for perfect 'cue.
- The most succulent pulled or chopped pork comes from the Boston butt (which is one half of a whole pork shoulder; the other half is the picnic shoulder). Bone-in is more economical, but even with the bone removed, this is still the best choice for smoking.
- Never allow flames to touch the meat—you're smoking, not grilling.
- Low and slow is the name of the game. Never increase the temperature of your grill or smoker to speed up cooking. The optimum smoker temperature is 225°. When the internal temperature of the meat reaches 190°, you're ready to go. If using a bone-in Boston butt, the shoulder bone should effortlessly pull away from the meat.

PEACH-CINNAMON ICE CREAM

freezeable • make ahead

Prep: 20 min., Cook: 20 min., Chill: 4 hrs., Freeze: 25 min.

Peach nectar is a sweet, intensely flavored drink that's usually found on the international food aisle, with the fruit juices, or with cocktail mixes.

> 4 cups peeled, diced fresh peaches (about 3 pounds)
> 1 cup peach nectar
> ½ cup sugar
> 3 egg yolks
> 4 cups milk
> 1 cup half-and-half
> 1 teaspoon lemon juice
> ½ teaspoon ground cinnamon
> Garnish: sliced fresh peaches

Combine first 3 ingredients in a medium bowl.

Process peach mixture, in batches, in a food processor until smooth, stopping to scrape down sides. Set aside.

Whisk together yolks and milk in a heavy saucepan over medium heat; cook, stirring constantly, 20 minutes or until mixture thickens and coats a spoon. Do not boil.

Remove from heat; whisk in peach mixture, half-and-half, lemon juice, and ground cinnamon. Cover and chill 4 hours.

Pour mixture into freezer container of a 6-quart electric ice-cream maker. Freeze according to manufacturer's instructions. (Instructions and times will vary.) Garnish, if desired. **Makes** 6 to 8 servings.

Note: For testing purposes only, we used a White Mountain 6-Quart Electric Ice Cream Freezer.

MADELAINE MILLER
COLUMBIA, SOUTH CAROLINA

Cherry Jewels

Sweet, juicy cherries, such as Bings, are ideal for eating out of hand or making Fresh Cherry Tart. Although the season is brief, look for these culinary gems in your grocery from June till mid-August. A cherry pitter, available at your local kitchen store, is a valuable gadget, preventing stained fingers and hands.

FRESH CHERRY TART

make ahead

Prep: 50 min., Bake: 6 min., Cook: 10 min., Chill: 2 hrs.

> 1⅓ cups graham cracker crumbs
> 3 tablespoons sugar
> 1 teaspoon ground cinnamon
> ⅓ cup butter, melted
> 2½ cups fresh cherries, pitted (about 1 pound)
> ⅔ cup sugar, divided
> 3 tablespoons cornstarch
> 3 tablespoons water
> ⅓ cup orange marmalade, divided
> 2 tablespoons butter or margarine
> 1 (8-ounce) container soft cream cheese

Stir together first 4 ingredients. Press mixture into bottom and up sides of a 13- x 4-inch tart pan with removable bottom.

Bake at 375° for 6 minutes. Cool in pan on a wire rack.

Bring cherries, ⅓ cup sugar, cornstarch, and 3 tablespoons water to a boil in a medium saucepan over medium heat, stirring constantly; boil, stirring constantly, 1 minute or until thickened and bubbly. Remove from heat; stir in 3 tablespoons orange marmalade and 2 tablespoons butter until melted. Cool; cover and chill at least 2 hours.

Stir together remaining ⅓ cup sugar, remaining orange marmalade, and cream cheese until blended. Spread evenly in crust, and top with chilled cherry mixture. **Makes** 8 to 10 servings.

JANET EILDERS
SIKESTON, MISSOURI

Simple and Fresh Brunch

Bring big flavor to your breakfast table with this easy-to-prepare menu for eight.

Brunch for a Bunch

Serves 8

Confetti Omelet Casserole

Breakfast Turkey Sausage Patties

Brown Sugar-Baked Pineapple

Sparkling Orange Punch

Breakfast is the most important meal of the day, so celebrate it in style. We've revised some classic morning favorites such as spicy sausage patties and cheesy egg casserole to lower the calories and fat but maintain the rich flavor. This spread is sure to please your guests, and they'll never guess it was so easy to prepare. It's a perfect way to treat your friends to good food and good health.

CONFETTI OMELET CASSEROLE

Prep: 20 min., Cook: 10 min., Bake: 45 min., Stand: 5 min.

- **6 bacon slices**
- **½ cup chopped onion**
- **4 cups egg substitute**
- **2 cups (8 ounces) 2% reduced-fat shredded sharp Cheddar cheese**
- **1 cup fat-free milk**
- **1 (4-ounce) jar chopped pimiento, drained**
- **2 tablespoons chopped fresh parsley**
- **½ teaspoon salt**
- **Vegetable cooking spray**
- **Garnish: fresh flat-leaf parsley sprigs**

Cook bacon in a medium skillet until crisp; remove bacon, and drain on paper towels, reserving 1 teaspoon drippings in skillet. Crumble bacon, and set aside.

Add ½ cup chopped onion to hot drippings in skillet, and sauté over medium heat 3 to 4 minutes or until tender.

Stir together crumbled bacon, onion, egg substitute, and next 5 ingredients in a large bowl. Pour egg mixture into a 13- x 9-inch baking dish coated with cooking spray.

Bake at 325° for 45 minutes or until set. Let stand 5 minutes before serving. Garnish, if desired. **Makes** 8 servings.

JEANNE STANTON HOTALING
AUGUSTA, GEORGIA

Per serving: Calories 194 (40% from fat); Fat 8.1g (sat 4.7g, mono 0.9g, poly 0.2g); Protein 22g; Carb 5.2g; Fiber 0.4g; Chol 26mg; Iron 2.6mg; Sodium 766mg; Calc 275mg

BREAKFAST TURKEY SAUSAGE PATTIES

freezeable • make ahead

Prep: 25 min., Chill: 8 hrs., Cook: 12 min. per batch

Freshly grated apple adds a tangy flavor to this spicy turkey sausage. We used a Fuji apple, but any other sweet, crisp apple or pear would make a delicious substitute.

- **1 large Fuji apple**
- **2 garlic cloves, minced**
- **1¼ pounds lean ground turkey**
- **½ cup chopped fresh parsley**
- **¼ cup finely chopped fresh sage**
- **1¾ teaspoons salt**
- **½ teaspoon dried crushed red pepper**
- **½ teaspoon black pepper**
- **1 large egg, beaten**
- **2 teaspoons olive oil**

Peel and core apple; coarsely shred apple with a hand grater. Place in a wire-mesh strainer; drain well, pressing gently with paper towels.

Combine apple, garlic, and next 7 ingredients in a bowl; stir until blended. Shape mixture into 16 patties (about 2 tablespoons each). Place patties on a wax paper-lined baking sheet. Cover and chill 8 hours or overnight.

Heat oil in a large nonstick skillet over medium heat. Cook patties, in batches, about 6 minutes on each side or until browned and done. **Makes** 8 servings.

Note: Make patties ahead by wrapping in wax paper and heavy-duty aluminum foil and freezing up to 2 weeks. Thaw frozen patties overnight in the refrigerator, and cook as directed.

Per serving: Calories 139 (45% from fat); Fat 7g (sat 1.6g, mono 1.1g, poly 0.2g); Protein 14g; Carb 4.5g; Fiber 0.8g; Chol 87mg; Iron 1.4mg; Sodium 604mg; Calc 43.5mg

BROWN SUGAR-BAKED PINEAPPLE

Prep: 10 min., Stand: 10 min., Broil: 17 min.

1 cup lemon juice
¾ cup honey
¼ cup firmly packed light brown sugar
2 fresh pineapples, peeled and cored
4 cups light vanilla ice cream

Stir together first 3 ingredients in a small bowl; let stand 10 minutes.
Cut each pineapple into 8 (¾- to 1-inch-thick) slices.
Place pineapple slices on an aluminum foil-lined baking sheet, and pour honey mixture evenly over top. Broil 3 inches from heat 15 to 17 minutes or until golden brown. Serve with ice cream. **Makes** 8 servings.

CELESTE STOVER
NEW ORLEANS, LOUISIANA

Per serving (2 pineapple slices and ½ cup ice cream): Calories 238 (13% from fat); Fat 3.6g (sat 2g, mono 0g, poly 0.1g); Protein 3.8g; Carb 52.3g; Fiber 1.8g; Chol 10mg; Iron 0.5mg; Sodium 50mg; Calc 124.3mg

Note: For nutritional analysis, we used Breyers All Natural Light Creamy Vanilla ice cream.

SPARKLING ORANGE PUNCH

make ahead

Prep: 5 min., Stand: 5 min., Chill: 2 hrs.

This punch adds fun and festivity to any meal.

4 cups boiling water
4 regular-size tea bags
½ cup sugar
1 (6-ounce) can orange juice concentrate, thawed
1 (750-milliliter) bottle sparkling wine or Champagne, chilled

Pour 4 cups boiling water over tea bags; cover and steep 5 minutes. Remove and discard tea bags. Stir in sugar and juice concentrate, stirring until sugar dissolves. Cover and chill 2 hours.
Stir together chilled tea mixture and sparkling wine. Serve immediately. **Makes** 8 servings.

Per (1-cup) serving: Calories 157 (0% from fat); Fat 0g (sat 0g, mono 0g, poly 0g); Protein 0g; Carb 24.5g; Fiber 0g; Chol 0mg; Iron 0mg; Sodium 2mg; Calc 3mg

what's for supper?

Quick Catfish Tonight

Tonight, serve a main dish that cooks in 10 minutes on the cooktop with a nice do-ahead slaw on the side. One skillet is all you need. Toast the bread first, remove it from the pan, cover with foil to keep warm, and then cook the fish in the same skillet.

Summer Supper

Serves 4

Quick Pan-fried Catfish
Broccoli-Squash Slaw
Lemon-Garlic Toast

QUICK PAN-FRIED CATFISH

fast fixin's

Prep: 15 min., Cook: 10 min.

Fish generally cooks 10 minutes per inch of thickness. If the catfish you buy is thicker, it will take longer to cook. Just lower the temperature slightly. Cook the prettiest side of the catfish first for picture-perfect results.

¾ cup all-purpose baking mix
½ cup yellow cornmeal
1 tablespoon Old Bay seasoning
4 (4- to 6-ounce) catfish fillets
½ cup Ranch dressing
3 tablespoons vegetable oil
Lemon wedges

Combine first 3 ingredients in a shallow bowl.
Pat catfish fillets dry with paper towels; brush both sides of each fillet evenly with Ranch dressing. Dredge in cornmeal mixture; lightly press cornmeal mixture onto fillets.

Cook catfish in hot vegetable oil in a large nonstick skillet over medium-high heat 3 to 5 minutes on each side or until fish just flakes with a fork. Serve immediately with lemon wedges. **Makes** 4 servings.

Note: For testing purposes only, we used Bisquick for all-purpose baking mix.

JANICE ELDER
CHARLOTTE, NORTH CAROLINA

BROCCOLI-SQUASH SLAW

make ahead

Prep: 20 min., Chill: 2 hrs.

Grate the lemon rind for Lemon-Garlic Toast before squeezing the juice for this recipe.

¼ cup mayonnaise
¼ cup honey
2 tablespoons fresh lemon juice
1 teaspoon salt
½ teaspoon black pepper
⅛ to ¼ teaspoon ground red pepper
1 (12-ounce) package broccoli slaw
2 medium-size yellow squash, cut in half lengthwise and thinly sliced
1 red bell pepper, chopped
½ cup chopped pecans, toasted

Whisk together first 6 ingredients in a small bowl. Combine broccoli slaw, squash, and bell pepper in a large bowl. Add half of mayonnaise mixture (about ¼ cup), tossing to coat. Cover and chill both slaw mixture and remaining mayonnaise mixture at least 2 hours or up to 24 hours.
Drain slaw mixture just before serving, discarding excess liquid; return slaw mixture to bowl. Add reserved half of mayonnaise mixture and pecans, tossing to coat. **Makes** 4 servings.

JANICE ELDER
CHARLOTTE, NORTH CAROLINA

LEMON-GARLIC TOAST

fast fixin's • make ahead

Prep: 15 min., Cook: 4 min.

- ¼ cup butter, softened
- 1½ teaspoons minced fresh parsley
- 1½ teaspoons grated lemon rind
- ⅛ teaspoon garlic powder
- 8 (¾-inch-thick) French bread slices

Stir together first 4 ingredients in a small bowl. Spread about ½ teaspoon mixture on both cut sides of each bread slice.

Heat a large nonstick skillet over medium-high heat until hot. Add bread slices, and cook 2 minutes on each side or until toasted. **Makes** 4 servings.

Note: Butter mixture can be made up to 2 days ahead. Cover and chill. To soften, microwave at LOW (20% power) for 20 seconds; stir. Microwave at LOW 5 to 10 more seconds, if necessary.

Potato Salad Like You've Never Had

Bring a heaping bowl of comfort to your warm-weather table with these terrific potato salads. We peeled and cubed the potatoes before cooking to save time.

SWEET POTATO SALAD

family favorite • make ahead

Prep: 20 min., Bake: 25 min.

- 2 pounds sweet potatoes, peeled and cut into 1-inch cubes
- Vegetable cooking spray
- ¾ teaspoon salt, divided
- 2 celery ribs, diced
- 1 jalapeño pepper, seeded and finely chopped
- ½ cup diced onion
- ⅓ cup diced green bell pepper
- 3 tablespoons brown sugar
- 2 tablespoons chopped fresh or 1 tablespoon dried parsley flakes
- 5 tablespoons white vinegar
- 1 tablespoon vegetable oil
- 1 teaspoon hot sauce
- 1 teaspoon prepared mustard
- 3 slices peppered or regular bacon, cooked and crumbled (optional)
- Garnish: fresh flat-leaf parsley sprigs

Arrange potatoes in an even layer in a 15- x 10-inch jelly-roll pan. Coat with cooking spray, and sprinkle with ½ teaspoon salt.

Bake at 400° for 25 minutes or just until tender. Let cool slightly.

Stir together remaining ¼ teaspoon salt, celery, and next 9 ingredients in a large bowl until blended. Add potatoes, and toss gently to coat. Sprinkle with crumbled bacon, if desired; garnish, if desired. Serve warm or chilled. **Makes** 4 to 6 servings.

PATTY HORN
MIDWEST CITY, OKLAHOMA

Test Kitchen Notebook

The kind of potato you use for a salad really makes a difference. I may like thinly sliced red potatoes for one recipe, and Yukon golds for another. Baking potatoes can get mealy. Other staff members favor all-purpose white potatoes, the large, slightly rounded potatoes found in supermarkets.

Vanessa McNeil

TEST KITCHEN SPECIALIST/FOOD STYLING

BACON POTATO SALAD

family favorite • make ahead

Prep: 15 min., Cook: 18 min., Chill: 1 hr.

Round white potatoes work well in this recipe. To lighten, use light mayonnaise and sour cream. To make ahead, peel and cut potatoes the night before, cover with water, and chill. (pictured on page 153)

- 6 to 8 medium potatoes (about 3 pounds), peeled and cut into 1-inch cubes
- ½ pound bacon, cooked and crumbled
- 6 green onions, chopped
- 2 celery ribs, finely chopped
- 2 tablespoons diced pimiento, drained
- ¾ teaspoon salt
- ¼ teaspoon pepper
- ½ cup mayonnaise
- ½ cup sour cream
- Garnishes: paprika, celery sticks

Cook potatoes in boiling water to cover in a Dutch oven over medium heat 15 to 18 minutes or until tender. Drain and let cool slightly.

Place potatoes in a large bowl. Add bacon, chopped green onions, and next 4 ingredients. Stir together mayonnaise and sour cream until blended. Pour over potato mixture, tossing gently to coat. Cover and chill at least 1 hour. Garnish, if desired. **Makes** 6 servings.

M. JANE WRIGHT
BIRMINGHAM, ALABAMA

Summer Living®

Plan an outdoor gathering with an array of scrumptious menus, including juicy burgers, slow-smoked barbecue, and fresh produce.

Savor a Sunset Supper

Take a cue from this couple, and treat your guests to dinner in a beautiful setting.

Cocktail Supper

Serves 8

Grilled Crostini With Olive Tapenade

Sewee Preserve's Seafood Salad with Dill Vinaigrette

Spicy Cheese Cocktail Biscuits

Citrus Bars

wine and beer

Laid-back entertaining in a gorgeous atmosphere is definitely the right kind of summer gathering—just ask Katherine and Dennis Avery of Mount Pleasant, South Carolina. "I'm a confirmed Lowcountry girl," declares a laughing Katherine, "so we decided to take our friends to the community dock at Sewee Preserve where everyone could enjoy a view of the marsh."

There, with the ever-changing tidal creeks and marsh, the shorebirds, a soft breeze, and a mist of rain, the couple served a relaxed menu. "Never fear going to Plan B," Katherine advises. "We wanted to set up several appetizer stations along the 900-foot-long boardwalk to the dock so we could enjoy each phase of the scenery and pace our enjoyment of the food. The rain meant we grabbed an umbrella and hurried to the gazebo-covered dock where we then served all the food." Just as guests were finishing the salad supper, the sun came out.

GRILLED CROSTINI WITH OLIVE TAPENADE

fast fixin's

Prep: 10 min., Grill: 6 min.

Grill the bread slices early the day of the gathering. Cool and store in zip-top plastic bags.

- **1 (12-ounce) French bread baguette**
- **3 tablespoons olive oil**
- **1 tablespoon balsamic vinegar**
- **1 garlic clove, minced**
- **¼ teaspoon pepper**
- **1 (7-ounce) container olive tapenade**
- **1 tablespoon chopped flat-leaf parsley**
- **Garnish: green onion strips**
- **¼ cup sliced green onions**

Slice bread into 24 (½-inch-thick) slices, discarding ends.

Whisk together olive oil and next 3 ingredients. Brush evenly on 1 cut side of each bread slice.

Grill bread slices over medium heat (300° to 350°) 2 to 3 minutes on each side.

Stir together olive tapenade and parsley; garnish, if desired. Place green onion slices in a small bowl. Serve tapenade and sliced green onions with bread. **Makes** 8 appetizer servings.

Note: For testing purposes only, we used Cantaré Olive Tapénade, which can be found in the deli section.

KATHERINE AVERY
MOUNT PLEASANT, SOUTH CAROLINA

SEWEE PRESERVE'S SEAFOOD SALAD

make ahead

Prep: 20 min., Broil: 13 min., Chill: 1 hr.

Our Foods staff decided this tasty recipe was worth the splurge to buy the crabmeat. Reserve the juice from the capers for the vinaigrette. Villa Maria Sauvignon Blanc, New Zealand (about $12) or Brancott Marlborough Sauvignon Blanc, New Zealand (about $10) would be excellent wines to partner with this salad.

- 1 pound unpeeled, cooked medium-large shrimp (about 24-30)
- 1 (1-pound) skinless flounder or grouper fillet
- 2 teaspoons olive oil
- ¼ teaspoon salt
- ¼ teaspoon pepper
- 1 pound fresh lump crabmeat, drained and picked
- ½ cup chopped red onion
- ¼ cup finely chopped dill pickle
- 2 tablespoons drained capers
- Dill Vinaigrette
- Watercress

Peel and devein shrimp; set aside.
Place fillet on a lightly greased rack in a broiler pan. Brush fillet with olive oil, and sprinkle evenly with salt and pepper. Broil 5 inches from heat 10 to 13 minutes or until fish flakes with a fork. Remove from pan, and cool.
Break cooled fish into large pieces, and place in a large bowl. Add shrimp, crabmeat, and next 3 ingredients; toss gently to combine. Drizzle with Dill Vinaigrette; toss gently to coat. Cover and chill at least 1 hour. Arrange seafood mixture on watercress. **Makes** 8 servings.

KATHERINE AVERY
MOUNT PLEASANT, SOUTH CAROLINA

DILL VINAIGRETTE:
fast fixin's

Prep: 10 min.

- ¼ cup red wine vinegar
- ¼ cup olive oil
- 2 tablespoons fresh lemon juice
- 2 tablespoons finely chopped sweet onion
- 2 tablespoons minced fresh dill
- 2 tablespoons minced dill pickle
- 2 teaspoons liquid from jarred capers
- ¾ teaspoon salt
- ¾ teaspoon coarsely ground black pepper
- ½ teaspoon sugar

Whisk together all ingredients. Cover and chill. **Makes** about ¾ cup.

SPICY CHEESE COCKTAIL BISCUITS

fast fixin's

Prep: 15 min., Bake: 15 min.

For best results, don't use preshredded Cheddar cheese—instead, grate your own. To give the biscuits a spicier flavor, use the larger amount of ground red pepper. Serve a sparkling white wine, such as Domaine Ste. Michelle Cuvée Brut, Washington (about $12), if you serve these cheese strawlike biscuits as appetizers.

- ½ cup butter, softened
- ½ (8-ounce) block sharp Cheddar cheese, shredded (about 1 cup)
- 1 cup all-purpose flour
- ¼ teaspoon salt
- ¼ to ½ teaspoon ground red pepper
- 28 pecan halves

Beat butter at medium speed with an electric mixer until creamy; gradually add cheese, beating well. Combine flour, salt, and red pepper; gradually add flour mixture to cheese mixture, beating well.

Shape dough into ½-inch balls; place on ungreased baking sheets. Press a pecan half into each ball to flatten.
Bake at 350° for 12 to 15 minutes. Cool 5 minutes; transfer to a wire rack to cool completely. **Makes** about 28 biscuits.

Note: For testing purposes only, we used Kraft Sharp Cheddar Cheese.

KATHERINE AVERY
MOUNT PLEASANT, SOUTH CAROLINA

CITRUS BARS

family favorite

Prep: 15 min., Bake: 52 min.

- 1 cup butter, softened
- 2¼ cups all-purpose flour, divided
- ½ cup powdered sugar
- 1¾ cups granulated sugar
- ⅓ cup fresh lemon juice
- 1 teaspoon finely grated orange rind
- ⅓ cup fresh orange juice
- 4 large eggs, beaten
- 1 teaspoon baking powder
- ¼ teaspoon salt
- 1 tablespoon powdered sugar
- Garnish: orange and lemon rind strips

Beat butter at medium speed with an electric mixer until creamy; add 2 cups flour and ½ cup powdered sugar. Beat until mixture forms a smooth dough. Press mixture into a lightly greased 13- x 9-inch pan.
Bake at 350° for 20 to 22 minutes or until lightly browned.
Whisk together remaining ¼ cup flour, granulated sugar, and next 6 ingredients; pour over baked crust.
Bake at 350° for 28 to 30 minutes or until set. Cool in pan on a wire rack. Sprinkle evenly with 1 tablespoon powdered sugar, and cut into bars. Garnish, if desired. **Makes** 2 dozen.

TONI THOMPSON
MOUNT PLEASANT, SOUTH CAROLINA

Backyard Smokehouse in Dallas

These tantalizing recipes would give any well-known barbecue joint a run for its money.

Residents of this east Dallas neighborhood see and smell smoke billowing behind neighbor Paul Bender's house regularly, but they don't call the fire department; they know he's cooking. Paul and his wife, Gina, are known as fabulous cooks. When Paul decided to build a covered smokehouse in his backyard, he pulled out all the stops.

This stone-and-cedar beauty includes a large smoking chamber, a built-in charcoal grill, work area, and room for entertaining. Our Foods staff awarded Paul's ribs, chicken, barbecue sauce, and rub their highest rating, and they're still talking about Bender barbecue. Now you can too.

BIG "D" SMOKED BABY BACK RIBS

Prep: 30 min., Stand: 30 min., Soak: 30 min., Smoke: 5 hrs.

> **3 slabs baby back pork ribs (about 6 pounds)**
> **¼ cup lemon juice**
> **¼ cup olive oil**
> **6 tablespoons Paul's Pork Ribs Rub (see following recipe)**
> **Hickory wood chunks**
> **4 to 6 (12-ounce) bottles dark beer**
> **2 cups Paul's Barbecue Sauce (recipe on facing page)**

Rinse ribs, and pat dry. Remove thin membrane from back of ribs by slicing into it with a knife and then pulling. (This makes ribs more tender and allows smoke and rub to penetrate meat better.)

Place lemon juice in a small bowl; add oil in a slow, steady stream, whisking constantly. Coat ribs evenly with lemon juice mixture. Sprinkle meat evenly with Paul's Pork Ribs Rub, and rub into meat. Let stand at room temperature 30 minutes.

Soak wood chunks in water for at least 30 minutes.

Prepare smoker according to manufacturer's directions, substituting beer for water in water pan. Bring internal temperature to 225° to 250°, and maintain temperature for 15 to 20 minutes. Drain wood chunks, and place on coals. Place rib slabs in a rib rack on upper cooking grate; cover with smoker lid.

Smoke ribs, maintaining the temperature inside smoker between 225° and 250°, for 4 hours and 30 minutes. Remove lid, baste with half of Paul's Barbecue Sauce, and, if necessary, add more beer to water pan. Cover with smoker lid, and smoke 30 more minutes. Cut meat into 3-rib sections, slicing between bones, and serve with remaining half of Paul's Barbecue Sauce. **Makes** 6 servings.

PAUL'S PORK RIBS RUB

fast fixin's • make ahead

Prep: 5 min.

> **1 cup Greek seasoning**
> **¼ cup garlic powder**
> **¼ cup paprika**
> **¼ cup firmly packed brown sugar**

Combine all ingredients. Store rub in an airtight container. **Makes** about 1¾ cups.

Note: For testing purposes only, we used Cavender's All Purpose Greek Seasoning.

Paul's Chicken Rub: Substitute 3 tablespoons dried oregano for the brown sugar, and store in an airtight container. **Makes** 1⅔ cups.

ROASTED CAMP CORN

family favorite

Prep: 30 min., Cook: 5 min., Grill: 25 min.

Serve with additional sweet pepper sauce and Creole seasoning, if desired. Paul likes to serve his corn with the charred inner husks peeled back but not removed.

> **6 ears fresh yellow corn with husks**
> **¼ cup butter**
> **1 teaspoon dried basil**
> **1 teaspoon sweet pepper sauce**
> **½ teaspoon Creole seasoning**
> **¼ teaspoon black pepper**

Remove heavy outer husks from corn; pull back (but do not remove) inner husks. Remove and discard silks; rinse corn, and dry with paper towels. Set aside.

Melt ¼ cup butter in a small saucepan over low heat. Stir in 1 teaspoon basil and next 3 ingredients, stirring until blended.

Brush corn evenly with butter mixture. Pull husks back over corn.

Grill corn, covered with grill lid, over high heat (400° to 500°) 25 minutes, making quarter turns every 6 to 7 minutes. Pull back husks before serving. **Makes** 6 servings.

Note: For testing purposes only, we used Pickapeppa Sauce for sweet pepper sauce.

PAUL'S BARBECUE SAUCE

make ahead

Prep: 20 min., Cook: 20 min.

This barbecue sauce is so darn good that it will be a permanent condiment in your refrigerator. Make an extra batch, and store in an airtight container up to 3 weeks.

- 2 tablespoons butter
- 1 tablespoon olive oil
- 1 medium onion, finely chopped
- ½ green bell pepper, finely chopped
- 4 garlic cloves, minced
- 3 medium jalapeño peppers, seeded and minced
- 1 cup firmly packed brown sugar
- 1 cup cider vinegar
- 1 cup chili sauce
- 1 cup bottled barbecue sauce
- 1 tablespoon mustard powder
- 1 tablespoon paprika
- 3 tablespoons fresh lemon juice
- 2 tablespoons Worcestershire sauce
- 2 tablespoons hot sauce
- 2 tablespoons molasses
- ¼ teaspoon salt

Melt butter with oil in a large Dutch oven over medium heat.

Add onion and next 3 ingredients, and sauté 5 to 6 minutes or until onion is tender.

Stir in brown sugar and remaining ingredients; bring to a boil. Reduce heat to medium-low, and simmer 10 minutes. Pour mixture through a wire-mesh strainer into a bowl, discarding solids. **Makes** about 3½ cups.

BIG "D" SMOKED CHICKEN

family favorite

Prep: 30 min.; Chill: 6 hrs.; Soak: 30 min.; Smoke: 3 hrs., 30 min.

Tender, moist, and loaded with flavor, the meat of this chicken just falls off the bone.

- 2 (5- to 5½-pound) whole chickens
- ½ cup lemon juice
- ½ cup olive oil
- 1 cup Paul's Chicken Rub (recipe on facing page)
- Hickory wood chunks
- 4 to 6 (12-ounce) bottles dark beer
- 2 cups Paul's Barbecue Sauce (recipe at left)

Rinse chickens, and pat dry.

Place lemon juice in a small bowl; add oil in a slow, steady stream, whisking constantly. Coat outside skin and inside cavities of chickens evenly with lemon juice mixture; sprinkle evenly with Paul's Chicken Rub, and rub into chickens. Wrap each chicken tightly with plastic wrap, and chill at least 6 hours. Soak wood chunks in water for at least 30 minutes.

Prepare smoker according to manufacturer's directions, substituting beer for water in water pan. Bring internal temperature to 225° to 250°, and maintain temperature for 15 to 20 minutes.

Drain hickory wood chunks, and place on coals. Place chickens, breast sides up, on upper cooking grate, and cover with smoker lid.

Smoke chickens, maintaining the temperature inside smoker between 225° and 250°, for 2 hours. Remove lid, baste with half of Paul's Barbecue Sauce, and, if necessary, add more beer to water pan. Cover with smoker lid; smoke 1 to 1½ more hours or until a meat thermometer inserted into thighs registers 180°. Serve with remaining half of Paul's Barbecue Sauce. **Makes** 8 servings.

TEXAS ROCKETS

Prep: 30 min., Chill: 30 min., Grill: 35 min.

You'll want to make more than one batch of these yummy appetizers. For less heat, look for jalapeño peppers with rounded tips.

- ½ pound chicken breast strips
- ¾ cup Italian dressing, divided
- ½ (8-ounce) package cream cheese, softened
- ⅛ teaspoon salt
- ⅛ teaspoon pepper
- 12 jalapeño peppers (about 3½ to 4 inches long)
- 12 thin bacon slices

Place chicken and ½ cup Italian dressing in a shallow dish or zip-top freezer bag; cover or seal, and chill 30 minutes.

Remove chicken from marinade, discarding marinade. Grill chicken, covered with grill lid, over medium heat (300° to 350°) 4 to 5 minutes on each side or until done, basting with remaining ¼ cup Italian dressing. Let chicken cool slightly, and finely chop.

Stir together chicken, cream cheese, salt, and pepper in a bowl.

Cut jalapeño peppers lengthwise down 1 side, leaving other side intact; remove seeds. Spoon 1½ to 2 tablespoons chicken mixture into cavity of each pepper. Wrap each pepper with 1 bacon slice, securing with 2 wooden picks.

Grill stuffed jalapeños, without grill lid, turning frequently, over medium heat 20 to 25 minutes or until bacon is crisp. **Makes** 1 dozen.

Add Flavor With Goat Cheese

Enjoy products from FireFly Farms or fresh selections from your supermarket in one of these dishes.

When Pablo Solanet and Mike Koch devised an exit strategy from their high-powered jobs in Washington, D.C., they chose the scenic route—a goat farm. They began FireFly Farms in Maryland's Allegheny Plateau in 2000, and two of their cheeses won awards the first year they were produced. Tasting FireFly Farms' cheeses inspired creativity in our Test Kitchens. We hope you like the results.

Test Kitchen Notebook

The excellence of Pablo and Mike's cheese may be partially explained by their loving care of the goats. "Our partner, who is an excellent farmer, thinks we're a little crazy the way we pamper the goats," Mike says with a laugh. The cheeses also demand a lot of care. They have to be turned every day and the amount of humidity is critical, as is the salting process.

In addition to fresh goat cheese, FireFly Farms produces excellent aged selections—a blue as well as Merry Goat Round. To order any of their products, visit **www.fireflyfarms.com** or call (301) 245-4630.

Donna Florio
SENIOR WRITER

ROASTED VEGETABLE-AND-GOAT CHEESE PIZZA

Prep: 30 min.; Bake: 1 hr., 15 min.

You can use more or less cheese depending on what you have available; substituting 2 (4-ounce) logs or most of an 11-ounce log works just fine.

- 1 medium-size sweet onion, cut into ¾-inch pieces
- 1 teaspoon olive oil
- 1 medium eggplant, peeled and cut into ¾-inch cubes
- 1 red bell pepper, cut into ¾-inch pieces
- 1 small zucchini, cut into ¾-inch cubes
- 1 teaspoon salt
- ½ teaspoon pepper
- 2 teaspoons chopped fresh thyme
- 1 tablespoon olive oil
- 1 (24-ounce) package prebaked pizza crusts
- 1 (7-ounce) container refrigerated prepared pesto sauce
- 1 (9-ounce) package goat cheese, crumbled
- ¼ cup pine nuts

Toss onion with 1 teaspoon oil; arrange on an aluminum foil-lined jelly-roll or broiler pan.
Bake at 425° for 20 minutes or until tender, stirring after 10 minutes.
Toss together eggplant and next 6 ingredients; add to onion on jelly-roll pan. Bake 30 more minutes, stirring at 10-minute intervals.
Place pizza crusts on 2 lightly greased baking sheets; spread pesto evenly over crusts, and arrange vegetables evenly over pesto. Sprinkle crumbled goat cheese and pine nuts over vegetables.
Bake pizzas at 425° for 25 minutes or until cheese is lightly browned. **Makes** 2 (12-inch) pizzas.

LIME-GOAT CHEESE CHEESECAKES

make ahead

Prep: 35 min.; Bake: 30 min.;
Stand: 1 hr., 10 min.; Chill: 8 hrs.

Bake not-too-sweet Lime-Goat Cheese Cheesecakes in muffin tins for individual servings.

- 2 tablespoons pistachios
- ½ cup graham cracker crumbs
- 3 tablespoons butter, melted
- 1 (8-ounce) package cream cheese, softened
- 1 (3-ounce) package cream cheese, softened
- 1 (4-ounce) package goat cheese, softened
- ⅓ cup honey
- 2 large eggs
- ½ teaspoon grated lime rind
- 1 tablespoon lime juice
- Garnish: fresh raspberries

Pulse 2 tablespoons pistachios in food processor just until finely chopped. Add ½ cup graham cracker crumbs and 3 tablespoons melted butter; pulse until well blended. Spoon mixture evenly into 12 lightly greased muffin pan cups; press firmly onto bottoms.
Bake at 325° for 5 minutes. Let cool on a wire rack.
Beat softened cream cheese and goat cheese at medium speed with a heavy-duty stand mixer until smooth; gradually add honey, beating until blended. Add eggs, 1 at a time, beating well after each addition. Stir in lime rind and

juice; pour batter evenly into prepared muffin pan.

Place muffin pan in a shallow broiler pan. Add hot water to broiler pan to a depth of ½ inch (halfway to top of muffin cups).

Bake at 300° for 20 to 25 minutes or until slightly firm in the center. Carefully remove from oven, and let stand in water bath for 10 minutes.

Remove muffin pan from water bath to wire rack, and let cool completely. Cover and chill 8 hours. Let stand at room temperature 1 hour before serving. Run a knife around edges to remove cheesecakes from pan. Garnish, if desired. **Makes** 1 dozen.

Note: To prevent the crumb mixture from getting on your hands, cover your fingers with plastic wrap when you press the mixture into the muffin cups. If you have one, a tart tamp also works well for this.

Summer-Fresh Produce

With markets and roadside stands piled high with colorful vegetables, there's no better time to discover new ways to serve them. These change-of-pace dishes—Green Beans With Blue Cheese and an oven-fried medley with dipping sauce—are definitely worth a try. For quick and even cooking, be sure to cut all vegetables in a recipe about the same size.

GARLICKY "FRIED" VEGETABLES

Prep: 35 min., Stand: 5 min., Bake: 35 min.

This assortment of crisp veggies bakes at a high oven temperature rather than being fried for their golden glow.

- 1 small green tomato, cut into ¼-inch-thick slices
- ⅛ teaspoon salt
- 1 small zucchini, cut into ¼-inch-thick slices
- ½ (8-ounce) container button mushrooms, stems removed
- ½ pound whole okra
- 1 medium-size red bell pepper, cut into strips
- 1 large garlic clove, minced
- 2 teaspoons Creole seasoning
- ¼ cup cornstarch, sifted
- 3 cups Japanese breadcrumbs (Panko)
- ¼ teaspoon salt
- ¼ teaspoon pepper
- 6 large egg whites
- Vegetable cooking spray
- Horseradish Sauce

Place tomato slices on paper towels; sprinkle with ⅛ teaspoon salt, and let stand 5 minutes.

Place tomatoes, zucchini, and next 4 ingredients in a large bowl. Sprinkle evenly with Creole seasoning and cornstarch; shake to remove excess.

Combine breadcrumbs, ¼ teaspoon salt, and pepper in a shallow bowl. Whisk 3 egg whites in a small bowl until frothy. Dip half of vegetables in egg whites, draining excess. Dredge vegetables, in batches, in breadcrumb mixture. Repeat procedure with remaining egg whites, vegetables, and breadcrumb mixture.

Arrange vegetables on wire racks coated with cooking spray; place racks in aluminum foil-lined pans. (Do not overlap vegetables.)

Bake at 400° for 30 to 35 minutes or until golden brown. Serve immediately with Horseradish Sauce. **Makes** 6 servings.

HORSERADISH SAUCE:
fast fixin's • make ahead

Prep: 5 min.

- ¾ cup sour cream
- 2 tablespoons buttermilk
- 2 teaspoons prepared horseradish
- ¼ teaspoon salt
- ¼ teaspoon pepper

Stir together all ingredients. Cover sauce, and chill until ready to serve. **Makes** ¾ cup.

GREEN BEANS WITH BLUE CHEESE

family favorite

Prep: 20 min., Cook: 12 min.

Toss frequently in order to distribute ingredients evenly.

- 1 pound fresh green beans, trimmed
- 1 cup chopped cooked ham
- ¾ cup crumbled blue cheese
- ⅓ cup chopped walnuts, toasted
- 1 teaspoon pepper

Cut trimmed green beans into 2-inch pieces.

Arrange beans in a steamer basket over boiling water. Cover and steam 5 minutes. Plunge beans into ice water to stop cooking process; drain.

Sauté 1 cup chopped ham in a large skillet over medium-high heat 2 minutes; add green beans, and sauté 3 minutes. Add crumbled blue cheese, and cook, stirring constantly, 2 minutes or until cheese is melted. Add chopped walnuts and pepper, tossing well. Serve immediately. **Makes** 6 servings.

LAURA TUTTLE
WICHITA, KANSAS

Gather for a Blueberry Bash

These neighbors celebrate their homegrown harvest with a backyard feast.

When garden designers Julie Foster and Leah Geis of Norcross, Georgia, started their former landscaping business, they never dreamed that their marketing strategy would start a summer tradition in their neighborhood. "To spread the word about our new partnership, we decided to have a blueberry bush sale," says Julie. "We posted flyers and couldn't sell the bushes fast enough. It was a big success."

It was so successful, in fact, that it inspired an annual neighborhood harvest party. "Even though Julie and I have separate businesses now," says Leah, "we still enjoy getting together with everyone for our own blueberry festival." This year, partygoers gathered at Julie's house, where they celebrated with yummy favorites, including pork tenderloin with fresh Blueberry Salsa and Julie's famous Frozen Blueberry Margaritas.

Grow Your Own

Blueberry bushes are easier to grow than you think. Julie and Leah suggest pairing two types for proper cross-pollination. "Look for Rabbiteye," says Leah, "and plant two different selections such as 'Tifblue' or 'Powderblue'."

CHILLED BLUEBERRY SOUP

fast fixin's • make ahead

Prep: 10 min., Cook: 5 min.

For a creamier soup, add a dollop of plain yogurt to each serving.

- **4 cups fresh blueberries**
- **1 cup orange juice**
- **½ cup sugar**
- **¼ teaspoon ground cinnamon**
- **⅛ teaspoon salt**
- **1 tablespoon fresh lemon juice**
- **1 pint half-and-half**
- **Garnish: mint sprigs**

Bring first 5 ingredients to a boil in a saucepan over medium-high heat, stirring often. Remove from heat, and cool slightly.

Process blueberry mixture and lemon juice in a blender or food processor until smooth, stopping to scrape down sides. Cover and chill until ready to serve.

Stir in half-and-half just before serving. Serve in stemmed glasses. Garnish, if desired. **Makes** 4 servings.

LAURA YATES
LITTLETON, MASSACHUSETTS

BLUEBERRY-RUM MARINATED PORK TENDERLOIN

make ahead

Prep: 10 min., Chill: 4 hrs., Grill: 26 min., Stand: 10 min.

Marinate the tenderloin up to 24 hours in advance to ease the preparation.

- **1 cup fresh blueberries**
- **¾ cup rum**
- **¼ cup lemon juice**
- **2 garlic cloves**
- **2 tablespoons brown sugar**
- **1 tablespoon chopped sweet onion**
- **1 tablespoon white vinegar**
- **1 (16-ounce) package pork tenderloins**
- **French bread slices, toasted**
- **Blueberry Salsa (recipe on facing page)**

Process first 7 ingredients in a blender or food processor until smooth, stopping to scrape down sides. Pour mixture into a large zip-top plastic freezer bag; add pork. Seal and chill at least 4 hours.

Remove pork from marinade, discarding marinade.

Grill pork, covered with grill lid, over medium heat (300° to 350°) 11 to 13 minutes on each side or until a meat thermometer inserted in thickest portion registers 155°. Remove from grill. Loosely cover pork with foil; let stand 10 minutes or until thermometer registers 160°. Cut pork into slices, and serve over toasted bread. Top with Blueberry Salsa. **Makes** 4 to 6 servings.

LAURA YATES
LITTLETON, MASSACHUSETTS

BLUEBERRY SALSA

fast fixin's • make ahead

Prep: 15 min.

This fruity salsa is a refreshing side to grilled meats and fish.

3 cups fresh blueberries, divided
¼ cup fresh lemon juice
3 tablespoons chopped fresh cilantro
2 jalapeño peppers, seeded and minced
⅓ cup diced red bell pepper
¼ cup chopped onion
½ teaspoon kosher salt

Coarsely chop 2 cups blueberries. Stir together chopped blueberries, remaining 1 cup whole blueberries, and remaining 6 ingredients in a large bowl. Cover and chill until ready to serve. **Makes** about 3 cups.

JULIE FOSTER
NORCROSS, GEORGIA

BERRY DELICIOUS SUMMER SALAD

fast fixin's

Prep: 5 min.

8 cups mixed salad greens
2 cups fresh blueberries
½ cup crumbled Gorgonzola or blue cheese
¼ cup chopped and toasted walnuts or pecans
Bottled vinaigrette

Toss together first 4 ingredients; drizzle with desired amount of vinaigrette, tossing gently to coat. **Makes** 6 to 8 servings.

Note: For testing purposes only, we used Newman's Own Light Raspberry & Walnut vinaigrette.

JULIE FOSTER
NORCROSS, GEORGIA

A Handful of Health

Whether you grow them at home or pick them up at the market, fresh blueberries have amazing health benefits that might surprise you.
■ Blueberries are one of the top sources of disease-fighting antioxidants in fruits and vegetables.
■ New research suggests that blueberries may play a role in reducing memory loss, good news for those at risk for Alzheimer's.
■ The pigment in blueberries is thought to improve eyesight.
■ Blueberries promote urinary tract health because they contain a bacteria-preventing component that helps guard against infection.
■ A cup of fresh blueberries equals about 80 calories, 4 grams of fiber, and a third of the daily recommendation for vitamin C, making blueberries the perfect snack.

BAKED BRIE WITH BLUEBERRY-GINGER TOPPING

Prep: 10 min., Cook: 5 min., Chill: 1 hr., Bake: 10 min.

1 cup fresh blueberries
¼ cup firmly packed brown sugar
1½ tablespoons cornstarch
2 tablespoons cider vinegar
2 tablespoons diced onion
1 tablespoon grated fresh ginger
1 (3-inch) cinnamon stick
⅛ teaspoon salt
1 (8-ounce) Brie round
Assorted crackers

Combine first 8 ingredients in a large saucepan. Bring to a boil over medium heat, and cook 1 minute. Remove and discard cinnamon stick. Cover and chill blueberry mixture at least 1 hour.
Place Brie round on an ungreased baking sheet.
Bake at 350° for 8 to 10 minutes or until cheese is soft. Transfer to a serving plate, and top evenly with chilled blueberry topping. Serve with crackers. **Makes** 8 to 10 appetizer servings.

LEAH GEIS
NORCROSS, GEORGIA

FROZEN BLUEBERRY MARGARITAS

fast fixin's

Prep: 15 min.

Dip glass rims in coarse-grained salt instead of sugar, if you prefer. Julie recommends straining the mixture before serving.

Fresh orange juice or lime juice (optional)
Blue or purple decorator sugar crystals (optional)
3 cups ice
⅓ cup tequila
2 cups fresh or frozen blueberries
1 (6-ounce) can frozen limeade concentrate
¼ cup powdered sugar
¼ cup orange liqueur

Dip rims of margarita glasses in orange juice, and dip in sugar crystals to coat, if desired.
Process ice and next 5 ingredients in a blender until smooth. Serve in prepared glasses. **Makes** about 5½ cups.

JULIE FOSTER
NORCROSS, GEORGIA

Casual Outdoor Get-together

These recipes have a hands-on time of 10 minutes or less, so you can join the party.

Backyard Cookout

Serves 8

Italian-Style Burgers with Tomato-Basil Mayonnaise

Slow Cooker Barbecue Beans

chips and salsa

sliced watermelon

Whether celebrating our nation's birthday or just rounding up friends and family for an easygoing afternoon meal, there's always a good reason to fire up the grill. You can't go wrong with burgers and beans. Round out the menu with chips, salsa, and watermelon.

"My husband and I swear by ground chuck for our Italian-Style Burgers," says reader Jennie Vieve Richardson, who prefers it over the leaner ground sirloin. Our Test Kitchens found that not only is ground chuck economical, it also makes a more tender burger.

ITALIAN-STYLE BURGERS

fast fixin's

Prep: 10 min., Grill: 12 min.

- **2 pounds ground chuck or ground round**
- **1 large egg**
- **¼ cup Italian-seasoned breadcrumbs**
- **2 teaspoons hot sauce**
- **1 teaspoon onion powder**
- **1 teaspoon garlic powder**
- **1 teaspoon salt**
- **1 teaspoon pepper**
- **8 hamburger buns**
- **Vegetable cooking spray**
- **Toppings: lettuce, tomato slices**
- **Tomato-Basil Mayonnaise**

Combine first 8 ingredients. Shape into 8 (4-ounce) patties.

Grill patties, covered with grill lid, over medium-high heat (350° to 400°) 5 minutes on each side or until beef is no longer pink.

Spray cut sides of buns with cooking spray; place buns, cut sides down, on cooking grate, and grill 2 minutes or until lightly browned. Serve hamburgers on buns with desired toppings and Tomato-Basil Mayonnaise. **Makes** 8 servings.

JENNIE VIEVE RICHARDSON
OXFORD, MISSISSIPPI

TOMATO-BASIL MAYONNAISE:

fast fixin's • make ahead

Prep: 5 min.

- **1½ cups mayonnaise**
- **½ cup fresh basil leaves**
- **2 tablespoons tomato sauce**

Process all ingredients in a blender or food processor until smooth, stopping to scrape down sides. Store in an airtight container in refrigerator up to 1 week. **Makes** about 1½ cups.

SLOW COOKER BARBECUE BEANS

make ahead

Prep: 5 min., Cook: 1 hr.

This recipe is perfect for leftover barbecue. Although it calls for pork, feel free to use chopped or shredded chicken, turkey, or brisket. If time is a concern, pick up meat from your favorite barbecue joint (just make sure you get it without sauce to prevent the beans from being too soupy).

- **½ pound chopped or shredded barbecue pork**
- **1 (32-ounce) can pork and beans, undrained**
- **1 (14½-ounce) can diced tomatoes with green peppers and onions, drained**
- **¼ cup spicy brown mustard**
- **3 tablespoons brown sugar**
- **2 tablespoons Worcestershire sauce**
- **1 tablespoon molasses (optional)**

Stir together first 6 ingredients, and, if desired, molasses in a 6-quart slow cooker. Cover and cook at HIGH 1 hour. (You can keep this recipe warm on LOW for up to 2 hours before serving.) **Makes** 8 servings.

DENISE HOOD
UNION GROVE, ALABAMA

Bake Up Some Fun

Cookies are welcome additions to any summer activity.

Keep these great snacks on hand for sweet treats that are ready in no time. The kids will have fun helping in the kitchen. Store cookies in an airtight container to keep them crisp. Tuck some in your backpack to celebrate the end of a hike, serve them with coffee to friends, or munch on one (or three) as you relax with a good book.

DOUBLE CHOCOLATE CHUNK COOKIES

family favorite

Prep: 30 min., Bake: 14 min. per batch

Semisweet chocolate chunks and milk chocolate candy bars pack these cookies with two kinds of chocolate. *(pictured on page 155)*

1 cup butter, softened
1 cup granulated sugar
1 cup firmly packed dark brown
    sugar
2 large eggs
1½ teaspoons vanilla extract
2½ cups uncooked quick-cooking
    oats
2 cups all-purpose flour
1 teaspoon baking powder
1 teaspoon baking soda
½ teaspoon salt
1 (11.5-ounce) package semisweet
    chocolate chunks
2 (1.55-ounce) milk chocolate
    candy bars, grated
1 cup chopped pecans, toasted

Beat butter and sugars at medium speed with an electric mixer until creamy. Add eggs and vanilla, beating until blended.

Pulse oats in a food processor to a fine powder. Combine oats, flour, and next 3 ingredients in a large bowl; gradually add to butter mixture, beating well. Stir in chocolate chunks, grated chocolate bars, and pecans. Drop dough by ¼ cupfuls onto lightly greased baking sheets.

Bake at 375° for 10 to 14 minutes or until desired degree of doneness. Remove cookies to wire racks to cool completely. **Makes** about 2½ dozen.

Note: For testing purposes only, we used Hershey's milk chocolate candy bars.

KATE KELLEY
BIRMINGHAM, ALABAMA

Test Kitchen *Notebook*

When making cookies, line baking sheets with parchment paper or special baking paper with a nonstick coating. The cookies won't stick, the liners minimize burning, and cleanup's a breeze.

Andria Scott Hurst

SENIOR WRITER

CRUNCHY OAT 'N' CEREAL COOKIES

family favorite

Prep: 20 min., Bake: 12 min. per batch

3½ cups all-purpose flour
1 teaspoon baking soda
½ teaspoon salt
1 cup butter, softened
1 cup granulated sugar
1 cup firmly packed brown sugar
1 large egg
1 teaspoon vanilla extract
½ cup vegetable oil
1 cup uncooked regular oats
1 cup crushed cornflakes cereal
½ cup sweetened flaked coconut
1 cup chopped toasted pecans
Powdered sugar

Combine flour, baking soda, and salt in a small bowl.

Beat butter, granulated sugar, and brown sugar at medium speed with a heavy-duty electric mixer 2 minutes or until well blended. Add egg and vanilla, beating until blended. Add oil, beating until blended. Add flour mixture, beating at low speed until blended. Add oats and next 3 ingredients, beating until blended.

Shape dough into 1-inch balls. Place on baking sheets, and flatten gently with tines of a fork.

Bake at 325° for 12 minutes or until edges are lightly browned. Remove to wire racks to cool completely. Sprinkle with powdered sugar. **Makes** about 8½ dozen.

STEFANIE BRANDON
FAYETTEVILLE, ARKANSAS

from our kitchen

A Taste of Summer

Herb-infused oils add a burst of bright flavor to light, summery meals. They're super-easy to make and will keep up to 1 week in the refrigerator. For best results, use a neutral oil such as canola, which readily absorbs delicate flavors.

Warm 1 cup of oil in a heavy saucepan over low heat; remove from heat, and stir in 1 cup of chopped fresh herbs such as basil, thyme, oregano, or chives. When adding more strongly flavored herbs, such as rosemary or sage, reduce the amount of herbs to ½ cup. Refrigerate overnight; pour the mixture through a wire-mesh strainer, discarding solids. Drizzle oil over sliced tomatoes and salad greens or grilled meats and fish. Toss with hot cooked pasta and Parmesan cheese, or season a quick skillet supper.

To add decorative sprigs of fresh herbs to the oil, do so just before serving; then remove the sprigs before returning to the refrigerator for food safety.

Tips and Tidbits

Pass the Peas, Please

Southern field peas are a farmers market favorite, especially when partnered with sweet-and-spicy chow-chow and crisp-crusted wedges of hot cornbread.

When shopping for fresh peas, choose flexible, well-filled pods with tender seeds. Many of our top-rated recipes combine the flavor and texture of several varieties such as Pink-eyed Peas, Crowder Peas, Lady Peas, or Black-eyed Peas.

Fresh peas are easily frozen. After shelling and washing, blanch peas in boiling water to cover for 2 minutes; cool immediately in ice water, and drain well. Package in airtight containers, leaving ½-inch headspace, or in zip-top plastic freezer bags, removing as much air as possible. Seal and freeze up to 6 months. Don't thaw frozen peas before cooking.

Wild About Blackberries

Fresh summer blackberries hold lots of delicious possibilities—from jewel-like jams and jellies to buttery, deep-dish cobblers. Blackberry Curd Filling is an irresistible treat we enjoy in both tarts and layer cakes. Unlike traditional curds that call for 30 minutes of cooking time, this easy recipe quickly thickens with a little cornstarch.

To prepare homemade miniature tart shells, unroll refrigerated piecrust on a lightly floured surface. Cut circular shapes using a 2½-inch round cutter; press into miniature muffin pans. Prick bottoms of shells; freeze shells 10 minutes. Bake at 450° for 6 to 8 minutes or until golden brown. Cool in pans on wire racks. Remove from pans when cooled.

Spoon curd evenly into shells; garnish with sweetened whipped cream, fresh mint, and sliced blackberries.

BLACKBERRY CURD FILLING

make ahead

Prep: 5 min., Cook: 8 min., Chill: 8 hrs.

Once chilled, fillings and sauces thickened with cornstarch will loosen when stirred. So, when ready to use, don't stir. Just spoon the curd directly into tart shells, or spoon and spread over cake layers.

1 cup sugar
3 tablespoons cornstarch
2 cups Blackberry Juice
3 large eggs
2 egg yolks
¼ cup butter

Combine sugar and cornstarch in a 3-quart saucepan; gradually whisk in Blackberry Juice. Whisk in eggs and egg yolks. Bring mixture to a boil (5 to 6 minutes) over medium heat, whisking constantly.

Cook, whisking constantly, 1 to 2 minutes or until a puddinglike thickness. Remove from heat, and whisk in butter. Cover, placing plastic wrap directly on curd, and chill 8 hours. **Makes** 3 cups.

BLACKBERRY JUICE:

fast fixin's • make ahead

Prep: 10 min., Cook: 8 min.

When fresh blackberries aren't available, substitute 2 (16-ounce) packages of frozen blackberries, thawed.

2 quarts fresh blackberries
½ cup water

Bring blackberries and water to a boil in a 3-quart saucepan. Reduce heat, and simmer 5 minutes or until blackberries are soft.

Mash blackberries with a potato masher or fork; pour through a large wire-mesh strainer into a bowl, using the back of a spoon to squeeze out the juice. Discard the pulp and seeds. **Makes** about 2 cups.

august

184   Cast-Iron Chefs *Three Southern chefs cook up some mouthwatering recipes using the region's favorite cookware*

186   Pasta: Toss It and Love It *Create fresh and flavorful dishes with a stash of pantry ingredients*

188   Top-Rated Menu Favorite Picnic Food *Easy nibbles that will get you out of the kitchen fast*

193   Quick & Easy Speedy and Scrumptious Desserts *Delectable treats that start with a simple hot fudge sauce*

194   Healthy & Light Smart Eating Starts With Good Taste *Enjoy a nutrient-packed dinner that fits with the new* Dietary Guidelines for Americans 2005

196   Taste of the South White Barbecue Sauce *Drizzle this true regional delicacy on barbecued chicken, pork, and more*

197   What's for Supper? It's on the Grill *Throw together an easy weeknight meal with short ingredient lists and low-fuss prep*

198   From Our Kitchen *Catfish, low-fat fish-frying tips, and more*

Cast-Iron Chefs

Three hot Southern chefs cook up restaurant-worthy recipes anyone can make.

Three chefs who come from different areas of the region were given the task to develop recipes that use chicken and incorporate at least five of the following ingredients: peas, beans, rice, tomatoes, melons, cilantro, basil, bacon, mayonnaise, green onions, lettuce, and corn.

Chef Hoover Alexander of Hoover's Cooking in Austin prefers a once-neglected skillet that he rescued from an auction. Chef Tom Condron of Upstream Restaurant in Charlotte believes the magic of a well-seasoned cast-iron skillet adds comfort to every recipe. Chef Sara Gibbs of Lynn's Paradise Cafe in Louisville fondly recalls the soul-warming grilled cheese sandwiches and fried cornbread prepared by her grandmother in the griddle-like skillet that she uses.

SARA'S GRILLED CHICKEN-CORNBREAD SALAD

chef recipe

Prep: 25 min., Cook: 5 min., Bake: 30 min.

- **4 applewood-smoked bacon slices**
- **1 (6-ounce) package cornbread mix**
- **Smoky Chicken Thighs**
- **1¼ cups mayonnaise**
- **¼ cup minced Vidalia or other sweet onion**
- **2 tablespoons finely sliced fresh basil**
- **2 tablespoons fresh lemon juice**
- **¼ teaspoon coarsely ground black pepper**
- **1 cup cooked fresh lima or butter beans**
- **1 cup cooked fresh corn kernels (about 2 ears)**
- **½ cup diced red bell pepper**
- **8 large tomatoes**

Cut bacon into ¼-inch pieces; cook in a 6½-inch cast-iron skillet until crisp. Remove bacon, and drain on paper towels, reserving 1 tablespoon drippings in skillet. Prepare cornbread batter according to package directions; pour batter into hot drippings in skillet.

Bake at 425° for 20 to 25 minutes or until golden brown; cool completely in skillet on a wire rack. Break or cut cornbread into small (about 1-inch) pieces; place on a baking sheet.

Bake cornbread pieces at 425° for 5 minutes or until lightly toasted.

Remove skin and bones from Smoky Chicken Thighs; cut meat into bite-size pieces.

Whisk together mayonnaise and next 4 ingredients in a large bowl. Gently fold chopped chicken, cornbread, bacon, lima beans, corn, and red bell pepper into mayonnaise mixture.

Cut a ¼-inch slice from tops of tomatoes; scoop out and discard pulp, leaving a ½-inch-thick shell. Spoon about ⅔ cup chicken mixture into each tomato. **Makes** 8 servings.

SMOKY CHICKEN THIGHS:

chef recipe

Prep: 15 min., Soak: 30 min., Stand: 30 min., Grill: 40 min.

- **1 cup hickory or pecan wood chips**
- **1 tablespoon chopped fresh basil**
- **1 tablespoon olive oil**
- **1 tablespoon fresh lemon juice**
- **½ teaspoon minced garlic**
- **¼ teaspoon salt**
- **3 pounds bone-in, skin-on chicken thighs**
- **Vegetable cooking spray**

Soak hickory or pecan wood chips in water at least 30 minutes. Drain.

Whisk together basil and next 4 ingredients in a shallow dish; add chicken. Cover and let stand 30 minutes at room temperature.

Prepare a hot fire by piling charcoal in center of grill; let burn 15 to 20 minutes or until coals are gray. Place wood chips on charcoal. Spray cold cooking grate with cooking spray; place on grill.

Remove chicken from marinade, discarding marinade; arrange chicken on cooking grate, and grill, covered with grill lid, 30 to 40 minutes or until a meat thermometer inserted into thickest portion registers 180°, turning occasionally. Remove chicken; let cool completely before slicing. **Makes** 4 servings.

CHEF SARA GIBBS
LYNN'S PARADISE CAFE
LOUISVILLE, KENTUCKY

HOOVER'S PICNIC SALAD WITH HONEY-MUSTARD DRESSING

chef recipe

Prep: 15 min., Chill: 4 hrs., Cook: 8 min., Fry: 6 min.

The chicken marinates in as little as 4 hours, but it's best when started the night before. This recipe easily doubles, but you'll need to fry the chicken in 2 batches.

- **2 skinned and boned chicken breasts (about 1 pound)**
- **¼ cup thinly sliced fresh basil**
- **2 cups mayonnaise**
- **½ cup milk**
- **2 teaspoons minced garlic**
- **4 teaspoons freshly ground black pepper, divided**
- **2 teaspoons salt, divided**
- **8 thick-cut bacon slices**
- **2 cups vegetable oil**
- **2 cups all-purpose flour**
- **1 head green leaf lettuce, chopped**
- **2 cups seeded and cubed watermelon, cantaloupe, or honeydew melon**
- **Honey-Mustard Dressing**
- **Garnish: fresh basil sprigs**

Butterfly chicken breasts by making a lengthwise cut horizontally through breasts to within ½ inch of other side.

Open breasts, and sprinkle evenly with sliced basil; place between 2 sheets of heavy-duty plastic wrap. Flatten chicken to ½-inch thickness using a cast-iron skillet or mallet.

Stir together mayonnaise, milk, garlic, 2 teaspoons pepper, and 1 teaspoon salt in a shallow dish; add chicken. Cover and chill chicken at least 4 hours or up to 24 hours.

Cook bacon slices in a large cast-iron skillet until crisp; remove bacon, and drain on paper towels, reserving drippings in skillet. Crumble bacon, and set aside. Add oil to drippings in skillet, and heat to 350°, stirring and scraping to release browned bits from bottom of skillet.

Combine flour, remaining 2 teaspoons black pepper, and remaining 1 teaspoon salt in a shallow dish. Remove chicken from marinade, discarding marinade. Scrape and discard excess marinade from chicken. Dredge chicken in flour mixture. Fry 2 to 3 minutes on each side or until golden brown and chicken is done.

Divide lettuce evenly between each of 2 serving plates. Top each with 1 cup melon, and drizzle with desired amount of Honey-Mustard Dressing. Cut chicken into thin slices, and place evenly on top of melon. Sprinkle with bacon, and garnish, if desired. Serve immediately. **Makes** 2 servings.

HONEY-MUSTARD DRESSING:
chef recipe • make ahead
Prep: 10 min., Chill: 4 hrs.

Prepare this dressing up to 2 days ahead or the morning before you serve it.

    1 cup mayonnaise
    3 tablespoons yellow mustard
    3 tablespoons honey
    2 tablespoons chopped fresh basil
    2 tablespoons vegetable oil
    2 teaspoons cider vinegar
    ½ teaspoon minced garlic
    ¼ teaspoon ground red pepper

Whisk together all ingredients; cover and chill at least 4 hours. **Makes** 1¾ cups.

CHEF HOOVER ALEXANDER
HOOVER'S COOKING
AUSTIN, TEXAS

TOM'S ROASTED CHICKEN WITH WILTED SALAD GREENS

chef recipe

Prep: 30 min.; Bake: 1 hr., 20 min.

Tom prefers the floral aroma and flavor of orange blossom honey, but any kind will work just fine. (*pictured on page 189*)

    ¼ cup unsalted butter
    6 pecan halves
    2 fresh basil leaves
    2 tablespoons chopped green
      onions
    1½ teaspoons honey
    1 (4-pound) whole roasting
      chicken
    1 lemon, halved
    1 teaspoon salt, divided
    1 teaspoon pepper, divided
    4 thick-cut applewood-smoked
      bacon slices
    12 garlic cloves, peeled
    2 tomatoes, each cut into 6 slices
    Wilted Salad Greens

Process first 5 ingredients in a food processor until smooth, stopping to scrape down sides. Set aside.

Remove and discard giblets from chicken cavity; rinse with cold water, and pat dry. Squeeze juice from 1 lemon half evenly over chicken; rub well with squeezed lemon half. Repeat procedure with remaining lemon half for inside cavity. Reserve lemon halves.

Loosen and lift skin from chicken breasts with fingers; spread pecan mixture evenly underneath. Carefully replace skin. Sprinkle ½ teaspoon salt and ½ teaspoon pepper evenly on skin; rub into skin. Sprinkle remaining ½ teaspoon salt and ½ teaspoon pepper inside cavity; rub into cavity. Place bacon slices evenly over skin of chicken breasts. Insert garlic cloves and reserved lemon halves in cavity of chicken. Place chicken, breast side up, in a 10-inch cast-iron skillet.

Bake at 400° for 20 minutes. Reduce oven temperature to 375°, and bake 55 to 60 minutes or until a meat thermometer inserted into chicken thigh registers 175°. Remove from oven, and let stand at room temperature until thermometer registers 180°.

Place 3 tomato slices in center of each of 4 large serving plates; top each evenly with Wilted Salad Greens. Cut chicken into pieces, cutting breasts into slices. Divide dark meat and breast meat evenly among servings, placing on top of greens on each plate; spoon about 1 tablespoon drippings from skillet over chicken on each plate. **Makes** 4 servings.

WILTED SALAD GREENS:
chef recipe • fast fixin's
Prep: 10 min., Cook: 10 min.

    1 cup thinly sliced Vidalia or other
      sweet onion
    3 tablespoons olive oil
    ½ cup pecan halves
    2 tablespoons red wine vinegar
    2 tablespoons honey
    10 cups mixed salad greens
    Salt and cracked pepper to taste

Sauté onion slices in hot oil in a medium skillet over medium heat 6 minutes or until tender and golden brown. Add pecans, and cook 2 minutes or until pecans are lightly toasted. Stir in vinegar and honey; remove from heat. Toss together salad greens and warm onion mixture in a large salad bowl just until greens are thoroughly warmed. Sprinkle with salt and pepper to taste. **Makes** 4 servings.

CHEF TOM CONDRON
UPSTREAM RESTAURANT
CHARLOTTE, NORTH CAROLINA

Test Kitchen *Notebook*

Sara's Grilled Chicken-Cornbread Salad is perfect for leftover grilled or smoked chicken. If time is short, pick up chicken (without sauce) from your favorite barbecue joint—just make sure you start with about 2 cups of chopped meat. When you shop, be sure to remember to buy ingredients needed for the cornbread mix.

Scott Jones
FOODS EDITOR

Pasta: Toss It and Love It

Keep a stash of pantry ingredients and fresh veggies on hand for these delish dishes.

With names like Sweet-Hot Asian Noodle Bowl and Roasted Red Pepper-Caesar Tortelloni, you know these recipes are totally tuned in to flavor and deliver the fresh feel you want on a hot day in August. (Actually, several of the dishes are equally good served hot, cold, or at room temperature.)

ROASTED RED PEPPER-CAESAR TORTELLONI

Prep: 20 min., Cook: 15 min.

Here's a tasty twist on a Caesar salad—including the croutons scattered on top.

- 2 (8-ounce) packages dried ricotta-and-asparagus tortelloni *
- 1½ cups bottled creamy Caesar dressing
- ½ teaspoon grated lemon rind
- 2 teaspoons fresh lemon juice
- ½ teaspoon Dijon mustard
- ¼ teaspoon freshly ground pepper
- ½ cup jarred roasted red bell peppers, cut into thin strips
- ¾ cup Caesar-style croutons

Cook pasta according to package directions; drain and set aside.

Stir together dressing and next 4 ingredients in a small microwave-safe bowl. Microwave at MEDIUM (50% power) 1 minute and 20 seconds to 1 minute and 30 seconds or until warm, stirring at 30-second intervals.

Combine hot cooked pasta and red pepper strips in a serving bowl. Pour dressing mixture evenly over pasta mixture. Top with croutons, and serve immediately. **Makes** 4 servings.

Note: For testing purposes only, we used Barilla Ricotta and Asparagus Tortelloni, Wishbone Creamy Caesar Dressing, and Cardini's Gourmet Cut Caesar Croutons.

*Substitute dried porcini mushroom tortelloni or refrigerated three-cheese tortellini, if desired.

SOUTHWESTERN FETTUCCINE ALFREDO

Prep: 20 min., Cook: 25 min.

Stir in chopped grilled chicken to make this a heartier main dish, or serve it as a side.

- 8 ounces uncooked fettuccine
- ¼ cup butter
- 1 cup fresh corn kernels (about 2 ears)
- 1 (4-ounce) can chopped green chiles
- 1 small jalapeño pepper, seeded and minced
- ½ teaspoon minced fresh garlic
- ¾ cup grated Parmesan cheese
- ¾ cup whipping cream
- ½ teaspoon salt
- ¼ teaspoon freshly ground pepper
- 1 tablespoon chopped fresh cilantro

Cook pasta according to package directions; drain.

Melt butter in a large saucepan over medium-high heat; add corn, and sauté 6 minutes or until tender. Stir in chiles,

---

How to Cook and Sauce Pasta

Big pot: Use one with a 6- to 8-quart capacity to cook 1 pound of pasta. We call this size pot a "large Dutch oven" in our recipes.

Lotta water: Fill the pot three-quarters full with water. Cover pot, and bring water to a rolling boil (large bubbles cover water's surface) over high heat.

Salt It?: We add about 1 tablespoon salt to cook 1 pound of pasta.

Down to business: Pour in the pasta, and stir with a wooden spoon. Bring water back to a rolling boil, and maintain it for remainder of cook time. Leave the pot uncovered. Stir the pasta two or three times during cooking.

Read the directions: Check package label for cooking times. A time range is given on the directions. Cook for the shorter time if the pasta will cook more, as in a casserole. Cook for the longer time if the pasta is to be sauced and eaten immediately. Taste test a piece near the end of cooking.

You're done: Drain pasta in a colander, and shake gently to remove most of the excess liquid. Rinse the pasta only if you are making a pasta salad. The starches that cling to the cooked pasta will help the sauce stick.

Sauce it: Pair the right pasta shape with the right sauce. Generally the wider or bigger the pasta, the chunkier, heartier, or thicker the sauce can be. Long, thin shapes typically work best with oil-based sauces, pesto, and basic tomato sauces. Filled pastas are great partners with smooth, light sauces or a simple drizzle of olive oil.

jalapeño pepper, and garlic; sauté 1 minute. Stir in Parmesan cheese and next 3 ingredients. Cook over medium-low heat, stirring often, until thoroughly heated. Stir in pasta. Sprinkle evenly with cilantro, and serve immediately. **Makes** 4 servings.

SWEET-HOT ASIAN NOODLE BOWL

Prep: 35 min., Cook: 15 min.

This dish is great cold, so plan to take leftovers to work. Store your bottle of dark sesame oil in the fridge. The oil will solidify, so let it come to room temperature before measuring.

- ¾ cup rice wine vinegar
- ⅓ cup lite soy sauce
- ⅓ cup honey
- 2 tablespoons minced fresh ginger
- 2 tablespoons dark sesame oil
- 1 tablespoon Asian chili-garlic sauce
- 16 ounces uncooked spaghetti
- 1 (15-ounce) can cut baby corn, rinsed and drained
- 1 (8-ounce) can sliced water chestnuts, rinsed and drained
- 1 large red bell pepper, thinly sliced
- 1 cup (about 4 ounces) thinly sliced snow peas
- ⅓ cup finely chopped green onions
- ¼ cup chopped fresh cilantro
- 1 tablespoon toasted sesame seeds (optional)

Whisk together first 6 ingredients in a medium bowl; set aside.

Cook spaghetti according to package directions in a large Dutch oven; drain and return pasta to Dutch oven.

Pour vinegar mixture over hot cooked pasta. Add baby corn and next 5 ingredients, and toss to combine. Sprinkle with sesame seeds, if desired. Serve hot or cold. **Makes** 8 servings.

Note: For testing purposes only, we used Lee Kum Kee Chili Garlic Sauce, found in the Asian section of large supermarkets.

JACKIE NEWGENT
NEW YORK, NEW YORK

TWO TOMATO LINGUINE

Prep: 25 min., Cook: 25 min.

The short 10-minute simmer time for the tomato sauce helps keep your kitchen cool. The mixture of chopped parsley, garlic, and grated lemon rind sprinkled over the pasta is called a gremolata.

- 6 tablespoons finely chopped fresh flat-leaf parsley, divided
- 4 teaspoons grated lemon rind, divided
- 1½ teaspoons minced fresh garlic, divided
- 12 ounces uncooked linguine
- 1 tablespoon olive oil
- 2 (14.5-ounce) cans petite diced tomatoes
- ½ teaspoon freshly ground pepper
- ¼ teaspoon salt
- 1 tablespoon fresh lemon juice
- 1 yellow tomato, seeded and chopped *
- Extra-virgin olive oil (optional)

Combine 4 tablespoons parsley, 3 teaspoons lemon rind, and ½ teaspoon garlic in a small bowl; set aside.

Cook pasta according to package directions in a large Dutch oven; drain. Return pasta to Dutch oven, and set aside.

Sauté remaining 1 teaspoon garlic in hot oil in a large nonstick skillet over medium-high heat 1 minute or until lightly browned. Stir in petite diced tomatoes, pepper, and salt. Bring to a boil; reduce heat to medium, and simmer, stirring occasionally, 10 minutes or until slightly thickened. Stir in remaining 2 tablespoons parsley, remaining 1 teaspoon lemon rind, and lemon juice.

Pour tomato sauce over hot cooked pasta, and toss to combine. Top each serving evenly with chopped yellow tomato and parsley mixture. Drizzle each serving evenly with olive oil, if desired. **Makes** 4 to 6 servings.

* Substitute ¾ cup yellow grape or cherry tomatoes, halved, or 1 red tomato, seeded and chopped, if desired.

PENNE WITH GREEK-STYLE TOMATO SAUCE

Prep: 35 min., Chill: 2 hrs., Cook: 15 min.

It's okay to skip seeding the tomatoes—just be aware that the watery substance surrounding the seeds may dilute flavors (see photo).

- 6 tomatoes (about 2 pounds), seeded and chopped
- 1 (12-ounce) jar marinated artichoke hearts, drained and chopped
- 1 (3.8-ounce) can sliced ripe black olives, drained
- ⅓ cup sliced green onions
- 1 (4-ounce) package feta cheese, crumbled into large pieces and divided
- ⅓ cup olive oil
- 2 tablespoons red wine vinegar
- 2 tablespoons chopped fresh parsley
- 1 tablespoon chopped fresh basil
- 1 teaspoon sugar
- 2 teaspoons Greek seasoning
- ¼ teaspoon salt
- ¼ teaspoon freshly ground pepper
- 12 ounces uncooked penne pasta

Place first 4 ingredients and half of crumbled feta cheese in a large bowl. Whisk together olive oil and next 7 ingredients. Pour over tomato mixture; stir to coat. Cover and chill 2 hours.

Cook pasta according to package directions in a large Dutch oven; drain. Return pasta to Dutch oven. Pour tomato mixture over hot cooked pasta, and toss to combine. Sprinkle with remaining half of crumbled feta cheese. **Makes** 6 to 8 servings.

LAURIE MARTIN
VESTAVIA HILLS, ALABAMA

Here's how to seed a tomato.

Favorite Picnic Food

This great meal gets you out of the kitchen fast.

Backyard Picnic

Serves 6

Honey-Pecan Chicken Strips

Old Bay Shrimp Salad

Bacon 'n' Onion Potato Salad

bakery cookies

Enjoy summer nights with friends and a few nibbles. All of these recipes bring special homemade touches to your menu and can be made ahead. Then just pick up some assorted sweet treats from the bakery for dessert.

HONEY-PECAN CHICKEN STRIPS

family favorite

Prep: 15 min., Chill: 2 hrs., Bake: 20 min.

- ½ teaspoon salt
- ½ teaspoon dried thyme
- ½ teaspoon ground red pepper
- ½ teaspoon ground black pepper
- 2 pounds chicken breast strips
- ¾ cup Dijon mustard, divided
- ¾ cup honey, divided
- 2 garlic cloves, minced
- 2 cups finely chopped pecans
- ½ teaspoon curry powder

Combine first 4 ingredients; sprinkle evenly over chicken in a shallow dish or zip-top freezer bag. Stir together ¼ cup mustard, ¼ cup honey, and garlic; pour over chicken. Cover or seal, and chill 2 hours.

Remove chicken from marinade, discarding marinade. Dredge chicken in pecans; place on a lightly greased rack in an aluminum foil-lined broiler pan.

Bake at 375° for 20 minutes or until chicken is done.

Stir together remaining ½ cup mustard, remaining ½ cup honey, and curry powder; serve sauce with chicken strips. **Makes** 6 servings.

OLD BAY SHRIMP SALAD

make ahead

Prep: 20 min., Cook: 2 min., Chill: 2 hrs.

- 3 quarts water
- ¼ cup Old Bay seasoning
- 2 pounds unpeeled, medium-size fresh shrimp
- ½ cup finely chopped celery
- ⅓ cup finely chopped onion
- ⅓ cup light mayonnaise
- 2 tablespoons lemon juice
- ¾ teaspoon Old Bay seasoning
- ¼ teaspoon seasoned pepper
- 8 green leaf lettuce leaves (optional)
- Assorted crackers (optional)

Bring 3 quarts water and ¼ cup Old Bay seasoning to a boil in a Dutch oven; add shrimp, and cook, stirring occasionally, 2 minutes or until shrimp turn pink. Drain. Pour into a 13- x 9-inch pan to cool. Peel shrimp, and devein, if desired; chop shrimp.

Stir together celery and next 5 ingredients; stir in shrimp. Cover and chill 2 hours. Serve on lettuce leaves with assorted crackers, if desired. **Makes** 6 to 8 servings.

CARRIE MCCORMICK
BELMONT, NORTH CAROLINA

Shrimp Rolls: Place 1 lettuce leaf on top of each of 8 (8-inch) flour tortillas. Top each evenly with ½ cup Old Bay Shrimp Salad and 3 or 4 avocado slices. Roll up tortillas, and secure with thick, round wooden picks. Cut in half. **Makes** 8 servings.

Shrimp Pitas: Cut 12 mini pita pockets in half. Stuff pockets with Old Bay Shrimp Salad. **Makes** 8 servings.

BACON 'N' ONION POTATO SALAD

make ahead

Prep: 15 min., Cook: 25 min., Chill: 1 hr.

- 4 pounds red potatoes
- 1 (8-ounce) container sour cream
- 1 cup light mayonnaise
- 3 tablespoons Creole mustard
- 1 teaspoon salt
- ½ teaspoon pepper
- 1 bunch green onions, chopped (about 1 cup)
- ¼ cup chopped fresh flat-leaf parsley
- 4 bacon slices, cooked and crumbled

Place potatoes and water to cover in a large Dutch oven; bring to a boil over medium-high heat. Cook 25 minutes or until potatoes are tender. Drain and let cool. Cut into ½-inch-thick slices.

Stir together sour cream and next 4 ingredients.

Stir together potatoes, sour cream mixture, green onions, and parsley in a large bowl. Cover and chill 1 hour or until ready to serve. Stir in bacon just before serving. **Makes** 6 to 8 servings.

Tom's Roasted Chicken With
Wilted Salad Greens, page 185

189

Grilled Pork Loin With Rosemary-
Breadcrumb Crust, page 200

Avocado Soup, page 200

Mixed Greens With Toasted
Almonds and Apple Cider
Vinaigrette, page 201

Caramel-Apple Muffins,
page 210

Speedy and Scrumptious Desserts

Go ahead and indulge. These delectable treats start with a simple hot fudge sauce that's great to keep on hand.

Yes, you do have time to prepare dessert on a weeknight. Make this yummy Hot Fudge Sauce—it's ready in about 15 minutes—and store it in your refrigerator. Then your family can enjoy a treat anytime by simply reheating the sauce in the microwave for 2 minutes. Once you have this rich, fudgy concoction on hand, use it as a base for the Chocolate-Peanut Butter Pizza, Chocolate Milk Shake, or the Banana-Berry Split. Bet you'll lick the spoon clean.

HOT FUDGE SAUCE

fast fixin's • make ahead
Prep: 5 min., Cook: 10 min.

Stir some of this sauce into your coffee, or use it as a fondue-type dip with fresh fruit.

- **1 (8-ounce) package unsweetened chocolate baking squares**
- **½ cup butter or margarine**
- **2 cups sugar**
- **1 cup milk**
- **1 teaspoon vanilla extract**
- **⅛ teaspoon salt**

Melt chocolate and butter in a large heavy saucepan over low heat, stirring constantly. Add sugar, stirring until dissolved. Add milk, and cook, stirring constantly, 2 to 3 minutes or until thoroughly heated. (Do not boil.) Remove from heat. Stir in vanilla and salt. Cover and chill leftover sauce up to 2 weeks. **Makes** 3¼ cups.

To reheat: Microwave sauce in a glass bowl at HIGH 1 minute. Stir and microwave at HIGH 1 more minute or until sauce is thoroughly heated.

LOUISE MAYER
RICHMOND, VIRGINIA

CHOCOLATE MILK SHAKE

family favorite • fast fixin's
Prep: 5 min.

This rich treat makes a decadent ending to any meal.

- **4 cups vanilla ice cream**
- **1½ cups milk**
- **⅓ cup Hot Fudge Sauce (recipe at left)**

Process all ingredients in a blender until smooth. Serve immediately. **Makes** about 5 (1-cup) servings.

CHOCOLATE-PEANUT BUTTER PIZZA

family favorite
Prep: 5 min., Bake: 25 min., Cool: 15 min.

Dust your fingertips with powdered sugar to spread the cookie dough without sticking.

- **1 (18-ounce) roll refrigerated sugar cookie dough**
- **½ cup creamy peanut butter**
- **1¼ cups milk chocolate-and-peanut butter morsels**
- **¼ cup miniature candy-coated chocolate pieces**
- **¼ cup chopped salted peanuts**
- **Hot Fudge Sauce (recipe below left)**

Spread dough evenly on bottom and up sides of a lightly greased 12-inch pizza pan.
Bake at 350° on bottom rack for 20 to 25 minutes or until golden brown. Remove from oven, and cool 15 minutes.
Spread peanut butter evenly on cookie. Sprinkle with morsels, chocolate pieces, and peanuts. Cut into 16 wedges, and place on individual plates. Drizzle with Hot Fudge Sauce. **Makes** 16 servings.

BANANA-BERRY SPLIT

family favorite • fast fixin's
Prep: 5 min.

- **2 bananas, sliced in half lengthwise**
- **6 scoops vanilla ice cream**
- **½ cup Hot Fudge Sauce (recipe at left)**
- **½ pint fresh blackberries**
- **½ pint fresh raspberries**
- **½ cup chopped salted peanuts**

Place 2 banana halves in a serving dish; add 3 scoops vanilla ice cream between banana halves. Top with half each of Hot Fudge Sauce, blackberries, raspberries, and chopped salted peanuts. Repeat procedure with remaining ingredients. **Makes** 2 to 4 servings.

Smart Eating Starts With Good Taste

A back-to-the-basics approach will lead to a healthier you.

Smart Supper

Serves 6

Jerk Turkey Tenderloin
With Raspberry-Chipotle Sauce

Easy Grilled Veggies

Romaine Salad With Cashews

Whole Wheat Popovers

Super Fast Strawberry Shortcake Parfaits

Iced Green Tea

Juicy turkey tenderloin with a sweet-and-spicy raspberry sauce, crispy salad greens topped with cashews, and a refreshing parfait will leave you feeling full of energy while packing in flavor and nutrients. Let these deliciously good-for-you recipes inspire smarter food choices. As a bonus, they fit perfectly into the new *Dietary Guidelines for Americans 2005*.

JERK TURKEY TENDERLOIN WITH RASPBERRY-CHIPOTLE SAUCE

Prep: 5 min., Chill: 1 hr., Grill: 20 min., Stand: 10 min.

If you can't find turkey tenderloins, substitute a boneless turkey breast instead.

2 tablespoons jerk seasoning
1½ pounds turkey tenderloins
1 tablespoon chopped fresh rosemary
1 cup raspberry-chipotle sauce
½ cup fresh orange juice

Rub seasoning evenly over tenderloins; sprinkle with rosemary, pressing into turkey. Cover and chill 1 hour.
Stir together raspberry-chipotle sauce and orange juice in a microwave-safe glass measuring cup. Microwave at HIGH 1 minute, stirring once. Reserve ½ cup sauce in a separate container.
Grill tenderloins, covered with grill lid, over medium-high heat (350° to 400°) 10 minutes on each side or until a meat thermometer inserted into thickest portion registers 170°, basting with reserved ½ cup sauce during the last 5 minutes. Let turkey stand 10 minutes before slicing. Serve with remaining sauce. **Makes** 6 servings.

Note: For testing purposes only, we used McCormick Caribbean Jerk Seasoning and Fischer and Wieser's The Original Roasted Raspberry Chipotle Sauce. The sauce can be found on the condiment aisle of large supermarkets or online at **www.jelly.com.** We loved the fresh flavor of the sauce, but you can omit it, if desired.

Per serving: Calories 233 (6% from fat); Fat 1.6g (sat 0g, mono 0g, poly 0g); Protein 28g; Carb 28.2g; Fiber 0.1g; Chol 45mg; Iron 1.5mg; Sodium 675mg; Calc 3mg

EASY GRILLED VEGGIES

Prep: 15 min., Grill: 17 min.

Bell peppers, tomatoes, and onions are low in calories and are exceptional sources of vitamins, minerals, and fiber.

1 large green bell pepper, cut into 2-inch pieces
1 large red bell pepper, cut into 2-inch pieces
1 large red onion, quartered
6 shallots, halved
2 tablespoons olive oil
1 teaspoon salt
1 teaspoon coarsely ground pepper
Vegetable cooking spray
2 pints grape or cherry tomatoes

Combine first 4 ingredients in a large bowl. Drizzle with oil, and sprinkle with salt and pepper, tossing to coat.
Grill vegetable mixture in a metal basket or grill wok coated with cooking spray, covered with grill lid, over medium-high heat (350° to 400°) 15 minutes or until vegetables are crisp-tender, stirring occasionally. Remove vegetables from basket; add tomatoes to

basket, and grill, covered, 1 to 2 minutes or until tomato skins begin to burst. **Makes** 6 servings.

Note: If you don't have a grill wok or basket, place a 24-inch piece of heavy-duty aluminum foil on grill cooking grate. Make several 1-inch slits evenly in foil. Arrange vegetables on foil. Proceed as directed.

Per serving: Calories 110 (36% from fat); Fat 5g (sat 0.7g, mono 3.4g, poly 0.6g); Protein 2.9g; Carb 16.6g; Fiber 2.5g; Chol 0mg; Iron 1.2mg; Sodium 405mg; Calc 17mg

ROMAINE SALAD WITH CASHEWS

fast fixin's

Prep: 15 min.

This simple salad is packed with heart-healthy ingredients such as olive oil, nuts, and beans.

¼ cup olive oil
2 tablespoons lemon juice
2 teaspoons Dijon mustard
⅛ teaspoon salt
⅛ teaspoon ground cumin
⅛ teaspoon ground cardamom (optional)
1 head romaine lettuce, torn
1 small red onion, thinly sliced
½ cup salted cashews, chopped✱
⅓ cup rinsed and drained chickpeas

Whisk together first 5 ingredients and, if desired, cardamom in a large bowl until blended. Add lettuce and remaining ingredients, tossing gently to coat. Serve immediately. **Makes** 6 servings.

✱Substitute pecans for cashews, if desired.

SHERRI WEIDEMANN
FALLSTON, MARYLAND

Per serving: Calories 176 (72% from fat); Fat 14.6g (sat 2.3g, mono 6.8g, poly 1.2g); Protein 3.6g; Carb 9.1g; Fiber 2.8g; Chol 0mg; Iron 1.6mg; Sodium 162mg; Calc 35mg

WHOLE WHEAT POPOVERS

family favorite

Prep: 10 min, Bake: 33 min., Stand: 3 min.

These light and airy popovers have a crisp crust and offer the healthy benefits of whole wheat flour. They are delicious on their own, but we also liked them dipped in olive oil (moderation is the key) or topped with honey or low-fat yogurt.

½ cup all-purpose flour
½ cup whole wheat flour
¼ teaspoon salt
1 cup 2% reduced-fat milk
2 large eggs
2 egg whites
1 tablespoon vegetable oil
Vegetable cooking spray

Combine first 3 ingredients in a medium bowl. Whisk together milk and next 3 ingredients. Whisk milk mixture into flour mixture, whisking until smooth.

Place popover pans or 6 (8-ounce) custard cups heavily coated with cooking spray in a 450° oven 3 minutes or until a drop of water sizzles when dropped in them. Remove pans from oven, and place on a baking sheet, filling cups half full with batter.

Bake at 425° for 30 minutes. Turn oven off; remove pans from oven. Cut a small slit in popover tops; return to oven. Let popovers stand in closed oven 3 minutes. Serve immediately. **Makes** 6 servings.

SUZAN L. WIENER
SPRING HILL, FLORIDA

Per serving: Calories 143 (32% from fat); Fat 5.1g (sat 1.2g, mono 2.3g, poly 1.1g); Protein 7.1g; Carb 17.4g; Fiber 1.5g; Chol 74mg; Iron 1.2mg; Sodium 161mg; Calc 64mg

Good-for-You Foods

The USDA's new food pyramid is still divided into categories, but now it has easier recommended serving sizes. Foods are listed in ounces, cups, or other basic measurements. These guidelines are designed to help folks achieve healthier lifestyles by targeting our unique nutrition needs and activity levels.
Whole grains: Consume at least 3 or more 1-ounce equivalents of whole grain foods per day. Examples of one serving: 1 slice of whole wheat bread, ½ cup cooked multigrain pasta or brown rice, or 1 cup dry cereal.
Fruits and vegetables: Choose a variety of fruits and vegetables each day. Aim for 2 cups of fruit and 2½ cups of vegetables. Choose vegetables from all five subgroups (orange, dark green, starchy, legumes, and other).
Meats and beans: Daily servings depend on the individual. Choose lean meat, poultry, fish, eggs, and legumes.
Milk and milk products: Consume 3 cups of fat-free or low-fat milk, cheese, or yogurt per day. One cup of milk is equal to 1½ ounces of cheese.
Fats: Most fat sources should come from fish such as salmon or tuna; nuts such as almonds, pecans, peanuts, and pistachios; and vegetable oils such as olive, canola, and peanut. Limit intake of saturated and trans fats such as butter, margarine, sour cream, shortening, and high-fat meats.

For more information about the *Dietary Guidelines for Americans 2005* or the "MyPyramid" Food Guidance System, see the following page, and visit **www.healthierus.gov/dietaryguidelines** or **www.mypyramid.gov.**

taste of the south
White Barbecue Sauce

The color spectrum of barbecue sauce is rich and diverse—one reason why sampling different styles from all over the South is so much fun and so delicious. Ask anyone the color of their favorite sauce, and you'll probably get answers such as brick red, mahogany, or caramel. Pose the same question to a resident of North Alabama, though, and you're sure to get only one answer: white.

"It's the only sauce we know here, because it's what everyone grows up on," says world barbecue champion Chris Lilly of Big Bob Gibson Bar-B-Q in Decatur, Alabama. Bob Gibson is credited with concocting white barbecue sauce in 1925. Today, this tangy, mayonnaise-based condiment, traditionally used to dress chicken, is as synonymous with the state of Alabama as legendary football coach Paul "Bear" Bryant.

SUPER FAST STRAWBERRY SHORTCAKE PARFAITS

family favorite

Prep: 10 min., Chill: 1 hr.

- **3 cups sliced fresh strawberries** ✱
- **2 tablespoons sugar**
- **1 (3.4-ounce) package vanilla instant pudding mix**
- **2 cups fat-free milk**
- **1½ cups angel food cake cubes (½ inch)**
- **2 tablespoons sliced almonds, toasted**
- **6 whole fresh strawberries**

Stir together sliced strawberries and sugar in a small bowl; cover and chill 1 hour.

Whisk pudding mix and milk 2 minutes or until smooth.

Divide 1 cup cake cubes among 6 parfait glasses. Top each with ¼ cup chilled strawberry mixture and 3 tablespoons pudding. Repeat procedure and layers with remaining cake cubes, strawberry mixture, and pudding. Sprinkle each parfait with 1 teaspoon almond slices, and top with 1 whole strawberry. **Makes** 6 servings.

✱Substitute frozen sliced strawberries, thawed, for fresh, if desired.

Per serving: Calories 172 (3% from fat); Fat 0.5g (sat 0.1g, mono 0.1g, poly 0.2g); Protein 4.3g; Carb 38.7g; Fiber 2.2g; Chol 2mg; Iron 0.9mg; Sodium 264mg; Calc 110mg

ICED GREEN TEA

fast fixin's

Prep: 10 min., Steep: 5 min.

Earthy-tasting green tea contains disease-fighting antioxidants, making it a nutritious alternative to soda.

- **4 cups boiling water**
- **8 regular-size green tea bags**
- **2 cups cold water**
- **½ cup no-calorie sweetener**

Pour 4 cups boiling water over tea bags; cover and steep 5 minutes. Remove tea bags from water, squeezing gently. Stir in 2 cups cold water and sweetener, stirring until sweetener dissolves. Serve tea over ice. **Makes** 6 servings.

Note: For testing purposes only, we used Celestial Seasonings Green Tea and Splenda for no-calorie sweetener.

Per 1-cup serving: Calories 0 (0% from fat); Fat 0g (sat 0g, mono 0g, poly 0g); Protein 0g; Carb 0g; Fiber 0g; Chol 0mg; Iron 0mg; Sodium 0mg; Calc 0mg

WHITE BARBECUE SAUCE

fast fixin's

Prep: 5 min.

If you prefer a thicker sauce, omit the water.

- **1½ cups mayonnaise**
- **¼ cup water**
- **¼ cup white wine vinegar**
- **1 tablespoon coarsely ground pepper**
- **1 tablespoon Creole mustard**
- **1 teaspoon salt**
- **1 teaspoon sugar**
- **2 garlic cloves, minced**
- **2 teaspoons prepared horseradish**

Whisk together all ingredients until blended. Store in the refrigerator up to 1 week. **Makes** 2 cups.

what's for supper?

It's on the Grill

Center tonight's meal around big, juicy pork chops.

Dinner off the Grill

Serves 4

Saucy Pork Chops
With Orange Slices

Basil Rice Pilaf

Grilled Asparagus

Throw some chops and asparagus on the grill for an easy weeknight meal.

SAUCY PORK CHOPS WITH ORANGE SLICES

family favorite

Prep: 10 min., Chill: 30 min., Grill: 22 min., Stand: 5 min.

Sweet orange marmalade is slightly less bitter than traditional orange marmalade. Either works fine in this recipe. If your chops are thinner than ours, reduce the grilling time.

 4 (1¼-inch-thick) bone-in pork rib
    chops or loin chops *
 ½ cup orange juice
 2 teaspoons soy sauce
 ¼ teaspoon dried crushed
    red pepper
 1 teaspoon salt
 ¾ teaspoon black pepper
 ¼ cup sweet orange marmalade
 ½ cup bottled barbecue sauce
 4 (¼-inch-thick) orange slices

Pierce pork chops with a fork several times on each side. Combine pork chops and next 3 ingredients in a large shallow dish or large zip-top freezer bag. Cover or seal, and chill for 30 minutes.
Remove chops from marinade, discarding marinade. Sprinkle chops evenly with salt and black pepper.
Stir together marmalade and barbecue sauce in a small bowl. Brush 1 side of pork chops evenly with half of marmalade mixture.
Grill chops, marmalade mixture side up and covered with grill lid, over medium-high heat (350° to 400°) 10 minutes. Turn pork chops, and brush evenly with remaining half of marmalade mixture. Grill 10 minutes or until done. Remove chops from grill, and let stand 5 minutes.
Grill orange slices, covered with grill lid, over medium-high heat 1 minute on each side. Serve with pork chops.
Makes 4 servings.

Note: For testing purposes only, we used Jack Daniel's Original No. 7 Barbecue Recipe Grilling Sauce.

*Substitute 4 (1¼-inch-thick) boneless pork loin chops, if desired. Reduce grilling time to 8 minutes on each side or until done.

BARBARA DEEM
CINCINNATI, OHIO

BASIL RICE PILAF

family favorite • fast fixin's

Prep: 10 min.

Grate the lemon rind for Grilled Asparagus before squeezing the juice for the pilaf.

 2 (8.8-ounce) pouches
    microwaveable rice pilaf
 2 tablespoons chopped fresh basil
 2 teaspoons fresh lemon juice
 2 teaspoons olive oil

Microwave rice pilaf according to package directions; spoon rice into a serving bowl.
Stir in basil, lemon juice, and olive oil; serve rice pilaf immediately. **Makes** 4 to 6 servings.

Note: For testing purposes only, we used Uncle Ben's Rice Pilaf Ready Rice for microwaveable rice pilaf.

GRILLED ASPARAGUS

family favorite • fast fixin's

Prep: 10 min., Grill: 4 min.

Our grilling time is for pencil-thin asparagus; increase the time for thicker spears.

 1 pound fresh asparagus
 1 tablespoon olive oil
 1 teaspoon balsamic vinegar
 ¼ teaspoon salt
 ¼ teaspoon pepper
 1 teaspoon grated lemon rind

Snap off and discard tough ends of asparagus.
Combine olive oil, balsamic vinegar, salt, and pepper in a shallow dish or large zip-top plastic bag; add asparagus, turning to coat.
Remove asparagus from oil mixture. Grill asparagus, covered with grill lid, over medium-high heat (350° to 400°) 2 to 4 minutes or until tender, turning once. Remove asparagus, and sprinkle evenly with grated lemon rind; serve immediately. **Makes** 4 servings.

JULIA MITCHELL
LEXINGTON, KENTUCKY

from our kitchen

Fresh fish is not only healthy and delicious, it's as quick and easy to cook as a boneless chicken breast and almost as versatile. In fact, many of the same cooking methods used for chicken—broiling, grilling, pan-frying, and poaching—work equally well with fish.

A general rule is to cook fish for 7 to 10 minutes per inch of thickness (3 to 5 minutes per ½ inch). When done, fish will start to flake and, like a boneless chicken breast, will turn in color from translucent to opaque. To check for doneness, slip a small knife under the fish, and gently lift. When starting to flake, the fish will break open, revealing an opaque color throughout.

During these hot summer months, fish makes a fabulous topping for a main-dish salad. Cut your favorite fillets (we used tilapia, a mild, firm fish) into 2-inch pieces. Sprinkle fillets with salt and pepper, coat lightly with vegetable cooking spray, and sauté in a hot nonstick skillet over medium-high heat 2 to 3 minutes or until fish begins to flake and is opaque throughout. Serve over mixed salad greens with your favorite dressing.

Low-Fat Frying
Here's a great way to duplicate the light and crispy taste of fried fish without the fat. Lightly coating the fillets, rather than the skillet, with vegetable cooking spray allows the oil to evenly cover the surface of the fish. The natural sugars found in paprika caramelize with the yellow cornmeal, producing a beautiful brown color. We used catfish fillets, but any mild-flavored fish will work equally well.

Tips and Tidbits

- A thin, flexible fish spatula is the perfect utensil for turning delicate fillets. Fish spatulas are available in a wide range of prices, but you don't need to pay more than $15 for a good one. Look for them in specialty stores and cookware catalogs.
- Fish steaks are thick, cross-sectional cuts from a large fish such as salmon or tuna that sometimes contain a small section of the backbone. Fillets are boneless, lengthwise cuts from the sides of a large or small fish.
- Always thaw frozen fish in your refrigerator, never at room temperature or under running water. When properly thawed, moisture remains in the flesh, preserving both the flavor and the texture. Allow 24 hours to thaw a 1-pound package of frozen fish.
- Before paying a premium price for fresh fish at the seafood counter, ask if it's been previously frozen.

Light and Crispy Pan-fried Catfish: Sprinkle 4 (6-ounce) catfish fillets evenly with salt and pepper to taste (or use a spicy seasoning blend, such as Creole or Caribbean jerk). Stir together ⅓ cup yellow cornmeal and 1 tablespoon paprika in a shallow dish. Dredge fillets in cornmeal mixture; coat lightly with vegetable cooking spray. Cook in a hot nonstick skillet over medium heat 3 to 4 minutes on each side or until fish begins to flake and is opaque throughout. **Makes** 4 servings. Prep: 5 min., Cook: 8 min.

Fresh Catch
Rather than shopping for a specific type of fish, see what looks the freshest. Truly fresh fish smells only faintly of the sea. It should be stored on ice in the display counter and should be well drained. Fish fillets and steaks should look moist and firm, with no discoloration or dryness around the edges.

If a recipe calls for a mild-flavored fish such as cod, you can easily substitute orange roughy or snapper. Bold-flavored fish, such as swordfish and tuna, are often interchangeable.

For more information about seafood and answers to specific questions about safety issues, call the USDA hotline at 1-888-723-3366.

A Case for Frozen Fish
Today's high-tech method of freezing seafood quickly locks in both moisture and flavor, providing a top-quality selection of fish year-round. Many large supermarkets and wholesale clubs offer an excellent variety of vacuum-packed fish fillets and steaks at reasonable prices. Look for packages that are clean and tightly sealed, have no signs of thawed juices, and are free of ice crystals and freezer burn.

september

200   Casual Family Gathering *Texas winemakers celebrate the harvest with some recipes for easy entertaining*

202   4 Speedy Suppers *Weeknight menus that will change the way you think about fast food*

204   Menu With a View *Enjoy fall with a delicious picnic dinner*

205   Top-Rated Menu One Sauce, Three Meals *Build a menu around a recipe that you can serve for breakfast, lunch, or dinner*

206   What's for Supper? Try Greek for a Fresh Change *Shortcuts and make-ahead tips let you breeze through this menu*

207   Blend the Easy Way *Grab your blender for a smooth and creamy tomato soup*

207   Quick & Easy Better Mac and Cheese, Please *Treat your family to the ultimate feel-good food*

208   Healthy & Light Simple Southern Salads *Lightened classics to fit your healthy lifestyle*

210   How Sweet It Is *This super-simple caramel frosting is a perfect match for our favorite fall treats—from fresh apple muffins to chocolate sheet cake*

211   Bake Sale Treats *Great goodies that will stand out in a crowd of confections*

212   Easy Game Day Get-together *Enjoy the big game with this winning football menu*

Cooking School®

213   Quick-and-Easy Favorites *Trim the time on one-dish dinners*

214   Dinner and a Movie *Italian food springs to life when a flick and friends are the backdrop for dinner*

215   Fruit and Spice Make It Nice *Boost the flavor of your family's everyday favorites*

217   Weeknight Wonders *Great recipes for your meal-planning arsenal*

219   Girls' Night Out *Food fit for an evening of fun*

220   Southern Hospitality With an International Accent *Enjoy a global buffet*

222   Soccer Night Solutions *Score big with these meal and snack selections*

222   Tweens' Turn to Cook *Recipes for your budding gourmet*

224   From Our Kitchen *Caramel creations, BLTs, and more*

Casual Family Gathering

These Texas winemakers toast the harvest with great food and good company.

Vineyard Menu

Serves 8

Grilled Shrimp With Bacon and Jalapeños

Avocado Soup

Grilled Pork Loin With Rosemary-Breadcrumb Crust

Mixed Greens With Toasted Almonds and Apple Cider Vinaigrette

Pecan Fudge Pie With Raspberry Sauce

Susan and Ed Auler have been producing some of the state's finest wines for more than 20 years at Fall Creek Vineyards in Tow, Texas. They're also great entertainers and share some of their favorites with us.

GRILLED SHRIMP WITH BACON AND JALAPEÑOS

Prep: 20 min., Soak: 30 min., Grill: 6 min.

If you're in a hurry, try the fully cooked bacon slices. Don't use flat, thin wooden picks—use thick, round ones.

- **16 thick, round wooden picks**
- **16 unpeeled, large fresh shrimp**
- **2 jalapeño peppers**
- **2 tablespoons olive oil**
- **¼ teaspoon salt**
- **⅛ teaspoon black pepper**
- **8 thick-cut bacon slices, halved**

Soak round wooden picks in water 30 minutes.

Peel shrimp, leaving tails on; devein, if desired. Set shrimp aside.

Cut each pepper lengthwise into 8 pieces; remove seeds.

Toss together shrimp, jalapeño peppers, olive oil, salt, and black pepper in a large bowl. Set aside.

Microwave bacon slices at HIGH 30 seconds.

Wrap 1 bacon slice half around 1 shrimp and 1 piece of jalapeño pepper. Secure with a wooden pick. Repeat procedure with remaining bacon slices, shrimp, and jalapeño pepper pieces.

Grill, without grill lid, over medium-high heat (350° to 400°) for 4 to 6 minutes or until shrimp turn pink, turning once. **Makes** 8 servings.

AVOCADO SOUP

make ahead

Prep: 15 min., Chill: 1 hr. *(pictured on page 191)*

- **4 avocados, peeled and quartered**
- **1 teaspoon salt**
- **1 teaspoon green hot sauce**
- **1 (14.5-ounce) can chicken broth**
- **1½ cups half-and-half**
- **1 (8-ounce) container sour cream**
- **¼ cup Johannisberg Riesling ✱**
- **3 tablespoons lime juice**
- **Garnish: thinly sliced green onions**

Process first 4 ingredients in a blender or food processor until smooth, stopping to scrape down sides.

Pour mixture into a large bowl; stir in half-and-half and next 3 ingredients until smooth. Place plastic wrap directly over soup; chill 1 hour. Garnish before serving, if desired. **Makes** 8 cups.

✱Substitute off-dry white wines such as Gewürztraminer or Chenin Blanc, if desired.

GRILLED PORK LOIN WITH ROSEMARY-BREADCRUMB CRUST

Prep: 30 min., Grill: 56 min., Stand: 10 min. *(pictured on pages 190-191)*

- **2 (3-pound) pork loins**
- **2 teaspoons salt**
- **1 teaspoon pepper**
- **¼ cup coarse-grained Dijon mustard**
- **½ cup olive oil**
- **2 cups soft breadcrumbs**
- **5 tablespoons finely chopped fresh rosemary**
- **¼ cup chopped garlic**
- **Garnishes: sliced fresh pears, fresh rosemary sprigs**

Sprinkle pork loins evenly with salt and pepper.

Stir together mustard and ¼ cup oil; spread evenly over pork. Stir together remaining oil and next 3 ingredients.

Light 1 side of grill, heating to medium-high heat (350° to 400°); leave other side unlit. Place pork over lit side, and grill, covered with grill lid, 8 minutes on each side or until browned. Remove pork from grill. Press breadcrumb mixture over the top of each pork loin. **Grill** over unlit side of grill, covered with grill lid, 35 to 40 minutes or until a meat thermometer inserted in thickest portion registers 155°. Remove from grill; cover and let stand 10 minutes or until thermometer registers 160°. Garnish, if desired. **Makes** 10 to 12 servings.

MIXED GREENS WITH TOASTED ALMONDS AND APPLE CIDER VINAIGRETTE

make ahead

Prep: 10 min., Chill: 2 hrs. *(pictured on page 191)*

> 1 large cucumber, thinly sliced
> ⅓ cup Apple Cider Vinaigrette
> 8 cups mixed salad greens
> 2 plum tomatoes, finely chopped
> 1 cup fresh blueberries
> ⅓ cup sliced almonds, toasted
> ½ cup (2 ounces) crumbled goat cheese

Combine cucumber and Apple Cider Vinaigrette; cover and chill 2 hours, stirring once. Remove and reserve cucumbers using a slotted spoon; reserve Apple Cider Vinaigrette.
Toss together salad greens, tomatoes, and blueberries. Sprinkle salad evenly with almonds and goat cheese before serving. Top with reserved marinated cucumber slices. Serve with reserved Apple Cider Vinaigrette. **Makes** 8 servings.

APPLE CIDER VINAIGRETTE:
fast fixin's
Prep: 10 min.

> ½ cup extra-virgin olive oil
> ¼ cup cider vinegar
> 4 teaspoons granulated sugar
> 1 tablespoon brown sugar
> 1 tablespoon balsamic vinegar
> 1 teaspoon Worcestershire sauce
> ½ teaspoon salt

Whisk together all ingredients until well combined. **Makes** 1 cup.

PECAN FUDGE PIE WITH RASPBERRY SAUCE

Prep: 20 min., Bake: 25 min.

The rich taste of chocolate mixed with pecans and drizzled with a flavorful raspberry sauce makes for a melt-in-your mouth dessert.

> ½ cup butter
> 2 (1-ounce) unsweetened chocolate squares
> 2 large eggs
> 1 cup granulated sugar
> ½ cup all-purpose flour
> 1 teaspoon vanilla extract
> ¼ teaspoon salt
> ⅔ cup chopped pecans, toasted
> Raspberry Sauce
> Toppings: powdered sugar, fresh raspberries

Melt butter and unsweetened chocolate squares in a small saucepan over low heat, stirring constantly; remove from heat.
Beat eggs at medium speed with an electric mixer 2 minutes. Gradually add 1 cup granulated sugar, beating until blended. Gradually add chocolate mixture, flour, vanilla, and salt, beating until blended. Stir in ⅔ cup chopped pecans.
Pour mixture into a lightly greased 9-inch pieplate.
Bake at 350° for 20 to 25 minutes or until center is firm. Serve pie warm with Raspberry Sauce and desired toppings. **Makes** 8 servings.

RASPBERRY SAUCE:
fast fixin's
Prep: 5 min., Cook: 13 min.

> 3 tablespoons pure maple syrup
> 2 tablespoons sugar
> 1 (16-ounce) package frozen raspberries (do not thaw)

Cook syrup and sugar in a saucepan over medium heat, stirring constantly, until sugar dissolves. Add raspberries, and cook, stirring constantly, 10 minutes or until thickened. Pour mixture through a fine wire-mesh strainer; press with back of a spoon against sides of strainer to squeeze out sauce, discarding solids. **Makes** 1 cup.

4 Speedy Suppers

These meals are so quick, you'll have them on the table before you can say "six o'clock."

FOUR EASY MEALS

Italian Tonight

(Serves 4)

One-Pot Pasta

Italian Tossed Salad

Basil-Garlic Bread

Weeknight Roast

(Serves 4)

Ginger-Glazed Pork Tenderloin

Sweet Carrots and Rice

Grill It

(Serves 4)

Raspberry-Barbecue Chicken

Sautéed Squash and Zucchini

Quick Parmesan Couscous

Southwest Supper

(page 204)

(Serves 6)

Tex-Mex Salisbury Steak

Cheesy Mashed Potatoes

Zesty Green Beans

Don't surrender to expensive take-out food. Consider these fresh and speedy menu ideas instead. We offer four effortless entrées—complete with easy side dishes—that will change the way you think about fast food. Most can be prepared in 20 minutes or less, allowing you to walk away from the kitchen as they bake and simmer. With these family-approved favorites, your weeknight meals will practically prepare themselves.

ONE-POT PASTA

family favorite

Prep: 10 min., Cook: 28 min.

This one-dish meal uses the convenience of your favorite prepared spaghetti sauce and refrigerated cheese-stuffed ravioli.

- 1 pound lean ground beef
- 1 small onion, diced
- 1 (8-ounce) package sliced fresh mushrooms
- 1 teaspoon vegetable oil
- 2 garlic cloves, minced
- 2 (26-ounce) jars tomato-and-basil pasta sauce
- 1 cup water
- 1 tablespoon dried Italian seasoning
- ½ teaspoon salt
- ¼ teaspoon pepper
- 1 (20-ounce) package refrigerated four-cheese ravioli
- 1 cup (4 ounces) shredded mozzarella cheese

Cook ground beef in a Dutch oven over medium-high heat, stirring until it crumbles and is no longer pink; drain. Wipe Dutch oven clean.

Sauté onion and mushrooms in hot oil over medium-high heat 8 minutes or until tender. Add garlic, and sauté 1 minute. Stir in beef, pasta sauce, 1 cup water, and next 3 ingredients.

Bring sauce to a boil; add ravioli. Reduce heat to medium-low, cover, and simmer, stirring occasionally, 8 to 10 minutes or until pasta is done. Stir in cheese. Serve immediately. **Makes** 4 servings.

Note: For testing purposes only, we used Classico Tomato & Basil pasta sauce and Buitoni Family Size Four Cheese Ravioli.

EDITH LYLE LESSLEY
HOMEWOOD, ALABAMA

ITALIAN TOSSED SALAD

fast fixin's

Prep: 10 min.

Toss together 1 (5-ounce) bag mixed salad greens, ½ cup (2 ounces) shredded mozzarella cheese, 1 (2.25-ounce) can drained sliced ripe black olives, 8 quartered baby carrots, and 1 sliced green onion. Drizzle with bottled balsamic vinaigrette or your favorite Italian salad dressing. **Makes** 4 servings.

MELISSA QUIÑONES
EUSTIS, FLORIDA

BASIL-GARLIC BREAD

fast fixin's

Prep: 10 min., Bake: 10 min.

Stir together ¼ cup melted butter, 1 teaspoon dried basil, and ¼ teaspoon garlic powder. Cut a 6-ounce Italian bread loaf in half horizontally; brush cut sides evenly with butter mixture. Wrap loaf in aluminum foil, and bake at 350° for 10 minutes or until thoroughly heated. **Makes** 4 servings.

MELODY LEE
DOTHAN, ALABAMA

GINGER-GLAZED PORK TENDERLOIN

Prep: 10 min., Bake: 25 min., Stand: 10 min.

- 1 (2-pound) package pork tenderloins
- ½ teaspoon salt
- ⅓ cup apricot preserves
- 3 garlic cloves, minced
- 1 tablespoon water
- 1 tablespoon soy sauce
- 1 tablespoon grated fresh ginger or 1 teaspoon ground ginger
- Garnish: green onion strips

Place pork tenderloins on a lightly greased rack in a foil-lined roasting pan. Sprinkle evenly with salt.
Combine preserves and next 4 ingredients. Spread evenly over pork.
Bake at 425° for 25 minutes or until a meat thermometer inserted in thickest portion registers 155°. Remove from oven; cover and let stand 10 minutes or until thermometer registers 160°. Garnish, if desired. **Makes** 6 servings.

VELITA WADDELL
WAXAHACHIE, TEXAS

Ginger-Glazed Pork Chops: Substitute 6 (½-inch-thick) bone-in pork chops (about 2½ pounds). Broil 6 inches from heat for 5 minutes. Reduce oven temperature to 425°. Bake 8 to 10 minutes or until a meat thermometer registers 155°. Remove from oven; cover and let stand 10 minutes or until thermometer registers 160°. **Makes** 6 servings. Prep: 8 min., Broil: 5 min., Bake: 10 min., Stand: 10 min.

SWEET CARROTS AND RICE

Prep: 5 min., Cook: 30 min.

Combine 1½ pounds baby carrots and 1 (14-ounce) can chicken broth in a skillet over medium-high heat. Bring to a boil; cook, stirring often, 12 to 15 minutes or until carrots are crisp-tender and broth is reduced to about ¼ cup. Stir in ⅓ cup apricot preserves, 2 tablespoons soy sauce, 2 teaspoons grated fresh ginger, and pepper to taste; cook, stirring constantly, 10 minutes or until mixture thickens and carrots are glazed. Serve over boil-in-bag or microwave-ready rice. **Makes** 4 servings.

RASPBERRY-BARBECUE CHICKEN

family favorite • fast fixin's

Prep: 5 min., Grill: 14 min.

Substitute any of our quick-to-make sauce variations at right for a spicy twist.

- 4 skinned and boned chicken breasts
- 1 teaspoon Creole seasoning
- Vegetable cooking spray
- Raspberry-Barbecue Sauce
- Garnish: fresh flat-leaf parsley sprigs

Sprinkle chicken evenly with Creole seasoning.
Spray cold cooking grate of a grill with cooking spray. Place cooking grate on grill; grill chicken, covered with grill lid, over medium-high heat (350° to 400°) 7 minutes on each side or until done, brushing Raspberry-Barbecue Sauce evenly on 1 side of chicken during the last 2 minutes of grilling. Serve with remaining sauce. Garnish, if desired. **Makes** 4 servings.

Note: For testing purposes only, we used Tony Chachere's Original Creole Seasoning.

RASPBERRY-BARBECUE SAUCE:

fast fixin's

Prep: 5 min., Cook: 7 min.

- 1 (10-ounce) jar seedless raspberry preserves
- ⅓ cup bottled barbecue sauce
- 2 tablespoons raspberry vinegar
- 2 tablespoons Dijon mustard
- 1½ teaspoons hot sauce

Bring first 4 ingredients to a boil in a small saucepan. Reduce heat to medium, and cook 2 minutes or until slightly thickened. Stir in hot sauce. **Makes** 1 cup.

Note: For testing purposes only, we used KC Masterpiece Original Barbecue Sauce.

Honey Mustard: Stir together 1 cup mayonnaise, 3 tablespoons Creole mustard, and 2 tablespoons honey. **Makes** about 1¼ cups. Prep: 5 min.

Simple Creole Sauce: Stir together 1½ cups mayonnaise, 3 tablespoons Creole mustard, and 1 finely chopped green onion. **Makes** about 1⅔ cups. Prep: 5 min.

Horseradish Sauce: Stir together 1 cup mayonnaise, 1 tablespoon cream-style horseradish, and 1 tablespoon Creole mustard. **Makes** about 1 cup. Prep: 5 min.

SAUTÉED SQUASH AND ZUCCHINI

fast fixin's

Prep: 10 min., Cook: 6 min.

Cut 2 medium-size yellow squash and 2 medium zucchini into ¼-inch-thick slices, and chop 1 small onion. Sauté vegetables in 1 tablespoon hot oil in a large skillet over medium-high heat 5 minutes. Add 1 minced garlic clove, and sauté 1 minute. Sprinkle mixture with salt and pepper to taste. **Makes** 4 servings.

QUICK PARMESAN COUSCOUS

fast fixin's

Prep: 5 min., Cook: 5 min., Stand: 5 min.

Bring 2 cups of chicken broth and 1 tablespoon butter to a boil. Stir in 1 (10-ounce) package plain, uncooked couscous; cover and remove from heat. Let stand 5 minutes. Stir in ⅓ cup grated Parmesan cheese, 1 tablespoon fresh lemon juice, 1 tablespoon olive oil, ¼ teaspoon salt, and ⅛ teaspoon freshly ground pepper. Fluff with a fork, and serve immediately. **Makes** 4 servings.

Note: For testing purposes only, we used DiGiorno Grated Parmesan Cheese.

Tex-Mex Salisbury Steak

family favorite

Prep: 20 min., Cook: 25 min.

> 1 pound ground round
> ½ pound hot or mild ground pork sausage
> 1 small onion, chopped
> 1 large egg
> ½ cup fine, dry breadcrumbs
> ¼ cup mild salsa
> 2 tablespoons taco seasoning mix
> 2 tablespoons chopped fresh cilantro, divided
> 1 (2.64-ounce) package country-style gravy mix
> 1 (14½-ounce) can reduced-sodium beef broth
> 1 (10-ounce) can diced tomatoes with green chiles, undrained
> Garnish: fresh cilantro sprigs

Combine first 7 ingredients and 1 tablespoon chopped cilantro. Shape mixture into 6 (⅓-inch-thick) patties. **Heat** a lightly greased large nonstick skillet over medium-high heat. Add patties; reduce heat to low, cover, and cook 8 to 10 minutes per side or until center is no longer pink. Remove from skillet. Wipe pan clean.
Whisk together gravy mix, broth, tomatoes with chiles, and remaining 1 tablespoon chopped cilantro. Cook over medium heat 1 minute or until thickened. Return patties to skillet, and cook until thoroughly heated. Garnish, if desired. **Makes** 6 servings.

PAM PACK
SEWICKLEY, PENNSYLVANIA

Cheesy Mashed Potatoes

family favorite • fast fixin's

Prep: 5 min., Cook: 13 min.

Cook 1 (22-ounce) package frozen mashed potatoes according to package directions. Stir in 1 cup (4 ounces) shredded Mexican four-cheese blend, 3 tablespoons butter, ½ teaspoon salt, and ¼ teaspoon pepper until smooth. Serve immediately. **Makes** 6 servings.

Zesty Green Beans

family favorite • fast fixin's

Prep: 10 min., Cook: 10 min.

Cook 1 pound fresh green beans, trimmed, in boiling water to cover 4 minutes or until crisp-tender; drain. Plunge beans into ice water to stop the cooking process; drain. Melt 1 tablespoon butter in a large skillet over medium-high heat. Add 1 minced garlic clove; sauté 1 minute. Stir in beans, ¼ teaspoon salt, and ¼ teaspoon pepper. Cook 4 minutes or until hot. Drizzle with 1 tablespoon fresh lemon juice just before serving. **Makes** 6 servings.

A Little Something Extra

Use the remaining ½ pound of pork sausage and leftover taco seasoning mix from the Tex-Mex Salisbury Steak recipe to make these delicious bonus recipes.

Breakfast Burritos

fast fixin's

Prep: 5 min., Cook: 13 min., Stand: 5 min.

Brown ½ pound hot or mild ground pork sausage and 1 tablespoon taco seasoning mix in a nonstick skillet. Add 6 lightly beaten large eggs, and cook, without stirring, until eggs begin to set on bottom. Draw a spatula across bottom of pan to form large curds. Continue to cook until eggs are thickened but still moist, about 5 minutes. Sprinkle evenly with ½ cup shredded Mexican four-cheese blend. Turn off heat, and cover. Let stand 5 minutes or until cheese melts. Spoon mixture evenly into 4 burrito-size flour tortillas, roll up tightly, and serve with salsa. **Makes** 4 servings.

Tex-Mex Popcorn

Toss 2 tablespoons taco seasoning mix with 2 (1.5-ounce) bags popped microwave popcorn.

Menu With a View

Picnic Supper

Serves 4

Giant Ham-and-Pepper Salad Sandwich

Mixed Fruit Pilaf

Praline Bars

Cranberry Lemonade

Nothing beats fall's fabulous weather. Rich blue skies, shimmery light, and trees flush with warm seasonal hues tempt us to get outside for inspiring adventures. What better way to take advantage of these glorious days than with a picnic? Grab a map and pack a basket with these tasty goodies.

Giant Ham-and-Pepper Salad Sandwich

fast fixin's

Prep: 15 min.

> 1 (16-ounce) round Italian bread loaf
> 3 tablespoons honey mustard
> 2 green onions, chopped
> 1 (3-ounce) package cream cheese, softened
> 1 tablespoon mayonnaise
> 1 pound deli ham, thinly sliced
> ¼ cup pickled sliced banana peppers, drained
> 1 (6-ounce) package Swiss cheese slices
> 4 (1-ounce) American cheese slices
> Tomato slices
> Lettuce leaves

Cut off top one-third of bread loaf, and spread cut side of top with honey mustard; set aside.

Scoop out soft center of remaining bread, leaving a ¼-inch-thick shell. (Reserve soft center of loaf for other uses, if desired.)

Stir together green onions, cream cheese, and mayonnaise; spread in bottom of bread shell. Layer with ham, peppers, and cheeses; cover with bread top, honey mustard side down. Wrap in aluminum foil or a zip-top plastic bag. Place tomato and lettuce in zip-top plastic bags. Surround with ice packs for transport to picnic.

Unwrap whole sandwich, add lettuce and tomato slices, and cut into 4 wedges. Serve on heavy paper towels or parchment paper. **Makes** 4 servings.

ZACK NICHOLS
BIRMINGHAM, ALABAMA

MIXED FRUIT PILAF

make ahead

Prep: 15 min., Cook: 30 min., Stand: 5 min.

- ½ cup chopped celery
- ¼ cup chopped onion
- 1 tablespoon olive oil
- 1 garlic clove, minced
- ½ cup dried mixed fruit, chopped
- 1 cup apple juice
- 1 cup chicken broth
- 1 teaspoon cumin seeds
- 1 teaspoon curry powder
- ¼ teaspoon ground allspice
- 1 teaspoon salt
- 1 cup uncooked bulgur wheat

Sauté celery and onion in hot oil in a 3-quart saucepan over medium-high heat 5 minutes or until onion is tender. Add garlic, and sauté 1 more minute.

Stir in dried fruit and next 6 ingredients. Bring to a boil; stir in bulgur wheat. Cover; reduce heat, and simmer, stirring occasionally, 15 minutes. Remove from heat, and let stand 5 minutes. **Makes** 6 servings.

Note: Pack Mixed Fruit Pilaf in a zip-top plastic bag or waterproof container, and chill to transport to the picnic. It can safely sit at room temperature 2 hours.

ADELYNE SMITH
DUNNVILLE, KENTUCKY

PRALINE BARS

Prep: 20 min., Cook: 5 min., Bake: 10 min.

A graham cracker sheet is a whole perforated but unbroken cracker stacked and wrapped.

- 15 graham cracker sheets
- ¾ cup chopped pecans
- 1¾ cups firmly packed brown sugar
- 1 cup butter or margarine
- ½ cup semisweet chocolate morsels
- ½ cup white chocolate morsels

Separate each graham cracker sheet into 4 crackers; place in a lightly greased 15- x 10-inch jelly-roll pan. Sprinkle chopped pecans over graham crackers.

Bring brown sugar and butter to a boil in a saucepan over medium-high heat. Boil 2 minutes. Pour brown sugar mixture over graham crackers in pan.

Bake at 350° for 10 minutes. Quickly remove graham crackers to wax paper, using a spatula, and let cool completely.

Microwave semisweet chocolate morsels in a microwave-safe bowl at HIGH 30 seconds. Stir and microwave at HIGH 30 more seconds or until smooth. Drizzle chocolate evenly over cooled bars. Repeat procedure with white chocolate morsels. **Makes** 60 bars.

BARBARA BRANDON
KILBOURNE, LOUISIANA

CRANBERRY LEMONADE

fast fixin's

Prep: 10 min.

- 5 cups water, divided
- ½ cup sugar
- 1 (6-ounce) can frozen lemonade concentrate, thawed
- 3 cups cranberry juice

Stir together 2 cups water and sugar in a small saucepan over medium heat, stirring until sugar dissolves.

Stir together sugar mixture, thawed lemonade concentrate, cranberry juice, and remaining 3 cups water. Chill until ready to serve. **Makes** 8 cups.

top-rated menu
One Sauce, Three Meals

Paulette Thomas of Edisto Island, South Carolina, sent us her signature recipe for Cajun Shrimp-and-Crab Sauce, and included three serving suggestions—for each meal of the day. We adapted her recipe to keep all the incredible flavor with just a fraction of the fat.

Cajun Supper

Serves 6

Cajun Shrimp-and-Crab Sauce with grits, pasta, or rice

Sautéed Green Beans

Lemon-Blueberry Layered Dessert

Cook's Notes

Try Cajun Shrimp-and-Crab Sauce anytime of day.

- **For breakfast,** spoon the mixture over toast points or hot cooked grits with a side of fresh fruit.
- **At lunch,** ladle the rich sauce into freshly baked pastry shells, and serve with a tossed green salad.
- **For an evening meal,** present the sauce over hot cooked pasta, grits, or rice. Follow package directions for the desired number of servings. Add a green vegetable, and you're set.

Cajun Shrimp-and-Crab Sauce

Prep: 20 min., Cook: 25 min.

- 1 pound unpeeled, medium-size fresh shrimp
- ½ (16-ounce) package andouille sausage
- 1 medium onion, chopped
- 1 green bell pepper, chopped
- 1 tablespoon olive oil
- 2 garlic cloves, minced
- 1 tablespoon all-purpose flour
- 1¾ cups chicken broth
- ½ pound fresh lump crabmeat, drained and picked
- ½ teaspoon Old Bay seasoning
- ¼ teaspoon celery seed
- ¼ teaspoon black pepper
- ⅛ teaspoon salt
- Hot cooked grits

Peel shrimp, and devein, if desired.
Cut sausage into ¼-inch-thick slices.
Cook sausage in a large skillet over medium-high heat 5 minutes or until golden brown. Remove sausage, and drain on paper towels, reserving drippings in pan. Set sausage aside.
Sauté onion and bell pepper in drippings and hot oil 8 minutes or until tender. Add garlic, and sauté 1 minute.
Whisk in flour, and cook, whisking constantly, 1 minute or until flour is browned.
Whisk in chicken broth. Bring to a boil; reduce heat, and simmer 2 minutes. Stir in shrimp, and cook, stirring occasionally, 4 minutes or just until shrimp turn pink. Stir in sausage, crabmeat, and next 4 ingredients; cook, stirring occasionally, until thoroughly heated. Serve immediately over hot cooked grits.
Makes 6 servings.

PAULETTE THOMAS
EDISTO ISLAND, SOUTH CAROLINA

Sautéed Green Beans

Prep: 10 min., Cook: 20 min.

- 2 pounds fresh green beans, trimmed
- 1 red bell pepper, sliced
- 2 tablespoons olive oil
- 2 garlic cloves, minced
- 1 teaspoon Creole seasoning

Cook green beans in boiling salted water to cover 8 to 10 minutes or until crisp-tender. Drain and plunge into ice water to stop the cooking process; drain.
Sauté sliced red bell pepper in 2 tablespoons hot oil in a large skillet over medium heat 5 minutes or until crisp-tender; add minced garlic, and sauté 2 more minutes. Add green beans; sprinkle with 1 teaspoon Creole seasoning, and cook, stirring constantly, until vegetable mixture is thoroughly heated.
Makes 6 servings.

Note: For testing purposes only, we used Tony Chachere's Creole Seasoning.

Lemon-Blueberry Layered Dessert

make ahead

Prep: 15 min., Chill: 4 hrs.

- 15 lemon cookies, coarsely crushed (about 2 cups)
- 1 (21-ounce) can blueberry pie filling
- 1 (8-ounce) container frozen whipped topping, thawed
- 1 (14-ounce) can sweetened condensed milk
- 1 (6-ounce) can frozen lemonade concentrate, thawed

Sprinkle 1 tablespoon crushed cookies into each of 8 (8-ounce) parfait glasses. Spoon 1½ tablespoons pie filling over cookies in each glass.
Spoon whipped topping into a bowl; fold in condensed milk and lemonade concentrate. Spoon 2 tablespoons whipped topping mixture over pie filling in each glass. Repeat layers once. Top evenly with remaining crushed cookies. Cover and chill 4 hours.
Makes 8 servings.

Note: For testing purposes only, we used Pepperidge Farm Lemon-Nut Homestyle Cookies.

what's for supper?
Try Greek for a Fresh Change

To jump-start this meal, we used a deli-prepared dip, dried and fresh herbs, and bottled salad dressing. The Tomato-Feta Salad can be made a day ahead; add 1 extra chopped tomato just before serving. Wrap any leftover Easy Greek Flank Steak tightly in foil, and refrigerate up to 2 days.

Easy Greek Supper

Serves 4 to 6

Quick Hummus Dip
Easy Greek Flank Steak
Sour Cream-Cucumber Sauce
Tomato-Feta Salad

Quick Hummus Dip

fast fixin's • make ahead

Prep: 5 min.

We freshened plain hummus dip from the deli by adding simple, on-hand ingredients. Serve as a dip with pieces of pita bread, red bell peppers, or pepperoncini salad peppers. You can also use as a spread for a pita sandwich.

- 2 (8-ounce) containers prepared hummus
- 4 teaspoons fresh lemon juice
- ½ teaspoon dried oregano
- Extra-virgin olive oil (optional)

Stir together first 3 ingredients. Cover and chill until ready to serve or up to 1 week. Drizzle with olive oil just before serving, if desired. **Makes** 2 cups.

KRIS WATSON
BIRMINGHAM, ALABAMA

EASY GREEK FLANK STEAK

Prep: 10 min., Grill: 20 min., Stand: 10 min.

1¾ pounds flank steak
2 tablespoons olive oil
1 tablespoon Greek seasoning
Sour Cream-Cucumber Sauce
  (optional)
Garnish: fresh flat-leaf parsley sprigs

Rub steak evenly with olive oil; sprinkle evenly with seasoning.
Grill steak, covered with grill lid, over medium-high heat (350° to 400°) 10 minutes on each side or to desired degree of doneness. Let stand 10 minutes; cut diagonally across the grain into thin strips. Serve with Sour Cream-Cucumber Sauce, if desired. Garnish, if desired. **Makes** 4 to 6 servings.

Note: For testing purposes only, we used Cavender's All Purpose Greek Seasoning.

SOUR CREAM-CUCUMBER SAUCE

make ahead

Prep: 10 min., Chill: 30 min.

1 cucumber, peeled and seeded
1 (8-ounce) container light sour cream
1 garlic clove, minced
½ teaspoon dried dill
½ teaspoon salt

Grate cucumber, and place in a colander, pressing to drain excess liquid. Place between paper towels, and pat dry.
Stir together cucumber and remaining ingredients. Cover and chill at least 30 minutes or up to 2 days. **Makes** 1½ cups.

TOMATO-FETA SALAD

make ahead

Prep: 15 min., Chill: 1 hr.

1 (4-ounce) package feta cheese
¼ cup Greek dressing
2 tablespoons chopped fresh parsley
6 plum tomatoes, chopped
½ cup sliced oil-cured ripe black olives
¼ cup chopped red onion

Break feta cheese into small pieces. Do not crumble.
Stir together dressing and parsley. Stir in feta and remaining ingredients. Cover and chill at least 1 hour or up to 2 days. Serve with a slotted spoon. **Makes** 4 to 6 servings.

Note: For testing purposes only, we used Ken's Steak House Greek dressing.

DOLORES VACCARO
PUEBLO, COLORADO

Tomato-Feta Lettuce Salad: Tear 1 small head iceberg lettuce and 1 small head romaine lettuce into bite-size pieces; toss together. Arrange lettuces evenly on 4 individual plates, and top evenly with chilled tomato mixture (do not use slotted spoon). Serve immediately.

Blend the Easy Way

Creamy soups, pureed vegetables, and fruit smoothies are easier to make than ever with a handheld, or immersion, blender. Place the straight, slender appliance—also called a stick blender—right into the pot or pitcher, and puree until the food mixture is smooth. The blade end can be detached and placed in the dishwasher.

CREAMY TOMATO SOUP WITH CRISPY CROUTONS

Prep: 10 min., Cook: 30 min., Cool: 10 min.

1 small onion, diced
2 tablespoons olive oil
3 garlic cloves, minced
2 (28-ounce) cans chopped tomatoes
1 (14-ounce) can chicken broth
1 (5-ounce) package Brie without
  rind, cut into pieces ＊
1 teaspoon salt
½ teaspoon freshly ground pepper
Chopped fresh basil (optional)
Crispy Croutons

Sauté onion in hot oil in a Dutch oven over medium-low heat 8 minutes or until tender; add garlic, and sauté 1 minute. Increase heat to medium-high; stir in tomatoes and chicken broth, and bring mixture to a boil. Simmer, stirring frequently, 10 minutes. Remove pan from heat. Allow mixture to cool 10 minutes; stir in Brie until melted.
Process soup with immersion blender until smooth.
Cook soup over medium-low heat until thoroughly heated. Stir in salt, pepper, and, if desired, basil. Serve with Crispy Croutons. **Makes** 6 to 8 servings.

Note: For testing purposes only, we used Alouette Crème de Brie.

＊Substitute 2 (3-ounce) packages cream cheese for Brie, if desired.

SUSAN MARTIN
BIRMINGHAM, ALABAMA

Crispy Croutons: Thinly slice 1 French bread baguette. Brush cut sides with olive oil; place on a baking sheet. Sprinkle with ¼ teaspoon salt and ¼ teaspoon pepper. Bake at 350° for 8 to 10 minutes or until golden. Prep: 5 min., Bake: 10 min.

quick & easy
Better Mac and Cheese, Please

Macaroni and cheese makes it to the top of the list of comfort foods. Most of the mac and cheese served these days comes from a boxed mix or the freezer, but it's easy to make it from scratch. Ten minutes is all you need to stir up the sauce. Once you've reached this point, the variations are endless. Mix in any type of shredded cheese, cooked pasta, salt, and pepper, and you're set. We recommend shredding block cheese with a grater for the creamiest results.

CREAMY MAC AND CHEESE

family favorite • fast fixin's

Prep: 10 min., Cook: 8 min.

- 1 (8-ounce) package elbow macaroni
- 1 (10-ounce) container refrigerated Alfredo sauce
- ½ cup milk
- ½ teaspoon freshly ground black pepper
- ¼ teaspoon salt
- ¼ teaspoon ground red pepper
- 1 (8-ounce) block Cheddar cheese, shredded

Prepare pasta according to package directions. Drain and keep warm.
Bring Alfredo sauce and next 4 ingredients to a boil in a large saucepan. Remove from heat. Stir in cheese until melted. Stir in cooked pasta. Serve immediately. **Makes** 2 to 3 main-dish or 4 to 6 side-dish servings.

TACO DINNER MAC AND CHEESE

family favorite

Prep: 15 min., Cook: 25 min.

- 1 (8-ounce) package elbow macaroni
- 1 pound ground beef
- 1 (1.25-ounce) envelope reduced-sodium taco seasoning mix
- ¾ cup water
- 2 tablespoons butter
- 2 tablespoons all-purpose flour
- 2 cups milk
- 1 (8-ounce) block sharp Cheddar cheese, shredded
- Toppings: chopped tomato, avocado, green onions, sour cream, salsa

Prepare pasta according to package directions. Drain and keep warm.
Brown ground beef in a nonstick skillet over medium-high heat, stirring until it crumbles and is no longer pink. Drain.
Return beef to skillet; stir in taco seasoning mix and ¾ cup water. Bring to a boil, and cook, stirring occasionally, 7 minutes or until most of the liquid

evaporates. Remove beef mixture from heat.
Melt butter in a large saucepan or Dutch oven over medium-low heat; whisk in flour until smooth. Cook, whisking constantly, 2 minutes. Gradually whisk in milk, and cook, whisking constantly, 5 minutes or until thickened. Remove from heat.
Stir in 1½ cups cheese, stirring until melted. Stir in cooked pasta and beef mixture. Sprinkle with remaining ½ cup cheese. Serve immediately with desired toppings. **Makes** 4 servings.

STEWART GORDON
CHARLESTON, SOUTH CAROLINA

HEARTY MAC AND CHEESE

family favorite

Prep: 15 min., Cook: 17 min.

- 1 (8-ounce) package elbow macaroni
- 1½ cups diced cooked ham
- ½ small onion, chopped
- Vegetable cooking spray
- 1 cup frozen green peas, thawed
- ¼ teaspoon salt
- ¼ teaspoon freshly ground black pepper
- ⅛ teaspoon ground red pepper
- 2 tablespoons butter
- 2 tablespoons all-purpose flour
- 2 cups milk
- 1 (8-ounce) block sharp Cheddar cheese, shredded

Prepare pasta according to package directions. Drain and keep warm.
Sauté ham and onion in a large nonstick skillet coated with cooking spray over medium-high heat 5 minutes; stir in peas and next 3 ingredients. Set aside.
Melt butter in a large saucepan over medium-low heat; whisk in flour until smooth. Cook, whisking constantly, 2 minutes. Gradually whisk in milk, and cook, whisking constantly, 5 minutes or until thickened. Remove from heat.
Stir in 1½ cups cheese, stirring until melted. Stir in cooked pasta and ham mixture. Sprinkle with remaining ½ cup cheese. Serve immediately. **Makes** 4 servings.

healthy & light
Simple Southern Salads

We've updated these Southern classic staples by simplifying the preparation and shortening and lightening the ingredient lists.

OVERNIGHT SLAW

make ahead

Prep: 15 min., Cook: 4 min., Chill: 8 hrs.

- 6 cups shredded cabbage (about 1¾ pounds)*
- 1 cup shredded red cabbage*
- ½ cup shredded carrot*
- ½ cup chopped red bell pepper
- 2 green onions, diagonally sliced
- 1½ tablespoons sugar
- 3 tablespoons white wine vinegar
- 3 tablespoons vegetable oil
- ½ teaspoon celery seed
- ½ teaspoon mustard seed
- 1 teaspoon coarse-grained Dijon mustard
- ¼ teaspoon salt
- ⅛ teaspoon pepper
- ½ (4-ounce) package crumbled feta cheese

Combine first 5 ingredients in a large bowl. Stir together sugar and next 7 ingredients in a small saucepan; bring to a boil. **Boil** 1 minute. Remove from heat; cool completely. Pour dressing over cabbage mixture; toss well. Cover and chill 8 hours. Toss with feta cheese just before serving. **Makes** 8 servings.

*Substitute 1 (16-ounce) package slaw mix, if desired.

CAROLYN WILLIAMS
NASHVILLE, TENNESSEE

Per (1-cup) serving: Calories 98 (62% from fat); Fat 7g (sat 1.5g, mono 3.5g, poly 1.7g); Protein 2.2g; Carb 7.7g; Fiber 0.7g; Chol 6mg; Iron 0.6mg; Sodium 188mg; Calc 70mg

EGG SALAD

make ahead

Prep: 15 min., Chill: 2 hrs.

If you prefer to leave out the dill, boost the flavor of this salad with an additional teaspoon of prepared yellow mustard.

- ¼ cup light mayonnaise
- 1 tablespoon chopped fresh dill
- 1 tablespoon grated onion
- 1 tablespoon dill pickle relish
- 1 tablespoon prepared yellow mustard
- ¼ teaspoon pepper
- ⅛ teaspoon salt
- 8 hard-cooked eggs, coarsely chopped

Stir together first 7 ingredients in a large bowl; gently stir in eggs. Cover and chill at least 2 hours or up to 2 days. **Makes** 5 servings.

BESS OSUCHA
MOUNT PLEASANT, SOUTH CAROLINA

Per (½-cup) serving: Calories 171 (67% from fat); Fat 12.6g (sat 3.2g, mono 3.3g, poly 1.2g); Protein 10.3g; Carb 3.5g; Fiber 0.3g; Chol 343mg; Iron 1.1mg; Sodium 320mg; Calc 44mg

GARLIC-HERB TWO-BEAN SALAD

make ahead

Prep: 15 min., Chill: 2 hrs.

- 1 (19-ounce) can chickpeas, rinsed and drained
- 1 (15-ounce) can kidney beans, rinsed and drained
- ½ cup diced red onion
- 2 garlic cloves, minced
- 1 jalapeño pepper, finely chopped
- 3 tablespoons chopped fresh cilantro
- ¼ cup olive oil
- 2 tablespoons red wine vinegar
- ½ teaspoon salt
- ¼ teaspoon pepper

Combine first 6 ingredients in a bowl. **Whisk** together oil and next 3 ingredients in a small bowl. Drizzle vinaigrette over bean mixture; toss gently. Cover and chill 2 hours. **Makes** 8 servings.

Per (½-cup) serving: Calories 158 (42% from fat); Fat 7.5g (sat 1g, mono 5.1g, poly 1g); Protein 4.6g; Carb 18.7g; Fiber 3.8g; Chol 0mg; Iron 1.3mg; Sodium 290mg; Calc 31mg

VANILLA-SCENTED FRUIT SALAD

fast fixin's

Prep: 15 min., Cook: 15 min.

For the best texture, choose crisp apples such as Granny Smith, Fuji, or McIntosh, and Bartlett or Bosc pears.

- ⅓ cup sugar
- ¼ cup water
- ¼ cup apple juice
- 1 teaspoon vanilla extract
- 2 cups coarsely chopped apple (about 2 medium)
- 2 cups coarsely chopped pear (about 3 medium)
- 1 cup red or green seedless grapes
- 2 teaspoons fresh lemon juice

Stir together first 3 ingredients in a small saucepan. Bring to a boil; reduce heat, and simmer, stirring occasionally, 12 minutes or until mixture is reduced. Remove pan from heat; stir in vanilla, and cool completely.
Combine apple and next 3 ingredients in a large bowl. Drizzle cooled syrup over fruit, gently tossing to coat. **Makes** 5 servings.

MARIANNE SELF
HELENA, ALABAMA

Per (1-cup) serving: Calories 165; Fat 0g (sat 0g, mono 0g, poly 0g); Protein 0.7g; Carb 43g; Fiber 4.6g; Chol 0mg; Iron 0.3mg; Sodium 3mg; Calc 16mg

CHUNKY CHICKEN PARMESAN SALAD

make ahead

Prep: 15 min., Chill: 2 hrs.

Serve with melon, berries, or crackers.

- 4 cups chopped cooked chicken breast
- ⅓ cup light mayonnaise
- ¼ cup freshly shredded Parmesan cheese
- 2 green onions, chopped
- 2 celery ribs, chopped
- 2 tablespoons chopped pecans, toasted
- ¼ teaspoon pepper
- ⅛ teaspoon salt
- Garnish: celery leaves

Stir together first 8 ingredients in a large bowl. Cover and chill 2 hours. Garnish, if desired. **Makes** 10 servings.

Note: For testing purposes only, we used BelGioioso Freshly Shredded Parmesan Cheese.

GRACIE WILTON
ALABASTER, ALABAMA

Per (½-cup) serving: Calories 140 (41% from fat); Fat 6.2g (sat 1.4g, mono 1.5g, poly 0.8g); Protein 18.4g; Carb 1.6g; Fiber 0.4g; Chol 52mg; Iron 0.7mg; Sodium 178mg; Calc 39mg

ROASTED CORN-AND-BLACK BEAN SALAD

chef recipe • make ahead

Prep: 15 min., Broil: 12 min., Stand: 10 min.

- 2 cups fresh corn kernels (about 3 ears) *
- 1 (15-ounce) can black beans, rinsed and drained
- 1 cup chopped tomato
- ⅓ cup lime juice
- ¼ cup red onion, finely chopped
- ½ jalapeño pepper, seeded and chopped
- 2 tablespoons chopped fresh cilantro
- 2 teaspoons hot sauce
- ½ teaspoon salt
- ½ teaspoon ground cumin
- ½ teaspoon ground coriander
- ½ teaspoon pepper

Place corn on an aluminum foil-lined baking sheet.
Broil corn 5 inches from heat 12 minutes or until lightly browned, stirring once. Remove from oven, and let stand 10 minutes.
Combine corn and remaining ingredients in a large bowl. Cover and chill until ready to serve. **Makes** 8 servings.

❋Substitute 2 cups frozen whole kernel corn, thawed, or 2 cups canned whole kernel corn, if desired.

ROBERT ST. JOHN
CRESCENT CITY GRILL
HATTIESBURG, MISSISSIPPI

Per (½-cup) serving: Calories 65 (8% from fat); Fat 0.7g (sat 0.1g, mono 0.2g, poly 0.3g); Protein 3g; Carb 15g; Fiber 3.3g; Chol 0mg; Iron 1mg; Sodium 212mg; Calc 19mg

How Sweet It Is

Use our easy caramel frosting for these delicious fall recipes. See "From Our Kitchen" on page 224 for preparation tips and serving suggestions.

CARAMEL-APPLE MUFFINS

freezeable • make ahead

Prep: 30 min., Cook: 4 min. per batch, Bake: 25 min.

Betty Moore of Owens Cross Roads, Alabama, sent us her recipe for Apple Bread, which was the inspiration for this moist and tender batter. See technique photos on page 224. *(pictured on page 192)*

> 1 (3-pound) bag small apples
> (12 to 14 apples)
> 2 cups sugar
> 1 cup vegetable oil
> 3 large eggs, lightly beaten
> 2 teaspoons vanilla extract
> 3 cups all-purpose flour
> 2 teaspoons ground cinnamon
> 1 teaspoon baking soda
> ½ teaspoon salt
> 2½ cups chopped pecans, toasted
> and divided
> Quick Caramel Frosting (recipe on
> opposite page)

Peel, core, and cut 4 apples into 24 (¼-inch-thick) rings. Sauté apple rings, in batches, in a lightly greased skillet over medium heat 1 to 2 minutes on each side or until lightly browned. Remove from skillet, and place 1 apple ring in the bottom of each of 24 lightly greased muffin pan cups.
Peel and finely chop enough remaining apples to equal 3 cups. Set aside.
Stir together sugar and next 3 ingredients in a large bowl.
Stir together flour and next 3 ingredients; add to sugar mixture, stirring just until blended. (Batter will be stiff.) Fold in finely chopped apples and 1 cup pecans.
Spoon batter over apple rings in muffin pan cups, filling cups three-fourths full.

Bake at 350° for 25 minutes or until a wooden pick inserted in center comes out clean. Remove muffins from pan, and cool, apple rings up, on a wire rack.
Press the handle of a wooden spoon gently into the center of each apple ring, forming a 1-inch-deep indentation in the muffins. Spoon warm Quick Caramel Frosting over muffins, filling indentations. Sprinkle with remaining 1½ cups chopped pecans. **Makes** 2 dozen.

Caramel-Apple Coffee Cakes: Omit apple rings, and prepare apple muffin batter as directed. Divide batter evenly between 2 greased and floured 8-inch round baking pans. Bake at 350° for 45 to 50 minutes or until a wooden pick inserted in center comes out clean. Remove from pans, and cool on wire racks. Spoon warm Quick Caramel Frosting over coffee cakes; sprinkle with remaining 1½ cups pecans. **Makes** 16 servings. Prep: 20 min., Bake: 50 min.

Apple Bread: Omit apple rings, Quick Caramel Frosting, and 1½ cups pecans on top. Prepare apple muffin batter as directed. Divide batter evenly between 2 greased and floured 9- x 5-inch loaf pans. Bake at 350° for 1 hour or until a wooden pick inserted in center comes out clean. Remove from pans, and cool on wire racks. **Makes** 2 (9-inch) loaves. Prep: 20 min., Bake: 1 hr.

CHOCOLATE-CARAMEL SHEET CAKE

freezeable • make ahead

Prep: 15 min., Bake: 25 min.

> 1 cup butter
> 1 cup water
> ¼ cup cocoa
> ½ cup buttermilk
> 2 large eggs
> 1 teaspoon baking soda
> 1 teaspoon vanilla extract
> 2 cups sugar
> 2 cups all-purpose flour
> ½ teaspoon salt
> Quick Caramel Frosting (recipe on
> opposite page)
> 1½ cups coarsely chopped pecans,
> toasted

Cook first 3 ingredients in a small saucepan over low heat, stirring constantly, until butter melts and mixture is smooth; remove from heat.
Beat buttermilk and next 3 ingredients at medium speed with an electric mixer until smooth; add cocoa mixture, beating until blended.
Combine sugar, flour, and salt; gradually add to buttermilk mixture, beating just until blended. (Batter will be thin.) Pour batter into a greased and floured 15- x 10-inch jelly-roll pan.
Bake at 350° for 20 to 25 minutes or until a wooden pick inserted in center comes out clean. Cool cake completely in pan on a wire rack.
Pour warm Quick Caramel Frosting over cake, spreading evenly to edges of pan. Sprinkle evenly with pecans. **Makes** 15 servings.

CARAMEL-PECAN CHEESECAKE BARS

freezeable • make ahead

Prep: 15 min., Bake: 48 min., Chill: 8 hrs.

See our tip in "From Our Kitchen" on page 224 for making cutting easier.

> 2 cups graham cracker
> crumbs
> ½ cup butter, melted
> 4 (8-ounce) packages cream
> cheese, softened
> ¾ cup sugar
> ¼ cup all-purpose flour
> 3 large eggs
> 1 tablespoon vanilla extract
> Quick Caramel-Pecan Frosting
> (recipe on opposite page)

Stir together graham cracker crumbs and butter; press into bottom of a lightly greased 13- x 9-inch pan.
Bake at 350° for 8 minutes. Remove from oven, and cool on a wire rack.
Beat cream cheese at medium speed with an electric mixer until smooth. Combine sugar and flour; gradually add to cream cheese, beating just until blended.
Add eggs, 1 at a time, beating until blended after each addition. Stir in vanilla. Pour mixture over prepared

crust, spreading evenly to edges of pan. **Bake** at 350° for 40 minutes or until set. Remove from oven, and cool on a wire rack.

Pour warm Quick Caramel-Pecan Frosting over cheesecake, spreading evenly to edges of pan. Cover and chill 8 hours. Cut into bars. **Makes** 2 dozen.

QUICK CARAMEL FROSTING

fast fixin's

Prep: 5 min., Cook: 10 min.

> 2 (14-ounce) cans sweetened condensed milk
> ½ cup firmly packed light brown sugar
> ½ cup butter
> 1 teaspoon vanilla extract

Place all ingredients in a heavy 3-quart saucepan; bring to a boil, stirring constantly, over medium-low heat. Cook, stirring constantly, 3 to 5 minutes or until mixture reaches a pudding-like thickness. Remove from heat. **Makes** 2½ cups.

Quick Caramel-Pecan Frosting: Prepare Quick Caramel Frosting as directed; remove from heat, and stir in 1½ cups chopped toasted pecans.

Quick Caramel-Coconut-Pecan Frosting: Prepare Quick Caramel Frosting as directed; stir in 1½ cups sweetened flaked coconut and 1½ cups chopped toasted pecans.

Bake Sale Treats

The bake sale booths at school fundraisers always draw a crowd. Visit a local party store for paper bags, take-out boxes, and bright tissue paper that will spark creative packaging ideas.

NO-BAKE PEANUT BUTTER CLUSTERS

make ahead

Prep: 25 min., Stand: 1 hr.

> 1 (24-ounce) package vanilla bark coating
> 1 (8-ounce) jar crunchy peanut butter
> 2 cups mini marshmallows
> 3 cups crisp rice cereal
> 3 cups toasted oat O-shaped cereal

Microwave bark in a large glass bowl at HIGH 2½ to 3 minutes, stirring mixture every 30 seconds until melted. **Stir** in peanut butter until blended. Add remaining ingredients, and stir until well coated.

Drop by heaping teaspoonfuls onto wax paper, and let stand 1 hour or until firm. Store in an airtight container. **Makes** about 6 dozen.

JOANNA L. HAY
ARCADIA, FLORIDA

CREAM CHEESE LADYBUGS

Prep: 30 min., Bake: 10 min. per batch

Calob Lindsey submitted the recipe for these very kid-friendly cookies in 1999 at the age of 8.

> 1 (8-ounce) package cream cheese, softened
> ¼ cup butter, softened
> 1¼ teaspoons red food coloring paste
> 1 teaspoon vanilla extract
> 1 egg yolk
> 1 (18.25-ounce) package white cake mix
> Chocolate candy sprinkles

Beat cream cheese and butter at medium speed with an electric mixer until blended. Add food coloring, vanilla, and egg yolk, beating well. Add cake mix, and beat until blended.
Shape a portion of the dough into 40 (1-inch) balls, and place on a lightly greased baking sheet. Shape remaining dough into 40 (¼-inch) balls; attach to larger balls on baking sheet. Gently press

a knife dipped in flour down center of each larger ball. Decorate body of ladybugs with chocolate candy sprinkles. **Bake** at 375° for 8 to 10 minutes. **Makes** about 3½ dozen.

CALOB LINDSEY
WHITNEY, TEXAS

TURTLE CAKE SQUARES

Prep: 20 min., Bake: 42 min.

Wrap cake squares in colorful plastic wrap, and tie with ribbon. Or bake in a disposable aluminum baking pan to sell whole.

> 1 (18.25-ounce) package devil's food cake mix
> 1¼ cups milk
> ½ cup vegetable oil
> 3 large eggs
> 1 (14-ounce) package caramels
> ¼ cup milk
> 1 cup semisweet chocolate morsels
> 1 cup chopped pecans, toasted

Beat cake mix and next 3 ingredients at medium speed with an electric mixer 2 minutes. Pour batter into a lightly greased 13- x 9-inch disposable aluminum pan.
Bake at 350° for 38 to 42 minutes or until a wooden pick inserted in center comes out clean.
Combine caramels and ¼ cup milk in a glass bowl. Microwave at HIGH 2½ to 3 minutes, stirring mixture every 30 seconds until smooth; pour half of mixture over baked cake. Sprinkle with chocolate morsels and pecans. Drizzle evenly with remaining caramel mixture. Cool completely on a wire rack. Cut into squares before serving. **Makes** 12 servings.

Note: For testing purposes only, we used Duncan Hines Devil's Food Cake Mix.

AMY STRAUTMAN
TUCSON, ARIZONA

SOUR CREAM COFFEE CAKES

freezeable • make ahead

Prep: 20 min., Bake: 45 min.

- **1 cup butter, softened**
- **2 cups sugar**
- **2 large eggs**
- **1 cup sour cream**
- **½ teaspoon vanilla extract**
- **2 cups all-purpose flour**
- **1 teaspoon baking powder**
- **¼ teaspoon salt**
- **1 cup chopped pecans**
- **¼ cup sugar**
- **1 teaspoon ground cinnamon**

Beat butter at medium speed with an electric mixer 2 minutes or until creamy. Gradually add sugar, beating 2 to 3 minutes. Add eggs, 1 at a time, beating until blended after each addition. Add sour cream and vanilla, beating until blended.

Combine flour, baking powder, and salt. Gradually stir by hand into butter mixture. Spoon half of cake batter evenly into 2 lightly greased 8½-inch-square disposable aluminum pans. (The batter will be very thick.)

Combine pecans, sugar, and cinnamon. Sprinkle half of pecan mixture evenly over cake batter in pans. Spoon remaining cake batter evenly over pecan mixture in each pan. Sprinkle evenly with remaining pecan mixture. **Bake** at 350° for 45 minutes. **Makes** 2 (8½-inch) cakes.

NORA HENSHAW
OKEMAH, OKLAHOMA

Mini Sour Cream Coffee Cakes:
Prepare batter and pecan mixture as directed above. Spoon a heaping ½ cup batter into each of 4 lightly greased mini (5¾- x 3¼- x 2-inch) aluminum loaf pans. Sprinkle half of pecan mixture evenly over batter in the 4 pans. Spoon remaining cake batter evenly over pecan mixture in pans. Sprinkle evenly with remaining pecan mixture. Place all 4 pans on a baking sheet. Bake at 350° for 1 hour. **Makes** 4 mini coffee cakes. Prep: 20 min., Bake: 1 hr.

Easy Game Day Get-together

Feeding the hungry football fans is easy. Grill hot dogs, and serve them with all the condiments. Set up a salsa bar for munching. Offer homemade Margarita Punch along with an assortment of soft drinks.

Fan Fare

Southwestern Salsa Dip

warm queso dip

hot dogs

tortilla and potato chips, pretzels

celery and carrot sticks

broccoli florets

purchased caramel corn and snack mixes

Margarita Punch

assorted soft drinks

SOUTHWESTERN SALSA DIP

make ahead

Prep: 10 min., Chill: 2 hrs.

Serve chilled or at room temperature with assorted tortilla chips.

- **¾ cup bottled salsa**
- **2 teaspoons olive oil**
- **¼ teaspoon salt**
- **2 drops hot sauce**
- **1 (15-ounce) can black beans, drained**

Stir together all ingredients in a medium bowl. Cover and chill at least 2 hours. **Makes** 1½ cups.

MARGARITA PUNCH

fast fixin's

Prep: 15 min., Cook: 3 min.

Offer this tangy beverage as a refreshing, nonalcoholic punch, or serve it with a side of tequila, and let guests mix their own cocktails.

- **1½ cups sugar**
- **2 tablespoons grated lemon rind**
- **2 tablespoons grated lime rind**
- **1 tablespoon grated orange rind**
- **2 cups fresh lemon juice (about 12 lemons)**
- **½ cup fresh lime juice (about 2 limes)**
- **⅔ cup fresh orange juice (about 3 oranges)**
- **1 cup water**
- **1 quart chilled water**
- **Tequila (optional)**
- **Garnishes: lemon and lime slices**

Combine first 8 ingredients in a saucepan. Bring to a boil; remove from heat, and let cool. Pour mixture into a pitcher; add 1 quart chilled water. Serve over ice, and, if desired, add 1 to 2 tablespoons or desired amount of tequila to each serving. Garnish, if desired. **Makes** 2 quarts.

Build a Hot Dog Bar

See how creative you can get with fun toppings. Use these suggestions to jump-start your grocery list.

Hot dogs
Hot dog buns
Yellow and Dijon mustards
Ketchup
Pickle relish
Chopped onions
Chili
Shredded Cheddar cheese
Shredded Swiss cheese
Sliced jalapeño peppers

Quick-and-Easy Favorites

Our Foods staff shares its best time-saving tricks in these recipes.

BUTTERMILK BAKED CHICKEN

family favorite

Prep: 20 min., Bake: 45 min.

- ¼ cup butter, melted
- 4 bone-in chicken breasts, skinned
- ½ teaspoon salt
- ½ teaspoon pepper
- 1½ cups buttermilk, divided
- ¾ cup all-purpose flour
- 1 (10¾-ounce) can CAMPBELL'S Cream of Mushroom Soup
- ¼ cup chopped fresh herbs (basil, flat-leaf parsley, and/or chives)
- Hot cooked rice

Pour butter evenly into a 13- x 9-inch baking dish.
Sprinkle chicken evenly with salt and pepper. Dip chicken in ½ cup buttermilk, and dredge in flour. Arrange chicken, breast sides down, in dish.
Bake at 425° for 25 minutes. Turn chicken, and bake 10 more minutes. Stir together remaining 1 cup buttermilk, soup, and herbs; pour over chicken, and bake 10 more minutes, shielding with aluminum foil to prevent excessive browning, if necessary. Serve over rice. **Makes** 4 servings.

BLT POTATO SALAD

make ahead

Prep: 20 min., Cook: 15 min., Chill: 3 hrs.

- 3 large baking potatoes (about 3½ pounds), peeled and chopped
- 1 cup HELLMANN'S Real Mayonnaise
- 3 tablespoons sweet pickle relish
- 2 tablespoons Dijon mustard
- 1 tablespoon chopped fresh parsley
- ¾ teaspoon salt
- ¾ teaspoon freshly ground pepper
- 1 cup grape tomatoes, halved
- 3 green onions, sliced
- 2 hard-cooked eggs, chopped
- 4 bacon slices, cooked and crumbled
- Lettuce leaves

Bring potatoes and salted water to cover to a boil in a Dutch oven. Boil 5 minutes or until tender. Drain and cool.
Stir together mayonnaise and next 5 ingredients in a large bowl; add cooked potatoes, tomatoes, green onions, and eggs, tossing gently until well blended. Cover and chill at least 3 hours. Stir in bacon just before serving. Serve on lettuce leaves. **Makes** 8 to 10 servings.

GRILLED CHEESE SANDWICHES WITH TOMATO, AVOCADO, AND BACON

fast fixin's

Prep: 15 min., Cook: 12 min.

- 8 bacon slices
- 2 large tomatoes, each cut into 4 slices
- ¼ teaspoon salt
- ¼ teaspoon pepper
- ¼ cup Ranch dressing
- 8 slices NATURE'S OWN Whitewheat Bread
- 4 (1-ounce) provolone cheese slices
- 4 (1-ounce) sharp Cheddar cheese slices
- 1 large avocado, cut into 8 slices
- Vegetable cooking spray

Prepare bacon according to package directions; drain and set aside. Sprinkle tomato slices evenly with salt and pepper.
Spread ½ tablespoon dressing on 1 side of each bread slice. Top each dressing-coated side of 4 bread slices with 1 provolone slice; top each remaining 4 bread slices with 1 Cheddar slice. Top each provolone slice with 2 tomato slices, 2 bacon slices, and 2 avocado slices.
Cook bread slices, cheese side up, on a hot nonstick electric griddle at 325° or in a hot nonstick skillet coated with cooking spray over medium heat 4 to 7 minutes or until browned.
Press together Cheddar cheese-topped bread slices and provolone-topped bread slices. Cut in half diagonally, and serve immediately. **Makes** 4 servings.

SOUTHERN-STYLE TURKEY COBB SALAD

Prep: 20 min., Cook: 3 min.

- ¼ pound fresh sugar snap peas
- 1 head iceberg lettuce, torn
- ½ cup (2 ounces) crumbled blue cheese
- 2 hard-cooked eggs, chopped
- 2 plum tomatoes, seeded and chopped
- 1 avocado, sliced
- 2 cups chopped cooked JENNIE-O TURKEY STORE Oven Ready Home Style Half Turkey
- 4 bacon slices, cooked and crumbled
- Freshly ground pepper
- Bottled light Ranch dressing

Cook peas in boiling water to cover 2 to 3 minutes or until crisp-tender; drain. Plunge into ice water to stop the cooking process; drain.
Divide lettuce evenly among 4 plates. Top evenly with peas, crumbled blue cheese, and next 4 ingredients. Sprinkle with crumbled bacon and pepper, and serve with dressing. **Makes** 4 servings.

PEAR CRISP

Prep: 15 min., Bake: 30 min.

- 4 large ripe pears, peeled and sliced
- 5 tablespoons SPLENDA No Calorie Sweetener, granular, divided
- 2 tablespoons orange juice
- ¼ cup all-purpose flour
- 2 tablespoons butter, melted
- 1 teaspoon pumpkin pie spice
- ¼ cup uncooked quick-cooking oats
- ¼ cup chopped pecans
- 2 cups fat-free, sugar-free vanilla ice cream

Toss together pears, 1 tablespoon no-calorie sweetener, and orange juice; spoon into a 9-inch pieplate or 4 (8-ounce) custard cups.
Stir together remaining 4 tablespoons no-calorie sweetener, flour, butter, and

pumpkin pie spice. Stir in oats and chopped pecans, and sprinkle evenly over pear mixture.
Bake at 375° for 25 to 30 minutes or until top is crisp and fruit is tender. Serve warm with ice cream. **Makes** 4 servings.

BLACK BEANS AND RICE

Prep: 25 min., Cook: 40 min.

The trick to this recipe is substituting canned black beans for dried beans and using pantry ingredients for big flavor.

- 2 cups uncooked MAHATMA Long-Grain White Rice
- 5 (15-ounce) cans black beans, divided
- 1 cup chopped onion
- ½ cup chopped green bell pepper
- ½ cup chopped red bell pepper
- 5 garlic cloves, minced
- 2 tablespoons seeded, minced jalapeño pepper
- 2 teaspoons olive oil
- 1 (14-ounce) can chicken broth
- 1 (6-ounce) can tomato paste
- 1 tablespoon red wine vinegar
- 1 teaspoon ground cumin
- 1 teaspoon dried crushed red pepper
- ¼ teaspoon black pepper
- Salt to taste
- Toppings: shredded Cheddar cheese, sour cream, chopped tomatoes, chopped fresh cilantro, chopped green onions, sliced jalapeño peppers

Cook rice according to package directions; keep hot.
Rinse and drain 3 cans black beans. (Do not drain other 2 cans.)
Sauté onion and next 4 ingredients in hot oil in a Dutch oven over medium-high heat 5 minutes or until tender. Stir in drained and undrained beans, chicken broth, and next 5 ingredients. Bring to a boil; reduce heat, and simmer uncovered, 30 minutes, stirring occasionally. Add salt to taste. Serve

with hot cooked rice and desired toppings. **Makes** 6 to 8 servings.

Dinner and a Movie

Italian Menu

Serves 8

Baked Ziti

— or —

Rigatoni With Sausage and Bell Peppers

tossed salad

Garlic Bread

Splendid Strawberries (double the recipe)

BAKED ZITI

Prep: 20 min., Cook: 25 min., Bake: 25 min., Stand: 10 min.

- ½ medium onion, chopped
- 1 tablespoon olive oil
- 2 garlic cloves, minced
- 1 pound lean ground beef
- 1 (26-ounce) jar tomato-and-basil pasta sauce
- ¾ teaspoon salt, divided
- 1 (16-ounce) box BARILLA Ziti Pasta
- 3 tablespoons butter
- 3 tablespoons all-purpose flour
- 3 cups milk
- 1 cup grated Parmesan cheese
- ½ teaspoon pepper
- 1 (8-ounce) package shredded mozzarella cheese

Sauté chopped onion in hot oil in a large skillet over medium-high heat 5 minutes or until tender. Add garlic, and sauté 1 minute. Add beef, and cook, stirring until beef crumbles and is no longer pink. Drain beef mixture, and return to pan. Stir in pasta sauce and ½ teaspoon salt. Set aside.

Cook pasta in a large Dutch oven according to package directions. Drain and return to Dutch oven.

Melt butter in a heavy saucepan over low heat; whisk in flour until smooth. Cook, whisking constantly, 1 minute. Gradually whisk in milk; cook over medium heat, whisking constantly, until mixture is thickened and bubbly. Stir in Parmesan cheese, remaining ¼ teaspoon salt, and pepper. Pour sauce over pasta in Dutch oven, stirring until pasta is evenly coated.

Transfer pasta mixture to a lightly greased 13- x 9-inch baking dish. Top evenly with beef mixture; sprinkle evenly with mozzarella cheese.

Bake at 350° for 20 to 25 minutes or until cheese is melted. Let stand 10 minutes before serving. **Makes** 8 to 10 servings.

RIGATONI WITH SAUSAGE AND BELL PEPPERS

Prep: 15 min., Cook: 20 min.

Invite friends into the kitchen to help chop the ingredients. Be sure to serve this piping hot.

- 1 (16-ounce) box BARILLA Rigatoni Pasta
- 1 pound mild Italian sausage
- ½ medium-size red onion, chopped
- ½ red bell pepper, cut into strips
- ½ green bell pepper, cut into strips
- 1 tablespoon olive oil
- 2 garlic cloves, minced
- ½ cup chicken broth
- ¼ teaspoon dried crushed red pepper
- ¼ teaspoon black pepper
- ¼ cup chopped fresh basil
- ¼ cup shredded Parmesan cheese

Cook pasta according to package directions; drain and set aside.

Cook sausage in a Dutch oven over medium-high heat, stirring until sausage crumbles and is no longer pink; drain.

Sauté onion and bell peppers in hot oil in Dutch oven over medium-high heat 6 minutes. Add garlic, and sauté 2 minutes. Stir in sausage, cooked pasta, chicken broth, crushed red pepper, and black pepper. Reduce heat to low, and cook, stirring occasionally, 5 minutes or until thoroughly heated. Transfer to a serving dish, and top evenly with basil and cheese. Serve immediately. **Makes** 8 servings.

GARLIC BREAD

fast fixin's

Prep: 10 min., Bake: 15 min.

- ½ cup butter, softened
- 2 large garlic cloves, pressed
- 4 teaspoons chopped fresh basil *
- ¼ teaspoon pepper
- 1 (16-ounce) French bread loaf, split horizontally
- 1 cup (4 ounces) shredded Italian six-cheese blend

Stir together first 4 ingredients in a small bowl until well blended; spread mixture evenly on cut sides of bread halves. Sprinkle evenly with cheese. Place on a baking sheet.

Bake at 375° for 15 minutes or until cheese is melted. **Makes** 8 servings.

***** Substitute ½ teaspoon dried Italian seasoning, if desired.

SPLENDID STRAWBERRIES

fast fixin's

Prep: 5 min., Cook: 1 min.

- 1 tablespoon butter
- 1 quart fresh strawberries, halved
- ¼ cup SPLENDA No Calorie Sweetener, granular
- 1 tablespoon balsamic vinegar
- Low-fat vanilla ice cream

Melt butter in a large skillet over medium-high heat. Stir in strawberries, no-caloric sweetener, and balsamic vinegar; cook 1 minute or until mixture is thoroughly heated. Serve over ice cream. **Makes** 4 servings.

Fruit and Spice Make It Nice

Add a little of this and a little of that, and before you know it, you've put a fresh twist on familiar dishes. Make beef, fish, vegetables, or even muffins special by adding a dash of spice or splash of fresh fruit flavor. These recipes will make tempting choices for any day of the week.

ORANGE-DATE MUFFINS

fast fixin's

Prep: 10 min., Bake: 15 min.

- 1 (16.6-ounce) package quick bread-and-muffin mix with dates
- 1 cup FLORIDA'S NATURAL Premium Brand Orange Juice
- ½ cup butter, melted
- 1 large egg, lightly beaten

Stir together all ingredients; spoon batter evenly into lightly greased muffin pans, filling three-fourths full.

Bake at 400° for 12 to 15 minutes or until golden. Remove muffins from pans immediately, and cool on wire racks. **Makes** 1 dozen.

Southern Living Cooking School

CHOCOLATE-COVERED CHERRY PIE

make ahead

Prep: 30 min., Bake: 30 min., Chill: 8 hrs.

Using a convenient ready-made crust allows time to dip cherries in chocolate for an eye-popping pie topper.

- 1 (12-ounce) package NESTLÉ TOLL HOUSE Semi-Sweet Chocolate Morsels
- ½ cup whipping cream
- ¼ cup butter, cut into pieces
- 1 (6-ounce) ready-made chocolate crumb piecrust
- 1 (21-ounce) can cherry pie filling
- 1 (8-ounce) package cream cheese, softened
- ⅓ cup powdered sugar
- 1 large egg
- ¼ teaspoon almond extract
- 16 maraschino cherries with stems
- 2 cups frozen whipped topping, thawed

Microwave morsels and cream in a microwave-safe bowl at MEDIUM (50% power) 1 to 2 minutes or until chocolate begins to melt. Whisk in butter until smooth. Let cool, whisking occasionally, 5 to 10 minutes or until mixture reaches spreading consistency. Spoon half of chocolate mixture into piecrust. Cover and chill remaining chocolate mixture.

Spoon cherry pie filling evenly over chocolate mixture in piecrust. Place piecrust on a baking sheet.

Beat cream cheese and next 3 ingredients at medium speed with an electric mixer until smooth. Pour cream cheese mixture evenly over cherry pie filling. (Pie shell will be very full but will not overflow when baking.)

Bake at 350° for 30 minutes or until center is set. Remove from oven, and cool on a wire rack. Cover and chill 8 hours.

Drain maraschino cherries on paper towels; pat dry.

Microwave reserved chocolate mixture at MEDIUM (50% power) 1 minute. Remove from microwave; stir until spreading consistency, reheating if necessary.

Dip cherries in chocolate mixture, and place on a baking sheet lined with wax paper; chill 15 minutes. Spread remaining chocolate mixture evenly over top of pie. Spoon 8 dollops of whipped topping around outer edge of pie; place 2 chocolate-covered cherries in center of each dollop. **Makes** 8 servings.

BAKED LEMON-DILL CATFISH

Prep: 20 min., Bake: 20 min.

Fresh lemon and dill add a delicious flavor to this Southern favorite.

- ½ cup HELLMANN'S Real Mayonnaise
- ¼ cup buttermilk
- 1 teaspoon grated lemon rind
- 3 tablespoons fresh lemon juice
- 2 tablespoons chopped fresh dill
- 1 garlic clove, minced
- 4 (4- to 6-ounce) catfish fillets
- 1 teaspoon salt
- ¼ teaspoon pepper
- 1 cup fine, dry breadcrumbs

Stir first 6 ingredients in a small bowl. Place half of mayonnaise mixture in another small bowl to serve with fish; cover and chill until ready to serve.

Rinse fillets, and pat dry with paper towels. Brush fillets evenly with remaining half of mayonnaise mixture; sprinkle evenly with salt and pepper. Dredge fillets in breadcrumbs. Arrange fillets on a lightly greased rack in an aluminum foil-lined broiler pan.

Bake at 425° for 20 minutes or until fish flakes with a fork and is opaque throughout. Serve immediately with chilled mayonnaise mixture. **Makes** 4 servings.

ORANGE TEA COOLER

fast fixin's • make ahead

Prep: 10 min., Steep: 5 min.

Your entire family will enjoy this refreshing orange juice sipper.

- 2 family-size tea bags or 5 regular-size tea bags
- 1¾ cups sugar
- 2 (2½-inch) cinnamon sticks
- 1 teaspoon whole cloves
- 1 quart boiling water
- 2½ cups FLORIDA'S NATURAL Premium Brand Orange Juice
- 2 cups water
- 1⅓ cups cranberry juice cocktail, chilled

Combine first 4 ingredients; stir in 1 quart boiling water. Cover and steep 5 minutes.

Pour mixture through a fine wire-mesh strainer into a large pitcher, discarding tea bags and spices. Stir in orange juice, 2 cups water, and cranberry juice. Chill. Serve over ice, if desired. **Makes** 4 quarts.

GINGER-MARINATED FLANK STEAK

Prep: 10 min., Chill: 8 hrs., Grill: 20 min., Stand: 5 min.

- ¼ cup vegetable oil
- ¼ cup soy sauce
- 2 tablespoons brown sugar
- 2 tablespoons lime juice
- 2 teaspoons ground ginger
- 1 teaspoon dried crushed red pepper
- 2 garlic cloves, chopped
- 1 (2-pound) BEEF Flank Steak

Combine first 7 ingredients in a shallow dish or large zip-top freezer bag; add steak, turning to coat. Cover or seal, and chill 8 hours, turning steak occasionally.

Remove steak from marinade, discarding marinade.

Grill, covered with grill lid, over medium-high heat (350° to 400°) 8 to 10 minutes on each side or to desired degree of doneness. Let stand 5 minutes; cut into thin slices diagonally across the grain. **Makes** 4 to 6 servings.

ROASTED FALL VEGETABLES

Prep: 20 min., Bake: 35 min.

These roasted veggies get their zing from ginger. You can also try them with ground cumin or Italian seasoning.

- PAM Original No-Stick Cooking Spray
- 3 medium-size sweet potatoes, peeled and cut into ½-inch cubes
- 1 medium-size red bell pepper, cut into ½-inch pieces
- 1 medium-size sweet onion, coarsely chopped
- 1 teaspoon salt
- 1 teaspoon ground ginger
- ¼ teaspoon pepper

Coat a 15- x 10-inch jelly-roll pan with cooking spray.
Place potatoes, bell pepper, and onion in pan; sprinkle evenly with salt, ginger, and pepper. Toss until vegetables are evenly coated with cooking spray.
Bake at 450° for 30 to 35 minutes or until potatoes are tender. **Makes** 6 servings.

Weeknight Wonders

In most kitchens, the refrigerator is a place of high esteem. Favorite drawings, notes, and invitations find their way there. We think these recipes are worthy of "fridge status"—you'll want to post them there for easy retrieval.

BEEFY PIZZA CASSEROLE

family favorite

Prep: 25 min., Cook: 12 min., Bake: 20 min.

In taste tests, our kitchen panel preferred the casserole with lean ground beef. We think this recipe will become on of your family's all-time favorites

- 2 pounds Ground BEEF
- 2 medium onions, chopped
- ½ cup chopped green bell pepper
- 4 teaspoons dried Italian seasoning, divided
- ¼ cup all-purpose flour
- 1 (26-ounce) jar tomato-and-basil pasta sauce
- 2 cups (8 ounces) shredded mozzarella cheese, divided
- 1 (13.8-ounce) can refrigerated pizza crust *
- 1 tablespoon olive oil
- 2 tablespoons grated Parmesan cheese

Cook first 3 ingredients and 3 teaspoons Italian seasoning in a large skillet over medium-high heat, stirring until beef crumbles and is no longer pink. Drain well, and return to skillet.
Add ¼ cup flour, stirring until blended. Stir in pasta sauce. Bring mixture to a boil over medium-high heat, stirring constantly. Spoon mixture into a lightly greased 13- x 9-inch baking dish. Sprinkle evenly with 1½ cups mozzarella cheese.
Unroll pizza crust, and place on top of cheese. (Tuck edges into baking dish, if necessary.) Brush with olive oil, and sprinkle evenly with remaining ½ cup mozzarella cheese, Parmesan cheese, and remaining 1 teaspoon Italian seasoning.
Bake at 425° for 15 to 20 minutes or until golden brown. **Makes** 8 servings.

*Substitute an 11.3-ounce refrigerated pizza crust, if desired.

SOUTHWESTERN SQUASH CASSEROLE

family favorite

Prep: 25 min., Bake: 20 min.

This updated version of squash casserole comes together quickly and easily. Crushed tortilla chips add a nice crunch, while the taco seasoning and green chiles add a nice, zippy flavor.

- 1 pound yellow squash, sliced
- 1 pound zucchini, sliced
- 1 cup water
- 1 (10¾-ounce) can CAMPBELL'S Cheddar Cheese Soup
- 1 cup crushed tortilla chips
- 1 (4.5-ounce) can chopped green chiles, undrained
- ¼ cup chopped onion
- 2 tablespoons taco seasoning
- 1 large egg, lightly beaten
- 1 cup (4 ounces) shredded Monterey Jack and Cheddar cheese blend

Place first 3 ingredients in a large microwave-safe glass bowl, and cover tightly with plastic wrap; pierce plastic wrap with a fork several times to vent. Microwave at HIGH 8 to 9 minutes or until vegetables are tender; drain. Press between layers of paper towels to remove excess moisture.
Stir together cooked vegetables, Cheddar cheese soup, and next 5 ingredients until well blended; spoon into a lightly greased 11- x 7-inch baking dish. Sprinkle evenly with cheese.
Bake at 450° for 20 minutes or until top is lightly browned. **Makes** 6 to 8 servings.

MOLASSES-GRILLED RIB-EYE STEAKS

family favorite

Prep: 10 min., Chill: 2 hrs., Grill: 14 min.

Serve this flavorful entrée with mashed potatoes and a salad.

½ cup molasses
¼ cup coarse-grained Dijon
    mustard
1 tablespoon olive oil
4 (8- to 10-ounce) boneless BEEF
    Rib-Eye Steaks
¾ teaspoon salt
¾ teaspoon pepper

Combine ½ cup molasses, ¼ cup mustard, and 1 tablespoon olive oil in a shallow dish or large zip-top plastic freezer bag. Add steaks; cover or seal, and chill at least 2 hours, turning occasionally. Remove steaks from marinade, discarding marinade. Sprinkle steaks evenly with salt and pepper.
Grill, covered with grill lid, over medium-high heat (350° to 400°) 5 to 7 minutes on each side or to desired degree of doneness. **Makes** 4 servings.

CRANBERRY-ORANGE SAUCE

fast fixin's • make ahead

Prep: 5 min., Cook: 15 min.

1 cup sugar
1 cup FLORIDA'S NATURAL
    Premium Brand Orange Juice
1 (12-ounce) bag fresh or frozen
    cranberries
1 (6-ounce) package sweetened
    dried cranberries
½ cup orange marmalade

Bring sugar and orange juice to a boil in a large saucepan over medium-high heat, stirring often; add fresh or frozen cranberries. Return to a boil. Reduce heat, and simmer, stirring often, 10 minutes or until cranberry skins begin to burst and mixture begins to thicken.
Remove from heat; stir in dried cranberries and orange marmalade. Let sauce cool; cover and chill until ready to serve. **Makes** about 4 cups.

Note: Sauce can be stored in an airtight container in the refrigerator up to 2 weeks.

BUTTERMILK CORN STICKS

Prep: 10 min., Bake: 12 min. per batch

2 cups self-rising cornmeal mix
¾ cup all-purpose flour
⅓ cup SPLENDA No Calorie
    Sweetener, granular
2 large eggs
2¼ cups fat-free buttermilk
⅓ cup butter, melted
Vegetable cooking spray

Combine first 3 ingredients; make a well in center of mixture. Whisk together eggs, 2¼ cups buttermilk, and ⅓ cup melted butter. Add to cornmeal mixture, stirring just until moistened.
Heat cast-iron corn stick pans in a 425° oven 5 minutes or until hot. Remove pans from oven, and coat evenly with cooking spray. Spoon batter into hot pans.
Bake at 425° for 10 to 12 minutes or until lightly browned. Remove from pans immediately. **Makes** 30 sticks.

SUCCOTASH RICE TOSS

Prep: 15 min., Cook: 30 min.

Jarred roasted red bell peppers update this classic Southern dish. Find them with other canned vegetables, or look in the Italian foods section.

2 cups frozen baby lima beans
1 (16-ounce) package frozen corn
    kernels
1 (3.5-ounce) bag SUCCESS White
    Rice
4 bacon slices
2 medium onions, chopped
2 teaspoons minced fresh garlic
¾ cup jarred, drained roasted red
    bell peppers, chopped
1½ teaspoons salt
1 teaspoon freshly ground pepper

Cook lima beans in boiling water to cover in a medium saucepan 9 minutes. Add corn, and cook 4 to 5 minutes or until beans are tender; drain and set aside.

Love These Turkey Sides

JENNIE-O TURKEY STORE Oven Ready Home Style Whole Turkey takes the guesswork out of roasting turkeys. The only thing we did to the bird was garnish with a little rosemary and sliced fresh apples. With turkey this easy, you're now able to enjoy a "real" meal during the week, dressed up with jazzy side dishes. The speedy side dishes offered below start with frozen foods and let fresh accents build on the convenience.

Lemon-Almond Green Beans: Melt 3 tablespoons butter in a large skillet over medium-high heat; add 6 thinly sliced green onions, and sauté 2 minutes. Add ¾ cup chicken broth, and bring to a boil. Add 2 (14-ounce) packages frozen whole green beans, 1 teaspoon seasoned pepper, and ¼ teaspoon salt; cook 5 to 7 minutes or until crisp-tender. Stir in 1 tablespoon grated lemon rind and ½ cup toasted slivered almonds. **Makes** 6 servings. Prep: 5 min., Cook: 10 min.

Garlic-Herb Mashed Potatoes: Prepare 1 (22-ounce) bag frozen mashed potatoes according to package directions. Stir in 1 (4-ounce) container garlic-and-herb spreadable cheese, ½ cup sour cream, ¼ cup chopped fresh parsley, ½ teaspoon seasoned pepper, and ¼ teaspoon salt. **Makes** 6 servings. Prep: 15 min.

Cook rice according to package directions; set aside.

Cook bacon in a Dutch oven until crisp; remove bacon, reserving 2 tablespoons drippings in Dutch oven. Crumble bacon.

Sauté chopped onions in hot drippings over medium-high heat 7 to 8 minutes or until tender. Add garlic, and sauté 1 minute. Stir in bean mixture, rice, roasted red peppers, salt, and pepper. Cook over medium heat, stirring often, until thoroughly heated. Top evenly with bacon. **Makes** 4 to 6 servings.

Girls' Night Out

What better treat is there than a no-fuss meal and the camaraderie of friends?

Fun With Friends

Serves 6

Tomato-Basil Dip

Balsamic-Marinated Chicken

Orange Rice Pilaf

Gingerbread

TOMATO-BASIL DIP

Prep: 10 min., Chill: 1 hr.

1 cup HELLMANN'S Real Mayonnaise
½ cup sour cream
½ cup chopped fresh basil
1 tablespoon tomato paste
1 tablespoon grated lemon rind
Assorted fresh vegetables

Stir together first 5 ingredients. Cover and chill at least 1 hour or up to 2 days. Serve with vegetables. **Makes** 1½ cups.

BALSAMIC-MARINATED CHICKEN

Prep: 10 min., Chill: 2 hrs., Cook: 16 min., Bake: 20 min.

Just brown the chicken, and pop it in the oven before your guests arrive. While it bakes, you can slice fresh oranges or pluck a few sprigs of rosemary for garnish.

2 tablespoons balsamic vinegar
1 tablespoon honey
¼ cup olive oil
2 teaspoons salt, divided
6 (6- to 8-ounce) PILGRIM'S PRIDE Boneless Skinless Chicken Breasts
½ teaspoon pepper

Combine first 3 ingredients and 1 teaspoon salt in a zip-top plastic freezer bag or large shallow dish, and add chicken. Seal or cover, and chill 2 hours, turning occasionally.

Remove chicken from marinade, discarding marinade. Sprinkle evenly with pepper and remaining 1 teaspoon salt.

Heat a large ungreased cast-iron skillet or grill skillet over medium-high heat until hot. Cook chicken, in batches, in hot skillet 3 to 4 minutes on each side or until browned. Place chicken in a 13- x 9-inch baking dish.

Bake at 350° for 20 minutes or until done. **Makes** 6 servings.

ORANGE RICE PILAF

make ahead

Prep: 15 min., Cook: 30 min.

½ cup chopped red bell pepper
6 green onions, sliced
1 tablespoon olive oil
1½ cups uncooked MAHATMA Long-Grain White Rice
3 cups chicken broth
1 tablespoon grated orange rind
½ teaspoon salt
¼ teaspoon pepper

Sauté bell pepper and green onions in hot oil in a medium saucepan over medium-high heat 5 to 7 minutes or until tender. Stir in rice, and sauté 1 minute. Stir in broth, and bring to a boil. Cover, reduce heat, and simmer 20 minutes or until rice is tender and liquid is absorbed. Stir in remaining ingredients. **Makes** 6 servings.

Tip: To make ahead, cook bell pepper, green onions, and rice according to directions. Refrigerate. At serving time, reheat in a microwave-safe serving dish covered loosely with plastic wrap; stir in orange rind, salt, and pepper just before serving.

GINGERBREAD

Prep: 15 min., Bake: 40 min.

1 cup DOMINO Granulated Sugar
½ cup applesauce
¼ cup butter, softened
¼ cup molasses
2 cups all-purpose flour
4 teaspoons ground ginger
1 teaspoon ground cinnamon
1 teaspoon baking soda
¼ teaspoon salt
1 cup fat-free buttermilk
2 large eggs, lightly beaten
Whipped cream (optional)

Beat first 4 ingredients at medium speed with an electric mixer until blended.

Stir together flour and next 4 ingredients in a medium bowl. Combine buttermilk and eggs in a separate bowl. Add both mixtures alternately to butter mixture, beginning and ending with flour mixture. Beat at low speed until blended after each addition. Pour batter into a lightly greased 10-inch cast-iron skillet.

Bake at 325° for 35 to 40 minutes or until a wooden pick inserted in center comes out clean. Serve with whipped cream, if desired. **Makes** 8 servings.

Southern Hospitality With An International Accent

Invite friends over to enjoy food and fun on a lazy Saturday or Sunday. We've planned a global buffet for a tasteful trek through dishes inspired by regional American, Mediterranean, and Mexican cuisines. You can mix and match these recipes to create a menu, or make the event a potluck party.

BERRY FREEZE

freezeable • make ahead

Prep: 15 min., Cook: 5 min., Stand: 25 min., Freeze: 8 hrs.

- 1½ cups DOMINO Granulated Sugar
- 1 cup water
- ½ cup loosely packed fresh mint leaves, torn
- 1 (64-ounce) bottle mixed berry juice

Bring sugar and 1 cup water to a boil in a small saucepan, stirring constantly. Boil, stirring constantly, 3 minutes or until sugar dissolves. Remove from heat; stir in mint. Let stand 5 minutes. Pour through a fine wire-mesh strainer into a large bowl; discard mint. Stir in berry juice.

Pour mixture into a 13- x 9-inch pan; freeze at least 8 hours. Let stand at room temperature 20 minutes. Process, in batches, in a food processor. Serve beverage immediately. **Makes** 10 to 12 servings.

FRESH FRUIT WITH LIME SYRUP

make ahead

Prep: 20 min., Cook: 5 min., Chill: 2 hrs.

- 1 cup water
- 1 tablespoon cornstarch
- 1 cup DOMINO Granulated Sugar
- 1 teaspoon grated lime rind
- ¼ cup fresh lime juice
- 1 pineapple, peeled, cored, and cut into 1-inch pieces
- 2 cups red seedless grapes, halved
- 3 kiwifruit, peeled and sliced
- 2 oranges, peeled and sectioned
- Garnish: fresh mint sprig

Whisk together 1 cup water and cornstarch in a small saucepan. Whisk in sugar, rind, and juice. Bring to a boil over low heat, whisking constantly; boil 1 minute. Cover and chill at least 2 hours.

Combine pineapple and next 3 ingredients in a large bowl; drizzle with chilled syrup, and garnish, if desired. Serve immediately. **Makes** 10 servings.

MEDITERRANEAN PASTA SALAD

Prep: 20 min., Chill: 2 hrs., Cook: 15 min.

- ¾ cup olive oil
- ⅓ cup loosely packed fresh flat-leaf parsley
- ⅓ cup balsamic vinegar
- 4 anchovy fillets
- 2 garlic cloves
- 1 tablespoon fresh lemon juice
- 1 teaspoon salt
- ½ teaspoon dry mustard
- ¼ teaspoon pepper
- 1 (16-ounce) box BARILLA Linguine

Process first 9 ingredients in a food processor until smooth, stopping to scrape down sides. Cover vinaigrette, and chill 2 hours.

Cook pasta according to package directions. Rinse with cold water; drain. Toss cooked pasta with vinaigrette. **Makes** 8 servings.

Mediterranean Antipasto Salad Platter: Prepare an additional recipe of the vinaigrette for Mediterranean Pasta Salad; do not add pasta. Marinate cooked green beans, pitted kalamata olives, and grape tomato halves in the vinaigrette 30 minutes; drain. Serve marinated items on a large platter with Mediterranean Pasta Salad, canned tuna, quartered hard-cooked eggs, drained capers, and red onions. Prep: 35 min.

GREEK-STYLE CHICKEN

family favorite

Prep: 20 min., Cook: 20 min., Bake: 30 min.

- ½ teaspoon salt
- ½ teaspoon pepper
- 1½ teaspoons Greek seasoning
- 4 (6- to 8-ounce) PILGRIM'S PRIDE Boneless Skinless Chicken Breasts
- 2 tablespoons olive oil
- 1 medium-size red bell pepper, chopped
- 1 small onion, thinly sliced
- ½ cup dry white wine
- ½ cup chicken broth
- 16 small pitted ripe black olives
- Hot cooked rice
- Chopped fresh flat-leaf parsley
- Garnish: fresh flat-leaf parsley sprig

Combine first 3 ingredients; sprinkle evenly over chicken.

Cook chicken in hot oil in a large ovenproof skillet over medium-high heat 5 minutes on each side or until browned. Remove chicken.

Add bell pepper and onion to skillet; sauté 5 minutes or until tender. Stir in wine and broth, stirring to loosen particles from bottom of pan. Stir in olives. Return chicken to skillet.

Bring to a boil. Remove skillet from heat. **Bake,** covered, at 350° for 30 minutes or until chicken is done. Combine rice and chopped parsley. Serve chicken over rice. Garnish, if desired. **Makes** 4 servings.

Brunch Fun

Here are a few ideas to get the brunch bunch actively involved.

■ Go global and have each guest bring a recipe to exchange from the theme country or region you've selected to showcase (or copy the recipes here for starters).

■ Make the party interactive; include salsa dance lessons if the menu features foods from Cuba, Mexico, or Puerto Rico.

■ Include theme music linked to your menu.

■ Share the theme with guests in advance, and ask each one to bring photos if they've visited the theme country or region.

■ Use maps as place mats.

SPICY HUEVOS RANCHEROS

Prep: 20 min., Cook: 12 min., Broil: 1 min.

Huevos rancheros, pronounced [WAY-vohs rahn-CHEH-rohs] is Spanish for "rancher's eggs." For brunch, set up a station at your cooktop, and have one person cook the tortillas while another does the eggs. They'll come out hot and cooked to order. Double or triple the recipe to accommodate your guests.

> 4 (6-inch) MISSION Corn Tortillas
> 2 tablespoons vegetable oil, divided
> 4 large eggs
> ½ cup (2 ounces) shredded Monterey Jack cheese with peppers
> 2 tablespoons chopped fresh cilantro
> 1 (8-ounce) jar peach salsa
> Garnishes: fresh fruit, cilantro sprigs

Cook tortillas in 2 batches in 1 tablespoon hot vegetable oil in a large nonstick skillet 2 minutes on each side or just until crisp. Drain on paper towels. Arrange tortillas in an even layer on an aluminum foil-lined baking sheet.

Break eggs in remaining 1 tablespoon hot oil in skillet, and cook 2 minutes on each side or to desired degree of doneness. Place 1 egg in center of each tortilla; top each evenly with cheese.

Broil 5½ inches from heat 1 minute or until cheese melts. Sprinkle with chopped cilantro. Top with salsa. Garnish, if desired. **Makes** 2 to 4 servings.

MAKE-AHEAD SPOON ROLLS

make ahead

Prep: 15 min., Stand: 5 min., Bake: 20 min.

The batter can be made ahead and stored in your refrigerator for up to 1 week, covered, for hot-from-the-oven rolls anytime.

> 1 (¼-ounce) envelope active dry yeast
> 1 teaspoon sugar
> 2 cups warm water (100° to 110°)
> 4 cups self-rising flour
> ¼ cup sugar
> ¾ cup butter, melted and cooled
> 1 large egg, lightly beaten
> Pinch of salt
> 2 teaspoons dried Italian seasoning
> ¼ teaspoon garlic powder
> PAM For Baking Spray

Combine first 3 ingredients in a large bowl; let mixture stand 5 minutes. Stir in flour and next 6 ingredients until blended. Spoon into muffin pans coated with baking spray, filling two-thirds full.

Bake at 400° for 20 minutes or until rolls are golden brown. **Makes** 2 dozen rolls.

TRIPLE-CHOCOLATE CAKE

Prep: 15 min., Bake: 1 hr., Stand: 10 min.

We used a half bag of the mini morsels in the cake batter for ease in slicing once baked. Sprinkle leftover morsels on ice cream or peanut butter sandwiches.

> 1 (18.25-ounce) package white cake mix with pudding
> 1 (3.9-ounce) package chocolate instant pudding mix
> ½ cup sugar
> ¾ cup vegetable oil
> ¾ cup water
> 4 large eggs
> 1 (8-ounce) container sour cream
> 1 cup (6 ounces) NESTLÉ TOLL HOUSE Semi-Sweet Chocolate Mini Morsels
> Chocolate Glaze

Combine first 3 ingredients in a large bowl, stirring with a whisk to remove large lumps. Add oil and next 3 ingredients, stirring until smooth. Stir in chocolate morsels. Pour batter into a greased and floured 12-cup Bundt pan.

Bake at 350° for 1 hour or until a long wooden pick inserted in center comes out clean.

Cool cake in pan on a wire rack 10 minutes; remove from pan, and let cool completely on wire rack. Spread with Chocolate Glaze. **Makes** 12 servings.

CHOCOLATE GLAZE:

fast fixin's

Prep: 10 min., Cook: 5 min.

> 1 cup (6 ounces) NESTLÉ TOLL HOUSE Semi-Sweet Chocolate Morsels
> 3 tablespoons butter
> ¼ cup milk
> 1½ cups powdered sugar

Whisk together first 3 ingredients in a heavy saucepan over low heat, and cook, whisking constantly, 5 minutes or until butter and chocolate melt. Remove pan from heat; whisk in powdered sugar until smooth and spreading consistency. **Makes** 1⅓ cups.

Soccer Night Solutions

Score big with these ideas for pregame meals or fuel on the way to the fields.

APPLE SPICE-RAISIN SNACK MIX

fast fixin's

Prep: 10 min., Bake: 14 min.

- 3 cups whole grain oat cereal squares
- 1 tablespoon sugar
- 2 teaspoons apple pie spice
- PAM Original No-Stick Cooking Spray
- 1 (11.5-ounce) can dry-roasted mixed nuts
- 1 cup raisins

Combine first 3 ingredients in a medium bowl. Coat cereal mixture evenly with cooking spray. Transfer to an aluminum foil-lined jelly-roll pan coated with cooking spray.

Bake at 350° for 7 minutes. Stir mixture, and coat evenly with cooking spray. Bake 7 more minutes. Stir in nuts and raisins. Cool. Store mixture in an airtight container. **Makes** about 6 cups.

CHICKEN-AND-SLAW WRAPS

fast fixin's • make ahead

Prep: 25 min.

- 2 (6-ounce) packages fully cooked chicken breast strips, chopped
- 1½ cups shredded coleslaw mix with carrots *
- ⅓ cup Ranch dressing
- ¼ cup sweet pickle relish
- 8 deli-style white Cheddar cheese slices (about 3 ounces)
- 4 MISSION Sundried Tomato Basil Wraps

Stir together first 4 ingredients.
Place 2 cheese slices in a single layer on 1 side of each wrap; top each evenly with about ¾ cup chicken mixture. Roll up, jelly-roll fashion, and wrap in plastic wrap, twisting ends of wrap to seal. Chill up to 8 hours, if desired. To serve, cut in half. **Makes** 4 servings.

*Substitute 1½ cups shredded lettuce for coleslaw mix.

OPEN-FACED MONTE CRISTO SANDWICHES

fast fixin's • family favorite

Prep: 10 min., Cook: 12 min., Broil: 3 min.

- 2 large eggs
- ½ cup milk
- 2 teaspoons prepared yellow mustard
- 6 slices NATURE'S OWN Whitewheat Bread
- 2 tablespoons butter
- 6 tablespoons strawberry jam
- 9 ounces thinly sliced deli turkey or chicken
- 9 ounces thinly sliced smoked deli ham
- 10 Swiss cheese slices

Whisk together first 3 ingredients in a shallow dish. Dip both sides of bread in egg mixture.
Melt 1 tablespoon butter in a large nonstick skillet over medium heat; add 3 bread slices, and cook 2 to 3 minutes on each side or until golden brown. Repeat with remaining 1 tablespoon butter and 3 bread slices.
Spread 1 tablespoon strawberry jam on 1 side of each bread slice; top each evenly with turkey, ham, and cheese. Place on a baking sheet.
Broil 5½ inches from heat 2 to 3 minutes or until cheese is melted. **Makes** 6 servings.

PEANUT BUTTER-CHOCOLATE CHIP COOKIES

family favorite

Prep: 20 min., Bake: 15 min. per batch

- ½ cup butter, softened
- ½ cup creamy peanut butter
- 1 teaspoon vanilla extract
- 1 (16-ounce) package dark brown sugar
- 2 large eggs
- 2 cups all-purpose flour
- 1 (10-ounce) package NESTLÉ TOLL HOUSE SWIRLED Milk Chocolate and Peanut Butter Morsels

Beat first 3 ingredients at medium speed with an electric mixer until creamy. Gradually add brown sugar; beat until well blended. Add eggs, beating until blended. Stir in flour and morsels.
Drop dough by level tablespoonfuls 2 inches apart onto parchment paper-lined baking sheets.
Bake at 350° for 13 to 15 minutes or until golden brown. Cool on baking sheets 1 minute; remove cookies to wire racks to cool completely. **Makes** about 6 dozen.

Note: Parchment paper makes cleanup a snap. Flip it over after the first use, and bake on it again. Cookies can also be baked on lightly greased baking sheets.

Tweens' Turn to Cook

They're not teens, and they're not children. Even so, they love the creativity and autonomy of the kitchen. Cooking is the perfect avenue for reinforcing basic math and life skills. It's also a way to build confidence and stir up some good old-fashioned fun.

FIESTA CHICKEN SALAD

fast fixin's

Prep: 20 min., Cook: 11 min.

- 1 pound PILGRIM'S PRIDE Boneless Skinless Chicken Breasts, cut into bite-size pieces
- 1 (1.12-ounce) package fajita seasoning
- ½ cup chopped onion
- Vegetable cooking spray
- 1 garlic clove, pressed
- ½ cup salsa
- Tortilla chips, coarsely crushed
- ½ head iceberg lettuce, shredded
- Toppings: shredded Cheddar cheese, light sour cream, salsa

Stir together chicken and fajita seasoning in a large bowl until evenly coated.
Sauté onion in a nonstick skillet coated with cooking spray over medium heat 4 minutes. Add chicken, and sauté over medium-high heat 4 minutes or until done. Add garlic; sauté 1 minute. Stir in ½ cup salsa. Cook over medium-high heat 2 minutes or until thoroughly heated.
Serve chicken mixture over tortilla chips and lettuce. Serve with desired toppings. **Makes** 4 servings.

PRONTO PORK FAJITAS

family favorite

Prep: 15 min., Stand: 15 min., Cook: 8 min.

- 1 pound boneless pork chops
- 2 tablespoons chopped fresh cilantro, divided
- 2 garlic cloves, pressed
- 2 teaspoons fajita seasoning
- 1 red bell pepper, cut into strips
- 1 medium onion, cut into strips
- 1 tablespoon vegetable oil
- 1 (10¾-ounce) can CAMPBELL'S Fiesta Nacho Cheese Soup
- 3 tablespoons fresh lime juice
- Warm corn tortillas
- Toppings: salsa, sour cream, guacamole

Slice pork diagonally across the grain into ¼-inch strips; toss with 1 tablespoon cilantro, garlic, and fajita seasoning. Let stand 15 minutes.
Sauté pork, bell pepper, and onion in hot oil in a large nonstick skillet over medium heat 4 to 5 minutes or until pork is done. Add soup, lime juice, and remaining 1 tablespoon cilantro, and cook until thoroughly heated. Serve in warm tortillas with desired toppings.
Makes 4 to 6 servings.

ROAST BEEF-CHEDDAR PANINI SANDWICHES

family favorite • fast fixin's

Prep: 5 min., Cook: 11 min.

If you don't have a panini press, place sandwiches in a hot skillet, and press with a smaller heavy pan. Cook until bread is golden brown; turn and cook until other side is golden brown and cheese is melted.

- 1 large onion, sliced
- 1 teaspoon sugar
- ½ teaspoon salt
- ½ cup prepared creamy horseradish sauce, divided
- 8 slices NATURE'S OWN 100% Whole Wheat Bread
- 1 pound deli roast beef slices
- 4 Cheddar, Swiss, or provolone cheese slices
- 1 tablespoon melted butter

Sauté first 3 ingredients in a lightly greased skillet over medium-high heat 8 minutes or until onion is tender.
Spread 1 tablespoon horseradish sauce on each of 4 bread slices; top evenly with roast beef, cooked onion, and cheese. Top with remaining bread slices. Brush melted butter on both sides of sandwich.
Cook in a preheated panini press 2 to 3 minutes or until golden brown. Serve with remaining horseradish sauce. **Makes** 4 servings.

CARAMEL-APPLE QUESADILLAS

family favorite • fast fixin's

Prep: 15 min., Cook: 16 min.

- 2 Granny Smith apples, peeled and thinly sliced
- ½ cup coarsely chopped walnuts
- 1 teaspoon cinnamon sugar
- 1 teaspoon lemon juice
- 3 tablespoons butter, divided
- ½ (8-ounce) package cream cheese, softened
- ¼ cup powdered sugar
- 4 MISSION Burrito Size Flour Tortillas
- ½ cup bottled caramel sauce
- Vanilla ice cream

Toss together first 4 ingredients.
Melt 1 tablespoon butter in a large nonstick skillet over medium-high heat; add apple mixture, and sauté 5 to 8 minutes or until apples are tender. Remove apple mixture from skillet; wipe skillet clean.
Stir together cream cheese and powdered sugar until smooth. Spread cream cheese mixture evenly on 1 side of each tortilla; top cream cheese mixture evenly with apple mixture. Fold tortillas in half over apple mixture.
Melt 1 tablespoon butter in skillet over medium heat. Cook 2 quesadillas 2 minutes on each side or until golden brown. Repeat procedure with remaining butter and quesadillas. Drizzle with caramel sauce, and top with vanilla ice cream. Serve immediately. **Makes** 4 servings.

from our kitchen

Bacon is a bargain when it comes to adding flavor to quick weeknight meals. Its smoky-sweet taste livens up everything from salad to pasta. This over-the-top version of the ultimate BLT layers a thick slice of hot, crusty garlic bread with butter, lettuce, fresh basil, vine-ripened tomatoes, and an irresistible tangle of crisp bacon strips. Serve open-faced with a sprinkling of freshly ground black pepper and a drizzle of your favorite salad dressing. Enjoy the two other bacon recipes at right, too.

Caramel Creations

Don't miss our fabulous recipe for Quick Caramel Frosting on page 211. For perfect results every time, just follow the tips below.

■ Cook the caramel mixture in a heavy saucepan, and stir with a wooden spoon rather than a whisk. A balloon whisk won't reach the edges of the pan, and the mixture will scorch.

■ Once the caramel mixture is removed from the heat, it cools down quickly—so go ahead and use it while it's still warm. If you'd like a thinner caramel, whisk in hot water, a tablespoon at a time, until mixture reaches the desired consistency.

■ We topped our muffins and cakes with a generous coating of caramel, but if you prefer less, just refrigerate leftovers. Store in airtight container up to 2 weeks.

■ If the caramel mixture starts to harden before you're ready to use it (or if it's been stored in the refrigerator), just warm over low heat for a few minutes or microwave at HIGH for 15-second intervals until soft.

■ Transform store-bought convenience products into fare worthy of company. Spoon Quick Caramel Frosting over hot apple pie, spread it over cheesecake, or sandwich it between chocolate wafers and roll the edges in chopped pecans.

■ To make cutting Caramel-Pecan Cheesecake Bars on page 210 extra easy, line the pan with lightly greased heavy-duty aluminum foil, allowing several inches to extend over sides. After baking and chilling, freeze for several hours. Lift from pan using foil; press foil sides down, and cut mixture while partially frozen into desired sizes and shapes.

Caramel-Apple Muffin Techniques

1

An apple corer is the secret to Caramel-Apple Muffins' perfectly shaped apple rings (page 210).

2

Use a wooden spoon with a slightly rounded end to create an indentation in the center of each muffin before adding frosting.

BLT Wraps

Prep: 20 min

1 cup mayonnaise
$^{1}/_{2}$ cup dried tomatoes in oil, drained and chopped
8 (10-inch) flour tortillas
1 large head iceberg lettuce, chopped
1 medium onion, thinly sliced (optional)
16 bacon slices, cooked and crumbled
1 teaspoon salt
1 teaspoon pepper

Combine mayonnaise and tomatoes in a small bowl. Spread evenly over 1 side of each tortilla, leaving a $^{1}/_{2}$-inch border.
Layer lettuce, onion, and bacon evenly over tortillas; sprinkle with salt and pepper. Roll tortillas; cut in half diagonally, and secure with wooden pick. **Makes** 8 wraps.

Bacon Pasta

12 to 15 bacon slices
$^{1}/_{2}$ cup sliced fresh mushrooms
2 garlic cloves, minced
16 ounces penne, cooked
1 cup grated Parmesan cheese
2 cups whipping cream
$^{1}/_{2}$ teaspoon pepper
$^{1}/_{2}$ cup sliced green onions

Cook bacon in a large skillet over medium heat until crisp; remove bacon, reserving 2 tablespoons drippings in skillet. Crumble bacon.
Sauté sliced mushrooms and garlic in reserved drippings 3 minutes or until tender. Stir in pasta, Parmesan cheese, whipping cream, and pepper; simmer over medium-low heat, stirring often, until sauce is thickened. Stir in bacon and sliced green onions; serve immediately. **Makes** 4 to 6 servings.

Grab-and-Go Grits

Plan ahead for breakfast on the run by spooning leftover grits into lightly greased microwave-safe cups. Cover with plastic wrap, and store in the refrigerator for up to 3 days. When ready to serve, just microwave at HIGH 1 to 2 minutes or until thoroughly heated.

Chalupa Dinner Bowl, page 238

Citrus-Pear Honey, page 230

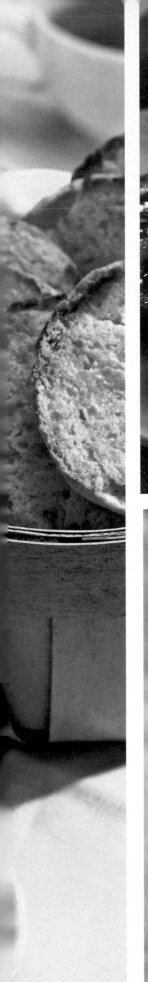

Savory Ham-and-Swiss Breakfast Pie, page 240

Yogurt with Mixed Fruit Granola and Orange Syrup, page 240

227

Fresh Apple Upside-Down Cake,
page 231

october

230 Try a Taste of Fall *Bring the fresh flavors of autumn to your table*

232 It's Great Pumpkin *Easy bake-and-take desserts*

233 Oven-Roasted Goodness *Delicious winter squash recipes packed with nutrition*

234 Taste of the South Make a Batch of Texas Chili *You don't have to live in the Lone Star State to enjoy a bowl of this tasty regional specialty*

235 Warm and Hearty Stews *Cook and carry these healthful dishes to your next gathering*

236 Cooking Up Cabbage *Try this versatile vegetable for a change of pace*

237 Supper Tonight *One-dish meals solve your dinner dilemma*

238 Healthy & Light The Season's Best Spices *Use warm, fragrant ingredients to give your dishes a tasty boost*

240 Top-Rated Menu Savor a Fall Breakfast *Enjoy this comforting menu anytime of the day*

241 What's for Supper? Keep on Grilling *You're in good company if you cook over fire year-round*

241 Quick & Easy Fast Asian Fare *Enjoy a speedy stir-fry full of products your taste buds will love*

242 From Our Kitchen *Pasta, Asian seasonings, and more*

Try a Taste of Fall

Apples and pears are ripe for the picking. Bring fresh flavors to the table with these simple recipes.

A handful of pantry ingredients turns a harvest of fragrant and juicy fruits into versatile desserts and side dishes. Warmly spiced Fresh Apple Upside-Down Cake is irresistible on a chilly autumn day. Topped with a round of refrigerated piecrust, Citrus-Pear Honey is quickly turned into a cobbler. Field Greens With Roasted Bacon-Wrapped Pears tastes equally good when made with pears and Parmesan or with apples and Cheddar. If you're lucky enough to have leftover Apple-Ginger Vinaigrette, drizzle it over a pan of hot roasted root vegetables or use it as a marinade for grilled chicken or pork.

FIELD GREENS WITH ROASTED BACON-WRAPPED PEARS

fast fixin's

Prep: 15 min., Bake: 10 min.

> 12 ready-to-serve bacon slices
> 3 large pears, peeled and quartered
> 6 cups mixed salad greens
> ⅔ cup pecans, toasted
> ⅔ cup shaved Parmesan cheese
> Apple-Ginger Vinaigrette

Wrap 1 slice of bacon around each pear quarter, and secure with a wooden pick. Place pear quarters on a wire rack in a 15- x 10-inch jelly-roll pan.
Bake pears at 350° for 10 minutes.
Arrange salad greens on 4 serving plates, and sprinkle evenly with pecans and Parmesan cheese. Place 3 pear quarters on each salad, and serve with Apple-Ginger Vinaigrette. **Makes** 4 servings.

Note: For testing purposes only, we used Oscar Mayer Ready to Serve Bacon.

APPLE-GINGER VINAIGRETTE:

fast fixin's

Prep: 10 min.

> ½ cup apple jelly, melted
> ⅓ cup cider vinegar
> 1 tablespoon Dijon mustard
> 2 tablespoons light brown sugar
> 3 tablespoons chopped fresh chives
> 2 teaspoons grated fresh ginger
> ¼ teaspoon salt
> 1 cup vegetable oil

Whisk together first 7 ingredients; gradually whisk in oil until well blended. **Makes** about 2 cups.

MARTHA JORDAN NEWBERRY
PALM BAY, FLORIDA

RASPBERRY-ALMOND PEAR TART

Prep: 20 min., Bake: 30 min., Cook: 5 min.

> ½ (15-ounce) package refrigerated piecrusts
> ⅓ cup seedless raspberry jam
> 6 tablespoons butter, softened and divided
> 4 large pears, peeled and quartered
> ¼ cup sugar
> 1 large egg
> ½ cup vanilla wafer crumbs
> ½ cup ground almonds, toasted
> ¼ teaspoon almond extract

Unroll piecrust, and fit into a 9-inch tart pan; trim excess.
Bake at 400° for 5 minutes; remove from oven, and cool completely on a wire rack. Spread raspberry jam evenly on bottom of prepared piecrust.
Melt 2 tablespoons butter in a large skillet over medium-high heat; add pears, and cook, stirring often, 5 minutes. Remove from heat, and arrange pear slices over raspberry jam.
Beat remaining 4 tablespoons butter at medium speed with an electric mixer until creamy; gradually add sugar, beating well. Add egg, beating until blended. Stir in vanilla wafer crumbs, almonds, and almond extract; spread evenly over pears.
Bake at 400° for 20 to 25 minutes or until browned; cool on a wire rack.
Makes 6 to 8 servings.

CITRUS-PEAR HONEY

fast fixin's • make ahead

Prep: 15 min., Cook: 15 min.

Deliciously syrupy, this breakfast treat is wonderful with everything from buttered toast and biscuits to waffles and French toast. (*pictured on page 226*)

> 2 tablespoons butter
> 6 large pears, peeled and quartered
> ½ cup sugar
> ⅓ cup honey
> 1 teaspoon grated orange rind
> ¼ cup orange juice

Melt butter in a Dutch oven over medium-high heat; stir in next 3 ingredients, and cook, stirring often, 10 to 15 minutes or until pears are tender and juices are slightly thickened and caramel colored. Remove from heat, and stir in orange rind and orange juice. Serve warm, or let cool, and store in an airtight container in the refrigerator for up to 2 weeks. **Makes** about 3 cups.

NANCY HAJEK
FAIRVIEW, TENNESSEE

Citrus-Pear Honey Cobbler: Double the ingredients for Citrus-Pear Honey, and prepare as directed in an ovenproof Dutch oven. Unroll ½ (15-ounce) package refrigerated piecrusts, and place on top of hot pear mixture in Dutch oven. Bake at 425° for 15 minutes or until crust is golden brown. **Makes** 8 servings. Prep: 25 min., Cook: 15 min., Bake: 15 min.

FRESH APPLE UPSIDE-DOWN CAKE

Prep: 20 min., Cook: 7 min., Bake: 30 min., Stand: 5 min.

Tart apples, such as Granny Smith, that hold their shape when cooked are best for this recipe. A small paring knife makes quick work of peeling the fruit. (pictured on page 228)

    ¾ cup butter, softened and
        divided
    2 cups sugar, divided
    3 large Granny Smith apples,
        peeled and cut into ½-inch-
        thick slices
    1 cup toasted chopped pecans,
        divided
    2 large eggs
    1½ cups all-purpose flour
    1 teaspoon baking powder
    1 teaspoon ground cinnamon
    ½ cup milk

Melt ¼ cup butter in a 10-inch cast-iron skillet over medium-high heat; add 1 cup sugar, and cook, stirring often, 2 minutes or until sugar is melted and begins to turn golden. Add apple slices, and cook, stirring often, 5 minutes or until apples have softened slightly and juices are thickened and syrupy. Remove skillet from heat, and sprinkle apple mixture with ½ cup pecans. Set aside.

Beat remaining ½ cup butter at medium speed with an electric mixer until creamy. Gradually add remaining 1 cup sugar, beating until light and fluffy. Add eggs, 1 at a time, beating just until blended after each addition.

Stir together flour, baking powder, and cinnamon; add to butter mixture alternately with milk, beating at low speed just until blended, beginning and ending with flour mixture. Stir in remaining ½ cup pecans. Spoon batter evenly over apple mixture in skillet.

Bake at 350° for 30 minutes or until a wooden pick inserted in center comes out clean. Cool in skillet 5 minutes; invert onto a serving plate. **Makes** 8 servings.

CRESCENT ROLL APPLES

Prep: 10 min., Bake: 45 min.

    1 (8-ounce) can refrigerated
        crescent rolls
    2 tablespoons butter, softened
    1 tablespoon sugar
    1 teaspoon ground cinnamon
    2 large Granny Smith apples,
        peeled and quartered
    1 (6-ounce) can frozen apple juice
        concentrate, thawed

Unroll crescent roll dough, and separate into triangles. Spread butter evenly over dough. Stir together sugar and cinnamon; sprinkle evenly over butter.

Wrap each apple quarter in 1 crescent roll dough triangle, and place in a lightly greased 13- x 9-inch baking dish. Pour apple juice concentrate evenly over rolls. **Bake** at 350° for 45 minutes or until golden brown and bubbly. **Makes** 8 servings.

NANCIE ALLEN
RUSSELLVILLE, ALABAMA

HOMEMADE APPLESAUCE

Prep: 20 min., Cook: 20 min.

For the best taste and texture, use at least two types of apples—such as Granny Smith and Gala— when making applesauce and pies.

    12 large apples, peeled and
        coarsely chopped
    1 cup sugar
    ½ lemon, sliced

Cook all 3 ingredients in a Dutch oven over medium heat, stirring often, 20 minutes or until the apples are tender and the juices are thickened. Remove and discard lemon slices. Serve applesauce warm; or let cool, and store in an airtight container in the refrigerator for up to 2 weeks. **Makes** about 6 cups.

Spiced Applesauce: Substitute ½ cup firmly packed brown sugar and ½ cup granulated sugar for 1 cup sugar. Omit lemon slices, and add 1 teaspoon ground cinnamon and ¼ teaspoon ground cloves; prepare as directed.

■ **Applesauce Turnovers:** Homemade Applesauce teams up with refrigerated piecrust rounds for quick and easy turnovers. Make as few or as many of these little pies as you'd like. Unroll the piecrust dough on a lightly floured surface, and cut circular shapes using a 4-inch round cutter. Lightly brush the edges of each circle with water. Spoon about 2 tablespoons of Homemade Applesauce in the center of each circle. Fold circles in half, pressing edges to seal. Place on a lightly greased baking sheet. Bake at 425° for 15 minutes or until golden brown.

■ **Quick Cranberry-Apple Chutney:** Stir together 2 cups Homemade Applesauce; 1 (10-ounce) jar jalapeño pepper jelly; 1 (6-ounce) package sweetened dried cranberries; and 1 small sweet onion, finely chopped, in a 3-quart saucepan. Bring to a boil over medium heat, and cook, stirring often, 10 minutes or until thickened. **Makes** about 3½ cups. Prep: 5 min., Cook: 10 min.

■ Quick Cranberry-Apple Chutney pairs perfectly with pork, chicken, or turkey. For a last-minute appetizer, combine equal parts softened cream cheese and shredded sharp Cheddar; shape and top with chutney.

■ **Applesauce Gingerbread:** Stir together 1 (14.5-ounce) package gingerbread mix, 1 cup Homemade Applesauce, ¾ cup water, and 1 large egg until blended; spoon evenly into a lightly greased 9-inch square pan. Bake at 350° for 30 minutes or until a wooden pick inserted in center comes out clean. **Makes** 9 servings. Prep: 5 min., Bake: 30 min.

■ Homemade Applesauce complements some of our favorite fall foods. Tuck a few spoonfuls into a baked sweet potato or a grilled cheese sandwich. Create a caramel-apple sundae or a breakfast parfait with yogurt and granola. Stir in a little chopped rosemary, and serve it as a side dish with pork chops or hash browns.

APPLE BROWN BETTY

Prep: 15 min., Bake: 45 min.

  4 cups soft white breadcrumbs
  1/3 cup butter, melted
  1 cup firmly packed brown sugar
  1 tablespoon ground cinnamon
  4 large Granny Smith apples,
    peeled and cut into
    1/4-inch-thick slices
  1 cup apple cider

Stir together breadcrumbs and butter.
Stir together brown sugar and cinnamon.
Place half of the apple slices in a lightly
greased 12- x 8-inch baking dish; sprinkle apples with half of brown sugar mixture and half of breadcrumb mixture.
Repeat procedure with remaining apples,
brown sugar mixture, and breadcrumb
mixture. Pour apple cider over top.
Bake at 350° for 45 minutes. **Makes**
6 servings.

SUZAN L. WIENER
SPRING HILL, FLORIDA

It's Great Pumpkin

Share the love of pumpkin with Mary
McClure of Barboursville, West Vir-
ginia. Every year she wins big at the
West Virginia Pumpkin Festival, held in
Milton. Try some of Mary's goodies.

PUMPKIN BREAD

freezeable • make ahead

Prep: 10 min., Bake: 1 hr.

  3 1/3 cups all-purpose flour
  3 cups sugar
  2 teaspoons baking soda
  1 1/2 teaspoons salt
  1 1/2 teaspoons ground cinnamon
  1 teaspoon ground nutmeg
  1 cup vegetable oil
  2/3 cup water
  4 large eggs
  1 (15-ounce) can pumpkin

Stir together all ingredients in a large
bowl until smooth. Divide batter evenly
among 3 greased and floured 9- x 5-
inch loafpans.
Bake at 350° for 50 minutes to 1 hour
or until a wooden pick inserted into
center of each loaf comes out clean.
Cool in pans on a wire rack 10 minutes.
Remove from pans, and cool completely on wire rack. **Makes** 3 loaves.

MARY MCCLURE
BARBOURSVILLE, WEST VIRGINIA

PUMPKIN FUDGE

Prep: 10 min., Cook: 15 min., Stand: 2 hrs.

Line pan with aluminum foil before you
begin to cook the fudge. Once the candy
thermometer reaches 234° and the remaining ingredients are added, quickly spoon the
fudge into the pan.

  3 cups sugar
  3/4 cup melted butter
  2/3 cup evaporated milk
  1/2 cup canned pumpkin
  2 tablespoons corn syrup
  1 teaspoon pumpkin pie spice
  1 (12-ounce) package white
    chocolate morsels
  1 (7-ounce) jar
    marshmallow cream
  1 cup chopped pecans, toasted
  1 teaspoon vanilla extract

Stir together first 6 ingredients in a
3 1/2-quart saucepan over medium-high
heat, and cook, stirring constantly, until
mixture comes to a boil. Cook, stirring
constantly, until a candy thermometer
registers 234° (soft-ball stage) or for
about 12 minutes.
Remove pan from heat; stir in remaining ingredients until well blended. Pour
into a greased aluminum foil-lined 9-
inch square pan. Let stand 2 hours or
until completely cool; cut fudge into
squares. **Makes** about 3 pounds.

MARY MCCLURE
BARBOURSVILLE, WEST VIRGINIA

PUMPKIN SPICE CAKE

Prep: 10 min., Bake: 30 min.

  4 large eggs
  2 cups sugar
  1 cup vegetable oil
  1 (15-ounce) can pumpkin
  2 cups all-purpose flour
  2 teaspoons baking
    powder
  2 teaspoons ground
    cinnamon
  1/2 teaspoon baking soda
  1/2 teaspoon salt
  1/2 teaspoon ground
    ginger
  1/4 teaspoon ground cloves
  Cream Cheese Frosting
  1/2 cup chopped walnuts,
    toasted

Combine first 4 ingredients in a large
bowl. Beat at medium speed with an
electric mixer until smooth.
Combine flour and next 6 ingredients.
Stir flour mixture into pumpkin mixture until well blended. Spread batter in
a lightly greased 15- x 10 1/2-inch jelly-
roll pan.
Bake at 350° for 25 to 30 minutes or
until lightly browned. Cool completely
in pan on a wire rack.
Spread Cream Cheese Frosting evenly
over cake; sprinkle with walnuts.
Makes 15 servings.

CREAM CHEESE FROSTING:
fast fixin's

Prep: 5 min.

  1 (3-ounce) package cream cheese,
    softened
  1/3 cup butter, softened
  1 teaspoon vanilla extract
  2 cups powdered sugar

Beat first 3 ingredients at medium
speed with an electric mixer until
creamy. Gradually beat in powdered
sugar until smooth. **Makes** 1 1/2 cups.

MARY MCCLURE
BARBOURSVILLE, WEST VIRGINIA

Oven-Roasted Goodness

Taste the wonders of winter squash with these fresh and flavorful dishes.

Never sacrifice rich flavor for good nutrition. Enjoy the best of both worlds with these recipes using winter squash, packed full of nutrients.

Roast your favorite type as directed. Then, serve it as a side dish, or use it as an ingredient in a soup or casserole. We even chopped roasted butternut squash into a hearty salad. You won't believe how great it tastes when drizzled with Blue Cheese Vinaigrette.

ROASTED WINTER SQUASH

Prep: 10 min., Bake: 35 min.

- **3 pounds butternut squash, acorn squash, or spaghetti squash**
- **1 tablespoon butter or margarine, melted**
- **½ tablespoon honey**
- **¼ teaspoon salt**
- **¼ teaspoon pepper**

Remove stem from squash. Cut squash in half lengthwise; remove and discard seeds. Cut each half into 4 wedges, and place on an aluminum foil-lined jelly-roll pan. (If using spaghetti squash, cut each half into 2 wedges.)

Stir together butter and honey until blended. Brush squash evenly with butter mixture; sprinkle evenly with salt and pepper.

Bake at 450° for 30 to 35 minutes or until tender, turning once. Cut skins from squash wedges, and discard. **Makes** 6 servings.

Per serving: Calories 108 (16% from fat); Fat 2.1g (sat 1g, mono 0.8g, poly 0.2g); Protein 1.8g; Carb 24g; Fiber 6.8g; Chol 5mg; Iron 1.5mg; Sodium 118mg; Calc 69mg

ROASTED BUTTERNUT SQUASH SALAD WITH BLUE CHEESE VINAIGRETTE

Prep: 20 min., Cook: 7 min.

- **1 small red onion, sliced**
- **1 teaspoon olive oil**
- **Roasted Winter Squash (see recipe at left; use 3 pounds butternut squash), cubed**
- **1 (6-ounce) package fresh baby spinach (about 8 cups)**
- **Blue Cheese Vinaigrette**
- **½ cup sweetened dried cranberries**
- **⅓ cup chopped pecans, toasted**
- **2 reduced-fat bacon slices, cooked and crumbled**

Sauté onion in hot oil in a large non-stick skillet over medium-high heat 5 minutes or until tender. Add roasted squash, and cook 1 to 2 minutes or just until warm. Remove from heat.

Toss spinach in a bowl with Blue Cheese Vinaigrette. Arrange baby spinach on a serving platter; top with squash mixture, cranberries, pecans, and bacon. **Makes** 6 servings.

Per serving (not including dressing): Calories 213 (38% from fat); Fat 8.9g (sat 2g, mono 4.6g, poly 1.8g); Protein 4g; Carb 35.5g; Fiber 8.3g; Chol 8mg; Iron 2.5mg; Sodium 203mg; Calc 111mg

BLUE CHEESE VINAIGRETTE:
fast fixin's • make ahead

Prep: 10 min.

This recipe easily doubles. Store in an air-tight container in the refrigerator for up to 2 weeks.

- **3 tablespoons crumbled blue cheese**
- **2 tablespoons water**
- **1½ tablespoons vegetable oil**
- **1 tablespoon white vinegar**
- **1 tablespoon lemon juice**
- **1 teaspoon Dijon mustard**
- **½ teaspoon dried oregano**
- **¼ teaspoon sugar**
- **¼ teaspoon freshly ground pepper**
- **Dash of salt**

Whisk together all ingredients. Cover and chill until ready to serve. **Makes** ½ cup (6 servings).

Per serving: Calories 54 (73% from fat); Fat 4.5g (sat 1.1, mono 1.8g, poly 1.5g); Protein 1g; Carb 2.8g; Fiber 0.1g; Chol 3mg; Iron 0.1mg; Sodium 98mg; Calc 23mg

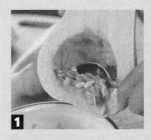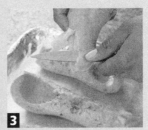

Roast with Ease

Roasting is a great way to enhance the flavor of winter squash. Follow the recipe for Roasted Winter Squash at left, and you'll have a great stand-alone side or the key ingredient for lots of delicious dishes.
1. After removing stem, cut squash in half lengthwise; discard seeds. Cut each half into 4 wedges. (If using spaghetti squash, cut each half into 2 wedges.) Place wedges on an aluminum foil-lined jelly-roll pan.
2. Brush squash with honey-butter mixture, and sprinkle with seasonings.
3. After roasting squash, cut skins from wedges, and discard.

BUTTERNUT SQUASH BAKE

Prep: 15 min., Bake: 40 min.

This easy dish has a soufflélike quality.

- Roasted Winter Squash (see recipe on previous page; use 3 pounds butternut squash), coarsely chopped
- ¾ cup egg substitute
- 2 tablespoons butter, melted
- 2 tablespoons frozen orange juice concentrate, thawed
- 2 tablespoons honey
- ⅛ teaspoon salt
- Dash of ground nutmeg

Toss together chopped roasted squash and remaining ingredients in a large bowl. Process mixture, in batches, in a blender or food processor until smooth, stopping to scrape down sides. Pour mixture into a lightly greased 1½-quart baking dish.

Bake at 350° for 35 to 40 minutes or until mixture is set. **Makes** 4 to 6 servings.

DOROTHY ROBERTS
HIAWASSEE, GEORGIA

Per serving: Calories 169 (34% from fat); Fat 6.9g (sat 3.1g, mono 2.6g, poly 0.8g); Protein 5.7g; Carb 24g; Fiber 5.5g; Chol 15mg; Iron 1.9mg; Sodium 250mg; Calc 100mg

CURRIED BUTTERNUT SQUASH SOUP

Prep: 15 min., Cook: 25 min.

For lower salt intake, use low-sodium chicken broth. Look for lite coconut milk on the Asian aisle of the supermarket.

- Roasted Winter Squash (see recipe on previous page; use 3 pounds butternut squash)
- ¾ pound unpeeled, medium-size fresh shrimp
- 1 (32-ounce) container chicken broth
- ½ cup lite coconut milk
- ½ teaspoon salt
- ½ teaspoon curry powder
- 2 tablespoons chopped fresh cilantro

Mash roasted squash with a potato masher or fork, and set aside.

Peel shrimp, and devein, if desired. Set aside.

Stir together broth and next 3 ingredients in a Dutch oven over medium heat, and cook, stirring occasionally, 20 minutes or until thoroughly heated. Remove from heat.

Process squash and broth mixture together, in batches, in a food processor or blender until smooth, stopping to scrape down sides. Return mixture to Dutch oven; add shrimp, and cook over medium heat until thoroughly heated and shrimp turn pink. Sprinkle each serving with cilantro. **Makes** 8 (1-cup) servings.

Per serving: Calories 136 (19% from fat); Fat 3g (sat 1.6g, mono 0.7g, poly 0.4g); Protein 11.6g; Carb 17.8g; Fiber 4.1g; Chol 68mg; Iron 2mg; Sodium 601mg; Calc 83mg

SPAGHETTI SQUASH SAUTÉ

fast fixin's

Prep: 15 min., Cook: 11 min.

Here's a fiber-rich alternative to potato hash browns.

- Roasted Winter Squash (see recipe on previous page; use 3 pounds spaghetti squash)
- ½ cup chopped onion
- 2 teaspoons olive oil, divided
- 2 garlic cloves, minced
- ¼ teaspoon salt
- ¼ teaspoon pepper

Rake stringy pulp from roasted spaghetti squash, using the tines of a fork, and place in a bowl. Set aside.

Sauté onion in 1 teaspoon hot oil in a large nonstick skillet over medium-high heat 5 minutes or until tender. Add garlic; sauté 1 minute.

Add squash, salt, pepper, and remaining 1 teaspoon oil to onion mixture in skillet, and cook, stirring occasionally, 5 minutes. Serve immediately. **Makes** 6 servings.

Per serving: Calories 113 (29% from fat); Fat 3.4g (sat 1.3g, mono 1.9g, poly 0.5g); Protein 1.9g; Carb 20g; Fiber 3.6g; Chol 5mg; Iron 0.8mg; Sodium 245mg; Calc 56mg

ROASTED ACORN SQUASH WITH CRANBERRY RELISH

fast fixin's

Prep: 10 min., Cook: 15 min.

- ⅓ cup apple cider
- ⅓ cup maple syrup
- 2 tablespoons butter
- ¼ teaspoon ground cinnamon
- ¼ teaspoon ground ginger
- ¼ teaspoon ground nutmeg
- 1 cup fresh cranberries
- ¼ cup chopped pecans, toasted
- Roasted Winter Squash (see recipe on previous page; use 3 medium acorn squash)

Bring first 6 ingredients to a boil in a small saucepan over medium heat. Reduce heat, and simmer 5 minutes.

Stir in cranberries, and simmer 8 minutes or until cranberry skins split. Remove from heat, and stir in pecans. Spoon cranberry mixture over warm squash wedges. **Makes** 6 servings.

FRANK MILLER
ARLINGTON, TEXAS

Per serving: Calories 241 (33% from fat); Fat 9.5g (sat 3.2g, mono 4.4g, poly 1.4g); Protein 2.3g; Carb 41g; Fiber 4.5g; Chol 15mg; Iron 1.9mg; Sodium 147mg; Calc 90mg

taste of the south
Make a Batch of Texas Chili

Associate Foods Editor Shannon Sliter Satterwhite has always had a passion for spicy food, but when she tried Texas chili for the first time, she found true love. Shannon's love affair with Southwestern flavor soon led her to the discovery of a rich, well-seasoned stew with chunks of tender beef in every bite—a style of chili that Texans have been making for generations.

The granddaddy of this Tex-Mex dish, chili con carne, is thought to have originated in the 1800s along the Texas cattle trails. Range cooks would commonly prepare a pot of fresh beef and wild-grown seasonings for the cowhands.

Before long, the popularity of this spicy stew spread like cheese on a hot burrito throughout the trail towns.

Texans take their chili seriously, and opinions vary widely on what makes a perfect bowl of "red." Some add a variety of meats, while others insist on beef. Many use commercial seasonings and powders for convenience, but purists grind their own chile peppers. Some cooks serve theirs with a side of pintos or other beans. The trick to any chili, however, is to slowly build flavor by letting your seasonings simmer awhile.

CHUNKY BEEF CHILI

freezeable

Prep: 25 min.; Cook: 1 hr., 45 min.

Replace spices you've had more than a year. Seasonings tend to dull in flavor the longer they sit on the shelf. Store them in a cool, dry place.

    4 pounds boneless chuck roast, cut
        into ½-inch pieces
    2 tablespoons chili powder
    2 (6-ounce) cans tomato paste
    1 (32-ounce) container beef broth
    2 (8-ounce) cans tomato sauce
    2 teaspoons granulated garlic
    1 teaspoon salt
    1 teaspoon ground oregano
    1 teaspoon ground cumin
    1 teaspoon paprika
    1 teaspoon onion powder
    ½ teaspoon ground black pepper
    ¼ teaspoon ground red pepper
    Cornbread sticks (optional)
    Toppings: crushed tortilla chips,
        sour cream, shredded cheese,
        chopped onion

Brown meat, in batches, in a Dutch oven over medium-high heat. Remove meat, reserving drippings in Dutch oven. Add chili powder to Dutch oven; cook, stirring constantly, 2 minutes. Stir in tomato paste; cook 5 minutes.
Return beef to Dutch oven. Stir in beef broth and next 9 ingredients; bring to a boil. Reduce heat to low, and simmer, uncovered, stirring occasionally, 1½ hours or until beef is tender. Serve with cornbread sticks, if desired, and desired toppings. **Makes** 9 cups.

Warm and Hearty Stews

This fall, take pleasure in eating well without a lot of fuss. These vitamin-packed stews are light on calories and will have you out of the kitchen in no time.

SLOW-COOKER BEEF STEW

family favorite • make ahead

Prep: 20 min.; Cook: 7 hrs., 30 min.

    2 pounds round steak, cut into
        1-inch pieces
    1 pound carrots, cut into 1-inch
        pieces*
    1 pound small red potatoes,
        quartered*
    1 (8-ounce) package sliced fresh
        mushrooms
    1 red bell pepper, diced**
    1 (14½-ounce) can diced
        tomatoes**
    1 (6-ounce) can tomato paste
    ¾ cup beef broth
    ⅓ cup red wine
    ¼ cup all-purpose flour
    2 garlic cloves, minced
    1½ teaspoons salt
    1 teaspoon pepper
    ½ teaspoon dried thyme

Combine all ingredients in a 6-quart slow cooker, and cook, covered, on LOW 7 hours and 30 minutes. **Makes** 8 (1¼-cup) servings.

*Substitute 2 (1-pound) packages frozen stew vegetables for carrots and potatoes, if desired.

**Substitute 1 (14½-ounce) can diced tomatoes with green peppers and onions for red bell pepper and diced tomatoes, if desired.

SHARON SMITH
OVERLAND PARK, KANSAS

Per serving: Calories 293 (23% from fat); Fat 7g (sat 2.6g, mono 2.9g, poly 0.43g); Protein 31g; Carb 26g; Fiber 4g; Chol 65mg; Iron 4.4mg; Sodium 702mg; Calc 42mg

CHICKEN-AND-VEGETABLE STEW

family favorite • make ahead

Prep: 10 min., Cook: 1 hr.

    1 (32-ounce) container fat-free
        chicken broth
    4 skinned, bone-in chicken breast
        halves (about 2¼ pounds)
    1 medium onion, chopped
    2 celery ribs, chopped
    1 (14-ounce) package frozen white
        corn
    1 (16-ounce) package frozen baby
        lima beans
    1 (14½-ounce) can crushed
        tomatoes
    ⅓ cup ketchup
    ¼ cup chopped country ham
    1 tablespoon sugar
    3 tablespoons red wine vinegar
    1 teaspoon Worcestershire sauce
    ½ to 1 teaspoon hot sauce
    1 teaspoon dried marjoram

Bring broth to a boil in a Dutch oven over medium-high heat. Add chicken, onion, and celery, and return to a boil. Reduce heat, and simmer 30 minutes or until chicken is tender. Remove chicken from pan, and let cool slightly.
Remove chicken from bones, discarding bones; shred chicken.
Add corn, next 9 ingredients, and chicken to Dutch oven. Bring to a boil; reduce heat, and simmer, stirring occasionally, 30 minutes or until beans are tender. **Makes** 8 (1¼-cup) servings.

BETTY M. POLLARD
HAMPTON, VIRGINIA

Per serving: Calories 289 (7% from fat); Fat 2g (sat 0.55g, mono 0.6g, poly 0.7g); Protein 33g; Carb 35g; Fiber 6g; Chol 62mg; Iron 2.8mg; Sodium 721mg; Calc 64mg

HEARTY HAM-AND-COLLARD STEW

family favorite • make ahead

Prep: 20 min.; Cook: 1 hr., 5 min.

- 1 large sweet onion, diced (about 1½ cups)
- 3 celery ribs, diced
- 1 (8-ounce) lean ham steak, diced
- 1 teaspoon vegetable oil
- 1 (14-ounce) can fat-free chicken broth
- 1 (29-ounce) can diced tomatoes
- 1 (1-pound) package fresh collard greens, washed, trimmed, and chopped
- 3 (16-ounce) cans pinto beans, rinsed and drained

Sauté diced onion, diced celery, and diced ham in hot vegetable oil in a large Dutch oven over medium-high heat 8 minutes or until onion is tender.
Stir in chicken broth, diced tomatoes, and chopped collard greens; bring to a boil. Cover, reduce heat, and simmer, stirring occasionally, 45 minutes.
Stir in beans, and simmer, stirring occasionally, 10 minutes or until thoroughly heated. **Makes** 8 (1½-cup) servings.

TONI ROCHE
LIZELLA, GEORGIA

Per serving: Calories 179 (12% from fat); Fat 2.4g (sat 0.1g, mono 0.27g, poly 0.4g); Protein 13g; Carb 26g; Fiber 8.8g; Chol 15mg; Iron 2.2mg; Sodium 748mg; Calc 141mg

Cooking Up Cabbage

Pick up a head of cabbage on your next trip to the supermarket, and we'll help you make it great. This affordable vegetable is easy to prepare and full of great flavor. Choose one that's heavy for its size with crisp, tightly packed leaves. Store a head of cabbage in a zip-top plastic bag in the refrigerator up to two weeks. When you're in a hurry, grab a bag of preshredded cabbage. Go ahead, and try cabbage tonight—it's good stuff.

FIESTA CABBAGE

Prep: 15 min., Cook: 25 min.

- 1 pound kielbasa, sliced into ¼-inch-thick slices *
- 1 medium-size red onion, diced
- 1 medium-size green bell pepper, diced
- 1 medium cabbage (about 2½ pounds), chopped into bite-size pieces
- 1 (14.5-ounce) can diced tomatoes, undrained
- 1 teaspoon salt
- ½ teaspoon pepper

Sauté kielbasa in a large nonstick skillet over medium-high heat until browned. Remove sausage with a slotted spoon, and drain on paper towels, reserving drippings in skillet. Set aside.
Sauté onion and bell pepper in hot drippings over medium-high heat 3 minutes. Stir in cabbage; cover and cook, stirring occasionally, 15 minutes or until vegetables are tender.
Stir in cooked sausage, tomatoes, salt, and pepper. Cook until thoroughly heated. **Makes** 6 servings.

*Substitute 1 pound ground pork sausage, if desired. Sauté vegetables in 2 tablespoons reserved drippings.

CODY WEST
HOLLIDAY, TEXAS

SCALLOPED CABBAGE

Prep: 15 min., Cook: 10 min., Bake: 30 min.

- 1 large cabbage (about 3 pounds), shredded
- 1¼ teaspoons salt, divided
- 2 cups boiling water
- 2 tablespoons butter
- 2 tablespoons all-purpose flour
- 1 cup milk
- ½ cup (2 ounces) shredded Cheddar cheese
- 3 tablespoons saltine cracker crumbs (optional)

Cook cabbage and 1 teaspoon salt in 2 cups boiling water 8 minutes. Remove from heat, and drain. Place cabbage in a lightly greased 2-quart baking dish.

Melt butter in a small saucepan over medium-high heat; whisk in flour. Slowly whisk in milk until smooth. Remove from heat, and whisk in remaining ¼ teaspoon salt and cheese, whisking until cheese is melted. Pour cheese mixture evenly over cabbage. Sprinkle evenly with cracker crumbs, if desired.
Bake, uncovered, at 350° for 30 minutes or until bubbly. **Makes** 6 servings.

PAULA S. BOYCE
CHARLOTTE, NORTH CAROLINA

BRAISED RED CABBAGE

Prep: 10 min., Cook: 50 min.

- 1 medium-size red cabbage (about 2½ pounds), shredded
- 2 Granny Smith apples, peeled and sliced
- ¼ cup butter
- ¼ cup dry red wine *
- 1 bay leaf
- 3 tablespoons brown sugar
- 1 teaspoon salt
- ¼ teaspoon pepper
- ¼ teaspoon ground cloves
- ½ cup chopped, toasted walnuts

Combine first 9 ingredients in a large saucepan. Cook over medium-high heat 5 minutes. Cover, reduce heat to low, and cook, stirring occasionally, 45 minutes or until liquid evaporates and cabbage is tender. Discard bay leaf.
Place cabbage mixture on serving dish; sprinkle evenly with toasted walnuts. **Makes** 6 servings.

*Substitute ¼ cup apple juice, if desired.

DELLA TAYLOR
JONESBOROUGH, TENNESSEE

Supper Tonight

Four fab recipes—pick one, serve with a salad, and dinner's done.

One-dish meals don't have to be blah. The flavor has been upped on these recipes, and each one keeps you well within your prep-time comfort zone and uses basic kitchen equipment. Sure, the first time you make each recipe you'll feel like a newbie, but after that you're on autopilot. Are the dishes good enough for company? You bet.

CAJUN SHRIMP CASSEROLE

freezeable • make ahead

Prep: 30 min., Cook: 16 min., Bake: 20 min.

This longer ingredient list is worth the effort for a special occasion meal. If you're not a fan of okra, you can leave it out of this dish.

- **2 pounds unpeeled, large fresh shrimp**
- **¼ cup butter**
- **1 small red onion, chopped ∗**
- **½ cup chopped red bell pepper ∗**
- **½ cup chopped yellow bell pepper ∗**
- **½ cup chopped green bell pepper ∗**
- **4 garlic cloves, minced**
- **2 cups fresh or frozen sliced okra**
- **1 tablespoon lemon juice**
- **1½ teaspoons salt**
- **1 (10¾-ounce) can cream of shrimp soup ∗∗**
- **½ cup dry white wine**
- **1 tablespoon soy sauce**
- **½ teaspoon cayenne pepper**
- **3 cups cooked long-grain rice**
- **¼ cup grated Parmesan cheese**
- **Garnishes: quartered lemon slices, fresh flat-leaf parsley sprigs**

Peel shrimp; devein, if desired.

Melt ¼ cup butter in large skillet over medium-high heat. Add onion and next 3 ingredients; sauté 7 minutes or until tender. Add garlic, and sauté 1 minute. Stir in okra, lemon juice, and salt; sauté 5 minutes. Add shrimp, and cook 3 minutes or until shrimp turn pink. Stir in soup and next 4 ingredients until blended. Pour into a lightly greased 11- x 7-inch baking dish. Sprinkle evenly with Parmesan cheese.

Bake at 350° for 15 to 20 minutes or until casserole is bubbly and cheese is lightly browned. Garnish, if desired. **Makes** 6 servings.

Note: Unbaked casserole can be made one day in advance. Cover and refrigerate. Let stand at room temperature 30 minutes before baking as directed. To freeze unbaked casserole, prepare as directed, omitting Parmesan cheese. Cover tightly, and freeze. Let stand at room temperature 30 minutes before baking. Bake, covered, at 350° for 50 minutes. Uncover; sprinkle evenly with Parmesan cheese, and bake 10 more minutes or until cheese is lightly browned.

∗Substitute 1 (10-ounce) package frozen onions and peppers for fresh onion and bell peppers, if desired.

∗∗Substitute 1 (10¾-ounce) can cream of mushroom soup for cream of shrimp soup, if desired.

ELAINE JEANSONNE
COTTONPORT, LOUISIANA

SAUSAGE-AND-CHICKEN CASSOULET

Prep: 25 min., Cook: 20 min., Bake: 35 min., Stand: 10 min.

A *cassoulet* is a French dish of beans, sausages, and meat that's covered and slowly cooked. Our version is covered with a corn-bread crust. Check your cookware information to make sure your skillet's handle is ovenproof up to 400° or higher. If not—just prep in a traditional skillet and then bake in a casserole dish that holds 2¼ to 3 quarts. (You can measure your dish capacity using water if the dish is not labeled.)

- **1 (16-ounce) package smoked sausage, sliced**
- **1 pound uncooked chicken breast strips, chopped**
- **1 (15.8-ounce) can great Northern beans, rinsed and drained**
- **1 (14.5-ounce) can diced tomatoes with onion and garlic, drained**
- **1 (14-ounce) can chicken broth**
- **1½ teaspoons dried thyme**
- **1 (6-ounce) package buttermilk cornbread mix**
- **⅔ cup water or milk**

Cook sausage in a 2¼- to 3-quart ovenproof skillet over medium heat 8 minutes or until browned. Remove sausage from skillet, and drain on paper towels, reserving drippings in skillet. Set sausage aside.

Cook chicken in hot drippings in skillet over medium-high heat 5 minutes or until brown.

Return sausage to skillet with chicken. Stir in beans and next 3 ingredients. Bring to a boil.

Stir together cornbread mix and ⅔ cup water. Pour evenly over hot sausage mixture in skillet.

Bake at 400° for 30 to 35 minutes or until golden. Let stand 10 minutes before serving. **Makes** 6 servings.

Note: For testing purposes only, we used Martha White Buttermilk Cornbread Mix. We also used a Le Creuset 2¼-quart (8½-inch-diameter x 3-inch-deep) Saucier Pan at one testing and a hand-me-down 3-quart (10-inch-diameter x 3-inch-deep) cast-iron skillet at another testing. Both skillets worked fine.

CHALUPA DINNER BOWL

Prep: 30 min., Cook: 11 hrs., Bake: 5 min.

Serve this pork and bean mixture spooned over cornbread or rolled up burrito style in flour tortillas. Make hearty nachos, quesadillas, or tacos with it too. *(pictured on page 225)*

- **1 pound dried pinto beans**
- **1 (3½-pound) bone-in pork loin roast**
- **2 (4-ounce) cans chopped green chiles**
- **2 garlic cloves, chopped**
- **1 tablespoon chili powder**
- **2 teaspoons salt**
- **1 teaspoon dried oregano**
- **1 teaspoon ground cumin**
- **1 (32-ounce) container chicken broth**
- **1 (10-ounce) can diced tomatoes and green chiles with lime juice and cilantro**
- **8 taco salad shells**
- **1 small head iceberg lettuce, shredded**
- **Toppings: shredded Monterey Jack cheese, pickled jalapeño slices, halved grape tomatoes, sour cream, chopped avocado**

Rinse and sort beans according to package directions. Place pinto beans in a 6-quart slow cooker; add roast and next 6 ingredients. Pour chicken broth over roast.

Cover and cook on HIGH 1 hour; reduce to LOW, and cook 9 hours. Or, cover and cook on HIGH 6 hours. Remove bones and fat from roast; pull roast into large pieces with 2 forks. Stir in diced tomatoes and green chiles. Cook, uncovered, on HIGH 1 more hour or until liquid is slightly thickened.

Heat taco salad shells according to package directions; place shredded lettuce evenly into shells. Spoon about 1 cup pork-and-bean mixture into each shell using a slotted spoon. Serve with desired toppings. **Makes** 8 servings.

Note: For testing purposes only, we used RO*TEL Mexican Festival tomatoes and a Rival Recipe Smart-Pot slow cooker. Times may vary depending on the slow cooker used.

NORA HENSHAW
OKEMAH, OKLAHOMA

SHORTCUT GREEK SHEPHERD'S PIE

Prep: 30 min., Cook: 20 min., Bake: 25 min.

Pasta sauce from a jar and frozen mashed potatoes speed up this meal. Serve with iceberg lettuce wedges drizzled with Greek dressing and sprinkled with chopped plum tomatoes.

- **1½ pounds lean ground beef**
- **2 medium zucchini, thinly sliced**
- **1 medium onion, chopped**
- **2 garlic cloves, minced**
- **1 (25-ounce) jar pasta sauce with roasted red peppers**
- **3 teaspoons Greek seasoning, divided**
- **1 (20-ounce) package frozen mashed potatoes**
- **1 (4-ounce) package feta cheese, crumbled**
- **½ teaspoon grated lemon rind**
- **1 tablespoon fresh lemon juice**

Cook ground beef in a large nonstick skillet, stirring until beef crumbles and is no longer pink; drain.

Cook zucchini, onion, and garlic in skillet, stirring occasionally, 6 to 7 minutes or until vegetables are tender. Add ground beef; stir in pasta sauce and 2½ teaspoons Greek seasoning. Cook over low heat 3 to 5 minutes or until thoroughly heated. Pour beef mixture into a lightly greased 3-quart round baking dish.

Prepare frozen mashed potatoes according to package directions. Stir together mashed potatoes, remaining ½ teaspoon Greek seasoning, crumbled feta cheese, lemon rind, and lemon juice. Spoon potato mixture evenly over beef mixture; smooth with back of spoon to cover beef mixture completely. **Bake** at 400° for 25 minutes or until potatoes are lightly browned. **Makes** 8 servings.

Note: For testing purposes only, we used Emeril's Roasted Red Pepper pasta sauce.

CAMILLA V. SAULSBURY
BLOOMINGTON, INDIANA

healthy & light
The Season's Best Spices

Give these sweet and savory dishes a tasty boost by adding nutmeg, cinnamon, allspice, and cloves. These sweet spices, as they are sometimes called, will add a cool-weather touch to your meal while offering up a wonderful aroma. Spices are an easy way to flavor your food without additional calories or fat. So experiment today, and enjoy delicious, exotic new tastes.

AROMATIC CURRY-AND-SPICE CHICKEN

Prep: 20 min., Cook: 46 min.

- **1½ cups uncooked brown rice**
- **6 (6-ounce) skinned and boned chicken breasts**
- **¾ teaspoon salt, divided**
- **½ teaspoon pepper**
- **2 medium-size sweet onions, chopped**
- **2 medium-size green bell peppers, chopped**
- **4 teaspoons vegetable oil, divided**
- **2 garlic cloves, minced**
- **2 (14½-ounce) cans petite diced tomatoes**
- **1 tablespoon curry powder**
- **⅛ teaspoon ground cloves**
- **1 (3-inch) cinnamon stick**
- **¼ cup golden raisins**
- **3 tablespoons chopped fresh cilantro**
- **¼ cup slivered almonds, toasted**

Prepare rice according to package directions, omitting salt and fat. Keep rice warm.

Sprinkle chicken evenly with ½ teaspoon salt and pepper; set aside.

Sauté chopped onions and bell peppers in 2 teaspoons hot oil in a large nonstick skillet over medium-high heat 8 minutes or until tender. Add garlic; sauté 1 minute.

Transfer onion mixture to a medium bowl; stir in remaining ¼ teaspoon salt, tomatoes, and next 4 ingredients. Wipe skillet clean.

Cook chicken in remaining 2 teaspoons hot oil in skillet over medium-high heat 6 minutes on each side or until browned. Pour tomato mixture evenly over chicken. Cover, reduce heat to medium low, and simmer 15 minutes. Uncover and simmer 10 minutes or until mixture is thickened and chicken is tender. Remove and discard cinnamon stick. Stir in cilantro, and top with almonds. Serve over brown rice. **Makes** 6 servings.

Per serving (1 chicken breast, about 1 cup sauce, ½ cup rice): Calories 436 (19% from fat); Fat 9.2g (sat 1.2g, mono 4.6g, poly 2.4g); Protein 45.2g; Carb 42.6g; Fiber 6.3g; Chol 99mg; Iron 2.9mg; Sodium 588mg; Calc 91mg

CREAMY SHRIMP-AND-SPINACH PASTA

Prep: 20 min., Cook: 30 min.

Freshly grated nutmeg gives this lightened creamy white sauce extra flavor.

- **12 ounces uncooked ziti pasta**
- **1 (6-ounce) package fresh baby spinach**
- **1 tablespoon butter**
- **1 (8-ounce) package sliced fresh baby portobello mushrooms**
- **1 large white onion, chopped**
- **2 teaspoons minced fresh garlic**
- **1 cup reduced-sodium chicken broth**
- **¼ cup dry white wine***
- **6 ounces ⅓-less-fat cream cheese**
- **½ teaspoon salt**
- **¼ teaspoon plus ⅛ teaspoon freshly grated nutmeg**
- **¼ teaspoon freshly ground black pepper**
- **1 pound peeled cooked medium shrimp, tails removed (about 41 to 50 shrimp)**
- **⅓ cup grated Parmesan cheese**

Cook pasta according to package directions, omitting salt and fat. Drain; return to pan. Stir in spinach; toss until spinach wilts. Set aside.

Melt 1 tablespoon butter in a large nonstick skillet over medium-high heat. Add mushrooms, and cook, stirring occasionally, 8 minutes or until

browned. Add onion, and sauté over medium heat 10 minutes or until tender. Add garlic; sauté 1 minute.

Stir in chicken broth and white wine. Increase heat to medium-high, and cook, stirring often, 8 minutes or until mixture thickens slightly. Reduce heat to medium. Stir in cream cheese and next 3 ingredients until smooth. Add shrimp, and cook until thoroughly heated. Pour shrimp mixture over pasta mixture; toss to combine. Sprinkle evenly with grated Parmesan cheese, and serve immediately. **Makes** 6 servings.

* Substitute ¼ cup reduced-sodium chicken broth, if desired.

Per (1⅓-cup) serving: Calories 427 (24% from fat); Fat 11.6g (sat 2.2g, mono 1.4g, poly 0.7g); Protein 30.4g; Carb 50.3g; Fiber 3.4g; Chol 144mg; Iron 4.8mg; Sodium 522mg; Calc 159mg

BROWN SUGAR BREAD PUDDING WITH CRÈME ANGLAISE

Prep: 30 min., Stand: 10 min., Bake: 35 min.

We prefer fresh French bread from the bakery to achieve the crispiest top and softest center. Save the egg yolks from the separated eggs for the Crème Anglaise.

- **4 egg whites**
- **1 large egg**
- **1¼ cups 2% reduced-fat milk**
- **¾ cup evaporated fat-free milk**
- **½ cup firmly packed light brown sugar**
- **1 teaspoon ground cinnamon**
- **¼ teaspoon ground nutmeg**
- **⅛ teaspoon salt**
- **⅛ teaspoon ground allspice**
- **2 teaspoons vanilla extract**
- **1 (12-ounce) French bread loaf, cut into 1-inch cubes (about 8 cups)**
- **Vegetable cooking spray**
- **4 teaspoons light brown sugar**
- **½ tablespoon butter, cut into small pieces**
- **¼ cup sliced almonds, toasted**
- **Crème Anglaise**
- **Garnish: cinnamon sticks**

Whisk together egg whites and egg in a medium bowl until blended. Whisk in reduced-fat milk and next 7 ingredients.

Arrange bread cubes in an 8-inch square pan coated with cooking spray. Pour egg mixture evenly over bread. Sprinkle evenly with 4 teaspoons brown sugar, butter, and almonds. Press down gently on bread cubes, and let stand 10 minutes.

Bake at 350° for 30 to 35 minutes or until a knife inserted in center comes out clean. Serve warm with 2 tablespoons chilled Crème Anglaise per serving. Garnish, if desired. **Makes** 9 servings.

Per 1 serving bread pudding and 2 tablespoons Crème Anglaise: Calories 261 (21% from fat); Fat 6g (sat 2g, mono 2.6g, poly 0.9g); Protein 10.2g; Carb 39.6g; Fiber 1.6g; Chol 81mg; Iron 1.4mg; Sodium 363mg; Calc 183mg

CRÈME ANGLAISE:
make ahead

Prep: 10 min., Cook: 8 min., Chill: 4 hrs.

We prepared our Crème Anglaise with milk instead of heavy cream to reduce the fat and calories. So expect a slightly thinner consistency but the same delicious flavor. Store leftover sauce in an airtight container in the refrigerator up to 1 week, and serve over fresh berries.

- **1¾ cups 2% reduced-fat milk**
- **⅓ cup sugar**
- **4 egg yolks**
- **1 teaspoon vanilla extract**
- **2 tablespoons bourbon**

Heat milk in a medium saucepan over medium heat just until bubbles and steam appear (do not boil). Remove from heat.

Whisk together sugar and egg yolks in a medium bowl until blended. Gradually add heated milk to egg yolk mixture, whisking constantly. Return mixture to saucepan. Cook over medium heat, whisking constantly, 6 minutes or until mixture thinly coats the back of a spoon. Pour mixture into a bowl. Stir in vanilla. Place plastic wrap directly on surface of mixture, and chill at least 4 hours. (Mixture will thicken slightly as it cools.) Stir in bourbon before serving. **Makes** 2 cups.

Per 2 tablespoons: Calories 47 (30% from fat); Fat 1.6g (sat 0.7g, mono 0.6g, poly 0.2g); Protein 1.6g; Carb 5.6g; Fiber 0g; Chol 53mg; Iron 0.1mg; Sodium 15mg; Calc 38mg

Savor a Fall Breakfast

Try these dishes when it's your turn to host friends.

Autumn Brunch

Serves 8

Savory Ham-and-Swiss Breakfast Pie

Orange Syrup, yogurt, and Mixed Fruit Granola

It doesn't matter the time of day, breakfast food is always a warm, comforting choice. It's also less expensive than a dinner menu with pricey entrées. These easy, make-ahead recipes will move to the top of your list for casual gathering ideas.

SAVORY HAM-AND-SWISS BREAKFAST PIE

Prep: 20 min., Cook: 15 min., Stand: 20 min., Bake: 55 min. *(pictured on page 227)*

- 1⅔ cups water
- 1 cup whipping cream
- 2 garlic cloves, pressed
- 2 tablespoons butter
- 1 teaspoon salt
- ¼ teaspoon pepper
- ⅔ cup uncooked quick-cooking grits
- 1¼ cups (5 ounces) shredded Swiss cheese, divided
- 8 large eggs, divided
- ½ pound cooked ham, diced
- 4 green onions, chopped
- ½ cup milk
- Garnish: chives

Bring first 6 ingredients to a boil in a saucepan; gradually whisk in grits. Cover, reduce heat, and simmer, whisking occasionally, 5 to 7 minutes. Add ½ cup cheese, stirring until cheese melts. Remove from heat; let stand 10 minutes. Lightly beat 2 eggs, and stir into grits mixture; pour into a greased 10-inch deep-dish pieplate.

Bake at 350° for 20 minutes; remove from oven. Increase temperature to 400°.

Sauté ham and onions in a nonstick skillet over medium-high heat 5 minutes or until onion is tender. Layer ham mixture evenly over grits crust. Whisk together milk and remaining 6 eggs; pour over ham mixture. Sprinkle remaining ¾ cup cheese evenly over egg mixture.

Bake at 400° for 35 minutes. Let stand 10 minutes, and cut into wedges. Garnish, if desired. **Makes** 8 servings.

ORANGE SYRUP

fast fixin's

Prep: 10 min., Cook: 5 min.

Drizzle this over ice cream, pound cake, pancakes, or waffles. *(pictured on page 227)*

- 1 cup sugar
- 2 teaspoons grated orange rind
- ½ cup orange juice
- 1 tablespoon lemon juice
- 1 tablespoon corn syrup
- ½ teaspoon vanilla extract
- 2 tablespoons orange liqueur (optional)
- Fat-free yogurt, orange segments, and Mixed Fruit Granola (recipe at right)

Combine first 6 ingredients and, if desired, orange liqueur in a heavy saucepan; bring to a boil over medium heat. Reduce heat, and simmer, stirring occasionally, 5 minutes or until sugar dissolves.

Top fat-free yogurt with orange segments and Mixed Fruit Granola; drizzle with syrup. **Makes** 1¾ cups.

MIXED FRUIT GRANOLA

make ahead

Prep: 10 min., Cook: 5 min., Bake: 30 min.

This makes a good high-fiber snack for a quick pick-me-up. *(pictured on page 227)*

- 3 cups uncooked regular oats
- ¼ cup wheat germ
- ¼ cup sunflower seed kernels
- ¼ cup chopped pecans
- 2 tablespoons sesame seeds
- ½ cup butter
- ½ cup firmly packed brown sugar
- 2 tablespoons corn syrup
- 1 teaspoon vanilla extract
- 1 cup chopped dried mixed fruit

Combine first 5 ingredients in a bowl. Set oats mixture aside.

Cook butter and brown sugar in a medium saucepan over medium heat, stirring constantly, until butter is melted and sugar is dissolved. Stir in corn syrup. Remove from heat, and stir in vanilla.

Pour sugar mixture evenly over oats mixture, tossing to coat well. Spread mixture evenly in a lightly greased jelly-roll or broiler pan.

Bake at 350° for 25 to 30 minutes, stirring 3 times. Cool completely. Stir in dried fruit. **Makes** about 4 cups.

Note: Store in an airtight container up to 2 weeks.

SUSAN CEARLEY
PIPE CREEK, TEXAS

Keep on Grilling

Fall Supper

Serves 4 to 6

Grilled Balsamic Pork Tenderloin

Speedy Rosemary Green Beans

Lemony Apple Salad

A nip in the air never stops a Southerner from firing up the grill for a great supper.

GRILLED BALSAMIC PORK TENDERLOIN

Prep: 10 min., Chill: 8 hrs., Grill: 24 min., Stand: 10 min.

Place the pork in the marinade the night before you plan to serve it. A few tablespoons of honey are also nice in this marinade. We omitted them here because of the honey in the Lemony Apple Salad.

¼ cup balsamic vinegar
2 garlic cloves, minced
½ teaspoon dried crushed red pepper
1 (2-pound) package pork tenderloins
1 teaspoon salt
1 teaspoon freshly ground black pepper
Garnish: rosemary sprigs

Combine first 3 ingredients in a shallow dish or large zip-top freezer bag; add pork. Cover or seal, and chill 8 hours. Remove pork from marinade; discard marinade. Sprinkle with salt and black pepper.

Grill, covered with grill lid, over medium-high heat (350° to 400°) 8 to 12 minutes on each side or until a meat thermometer inserted into thickest portion registers 155°. Remove from grill,

and let stand 10 minutes or until thermometer registers 160°. Slice pork, and garnish, if desired. **Makes** 6 servings.

JANICE ELDER
CHARLOTTE, NORTH CAROLINA

SPEEDY ROSEMARY GREEN BEANS

fast fixin's

Prep: 5 min., Cook: 8 min.

1 (16-ounce) package frozen cut green beans (do not thaw)
2 tablespoons butter
2 tablespoons water
1 teaspoon chopped fresh or ½ teaspoon dried rosemary
¼ teaspoon salt
¼ teaspoon pepper

Stir together all ingredients in a 1-quart microwave-safe bowl. Microwave, covered with plastic wrap, at HIGH 8 minutes or until beans are crisp-tender, stirring after 4 minutes. Serve with a slotted spoon. **Makes** 4 to 6 servings.

LEMONY APPLE SALAD

fast fixin's

Prep: 30 min.

¼ cup mayonnaise
½ teaspoon grated lemon rind
2 tablespoons lemon juice
2 tablespoons honey
¼ teaspoon salt
2 Red Delicious apples, cored and chopped
1 Granny Smith apple, cored and chopped
¼ cup diced celery
¼ cup raisins
¼ cup chopped pecans, toasted

Stir together first 5 ingredients in a large bowl. Stir in apples, celery, and raisins. Cover and chill until ready to serve. Sprinkle with chopped pecans just before serving. **Makes** 6 servings.

Fast Asian Fare

STIR-FRY PORK

Prep: 25 min., Stand: 10 min., Cook: 8 min.

See "From Our Kitchen" on page 242 for a list of Asian products your taste buds will love.

8 ounces uncooked thin spaghetti or vermicelli
1 pound boneless pork loin chops
⅓ cup hoisin sauce
4 garlic cloves, pressed
3 tablespoons lite soy sauce
1 tablespoon rice vinegar
2 teaspoons sesame oil
1 teaspoon grated fresh ginger
1 (10-ounce) package fresh spinach
1 (8-ounce) can sliced water chestnuts, rinsed and drained
2 cups packaged shredded or matchstick carrots
4 green onions, sliced
¼ to ½ teaspoon dried crushed red pepper
1 tablespoon vegetable oil
Lite soy sauce (optional)

Prepare pasta according to package directions. Drain and keep warm.

Trim fat from pork chops, and cut into thin strips; place in a shallow dish.

Whisk together hoisin sauce and next 5 ingredients. Pour half of hoisin sauce mixture over pork, turning to coat. Let stand 10 minutes.

Sauté pork mixture in a large nonstick skillet over medium-high heat 2 to 3 minutes or until pork is done. Remove pork from skillet.

Sauté spinach and next 4 ingredients in hot oil over medium-high heat 3 minutes or until spinach is wilted. Stir in pasta, pork, and remaining hoisin sauce mixture, and cook, stirring constantly, 2 minutes or until thoroughly heated. Serve with lite soy sauce, if desired. **Makes** 4 to 6 servings.

SHELLY NAWROCKI
OCALA, FLORIDA

from our kitchen

Top Pasta Picks

The perfect make-ahead dish for casual entertaining, pasta salad is a crowd-pleaser any time of year. Test Kitchens Specialist Vanessa McNeil Rocchio created this colorful Confetti Pasta Salad. Versatile enough to serve with almost any entrée, it's one of our favorites.

Mix and match the ingredients according to what's on hand. Red or green bell peppers can be substituted for yellow, broccoli for spinach, or fresh basil for dill. For a quick and satisfying main dish, Vanessa adds grilled chicken or boiled shrimp. We used shell pasta, but any small type, such as orzo, will work well.

CONFETTI PASTA SALAD

fast fixin's • make ahead

Prep: 20 min.

This salad tastes great the minute it's made but will become more strongly flavored if allowed to chill a few hours before serving. When making ahead, add the cheese just before serving.

8 ounces uncooked small shell pasta
1 pint grape tomatoes, halved
2 cups coarsely chopped fresh spinach
1 yellow bell pepper, chopped
¼ cup finely chopped red onion
3 tablespoons chopped fresh dill
Fresh Lemon Vinaigrette
1 (4-ounce) package crumbled feta cheese

Cook pasta according to package directions; drain. Toss pasta with tomatoes and remaining ingredients. Serve immediately, or cover and chill up to 8 hours. **Makes** 4 to 6 servings.

Fresh Lemon Vinaigrette: Whisk together ¼ cup fresh lemon juice; ¼ cup olive oil; 2 tablespoons red wine vinegar; 2 garlic cloves, pressed; 1 teaspoon salt; and ½ teaspoon pepper. **Makes** about ⅔ cup. Prep: 5 min.

Pasta Tips and Tidbits

■ Inserts, made of perforated stainless steel, are a quick and easy way to safely drain pasta after cooking. Fill the pot three-quarters full with water, and then place the insert in the pot. When the pasta's ready, simply lift out the insert for perfectly drained pasta. The pasta insert is also great for cooking corn on the cob or boiling potatoes.

■ Use a pot large enough to hold three times the volume of pasta you're going to cook. This ratio allows the pasta to cook evenly. Add the pasta to briskly boiling water, and stir it immediately to prevent it from clumping together.

■ Cook pasta up to two days ahead, and drain. Toss with a few drops of olive oil, and cool. Place in a zip-top freezer bag, and refrigerate until ready to use.

■ When making pasta salads, always undercook the pasta a minute or two. This will allow it to absorb the dressing but still retain a firm texture as it chills.

■ To freshen plastic storage containers and remove the residue left by oily salad dressings and tomato-based pasta sauces, scrub with a paste of baking soda and water.

■ Inexpensive pasta forks are terrific for loosening and then serving long strands of pasta such as spaghetti or fettuccine.

■ To prevent filled pastas such as ravioli or tortellini from breaking open when cooking, add to gently boiling water, and simmer.

Asian Seasonings

Here are some Asian products your taste buds will love. For a great recipe incorporating some of these ingredients, see previous page.

• **Coconut milk:** Don't confuse sweetened cream of coconut, used for desserts and mixed drinks, with unsweetened coconut milk.

• **Dark sesame oil:** Adding a splash of this strong-flavored oil just before serving a dish adds a real kick. Store opened bottles in the refrigerator up to 6 months; bring to room temperature before using.

• **Fish sauce:** a pungent, salty liquid that's used for flavoring. Store in refrigerator up to 3 months.

• **Fresh ginger:** It's okay to break off the size you need to purchase. Store tightly wrapped, unpeeled ginger in the refrigerator for 3 weeks, or freeze up to 6 months.

• **Hoisin sauce:** a mixture of soybeans, garlic, chile peppers, and various spices. Store in the refrigerator up to 6 months.

• **Light sesame oil:** has a nutty flavor and can be used for salad dressings, sauces, and sautéing. It's high in polyunsaturated fats and has a smoke point of 420°, which makes it perfect for frying.

• **Red curry paste:** a blend of red chiles, lemon grass, ginger, and cilantro. Store in the refrigerator up to 3 months.

• **Rice vinegar:** made from fermented rice; use like any other vinegar.

• **Soy sauce:** used for flavoring everything from meats to marinades; store at room temperature or in refrigerator up to 6 months.

november

244   Gather Together *Enjoy a Thanksgiving menu with a Carolina twist*

246   What's for Supper? Love the Leftovers *Great ways to use your seemingly inexhaustible supply of Thanksgiving turkey*

247   Simple Southwestern Casserole Starts the Fun *Serve a supper with a little kick*

248   Top-Rated Menu Easy, Elegant Dinner *No-fuss recipes make entertaining during this busy season a snap*

249   Make-Ahead Appetizer *Try this flavorful Southwest Cheesecake sure to get rave reviews*

250   Cook With Confidence *Turkey tips and special side dishes*

251   Stir-and-Bake Breads *Amazingly easy recipes made without yeast*

252   Quick & Easy Microwave Magic *Enjoy a speedy lasagna dinner*

253   Deep Chocolate Brownies *Satisfy your craving for a sweet little snack*

254   Soup for Supper *Grab a bowl for a hearty meal*

255   Soufflés: Here's the Trick *Secrets to putting together an impressive dessert*

256   Healthy & Light Good News: Five-Ingredient Southern Recipes *Taste and ease are abundant in this delicious dinner for four*

257   Enjoy a Cup of Hot Tea *Sample some hot sippers on a cold winter day*

Holiday Dinners®

258   Pack-and-Go Supper Club *All the ingredients for a dazzling dinner*

260   Three Yummy Desserts *Sweet endings for Thanksgiving celebrations*

270   Kitchen Shortcuts *Our Foods staff's favorite holiday secrets*

270   Ultimate Mashed Potatoes *Multiple choices for comfort food at its finest*

272   Gather Around the Table *Fresh take on a Hanukkah menu*

272   Bake the Best Cheesecake *Discover baking tips and irresistible recipes from an expert*

274   Party Favors in a Flash *Send your guests home with a Sweet Spice Blend*

274   Hats Off to This Celebration *Tea party treats*

276   A Buffet Built on Comfort *Menu for a casual gathering*

278   We're Glad You're Here *Welcome guests to a South Beach supper*

280   Cheers to an Easy, Gorgeous Party *Ring in the New Year*

282   Pop the Cork *Champagne and chocolate pair divinely*

282   At Play in the Kitchen *Get the kids cooking*

284   From Our Kitchen *An herb mix, honey mustard, and more*

Gather Together

This family adds a Carolina twist to the traditional Thanksgiving menu.

Carolina Celebration

Serves 8 to 10

Grilled Oysters With Paul's Cocktail Sauce

Roasted Turkey

Barbecued Pork Tenderloin

Maple-Sweet Potato Casserole

Creamy-and-Crunchy Green Bean Casserole

steamed carrots

Cranberry Relish Salad

Coconut Layer Cake

Oysters roast on a pit, and vinegar-mopped barbecue sizzles on the grill. In the presence of 50-year-old azaleas, a late-blooming hibiscus, and turning fall leaves, you can sniff the salty air from the Newport River.

At the Geer family Thanksgiving, you can't miss the old ballast stone fireplace. The cabin that it heated has been torn down, yet the fireplace and the spirited memories of past Thanksgiving celebrations at "The Camp," as the family calls it, still live. The place, built by Webb Geer's grandparents, now hosts Webb and Laura's Thanksgiving celebration in Morehead City, North Carolina.

"We built our house and patio around the remaining fireplace and landscape with hopes that our families would once again have a meaningful place to gather for this day of thanks," Laura tells us.

And, wow, do they gather. Everyone brings something delicious to the table. Webb's grandmother, Lois Davis Webb, has passed many of her recipes on to others to make and bring, especially her desserts. (See "Three Yummy Desserts" on page 260.)

GRILLED OYSTERS WITH PAUL'S COCKTAIL SAUCE

fast fixin's

Prep: 5 min., Grill: 20 min.

2 dozen fresh oysters (in the shell)
Paul's Cocktail Sauce

Grill oysters, covered with grill lid, over medium heat (300° to 350°) 20 minutes or until oysters open. Serve with Paul's Cocktail Sauce. **Makes** 2 dozen oysters.

PAUL'S COCKTAIL SAUCE:
Prep: 10 min., Chill: 30 min.

1 (12-ounce) jar chili sauce
½ cup cider or white vinegar
2 teaspoons pepper
2 teaspoons Worcestershire sauce
1 teaspoon lemon juice

Stir together all ingredients. Cover and chill 30 minutes. **Makes** 1½ cups.

PAUL GEER
BEAUFORT, NORTH CAROLINA

ROASTED TURKEY

family favorite

Prep: 30 min.; Bake: 2 hrs., 45 min.; Stand: 20 min.

The addition of chicken broth to the roasting pan will keep the turkey moist and yield drippings to make gravy. *(pictured on page 261)*

1 (14-pound) frozen whole turkey, thawed ✱
½ cup butter, softened
1 teaspoon rubbed sage
1 teaspoon salt
½ teaspoon pepper
1 (32-ounce) container chicken broth
Garnishes: Red Globe grapes, fresh sage leaves, orange wedges

Remove and discard giblets and neck from turkey. Rinse turkey with cold water; pat dry.

Loosen skin from turkey breast without totally detaching skin. Stir together ½ cup butter, 1 teaspoon sage, salt, and pepper. Rub half of butter mixture (about ¼ cup) evenly over turkey breast under skin; replace skin.

Place turkey, breast side up, on a lightly greased wire rack in an aluminum foil-lined roasting pan. Rub entire turkey evenly with remaining half of butter mixture. Pour chicken broth into bottom of roasting pan.

Bake at 350° for 2 hours and 45 minutes or until a meat thermometer inserted into thigh registers 180°. (Prevent overcooking turkey by checking for doneness after 2 hours.) Remove turkey from roasting pan, and let stand 20 minutes before slicing. Garnish, if desired. **Makes** 12 servings.

Note: To loosen skin from turkey, grasp edge of turkey skin with one hand, lifting skin up and pulling it back. Slide fingers of other hand between skin and meat to separate. Wear disposable rubber gloves, or wrap fingers in plastic wrap, if desired.

✱Substitute 1 (14-pound) whole fresh turkey, if desired.

LAURA GEER
MOREHEAD CITY, NORTH CAROLINA

BARBECUED PORK TENDERLOIN

Prep: 15 min., Cook: 35 min., Grill: 24 min., Stand: 10 min. *(pictured on page 261)*

**3 cups apple cider vinegar
¼ cup ketchup
1 tablespoon dried crushed red
   pepper
1 tablespoon hot sauce
1 tablespoon Worcestershire
   sauce
¼ teaspoon black pepper
2 (2-pound) packages pork
   tenderloin**

Bring first 6 ingredients to a boil in a large saucepan over medium-high heat. Reduce heat to low, and simmer 30 minutes. Reserve 1 cup mixture.

Grill pork, without grill lid, over medium-high heat (350° to 400°) 10 to 12 minutes on each side or until a meat thermometer inserted in thickest portion of tenderloin registers 155°, basting often with remaining vinegar mixture. Remove from grill, and let stand 10 minutes or until temperature registers 160°. Serve with reserved vinegar mixture. **Makes** 12 servings.

Note: For testing purposes only, we used Texas Pete Hot Sauce.

WEBB GEER
MOREHEAD CITY, NORTH CAROLINA

MAPLE-SWEET POTATO CASSEROLE

family favorite

Prep: 20 min., Cook: 20 min., Bake: 28 min.

A ricer is a kitchen utensil that resembles a large garlic press. Pressing the potatoes through it removes the stringy portion, leaving them smooth and fluffy. *(pictured on page 261)*

**7 medium-size sweet potatoes,
   peeled and cubed (about
   7 pounds)
1 teaspoon salt
¼ cup butter, cut up
¼ cup dark firmly packed brown
   sugar
¼ cup pure maple syrup
2 cups miniature marshmallows**

Bring sweet potatoes, salt, and water to cover to a boil in a large Dutch oven. Boil 15 to 20 minutes or until tender; drain.
Mash potatoes, or press though a ricer; stir in butter, brown sugar, and maple syrup. Spoon mixture into a lightly greased 11- x 7-inch baking dish.
Bake at 350° for 20 minutes. Top evenly with marshmallows, and bake 8 more minutes or until marshmallows are puffed and golden. **Makes** 8 to 10 servings.

PETE KUMPEL
MOREHEAD CITY, NORTH CAROLINA

CREAMY-AND-CRUNCHY GREEN BEAN CASSEROLE

family favorite

Prep: 10 min., Cook: 10 min., Bake: 35 min. *(pictured on page 261)*

**¼ cup butter
1 large onion, chopped
2 (10¾-ounce) cans cream of
   mushroom soup
2 (16-ounce) packages frozen
   French-cut green beans,
   thawed
1 (14-ounce) can bean sprouts,
   rinsed and drained
2 (8-ounce) cans diced water
   chestnuts, drained
¼ teaspoon salt
1 cup (4 ounces) shredded sharp
   Cheddar cheese
2 (2.8-ounce) cans French fried
   onions**

Melt butter in a Dutch oven over medium-high heat; add onion, and sauté 8 minutes or until tender. Stir in soup, and bring to a boil. Stir in beans and next 3 ingredients. Spoon into a lightly greased 13- x 9-inch baking dish. Sprinkle evenly with shredded Cheddar cheese.
Bake, covered, at 375° for 25 minutes. Uncover and sprinkle evenly with French fried onions, and bake 10 more minutes or until bubbly. **Makes** 8 servings.

ANN BRINSON
KINSTON, NORTH CAROLINA

CRANBERRY RELISH SALAD

make ahead

Prep: 45 min.; Chill: 8 hrs., 30 min. *(pictured on page 261)*

**2 (3-ounce) packages cherry-
   flavored gelatin
2 cups boiling water
1 cup sugar
1 cup cold water
1 (12-ounce) package fresh or
   thawed frozen cranberries
1 cup pecans, toasted
3 Red Delicious apples, peeled and
   quartered
3 oranges, peeled and sectioned
1 (8¼-ounce) can crushed
   pineapple in heavy syrup,
   undrained
Toppings: sweetened whipped
   cream, toasted chopped pecans**

Stir together gelatin, 2 cups boiling water, and 1 cup sugar in a large bowl 2 minutes or until gelatin and sugar dissolve. Add 1 cup cold water, and chill 30 minutes or until consistency of unbeaten egg white.
Process cranberries and pecans in a food processor 30 seconds or until coarsely chopped, stopping to scrape down sides. Place in a mixing bowl.
Process apples and oranges in a food processor 30 to 45 seconds or until coarsely chopped, stopping to scrape down sides. Add to cranberry mixture in bowl. Stir in pineapple.
Stir fruit mixture into chilled gelatin mixture. Spoon into a lightly greased 10- to 12-cup bowl; cover and chill 8 hours or until firm. Invert onto a serving plate, and serve with desired toppings. **Makes** 10 servings.

ROSEMARY KUMPEL
MOREHEAD CITY, NORTH CAROLINA

COCONUT LAYER CAKE

Prep: 45 min., Bake: 20 min.

The frozen flaked coconut provides the cake's moist texture.

- ⅔ cup butter or shortening, softened
- 1⅔ cups sugar
- 3 large eggs
- 2½ cups all-purpose flour
- 1½ teaspoons baking powder
- 1 teaspoon salt
- 1½ cups milk
- 1 teaspoon vanilla extract
- ¼ cup freshly squeezed orange juice (juice of 1 orange)
- 2 teaspoons sugar
- Satin Icing
- 2 (6-ounce) packages frozen grated coconut, thawed

Beat butter at medium speed with an electric mixer until fluffy; gradually add 1⅔ cups sugar, beating well. Add eggs, 1 at a time, beating until blended after each addition.

Combine flour, baking powder, and salt; add to butter mixture alternately with milk, beating at low speed until blended, beginning and ending with flour mixture. Stir in vanilla. Pour batter into 3 greased and floured 8-inch round cakepans.

Bake at 350° for 18 to 20 minutes or until a wooden pick inserted in center comes out clean. Cool in pans on wire racks about 10 minutes; remove from pans, and cool completely on wire racks.

Stir together orange juice and 2 teaspoons sugar. Microwave at HIGH 1 minute or until sugar dissolves. Drizzle evenly over tops of cake layers.

Spread ½ cup Satin Icing between layers. Spread remaining Satin Icing on top and sides of cake. Lightly press coconut between layers of paper towels to remove excess moisture. Sprinkle coconut on top and sides of cake; press slightly. **Makes** 12 servings.

SATIN ICING:
fast fixin's

Prep: 10 min., Cook: 7 min.

Improvise a double boiler to make the icing by placing a metal bowl on top of a saucepan with boiling water. The bowl will be hot, so make sure you use hot pads. Water should not touch the bottom of the bowl, and be careful that no water splashes into the icing.

- 2 large egg whites
- 1 cup sugar
- ¼ cup water
- 3 tablespoons light corn syrup
- ¼ teaspoon cream of tartar
- ⅛ teaspoon salt
- 1 teaspoon vanilla extract

Combine first 6 ingredients in top of a large double boiler; beat at low speed with a handheld electric mixer until blended. Place over boiling water, beating at high speed 7 minutes; remove from heat. Add vanilla, and beat to spreading consistency. Spread immediately over cooled cake. **Makes** about 5½ cups.

LOIS DAVIS WEBB
MOREHEAD CITY, NORTH CAROLINA

what's for supper?
Love the Leftovers

We challenged Test Kitchens professional Alyssa Porubcan to turn holiday leftovers into divine new recipes. One idea, Next-Day Turkey Dinner Bake, comes from her mom. It's so good our Foods staff came back for seconds. To make sure leftovers are safe to eat the next day, Alyssa reminds us to chill hot foods within two hours of removing them from the oven or cooktop. Re-refrigerate cold foods within two hours. Use leftovers within four days, except for gravy, which should be used within two days.

NEXT-DAY TURKEY DINNER BAKE

family favorite

Prep: 15 min.; Bake: 1 hr., 15 min.; Stand: 5 min.

If the mashed potatoes won't spread, warm them slightly in the microwave with a little milk. After the big meal, large amounts of leftovers, such as cornbread dressing, should be divided into smaller portions (2 to 4 servings) so they'll chill more quickly in the fridge.

- 2½ cups coarsely chopped cooked turkey
- 2½ cups prepared cornbread dressing
- 1½ cups chilled prepared turkey gravy
- 3 cups prepared mashed potatoes
- ½ tablespoon butter

Layer a lightly greased 8-inch square baking dish with turkey, dressing, and gravy. Spread mashed potatoes evenly over gravy, sealing to edges. Dot evenly with butter.

Bake at 325° for 1 hour and 15 minutes. Let casserole stand 5 minutes before serving. **Makes** 6 servings.

RUTH OUVERSON
MONTROSE, MINNESOTA

MAIN DISH TURKEY SALAD WITH CRANBERRY VINAIGRETTE AND GARLIC CROUTONS

fast fixin's

Prep: 15 min.

- 1 head romaine lettuce, torn
- 2 cups coarsely chopped cooked turkey
- 4 bacon slices, cooked and crumbled
- 1 medium Granny Smith or Braeburn apple, thinly sliced
- 1 cup Garlic Croutons
- Cranberry Vinaigrette

Toss together first 4 ingredients in a large serving bowl. Top salad with Garlic Croutons, and serve with Cranberry Vinaigrette. **Makes** 4 servings.

GARLIC CROUTONS:
make ahead

Prep: 10 min., Cook: 2 min., Bake: 25 min.

- ¼ cup butter
- 2 large garlic cloves, pressed
- ¾ teaspoon ground red pepper
- 4 large dinner yeast rolls, cubed (about 3¼ cups cubes)

Melt butter in a large nonstick skillet over medium-high heat. Add garlic and red pepper; sauté 30 seconds. Remove from heat; stir in bread cubes until evenly coated.

Spread bread cubes in an even layer on a lightly greased aluminum foil-lined jelly-roll pan.

Bake at 300° for 20 to 25 minutes or until browned and crisp, stirring occasionally. Spread in a single layer on wax paper to cool completely. Store in an airtight container up to 1 week. **Makes** about 3 cups.

CRANBERRY VINAIGRETTE:
fast fixin's

Prep: 10 min.

Balsamic vinegar gives this dressing a rich reddish-brown color.

- ½ cup whole-berry cranberry sauce
- 2 tablespoons balsamic vinegar
- ½ teaspoon grated orange rind
- 2 tablespoons fresh orange juice
- 1½ teaspoons Dijon mustard
- ½ teaspoon honey
- ⅛ teaspoon salt
- ¼ cup olive oil

Stir together first 7 ingredients until blended. Stir in olive oil, 1 tablespoon at a time, until well blended. **Makes** about 1 cup.

Simple Southwestern Casserole Starts the Fun

Serve something with a little kick this season. These recipes will bring a welcome change from standard fare.

TEXAS-STYLE ENCHILADA CASSEROLE
family favorite

Prep: 10 min., Cook: 6 min., Bake: 25 min.

- 1 pound ground chuck
- ½ medium-size red onion, chopped
- 1 (4-ounce) can diced green chiles
- 12 (6-inch) corn tortillas, cut into 1-inch pieces
- 1 (10¾-ounce) can cream of mushroom soup
- 1 (2¼-ounce) can sliced ripe black olives
- 1 cup mild enchilada sauce
- ½ cup sour cream
- 1 (8-ounce) block sharp Cheddar cheese, shredded and divided

Toppings: shredded lettuce, diced tomato, finely chopped red onion

Cook first 3 ingredients in a large skillet over medium-high heat, stirring until beef crumbles and is no longer pink. Drain well.

Place beef mixture in a large bowl. Stir in tortilla pieces, next 4 ingredients, and 1 cup cheese; spoon mixture into a lightly greased 11- x 7-inch baking dish. Sprinkle evenly with remaining 1 cup cheese.

Bake at 400° for 20 to 25 minutes or until bubbly. Serve casserole with desired toppings. **Makes** 6 servings.

KAREN MCABEE
FORT WORTH, TEXAS

Lightened Texas-Style Enchilada Casserole: Substitute 1 pound ground sirloin, 1 (10¾-ounce) can 98% fat-free cream of mushroom soup, ½ cup light sour cream, and 1 (8-ounce) block 2% reduced-fat sharp Cheddar cheese. Proceed as directed.

ANN SCATES
BETHALTO, ILLINOIS

CILANTRO-LIME SOUR CREAM DIP

Prep: 5 min.

- ½ cup sour cream
- 2 green onions, thinly sliced
- 2 tablespoons chopped fresh cilantro
- 1 teaspoon grated lime rind
- 1 teaspoon fresh lime juice
- ¼ teaspoon salt
- ⅛ teaspoon pepper

Stir together all ingredients. Cover and chill until ready to serve. **Makes** ¾ cup.

CREAMY CHIPOTLE-BLACK BEAN DIP

Prep: 5 min.

- ½ cup sour cream
- ½ cup prepared black bean dip
- 1 teaspoon minced chipotle peppers in adobo sauce
- 1 teaspoon adobo sauce from can
- ¼ teaspoon salt

Stir together all ingredients. Cover and chill until ready to serve. **Makes** 1 cup.

"SALSAFIED" SOUR CREAM DIP

Prep: 5 min.

- ¼ cup sour cream
- ¼ cup salsa
- 1 tablespoon chopped fresh cilantro
- ½ teaspoon ground cumin

Stir together all ingredients. Cover and chill until ready to serve. **Makes** ½ cup.

Easy, Elegant Dinner

No-fuss recipes make holiday entertaining a breeze.

Holiday Dinner

Serves 10

Rosemary-Thyme Rib Roast
Potato-and-Gruyère Casserole
Strawberry-Cranberry-Orange Salad

This menu is ideal for busy schedules. In fact, the Rosemary-Thyme Rib Roast and the Potato-and-Gruyère Casserole can be baked at the same time. Just pop the casserole in the oven during the last hour of cooking the roast.

ROSEMARY-THYME RIB ROAST

Prep: 25 min., Bake: 3 hrs., Stand: 15 min.

If you can't find a boneless rib roast, buy a 6-pound bone-in roast and have the butcher remove the bone for you.

> 1 tablespoon salt
> 2 tablespoons coarsely ground pepper
> 1 (4½-pound) boneless beef rib roast
> 4 garlic cloves, minced
> 1 tablespoon dried rosemary
> 1 teaspoon dried thyme
> 1½ cups dry red wine
> 1½ cups red wine vinegar
> ½ cup olive oil
> Garnishes: fresh rosemary sprigs, fresh thyme sprigs

Combine salt and pepper; rub evenly over roast.

Brown roast on all sides in a large skillet over medium-high heat. Remove skillet from heat, and let roast cool slightly.

Combine garlic, dried rosemary, and dried thyme. Rub mixture evenly over roast; place on a lightly greased rack in an aluminum foil-lined roasting pan.

Stir together wine, vinegar, and oil. Gradually pour wine mixture over roast.

Bake at 250° for 2 hours; increase oven temperature to 350°, and bake 1 more hour or until a meat thermometer inserted into thickest portion registers 145° (medium rare) or to desired degree of doneness. Remove roast from oven, and let stand 15 minutes before slicing. Garnish, if desired. **Makes** 8 to 10 servings.

POTATO-AND-GRUYÈRE CASSEROLE

Prep: 20 min.; Cook: 30 min.; Bake: 1 hr., 15 min.

Gruyère cheese is known for its rich, nutty flavor. You can also substitute Swiss or Cheddar cheese.

> 12 medium Yukon gold potatoes (about 4 pounds)
> 2 teaspoons salt, divided
> 2 tablespoons butter or margarine
> 1 large sweet onion, chopped
> ½ teaspoon pepper
> 2 cups (8 ounces) shredded Gruyère cheese *
> Cream Sauce

Peel and thinly slice potatoes.

Bring potatoes, 1 teaspoon salt, and water to cover to a boil in a Dutch oven; cook 8 to 10 minutes. Remove from heat; drain and set aside.

Melt butter in a large skillet over medium-high heat; add chopped onion, and sauté 12 to 15 minutes or until golden brown.

Layer half of potatoes in a lightly greased 13- x 9-inch baking dish or 2 (8-inch) square baking dishes; sprinkle with ½ teaspoon salt and ¼ teaspoon pepper. Top with half each of onions, Gruyère cheese, and Cream Sauce. Repeat layers, ending with Cream Sauce.

Bake at 350° for 1 hour and 15 minutes or until golden brown. **Makes** 10 to 12 servings.

* Substitute 1 (8-ounce) block Swiss cheese, shredded, or 1 (8-ounce) block sharp white Cheddar cheese, shredded, if desired.

CREAM SAUCE:
fast fixin's

Prep: 5 min., Cook: 25 min.

> ¼ cup butter or margarine
> ⅓ cup all-purpose flour
> 2½ cups milk
> 1 cup dry white wine
> ¼ teaspoon salt

Melt butter in a heavy saucepan over low heat; whisk in flour until smooth. Cook, whisking constantly, 1 minute. Gradually whisk in milk and wine; cook over medium heat, whisking constantly, 18 to 20 minutes or until mixture is thickened and bubbly. Stir in salt. **Makes** 3½ cups.

STRAWBERRY-CRANBERRY-ORANGE SALAD

fast fixin's • make ahead

Prep: 30 min.

The salad dressing can be made ahead and refrigerated up to 1 week.

- ½ cup olive oil
- ½ cup orange juice
- ¼ cup cranberry-orange crushed fruit
- 1 small shallot, peeled and chopped
- 2 tablespoons balsamic vinegar
- ¼ teaspoon salt
- ⅛ to ¼ teaspoon ground red pepper
- ¼ teaspoon freshly ground black pepper
- 2 (5-ounce) packages gourmet mixed salad greens
- 2 cups sliced fresh strawberries
- ½ cup sweetened dried cranberries, chopped
- 2 large navel oranges, peeled and sectioned
- ½ cup slivered almonds, toasted

Process first 8 ingredients in a blender until smooth, stopping to scrape down sides.
Place salad greens and next 3 ingredients in a large bowl, and gently toss. Sprinkle with slivered almonds. Serve with vinaigrette. **Makes** 8 to 10 servings.

Note: For testing purposes only, we used Ocean Spray Cran-Fruit Crushed Fruit For Chicken (Cranberry Orange).

GLORIA PLEASANTS
WILLIAMSBURG, VIRGINIA

Make-Ahead Appetizer

Try Southwest Cheesecake, which yields big, flavor-packed results and is worth every moment of effort.

SOUTHWEST CHEESECAKE

make ahead

Prep: 20 min., Bake: 52 min., Stand: 10 min., Chill: 3 hrs.

Your favorite white or yellow tortilla chips will work just fine in this recipe. Sparkling wine or the crisp acidity of a Sauvignon Blanc or Pinot Grigio creates an ideal pairing.

- 1½ cups finely crushed blue tortilla chips
- ¼ cup butter, softened
- 2 (8-ounce) packages cream cheese, softened
- 2 cups (8 ounces) shredded Monterey Jack cheese
- ¼ teaspoon salt
- 3 (8-ounce) containers sour cream, divided
- 3 large eggs
- 1 cup thick and chunky salsa
- 1 (4-ounce) can chopped green chiles, drained
- 1 cup fresh or frozen guacamole (thawed)
- 1 medium-size tomato, seeded and diced
- Tortilla chips or crackers

Combine crushed tortilla chips and ¼ cup softened butter, and press into bottom of a lightly greased 9-inch springform pan.
Bake at 350° for 12 minutes. Cool in pan on a wire rack.
Beat cream cheese, shredded cheese, and salt at medium speed with an electric mixer 3 minutes or until fluffy. Add 1 container sour cream, beating until blended. Add eggs, 1 at a time, beating until blended after each addition. Stir in salsa and chiles. Pour over prepared crust.

Crust Pointers

If you don't have a food processor to crush the chips, use a rolling pin and a large zip-top plastic bag. Keep a small portion of the bag unsealed to allow air to escape.

Press the tortilla chip-and-butter mixture on the bottom of a 9-inch springform pan. Once baked, a colorful and sturdy crust forms.

Bake at 350° for 40 minutes or until center is almost set. Remove pan from oven; let stand 10 minutes on a wire rack. Gently run a knife around edge of pan to loosen sides. Remove sides of pan; let cheesecake cool completely.
Stir together remaining 2 containers sour cream until smooth; spread evenly over top of cooled cheesecake. Cover and chill at least 3 hours or up to 1 day. Spread evenly with guacamole; sprinkle with diced tomatoes before serving. Serve with tortilla chips. **Makes** 25 appetizer servings.

SHARLA SANDERSON
ABERDEEN, MISSISSIPPI

Cook With Confidence

Follow our turkey tips and try some of these sure-to-please recipes.

Thanksgiving Day's crowning glory is turkey and those special family side dishes. The meal only comes out perfectly, however, if you do a little advance strategizing. Once you've decided on your menu, think through how to cook it. If all of your dishes have to go in the oven—and at different temperatures and times—you might have trouble. Modify your menu so that you get the turkey done first; then choreograph the rest of your prep time so that all your dishes come out together. Follow these turkey tips for great holiday gatherings.

Turkey Tricks

It can take two to three days to thaw a frozen turkey. So, buy it ahead of time while the selection is still good, and plan when and how you'll thaw it. Find defrosting charts attached to the turkey, or you can visit **www.butterball.com**.

After the turkey thaws, stick your hand into the cavity and pull out the neck and giblets. They're usually wrapped in paper. If you forget this step and find these after you've finished cooking, your turkey is still safe to eat; just pull 'em out, enjoy a laugh about it, and go on.

Once you remove the turkey from the oven, cover it loosely with foil to allow the bird to rest. The juices absorb back into the turkey, and it carves easily. This resting is prime oven time for additional casseroles or dessert.

Essential Gadgets

- A bulb baster makes gathering pan drippings for basting the bird easy.
- Turkey lifters help you move the hot bird safely from the roasting pan to the serving platter or carving board.
- A timer/thermometer guarantees a completely done turkey that is moist, tender, and never overcooked. A turkey breast should cook to 170°; turkey thighs (or dark meat) should cook to 180°.
- Replacement racks for roasting pans are inexpensive and available at grocery stores.
- At the supermarket, pick up an aluminum foil oven liner (such as the ones made by Hefty) for easy cleanup. Simply slide the flat sheet under the heating element on the bottom of an electric oven to catch spills and drips. They work well on the bottom of gas ovens too. (Check your oven manual and package directions to see if they'll work in your oven.)

AU GRATIN POTATO CASSEROLE

family favorite • make ahead

Prep: 10 min.; Bake: 1 hr., 20 min.

You can make this ahead, refrigerate it, and then bake it while the turkey rests. It's smart to let chilled casseroles come to room temperature before you bake them.

- 1 (32-ounce) package frozen Southern-style hash browns
- 1 (16-ounce) container sour cream
- 2 cups (8 ounces) shredded Cheddar cheese
- 1 (10¾-ounce) can cream of mushroom soup
- 1 small onion, finely chopped
- ¼ teaspoon pepper
- 2 cups crushed cornflakes cereal
- ¼ cup melted butter

Stir together first 6 ingredients.
Spoon potato mixture into a lightly greased 13- x 9-inch baking dish. Sprinkle evenly with crushed cornflakes, and drizzle evenly with butter.
Bake at 325° for 1 hour and 20 minutes or until bubbly. **Makes** 10 to 12 servings.

Note: For testing purposes only, we used Ore-Ida Southern Style Hash Browns.

CHRIS BRYANT
JOHNSON CITY, TENNESSEE

EASY-DOES-IT MASHED SWEET POTATOES

Prep: 20 min., Stand: 15 min., Cook: 2 hrs.

Use your microwave to easily cook sweet potatoes, and then tap your slow cooker to hold the mashed sweet potatoes at the perfect serving temperature. You can use the same procedure for your favorite mashed potato recipe with white potatoes.

To cook 5 pounds sweet potatoes (about 6 medium) in the microwave, pierce sweet potatoes several times with tines of a fork. Place in a large microwave-safe bowl; cover with damp paper towels. Microwave at HIGH 15 minutes or until tender, turning every 5 minutes. Let stand 15 minutes. Peel and mash sweet potatoes with a potato masher or a handheld mixer until smooth. Stir in ½ cup butter, cut up; ½ cup maple syrup; ½ cup firmly packed brown sugar; 1 teaspoon ground cinnamon; ¾ teaspoon ground nutmeg; ¾ teaspoon ground ginger; and ½ teaspoon salt. Stir until butter melts. Transfer to a 4-quart slow cooker. Cover and cook on LOW 2 hours or until thoroughly heated; serve immediately. Sweet potatoes may be kept warm on LOW up to 4 more hours, stirring every 30 minutes. **Makes** about 10 servings.

PRALINE-APPLE PIE

make ahead

Prep: 25 min., Bake: 45 min., Cook: 5 min., Stand: 5 min.

Make this pie the morning of your gathering. After it cools, pour the luscious praline topping over the crust. If your family likes to enjoy dessert after dinner settles, put the pie in the oven when you sit down to eat your meal, and serve it warm later. *(pictured on page 1)*

1 (15-ounce) package refrigerated piecrusts
½ cup granulated sugar
⅓ cup all-purpose flour
½ teaspoon ground cinnamon
6 cups peeled, sliced Rome or other cooking apples
2 tablespoons butter, cut up
2 teaspoons lemon juice
¼ cup butter
½ cup firmly packed light brown sugar
2 tablespoons whipping cream
½ cup chopped pecans

Fit 1 piecrust into a 9-inch pieplate according to package directions.
Stir together granulated sugar, flour, and cinnamon. Stir in apples; spoon mixture into crust. Dot with 2 tablespoons butter; sprinkle evenly with lemon juice. Top with remaining piecrust; fold edges under, and crimp. Cut several slits in top.
Bake pie at 400° for 45 minutes on lower oven rack, shielding with aluminum foil after 30 minutes to prevent excessive browning. Remove from oven; let cool.

Melt ¼ cup butter in a small saucepan; stir in brown sugar and whipping cream. Bring to a boil over medium heat, stirring constantly; cook 1 minute, and remove from heat. Stir in pecans, and let stand 5 minutes. Slowly drizzle mixture over pie. **Makes** 8 servings.

BOB GORHAM
WINTER HAVEN, FLORIDA

Holiday Hotlines

Here's the insider's list of toll-free telephone numbers and Web sites for quick answers to last-minute questions about roasting turkeys, baking, and food safety issues.

■ **USDA Meat & Poultry Hotline:** 1-800-535-4555
■ **FDA Center for Food Safety:** 1-888-723-3366
■ **Butterball Turkey Talk Line:** 1-800-288-8372 or **www.butterball.com**
■ **The Reynolds Kitchen Tips Line:** 1-800-745-4000 or **www.reynoldskitchens.com**
■ **Fleischmann's Yeast:** 1-800-777-4959 or **www.fleischmanns.com**
■ **Betty Crocker (General Mills):** 1-888-275-2388 or **www.bettycrocker.com**
■ **Nestlé Baking:** 1-800-637-8537 or **www.verybestbaking.com**
■ **Ocean Spray:** 1-800-662-3263 or **www.oceanspray.com**

Stir-and-Bake Breads

On a cold day—or on any day, nothing smells better than fresh-baked bread. Ready for the oven in minutes, these amazingly easy recipes are made without yeast.

CREAM CHEESE-PUMPKIN BREAD

Prep: 20 min.; Bake: 1 hr., 15 min.; Stand: 10 min.

A spoon and a whisk are all you need to quickly mix up a bowl of batter.

3½ cups all-purpose flour
3 cups sugar
2 teaspoons ground cinnamon
1½ teaspoons baking soda
1 teaspoon ground nutmeg
½ teaspoon salt
2 cups canned unsweetened pumpkin
1 cup vegetable oil
⅔ cup water
4 large eggs
Cream Cheese Filling

Stir together first 6 ingredients in a large bowl. Whisk together pumpkin and next 3 ingredients; add to flour mixture, whisking just until dry ingredients are moistened. Spoon 3 cups of batter into each of 2 greased and floured 9- x 5-inch loafpans. Spoon Cream Cheese Filling evenly over batter. Spoon remaining batter evenly over Cream Cheese Filling.
Bake at 350° for 1 hour and 15 minutes or until a wooden pick inserted in center of bread comes out clean. Let cool in pans 10 minutes. Remove bread from pan, and cool completely on a wire rack. **Makes** 2 (9-inch) loaves.

CREAM CHEESE FILLING:
fast fixin's
Prep: 5 min.

1 (8-ounce) package cream cheese, softened
½ cup sugar
½ cup chopped pecans, toasted
1 large egg

Stir together all ingredients. **Makes** about 2 cups.

LORI TRUMBO
CENTRALIA, ILLINOIS

ICE-CREAM BREAD

Prep: 5 min., Bake: 45 min.

This two-ingredient bread is terrific anytime of day. Pop it in the oven while you're preparing supper, or serve it for afternoon tea. If you're lucky enough to have leftovers, toast a few slices for breakfast and serve with butter and jam.

- **1 pint (2 cups) ice cream, softened**
- **1½ cups self-rising flour**

Stir together ice cream and flour, stirring just until flour is moistened. Spoon batter into a greased and floured 8- x 4-inch loafpan.
Bake at 350° for 40 to 45 minutes or until a wooden pick inserted in center of bread comes out clean. Remove from pan, and cool on a wire rack. **Makes** 1 (8-inch) loaf.

Note: Batter can also be divided evenly between 2 greased and floured 5- x 3-inch loafpans. Bake at 350° for 20 to 25 minutes or until a wooden pick inserted in center of bread comes out clean.

SWEET POTATO CORNBREAD

fast fixin's

Prep: 5 min., Bake: 25 min.

Be sure to use self-rising cornmeal mix or your bread will be flat and hard.

- **2 cups self-rising cornmeal mix**
- **¼ cup sugar**
- **1 teaspoon ground cinnamon**
- **1½ cups milk**
- **1 cup mashed cooked sweet potato**
- **¼ cup butter, melted**
- **1 large egg, beaten**

Whisk together all ingredients, whisking just until dry ingredients are moistened. Spoon batter into a greased 8-inch cast-iron skillet or pan.
Bake at 425° for 20 to 25 minutes or until a wooden pick inserted in center comes out clean. **Makes** 6 servings.

Note: For testing purposes only, we used White Lily Self-Rising Buttermilk Cornmeal Mix.

CHRISTY WHITE
OXFORD, MISSISSIPPI

.

SUN-DRIED TOMATO-HERB BREAD

Prep: 10 min., Bake: 30 min.

- **2 cups all-purpose flour**
- **1 tablespoon baking powder**
- **½ teaspoon salt**
- **¼ teaspoon pepper**
- **½ cup grated Parmesan cheese**
- **¼ cup finely chopped sun-dried tomatoes**
- **1 teaspoon dried oregano**
- **1 cup milk**
- **1 large egg**
- **¼ cup olive oil**

Stir together first 7 ingredients in a large bowl.
Whisk together milk, egg, and olive oil; add to flour mixture, stirring just until dry ingredients are moistened. Spoon batter into a greased and floured 8- x 4-inch loafpan.
Bake at 375° for 25 to 30 minutes or until a wooden pick inserted in center

of bread comes out clean. Remove from pan, and cool on a wire rack. **Makes** 1 (8-inch) loaf.

KATE STEWART ROVNER
PLANO, TEXAS

quick & easy
Microwave Magic

Speedy Lasagna amazed our staff with its moist layers, tender noodles, and perfectly melted cheese. These recipes were tested in an 1,100-watt oven. Check the manufacturer's instructions on your model for its wattage.

SPEEDY LASAGNA

family favorite

Prep: 15 min., Cook: 40 min., Stand: 5 min.

You'll need a microwave-safe colander to cook and drain the sausage for the lasagna. If you don't have one, brown the sausage on the cooktop, drain, and continue the recipe as directed.

- **1 pound Italian sausage, casings removed**
- **1 (26-ounce) jar spaghetti sauce with onions and roasted garlic**
- **1 tablespoon chopped fresh or 1 teaspoon dried basil**
- **½ teaspoon pepper**
- **6 no-cook lasagna noodles**
- **2 cups ricotta cheese**
- **2 cups shredded mozzarella cheese**
- **¾ cup grated Parmesan cheese**

Crumble sausage into a plastic colander; place over a large microwave-safe bowl. Microwave at HIGH 1 minute, and stir. Microwave at HIGH 3 to 3½ minutes more, stirring every 30 seconds, or until sausage is done and no longer pink. Drain well on paper towels. Discard drippings. Rinse and wipe bowl clean.

Stir together sausage, spaghetti sauce, basil, and pepper in a large bowl.

Spread one-third sausage mixture in a lightly greased 11- x 7-inch microwave-safe baking dish; top with 3 noodles, 1 cup ricotta cheese, and 1 cup mozzarella cheese. Repeat layers.

Top evenly with remaining sausage mixture and grated Parmesan cheese. Cover with double-thickness plastic wrap, and microwave at MEDIUM (50% power) 30 to 35 minutes. Using an oven mitt, carefully lift 1 corner of plastic wrap to allow steam to escape, and let stand in microwave 5 minutes before serving. **Makes** 6 servings.

SHIRLEY CARTER
WALLS, MISSISSIPPI

GARLIC BUTTER SAUCE

fast fixin's

Prep: 5 min.

Serve over meat, rice, and vegetables or with bread.

> **3 tablespoons butter**
> **1 garlic clove, minced**
> **Salt and pepper to taste**

Microwave all ingredients in a microwave-safe measuring cup at HIGH 30 seconds; stir. Continue to microwave sauce at HIGH, stirring at 15-second intervals, until butter is melted. **Makes** 3 tablespoons.

LORI WOLZ
HOPE MILLS, NORTH CAROLINA

Deep Chocolate Brownies

We all enjoy a treat now and then, and a brownie can satisfy that craving. Not only will a bite of chocolate melt away your yearning for a sweet snack, but if you use dark chocolate when baking, you may also enjoy some health benefits.

FUDGY BITTERSWEET BROWNIES

Prep: 20 min., Cook: 5 min., Cool: 10 min., Bake: 25 min.

> **¾ cup all-purpose flour**
> **¼ teaspoon baking powder**
> **¼ teaspoon salt**
> **3 (1-ounce) unsweetened chocolate squares**
> **½ cup butter**
> **1 cup sugar**
> **2 large eggs**
> **1 teaspoon vanilla extract**
> **¾ cup chopped pecans, toasted and divided ✱**

Combine flour, baking powder, and salt. Set aside.

Melt chocolate and butter in a small saucepan over low heat, stirring often until smooth. Cool 10 minutes.

Beat sugar and eggs with an electric mixer until blended. Add chocolate mixture and vanilla, beating until blended. Add flour mixture and ½ cup chopped nuts, beating until blended.

Spread batter in a lightly greased 8-inch square pan; sprinkle evenly with remaining ¼ cup nuts.

Bake at 350° for 20 to 25 minutes or until a wooden pick inserted in center comes out clean. **Makes** 9 servings.

✱Substitute ¾ cup chopped, salted pistachios for pecans, if desired.

SHIRLEY AWOOD GLAAB
HATTIESBURG, MISSISSIPPI

Time-Saving Strategies

Today's new and improved microwaves provide a speedy shortcut for many recipes. Follow the manufacturer's instructions to bake potatoes, cook frozen vegetables, soften butter, and melt chocolate morsels. Various ovens cook at different wattages. Place this timetable on the inside of your cupboard, and use it as a handy reference. Be sure to use microwave-safe containers, and cover them to avoid splatters. Start with the shortest time listed, and then add time as needed.

Melting Butter and Chocolate

■ **Butter:** Place in a microwave-safe glass measuring cup; microwave at HIGH, stirring after shortest time, until melted. For ½ cup or larger, cut sticks of butter in half.

1 to 2 tablespoons	35 to 40 seconds
¼ cup to ½ cup	40 to 45 seconds
¾ cup	40 to 50 seconds
1 cup	50 to 60 seconds

■ **Chocolate morsels:** Place in a microwave-safe glass measuring cup; microwave at HIGH, stirring after 30 seconds, until melted.

¼ cup to 1 cup	50 to 60 seconds

■ **Chocolate baking squares:** Place in a microwave-safe glass measuring cup; microwave at HIGH, stirring every 30 seconds, until melted.

1-ounce baking square	30 to 40 seconds
2-ounce baking square	60 to 90 seconds

MINT TRUFFLE BROWNIE SQUARES

Prep: 30 min.; Bake: 30 min.; Cool: 20 min.;
Chill: 3 hrs., 30 min.

Serve these candylike brownies as after-
dinner "mints" with coffee.

- ½ cup butter, softened
- 1 cup sugar
- 2 large eggs
- 1½ teaspoons vanilla extract
- ¾ cup all-purpose flour
- 6 tablespoons cocoa
- ¼ teaspoon salt
- ⅔ cup chopped macadamia nuts
   (optional)
- 1¾ cups semisweet chocolate
   morsels
- 2 tablespoons butter
- ½ cup whipping cream
- ½ teaspoon peppermint
   extract
- 3 tablespoons chopped
   macadamia nuts (optional)

Beat ½ cup softened butter and sugar
at medium speed with an electric mixer
until fluffy. Add eggs, 1 at a time, beating until blended after each addition.
Stir in vanilla.
Combine flour, cocoa, and salt. Gradually add to butter mixture, beating just
until blended. Stir in ⅔ cup nuts, if
desired. Spread batter evenly (it will be
thick) into a greased 11- x 7-inch baking dish.
Bake at 350° for 25 to 30 minutes or
until mixture is set and a wooden pick
inserted in center comes out clean.
Cool in pan on a wire rack 15 to 20
minutes.
Microwave morsels, 2 tablespoons
butter, and cream in a microwave-safe
glass bowl at HIGH 1 minute (if you
have a lower wattage microwave oven,
add an additional 20 to 30 seconds); let
stand 30 seconds. Whisk in peppermint
extract until smooth. Spread chocolate
mixture over brownie layer. Cover and
chill 30 minutes.
Sprinkle with 3 tablespoons nuts, if
desired. Chill 2 to 3 hours or until set.
Cut into 1-inch squares, and place in
small foil candy cups. **Makes** about
6 dozen.

CATHERINE HARDY
SALT LAKE CITY, UTAH

Soup for Supper

Sometimes foods spark your memory
as much as your appetite. Our readers shared these hearty recipes, along
with their personal anecdotes.

MAMA'S MEXICAN MINESTRONE

family favorite

Prep: 30 min., Bake: 10 min., Cook: 25 min.

Linda Morten turned this delicious soup into
a teaching tool by adding stories about
Mexico and Italy to the menu when ladling
bowls for her children. Fideos pasta can be
found in the ethnic aisle of the supermarket.

- 1 (7-ounce) package fideos
   pasta *
- 1¼ pounds (1-inch-thick) boneless
   sirloin steak
- 1 (1.25-ounce) envelope taco
   seasoning mix
- 1 small onion, chopped
- ½ medium-size green bell pepper,
   chopped
- Vegetable cooking spray
- 2 garlic cloves, minced
- 1 tablespoon chopped fresh basil
- 6¾ cups low-sodium beef broth
- 1 (10-ounce) can diced tomatoes
   and green chiles
- 1 (15-ounce) can kidney beans,
   rinsed and drained
- 2 small yellow squash or zucchini,
   chopped (about 2 cups)
- 1 (6-ounce) bag fresh baby
   spinach
- ¾ cup shredded Parmesan cheese

Spread pasta in a single layer in a 15- x
10-inch jelly-roll pan. Bake at 350° for 8
to 10 minutes or until lightly browned,
stirring once. Set aside.
Cut beef into ¼-inch-thick strips; cut
each strip into 1-inch pieces. Coat with
taco seasoning mix.
Cook beef, onion, and bell pepper in a
Dutch oven coated with cooking spray
over medium heat, stirring often, 6 to 8
minutes or until beef is browned. Add

garlic, and sauté 1 minute. Stir in basil;
cook, stirring constantly, 30 seconds.
Add toasted pasta, broth, and next 3
ingredients. Bring mixture to a boil over
medium-high heat, stirring occasionally. Reduce heat to low, and simmer,
stirring occasionally, 8 to 10 minutes or
until pasta is almost tender. Stir in
spinach. Sprinkle each serving with
shredded Parmesan cheese. **Makes** 16
(1-cup) servings.

✱Substitute 7 ounces angel hair or vermicelli pasta broken into 1-inch pieces
for fideos pasta, if desired.

LINDA MORTEN
KATY, TEXAS

CREAMY PIMIENTO CHEESE SOUP

Prep: 30 min., Cook: 30 min., Cool: 5 min.

Alana Chandler Steel concocted a taste of her
Southern roots when a new job landed her in
a city where pimiento cheese was hard to find.

- 1 tablespoon butter
- 1 medium onion, chopped
- 1 celery rib, chopped
- 1 medium-size sweet potato,
   peeled and chopped ✱
- 4 cups milk
- 1½ cups chicken broth
- 1 (4-ounce) jar sliced pimientos,
   drained and divided
- 1 cup (4 ounces) shredded sharp
   Cheddar cheese
- 1 (3-ounce) package cream cheese,
   cubed
- ¾ teaspoon salt
- ¼ teaspoon pepper
- ¼ teaspoon hot sauce

Melt butter in a large Dutch oven over
medium heat. Add onion and celery, and
sauté 5 minutes or until vegetables are
tender.
Add chopped sweet potato, milk, and
chicken broth; bring to a boil, stirring
occasionally. Reduce heat, and simmer,
stirring occasionally, 18 to 20 minutes or
until sweet potato is tender. Remove mixture from heat, and stir in half of the
pimientos. Add Cheddar cheese and next
4 ingredients, stirring until cheese melts.
Let cool 5 minutes.

Process cheese mixture, in batches, using a handheld blender, blender, or food processor until smooth, stopping to scrape down sides. Stir in remaining half of pimientos before serving. **Makes** about 7 cups.

*Substitute 1 medium potato, peeled and chopped, if desired.

Note: Our Test Kitchens professionals tested this soup using three different tools—a food processor, blender, and handheld blender. Though each worked well, the handheld blender produced the smoothest soup.

ALANA CHANDLER STEEL
RICHARDSON, TEXAS

Soufflés: Here's the Trick

SPICED SOUFFLÉS WITH LEMON WHIPPED CREAM

Prep: 20 min., Cook: 5 min., Stand: 20 min., Bake: 20 min. *(pictured on page 266)*

    Butter or margarine, softened
    Sugar
    ¼ cup butter or margarine
    ¼ cup all-purpose flour
    1¼ cups milk
    ⅔ cup sugar
    ¼ cup molasses
    2 teaspoons ground ginger
    1 teaspoon ground cinnamon
    ¼ teaspoon salt
    1 teaspoon vanilla extract
    5 large eggs, separated
    Lemon Whipped Cream

Grease bottom and sides of 8 (6-ounce) ramekins or custard cups evenly with butter. Lightly coat bottom and sides of ramekins evenly with sugar, shaking out excess. Place ramekins in a 13- x 9-inch pan or baking dish, and set aside.

7 Secrets to Soufflés

1. Preparing the dishes: The ramekins (round, straight-sided individual soufflé dishes) are buttered and sugared to give the soufflé mixture a rough surface to cling to as it rises. Place all ramekins in a pan for easy handling.

2. Separating eggs: Just a speck of yolk in the whites, and the soufflé will not rise to its fullest volume. Use the hands-on method to separate whites from yolks rather than to switch yolks from side to side in the cracked eggshell. Crack the egg into your hand, and let the whites drip through. The less time the shells are involved, the less chance there is to nick the yolk. For extra insurance, you can separate each white into a separate small bowl, and then combine with other whites. Use spotlessly clean glass or metal bowls.

3. Beating egg yolks: A stand mixer is not necessary for this recipe. These were made using a hand mixer. When egg yolks are thick and pale, you'll find the consistency will remind you of some cake batters or a 5-minute instant pudding just as it starts to set.

4. Blending ingredients: Be prepared to quickly combine the beaten yolks with the hot milk mixture without scrambling the eggs. Find a whisk that's sturdy and comfortable, and put a dampened cloth under the bowl so it won't move around the counter while mixing. Get a feel for lifting the saucepan with one hand and whisking with the other hand. Now, you're ready to temper. That's to rapidly whisk about one-fourth of the hot mixture into the yolks, and then whisk the warmed yolks into the remaining mixture in the saucepan.

5. Beating egg whites: Beat egg whites until soft peaks form. Overbeaten, stiff egg whites (beating until tall points form when beaters are lifted) are like a balloon bouquet, with each balloon maxed out with air. Each will burst if more air is added, and the bouquet will ultimately collapse. In a soufflé, the egg whites need to stretch when more air (actually steam) is pumped into the little bubbles you created by beating.

6. Folding in egg whites: To fold whites into yolks, cut down through the center of the mixture using a rubber spatula, scrape the bottom of the pan, come up the sides, and repeat. Do this delicately and quickly, and only just until most white specks disappear.

7. Baking tip: Now comes the most important step: While baking, don't open the oven or slam the cabinet doors; instead, it's the perfect time to adjourn to the living room.

Melt ¼ cup butter in a small saucepan over medium heat; whisk in flour. Cook, whisking constantly, 1 minute. Gradually whisk in milk, whisking constantly until thickened. Remove from heat. Whisk in ⅔ cup sugar and next 5 ingredients.

Beat egg yolks at high speed with an electric mixer 4 to 5 minutes or until thick and pale. Gradually whisk about one-fourth of hot mixture into yolks; add to remaining hot mixture, whisking constantly. Cook over medium heat 1 minute. Remove from heat, and let stand 20 minutes.

Beat egg whites at high speed with an electric mixer until soft peaks form. Gently fold egg whites into milk mixture. Spoon into each ramekin, filling to top.

Bake at 400° for 18 to 20 minutes or until puffed and set. Serve immediately with Lemon Whipped Cream. **Makes** 8 servings.

LEMON WHIPPED CREAM:
Prep: 5 min.

    1 cup whipping cream
    2 tablespoons sugar
    1 tablespoon grated lemon
       rind
    1 tablespoon fresh lemon juice

Beat whipping cream at high speed until foamy; gradually add sugar, lemon rind, and lemon juice, beating until soft peaks form. **Makes** 2 cups.

Good News: Five-Ingredient Southern Recipes

Serve this full-flavored menu for an easy meal on the weekend.

Dinner for Four

Crispy Oven-Fried Catfish

Ranch Potatoes

Pecan Broccoli

Rosemary-Roasted Cherry Tomatoes

S'mores Sundaes

Capture the robust flavors of our region with only five main ingredients (not including salt, pepper, water, and cooking spray). You'll consume a fraction of the fat and calories and an abundance of vitamins and minerals.

You've told us that taste and ease are the most important issues when cooking for your family (especially when you are in a hurry), so let this menu inspire you to get back in the kitchen and try these quick and convenient favorites.

CRISPY OVEN-FRIED CATFISH

Prep: 10 min., Chill: 20 min., Bake: 35 min.

Using a salt-free seasoning allows you to control the amount of salt in this dish while adding flavor at the same time.

- 1 cup low-fat buttermilk
- 4 (6-ounce) catfish fillets
- 2½ teaspoons salt-free Creole seasoning
- ½ teaspoon salt
- 3 cups cornflakes cereal, crushed
- Vegetable cooking spray
- Lemon wedges

Place 1 cup low-fat buttermilk in a large zip-top freezer bag; add 4 (6-ounce) catfish fillets, turning to coat. Seal and chill 20 minutes, turning once.

Remove catfish fillets from buttermilk, discarding buttermilk. Sprinkle catfish fillets evenly with 2½ teaspoons salt-free Creole seasoning and ½ teaspoon salt. **Place** crushed cornflakes in a shallow dish. Dredge catfish fillets in cornflakes, pressing cornflakes gently onto each fillet. Place fillets on a rack coated with cooking spray in a roasting pan. **Bake** catfish fillets at 425° for 30 to 35 minutes or until fish flakes with a fork. Serve catfish fillets immediately with lemon wedges. **Makes** 4 servings.

Note: For testing purposes only, we used The Spice Hunter Cajun Creole Seasoning Salt Free.

LINDSEY MCCLAIN
SAN ANTONIO, TEXAS

Per serving: Calories 321 (37% from fat); Fat 13.1g (sat 3.1g, mono 6.2g, poly 2.7g); Protein 28.6g; Carb 21.4g; Fiber 1.2g; Chol 81mg; Iron 5.3mg; Sodium 472mg; Calc 36mg

RANCH POTATOES

Prep: 10 min., Cook: 25 min.

It's possible to fit rich and creamy mashed potatoes into a healthful diet. For more mashed potato recipes, see "Ultimate Mashed Potatoes" on page 270.

- 1½ pounds Yukon gold potatoes (about 4 medium)
- 2 tablespoons light butter
- ¼ teaspoon salt
- ½ teaspoon pepper
- ⅓ cup reduced-fat Ranch dressing
- 2 turkey bacon slices, cooked and crumbled

Bring potatoes and water to cover to a boil in a large Dutch oven; boil 15 to 20 minutes or until tender. Drain; peel, if desired.

Beat potatoes at low speed with an electric mixer just until mashed. Add butter, salt, and pepper, beating until butter is melted. Gradually add dressing, beating just until smooth. Top with crumbled bacon; serve immediately. **Makes** 4 servings.

Per (⅔-cup) serving: Calories 189 (28% from fat); Fat 5.9g (sat 2.4g, mono 0.5g, poly 0.4g); Protein 4.4g; Carb 30.3g; Fiber 4.2g; Chol 16mg; Iron 1.1mg; Sodium 456mg; Calc 19mg

PECAN BROCCOLI

fast fixin's

Prep: 5 min., Cook: 10 min.

Pecans contribute heart-healthy, unsaturated fat to this recipe. However, because broccoli is such a low-calorie food, the fat percentage for this recipe is slightly higher than others.

- **1 (12-ounce) package fresh broccoli florets**
- **1 tablespoon light butter**
- **3 tablespoons chopped pecans, toasted**
- **¼ teaspoon salt**
- **¼ teaspoon pepper**

Arrange broccoli in a steamer basket over boiling water. Cover and steam 4 minutes or until crisp-tender. Plunge broccoli into ice water to stop the cooking process; drain.

Heat butter in a large nonstick skillet over medium heat 2 to 3 minutes or until melted. Add broccoli, pecans, salt, and pepper. Cook, stirring gently, 2 to 3 minutes or until thoroughly heated. **Makes** 4 servings.

Per (¾-cup) serving: Calories 75 (70% from fat); Fat 5.8g (sat 1.4g, mono 2.3g, poly 1.4g); Protein 3.3g; Carb 5.3g; Fiber 3g; Chol 5mg; Iron 0.9mg; Sodium 188mg; Calc 45mg

ROSEMARY-ROASTED CHERRY TOMATOES

fast fixin's

Prep: 5 min., Bake: 15 min.

Fragrant rosemary boosts the flavor of these tomatoes. If you can't find cherry tomatoes, substitute winter tomatoes, such as Roma.

- **2 pints cherry tomatoes**
- **1 teaspoon olive oil**
- **1½ teaspoons chopped fresh rosemary**
- **2 garlic cloves, minced**
- **¼ teaspoon salt**
- **¼ teaspoon pepper**
- **Vegetable cooking spray**

Combine first 6 ingredients in a zip-top freezer bag. Gently shake until tomatoes are well coated. Transfer to an aluminum foil-lined jelly-roll pan coated with cooking spray.

Bake at 425°, stirring occasionally, 15 minutes or until tomatoes begin to burst. **Makes** 4 servings.

NICOLE MCGLAUGHLIN
MOUNT PLEASANT, SOUTH CAROLINA

Per (¾-cup) serving: Calories 44 (29% from fat); Fat 1.6g (sat 0.2g, mono 0.9g, poly 0.3g); Protein 1.4g; Carb 7.6g; Fiber 1.7g; Chol 0mg; Iron 0.7mg; Sodium 161mg; Calc 12mg

S'MORES SUNDAES

make ahead

Prep: 10 min., Freeze: 1 hr.

- **2 cups low-fat chocolate chunk ice cream, slightly softened**
- **20 graham cracker sticks, crushed**
- **¼ cup marshmallow cream**
- **4 teaspoons semisweet chocolate mini-morsels**
- **8 whole graham cracker sticks**

Stir together softened ice cream and crushed graham crackers in a small bowl. Freeze 1 hour or until firm.

Spoon ice-cream mixture into 4 bowls; top evenly with marshmallow cream and chocolate morsels. Serve each with 2 graham cracker sticks. **Makes** 4 servings.

Note: For testing purposes, we used Healthy Choice Chocolate Chocolate Chunk Premium Low Fat Ice Cream and Honey Maid Grahams Honey Sticks.

HOLLY LOLLAR
BIRMINGHAM, ALABAMA

Per (½-cup) serving: Calories 217 (26% from fat); Fat 6.1g (sat 2.9g, mono 0.9g, poly 0g); Protein 4.2g; Carb 35.8g; Fiber 1.7g; Chol 20mg; Iron 0.7mg; Sodium 135mg; Calc 61mg

Enjoy a Cup of Hot Tea

Iced tea has been called the "house wine" of the South. Who thought that Southerners would enjoy their favorite beverage served hot? Try our simple tips and this delicious recipe for hot tea.

VERLA'S HOT TEA

fast fixin's

Prep: 5 min.

This recipe is created from a blend of three different flavors.

- **¼ cup sugar**
- **3 cups boiling water**
- **2 regular-size Earl Grey tea bags**
- **2 regular-size Irish Breakfast tea bags**
- **2 regular-size raspberry-flavored tea bags**

Stir together sugar and 3 cups boiling water until sugar dissolves. Pour mixture over tea bags. Cover and steep 4 minutes; discard tea bags. (Do not squeeze bags.) Serve immediately. **Makes** 3 cups.

FRED THOMPSON
RALEIGH, NORTH CAROLINA

Brewing Help

- A general rule of thumb is 6 ounces of boiling water for each tea bag (or 1 tablespoon loose leaves).
- Bring water to a soft, rolling boil rather than a full boil, which destroys the delicacy of the tea.
- Whether you use loose leaves or bags, never squeeze the tea after steeping. This releases tannins, a chemical compound found in the leaves that imparts an unpleasant astringent quality to the tea.
- When it comes to loose tea, the higher the quality, the less you'll need. More expensive teas generally have more leaves, while less expensive teas tend to have more stems (which cause bitterness).
- For more information on tearooms around the South, contact the Southern Tea Society at (864) 284-9580.

Holiday Dinners.

*Grab a fork, and come with us. Whether it's a
fabulous party or the ultimate mashed potatoes,
we're serving up tips, tricks, and good fun.*

Pack-and-Go Supper Club

A Dazzling Dinner

Serves 10

Baked Honey-Raisin Brie

Spiced-and-Stuffed Pork Loin With
Cider Sauce

Caramelized Onions

Cranberry-and-Toasted Pecan
Couscous

Balsamic-Browned Butter Asparagus

Berry Bread Pudding With Vanilla
Cream Sauce

One day a month, this group of
friends packs up ingredients and
cooking equipment and convenes at one
home to cook, laugh, and learn about
food and each other. "The best way to
describe the style of our gatherings," tells
Kristen Ohlenforst, founder of this Dallas supper club, "is a cross between a
food television show and a sitcom about
six girls in first jobs and graduate school
living in the big city." There's always a
theme to the menu, and they never shy
away from a challenging recipe.

BAKED HONEY-RAISIN BRIE

make ahead

Prep: 10 min., Stand: 5 min., Bake: 15 min.

Bake this appetizer ahead, cover with nonstick aluminum foil, and take to the party.
Toss pear slices (and apple slices, if desired)
in lemon juice diluted slightly with water to
prevent browning, or cut and serve fruit
immediately when you get there.

¼ cup orange liqueur
1 cup golden raisins
2 (8-ounce) Brie rounds
3 tablespoons honey
Pear slices, assorted crackers

Microwave orange liqueur at HIGH 1
minute in microwave-safe bowl; add
raisins, and let stand 5 minutes.
Trim rind from top of Brie rounds, leaving a ½-inch border on tops. Place Brie
rounds in 9-inch pieplates or ovenproof
plates. Spoon raisin mixture evenly on
Brie rounds, and drizzle with honey.
Bake at 350° for 12 to 15 minutes or
until cheese melts. Serve immediately
with pear slices and crackers. **Makes**
10 servings.

KAREN MACY SCHEPIS
DALLAS, TEXAS

SPICED-AND-STUFFED PORK LOIN WITH CIDER SAUCE

Prep: 30 min., Cook: 10 min., Stand: 20 min.,
Bake: 50 min.

1 tablespoon butter
½ cup finely chopped onion
⅛ teaspoon pepper
1 cup apple cider
**½ cup peeled and diced Granny
   Smith apple**
½ cup chopped dried apricots
1 teaspoon rubbed sage
2 cups cornbread stuffing mix
**2 (3-pound) boneless pork loin
   roasts, trimmed**
2 tablespoons olive oil, divided
Spice Rub
**2 Granny Smith apples, cut into
   wedges**
Cider Sauce

Melt butter in a large nonstick skillet
over medium heat. Add onion and pepper, and sauté 6 to 8 minutes or until
tender. Add cider and next 3 ingredients, and bring to a boil; reduce heat,
and simmer 2 minutes. Remove from
heat, and let stand 5 minutes. Stir in
stuffing mix, and set aside.
Butterfly 1 pork loin by making a horizontal cut (about one-third down from

top) into 1 side of pork, cutting to within ½ inch of other side. (Do not cut all the way through roast.)

Unfold top cut piece, open, and lay flat. Butterfly and repeat procedure on opposite side of remaining two-thirds portion of pork loin, beginning at top or bottom of inside cut.

Place pork between 2 sheets of heavy-duty plastic wrap; flatten to ½-inch thickness using a mallet or rolling pin. Rub pork loin completely with 1 tablespoon olive oil, and sprinkle both sides evenly with half of Spice Rub. Spread half of stuffing mixture on pork, leaving a ½-inch border. Roll up roast, and tie with kitchen string at 2-inch intervals.

Repeat with remaining pork loin, oil, Spice Rub, and stuffing mixture.

Arrange apple wedges in a single layer in the bottom of a 13- x 9-inch roasting pan. Place roasts, seam sides down, on apples.

Bake at 450° for 25 minutes. Reduce temperature to 425°; bake 25 more minutes or until a meat thermometer inserted into thickest portion registers 155°. Remove from oven; let stand 15 minutes or until thermometer reaches 160° before slicing. Discard apples. Serve pork with Cider Sauce. **Makes** 10 servings.

Note: For testing purposes only, we used Pepperidge Farm Cornbread Stuffing mix.

SPICE RUB:
fast fixin's
Prep: 10 min.

- 2 teaspoons ground cumin
- 1 teaspoon ground cinnamon
- 1 teaspoon garlic powder
- 1 teaspoon salt
- ½ teaspoon ground ginger
- ½ teaspoon ground red pepper
- ½ teaspoon black pepper
- ¼ teaspoon ground cloves

Combine all ingredients. **Makes** about 2 tablespoons.

CIDER SAUCE:
fast fixin's
Prep: 10 min., Cook: 5 min.

- 1 (14-ounce) can chicken broth
- 1 cup apple cider
- 1 tablespoon cornstarch
- ⅛ teaspoon pepper
- 1 tablespoon butter

Whisk together first 4 ingredients in a saucepan until smooth. Bring to a boil over medium-high heat; boil, whisking constantly, 1 minute. Whisk in butter. Serve immediately. **Makes** 2½ cups.

KRISTEN OHLENFORST
DALLAS, TEXAS

CARAMELIZED ONIONS
make ahead
Prep: 25 min., Cook: 50 min.

Make these the day before, and reheat.

- 2 tablespoons butter
- 3 large yellow onions, thinly sliced

Melt butter in a large skillet over low heat. Add onions; cover and cook 30 minutes, stirring once. Uncover, increase heat to medium-high, and cook, stirring constantly, 20 minutes or until onions are caramel colored. **Makes** 10 servings.

KRISTEN OHLENFORST
DALLAS, TEXAS

CRANBERRY-AND-TOASTED PECAN COUSCOUS
make ahead
Prep: 5 min., Stand: 25 min., Cook: 5 min.

Measure all ingredients, soak the dried cranberries, and toast the pecans ahead. Cook the recipe when you arrive.

- ½ cup port
- 1 cup dried cranberries
- 1 (32-ounce) container fat-free low-sodium chicken broth
- 2 cups uncooked couscous
- 1 cup chopped pecans, toasted

Microwave ½ cup port at HIGH in a microwave-safe bowl 1 minute; add cranberries, and let stand 15 minutes.

Bring chicken broth to a boil in a medium saucepan. Stir in couscous and cranberry mixture. Cover and remove pan from heat; let stand 10 minutes. Fluff couscous with a fork. Sprinkle with pecans, and serve immediately. **Makes** 10 servings.

KAREN MACY SCHEPIS
DALLAS, TEXAS

We Were Inspired

Our Test Kitchens used the Spice Rub recipe (see above) on the Apricot-Glazed-and-Spiced Pork Loin featured on page 1. Simply rub 1 (3-pound) boneless pork loin roast on all sides with 1 tablespoon olive oil, and sprinkle evenly with 1 tablespoon Spice Rub. Place roast on a rack in an aluminum foil-lined broiler pan. Bake at 450° for 50 minutes. Brush pork with a mixture of ⅓ cup apricot preserves and ⅓ cup chopped dried apricots. Bake 8 more minutes or until a meat thermometer inserted into thickest portion registers 155°. Remove from oven, and let stand 15 minutes or until thermometer reaches 160° before slicing. **Makes** 8 to 10 servings. Prep: 15 min., Bake: 58 min., Stand: 15 min.

BALSAMIC-BROWNED BUTTER ASPARAGUS

fast fixin's

Prep: 10 min., Bake: 15 min., Cook: 4 min.

The secret to browning butter without burning it is to use smell as a test for doneness—it should have a nutty aroma. *(pictured on page 1)*

> **4 pounds fresh asparagus**
> **2 tablespoons extra-virgin olive oil**
> **½ teaspoon kosher salt**
> **¼ teaspoon cracked black pepper**
> **¼ cup butter**
> **4 teaspoons lite soy sauce**
> **2 teaspoons balsamic vinegar**

Snap off and discard tough ends of asparagus.

Arrange asparagus evenly on a lightly greased 15- x 10-inch jelly-roll pan. Drizzle with olive oil, and sprinkle with salt and pepper; toss to coat.

Bake asparagus at 400° for 15 minutes or just until tender.

Melt butter in a large skillet over medium heat. Cook, stirring occasionally, 4 minutes or until butter is lightly browned. Remove from heat; stir in soy sauce and balsamic vinegar. Drizzle over asparagus, tossing to coat. Serve immediately. **Makes** 10 servings.

KRISTEN OHLENFORST
DALLAS, TEXAS

Smart Tabletop Strategies

Consider using place mats to show off a beautiful table. You can also borrow place settings (to make the 10 needed) and place them at either end of the table. Use red goblets to unify the look. Create a fresh centerpiece by alternating cranberry-and-poinsettia-filled glass candleholders with pillar candles on pewter-like candle coasters.

BERRY BREAD PUDDING WITH VANILLA CREAM SAUCE

Prep: 30 min., Stand: 50 min., Bake: 1 hr.

Make the sauce the day before, and reheat in the microwave. Assemble the bread pudding when the roast comes out of the oven, and bake it while you have dinner. *(pictured on page 267)*

> **1 (16-ounce) French bread loaf, cubed**
> **1 cup frozen raspberries (do not thaw)**
> **1 cup frozen blackberries (do not thaw)**
> **4 large eggs, lightly beaten**
> **2¾ cups milk**
> **1 cup sugar**
> **¼ cup butter, melted**
> **1 teaspoon ground cinnamon**
> **1 teaspoon ground nutmeg**
> **1 teaspoon vanilla extract**
> **2 tablespoons melted butter**
> **2 tablespoons sugar**
> **Vanilla Cream Sauce**
> **Garnishes: fresh raspberries, powdered sugar**

Arrange half of bread pieces in a lightly greased 11- x 7-inch baking dish. Arrange frozen berries in a single layer over bread. Top with remaining bread pieces.

Whisk eggs and next 6 ingredients until smooth. Slowly pour egg mixture over bread, pressing down with a wooden spoon until bread absorbs mixture. Let stand 20 minutes.

Bake, covered, at 350° for 30 minutes. Uncover, brush evenly with 2 tablespoons melted butter; sprinkle evenly with 2 tablespoons sugar, and bake 30 more minutes or until set. Remove from oven, and let stand 30 minutes. Serve with Vanilla Cream Sauce. Garnish, if desired. **Makes** 10 servings.

VANILLA CREAM SAUCE:
fast fixin's

Prep: 10 min., Cook: 5 min.

> **2 cups whipping cream**
> **1 cup sugar**
> **2 tablespoons all-purpose flour**
> **½ cup butter**
> **1 teaspoon vanilla extract**

Stir first 3 ingredients together in a saucepan. Add butter, and cook, stirring constantly, over medium heat until butter is melted and mixture begins to boil. Cook, stirring constantly, 3 minutes or until mixture is slightly thickened. Remove from heat, and stir in vanilla. Serve warm. **Makes** 2½ cups.

JENNIFER BOURLAND
DALLAS, TEXAS

Three Yummy Desserts

Sweet treats almost too numerous to count are brought to Laura and Webb Geer's Thanksgiving Day celebration in Morehead City, North Carolina (see "Gather Together" on page 244). Many of the recipes come from Webb's grandmother, Lois "Granny" Davis Webb. Here are two of her best and one from a family friend for you to try.

Yummy Desserts Tote 'Em Tips

■ Place the Caramel-Pecan Pie in a box or roasting pan; then tuck a ring of scrunched paper towels around the base of the pieplate to prevent sliding and to softly cushion the crust's edge.
■ Cover the pan of Pumpkin Crisp with aluminum foil; then wrap the entire dish in about ½-inch thickness of newspaper to help retain the heat.
■ Place a tall, narrow drinking glass in the center hole of Granny's Pound Cake; then loosely cover with foil. The glass will help hold the foil above the cake without disturbing the sprinkling of powdered sugar.

(Top, right) Roasted Turkey, page 244; dressing; steamed carrots; Creamy-and-Crunchy Green Bean Casserole, page 245; Barbecued Pork Tenderloin, page 245; Maple-Sweet Potato Casserole, page 245; Cranberry-Relish Salad, page 245

Peppered Beef Tenderloin With
Portobello-Marsala Sauce,
page 280

Potato-Leek Gratin, page 281

Chocolate Fondue, page 281

Grilled Sweet Guava
Chicken, page 278

Rum Cake, page 279

Southwest Mashed Sweet Potatoes, page 271; Three-Potato Mash, page 271; Simple Mashed Potatoes, page 271

Chocolate-Cherry
Surprise Cheesecake,
page 273

Spiced Soufflés With Lemon
Whipped Cream, page 255

Berry Bread Pudding With
Vanilla Cream Sauce, page 260

Caramel-Pecan Pie, page 269

CARAMEL-PECAN PIE

Prep: 20 min., Bake: 38 min., Cook: 7 min.
(pictured on opposite page)

- ½ (15-ounce) package refrigerated piecrusts
- 28 caramels
- ¼ cup butter
- ¼ cup water
- ¾ cup sugar
- 2 large eggs
- ½ teaspoon vanilla extract
- ¼ teaspoon salt
- 1 cup coarsely chopped pecans, toasted
- Chocolate-Dipped Pecans (optional)

Fit piecrust into a 9-inch pieplate according to package directions; fold edges under, and crimp. Prick bottom and sides of piecrust with a fork.

Bake piecrust at 400° for 6 to 8 minutes or until lightly browned; cool on a wire rack.

Combine caramels, butter, and ¼ cup water in a large saucepan over medium heat. Cook, stirring constantly, 5 to 7 minutes or until caramels and butter are melted; remove from heat.

Stir together sugar and next 3 ingredients. Stir into caramel mixture until thoroughly combined. Stir in pecans. Pour into prepared crust.

Bake pie at 400° for 10 minutes. Reduce heat to 350°, and bake 20 more minutes, shielding edges of crust with aluminum foil to prevent excessive browning. Remove pie to wire rack to cool. Top pie with Chocolate-Dipped Pecans, if desired. **Makes** 8 servings.

CHOCOLATE-DIPPED PECANS:
fast fixin's
Prep: 20 min.

- 1 (6-ounce) package semisweet chocolate morsels
- 20 pecan halves, toasted

Microwave chocolate morsels in a microwave-safe bowl at HIGH for 1 to 1½ minutes or until melted, stirring at 30-second intervals.

Dip half of each pecan in melted chocolate; place on a wax paper-lined baking sheet. Let cool completely. Store in a single layer in an airtight container for up to 2 days. **Makes** 20 pecans.

LOIS DAVIS WEBB
MOREHEAD CITY, NORTH CAROLINA

GRANNY'S POUND CAKE

family favorite

Prep: 15 min.; Bake: 1 hr., 20 min.;
Stand: 15 min.

- 1 cup butter, softened
- ½ cup shortening
- 3 cups granulated sugar
- 5 large eggs
- 3 cups all-purpose flour
- 1 teaspoon salt
- 1 cup milk
- 2 teaspoons vanilla extract
- Powdered sugar

Beat butter and shortening at medium speed with an electric mixer until creamy. Gradually add 3 cups granulated sugar, beating at medium speed until light and fluffy. Add eggs, 1 at a time, beating after each addition just until the yellow disappears.

Stir together flour and salt; add to butter mixture alternately with milk, beginning and ending with flour mixture. Beat at low speed just until blended after each addition. Beat in vanilla just until blended. Pour batter into a greased and floured 12-cup Bundt pan.

Bake at 325° for 1 hour and 15 minutes to 1 hour and 20 minutes or until a long wooden pick inserted in center of cake comes out clean. Cool in pan on a wire rack 10 to 15 minutes. Remove from pan; cool completely on wire rack. Dust cake evenly with powdered sugar. **Makes** 10 to 12 servings.

LOIS DAVIS WEBB
MOREHEAD CITY, NORTH CAROLINA

PUMPKIN CRISP

Prep: 15 min.; Bake: 1 hr., 5 min.; Stand: 10 min.

One of our Foods staffers, who shall remain anonymous, ate half a pan of this easy and fabulous dessert.

- 1 (15-ounce) can pumpkin
- 1 cup evaporated milk
- 1 cup sugar
- 1 teaspoon vanilla extract
- ½ teaspoon ground cinnamon
- 1 (18.25-ounce) package butter-flavored yellow cake mix
- 1 cup chopped pecans
- 1 cup butter, melted
- Whipped Cream (optional)
- Ground nutmeg (optional)

Stir together first 5 ingredients. Pour into a lightly greased 13- x 9-inch baking dish. Sprinkle cake mix evenly over pumpkin mixture; sprinkle evenly with pecans. Drizzle butter evenly over pecans.

Bake at 350° for 1 hour to 1 hour and 5 minutes or until golden brown. Remove from oven, and let stand 10 minutes before serving. Serve warm or at room temperature with Whipped Cream, if desired. Sprinkle with nutmeg, if desired. **Makes** 8 to 10 servings.

Note: For testing purposes only, we used Betty Crocker Super Moist Butter Recipe Yellow Cake Mix.

WHIPPED CREAM:
fast fixin's
Prep: 5 min.

- 1 (8-ounce) carton whipping cream
- 2 tablespoons powdered sugar
- Dash of ground nutmeg

Beat cream at low speed with an electric mixer until foamy; increase speed to medium-high, and gradually add sugar and nutmeg, beating until soft peaks form. **Makes** 2 cups.

ANN GOELLNER
BEAUFORT, NORTH CAROLINA

Kitchen Shortcuts

Sometimes, it's the small things that make a difference. Here, our Foods staff shares a collage of ideas—from taking it easy with a reader's slow-cooker dressing to spiffing up a commercial cranberry sauce. Each is designed to de-stress you, yet impress your guests.

SLOW-COOKER CORNBREAD DRESSING

make ahead

Prep: 15 min., Cook: 4 hrs.

When you have more electrical outlets than oven space, take a cue from Linda Riise of Fort Worth, who makes Slow-Cooker Cornbread Dressing. It received one of our highest ratings.

- 4½ cups cornbread crumbs
- 1 (16-ounce) package herb stuffing mix
- 2 (10¾-ounce) cans cream of chicken soup
- 2 (14-ounce) cans low-sodium chicken broth
- 1 medium onion, chopped
- ½ cup chopped celery
- 4 large eggs
- 1 tablespoon rubbed sage
- ½ teaspoon salt
- ½ teaspoon pepper
- 2 tablespoons butter, cut up

Stir together first 10 ingredients in a large bowl.

Pour cornbread mixture into a lightly greased 5½- or 6-quart slow cooker. Dot with butter.

Cook, covered, on LOW 4 hours or until cooked through and set. **Makes** 12 to 16 servings.

Note: For testing purposes only, we used Pepperidge Farm Herb Seasoned Stuffing mix. We also used 2 (7.5-ounce) packages Martha White Yellow Cornbread Mix prepared according to package directions in 8-inch square pans. The baked cornbread made 7 cups crumbs; just freeze the rest.

ORANGE 'N' JELLIED CRANBERRY SAUCE STACKS

fast fixin's

Prep: 10 min.

The winner of our in-house gussy-up-cranberry-sauce-for-company contest was Alyssa Porubcan, who beat out the other Test Kitchens professionals (it was a close call). Serve these individually, or arrange stacks on a platter for a buffet-style service. For the best presentation, choose an orange that has the same diameter as the cranberry sauce.

- 1 (16-ounce) can jellied cranberry sauce
- 4 (¼-inch-thick) fresh navel orange slices
- Garnishes: fresh cranberries, mint sprigs

Remove cranberry sauce gently from can, leaving cylinder intact. Cut sauce crosswise into 4 equal portions, and place each on a small plate. Top each portion with 1 orange slice. Garnish, if desired. **Makes** 4 servings.

A Speedy Idea

For the Quick Orange-Cranberry Sauce pictured on page 1, cook 1 (12-ounce) bag fresh or frozen cranberries, 1 cup sugar, and ½ cup orange juice in a saucepan over medium-high heat 5 minutes or until cranberries pop. Serve warm, or refrigerate and serve cold.

In a Pinch

Try this recipe to make gravy in a hurry—it was developed by Test Kitchens pro Pam Lolley.
Quick Herbed Turkey Gravy:
Prepare 1 (1.2-ounce) package Knorr Roasted Turkey Gravy Mix according to package directions, stirring in ½ teaspoon chopped fresh sage, ½ teaspoon chopped fresh thyme, and ¼ teaspoon pepper before bringing to a boil. Proceed as directed on the package. **Makes** 1¼ cups. Prep: 10 min., Cook: 8 min.

Ultimate Mashed Potatoes

You may think that mashed potatoes are a pretty straightforward comfort food. When it comes down to it, however, the possibilities are endless. Skins on or off? Skim milk, half-and-half, or whipping cream? Butter or olive oil? Cream cheese or sour cream?

The following recipes offer lots of choices. Each received high ratings from our Test Kitchens. In addition, each was tested with a potato masher, an electric mixer, and a potato ricer. After making inquiries, we discovered more cooks own mashers or mixers than ricers. That's why we list a potato masher or electric mixer in the method. A ricer, which resembles a big garlic press, forces the cooked pulp through tiny holes. This causes the potatoes to resemble grains of rice.

We know that no matter how you mash them, you'll enjoy these potatoes as much as we do.

SIMPLE MASHED POTATOES

family favorite

Prep: 10 min., Cook: 35 min.

Using the paddle attachment in your stand mixer makes quick work of mashing the potatoes. Be sure not to overmix. (pictured on page 265)

> 2½ pounds Yukon gold potatoes *****
> ¼ cup butter
> 1 teaspoon salt
> ½ teaspoon pepper
> ¾ cup whipping cream
> Garnish: pats of butter

Bring potatoes and cold water to cover to a boil in a large Dutch oven; boil 25 minutes or until tender. Drain; peel, if desired.
Beat potatoes at low speed with an electric mixer just until mashed. Add ¼ cup butter, salt, and pepper, beating until butter is melted. Gradually add cream, beating just until smooth. Serve immediately. Garnish, if desired. **Makes** 4 to 6 servings.

* Substitute red or russet potatoes, if desired.

SOUTHWEST MASHED SWEET POTATOES

fast fixin's • make ahead

Prep: 10 min., Cook: 20 min. (pictured on page 265)

> 5 to 6 medium-size sweet potatoes (about 3½ pounds)
> 1 cup sour cream
> ½ cup butter, softened
> 1 (4-ounce) can chopped green chiles
> ¾ teaspoon salt
> ¼ teaspoon pepper
> Garnish: fresh jalapeño slices

Peel potatoes; cut into 1-inch pieces.
Bring potatoes and cold water to cover to a boil in a large saucepan, and boil 12 minutes or until tender.

Drain and return potatoes to pan. Add sour cream and next 4 ingredients. Mash with a potato masher or fork until smooth. Garnish, if desired. Serve warm. **Makes** 8 to 10 servings.

Note: To make ahead, place prepared Southwest Mashed Sweet Potatoes in a lightly greased 11- x 7-inch baking dish; cover and chill up to 2 days. When ready to serve, let stand at room temperature 45 minutes; top with 1 tablespoon cut up butter, and bake, uncovered, at 350° for 35 minutes or until thoroughly heated.

TERRI MATHEWS
LEEDS, ALABAMA

Potato Facts

- **Sweet potatoes** are dark-skinned with a deep orange flesh that's moist when cooked. These are often confused with yams, which are seldom grown in the United States.
- **Russets,** also known as baking potatoes, have rough brown skin and are oblong in shape. Choose these high-in-starch and low-in-moisture potatoes for light and fluffy results.
- **Yukon golds** possess golden skin and yellow, waxy flesh with a firm but creamy texture that has a buttery taste. Golds are a good balance starchwise; in texture, they fall between russets and round reds. This makes them a favorite among many chefs.
- **Round reds,** also called boiling potatoes, have red skin, a round shape, and waxy flesh with less starch than russets. Reds become very creamy when mashed. Try not to overwork these potatoes, or they can become sticky.

THREE-POTATO MASH

family favorite

Prep: 7 min., Cook: 50 min., Bake: 30 min. (pictured on page 265)

> 2 medium-size red potatoes (about ¾ pound)
> 2 medium-size baking potatoes (about 1 pound)
> 2 medium-size Yukon gold potatoes (about ¾ pound)
> 1½ cups sour cream
> 6 tablespoons butter, melted
> 3 green onions, thinly sliced
> 1 teaspoon salt
> 1 teaspoon pepper
> ½ (8-ounce) block sharp Cheddar cheese, shredded
> 2 tablespoons cold butter, cut up
> ⅛ teaspoon paprika
> Garnish: green onion fans

Bring potatoes and cold water to cover to a boil in a large Dutch oven; boil 35 to 40 minutes or until tender. Drain and cool. Peel potatoes, and mash with a potato masher or fork until smooth.
Stir in sour cream and next 4 ingredients; fold in cheese. Spoon into a lightly greased 2-quart baking dish. Top evenly with 2 tablespoons cold butter, and sprinkle evenly with paprika.
Bake, uncovered, at 350° for 30 minutes. Garnish, if desired. **Makes** 6 servings.

LISA BLACKBURN
WEIRSDALE, FLORIDA

Green Onion Fans: Cut off root end and most of top portion. Slice into 2-inch lengths; place on a cutting board. Using a sharp knife, cut several slits at both ends of each piece, cutting almost to but not through the center. Place in ice water; refrigerate until ends curl.

Gather Around the Table

Try a fresh take on a Hanukkah menu.

Even though the holidays are all about tradition, we often shape them to suit our lifestyles. Jennifer and Lee Engel of Roswell, Georgia, share a meal—without the usual brisket—with friends and family. Some traditions can't be broken, though, and for Jennifer this means latkes. The potato pancakes, crunchy on the outside and moist on the inside, are usually served alongside brisket.

CRANBERRY CHICKEN

family favorite

Prep: 8 min., Bake: 1 hr.

  4 pounds chicken pieces
     (3 breasts, 3 thighs,
     3 drumsticks)
  1 (1-ounce) envelope dry onion
     soup mix
  1 (16-ounce) can whole-berry
     cranberry sauce
  1 cup spicy-sweet French dressing

Rinse chicken with cold water; pat dry. Place chicken in a single layer in a lightly greased 13- x 9-inch baking dish. Sprinkle soup mix evenly over chicken. Stir cranberry sauce, and spoon over chicken; top evenly with dressing. Cover with aluminum foil.
Bake at 400° for 40 minutes; remove foil, reduce temperature to 350°, and bake for 20 more minutes. **Makes** 6 servings.

Note: For testing purposes only, we used Kraft Catalina dressing.

SIMPLE POTATO LATKES

Prep: 10 min., Fry: 8 min. per batch

Squeezing the mixture with your hands removes excess liquid before dropping it into the hot oil. This will ensure crisp latkes and keep the oil from splattering.

  3 large baking potatoes (about
     2¼ pounds)
  1 large onion, quartered
  2 large eggs, lightly beaten
  ¼ cup all-purpose flour
  2 teaspoons salt
  1 teaspoon pepper
  Vegetable oil
  Applesauce

Scrub baking potatoes; do not peel. Shred potatoes and onion in a food processor; drain, pressing between paper towels.
Place potatoes and onion in a large bowl; stir in eggs and next 3 ingredients until combined.
Pour oil to a depth of ½ inch in a large heavy skillet over medium-high heat; heat oil to 350°. Squeeze about ¼ cup potato mixture firmly in hand to remove excess liquid; carefully drop into hot oil. Fry, in batches, 3 to 4 minutes on each side or until golden. Drain on paper towels. Place drained latkes on a wire rack on an aluminum foil-lined baking sheet. Keep warm in a 200° oven up to 30 minutes. Serve with applesauce. **Makes** about 20 latkes.

Kosher Wines

Sweet Concord grape wine is no longer the only choice to serve with your holiday meal. Kosher winemakers around the world produce sparkling wines, Chenin Blanc, Shiraz, and other varietals. Look for producers such as Baron Herzog, Mouton Cadet, Yarden, and Alfasi, which are widely available, or ask your wine merchant for other suggestions. In many cases, you can also buy wine online.

Bake the Best Cheesecake

"Daddy Yum-Yum" is his nickname, and cheesecake-baking is his game. "I can crank them out," exclaims Jude Washington. "Once, I baked 60 cheesecakes in two days for family and friends. What can I say—I have a big family and lots of friends!"

Chatting with Jude, who is now a deputy sheriff in Birmingham, Alabama, is a real treat. Each holiday season, Jude makes about 40 cheesecakes for family and friends. He amazingly bakes more than 140 different flavors and knows each recipe by heart. There's good news for us—he has divulged a couple of his recipes along with some baking tips. Go ahead, and indulge.

CHOCOLATE-CHERRY SURPRISE CHEESECAKE

Prep: 30 min.; Cook: 5 min.; Cool: 5 min.; Bake: 1 hr., 35 min.; Stand: 15 min.; Chill: 8 hrs.

This cheesecake has a scrumptious home-made fudge brownie crust. *(pictured on page 266)*

- ½ cup butter
- 4 (1-ounce) unsweetened chocolate baking squares
- 2¼ cups sugar, divided
- 5 large eggs, divided
- ¼ cup milk
- 2 teaspoons vanilla extract, divided
- 1 cup all-purpose flour
- ½ teaspoon salt
- 3 (8-ounce) packages cream cheese, softened
- ½ cup sour cream
- 2 (1-ounce) semisweet chocolate baking squares, melted
- 1 cup canned cherry pie filling
- Toppings: canned cherry pie filling, sweetened whipped cream, milk chocolate kisses

Melt butter and unsweetened chocolate squares in a 3-quart heavy saucepan over low heat, stirring constantly. Remove from heat, and cool 5 minutes. Stir in 1½ cups sugar. Add 2 eggs, 1 at a time, blending well after each addition. Add milk and 1 teaspoon vanilla. Add flour and salt, stirring until mixture is well blended. Spread mixture evenly into a lightly greased 9-inch springform pan.

Bake at 325° for 25 minutes. Remove from oven, and cool in pan on a wire rack. Reduce oven temperature to 300°.

Beat cream cheese and remaining ¾ cup sugar at medium speed with an electric mixer until smooth. Add remaining 1 teaspoon vanilla, beating just until blended. Add remaining 3 eggs, 1 at a time, beating at low speed just until blended after each addition. Add sour cream and melted semisweet chocolate squares, beating just until blended.

Spoon cherry pie filling evenly over prepared crust. Pour chocolate cheesecake mixture over cherry pie filling.

Bake at 300° for 1 hour and 5 minutes to 1 hour and 10 minutes or until edges of cheesecake are set. (Center of cheesecake will not appear set.) Turn oven off; let cheesecake stand in oven 15 minutes. Remove cheesecake from oven; gently run a knife around edge of cheesecake to loosen. Cool completely on a wire rack. Cover and chill 8 hours. Release and remove sides of pan; serve with desired toppings. **Makes** 10 to 12 servings.

IRISH STRAWBERRY-AND-CREAM CHEESECAKE

Prep: 20 min.; Bake: 1 hr., 5 min.; Stand: 15 min.; Chill: 8 hrs.

- 1 cup graham cracker crumbs
- 3 tablespoons butter, melted
- 3 tablespoons sugar
- 4 (8-ounce) packages cream cheese, softened
- 1 cup sugar
- 3 tablespoons all-purpose flour
- 2 teaspoons vanilla extract
- ¼ cup Irish cream liqueur
- 4 large eggs
- 1¼ cups sour cream, divided
- 3 tablespoons strawberry preserves
- Garnish: whole strawberries

Stir together first 3 ingredients; press mixture into bottom of a lightly greased 9-inch springform pan.

Bake crust at 325° for 10 minutes. Cool on a wire rack. Reduce oven temperature to 300°.

Beat cream cheese, 1 cup sugar, and 3 tablespoons flour at medium speed with an electric mixer until smooth. Gradually add vanilla and Irish cream liqueur, beating just until blended. Add eggs, 1 at a time, beating at low speed just until blended after each addition. Add ¾ cup sour cream, beating just until blended.

Pour half of batter into prepared crust. Dollop strawberry preserves over batter; gently swirl batter with a knife to create a marbled effect. Top with remaining batter.

Bake at 300° for 55 minutes or until edges of cheesecake are set. (Center of cheesecake will not appear set.) Turn oven off; let cheesecake stand in oven 15 minutes. Remove cheesecake from oven; gently run a knife around edge of cheesecake to loosen. Cool completely on a wire rack. Cover and chill 8 hours. **Release** and remove sides of pan. Spread remaining ½ cup sour cream evenly over top of cheesecake; garnish, if desired. **Makes** 10 to 12 servings.

Note: For testing purposes only, we used Baileys Irish Cream.

Jude Washington's Tips for Great Cheesecakes

■ **On cream cheese:** "I use Original Philadelphia Cream Cheese, and let it stand at room temperature at least one hour to soften. You can use the microwave [to soften]; just make sure to use the defrost power level."

■ **About the mixer:** "I've had my hand mixer since 1998, and I actually don't want a stand mixer. If the cream cheese is soft, there's really not much mixing to making a cheesecake. In fact, never beat at high speed—that increases the chances of cracks on the top."

■ **Which pans to use:** "I prefer either the dull- or shiny-finished silver springform pans. The crust often burns when baked in a pan with a dark finish."

■ **If the cheesecake cracks:** "Mine usually don't crack, but if one does, I just cover it up with a topping. It still tastes great."

■ **On slicing the cake:** "Use a knife dipped in hot water to cut the cake. Wipe off the knife after each cut. Or put the cake in the freezer until almost frozen; it will then cut cleanly."

Party Favors in a Flash

End an evening among friends with this memento. We created a six-ingredient Sweet Spice Blend and put it to good use in three delicious recipes. See "Just 4 Steps" at right for packaging inspiration. And for more spice ideas, see "From Our Kitchen" on page 284.

SWEET SPICE BLEND

fast fixin's

Prep: 5 min.

A 2-ounce jar of ground cardamom will cost about $8—you can use cinnamon in its place.

    2 tablespoons light brown sugar
    2 tablespoons ground cinnamon
    4 teaspoons dried ground ginger
    1 teaspoon ground nutmeg
    ½ teaspoon ground cloves
    ½ teaspoon ground cardamom

Combine all ingredients in a small bowl. Store in an airtight container. **Makes** 6 tablespoons.

HONEY-SPICE BUTTER

fast fixin's

Prep: 5 min.

Serve this versatile spread with pancakes, biscuits, or sweet potatoes; or stir into oatmeal for a flavorful twist.

    ½ cup butter, softened
    2 tablespoons honey
    ¾ teaspoon Sweet Spice Blend
       (recipe above)

Stir together all ingredients until mixture is smooth. **Makes** about ½ cup.

SPICED-GLAZED CARROTS

fast fixin's

Prep: 10 min., Cook: 15 min.

This recipe easily doubles.

    1 pound baby carrots
    3 tablespoons apricot preserves
    1 tablespoon butter
    1 teaspoon cider vinegar
    ¼ teaspoon salt
    ¼ teaspoon Sweet Spice Blend
       (recipe at left)

Arrange carrots in a steamer basket over boiling water. Cover and steam 7 to 9 minutes or until crisp-tender. Remove from heat.
Stir together 3 tablespoons apricot preserves and next 4 ingredients in a medium skillet over medium heat until blended. Stir in carrots, and cook until thoroughly heated. Serve immediately. **Makes** 4 servings.

SUGAR-AND-SPICE NUTS

make ahead

Prep: 15 min., Bake: 55 min.

Use 1 pound of your favorite combination of raw nuts to make this addictive snack.

    ¾ cup sugar
    1 tablespoon Sweet Spice Blend
       (recipe above, left)
    ¾ teaspoon salt
    1 egg white
    1 tablespoon water
    1 pound pecan halves *

Combine first 3 ingredients in a medium bowl; set aside.
Beat egg white and 1 tablespoon water in a medium bowl using a handheld egg beater or a wire whisk until foamy. (No liquid should remain.) Add pecans, stirring until evenly coated.
Add pecans to sugar mixture, stirring until coated. Place pecans in a single layer on a buttered 15- x 10-inch jelly-roll pan.

Bake at 275° for 50 to 55 minutes, stirring every 15 minutes. Spread immediately in a single layer on wax paper; cool completely. Store in an airtight container. **Makes** about 5 cups.

*Substitute whole almonds or walnut halves, if desired.

Just 4 Steps

■ Make the spice blend (multiply the recipe by the number of recipients), and divide between small glass jars. Use a funnel to fill narrow-mouthed jars.
■ Label each jar using a gift tag; secure tags to jars with decorative ribbon.
■ Copy the recipe onto a gift card. Roll up each recipe page, and tie with ribbon.
■ Arrange jars of Sweet Spice Blend and scrolls of recipes on a table in the entryway so guests can take one on their way out.

Hats Off to This Celebration

Our thanks go to Dixie Spivey with the Charlotte Herb Guild in North Carolina for inviting us to attend the guild's fabulous annual Tea Parties. We sorted through members' fantastic recipes and picked our favorites to share with you. This soiree is big—at least 100 partygoers sit at beautifully decorated dining tables to enjoy more than 50 great appetizers and desserts, plus three specially selected teas. This year marks the 10th year of the event.

LAYERED SUN-DRIED-TOMATO-AND-BASIL SPREAD

make ahead

Prep: 25 min., Chill: 8 hrs.

Make this recipe up to 3 days before the party.

- **2 (8-ounce) packages cream cheese, softened**
- **¾ cup butter, softened**
- **1 teaspoon salt, divided**
- **¼ teaspoon pepper**
- **1⅓ cups sun-dried tomatoes in oil, drained**
- **2 (3-ounce) packages cream cheese, softened and divided**
- **⅓ cup tomato paste**
- **4 garlic cloves, chopped**
- **1½ cups firmly packed fresh basil**
- **¼ cup pine nuts**
- **2 tablespoons olive oil**
- **2 tablespoons fresh lemon juice**
- **¼ cup grated Parmesan cheese**
- **Vegetable cooking spray**
- **Garnishes: fresh rosemary sprigs, sun-dried tomatoes**
- **Crackers or baguette slices**

Beat 2 (8-ounce) packages cream cheese, butter, ½ teaspoon salt, and pepper at medium speed with an electric mixer until creamy. Set aside.

Process dried tomatoes in a food processor until chopped. Add 1 (3-ounce) package cream cheese, tomato paste, and ¼ teaspoon salt; process until smooth, stopping to scrape down sides. Spoon into a bowl, and set aside. Wipe container of food processor clean.

Process garlic and next 4 ingredients in food processor until chopped. Add Parmesan cheese, remaining 3-ounce package cream cheese, and remaining ¼ teaspoon salt; pulse just until blended, stopping to scrape down sides.

Spray a 6-inch springform pan with cooking spray. Spread ½ cup butter mixture evenly on bottom of springform pan. Layer with half of tomato mixture, ½ cup butter mixture, and half of basil mixture; top with ½ cup butter mixture. Repeat layers with remaining tomato mixture, ½ cup butter mixture, and remaining basil mixture. Top with remaining butter mixture. Cover with plastic wrap; chill at least 8 hours.

Run a knife gently around edge of pan to loosen sides. Remove sides of pan; carefully remove bottom of pan, and place layered spread on a serving tray. Garnish, if desired. Serve with crackers or baguette slices. **Makes** 20 servings.

BRENDA DILLS
CHARLOTTE, NORTH CAROLINA

LEMON-BASIL SNAPS

Prep: 15 min., Chill 1 hr., Bake: 12 min. per batch

Chilling the dough will help cookies hold their shape while baking. We don't recommend substituting dried basil in this scrumptious recipe.

- **¾ cup butter, softened**
- **¾ cup sugar**
- **1 large egg**
- **1 tablespoon grated lemon rind**
- **1 tablespoon fresh lemon juice**
- **⅓ cup minced fresh lemon basil leaves** ✱
- **2 cups all-purpose flour**
- **½ teaspoon baking soda**
- **¼ teaspoon salt**
- **⅓ cup finely chopped pistachio nuts**
- **3 tablespoons sugar**

Beat butter at medium speed with an electric mixer until fluffy; add ¾ cup sugar, beating well. Add egg and next 3 ingredients, beating until blended.

Combine flour, baking soda, and salt; gradually add to butter mixture, beating until blended. Cover and chill 1 hour.

Combine nuts and 3 tablespoons sugar in a shallow bowl.

Shape dough into 1-inch balls; roll in nut mixture, and place 2 inches apart on ungreased baking sheets. Flatten slightly with hands or bottom of a glass.

Bake at 350° for 10 to 12 minutes or until golden brown. Remove to wire racks to cool. **Makes** 3 dozen.

✱ Substitute fresh sweet basil, if desired.

DOROTHY HOWELL
CHARLOTTE, NORTH CAROLINA

CHERRY-TARRAGON CHICKEN SALAD

make ahead

Prep: 15 min., Cook: 15 min., Chill: 2 hrs.

Look for dried cherries on a hanging rack in the produce department or with the other dried fruit in your grocery store.

- **1 cup fresh orange juice**
- **½ cup dried cherries**
- **4 cups chopped cooked chicken**
- **⅓ cup mayonnaise**
- **¼ cup sour cream**
- **2 teaspoons fresh tarragon**
- **1 teaspoon grated orange rind**
- **½ teaspoon salt, divided**
- **¼ teaspoon pepper**
- **Crackers**

Bring juice and cherries to a boil in a medium saucepan over medium-high heat. Reduce heat, and simmer, stirring occasionally, 10 to 12 minutes or until liquid is reduced to ¼ cup. Remove from heat, and cool slightly. Pour mixture into a large bowl; stir in chicken and next 6 ingredients, tossing to coat. Cover and chill at least 2 hours. Serve with crackers. **Makes** 6 to 8 servings.

HOLLY JEFFRIES
CHARLOTTE, NORTH CAROLINA

Savvy Idea from the Herb Guild

When serving buffet style to a large number of people, place a recipe card next to each dish so that guests can easily compare their dietary limitations to the list of ingredients.

A Buffet Built on Comfort

The faculty and staff of Emory & Henry College give this gathering high marks.

A Casual, Comfortable Buffet

Serves 10 to 12
We don't feature all of Greg's great recipes here, but this list shows how to structure a similar buffet with your favorite dishes.

Whiskey Punch, wine, and assorted soft drinks

ham with rolls or muffins

Broccoli Casserole

Squash Casserole

Broccoli Slaw

Nutty Wild Rice

homemade bread

banana bread

pimiento cheese sandwiches

peanut butter-and-jelly sandwiches for children

macaroni and cheese for children

pound cake

Tucked beneath a bright moon in the blue-gray mountains of Glade Spring, Virginia, a friendly brick home twinkles like a Christmas card. Luminarias light the walk, and a brass quintet welcomes visitors with "Joy to the World."

Now in his sixth year as host of the Emory & Henry College faculty and staff holiday social, Greg McMillan has abandoned a traditional menu of appetizers and cheese balls "which are great," he says, "but not enough to make a supper."

"I asked myself, 'How can I make this party different, more special?'" he recalls. "I turned to comfort foods—casseroles, more substantial dishes. This party is about community. We want people to come and stay awhile and talk. It's like a family here."

As the moon rises, chatty guests pack into the kitchen, dining room, and living room. Greg speaks to everyone at the party, beaming. "I get a lot of energy from being around people," he says. "Entertaining is part of my personality."

WHISKEY PUNCH

fast fixin's • make ahead

Prep: 20 min.

Greg found the original recipe for this potent punch in a local Episcopal church cookbook and later learned that it was included as a joke. He tinkered with the proportions, and the punch is now a staple at the party.

> 2 liters whiskey or bourbon
> ½ liter dark rum
> 1¼ cups sugar
> 7 cups strong-brewed tea
> 3½ cups fresh lemon juice or
>   4 (7.5-ounce) bottles frozen
>   lemon juice, thawed
> 2 quarts orange juice

Stir together all ingredients in a large crock or food-safe container. Cover mixture, and chill up to 3 days before serving. **Makes** 32 cups.

Note: For strong-brewed tea, pour 5 cups boiling water over 2 family-size tea bags; cover and steep 5 minutes. Remove tea bags from water, squeezing gently. Add 2 cups cold water.

BROCCOLI CASSEROLE

Prep: 15 min., Cook: 7 min., Bake: 50 min., Stand: 10 min.

> 2 (16-ounce) packages fresh
>   broccoli florets
> ½ cup water
> 2 tablespoons butter or margarine
> 1 small onion, chopped
> Cheddar Cheese Cream Sauce
> 2 (8-ounce) cans sliced water
>   chestnuts
> ½ teaspoon salt
> 2 (2-ounce) jars diced pimientos,
>   drained (optional)
> 1 cup shredded Cheddar cheese

Place half of broccoli florets in an 11- x 7-inch baking dish. Add ¼ cup water, and microwave at HIGH 7 minutes or until tender; drain. Repeat with remaining half of broccoli and ¼ cup water. Set aside.

Melt butter in a large skillet over medium heat; add onion, and sauté 7 minutes or until tender.

Combine broccoli, onion, Cheddar Cheese Cream Sauce, sliced water chestnuts, salt, and, if desired, pimientos. Spoon mixture into a lightly greased 13- x 9-inch baking dish.

Bake at 350° for 15 minutes. Sprinkle evenly with Cheddar cheese; bake 30 to 35 more minutes or until set. Let stand 10 minutes before serving. **Makes** 10 to 12 servings.

CHEDDAR CHEESE CREAM SAUCE:

Prep: 25 min., Cook: 15 min.

- 6 tablespoons butter or margarine, melted
- 6 tablespoons all-purpose flour
- 3 cups milk
- ½ teaspoon salt
- ¼ teaspoon ground red pepper
- 1 cup shredded Cheddar cheese
- 2 large eggs

Melt butter in a heavy saucepan over medium heat; whisk in flour until smooth. Gradually whisk in milk, salt, and red pepper.

Bring mixture to a boil over medium-high heat, whisking constantly. Boil, whisking constantly, 1 minute. Remove from heat, and stir in cheese until melted and blended.

Beat eggs with a fork until thick and pale. Gradually stir about one-fourth hot milk mixture into eggs; add egg mixture to remaining hot milk mixture, stirring constantly. **Makes** 4 cups.

You Can Do It

Greg's planning makes the party work. He makes the casseroles the week of the event and freezes them. He and many of the guests are vegetarians, so the casseroles are vegetable-based. Meat lovers cut into a ham his mom carves. The ham is served with rolls or split muffins. The make-ahead sides are simple to do yet highly flavorful. A lovely cake is usually the centerpiece of the buffet. Some guests bring their favorite dishes and desserts, and Greg anticipates space for these platters too. He transforms his dining room table into the buffet and serves punch and wine from the sideboard. Beer, soft drinks, and juice boxes are iced down in the kitchen in galvanized tubs.

SQUASH CASSEROLE

freezeable • make ahead

Prep: 40 min., Cook: 10 min., Bake: 50 min., Stand: 10 min.

The luscious Swiss Cheese Cream Sauce takes a few extra minutes to make, but the rich results are worth the effort. Greg makes this casserole up to a day ahead of the party or freezes it earlier in the week.

- 2 tablespoons butter or margarine
- 3 pounds yellow squash, thinly sliced
- 1 small onion, chopped
- 1¼ teaspoons salt
- ½ teaspoon pepper
- 2 (8-ounce) cans sliced or chopped water chestnuts, drained
- Swiss Cheese Cream Sauce
- 2 (2-ounce) jars diced pimientos, drained (optional)
- Buttery Parmesan Topping

Melt butter in a large skillet over medium heat; add squash and next 3 ingredients, and sauté 10 minutes or until vegetables are tender.

Stir in water chestnuts, Swiss Cheese Cream Sauce, and, if desired, diced pimientos. Spoon squash mixture into a lightly greased 13- x 9-inch baking dish.

Bake at 350° for 15 minutes. Sprinkle evenly with Buttery Parmesan Topping; bake 30 to 35 more minutes or until set and golden brown. Let stand 10 minutes before serving. **Makes** 10 to 12 servings.

SWISS CHEESE CREAM SAUCE:

Prep: 25 min., Cook: 15 min.

- 6 tablespoons butter or margarine, melted
- 6 tablespoons all-purpose flour
- 3 cups milk
- ½ teaspoon salt
- 1 cup shredded Swiss cheese
- 2 large eggs

Melt butter in a heavy saucepan over medium heat; whisk in flour until smooth. Gradually whisk in milk and salt.

Bring mixture to a boil over medium-high heat, whisking constantly. Boil, whisking constantly, 1 minute. Remove from heat, and stir in cheese until melted and blended.

Beat eggs with a fork until thick and pale. Gradually stir about one-fourth hot milk mixture into eggs; add egg mixture to remaining hot milk mixture, stirring constantly. **Makes** 4 cups.

BUTTERY PARMESAN TOPPING:

Prep: 10 min.

- 8 white bread slices, cut into ¼-inch cubes
- ½ cup grated Parmesan cheese
- ½ cup butter or margarine, melted
- 2 tablespoons dried parsley flakes

Pulse bread cubes in a food processor until mixture resembles fine crumbs. Transfer breadcrumbs to a large bowl. Stir in Parmesan cheese, butter, and parsley. **Makes** 3 cups.

BROCCOLI SLAW

fast fixin's • make ahead

Prep: 20 min.

This is a terrific dish to take to a potluck after a busy day because you can make it the night before. We love the fresh taste.

- **1 (12-ounce) package fresh broccoli slaw**
- **1 cup red seedless grapes, halved**
- **1 Granny Smith apple, diced**
- **1 cup Vidalia onion dressing or poppy seed dressing**
- **2 oranges, peeled and sectioned**
- **Toasted chopped pecans (optional)**

Stir together first 5 ingredients in a large bowl. Top with chopped pecans, if desired. **Makes** 8 servings.

NUTTY WILD RICE

make ahead

Prep: 25 min., Chill: 2 hrs.

Leave out the green onions until the day you serve the dish so they won't overpower the other flavors.

- **1 (6-ounce) package long-grain and wild rice mix**
- **1 cup dried cherries or raisins**
- **4 green onions, chopped**
- **⅓ cup fresh orange juice (about 1 orange)**
- **¼ cup olive oil**
- **2 tablespoons chopped fresh mint**
- **¼ teaspoon pepper**
- **1 cup pecan halves, toasted**

Prepare rice according to package directions. Add dried cherries and next 5 ingredients; toss. Cover and chill at least 2 hours; top with toasted pecan halves before serving. **Makes** 8 to 10 servings.

We're Glad You're Here

Greet your out-of-town company with this Latin-inspired menu.

South Beach Supper

Serves 8

Grilled Sweet Guava Chicken

The Ultimate White Rice

mixed salad greens

Rum Cake

We looked to the Miami masters of fun, good times, and easy-to-do Cuban foods—Raul Musibay, Jorge Castillo, and Glenn Lindgren—to help us with a dinner that will re-energize travel-weary guests. These brothers-in-law call themselves the Three Guys From Miami, and we've adapted recipes from their cookbook, *Three Guys From Miami Cook Cuban* (Gibbs Smith Publisher, 2004, www.icuban.com), for you to try. The main dish takes you outdoors to grill chicken. Dessert is a very relaxing and potent Rum Cake. As Raul tells it, entertaining company should be "No rush! Laugh and have a good time, do a little salsa [dancing], or whatever it is at your house. Greet everyone with a smile, and be happy." Some good words to set the mood in your home.

GRILLED SWEET GUAVA CHICKEN

Prep: 20 min.; Chill: 8 hrs.; Grill: 1 hr., 10 min.

Ask your butcher to cut chickens in half for you, or you can substitute chicken breasts and leg quarters. Most grills have hot and cooler spots, so plan to rotate the chicken from one area to another for more even cooking. *(pictured on page 264)*

- **2 (3½-pound) whole chickens ✱**
- **2 tablespoons ground cumin**
- **1 teaspoon salt**
- **¼ teaspoon pepper**
- **½ cup olive oil**
- **⅓ cup fresh lime juice**
- **6 garlic cloves, pressed**
- **Guava Glaze**
- **Garnishes: lemon half, lime half, sliced papaya**

Cut each whole chicken in half, and set aside.
Stir together cumin, salt, and pepper in a small bowl.

Combine 4 teaspoons cumin mixture, olive oil, lime juice, and garlic in a shallow dish or large zip-top freezer bag; reserve remaining cumin mixture. Add chicken to dish or bag; cover or seal, and chill 8 hours or up to 24 hours, turning occasionally.

Light 1 side of grill, heating to high heat (400° to 500°); leave the other side unlit. Remove chicken from marinade, discarding marinade. Pat dry with paper towels. Rub reserved cumin mixture over chicken. Arrange, skin side up, on unlit side of grill, and grill, covered with grill lid, 40 minutes or until a meat thermometer inserted into thickest portion of thigh and breast registers 150°.

Brush chicken with Guava Glaze. Grill, covered with grill lid, 30 more minutes or until meat thermometer inserted into thickest portion of thigh registers 180° and thickest portion of breast registers 170°, brushing every 10 minutes with glaze. Cut chicken halves in half between breast and thigh to make 8 serving-size pieces. Garnish, if desired. **Makes** 8 servings.

*Substitute 4 bone-in, skin-on chicken breasts and 4 chicken leg quarters, if desired.

Guava Glaze:
fast fixin's
Prep: 5 min., Cook: 10 min.

Look for guava jelly in the jelly or ethnic aisles of the grocery store, or order it from **www.cubanfoodmarket.com.**

- ¼ cup firmly packed light brown sugar
- ¼ cup guava jelly
- ¼ cup apple juice
- ¼ cup fresh lemon juice

Bring all ingredients to a boil in a small saucepan over medium-high heat. Reduce heat to medium-low; simmer 7 minutes or until glaze thickens and reduces slightly, stirring often. Remove from heat; cool. **Makes** about ⅔ cup.

Note: For testing purposes only, we used Palmalito Guava Jelly.

THE ULTIMATE WHITE RICE
Prep: 10 min., Cook: 30 min.

Rinsing the rice helps get rid of excess starch, resulting in light and fluffy—not sticky—rice.

- 3 cups uncooked converted white rice
- 4½ cups water
- 1½ tablespoons olive oil
- 1 large garlic clove, peeled
- 1½ teaspoons salt

Place rice in a fine wire-mesh strainer, and rinse under cold water until water runs clear; drain. Combine rinsed rice, 4½ cups water, and remaining ingredients in a large saucepan over medium-high heat; bring to a boil. Boil, uncovered, 3 minutes. Cover, reduce heat to low, and simmer 15 to 20 minutes or until water is absorbed. Fluff rice with a fork. Remove garlic clove, and serve immediately. **Makes** 8 servings.

Note: For testing purposes only, we used Uncle Ben's Converted Original Enriched Parboiled Long Grain Rice.

RUM CAKE
Prep: 20 min., Bake: 1 hr., Cool: 15 min., Stand: 45 min. *(pictured on page 265)*

- 1½ cups butter, softened
- 1½ cups granulated sugar
- 3 large eggs
- 1 egg yolk
- 2 teaspoons vanilla extract
- 2 tablespoons grated lemon rind
- ½ cup dark rum
- ¼ cup banana liqueur *
- 3 cups all-purpose flour
- 2 teaspoons baking powder
- ½ teaspoon baking soda
- ⅛ teaspoon salt
- 1 cup whipping cream
- Rum Syrup
- Powdered sugar

Beat butter and granulated sugar at medium speed with an electric mixer until light and fluffy. Add eggs, egg yolk, and vanilla, beating until blended. Add lemon rind, and beat until blended. Gradually add rum and banana liqueur, beating until blended. (Batter will look curdled.)

Stir together flour and next 3 ingredients; add to batter alternately with whipping cream, beginning and ending with flour mixture. Beat batter at low speed just until blended after each addition. Pour batter into a greased and floured 10-inch Bundt pan.

Bake at 350° for 55 to 60 minutes or until a long wooden pick inserted in center of cake comes out clean.

Cool in pan on a wire rack 15 minutes. Pierce cake multiple times using a metal or wooden skewer. Pour Rum Syrup evenly over cake. Let stand 45 minutes. Remove from pan; cool completely on a wire rack. Sprinkle evenly with powdered sugar before serving. **Makes** 10 to 12 servings.

*Substitute ¼ cup dark rum, if desired.

RUM SYRUP:
Prep: 5 min., Cook: 15 min., Cool: 10 min.

- 10 tablespoons butter
- ¾ cup sugar
- ¼ cup dark rum
- ¼ cup banana liqueur *

Melt butter in a 2-quart saucepan over medium-high heat; stir in remaining ingredients. Bring to a boil, stirring often; reduce heat to medium, and cook, stirring often, 8 to 10 minutes or until slightly thickened. Remove from heat, and cool 10 minutes. **Makes** about 1 cup.

*Substitute ¼ cup dark rum for banana liqueur, if desired.

Cheers to an Easy, Gorgeous Party

Ring in the New Year with a casual, smashing dinner.

Fabulous New Year's Menu

Serves 6 to 8

appetizer—host's choice

Cybil drizzles olive oil over hummus (purchased from her grocer's deli), sprinkles it with chopped olives, and serves it with pita chips or toasted baguette slices.

Peppered Beef Tenderloin With Portobello-Marsala Sauce

Potato-Leek Gratin

Autumn Salad With Maple-Cider Vinaigrette

white wine: Red Bicyclette Chardonnay

red wine: Yellow Tail Shiraz

sparkling wine: Domaine Ste. Michelle Cuvée Brut

Chocolate Fondue

Take your cue for hosting a small dinner party from Cybil and Broderick Talley of Atlanta. Cybil worked on our Foods staff for about three years before moving to Georgia. Their plan for a New Year's Eve gathering is casual with a touch of fancy—featuring beef tenderloin on the menu and low-fuss decorating.

PEPPERED BEEF TENDERLOIN WITH PORTOBELLO-MARSALA SAUCE

Prep: 5 min., Stand: 40 min., Broil: 15 min., Bake: 35 min.

Ask your butcher to trim the tenderloin, or do it yourself. Use a sharp, thin knife to cut away the top layer of fat and the thin (about 2-inch-wide) membrane called silver skin. *(pictured on page 262)*

**2 teaspoons freshly ground black pepper
1 teaspoon kosher salt
1 teaspoon lemon pepper
¼ teaspoon granulated garlic
¼ teaspoon dried thyme
1 (4-pound) beef tenderloin, trimmed
Portobello-Marsala Sauce
Garnishes: fresh thyme sprigs, roasted garlic bulbs**

Combine first 5 ingredients; pat mixture evenly over beef. Cover and let stand at room temperature 30 minutes. **Broil** 6 inches from heat 15 minutes on a lightly greased rack in a roasting pan; reduce oven temperature to 375°, and bake 30 to 35 minutes or until a meat thermometer inserted into thickest portion registers 140° or to desired degree of doneness. Remove from oven; let stand 10 minutes before slicing. Serve with Portobello-Marsala Sauce. Garnish, if desired. **Makes** 6 to 8 servings.

PORTOBELLO-MARSALA SAUCE:
Prep: 5 min., Cook: 35 min.

This sauce can be made the day before.

**3 tablespoons cold butter, divided
1 (8-ounce) package sliced baby portobello mushrooms *
3 garlic cloves, minced
2 large shallots, diced
2 cups Marsala wine
1 cup chicken broth**

Melt 1 tablespoon butter in a medium skillet over high heat; add mushrooms, and sauté 10 minutes or until mushrooms are browned and liquid is evaporated. **Add** 1 tablespoon butter, garlic, and shallots to skillet; sauté 5 minutes. Stir in Marsala and chicken broth, stirring to loosen browned bits from bottom of skillet. Bring to a boil, and cook 20 minutes or until reduced by two-thirds. Remove

---

Tips for Tenderloins

At a regular price of $20 or more per pound, beef tenderloin is a pricey investment for dinner. Buy it on sale up to one month before the party, and freeze it. (A great price is $10 to $15 per pound.) To freeze, triple-wrap tenderloin in plastic wrap, and then overwrap it in heavy-duty aluminum foil. To thaw, remove foil and two layers of plastic wrap, and refrigerate for about 24 hours.

As with any large cut of meat, let stand at room temperature 30 minutes for even cooking. Cooking beef tenderloin is a three-step process. First, the meat is broiled to sear the outside for appearance, flavor, and to help seal in the juices. Second, the oven temperature is reduced to 375° to slowly cook this lean cut of meat and avoid overcooking. Finally, the meat needs to stand 10 minutes. As meat cooks, the juices tend to move toward the center. Standing time allows the juices to redistribute throughout, making each piece juicy.

from heat, and stir in remaining 1 tablespoon butter. **Makes** 1½ cups.

* Substitute 1 (8-ounce) package sliced button mushrooms, if desired.

POTATO-LEEK GRATIN

Prep: 15 min., Cook: 10 min., Bake: 50 min., Stand: 10 min.

Leeks look like big green onions and taste like a cross between a mildly flavored onion and garlic. Cut off the root end and darker portions of the green leaves. Split in half lengthwise, and wash thoroughly before slicing. *(pictured on page 262)*

> 3 tablespoons butter
> 3 medium leeks, thinly sliced
> 3 garlic cloves, minced
> 3 tablespoons all-purpose flour
> 3½ cups milk
> 2 teaspoons kosher salt
> 1 teaspoon freshly ground pepper
> ⅛ teaspoon ground nutmeg
> ⅛ teaspoon dried thyme
> 2 cups (8 ounces) shredded Italian cheese blend
> 3 pounds baking potatoes, peeled and thinly sliced

Melt butter in a 3-quart saucepan over medium heat; add leeks, and sauté 5 minutes or until tender (do not brown). Add garlic; sauté 1 minute.
Whisk in flour; cook, whisking constantly, 1 minute. Gradually whisk in milk. Stir in 2 teaspoons salt and next 3 ingredients.
Cook over medium heat, whisking constantly, until mixture thickens. Remove from heat; stir in cheese until melted and smooth.
Layer half of potatoes in a lightly greased 13- x 9-inch baking dish; pour half of sauce evenly over potatoes in dish. Repeat layers, ending with sauce.
Bake, uncovered, at 375° for 50 minutes or until potatoes are golden brown and fork tender, shielding with aluminum foil to prevent excessive browning, if necessary. Remove from oven, and let stand 10 minutes. **Makes** 8 servings.

AUTUMN SALAD WITH MAPLE-CIDER VINAIGRETTE

fast fixin's
Prep: 10 min.

Place pear in a paper sack to speed ripening. The dressing and nuts can be made ahead.

> 1 (10-ounce) bag baby spinach
> 1 ripe Bartlett pear, cored and thinly sliced
> 1 small red onion, thinly sliced
> 1 (4-ounce) package crumbled blue cheese
> Sugared Curried Walnuts
> Maple-Cider Vinaigrette

Combine first 5 ingredients in a large bowl. Drizzle with Maple-Cider Vinaigrette, gently tossing to coat. **Makes** 8 servings.

SUGARED CURRIED WALNUTS:
fast fixin's • make ahead
Prep: 5 min., Bake: 10 min.

> 1 (6-ounce) package walnut halves *****
> 2 tablespoons butter, melted
> 3 tablespoons sugar
> ¼ teaspoon ground ginger
> ⅛ teaspoon curry powder
> ⅛ teaspoon kosher salt
> ⅛ teaspoon ground red pepper

Toss walnuts in melted butter. Stir together sugar and next 4 ingredients in a medium bowl; sprinkle over walnuts, tossing to coat. Spread in a single layer on a nonstick aluminum foil-lined pan.
Bake walnuts at 350° for 10 minutes. Cool in pan on a wire rack; separate walnuts with a fork. Store in an airtight container for up to 1 week. **Makes** 1½ cups.

* Substitute pecan halves, if desired.

MAPLE-CIDER VINAIGRETTE:
fast fixin's
Prep: 5 min.

> ⅓ cup cider vinegar
> 2 tablespoons pure maple syrup
> 1 tablespoon Dijon mustard
> ¼ teaspoon salt
> ¼ teaspoon pepper
> ⅔ cup olive oil

Whisk together first 5 ingredients. Gradually whisk in oil until completely blended. Cover and refrigerate up to 3 days. **Makes** 1⅓ cups.

CHOCOLATE FONDUE

Prep: 10 min.

Stir in additional heated whipping cream, 1 tablespoon at a time, if you want a thinner fondue. A fondue pot for chocolate is heated by a tea light or votive candle. *(pictured on page 263)*

> 1 cup whipping cream
> 3 (4-ounce) semisweet chocolate bars, chopped
> 2 tablespoons coffee liqueur or other flavored liqueur
> Assorted cookies, pretzel sticks, fruit, marshmallows

Microwave whipping cream and chocolate in a microwave-safe glass bowl at HIGH 1½ to 2 minutes, stirring every 30 seconds. Stir in liqueur.
Transfer to a fondue pot; keep warm, stirring occasionally. Serve with cookies, pretzels, fruit, and marshmallows. **Makes** 6 to 8 servings.

Simple, Pretty Decoration

The hot flower arrangement for this year is a glass vase filled with one or two basic flowers, such as euphorbia and star-of-Bethlehem. Strip leaves off flower stems below the water line for a professional look.

Pop the Cork

Champagne and chocolate—a divine pairing, right? It may seem like a crazy idea to combine them into a luscious chocolate sauce, but our Test Kitchens did it. This idea inspired others on our staff, and soon we had two cocktails to share with you.

WAYNE'S "FRENCH 75"

chef recipe • fast fixin's

Prep: 5 min.

This is definitely a sipping cocktail that's at its best when it's made with high-quality ingredients.

- 3 tablespoons brandy
- 1 tablespoon orange liqueur
- Crushed ice cubes
- 1 lemon wedge
- 1 small lemon rind twist
- ½ cup Champagne or sparkling wine

Combine first 3 ingredients in a cocktail shaker or martini shaker. Cover with lid, and shake 30 seconds or until thoroughly chilled. Remove lid, and strain into a martini glass. Squeeze juice from lemon wedge into glass; rub lemon rind twist around rim, and drop into glass. Add Champagne to brandy mixture, and serve immediately. **Makes** 1 serving.

Note: For testing purposes only, we used Cognac for brandy and Cointreau for orange liqueur.

WAYNE RUSSELL
CHEZ FONFON
BIRMINGHAM, ALABAMA

POMEGRANATE-CHAMPAGNE COCKTAIL

fast fixin's

Prep: 5 min.

Pomegranate juice is available in the refrigerated juice section or produce section of the grocery store. Turbinado is a raw, very coarse sugar with a mild brown sugar taste. Find it with other sugars. We found rock candy stirrers at an import store that carries wines and specialty food items.

- 1 turbinado sugar cube*
- 2 tablespoons pomegranate juice**
- ½ cup Champagne or sparkling wine, chilled

Place sugar cube in a Champagne flute; add 2 tablespoons pomegranate juice and ½ cup Champagne. Serve immediately. **Makes** 1 serving.

*Substitute 1 rock candy stirrer or granulated sugar cube, if desired.

**Substitute 2 tablespoons cranberry juice cocktail, if desired. Omit sugar cube.

CHAMPAGNE-CHOCOLATE SAUCE

fast fixin's

Prep: 10 min.

- 2 (6-ounce) dark chocolate candy bars, finely chopped
- 1 tablespoon butter
- ½ cup Champagne or sparkling wine

Microwave chocolate and butter in a 2-quart microwave-safe bowl at HIGH 1 minute or just until chocolate begins to melt, stirring after 30 seconds. Whisk in Champagne, whisking until chocolate melts and mixture is smooth (mixture may appear broken, but continue to whisk until smooth). **Makes** about 1¾ cups.

Note: For testing purposes only, we used Hershey's Special Dark Chocolate candy bars.

At Play in the Kitchen

Helen DeFrance and Leslie Carpenter always make cooking a family affair. They are so enthusiastic about the importance of a family bonding over food, they hold a series of cooking classes, called Kids Are Cooking.

CRISPY BROWN SUGAR BACON

family favorite

Prep: 15 min., Bake: 25 min.

Twist the bacon for a texture that's crisp on the ends and chewy in the center.

**1 pound hickory-smoked bacon
    slices
1 cup firmly packed light brown
    sugar
1 tablespoon cracked black pepper**

Cut bacon slices in half.

Combine sugar and pepper in a shallow dish. Dredge bacon in sugar mixture, shaking off excess.

Twist each bacon slice, if desired. Place bacon in a single layer on a lightly greased baking rack in an aluminum foil-lined baking pan.

Bake at 425° for 20 to 25 minutes or until crisp. Allow bacon to cool before serving. **Makes** 6 servings.

CHEDDAR CHEESE GRITS CASSEROLE

family favorite

Prep: 15 min., Cook: 10 min., Bake: 40 min.

**4 cups milk
¼ cup butter
1 cup uncooked quick-cooking
    grits
1 large egg, lightly beaten
1 teaspoon salt
½ teaspoon pepper
2 cups (8 ounces) shredded sharp
    Cheddar cheese
¼ cup grated Parmesan
    cheese
Garnish: parsley sprigs**

Bring milk just to a boil in a large saucepan over medium-high heat; gradually whisk in butter and grits. Reduce heat, and simmer, whisking constantly, 5 to 7 minutes or until grits are done. Remove from heat.

Stir in egg and next 3 ingredients. Pour into a lightly greased 11- x 7-inch

baking dish. Sprinkle evenly with grated Parmesan cheese.

Bake, covered, at 350° for 35 to 40 minutes or until mixture is set. Serve immediately. Garnish, if desired. **Makes** 6 servings.

FRUITINI

family favorite • fast fixin's

Prep: 20 min.

**1 banana, peeled and sliced
    (about ½ cup)
½ cantaloupe, cut into ½-inch
    cubes (about 3 cups)
½ pound grapes, halved (about
    1 cup)
2 kiwifruit, peeled and sliced
1 navel orange, peeled and
    sectioned
10 strawberries, sliced
¼ cup powdered sugar, divided
⅓ cup fresh lemon juice, divided
    (about 2 lemons)**

Toss together first 6 ingredients, 2 tablespoons powdered sugar, and 1 tablespoon lemon juice in a large bowl.

Pour remaining lemon juice into a saucer. Dip rims of 6 parfait, wine, or martini glasses in remaining lemon juice; dip rims in remaining 2 tablespoons powdered sugar.

Fill glasses with fruit mixture. **Makes** 6 servings.

Cooks' Notes

Here are a few of Helen and Leslie's tips for getting children involved in the kitchen.

■ Plan ahead. Everyone loves to make cookies, so freeze a few batches of dough to have on hand. In a moment's notice, you're ready to bake a dozen.

■ Use the microwave. It's great for softening brown sugar and butter. It's also useful for extracting maximum juice from lemons and limes. Slice fruit in half, and microwave at HIGH for 15 to 20 seconds.

■ Buy a roll of parchment paper. This virtually nonstick paper is perfect for wrapping and rolling out cookie dough, as well as lining baking sheets.

OVERNIGHT OVEN-BAKED FRENCH TOAST

family favorite

Prep: 15 min., Chill: 8 hrs., Bake: 45 min.

Dust with powdered sugar just before serving.

**1 (16-ounce) French bread loaf
¼ cup butter, softened
4 large eggs
1 cup milk
¼ cup sugar
2 tablespoons maple syrup
1 teaspoon vanilla extract
½ teaspoon salt**

Cut bread loaf into about 10 (¾-inch-thick) slices.

Spread butter evenly over 1 cut side of each bread slice.

Arrange bread, butter side up, in an ungreased 13- x 9-inch baking dish.

Whisk together eggs and next 5 ingredients; pour over bread, pressing slices down. Cover and chill 8 hours.

Remove bread slices from baking dish, and place on two lightly greased baking sheets.

Bake, uncovered, at 350° for 45 minutes or until golden. **Makes** 8 servings.

from our kitchen

Gifts of Good Taste

Homemade treats are always welcome, especially during the hectic holiday season when all of us do a lot of last-minute entertaining. Festive jars of Sweet-Hot Honey Mustard and Italian Parmesan Herb Mix are two easy-to-make favorites that you can use in dozens of different ways. Our gifts are packaged in recycled jelly jars; colorful labels made with inexpensive holiday scrapbook stickers from a crafts store identify the tasty treats.

Made with Sweet-Hot Honey Mustard, Cranberry-Pecan Chicken Salad (see recipe below, right) is great to keep on hand for casual get-togethers. Serve it as a luncheon entrée or in miniature tart shells for a quick appetizer. For gift giving, pack the mustard into pretty jars, and deliver to family and friends with a fresh loaf of bakery bread.

Pack Holiday Herb Butter into colorful pottery crocks, or mold it into festive shapes using cookie cutters. Plastic candy molds, sold at crafts stores, are perfect for shaping individual portions.

To make the Christmas tree shape pictured, place a tree-shaped cookie cutter on a plate lined with wax paper; fill with butter, and garnish with pink peppercorns. Freeze four hours or until firm enough to remove from mold. Place in a zip-top freezer bag, and freeze up to one month.

ITALIAN PARMESAN HERB MIX

fast fixin's

Prep: 5 min.

This is one of our most versatile seasoning blends. Toss the mix with hot cooked pasta, steamed vegetables, or a bag of microwave popcorn. Sprinkle it over French bread and croutons; or dip frozen roll dough and biscuits into melted butter, and dredge with the mixture before baking. Combined with an equal amount of fresh, soft breadcrumbs, it makes an irresistibly crisp coating for pan-fried chicken cutlets and pork chops or a flavorful binder for homemade meatballs and meat loaf.

1 (8-ounce) container grated Parmesan cheese
3 tablespoons dried Italian seasoning
3 tablespoons dried parsley flakes
1 tablespoon granulated garlic
½ teaspoon ground red pepper

Stir together all ingredients. Package mixture in airtight containers, and store in refrigerator up to 6 weeks. **Makes** about 2 cups.

Holiday Herb Butter: Stir together 1 cup softened butter and ¼ cup Italian Parmesan Herb Mix. **Makes** 1 cup. Prep: 5 min.

SWEET-HOT HONEY MUSTARD

make ahead

Prep: 5 min., Cook: 12 min.

This is a delicious complement to holiday ham and turkey. Spread it on a grilled chicken sandwich or over the crust of a quiche before adding the filling. Straight from the jar, it makes a bold and spicy dip for egg rolls. Look for bargains on packets of dry mustard at wholesale clubs and specialty markets, or order online at **www.penzeys.com**.

2 cups sugar
1½ cups dry mustard
2 cups white vinegar
3 large eggs, lightly beaten
½ cup honey

Whisk together sugar and mustard in a heavy 3-quart saucepan; gradually whisk in vinegar and eggs until blended.

Cook mustard mixture over medium heat, whisking constantly, 10 to 12 minutes or until smooth and thickened. Remove from heat, and whisk in honey. Let cool, and store in airtight containers in the refrigerator for up to 1 month. **Makes** 4 cups.

Cranberry-Pecan Chicken Salad: Stir together 8 cups chopped cooked chicken; 3 celery ribs, diced; 5 green onions, thinly sliced; 1½ cups chopped, toasted pecans; 1 (6-ounce) package sweetened dried cranberries; 1 cup mayonnaise; and ½ cup Sweet-Hot Honey Mustard. Season with salt and pepper to taste. Cover and chill salad up to 3 days. **Makes** 6 to 8 servings. Prep: 20 min.

december

286   Can't-Miss Cakes *Bake up these festive and delicious holiday treats*

289   Healthy & Light Lightened and Luscious *Enjoy the great flavor of these traditional Southern Living dishes without the extra fat*

290   Fix and Freeze Ground Beef *Hearty, make-ahead meals for the busy season*

291   Winter Fruit Salads *Two classics that bring out cold-weather flavor*

291   Special-Occasion Salad *This great side is sure to be a knockout at your next gathering*

292   Stir Up a Quick Side *Add a little color to your holiday table with these succulent, good-for-you veggies*

292   Quick & Easy Fast Dishes for Busy Days *Time-saving convenience products lighten the workload and produce tasty results*

293   Comfort Foods Made Easy *These dishes prove that a soup and sandwich supper doesn't have to be boring*

294   Spice Up Your Christmas *This menu boasts bright tropical colors and flavorful foods*

Christmas All Through the House

296   Beautiful Buffets *Adapt these recipes to fit any size gathering*

300   Garlands and Goodies *Set out these tasty snacks to get the decorating party started*

306   Come Over for Coffee *Invite guests for some flavorful java*

307   Have a Cookie *Share some fun in the kitchen baking up these holiday bites*

309   Top-Rated Menu Simply Splendid *Throw a big party with a few signature dishes*

310   Make-Ahead Appetizers *Get set to entertain with these freezeable starters*

311   Hearty Casseroles *Whip up these handy-to-have dinners*

312   What's for Supper? Crusted Baked Chicken *This recipe is great for weeknight dinners or dinner with friends*

313   Fresh Ways With Cranberries *Great recipes for this versatile fruit*

314   From Our Kitchen *Cakepans, packaging ideas, and more*

Can't-Miss Cakes

Share the magic of Christmas with these easy-to-make treats.

'Tis the season for oven-baked goodies, and these are some of our best. Whether you need a sleigh full of small gifts or one spectacular offering for a special gathering of family and friends, you're sure to find the perfect recipe here. Simple packaging ideas make these cakes as festive as they are delicious.

PRALINE PECANS

freezeable • make ahead

Prep: 5 min., Cook: 15 min., Stand: 20 min.

Pralines are best made when the weather is dry—humidity tends to make them grainy. Be sure to use a heavy saucepan, and work quickly when spooning the mixture onto the wax paper.

- 1½ cups granulated sugar
- ¾ cup firmly packed brown sugar
- ½ cup butter
- ½ cup milk
- 2 tablespoons corn syrup
- 5 cups toasted pecan halves

Stir together first 5 ingredients in a heavy 3-quart saucepan. Bring to a boil over medium heat, stirring constantly. Boil, stirring constantly, 7 to 8 minutes or until a candy thermometer registers 234°.

Remove from heat, and vigorously stir in pecans. Spoon pecan mixture onto wax paper, spreading in an even layer. Let stand 20 minutes or until firm. Break praline-coated pecans apart into pieces. Store in an airtight container at room temperature up to 1 week. Freeze in an airtight container or zip-top freezer bag for up to 1 month. **Makes** about 8 cups.

PRALINE-PECAN CAKES

freezeable • make ahead

Prep: 30 min., Bake: 35 min., Stand: 15 min.

Use the small disposable foil pans, available at the supermarket, for this recipe; the shiny surface (which reflects heat away from the pan) and the shorter bake time ensure the praline coating doesn't overbrown. Be sure to generously butter the pans before sprinkling with pecans. We used about ¼ cup of softened butter to grease 9 (5- x 3-inch) pans. *(pictured on cover)*

- 4 cups finely chopped Praline Pecans
- 1 recipe Sour Cream-Pecan Cake Batter

Sprinkle Praline Pecans evenly into 9 buttered 5- x 3-inch disposable foil loaf-pans; shake to coat bottoms and sides of pans. Spoon batter evenly into prepared pans (a little less than 1 cup batter in each pan).

Bake at 325° for 28 to 35 minutes or until a wooden pick inserted in center comes out clean. Cool in pans on wire racks 15 minutes; remove from pans, and let cool completely on wire racks. **Makes** 9 (5-inch) loaves.

SOUR CREAM CAKE BATTER

Prep: 15 min.

- 1 cup butter, softened
- 2½ cups sugar
- 6 large eggs
- 3 cups all-purpose flour
- ¼ teaspoon baking soda
- 1 (8-ounce) container sour cream
- 2 teaspoons vanilla extract

Beat butter at medium speed with an electric mixer until creamy. Gradually add sugar, beating until light and fluffy. Add eggs, 1 at a time, beating just until blended after each addition.

Stir together flour and baking soda. Add to butter mixture alternately with sour cream, beating at low speed just until blended, beginning and ending with flour mixture. Stir in vanilla. Use batter immediately, following baking directions in box on opposite page for desired cake. **Makes** about 7 cups.

Chocolate-Red Velvet Cake Batter: Prepare Sour Cream Cake Batter as directed, stirring 3 tablespoons unsweetened cocoa into the flour mixture. After preparing batter as directed, stir in 2 (1-ounce) bottles red food coloring. Use batter immediately, following directions for desired cake.

Sour Cream-Pecan Cake Batter: Prepare Sour Cream Cake Batter as directed, substituting 1¼ cups firmly packed brown sugar and 1¼ cups granulated sugar for 2½ cups sugar. After preparing batter as directed, stir in 1½ cups chopped, toasted pecans. Use batter immediately, following directions for desired cake.

Holidays on Ice: Freezing Tips

You can bake these cakes and brownies weeks ahead of the hectic holiday season. Place baked, completely cooled cakes in large zip-top freezer bags, and freeze up to 1 month.

Cool brownies completely; arrange in a single layer in an airtight container, and freeze up to 1 month. Cover with wax paper, and repeat layers as needed, leaving enough air space at the top to allow the container to close easily.

Sour Cream Cake Batter can be baked in lots of different shapes and sizes—just use these tips and times as a guideline, and be sure to grease and flour your pans. With smaller muffin pans and molds, such as the fluted brioche pan, we found it easier to use a vegetable cooking spray with flour. Check for doneness at the minimum time range, continuing to bake, if necessary, until a wooden pick inserted in the center of the cake comes out clean. Variations with added fruit and nuts will require the maximum time and yield more cakes.

- Bake at 325° in 1 (12-cup) tube pan for 1 hour and 15 minutes to 1 hour and 30 minutes.
- Bake at 325° in 3 (8- x 4-inch) loafpans for 55 to 65 minutes.
- Bake at 325° in 7 to 9 (5- x 3-inch) loafpans for 25 to 35 minutes.
- Bake at 325° in baby Bundt pans for 25 to 30 minutes. **Makes** 14 to 16 baby Bundt cakes. (Spoon ½ cup batter in each 1-cup mold.)
- Bake at 350° in muffin pans for 23 to 28 minutes. **Makes** 32 to 38 cupcakes.
- Bake at 350° in miniature muffin pans for 9 to 11 minutes. **Makes** about 9 to 10 dozen miniature cupcakes.

Cranberry-Pecan Cake Batter: Soak 1 (6-ounce) package sweetened dried cranberries in boiling water to cover for 10 minutes. Drain well, and press gently between paper towels. Pulse 4 or 5 times in a food processor or until finely chopped. Prepare Sour Cream Cake Batter as directed. Stir finely chopped cranberries; 1 cup finely chopped, toasted pecans; and 2 tablespoons grated orange rind into prepared cake batter. Use batter immediately, following directions for desired cake.

Lemon-Poppy Seed Cake Batter: Prepare Sour Cream Cake Batter as directed; stir in 3 tablespoons grated lemon rind and 2 tablespoons poppy seeds. Use batter immediately, following directions for desired cake.

FLUTED CHOCOLATE-RED VELVET CAKES

freezeable • make ahead

Prep: 30 min., Bake: 50 min., Stand: 10 min.

See "From Our Kitchen" on page 314 for information on brioche pans. *(pictured on cover)*

1 recipe Chocolate-Red Velvet
  Cake Batter
Vanilla Glaze
Garnishes: fresh mint sprigs,
  raspberry candies

Spoon cake batter evenly into 3 greased and floured 8-inch brioche pans. Bake at 325° for 50 minutes or until a wooden pick inserted in center comes out clean.
Cool in pans on wire racks 10 minutes; remove from pans, and let cool completely on wire racks.
Spoon Vanilla Glaze evenly over top of cakes. Garnish, if desired. **Makes** 3 cakes.

CHOCOLATE-RED VELVET LAYER CAKE

freezeable • make ahead

Prep: 30 min., Bake: 20 min., Stand: 10 min.

We baked our cake layers in 6 (8-inch) disposable foil cake pans, so we could fill all the pans at once. This way, if you need to bake the cake layers in batches, the second batch will be ready to put in the oven as soon as the first one is done. To allow the heat to circulate for even baking, space pans at least 2 inches apart from one another and away from the inside walls of the oven. Although the pans are disposable, they can be washed and reused.

1 recipe Chocolate-Red Velvet
  Cake Batter
1½ recipes Cream Cheese Frosting
Garnishes: fresh mint sprigs,
  raspberry candies

Spoon cake batter evenly into 6 greased and floured 8-inch round foil cakepans. Bake at 350° for 18 to 20 minutes or until a wooden pick inserted in center comes out clean.
Cool in pans on wire racks 10 minutes; remove from pans, and let cool completely on wire racks.
Spread Cream Cheese Frosting between layers and on top and sides of cake. Garnish, if desired. **Makes** 16 servings.

CREAM CHEESE FROSTING

fast fixin's

Prep: 15 min.

2 (8-ounce) packages cream
  cheese, softened
½ cup butter, softened
2 (16-ounce) packages powdered
  sugar
2 teaspoons vanilla extract

Beat cream cheese and butter at medium speed with an electric mixer until creamy. Gradually add powdered sugar, beating until light and fluffy. Stir in vanilla. **Makes** about 5 cups.

Chocolate Glaze: Melt 1 (12-ounce) package semisweet chocolate morsels and ½ cup whipping cream in a 2-quart microwave-safe bowl at MEDIUM (50% power) 2½ to 3 minutes or until chocolate morsels begin to melt. Whisk until chocolate morsels melt and mixture is smooth. **Makes** about 2 cups. Prep: 5 min.

Vanilla Glaze: Stir together 1 (16-ounce) package powdered sugar, 5 tablespoons milk, and 2 teaspoons vanilla extract just until powdered sugar is moistened and mixture is smooth. Add an additional tablespoon of milk, if needed. Use immediately. **Makes** about 1½ cups. Prep: 5 min.

Note: We kept this glaze very thick so that it wouldn't drip all the way down the sides of the Fluted Chocolate-Red Velvet Cakes, but feel free to make it a little thinner if you'd like to drizzle it over other cakes.

CHOCOLATE FUDGE BROWNIES

freezeable • make ahead

Prep: 15 min., Bake: 40 min.

This basic brownie recipe is one of our favorites and offers lots of options. If you're a fan of nuts, stir 1 cup chopped, toasted pecans into the batter. After baking, sift a little powdered sugar over the top, or spread with our deliciously rich Chocolate Glaze (recipe on page 287). To easily remove and cut brownies, line the pan with greased and floured heavy-duty aluminum foil, allowing several inches to extend over sides. After baking and cooling, lift the block of brownies from the pan using the foil. Press down the foil sides, and cut brownies.

4 (1-ounce) unsweetened chocolate baking squares
1 cup butter, softened
2 cups sugar
4 large eggs
1 cup all-purpose flour
1 teaspoon vanilla extract
1 cup semisweet chocolate morsels

Microwave chocolate squares in a small microwave-safe bowl at MEDIUM (50% power) 1½ minutes, stirring at 30-second intervals until melted. Stir until smooth.

Beat butter and sugar at medium speed with an electric mixer until light and fluffy. Add eggs, 1 at a time, beating just until blended after each addition. Add melted chocolate, beating just until blended.

Add flour, beating at low speed just until blended. Stir in vanilla and chocolate morsels. Spread batter into a greased and floured 13- x 9-inch pan.

Bake at 350° for 35 to 40 minutes or until center is set. Cool completely on a wire rack. Cut into squares. **Makes** 32 brownies.

Praline-Pecan Brownies: Prepare and bake Chocolate Fudge Brownies as directed; cool completely. Spread uncut brownies evenly with Chocolate Glaze (recipe on page 287); sprinkle evenly with 2 cups coarsely chopped Praline Pecans (recipe on page 286). **Makes** 32 brownies. Prep: 15 min., Bake: 40 min.

Caramel-Coconut-Pecan Brownies: Prepare batter for Chocolate Fudge Brownies as directed; spread batter into a greased and floured 13- x 9-inch pan. Sprinkle batter evenly with 2 cups sweetened flaked coconut, 1 (12-ounce) package semisweet chocolate morsels, and 1½ cups chopped pecans. Drizzle evenly with 1 (14-ounce) can sweetened condensed milk. Bake at 350° for 50 to 55 minutes or until golden brown and center is set. **Makes** 32 brownies. Prep: 20 min., Bake: 55 min.

Peppermint Brownie Tarts: Prepare batter for Chocolate Fudge Brownies as directed. Divide batter evenly between 2 greased and floured 9-inch tart pans with removable bottoms. Bake at 350° for 20 minutes or until center is set. Cool completely on wire racks.

Beat ½ cup softened butter at medium speed with an electric mixer until creamy; gradually add 1 (16-ounce) package powdered sugar alternately with ⅓ cup milk, beating at low speed after each addition. Stir in ¼ teaspoon peppermint oil. Divide butter mixture between each tart, spreading evenly over cooled brownie in pans; cover and chill 1 hour or until firm. Divide 1 recipe Chocolate Glaze (recipe on page 287) evenly between each tart, spreading over chilled butter mixture in pans. Sprinkle ½ cup crushed peppermint candy canes around outer edge of each tart. **Makes** 2 (9-inch) tarts. Prep: 30 min., Bake: 20 min.

Chocolate Fudge Cheesecake: Sprinkle ½ cup toasted chopped pecans evenly over the bottom of each of 2 greased and floured 9-inch springform pans. Prepare Chocolate Fudge Brownie batter as directed. Divide batter evenly between pans, spreading over chopped pecans.

Beat 4 (8-ounce) packages softened cream cheese at medium speed with an electric mixer until smooth; add 1¾ cups sugar, beating until blended. Add 7 large eggs, 1 at a time, beating just until blended after each addition. Stir in 2 teaspoons vanilla extract. Divide cream cheese mixture evenly between each pan, spreading over brownie batter.

Bake at 325° for 1 hour and 15 minutes or until set. Remove from oven, and cool completely on wire racks. Spread top of each cooled cheesecake with 1 recipe Chocolate Glaze (recipe on page 287); cover and chill 8 hours. Remove sides of pans before serving. Garnish with fresh mint sprigs and sliced strawberries, if desired. **Makes** 2 (9-inch) cheesecakes. Prep: 30 min.; Bake: 1 hr., 15 min.; Chill: 8 hrs.

Note: We topped each cheesecake with 1 full recipe of Chocolate Glaze. If you'd like a thinner layer of chocolate on top, divide 1 recipe of glaze between the two cheesecakes.

CINNAMON-PECAN CRUMB CAKES

freezeable • make ahead

Prep: 15 min., Stand: 30 min., Bake: 55 min.

Lining the pans with greased and floured heavy-duty aluminum foil makes these cakes easy to remove without inverting the pan and losing the crumb topping. Leave extra foil extending above the pan to lift out the cakes.

1 cup butter, melted
¾ cup firmly packed brown sugar
½ cup granulated sugar
1 tablespoon ground cinnamon
¼ teaspoon salt
3 cups all-purpose flour
2 cups chopped pecans
1 recipe Sour Cream Cake Batter (recipe on page 286)

Stir together first 5 ingredients in a large bowl; add flour and pecans, stirring until blended. Let stand 30 minutes or until mixture is firm enough to crumble into small pieces.

Spoon cake batter evenly into 2 greased and floured aluminum foil-lined 9- x 2-inch round cakepans. Sprinkle crumbled pecan mixture evenly over cake batter. Bake at 350° for 45 to 55 minutes or until a wooden pick inserted in center comes out clean. Cool completely on wire racks. **Makes** 2 (9-inch) cakes.

Lightened and Luscious

Enjoy the luscious flavors of Christmas with these traditional *Southern Living* recipes that have been lightened. We whittled down the fat but not the flavor in these dishes.

Healthy Holiday Supper
Serves 6

Molasses-Coffee Turkey Breast

Roasted Potato-and-Bacon Salad

Sugar-and-Spice Acorn Squash

Gingered Green Beans

Mocha-Pecan Mud Pie

MOLASSES-COFFEE TURKEY BREAST

Prep: 15 min.; Bake: 2 hrs., 30 min.; Stand: 15 min.

Roast the turkey with the skin on to lock in the flavors and keep the meat moist and tender. Basting throughout the cooking process also ensures juiciness because it keeps the skin from becoming dry and brittle. Remove the skin before serving for an incredible low-fat and low-calorie dish.

- **1 (10-ounce) jar apricot spreadable fruit**
- **¾ cup strong-brewed coffee**
- **¾ cup molasses**
- **2 tablespoons cider vinegar**
- **1 tablespoon Dijon mustard**
- **½ teaspoon salt**
- **1 (5-pound) bone-in turkey breast**
- **Vegetable cooking spray**

Stir together first 6 ingredients until blended. Reserve 1 cup molasses-coffee sauce in a microwave-safe small bowl; set aside.

Place turkey in an 11- x 7-inch baking dish coated with cooking spray. Pour remaining molasses-coffee sauce evenly over turkey. Cover loosely with aluminum foil.

Bake at 350° for 1 hour; uncover and bake 1 to 1½ more hours or until a meat thermometer inserted into the thickest portion registers 170°, basting with molasses-coffee sauce every 15 minutes. Remove from oven, and let stand 15 minutes. Remove and discard skin. Serve with 1 cup reserved molasses-coffee sauce heated in the microwave at HIGH 30 seconds or until warm. **Makes** 12 servings.

Note: For testing purposes only, we used Polaner All Fruit Spreadable Fruit.

Per serving (about 5½ ounces of meat): Calories 209 (5% from fat); Fat 1g (sat 0.3g, mono 0.2g, poly 0.3g); Protein 40g; Carb 7.3g; Fiber 0g; Chol 110mg; Iron 2.3mg; Sodium 104mg; Calc 27mg

ROASTED POTATO-AND-BACON SALAD

Prep: 20 min., Bake: 50 min., Cook: 10 min.

We cut out some of the extra calories and fat in this warm spinach salad by using less oil and switching to turkey bacon. The results were incredible and this updated dish is now a favorite in our Test Kitchens.

- **2 pounds new potatoes, quartered**
- **2 teaspoons olive oil**
- **2 tablespoons chopped fresh rosemary**
- **1 teaspoon salt, divided**
- **1 teaspoon freshly ground pepper, divided**
- **Vegetable cooking spray**
- **8 turkey bacon slices**
- **¼ cup red wine vinegar**
- **3 tablespoons olive oil**
- **1 tablespoon sugar**
- **2 garlic cloves, pressed**
- **1 (6-ounce) package fresh spinach**
- **1 (5-ounce) package mixed salad greens**
- **¼ cup freshly shredded Parmesan cheese**

Combine potatoes, 2 teaspoons oil, rosemary, ½ teaspoon salt, and ½ teaspoon pepper, tossing gently, and spread in a 15- x 10-inch jelly-roll pan coated with cooking spray.

Bake at 400° for 40 to 50 minutes or until potatoes are tender and lightly browned. Sprinkle evenly with ¼ teaspoon salt and ¼ teaspoon pepper; keep warm.

Cook bacon in a large skillet until crisp; remove bacon, and drain on paper towels, reserving drippings in skillet. Crumble bacon, and set aside.

Whisk together vinegar, next 3 ingredients, remaining ¼ teaspoon salt, and remaining ¼ teaspoon pepper in skillet; cook over medium heat, whisking occasionally, 3 to 4 minutes or until thoroughly heated.

Combine spinach and mixed greens; drizzle with warm dressing, tossing to coat. Top with potatoes, bacon, and Parmesan cheese; serve immediately. **Makes** 8 servings.

Per serving: Calories 202 (43% from fat); Fat 10g (sat 2.1g, mono 5.9g, poly 1.4g); Protein 6.1g; Carb 23.3g; Fiber 3.5g; Chol 14mg; Iron 2.2mg; Sodium 554mg; Calc 78mg

SUGAR-AND-SPICE ACORN SQUASH

Prep: 10 min., Bake: 52 min.

A touch of brown sugar and nutmeg brings out the natural sweetness in the squash and makes it a perfect accompaniment with any entrée.

- **2 large acorn squash (about 2 pounds each)**
- **¼ teaspoon salt**
- **¼ teaspoon pepper**
- **Vegetable cooking spray**
- **¼ cup light butter, melted**
- **¼ cup firmly packed brown sugar**
- **¼ teaspoon ground nutmeg**

Cut each squash in quarters lengthwise; remove and discard seeds and membranes. Sprinkle evenly with salt and pepper. Place cut sides down on an aluminum foil-lined baking sheet coated with cooking spray.

Bake at 400° for 45 minutes or until squash is tender.

Combine butter, brown sugar, and nutmeg. Turn squash, cut sides up, on baking sheet; sprinkle evenly with butter mixture. Bake 5 to 7 more minutes or until brown. **Makes** 8 servings.

Per serving: Calories 120 (21% from fat); Fat 3.2g (sat 2.1g, mono 0g, poly 0.1g); Protein 1.9g; Carb 24.5g; Fiber 2.6g; Chol 10mg; Iron 1.3mg; Sodium 117mg; Calc 62mg

GINGERED GREEN BEANS

fast fixin's

Prep: 15 min., Cook: 15 min.

Look for fresh ginger (also called gingerroot) in the specialty produce section of your grocery store. Peel it with a vegetable peeler, and mince with a sharp knife. Leftover ginger can be frozen up to one month.

3 cups low-sodium fat-free chicken broth
1 pound fresh green beans, trimmed
1 tablespoon butter
1 small sweet onion, diced
2 garlic cloves, minced
2 tablespoons peeled and minced fresh ginger
¼ teaspoon salt
½ teaspoon seasoned pepper

Bring broth to a boil in a large saucepan over medium-high heat. Add green beans, and cook 4 to 6 minutes or until crisp-tender; drain.
Melt butter in a large nonstick skillet over medium-high heat. Add onion, garlic, and ginger; sauté 2 minutes. Add beans, salt, and pepper; sauté 1 minute or until thoroughly heated. **Makes** 6 servings.

Per serving: Calories 59 (28% from fat); Fat 2g (sat 1g, mono 0.8g, poly 0.1g); Protein 3.3g; Carb 8.5g; Fiber 1.3g; Chol 5mg; Iron 0.9mg; Sodium 428mg; Calc 36mg

---

Quick-Fix Desserts

If you're short on time during the holidays—like most of us—here's a list of items you can pick up at the market and have on-hand for unexpected guests.

■ Serve slightly warmed chocolate sauce as fondue. Strawberries, pineapple chunks, and marshmallows make delightful dippers.
■ Blend a few tablespoons of fudge sauce into softened vanilla ice cream for a rich, thick milk shake.
■ Melt vanilla ice cream in the microwave as a quick sauce for fresh fruit.

MOCHA-PECAN MUD PIE

Prep: 15 min.; Bake: 10 min.; Freeze: 8 hrs., 10 min.

Round out your meal with a slice of decadent ice-cream pie. This dessert is so rich, your guests will never know it was lightened.

½ cup chopped pecans
Vegetable cooking spray
1 teaspoon sugar
1 pint light coffee ice cream, softened
1 pint light chocolate ice cream, softened
1 cup coarsely chopped reduced-fat cream-filled chocolate sandwich cookies, divided (about 10 cookies)
1 (6-ounce) ready-made chocolate crumb piecrust
2 tablespoons light chocolate syrup

Place pecans in a single layer on a baking sheet coated with cooking spray; sprinkle evenly with sugar.
Bake at 350° for 8 to 10 minutes or until lightly toasted. Cool.
Stir together ice creams, ³⁄₄ cup cookie chunks, and ¹⁄₃ cup pecans; spoon into crust. Freeze 10 minutes. Press remaining cookie chunks and pecans evenly on top. Cover with plastic wrap, and freeze 8 hours. Drizzle individual slices evenly with chocolate syrup. **Makes** 9 servings.

Note: For testing purposes only, we used Keebler Chocolate Ready Crust and Häagen-Dazs Light Coffee Ice Cream.

Per serving: Calories 327 (39% from fat); Fat 14.5g (sat 4.4g, mono 3.6g, poly 1.8g); Protein 5.4g; Carb 45.8g; Fiber 1.9g; Chol 2mg; Iron 1.3mg; Sodium 190mg; Calc 41mg

---

Fix 'n' Freeze Ground Beef

Cook and freeze several batches of Ground Beef-Tomato Sauce to get ahead on weeknight meals. Thaw frozen sauce in the refrigerator, microwave, or a saucepan over low heat. Bring the sauce to a boil before serving or using in a recipe.

GROUND BEEF-TOMATO SAUCE

freezeable • make ahead

Prep: 5 min., Cook: 35 min., Cool: 10 min.

Spoon the desired amount of cooled sauce into zip-top freezer bags; press out the air, and seal. Flatten the bags to freeze them, and they'll easily stack.

3 pounds lean ground beef
1 large onion, chopped
1 green bell pepper, chopped
2 (8-ounce) cans basil, garlic, and oregano tomato sauce
1 (8-ounce) can tomato sauce
1 (6-ounce) can tomato paste
1 teaspoon salt
1 teaspoon dried crushed red pepper

Cook first 3 ingredients in a Dutch oven over medium-high heat, stirring until beef crumbles and is no longer pink; drain. Return beef mixture to Dutch oven.
Stir in tomato sauces and remaining ingredients. Cover and simmer, stirring occasionally, 20 minutes. Remove from heat, and cool 10 minutes.
Spoon beef mixture into zip-top plastic freezer bags; seal and freeze up to 2 months. **Makes** about 8 cups.

DAVID BOMBA
CANTON, MISSISSIPPI

CHIMICHANGAS

Prep: 12 min., Cook: 20 min.,
Fry: 4 min. per batch

These meat- and bean-filled wraps are simply deep-fried burritos.

2½ cups Ground Beef-Tomato Sauce, thawed
1 (16-ounce) can refried beans
2 teaspoons chili powder
1 teaspoon ground cumin
10 (9-inch) flour tortillas
1 (10-ounce) can diced tomatoes and green chiles, drained
1 (8-ounce) can tomato sauce
Vegetable oil
1 (8-ounce) package shredded Mexican four-cheese blend
Garnish: chopped fresh cilantro

Stir together first 4 ingredients in a medium saucepan. Cook over medium heat, stirring occasionally, 10 minutes.

Spoon about ⅓ cup sauce mixture just below center of 1 tortilla. Fold bottom third of tortilla up and over mixture, just until covered. Fold left side of tortilla over mixture; repeat with right side. Roll up, and secure with wooden picks. Repeat with remaining sauce mixture and tortillas; set chimichangas aside.

Stir together diced tomatoes and green chiles and tomato sauce in a saucepan. Bring to a boil; reduce heat, and simmer 5 minutes. Keep warm.

Pour oil to a depth of 1 inch into a Dutch oven; heat to 375°. Fry chimichangas, in batches, 2 minutes on each side or until golden. Drain on wire racks over paper towels. Remove wooden picks.

Arrange chimichangas on a platter. Spoon hot tomato mixture over tops, and sprinkle evenly with shredded cheese. Garnish, if desired. **Makes** 5 servings.

ELIZABETH GRIFFIN
LITTLE ROCK, ARKANSAS

Winter Fruit Salads

Don't despair. You can still have a good salad this time of year. Two readers share their recipes.

HARVEST CRUNCH SALAD

fast fixin's • make ahead

Prep: 25 min.

- 3 large Anjou pears, cut into bite-size pieces
- ½ cup dried cranberries
- 2 tablespoons lemon juice
- 1 (8-ounce) package cream cheese, softened
- 1 (6-ounce) container vanilla yogurt
- ½ teaspoon ground cinnamon
- 2 cups low-fat granola
- ½ cup fat-free caramel ice-cream topping

Place pears and cranberries in a bowl. Sprinkle with lemon juice; gently toss.

Beat cream cheese in a large bowl at medium speed with an electric mixer until fluffy. Add yogurt and cinnamon, beating at low speed until blended. Fold half of cream cheese mixture into pear mixture.

Layer half each of pear mixture and granola in a large serving bowl. Spread cream cheese mixture on top, and drizzle with half of the caramel topping. Repeat layers, omitting cream cheese layer. Serve immediately, or chill 2 hours, if desired. Refrigerate any leftovers. **Makes** 6 to 8 servings.

SHELLY PLATEN
AMHERST, WISCONSIN

MANDARIN ORANGE-AND-ALMOND SALAD

fast fixin's • make ahead

Prep: 10 min.

- 1 bunch Green Leaf lettuce
- 1 bunch Red Leaf lettuce
- 2 (11-ounce) cans mandarin oranges, drained and chilled
- 1 cup sliced almonds
- Celery Seed Dressing

Tear lettuce into bite-size pieces. Add oranges and almonds; toss gently.

Add desired amount of Celery Seed Dressing just before serving, gently tossing to coat. **Makes** 4 to 6 servings.

CELERY SEED DRESSING:

Prep: 10 min.

- ½ cup vegetable oil
- ¼ cup red wine vinegar
- 5 tablespoons sugar
- 2 garlic cloves, minced
- 1 teaspoon finely chopped onion
- ½ teaspoon prepared mustard
- ½ teaspoon celery seeds

Whisk together all ingredients. **Makes** 1 cup.

LORI COOK
WICHITA FALLS, TEXAS

Special-Occasion Salad

This dressed-up recipe is bursting with flavor.

SPINACH-ENDIVE SALAD WITH WARM VINAIGRETTE

fast fixin's

Prep: 15 min., Cook: 12 min.

If apple-smoked bacon is not available, your favorite kind will work just fine.

- 4 apple-smoked bacon slices
- ¼ cup balsamic vinegar
- 4 teaspoons Dijon mustard
- ½ cup crumbled blue cheese (optional)
- ¼ medium-size red onion, thinly sliced
- 2 teaspoons chopped fresh parsley
- ½ teaspoon salt
- ½ teaspoon freshly ground pepper
- 1 (10-ounce) package fresh baby spinach
- 1 head Belgian endive, cut into 8 slices lengthwise *
- Crumbled blue cheese (optional)

Cook bacon in a large skillet until crisp; remove bacon, and drain on paper towels, reserving ¼ cup drippings in skillet. Crumble bacon, and set aside.

Combine vinegar, mustard, and, if desired, ½ cup crumbled blue cheese, stirring until blue cheese is smooth.

Add vinegar mixture and onion to hot bacon drippings in skillet over medium heat, stirring to coat. Add crumbled bacon, parsley, salt, and pepper. Add spinach and endive; toss in skillet just until combined. Serve immediately. Top with additional crumbled blue cheese, if desired. **Makes** 6 servings.

*Substitute ½ (10-ounce) package fresh baby spinach, if desired.

SUZY STENSRUD
NEW ORLEANS, LOUISIANA

Stir Up a Quick Side

A dd a little color to your holiday plate with these succulent recipes.

QUICK PARMESAN SPINACH

Prep: 2 min., Cook: 8 min.

2 garlic cloves, pressed
2 teaspoons olive oil
Vegetable cooking spray
3 (10-ounce) packages fresh spinach
¼ teaspoon salt
¼ teaspoon ground red pepper
1 tablespoon fresh lemon juice
2 tablespoons freshly grated
   Parmesan cheese

Sauté garlic in hot oil in a large skillet coated with cooking spray over medium-high heat 1 minute. Add spinach, 1 handful at a time, and sauté just until spinach begins to wilt. Add salt, red pepper, and lemon juice, gently tossing to coat. Remove from heat, and sprinkle evenly with Parmesan cheese. **Makes** 6 servings.

Per serving: Calories 58 (37% from fat); Fat 2.8g (sat 0.6g, mono 1.1g, poly 0.4g); Protein 5.1g; Carb 5.6g; Fiber 3.2g; Chol 2mg; Iron 3.9mg; Sodium 250mg; Calc 176mg

BROCCOLI WITH ALMOND-LEMON DIP

Prep: 5 min., Chill: 8 hrs., Cook: 3 min.

½ cup slivered almonds, toasted
1¼ cups light sour cream
1 tablespoon grated lemon rind
1 tablespoon fresh lemon juice
½ teaspoon salt
½ teaspoon pepper
2 (12-ounce) packages fresh
   broccoli florets

Pulse almonds in a food processor until finely ground. Stir together ground almonds, sour cream, and next 4 ingredients. Cover and chill 8 hours.
Cook broccoli in boiling water to cover 3 minutes or until crisp-tender. Plunge into ice water to stop the cooking process; drain. Cover and chill until ready to serve. Serve with almond-lemon dip. **Makes** 12 to 15 servings.

AMY WESTMORELAND
SCOTTSBORO, ALABAMA

Per serving: Calories 64 (49% from fat); Fat 3.8g (sat 1.2g, mono 1.5g, poly 0.6g); Protein 3g; Carb 6g; Fiber 1.8g; Chol 7mg; Iron 0.6mg; Sodium 110mg; Calc 60mg

COLLARD, RAISIN, AND PECAN SAUTÉ

Prep: 15 min., Cook: 30 min.

1 medium-size sweet onion, diced
   (about 1 cup)
3 garlic cloves, chopped
1 tablespoon olive oil
2 (16-ounce) packages frozen
   collard greens, thawed and
   drained
½ cup golden raisins
¼ teaspoon salt
½ teaspoon freshly ground black
   pepper
2 cups fat-free chicken broth
¼ cup chopped pecans, toasted
3 bacon slices, cooked and
   crumbled (optional)

Sauté onion and garlic in hot oil in a large nonstick skillet over medium-high heat 5 minutes or until golden. Stir in greens and next 3 ingredients.
Stir in broth. Bring to a boil; reduce heat, and simmer 20 minutes or until greens are tender, stirring occasionally. Stir in pecans; sprinkle with bacon, if desired. Serve immediately. **Makes** 6 servings.

LILLIAN KAYTE
GAINESVILLE, FLORIDA

Per serving (not including bacon): Calories 140 (40% from fat); Fat 6.3g (sat 0.7g, mono 3.7g, poly 1.5g); Protein 5.3g; Carb 18.5g; Fiber 4.5g; Chol 0mg; Iron 1.3mg; Sodium 173mg; Calc 151mg

quick & easy
Fast Dishes
for Busy Days

T ime-saving convenience products lighten your workload and make it easy to put a tasty meal on the table.

EASY BRUNSWICK STEW

Prep: 20 min., Cook: 40 min.

1 (1-pound, 4-ounce) package
   refrigerated diced potatoes
3 cups chicken broth
½ teaspoon pepper
1 (28-ounce) can diced tomatoes,
   undrained
1 (16-ounce) package frozen
   shoepeg corn
1 (15-ounce) can lima beans,
   drained
1 pound shredded pork barbecue
   with sauce *

Bring potatoes and broth to a boil in a large Dutch oven over medium-high heat; stir in pepper. Reduce heat to medium, and boil 5 minutes. Stir in tomatoes and remaining ingredients; reduce heat to medium-low, and cook, covered, 30 minutes or until thoroughly heated. **Makes** 12 cups.

* Substitute 1 (18-ounce) container refrigerated shredded pork barbecue, if desired.

JANICE PURVIS
DUBLIN, GEORGIA

CHEESY MAC 'N' CHICKEN SOUP

family favorite

Prep: 10 min., Cook: 30 min.

1 small onion, diced
1 celery rib, diced
1 teaspoon vegetable oil
1 (32-ounce) container low-
   sodium chicken broth
1 (20-ounce) package frozen
   macaroni and cheese
1 (16-ounce) package frozen
   mixed vegetables
1 (16-ounce) package pasteurized
   prepared cheese product,
   cubed
1 (10¾-ounce) can cream of
   chicken soup
2 cups chopped cooked chicken

Sauté onion and celery in hot oil in a large Dutch oven over medium-high heat 5 minutes or until vegetables are tender. Stir in chicken broth and remaining ingredients. Bring to a boil, stirring occasionally. Reduce heat to low, and simmer, stirring occasionally, 20 minutes or until cheese is melted and mixture is blended and thoroughly heated. **Makes** 12 cups.

Note: For testing purposes only, we used Stouffer's Macaroni and Cheese.

ANN HEATHERLY
RUSSELLVILLE, ALABAMA

BEEF RAVIOLI IN BASIL-CREAM SAUCE

fast fixin's

Prep: 10 min., Cook: 15 min.

- 1 (24-ounce) package frozen beef ravioli
- 2 tablespoons butter
- 1 (8-ounce) package sliced fresh mushrooms
- 3 green onions, chopped
- 2 garlic cloves, minced
- 1 teaspoon dried Italian seasoning
- 1 (10-ounce) can diced mild tomatoes and green chiles, drained
- 2 tablespoons chopped fresh basil
- 1 cup whipping cream
- ½ cup grated Parmesan cheese
- ½ teaspoon salt

Prepare ravioli in a large Dutch oven according to package directions; drain and keep warm.

Melt butter in Dutch oven over medium-high heat. Add mushrooms and next 3 ingredients; sauté over medium-high heat 6 minutes or until mushrooms are tender. Stir in diced tomatoes and green chiles, basil, and cream; bring to a boil. Reduce heat, and simmer, stirring occasionally, 5 minutes. Stir in Parmesan cheese; add salt. Stir in cooked ravioli, tossing to coat. **Makes** 4 servings.

Note: For testing purposes only, we used Rosina Celentano Beef Ravioli.

DOROTHY GOODSON SNOWDEN
MARIETTA, GEORGIA

Comfort Foods Made Easy

A soup and sandwich supper doesn't have to be boring. We've jazzed up tomato soup with roasted red pepper and cream, then paired it with the Southern version of a Monte Cristo sandwich. This classic French ham and cheese is dipped in batter and grilled; we added brown sugar and pecans for regional flavor. You can choose your favorite style of bread, but our Foods staff was partial to sourdough and whole grain.

We tried to lighten the soup using milk and fat-free half-and-half, but those products tend to curdle. This is a rich duo—enjoy them on a day when you've walked an extra block. We think they're worth the splurge.

CREAMY BELL PEPPER 'N' TOMATO SOUP

Prep: 10 min., Cook: 40 min., Cool: 10 min.

- 2 tablespoons butter or margarine
- 2 garlic cloves, finely chopped
- 2 (28-ounce) cans crushed tomatoes
- 1 (14-ounce) can chicken broth
- 3 or 4 whole roasted red bell pepper (from jar), drained
- 1 tablespoon sugar
- 1 (0.75 ounce) package savory tomato pasta sauce mix
- 2 cups half-and-half
- ¼ teaspoon ground red pepper
- Garnish: freshly grated Parmesan cheese

Melt butter in a large Dutch oven over medium heat; add garlic, and sauté 2 minutes or until slightly golden. Stir in crushed tomatoes and next 4 ingredients; cook, stirring occasionally, over medium heat 30 minutes. Remove from heat, and let cool 10 minutes.

Process mixture, in small batches, in a blender or food processor until smooth, stopping to scrape down sides. Return mixture to Dutch oven.

Stir in half-and-half, and simmer, stirring occasionally, over low heat; stir in ground red pepper. Garnish, if desired. **Makes** 11 cups.

Note: For testing purposes only, we used Spice Islands Savory Tomato Pasta Sauce Blend.

GRILLED CHEESE-AND-HAM SANDWICHES

family favorite

Prep: 10 min., Cook: 8 min. per batch

- ¼ cup spicy mustard
- 12 sourdough or whole grain bread slices
- 6 (1-ounce) processed American cheese slices
- 6 (1-ounce) Swiss cheese slices
- 6 (1-ounce) cooked ham slices
- 2 large eggs
- 1 cup milk
- ½ cup finely ground pecans
- ¼ cup firmly packed light brown sugar
- ¼ cup butter or margarine

Spread mustard evenly on 1 side of 6 bread slices. Top with 1 slice each of cheeses and ham; top with remaining 6 bread slices.

Whisk together eggs and next 3 ingredients in a shallow dish until blended. Dip both sides of each sandwich in egg mixture.

Melt 2 tablespoons butter in a heavy nonstick skillet over medium-low heat. Add 3 sandwiches, and cook 3 to 4 minutes on each side or until bread lightly browns and cheese begins to melt. Repeat procedure with remaining 2 tablespoons butter and 3 sandwiches. Serve immediately. **Makes** 6 sandwiches.

Spice Up Your Christmas

Join the Suarez family for slow-cooked pork, black beans, rice, and other traditional holiday favorites.

Cuban Celebration

Serves 8

Ham With Garlic and Orange

Yuca With Garlic-Lime Mojo

Cuban Black Beans

Mojito

Buñuelos

There's nothing quite like bright tropical colors and flavorful foods to define a Cuban holiday celebration. When Cuban-born Yolanda and Emilio Suarez started their family in Miami, they were determined to make sure that their first-generation American-born children, Vicky and Isabel, grew up knowing as much about their heritage as possible.

The Roasting Tradition

Many Cuban families traditionally prepare a Lechon *(pronounced Leh-CHONE)*, a whole suckling pig roasted slowly in either a Chinese box or pit. For a more manageable cut of pork, see our recipe for Ham With Garlic and Orange. It uses a fresh (not cured or smoked) ham. Be sure to call your supermarket's meat department to ensure that they carry fresh hams. If not, call a week ahead to order one.

HAM WITH GARLIC AND ORANGE

Prep: 15 min., Chill: 8 hrs., Bake: 7 hrs., Stand: 20 min.

- **1 (15- to 18-pound) fresh ham (not cured or smoked)**
- **1 tablespoon salt**
- **½ cup chopped fresh or 1 (4-ounce) jar minced garlic**
- **2 teaspoons pepper**
- **2 teaspoons dried oregano**
- **½ cup fresh lime juice**
- **½ cup fresh orange juice**

Place ham in an aluminum foil-lined roasting pan. Cut 4 or 5 (1-inch-deep) slits across top of ham. Sprinkle evenly with salt.

Stir together garlic and next 4 ingredients. Pour mixture evenly over ham, rubbing mixture into slits. Cover and chill 8 hours.

Bake, uncovered, at 350° for 7 hours or until a meat thermometer inserted into thickest portion registers 185°. Let stand 20 minutes before slicing. **Makes** 18 servings.

Citrus-and-Garlic Pork Roast: Substitute 1 (6-pound) bone-in pork shoulder roast (Boston butt) for fresh ham. Reduce garlic to 3 tablespoons. Reduce oven temperature to 325°. Proceed as directed, baking for 4½ hours or until meat thermometer inserted into thickest portion registers 175°. Remove from oven, and let stand until thermometer reaches 185°. **Makes** 6 to 8 servings. Prep: 15 min.; Chill: 8 hrs.; Bake: 4 hrs., 30 min.

YUCA WITH GARLIC-LIME MOJO

Prep: 15 min., Cook: 35 min.

Pronounced YOO-kuh, this starchy root vegetable tastes similar to red potatoes. Check the produce section of your grocery store for yuca, which looks like a large, dark sweet potato with a thick, brown skin. Mojo *(pronounced Mo-Ho)* is a sort of vinaigrette flavored with garlic and lime or orange juice.

- **2 pounds yuca, peeled, halved, and cut into 3- to 4-inch pieces ✱**
- **3 teaspoons salt, divided**
- **6 garlic cloves, pressed**
- **1 large sweet onion, finely chopped**
- **½ cup extra-virgin olive oil**
- **⅓ cup fresh lime juice**
- **Sliced onion rings (optional)**

Bring yuca with water to cover and 2 teaspoons salt to a boil in a large Dutch oven over medium-high heat. Cover, reduce heat to medium-low, and simmer 25 minutes or until tender. Drain well. Transfer yuca to a large bowl or serving platter, and keep warm.

Stir together remaining 1 teaspoon salt, garlic, and next 3 ingredients in a saucepan over medium heat, and cook, stirring occasionally, 8 to 10 minutes or until onion is translucent. Spoon garlic mixture evenly over yuca; top with onion rings, if desired, and serve immediately. **Makes** 8 servings.

YOLANDA MELLON
MIAMI, FLORIDA

✱ Substitute 1 (24-ounce) package frozen yuca, thawed, for fresh, if desired. Order online at **www.melissas.com**.

Cubanelle Chile Peppers

These are similar to banana peppers but are light green in color. (Green bell or Anaheim peppers are good substitutes.) They're about 4 to 5 inches long and have a sweet, mild flavor. Refrigerate green Cubanelles, unwashed, in a plastic bag for up to one week. Red Cubanelles will keep for only a few days.

CUBAN BLACK BEANS

Prep: 15 min.; Cook: 2 hrs., 40 min.; Stand: 5 min.

This authentic recipe for frijoles negros calls for grinding dried whole oregano and cumin seed. If you prefer, you can substitute 2 teaspoons each of ground oregano and cumin.

- **2 pounds dried black beans**
- **14 cups water**
- **1 large or 2 small bay leaves**
- **3 garlic cloves, pressed**
- **2 teaspoons dried whole oregano**
- **2 teaspoons cumin seeds**
- **3½ teaspoons salt**
- **2 Cubanelle chile peppers, seeded and chopped (about 1 cup)***
- **2 tablespoons extra-virgin olive oil**
- **2 large onions, chopped**
- **Hot cooked rice**
- **Extra-virgin olive oil**
- **Sherry or red wine vinegar**

Rinse and sort beans according to package directions. Place beans in a large Dutch oven; cover with cold water, and let stand overnight. Drain beans, and return to Dutch oven. Add 14 cups water, bay leaves, and garlic; bring to a boil over medium-high heat. Cover, reduce heat to medium-low, and simmer, stirring occasionally, 2 hours or until beans are tender.

Process oregano, cumin seeds, and salt in an electric spice grinder until ground and blended.

Sauté chiles in 2 tablespoons hot oil over medium-high heat in a large skillet

5 minutes; add onions, and sauté 5 minutes or until tender. Stir onion mixture and oregano mixture into beans in Dutch oven, and simmer, stirring occasionally, 30 minutes.

Remove and discard bay leaf. Cover and let stand 5 minutes. (For a thicker consistency, remove 1 cup bean mixture, and mash with a fork; return to pan.) Serve over hot cooked rice, drizzling with additional olive oil and vinegar. **Makes** 12 servings.

Note: If you don't have an electric spice grinder, crush and grind seeds and salt with a pestle in a mortar bowl or place in a zip-top freezer bag, seal, and pound with the flat side of a meat mallet.

*Substitute 1 large green bell pepper, if desired.

NEIDA GONZALEZ
MIAMI, FLORIDA

MOJITO

fast fixin's

Prep: 5 min.

The mojito (*pronounced moe-HEE-toe*) is, without a doubt, Cuba's signature libation. A frequent visitor to the tropics, Ernest Hemingway named this his beverage of choice.

- **10 fresh mint leaves**
- **2 tablespoons sugar**
- **Juice from ½ lime (about 2 tablespoons)**
- **¼ cup light rum**
- **Ice cubes**
- **Splash of club soda**

Combine mint leaves, sugar, and lime juice in a small mortar bowl; crush mint using a pestle. Transfer mint mixture to a tall glass.

Add rum and stir; add ice cubes. Add a splash of club soda.

Note: If you don't have a mortar and pestle, simply crush the mint leaves in your glass with the sugar and lime juice, using the back of a spoon. **Makes** 1 serving.

BUÑUELOS

Prep: 30 min., Cook: 25 min., Fry: 6 min. per batch

In addition to powdered sugar, these Cuban fritters (*pronounced boo-NWAY-lohs*) can also be served with syrup or honey. If you have one, a box grater makes quick work of grating the sweet potatoes and malanga.

- **1 pound sweet potatoes**
- **1 pound malanga, peeled and cut into 4-inch chunks**
- **2 teaspoons salt, divided**
- **1 cup all-purpose flour**
- **½ teaspoon baking soda**
- **2 egg yolks, beaten**
- **⅛ teaspoon anise extract (optional)**
- **All-purpose flour**
- **Vegetable oil**
- **Powdered sugar**

Bring sweet potatoes and malanga with 1 teaspoon salt in water to cover to a boil in a large Dutch oven over medium-high heat. Cover, reduce heat to medium, and simmer 20 minutes or just until tender. (Do not cook until mushy.) Drain well. Cool; peel sweet potatoes. Grate cooked malanga and sweet potatoes in a large bowl.

Stir together 1 cup flour, baking soda, and remaining 1 teaspoon salt in a large bowl. Stir in beaten egg yolks; gently stir in grated sweet potatoes and malanga; if desired, stir in anise extract. Divide dough into 24 equal pieces. With floured hands, roll each piece into a ball; roll each ball into an 8-inch rope on a floured surface, adding additional flour to hands and surface as needed. Shape each rope into a figure 8, pinching ends together.

Pour oil to a depth of 2 inches in a Dutch oven; heat to 375°. Fry buñuelos, in batches, 3 minutes on each side or until golden brown. Drain well on paper towels. Sprinkle with powdered sugar, and serve immediately. **Makes** 2 dozen.

YOLANDA MELLON
MIAMI, FLORIDA

Christmas All Through the House

Within these pages, we share easy-going recipes and simple decorations.

Beautiful Buffets

These recipes can be adapted to fit any size party.

A Fabulous Affair

Serves 24

All 3 salsas

2 recipes Tuscan Pork Loin and 1 recipe Herbed Roast Beef

3 recipes Golden Buttermilk Mashed Potatoes (page 298)

3 recipes Roasted Asparagus (page 298)

1 Mama Dip's Carrot Cake (page 299)

2 recipes Mascarpone Pecan Pie (page 299)

2 batches Chocolate-Dipped Cookies (page 299)

A Smaller Gathering

Serves 12

2 of the 3 salsas

1 recipe Herbed Roast Beef or 2 recipes Tuscan Pork Loin

2 recipes Golden Buttermilk Mashed Potatoes (page 298)

2 recipes Roasted Asparagus (page 298)

1 Mama Dip's Carrot Cake (page 299)

1 recipe Mascarpone Pecan Pie (page 299)

1 batch Chocolate-Dipped Cookies (page 299)

An Intimate Party

Serves 8

Make 1 recipe each of salsa, pork loin, mashed potatoes, and asparagus. Choose one dessert selection.

Think location, location, location when you set up your next holiday party. Find three or more fabulous settings in your home to serve each course. A perky salsa bar sits on a kitchen island. The main course is spread on a table near the fireplace, and desserts stand in all their glory on a sideboard in the dining room. No sideboard? Consider using the dresser in a roomy bedroom. The idea is to keep guests moving from one place to the next and re-energizing the conversation with each new destination. The bigger the party and the more guests you have, the more stations you need to set up. Using our tips, you can plan for 24 as easily as 8. The choice is yours.

TUSCAN PORK LOIN

Prep: 25 min., Bake: 30 min., Stand: 10 min.

This recipe calls for dried pesto seasoning, which is found on the spice aisle of the supermarket. Do not confuse this seasoning with prepared pesto sauce, which is a refrigerated product. You can also substitute dried Italian seasoning.

- 1 (4-pound) boneless pork loin roast
- 1 (8-ounce) package cream cheese, softened
- 1 tablespoon dried pesto seasoning
- ½ cup loosely packed fresh spinach leaves
- 6 bacon slices, cooked and drained
- ½ (12-ounce) jar roasted red bell peppers, drained
- 1 teaspoon salt
- 1 teaspoon paprika
- ½ teaspoon pepper
- Fresh spinach leaves

Slice pork lengthwise, cutting down center, to but not through other side. Open halves, and cut down center of each half, cutting to but not through other sides. Open into a rectangle. Place plastic wrap over pork, and pound to an even thickness with a meat mallet or rolling pin.

Spread cream cheese evenly down center of pork lengthwise. Sprinkle cream cheese evenly with dried pesto seasoning.

Arrange spinach over cream cheese, and top with bacon and red pepper.

Roll up pork, starting with 1 long side. Secure at 2-inch intervals with kitchen string. Rub pork roll with salt, paprika, and pepper. Place seam side down on a lightly greased rack on an aluminum foil-lined pan.

Bake at 425° for 30 minutes or until a meat thermometer inserted into thickest portion registers 155°. Remove from oven. Let stand 10 minutes.

Remove string from pork; cut into ½-inch slices. Serve pork slices on a bed of fresh spinach leaves. **Makes** 8 to 10 servings.

Note: For testing purposes only, we used McCormick Gourmet Collection Pesto Seasoning.

MARY LOU COOK
WELCHES, OREGON

HERBED ROAST BEEF

Prep: 10 min., Bake: 3 hrs., Stand: 10 min., Cook: 10 min.

The gravy for this recipe calls for a dry red wine. We recommend either Merlot or Cabernet Sauvignon.

¼ cup all-purpose flour
2 tablespoons dry mustard
1½ tablespoons chopped fresh rosemary
2 teaspoons seasoned salt
2 teaspoons seasoned pepper
1 (8-pound) rolled boneless rib roast
1 cup dry red wine
2 cups beef broth
½ cup water

Combine first 5 ingredients. Reserve 3 tablespoons flour mixture. Pat remaining flour mixture evenly over roast.

Place roast, fat side up, on a rack in a shallow roasting pan.

Bake, uncovered, at 325° for 3 hours or until a meat thermometer registers 135° or until desired degree of doneness.

Remove roast from pan, reserving drippings. Let stand 10 minutes for temperature to rise to 145° before serving.

Whisk together reserved 3 tablespoons flour mixture, ½ cup pan drippings (adding additional water, if necessary, to equal ½ cup), wine, broth, and ½ cup water in a saucepan over medium heat. Cook, stirring occasionally, until thick and bubbly. Serve over roast. **Makes** 16 servings.

RON POOLE
SALUDA, NORTH CAROLINA

BLACK BEAN-AND-MANGO SALSA

make ahead

Prep: 15 min., Chill: 1 hr.

1 (15-ounce) can black beans, rinsed and drained
1 mango, peeled and chopped
1 small green bell pepper, chopped
2 plum tomatoes, seeded and chopped
4 green onions, chopped
¼ cup Italian vinaigrette dressing
1 tablespoon fresh lime juice
2 teaspoons chopped fresh cilantro
½ teaspoon garlic salt
½ teaspoon seasoned pepper
½ teaspoon chili powder
½ teaspoon hot sauce
Assorted tortilla chips

Stir together first 12 ingredients in a medium bowl; cover and chill 1 hour or up to 24 hours. Serve with tortilla chips. **Makes** 8 appetizer servings.

Black Bean-and-Corn Salsa: Substitute 1 (11-ounce) can shoepeg corn, drained, for mango. Proceed as directed.

GOLDEN BUTTERMILK MASHED POTATOES

family favorite

Prep: 20 min., Cook: 30 min.

You won't need a mixer here—just mash these with a fork. The recipe calls for cooking the potatoes an additional 30 seconds after they've been drained. This allows excess water to steam off, creating fluffier mashed potatoes.

- **4 garlic cloves, minced**
- **2 tablespoons olive oil**
- **6 cups water**
- **2 pounds baking potatoes, peeled and cubed**
- **1 pound sweet potatoes, peeled and cubed**
- **1 teaspoon salt**
- **¾ cup buttermilk**
- **¼ cup butter**
- **¾ teaspoon salt**
- **½ teaspoon pepper**

Cook garlic in hot oil in a Dutch oven, stirring occasionally, over medium heat 3 minutes. Add 6 cups water and next 3 ingredients; bring to a boil. Reduce heat, cover, and cook 20 minutes or until tender.
Drain potatoes, and return to Dutch oven. Cook, stirring constantly, over medium heat 30 seconds. Remove from heat.
Add buttermilk and remaining ingredients; mash with a large fork to desired consistency. Serve immediately. **Makes** 6 to 8 servings.

JULIA MITCHELL
LEXINGTON, KENTUCKY

AVOCADO-FETA SALSA

fast fixin's

Prep: 20 min.

Make this salsa shortly before serving for best results. Avoid refrigerating it—the texture of the tomatoes will soften.

- **4 plum tomatoes, chopped**
- **2 tablespoons finely chopped red onion**
- **2 garlic cloves, minced**
- **1 (4-ounce) package crumbled feta cheese**
- **1 tablespoon chopped fresh parsley**
- **3 tablespoons red wine vinegar**
- **2 tablespoons olive oil**
- **½ teaspoon dried oregano**
- **½ teaspoon salt**
- **2 avocados, chopped**
- **Assorted tortilla chips**

Stir together first 9 ingredients. Gently stir in avocado just before serving. Serve with assorted tortilla chips. **Makes** 8 appetizer servings.

SUZANNE PAULSEN
LAUREL, MISSISSIPPI

ROASTED ASPARAGUS

fast fixin's

Prep: 10 min., Bake: 7 min.

- **2 pounds medium-size fresh asparagus spears, trimmed**
- **Vegetable cooking spray**
- **½ cup pine nuts, toasted**
- **1 plum tomato, seeded and chopped**

Spray asparagus lightly with cooking spray, and arrange asparagus in an aluminum foil-lined pan.
Bake at 425° for 7 minutes.
Sprinkle asparagus with pine nuts and tomato. **Makes** 8 servings.

MARY LOU COOK
WELCHES, OREGON

Holiday Party Decorating Stress-Buster

Start decorating with what you have. You don't have to spend a small fortune to lavish your rooms with holiday style. Use items you already have in different ways.
- Arrange flowers in pitchers and gravy boats on your table.
- Place votive candles and jingle bells together in wineglasses, and arrange them on a buffet or across a mantel.
- Use ribbon and fabric remnants to trim fresh garlands, trees, and wreaths with color.

ZUCCHINI-CARROT SALSA

fast fixin's

Prep: 15 min.

This mild salsa can be made the day before the party. It also makes a hearty sandwich spread when served with a slotted spoon.

- **3 small zucchini, diced**
- **2 medium carrots, diced**
- **1 tablespoon minced red onion**
- **1 (11-ounce) can sweet whole kernel corn, drained**
- **2 tablespoons olive oil**
- **2 tablespoons red wine vinegar**
- **1½ tablespoons chopped fresh parsley**
- **1 tablespoon fresh lime juice**
- **½ teaspoon sugar**
- **½ teaspoon salt**
- **¼ teaspoon ground red pepper**
- **¼ teaspoon black pepper**
- **Assorted tortilla chips**

Toss together first 12 ingredients in a large bowl. Cover and chill 1 hour, if desired, or up to 24 hours. Serve with assorted tortilla chips. **Makes** 8 appetizer servings.

MAMA DIP'S CARROT CAKE

freezeable • make ahead

Prep: 30 min., Bake: 40 min., Stand: 10 min.

This recipe from Chapel Hill, North Carolina, restaurateur Mildred "Mama Dip" Council is one of the best carrot cakes we've tested. The cake layers can be made ahead and frozen up to one month.

2¼ cups self-rising flour
1 teaspoon baking soda
1½ teaspoons ground cinnamon
2 cups sugar
1½ cups vegetable oil
4 large eggs
3 cups grated carrots
2 cups finely chopped walnuts, divided
Cream Cheese Frosting
Garnishes: walnut halves, carrot strips

Sift together flour, baking soda, and cinnamon; set aside.

Line 3 lightly greased 9-inch round cakepans with parchment paper; lightly grease parchment paper.

Beat sugar and oil at medium speed with an electric mixer until smooth.

Add eggs, 1 at a time, beating until blended after each addition. Add flour mixture, beating at low speed just until blended. Fold in carrots and 1 cup chopped walnuts. Spoon batter evenly into prepared pans.

Bake at 350° for 35 to 40 minutes or until a wooden pick inserted in center comes out clean. Cool in pans on wire racks 10 minutes; remove from pans, and cool completely on wire racks.

Spread Cream Cheese Frosting between layers and on top and sides of cake; press remaining 1 cup finely chopped walnuts evenly on sides of cake. Garnish, if desired. **Makes** 12 servings.

MILDRED "MAMA DIP" COUNCIL
MAMA DIP'S RESTAURANT
CHAPEL HILL, NORTH CAROLINA

CREAM CHEESE FROSTING:

fast fixin's • make ahead

Prep: 10 min.

2 (8-ounce) packages cream cheese, softened
½ cup butter, softened
1 (16-ounce) package powdered sugar
1 teaspoon vanilla extract

Beat cream cheese and butter at medium speed with an electric mixer until fluffy; gradually add sugar, beating well. Stir in vanilla. **Makes** 4 cups.

CHOCOLATE-DIPPED COOKIES

Prep: 15 min., Stand: 30 min.

Shortbread cookies are available in shapes such as petticoat tails and sticks. Use your favorite, or a variety, for this recipe.

4 (1-ounce) semisweet chocolate baking squares
2 tablespoons butter
½ tablespoon shortening
3 (5.3-ounce) boxes shortbread cookies
Toppings: finely chopped toasted pecans, crushed hard peppermint candies, toasted sweetened flaked coconut, red or green candy sprinkles

Microwave chocolate, butter, and shortening in a small microwave-safe bowl at HIGH 1 minute, stirring at 15-second intervals. Stir until smooth. (Higher wattage microwaves may need less time.)

Dip ends of cookies in melted chocolate, and roll in desired toppings. Place on a wax paper-lined baking sheet, and let stand 30 minutes or until firm. **Makes** about 2 dozen.

Note: For testing purposes only, we used Walker's Pure Butter Shortbread cookies and Crisco shortening.

MASCARPONE PECAN PIE

make ahead

Prep: 15 min., Bake: 1 hr., Chill: 6 hrs.

If you prefer to use your own 9-inch pieplates, transfer the frozen piecrusts to the pieplates before filling and baking.

1 (8-ounce) package cream cheese, softened
1 (8-ounce) container mascarpone cheese *
1½ cups sugar, divided
1 teaspoon lemon juice
5 eggs, divided
2 frozen unbaked (9-inch) deep-dish piecrusts
1 cup light corn syrup
1½ cups chopped pecans

Beat cheeses, 1 cup sugar, and lemon juice at medium speed with an electric mixer until smooth. Add 2 eggs, 1 at a time, blending well after each addition. Spread cheese mixture evenly into frozen crusts.

Whisk together remaining 3 eggs, remaining ½ cup sugar, and corn syrup in a medium bowl. Stir in pecans. Gently pour pecan mixture evenly over cream cheese mixture in crusts.

Bake at 350° for 20 minutes; reduce heat to 325°, and bake 40 more minutes or until set. Cool to room temperature; cover and chill at least 6 hours or overnight. **Makes** 16 servings.

* Substitute 1 (8-ounce) package cream cheese, softened, for mascarpone cheese, if desired.

BETH ROYALS
RICHMOND, VIRGINIA

Garlands and Goodies

Start a garland-making tradition with friends and family.

Deck the Halls With Appetizers

Serves 8 to 10

Chicken Fingers With Honey-Mustard Sauce

Sausage-Stuffed Mushrooms

Pinecone Cheese Ball

Spicy Chipotle-Barbecue Sausage Bites

Bourbon-Mustard Glazed Sausage Bites

Sweet-and-Sour Sausage Bites

Asian Snack Mix

Whip up some of these tasty snacks to get the decorating party started.

CHICKEN FINGERS WITH HONEY-MUSTARD SAUCE

fast fixin's

Prep: 5 min.

For an easy appetizer, serve sauce with 2 pounds fried chicken strips from the deli or 1 (28-ounce) bag frozen chicken strips, cooked according to package directions.

> ¾ cup Dijon mustard
> ½ cup mayonnaise
> ¼ cup honey
> ¼ teaspoon ground red pepper
> ⅛ teaspoon garlic salt
> 2 pounds deli fried chicken fingers

Stir together first 5 ingredients. Serve with fried chicken fingers. **Makes** 6 to 8 appetizer servings.

SAUSAGE-STUFFED MUSHROOMS

make ahead

Prep: 25 min., Cook: 20 min., Bake: 30 min.

If these are made ahead and chilled, the baking time will be closer to 30 minutes.

> 2 (16-ounce) packages fresh whole mushrooms
> 1 (12-ounce) package reduced-fat ground pork sausage
> 2 tablespoons butter or margarine
> 1 medium onion, finely chopped (about 1½ cups)
> 2 cups herb stuffing mix
> ¾ cup mayonnaise

Clean mushrooms. Remove and finely chop stems to equal about 2 cups; set stems and mushroom caps aside.

Cook sausage in a large nonstick skillet over medium-high heat, stirring until it crumbles and is no longer pink. Remove sausage, and drain on paper towels. Set aside.

Melt butter in skillet over medium-high heat; add onion and chopped mushroom stems, and sauté 10 minutes.

Stir together onion mixture, sausage, stuffing mix, and mayonnaise in a large bowl. (Mixture will be a little stiff.) Spoon generously into mushroom caps. If desired, cover with plastic wrap, and chill up to 8 hours.

Bake, uncovered, at 350° on a wire rack in a jelly-roll pan for 20 to 30 minutes or until thoroughly heated. Transfer to a serving platter. **Makes** 3 dozen.

PINECONE CHEESE BALL

make ahead

Prep: 10 min., Chill: 2 hrs.

> 1 (8-ounce) package cream cheese, softened
> 1 (3-ounce) package cream cheese, softened
> 2 (3-ounce) cans deviled ham
> 1 (0.7-ounce) envelope Italian dressing mix
> 1 (6-ounce) can whole smoked or unsalted almonds
> Assorted crackers and fresh vegetables
> Garnish: fresh rosemary sprigs

Combine first 4 ingredients until well blended. Cover and chill 1 hour.

Form mixture into a pinecone shape, using hands and plastic wrap. Starting at the bottom, press almonds into cheese mixture at slight angles, forming overlapping rows to resemble a pinecone. Cover loosely, and chill 1 hour. Serve with crackers and vegetables. Garnish, if desired. **Makes** 8 to 10 appetizer servings.

Note: For testing purposes only, we used Hormel Cure 81 Deviled Ham.

BARRET BURGER
CAMDEN, ARKANSAS

Story continues on page 305

Chocolate-Coffee Cheesecake
With Mocha Sauce, page 316

Herb-Grilled Chicken With
Watermelon-Feta Salad, page 320

Crispy Coconut Chicken
Dippers With Wowee Maui
Mustard, page 324

Cuban Mojo Chicken With Mandarin-
Black Bean Salad, page 318

Chocolate Cake IV, page 322

SPICY CHIPOTLE-BARBECUE SAUSAGE BITES

fast fixin's • make ahead

Prep: 5 min., Cook: 20 min.

**1 (28-ounce) bottle barbecue
    sauce**
1 (18-ounce) jar cherry preserves
**3 canned chipotle peppers in
    adobo sauce, undrained**
½ cup water
**1 tablespoon adobo sauce from
    can**
**2 (16-ounce) packages cocktail-
    size smoked sausages**

Whisk together first 5 ingredients in a Dutch oven over medium-high heat. Bring to a boil; add sausages, and return to a boil. Reduce heat to medium, and simmer, stirring occasionally, 15 minutes. Keep warm in a slow cooker on LOW, if desired. **Makes** 12 to 14 appetizer servings.

Spicy Chipotle-Barbecue Meatballs: Substitute 1 (32-ounce) package frozen meatballs for sausages. Increase water to 1½ cups. Proceed as directed, increasing simmer time to 45 minutes. **Makes** 12 to 14 appetizer servings. Prep: 5 min., Cook: 50 min.

How Kids Can Help

If your kids are too young to handle needles, here are other ways they can help make garlands.
■ Have them count the orange slices and kumquats, and then put them in bowls. An adult or older child can do the threading.
■ Let young kids thread large, colorful beads (instead of kumquats) onto strands of ribbon to add to the garland.

Garland Basics

Keep the materials simple, and you'll never buy your garland from the tree lot again. We used a combination of rosemary and lemon leaf. You can use any evergreen leaves; remember, the heartier, the better. Magnolia is also an accessible option that dries beautifully.

Start with a length of ¾-inch-wide jute rope, which can be purchased at any home-improvement or hardware store. Wire together bunches of greenery—the number of bunches will depend on the length of rope. A 25-inch garland can take as many as 40 bunches for a plush finished product. Wire them onto the rope using florist wire. Continue until the rope is completely covered.

BOURBON-MUSTARD GLAZED SAUSAGE BITES

fast fixin's

Prep: 5 min., Cook: 20 min.

1 (12-ounce) bottle chili sauce
1 (8-ounce) jar Dijon mustard
½ cup water
⅔ cup bourbon
**½ cup firmly packed dark brown
    sugar**
**2 (16-ounce) packages cocktail-
    size smoked sausages**

Whisk together first 5 ingredients in a Dutch oven over medium-high heat. Bring to a boil; add sausages, and return to a boil. Reduce heat to medium, and simmer, stirring occasionally, 15 minutes. Keep warm in a slow cooker on LOW, if desired. **Makes** 12 to 14 appetizer servings.

Bourbon-Mustard Glazed Meatballs: Substitute 1 (32-ounce) package frozen meatballs for sausages. Increase water to 1 cup. Proceed as directed, increasing simmer time to 35 minutes. **Makes** 12 to 14 appetizer servings. Prep: 5 min., Cook: 40 min.

SWEET-AND-SOUR SAUSAGE BITES

fast fixin's

Prep: 5 min., Cook: 20 min.

Chili-garlic sauce can be found in the ethnic foods aisle of large supermarkets.

2 (18-ounce) jars apricot preserves
1 (12-ounce) bottle chili sauce
3 tablespoons white vinegar
2 tablespoons chili-garlic sauce
**2 (16-ounce) packages cocktail-
    size smoked sausages**

Whisk together first 4 ingredients in a Dutch oven over medium-high heat. Bring to a boil; add sausages, and return to a boil. Reduce heat to medium, and simmer, stirring occasionally, 15 minutes. Keep warm in a slow cooker on LOW, if desired. **Makes** 12 to 14 appetizer servings.

Sweet-and-Sour Meatballs: Substitute 1 (32-ounce) package frozen meatballs for sausages. Add 1 cup water. Proceed as directed, increasing simmer time to 30 minutes. **Makes** 12 to 14 appetizer servings. Prep: 5 min., Cook: 35 min.

ASIAN SNACK MIX

Prep: 10 min., Bake: 1 hr.

- ¾ cup butter, melted
- 2 tablespoons brown sugar
- 2 tablespoons soy or teriyaki sauce
- 2 tablespoons ketchup
- 1 teaspoon onion powder
- ¾ teaspoon garlic powder
- ¼ teaspoon ground ginger
- ¼ teaspoon ground red pepper
- ¼ teaspoon prepared brown mustard
- 1 tablespoon dark sesame oil (optional)
- 4 cups rice cereal squares
- 4 cups wheat cereal squares
- 1 (3-ounce) can chow mein noodles
- 2 cups salted cashew halves
- 3 (2.29-ounce) cans wasabi peas

Combine first 9 ingredients, and, if desired, sesame oil in a medium bowl until well blended.

Combine rice cereal squares and next 4 ingredients in a large bowl. Slowly stir in butter mixture, tossing to coat. Spread mixture in an even layer in 2 (15- x 10-inch) jelly-roll pans.

Bake at 250° for 1 hour, stirring every 15 minutes. Cool in pans 10 minutes; spread mixture on paper towels to cool completely. **Makes** 12 cups.

Note: For testing purposes only, we used Rice Chex and Wheat Chex cereals. Wasabi peas can be found in the ethnic foods aisle of large supermarkets.

JEREMY BAZATA
PANAMA CITY, FLORIDA

Come Over for Coffee

Love the idea of holiday entertaining but dislike preparing an entire menu? Here's an easy solution: Become a barista for a day. A pot of piping hot coffee is the main attraction at this gathering, while sweets and flavorful syrups, creams, and spices give your servings a special touch. Now that's the perfect excuse for a second cup!

Pour hot coffee in carafes, and give guests plenty of ways to sweeten and flavor their java. Fill several small bowls with your favorite ground spices, such as nutmeg, cocoa, and cinnamon. Fill glass mugs and bowls with white and brown sugar cubes—and don't forget the swizzle sticks for easy stirring.

Skip the doughnuts, and serve cookies instead. At our party, we set out plates of biscotti, shortbread bites, and pirouette cookies.

Quick Tip: Right before your get-together, wash your coffee mugs in a dishwasher and push the "warm dry" button, so the mugs are nice and toasty when the cycle is over. Hand guests a warm mug for their coffee; they'll appreciate the gesture.

More Stir-ins for Your Coffee Bar

chocolate syrup

liqueurs

powdered sugar

flavored syrups

chocolate-dipped cinnamon sticks

rock candy sticks

peppermint sticks

whipped cream

Brew a Better Cup

■ For the best-tasting coffee, grind fresh, whole coffee beans right before you brew them.

■ Clean coffeepots and carafes with coffeepot cleaner. Ordinary dishwashing soap can leave a residue and affect the taste of your coffee.

■ When making flavored coffee, add a few grains of salt to the grinds in the filter. This brings out the flavor even more.

MOCHA CAFÉ AU LAIT

fast fixin's

Prep: 5 min., Cook: 8 min.

To make chocolate sprinkles, use a mini-grater to grate your favorite dark or milk chocolate bar.

- 2 cups milk
- 6 ounces milk chocolate candy bars, chopped
- 1½ teaspoons vanilla extract, divided
- 3 cups freshly brewed coffee
- ½ cup whipping cream
- 1 tablespoon powdered sugar
- Garnish: semisweet chocolate shavings

Stir together milk, chopped chocolate, and 1 teaspoon vanilla in a medium saucepan over low heat. Cook, stirring constantly, 8 minutes or until mixture begins to bubble around edges and chocolate is melted and smooth. Stir in coffee. Remove from heat, and set aside.

Beat cream, powdered sugar, and remaining ½ teaspoon vanilla at high speed with an electric mixer until soft peaks form.

Pour hot coffee mixture into mugs. Top with whipped cream; garnish, if desired. **Makes** about 6 cups.

SPICED COFFEE

fast fixin's

Prep: 5 min.

- **10 tablespoons ground coffee**
- **1 teaspoon ground cinnamon**
- **¼ teaspoon ground nutmeg**
- **6 cups water**
- **½ cup whipping cream**
- **3 tablespoons powdered sugar**
- **⅛ teaspoon ground nutmeg**

Combine coffee, cinnamon, and nutmeg in a coffee filter. Brew with 6 cups water in a coffeemaker, according to manufacturer's instructions.

Beat cream, powdered sugar, and nutmeg at high speed with an electric mixer until soft peaks form.

Pour coffee into mugs, and top with whipped cream. **Makes** 7 cups.

BEBE MAY
PENSACOLA, FLORIDA

Gifts to Go

For a fun take on a party favor, ask each guest to bring a cute holiday mug to your gathering. Choose names to see who gets each mug—or put them all on a table, and let everyone choose a favorite cup as she leaves.

Have a Cookie

For one day, let this be your holiday motto: the more, the merrier. Put on a colorful apron (kids too!), and line up those baking sheets and mixing bowls. We have five delicious recipes that give new flavors to your favorite holiday bites.

SHORTBREAD THUMBELINAS

family favorite

Prep: 25 min., Chill: 1 hr.,
Bake: 14 min. per batch

- **2½ cups all-purpose flour**
- **1 cup finely chopped, toasted almonds, divided**
- **¼ teaspoon salt**
- **1¼ cups butter, softened**
- **1 cup powdered sugar, sifted**
- **1 teaspoon vanilla extract**
- **Chocolate Filling**

Combine flour, ½ cup almonds, and salt; set aside.

Beat butter at medium speed with an electric mixer until creamy; gradually add powdered sugar, beating until light and fluffy.

Add flour mixture to butter mixture gradually, beating just until blended. Stir in vanilla.

Cover dough, and chill 1 hour.

Shape dough into 1-inch balls; roll balls in remaining ½ cup almonds. Place about 1 inch apart on lightly greased baking sheets; gently press an indentation into center of each cookie with thumb.

Bake at 350° for 14 minutes or until set; remove from pans to wire racks to cool completely.

Spoon or pipe about ½ teaspoon Chocolate Filling into indentation of each cooled cookie. **Makes** about 3 dozen.

CHOCOLATE FILLING:
fast fixin's

Prep: 5 min., Cool: 28 min.

- **¾ cup semisweet chocolate morsels**
- **3 tablespoons whipping cream**

Combine chocolate morsels and cream in a microwave-safe glass measuring cup. Microwave at HIGH 30 seconds. Whisk until smooth. Cool 20 minutes, and stir well; cool 8 more minutes. **Makes** about 1 cup.

MOCHA SHORTBREAD

Prep: 25 min., Bake: 20 min. per batch

If you have only salted butter, use it and omit the ¼ teaspoon salt.

- **1¼ cups all-purpose flour**
- **¼ cup cornstarch**
- **¼ cup unsweetened cocoa**
- **1½ teaspoons instant coffee granules**
- **¼ teaspoon salt**
- **1 cup unsalted butter**
- **1 cup powdered sugar**
- **2 (2-ounce) squares almond bark, chopped**
- **2 (1-ounce) squares semisweet chocolate, chopped**

Sift together first 5 ingredients; set aside.

Beat butter and sugar at medium speed with an electric mixer until light and fluffy.

Add flour mixture to butter mixture, beating until blended. (Dough will be sticky.)

Divide dough equally into thirds. Place 1 dough portion onto a parchment paper-lined baking sheet; cover with wax paper and roll or pat into a 6-inch circle (about ¼ inch thick). Repeat procedure with remaining 2 dough portions.

Remove wax paper, and bake at 350° for 18 to 20 minutes. Remove from oven, and cut each shortbread evenly into 8 wedges. Let cool on baking sheets on wire racks.

Microwave almond bark in a microwave-safe bowl at HIGH 30 seconds; stir well. Microwave in additional 10-second intervals, stirring after each interval until bark melts. Drizzle bark evenly over shortbread wedges. Repeat procedure with semisweet chocolate. **Makes** 2 dozen.

ANGEL COOKIES

Prep: 45 min., Chill: 8 hrs.,
Bake: 8 min. per batch

Use any shape cookie cutter; just be aware that your choice may affect the yield.

2 cups all-purpose flour
2 teaspoons baking powder
½ teaspoon salt
¼ cup butter, softened
¼ cup shortening
¾ cup sugar
2 large eggs
1 teaspoon grated lemon rind
    (optional)
1 teaspoon vanilla extract
Buttercream Frosting*

Combine flour, baking powder, and salt; set aside.
Beat butter, shortening, and sugar at medium speed with an electric mixer until blended. Add eggs, 1 at a time, beating until blended after each addition. Stir in lemon rind, if desired, and vanilla.
Add flour mixture to sugar mixture, beating until blended. Cover and chill 8 hours.
Roll dough to ¼-inch thickness on a lightly floured surface; cut with a 3-inch angel cookie cutter. Place on lightly greased baking sheets.
Bake at 350° for 8 minutes or just until edges begin to brown. Remove to wire racks to cool. Decorate as desired with Buttercream Frosting. **Makes** about 3 dozen.

*Substitute 1 can of ready-to-spread cream cheese frosting, if desired.

BUTTERCREAM FROSTING:

Prep: 5 min.

2 cups powdered sugar
¼ cup butter, softened
2 tablespoons milk
½ teaspoon vanilla extract

Beat powdered sugar and butter at low speed with an electric mixer until blended; stir in milk and vanilla. **Makes** about 1¼ cups.

CHOCOLATE AND MINT COOKIES

Prep: 15 min., Bake: 12 min. per batch

1¾ cups all-purpose flour
½ teaspoon salt
½ teaspoon baking powder
½ teaspoon baking soda
½ cup unsalted butter,
    softened
¾ cup firmly packed light brown
    sugar
¼ cup granulated sugar
1 large egg
2 teaspoons vanilla extract
½ cup milk chocolate morsels
½ cup semisweet mini-morsels
½ (3-ounce) mint chocolate bar,
    chopped

Combine first 4 ingredients, and set aside.
Beat butter at medium speed with an electric mixer 3 minutes. Add sugars, and beat 2 to 3 minutes or until light and fluffy. Add egg and vanilla, beating until well blended.

Add flour mixture to butter mixture, beating well. Stir in morsels and chopped mint chocolate.
Drop dough by heaping tablespoonfuls onto lightly greased baking sheets.
Bake at 350° for 10 to 12 minutes or until light golden brown. Remove cookies to wire racks. Cool completely. **Makes** about 2½ dozen.

Note: For testing purposes only, we used Ghirardelli Mint Chocolate.

CRANBERRY-WHITE CHOCOLATE COOKIES

Prep: 15 min., Bake: 12 min. per batch

2½ cups all-purpose flour
1 teaspoon baking powder
¼ teaspoon salt
⅛ teaspoon baking soda
½ cup butter, softened
1⅓ cups sugar
2 large eggs
1½ cups white chocolate morsels
1 (6-ounce) package sweetened
    dried cranberries

Combine first 4 ingredients; set aside.
Beat butter at medium speed with an electric mixer until creamy; gradually add sugar, beating well. Add eggs, 1 at a time, beating until blended after each addition.
Add flour mixture to butter mixture gradually, beating at low speed until blended. Stir in white chocolate morsels and cranberries.
Drop dough by heaping tablespoonfuls onto lightly greased baking sheets.
Bake at 350° for 10 to 12 minutes or until lightly browned on bottom. Remove to wire racks to cool. **Makes** about 3 dozen.

Note: For testing purposes only, we used Craisins for sweetened dried cranberries.

Extra Fun for Little Helpers

▪ Let their imaginations run wild when decorating frosted cookies. Set out bowls of colorful candies and sprinkles.
▪ Set up a side table of Christmas coloring books, crayons, paper, and stickers. When the cookies are baking (and boredom sets in), kids can stay occupied at a crafts corner.
▪ Make giving an exciting activity. As you bake, ask youngsters to decide which cookies should go to which family members, friends, and charities. Ask them to create tags from construction paper to tie on the gift boxes.

Simply Splendid

Throw a party that lives big with only a few carefully chosen items.

Simple Sandwich Supper

Serves 8 to 10

Beef Tenderloin With Horseradish Cream

Blue Cheese Biscuits

vegetable and relish tray

Mulled Pomegranate Cider

Sometimes a tasty finger sandwich, a warm beverage, and a rich dessert are all you need for a grand get-together. All that's left is to pick up a vegetable tray at the supermarket, and transfer the items to your favorite platter. You could also add marinated olives or relishes to accompany the menu. We love these flavors together, and they satisfy the most discerning palates.

BEEF TENDERLOIN WITH HORSERADISH CREAM

Prep: 10 min., Grill: 20 min., Stand: 10 min.

Serve these tasty sandwiches alongside the Mulled Pomegrante Cider for an exquiste party meal.

2 (8-ounce) beef tenderloin steaks (about 1½ inches thick)
½ teaspoon salt
½ teaspoon seasoned pepper
1 recipe Blue Cheese Biscuits
Horseradish Cream

Sprinkle steaks evenly with salt and seasoned pepper. Grill, covered with grill lid, over medium-high heat (350° to 400°) 10 minutes on each side or until desired degree of doneness. Remove steaks from grill; cover steaks with aluminum foil, and let stand 10 minutes.

Cut steaks into thin slices. Cut Blue Cheese Biscuits or desired bread in half. Divide and place beef slices evenly on the cut sides of biscuits; top with Horseradish Cream. Top with remaining biscuit halves. (Or serve the cream on the side, and let guests make their own sandwiches.) **Makes** 8 to 10 appetizer servings.

HORSERADISH CREAM:
Prep: 5 min., Chill: 1 hr.

½ cup sour cream
1½ teaspoons prepared horseradish
1½ teaspoons Dijon mustard

Stir together all ingredients. Cover and chill at least 1 hour.

BLUE CHEESE BISCUITS

Prep: 10 min., Bake: 18 min.

Pair these biscuits with Beef Tenderloin With Horseradish Cream for a flavorful appetizer.

2 cups self-rising flour
1 (8-ounce) container sour cream
½ cup butter, melted
1 (4-ounce) package crumbled blue cheese

Stir together all ingredients just until blended.

Turn dough out onto a lightly floured surface. Pat dough to ¾-inch thickness; cut with a 2-inch round cutter. Place on a lightly greased baking sheet.
Bake at 425° for 15 to 18 minutes or until biscuits are lightly browned.
Makes 12 biscuits.

MULLED POMEGRANATE CIDER

Prep: 10 min., Cook: 25 min.

The sweetness of a beverage is less pronounced at lower temperatures. If you're serving this beverage over ice, use 2 cups of sugar; if serving it hot, use 1½ cups sugar.

5 (3-inch) cinnamon sticks, halved
1 tablespoon whole cloves
1½ to 2 cups sugar
2 quarts water
2 (16-ounce) bottles pomegranate juice ＊
¼ cup fresh lemon juice
1 cup orange juice

Place cinnamon sticks and cloves in center of an 8-inch square of cheesecloth; tie with string.
Bring spice bag, sugar, and next 3 ingredients to a boil in a Dutch oven, stirring occasionally. Reduce heat, and simmer, uncovered, 10 minutes.
Remove and discard spice bag; stir in orange juice. Serve hot or cold. **Makes** 3¼ quarts.

Note: For testing purposes only, we used POM Wonderful Pomegranate Juice, which can be found in the refrigerated produce section of large supermarkets.

＊Substitute 1 (32-ounce) bottle cranberry juice cocktail, if desired.

Wine selection

Pair this menu with Columbia Crest Cabernet Sauvignon or Woodbridge Cabernet Sauvignon or Merlot.

Make-Ahead Appetizers

Whether the gathering is planned or impromptu, you'll be set to entertain this season with these ready-and-waiting treasures.

Make-ahead ease meets hard-working flavor head-on with these sensational starters. Fix them on a leisurely Sunday, and freeze for later use. Tackling the prep work in advance gives you breathing room for all the other fun cooking when company's coming.

Company's Coming Christmas Cocktails

Serves 8 to 10

Mushroom Turnovers

Cranberry Meatballs

Creamy Olive Spread with pita chips

wine and beer

MUSHROOM TURNOVERS

freezeable • make ahead

Prep: 30 min., Chill: 1 hr., Cook: 15 min., Bake: 20 min.

> 1½ (8-ounce) packages cream cheese, softened
> 2¼ cups all-purpose flour
> ¾ cup butter, softened
> 3 tablespoons butter
> 1 cup chopped onion
> 1 pound fresh mushrooms, chopped
> ¼ teaspoon dried thyme
> ¼ teaspoon salt
> ½ teaspoon pepper
> 2 tablespoons all-purpose flour
> ¼ cup sour cream
> 3 tablespoons sherry
> 1 tablespoon butter, melted

Combine first 3 ingredients. Shape dough into a ball; cover and chill 1 hour.

Melt 3 tablespoons butter in a large skillet over medium heat; add onion, and sauté 12 minutes or until onion is golden. Stir in mushrooms, and sauté 3 minutes. Stir in thyme, salt, and pepper. Sprinkle 2 tablespoons flour evenly over mushroom mixture. Stir in sour cream and sherry. Remove from heat, and set aside.

Pat or roll chilled dough to ⅛-inch thickness on a lightly floured surface; cut with a 3-inch round cutter.

Spoon 1 teaspoon mushroom mixture on half of each dough circle; fold dough over filling. Press edges together with a fork to seal. Place on an ungreased baking sheet.

Bake at 400° for 15 to 20 minutes or until edges are lightly browned; brush tops with 1 tablespoon melted butter.

Makes 3½ dozen appetizer servings.

Note: To make ahead, place unbaked turnovers in a single layer on baking sheets, and freeze. Transfer frozen turnovers to large zip-top freezer bags; seal and freeze up to 1 month. Place frozen turnovers on ungreased baking sheet. Bake as directed.

ROSEMARIE CAVANAGH
STATEN ISLAND, NEW YORK

CRANBERRY MEATBALLS

freezeable • make ahead

Prep: 30 min., Cook: 40 min.

> 2 pounds ground chuck
> 2 large eggs
> ⅓ cup dry breadcrumbs
> 1 teaspoon salt
> ½ teaspoon pepper
> ½ teaspoon garlic powder
> ½ teaspoon onion powder
> ½ teaspoon dried thyme
> 1 (16-ounce) can cranberry sauce
> 1 (12-ounce) jar chili sauce
> ¼ cup orange marmalade
> ¼ cup water
> 2 tablespoons soy sauce
> 2 tablespoons red wine vinegar
> 1 teaspoon dried crushed red pepper

Combine first 8 ingredients in a large bowl. Shape mixture into about 54 (1-inch) balls.

Cook meatballs, in batches, in a large skillet over medium-high heat until browned (about 5 minutes); remove from pan, and drain on paper towels.

Stir together cranberry sauce and next 6 ingredients in a large Dutch oven over medium heat, and cook, whisking occasionally, 5 minutes or until smooth. Add meatballs; reduce heat to low, and cook, stirring occasionally, 15 to 20 minutes or until centers are no longer pink. **Makes** about 4½ dozen.

JANE RABEY
DACULA, GEORGIA

Note: To make ahead, place cooked meatballs in a zip-top freezer bag, and freeze up to 1 month. Thaw in refrigerator, and cook, stirring occasionally, until thoroughly heated.

CREAMY OLIVE SPREAD

freezeable • make ahead

Prep: 10 min.

- 2 (8-ounce) packages cream cheese, softened
- 1 (4.25-ounce) can chopped ripe black olives
- ½ cup chopped pimiento-stuffed olives
- 1 garlic clove, minced
- 2 tablespoons olive oil
- 2 tablespoons fresh lemon juice
- ¼ teaspoon salt (optional)
- Pita chips

Stir together first 6 ingredients and, if desired, salt. Serve with pita chips. **Makes** about 2¾ cups.

Note: To make ahead, place spread in an airtight container, and chill up to 1 week or freeze up to 2 weeks. Thaw in refrigerator. Let stand at room temperature 30 minutes, and stir before serving.

MAGGI HOOVER
EDMONDS, WASHINGTON

Hearty Casseroles

Casseroles are just plain handy. Both of these recipes marry familiar ingredients with more international accents such as curry powder and poblano chile peppers.

Make the Cheesy Chicken Curry Casserole ahead and freeze up to a month (we've even included reheating instructions). The Zesty Poblano-and-Cheese Casserole is similar to chiles rellenos, a classic Tex-Mex comfort food,

only in casserole form. Make this the day you plan to serve it because it doesn't freeze well. You can substitute bell peppers for the poblano chile peppers, but the flavor won't be as full-bodied. Poblanos are low on the heat scale with a wonderfully rich and almost smoky flavor, whereas bell peppers are much sweeter and milder. Regardless of the pepper, removing the seeds always reduces the heat.

CHEESY CHICKEN CURRY CASSEROLE

freezeable • make ahead

Prep: 15 min., Bake: 40 min., Stand: 5 min.

- 2 cups chopped cooked chicken
- 2 cups broccoli florets, cooked
- 1 (10¾-ounce) can cream of chicken soup, undiluted
- 1 (8-ounce) container sour cream
- 1 cup (4 ounces) shredded Cheddar cheese
- ¾ cup milk
- 1 teaspoon curry powder
- ½ teaspoon ground black pepper
- ¼ teaspoon garlic powder
- ⅛ teaspoon ground red pepper (optional)
- ½ cup fine, dry breadcrumbs
- 2 tablespoons butter or margarine, melted

Combine first 9 ingredients and red pepper, if desired. Spoon into a lightly greased 11- x 7-inch baking dish.
Bake at 350° for 30 minutes or until hot and bubbly. Stir together breadcrumbs and melted butter; sprinkle over casserole, and bake 10 more minutes. Let stand 5 minutes before serving. **Makes** 6 servings.

Note: Freeze unbaked casserole, omitting breadcrumbs and butter, for up to 1 month, if desired. Allow to stand at room temperature 1 hour. Bake at 350° for 1 hour and 30 minutes or until hot and bubbly. Stir together breadcrumbs and melted butter; sprinkle over casserole, and bake 10 more minutes. Let stand 5 minutes before serving.

TERESA STOKES
BIRMINGHAM, ALABAMA

ZESTY POBLANO-AND-CHEESE CASSEROLE

Prep: 25 min., Broil: 16 min., Bake: 30 min., Stand: 10 min.

- 4 to 6 large poblano chile peppers *
- 1 (16-ounce) container ricotta cheese
- 1½ cups (6 ounces) shredded Monterey Jack cheese
- 1½ cups (6 ounces) shredded mozzarella cheese
- 2 large eggs, lightly beaten
- 1 teaspoon salt
- ½ teaspoon pepper
- ¼ teaspoon dried oregano
- ¼ teaspoon dried thyme
- ¾ cup marinara sauce
- ⅓ cup grated Parmesan cheese

Broil chile peppers on an aluminum foil-lined baking sheet 5 inches from heat about 8 minutes on each side or until peppers look blistered.
Place peppers in a zip-top plastic freezer bag; seal bag and let stand 10 minutes.
Peel peppers, and remove and discard seeds; pat dry with paper towels. Cut into ½-inch strips; set aside.
Stir together ricotta cheese and next 7 ingredients.
Layer one-third each of chile pepper strips, cheese mixture, and marinara sauce into a lightly greased 9-inch square baking dish; repeat layers twice. Sprinkle with Parmesan cheese.
Bake at 350° for 30 minutes or until golden. **Makes** 6 servings.

*Substitute 6 to 8 red, yellow, or green bell peppers for poblano chile peppers, if desired.

BEATRIZ SWIRSKY
SUNRISE, FLORIDA

Crusted Baked Chicken

This versatile adult-, kid-, and company-friendly recipe is ideal for the season.

Company's Coming Supper

Serves 4

Baked Pecan Chicken With Creamy Mushroom-Artichoke Sauce

Rosemary Baked Vegetables

romaine lettuce salad with Red Delicious apple slices

Apricot Vinaigrette

bakery brownies

O ur Baked Pecan Chicken can be served in four different ways during December. For weeknights, serve with the salad idea from the menu box. For company, pair with Creamy Mushroom-Artichoke Sauce, the salad, and Rosemary Baked Vegetables. Planning an open house? Slice the crunchy-coated chicken into strips and serve with honey-mustard and barbecue sauce. For entertaining holiday houseguests, serve the separate dishes as a salad. Make each one the day before. To serve, arrange romaine lettuce and apple slices on individual plates, top with the baked vegetables and chicken, and drizzle with warmed Apricot Vinaigrette. Enjoy!

BAKED PECAN CHICKEN

family favorite

Prep: 10 min., Bake: 25 min.

Baked Pecan Chicken is a hit whether served with Creamy Mushroom-Artichoke Sauce for grown-ups or in strips with ketchup and mustard for kids.

- 1½ cups finely chopped pecans, toasted
- 2 tablespoons chopped parsley
- 1½ teaspoons salt
- 2 egg whites
- 4 skinned and boned chicken breasts
- Creamy Mushroom-Artichoke Sauce (optional)

Combine first 3 ingredients in a shallow bowl.

Beat egg whites with a fork just until foamy. Dip both sides of chicken in egg; dredge in pecan mixture. Arrange chicken breasts on a lightly greased aluminum foil-lined baking sheet.

Bake at 400° for 20 to 25 minutes or until chicken is done. Serve with Creamy Mushroom-Artichoke Sauce, if desired. **Makes** 4 servings.

CYNTHIA FOUSE
ROSWELL, GEORGIA

CREAMY MUSHROOM-ARTICHOKE SAUCE

fast fixin's

Prep: 15 min., Cook: 12 min.

- 2 tablespoons butter
- 1 tablespoon vegetable oil
- 1 (8-ounce) package sliced mushrooms
- ½ cup chopped onion (about ½ onion)
- 2 garlic cloves, minced
- ¾ cup chicken broth
- 1 (8-ounce) package cream cheese, softened ∗
- 1 (14-ounce) can artichoke hearts, drained and coarsely chopped
- 2 tablespoons fresh lemon juice
- ⅛ to ¼ teaspoon ground red pepper

Melt butter with oil in a large skillet over medium heat; add mushrooms, onion, and garlic, and sauté 5 to 7 minutes or until tender. Stir in chicken broth and cream cheese, and cook, stirring constantly, 2 to 3 minutes or until cream cheese melts. Stir in artichoke hearts, lemon juice, and red pepper. Reduce heat to low, and cook 2 minutes or until mixture is hot. **Makes** about 2½ cups.

∗Substitute 1 (8-ounce) package ⅓-less-fat cream cheese, if desired.

CYNTHIA FOUSE
ROSWELL, GEORGIA

APRICOT VINAIGRETTE

fast fixin's

Prep: 5 min.

- 1 (10-ounce) jar apricot fruit spread or preserves
- ⅓ cup seasoned rice wine vinegar
- 3 tablespoons olive oil

Microwave apricot spread in a microwave-safe bowl at MEDIUM-LOW (30% power) 1 minute or until melted. Whisk in vinegar and olive oil until blended; cool. Serve at room temperature. **Makes** about 1¾ cups.

ROSEMARY BAKED VEGETABLES

Prep: 15 min., Bake: 45 min.

The recipe calls for an entire bulb of garlic. Remove any loose paper-like skin before cutting off the top. Once garlic is cooked, squeeze the bulb, releasing the individual cloves of just-cooked garlic. Left whole, the cooked cloves will have a milder flavor than if pressed or chopped.

- 3 red potatoes, cut into 1-inch pieces (about 1 pound)
- 12 baby carrots
- 1 medium-size sweet potato, peeled and cut into 1-inch pieces
- 1 large or 2 small zucchini, cut into 1-inch pieces
- 1 onion, quartered
- 1 garlic bulb, pointed end cut off
- ¼ cup olive oil
- 1 teaspoon crushed dried rosemary
- ½ teaspoon salt

Toss together all ingredients, and place in a single layer in a 15- x 10-inch jelly-roll pan.
Bake at 400° for 45 minutes or until tender. Carefully squeeze pulp from garlic bulb, discarding husk. Stir together garlic and vegetables. **Makes** 4 servings.

JESSIE LITTRELL
MOYIE SPRINGS, IDAHO

Fresh Ways With Cranberries

One sure sign that the holidays are here is that cranberries are popping up everywhere. They're versatile, good for you, and a popular ingredient. Try Cranberry Muffins with golden raisins for breakfast on the go. For an entrée, choose Holiday Pork Chops dressed up with a stuffing of dried cranberries.

HOLIDAY PORK CHOPS

Prep: 20 min., Cook: 16 min., Stand: 15 min., Bake: 25 min.

- 1 tablespoon butter
- ½ cup chopped onion
- ½ cup chopped celery
- 1 cup fresh breadcrumbs
- ½ cup sweetened, dried cranberries, coarsely chopped
- ¼ cup chicken broth
- 1 tablespoon chopped fresh parsley
- 1 teaspoon grated orange rind
- 1 teaspoon salt
- ¼ teaspoon ground sage
- 1 (4-pound) boneless pork loin roast (about 9 inches long), trimmed *
- 3 tablespoons dried steak seasoning
- 2 tablespoons olive oil

Melt butter in a large ovenproof skillet over medium-high heat; add onion and celery. Sauté 8 to 10 minutes or until vegetables are tender and liquid evaporates. Remove from heat. Stir in breadcrumbs, cranberries, and next 5 ingredients. Let stand 10 minutes. Spoon breadcrumb mixture into a large zip-top plastic bag; set aside. Wipe skillet clean.
Cut pork loin into 6 (1½-inch-thick) chops. Cut a 1½-inch slit in 1 side of each chop, cutting to, but not through other side (about 1½ to 2 inches), to form a pocket.
Snip 1 corner of bag, and pipe breadcrumb mixture evenly into slits in pork. Rub both sides of stuffed chops evenly with steak seasoning.
Cook chops in hot oil in ovenproof skillet over medium-high heat 2 to 3 minutes on each side or until chops are browned. Cover skillet with lid or aluminum foil. Bake at 350° for 20 to 25 minutes or until a meat thermometer inserted in pork registers 155°. Remove from oven, and let stand 5 minutes or until thermometer registers 160°. **Makes** 6 servings.

Note: For testing purposes only, we used McCormick Grill Mates Montreal Steak Seasoning.

*Substitute 6 (1½-inch-thick) boneless pork chops for pork loin roast, if desired.

BETSY SPAELAFORA
FAIRFIELD, OHIO

CRANBERRY MUFFINS

freezeable • make ahead

Prep: 15 min., Bake: 20 min.

You can freeze these muffins in a zip-top freezer bag up to a month. Thaw at room temperature or microwave frozen muffins 15 to 30 seconds at HIGH.

- 3 tablespoons sugar
- ¼ cup orange juice
- ½ cup cranberries
- ⅓ cup golden raisins
- 1⅓ cups all-purpose flour
- ½ cup cornmeal
- ½ cup sugar
- 2 teaspoons baking powder
- ¾ cup buttermilk
- 3 tablespoons butter, melted
- 1 egg, lightly beaten

Combine sugar and orange juice, stirring until sugar dissolves. Stir in cranberries and raisins.
Combine flour and next 3 ingredients in a large bowl; make a well in center of mixture. Stir together buttermilk, melted butter, and egg; add to dry ingredients, and stir just until moistened. Gently fold in cranberry mixture. Spoon muffin batter evenly into 10 lightly greased muffin cups in muffin pan, filling two-thirds full. Fill remaining 2 muffin cups with water.
Bake at 425° for 20 minutes or until muffins are lightly browned and a wooden pick inserted in center comes out clean. Remove muffins from pans immediately, and let cool completely on wire racks. **Makes** 10 muffins.

CHARLOTTE BRYANT
GREENSBURG, KENTUCKY

from our kitchen

Dressed for the Holidays

Disposable foil pans, available at the supermarket, come in a variety of sizes and patterns that are perfect for baking and delivering homemade treats. We used a glue gun to attach colorful strips of holiday ribbon to loaf pans of Cranberry-Pecan Cake (recipe page 287/photo below). For a festive glow, drizzle cooled cakes with Vanilla Glaze (page 287), and garnish with additional chopped sweetened dried cranberries, toasted pecans, and sugared orange rind. (To make sugared citrus rind, toss together equal amounts of grated citrus rind and granulated sugar.)

■ To easily release cakes from shaped pans, be sure to grease all the flutes and crevices. Use a pastry brush to generously coat the bottom and sides of the pan with a solid vegetable shortening such as Crisco. Lightly sprinkle with flour, tilting and tapping the pans so the flour completely covers the greased surfaces; invert the pans, and gently tap out any excess flour.

■ Before removing the cakes from the pan after baking, cool according to recipe directions. Invert the pan over a wire rack, gently shaking the pan to release the cakes. If needed, use the blade of a small icing spatula to loosen the sides of the cakes from the pan.

■ With smaller muffin pans and molds, such as the fluted brioche pan, we found it easier to use a vegetable cooking spray with flour, such as PAM For Baking, Crisco Flour No-Stick Spray, or Baker's Joy Original No-Stick Baking Spray With Flour.

Tiny Temptations

Iced with Cream Cheese Frosting (page 287), bite-size Chocolate-Red Velvet Cupcakes (page 287) are sure to delight children of all ages. Sprinkle with sparkling sugar, crushed peppermints, or decorative candies, and then package the treats in miniature muffin pans. Tie on a ribbon and some candy canes, and slip the pan inside a cellophane gift bag so all the goodies shine through.

Lasting Impressions

We had great fun testing our Christmas cake batters in different sizes and shapes. At right we list some of our favorite pans. They're available in kitchen shops in the region (such as Williams-Sonoma, 1-800-541-2233 or www.williams-sonoma.com), in discount

department stores (such as Target), through mail-order catalogs, and on Web sites (such as **www.amazon.com** and **www.cooking.com**). You'll find baking instructions included on the packaging with most pans.

■ Fluted brioche molds, traditionally used to bake the rich and buttery French yeast bread known as brioche, are also perfect for baking fanciful cakes such as the Fluted Chocolate-Red Velvet Cakes (page 287) on our cover. Sold in a variety of sizes, we chose the 8-inch brioche molds for our cakes. Because we used nonstick molds with a dark outer surface, we covered the whole outside of the mold with aluminum foil. The shiny side of the foil reflects the heat away from the sides of the mold for a lighter, bright red crust.

■ NordicWare makes a multi-mini Bundt cakepan that has two each of three different shapes. Dust the finished cakes with powdered sugar to accent the molded designs.

■ The Bundt brownie pan is also the perfect size for cupcakes. We garnished ours with a dollop of whipped cream, raspberry candies, and fresh mint.

■ During our testing, we also experimented with the new flexible silicone bakeware and were disappointed with the results. We found the batters baked unevenly, and the cakes were difficult to remove from the pans when done.

Southern Living®
cook-off 2005 winners

316   **Southern Desserts**
- *Grand Prize/Category Winner* Chocolate-Coffee Cheesecake With Mocha Sauce
- Decadent Banana Cake With Coconut-Cream Cheese Frosting
- Southern Peach-and-Blueberry Shortcakes

318   **Healthy & Good for You**
- *Category Winner* Cuban Mojo Chicken With Mandarin-Black Bean Salad
- White Bean Soup With Gremolata
- Toasted Pecan, Cranberry, and Gorgonzola Turkey Burgers

320   **Easy Entrées**
- *Category Winner* Herb-Grilled Chicken With Watermelon-Feta Salad
- Pané Chicken With Sweet-'n'-Spicy Red Pepper Sauce
- Southwestern Chicken-Corn Cakes

322   **Your Best Recipe**
- *Category Winner* Chocolate Cake IV
- Pimiento Cheese-Stuffed Fried Chicken
- Double Whammie Yeast Rolls

324   **Kids Love It!**
- *Category Winner* Crispy Coconut Chicken Dippers With Wowee Maui Mustard
- Sloppy José Sandwiches With Cilantro Slaw
- Crispy Ginger-and-Garlic Asian Turkey Lettuce Wraps

325   **Brand Winners**
- Hearty Healthy Breakfast Casserole
- Tex-Mex Chicken-and-Bacon Pizza
- Souffleeta
- Sour Cream-Blueberry Morning Pancakes With Wild Blueberry-and-Peach Topping
- The Ultimate No-Bake Cheesecake Banana Pudding With Caramel Syrup
- Texas Best Fried Shrimp
- Southern-Style Fish Tacos
- Margarita Marinated Chicken With Mango Salsa
- Spicy Baked Beans
- My Best Tuna Salad
- Cuban Pulled Pork Tortilla Pie With Snappy Mango Salsa
- Tex-Mex Grilled Beef "Tenders," Corn and Tomatoes With Chipotle-Lime Cream
- Fried Green Tomato Po' Boys
- Maple-Mustard-Glazed Balsamic Steaks With Blue Pecan Confetti

Cook-Off 2005 Winners

You'll love these prizewinning recipes from our fourth annual Cook-Off.

The *Southern Living* Foods Staff strives to make every recipe we publish one you'd be proud to serve to family and friends. So we want our Cook-Off finalists' recipes to embody the "best of the best" in recipe quality. Several factors decide a winning recipe. Not only does it have to taste good, but it also has to be well written so that we can accurately re-create it for our tasting. Eventually, we pare down thousands of recipes to 15 and let the judges decide which of them is worth a cool $100,000. This year's grand prize winner, Sharon Collison, delivered taste, accuracy, and, to quote one of the judges, "a perfectly executed" performance at the contest. We salute her efforts—and her cheesecake. In our eyes, every one of these recipes is a winner.

Note: To enter the contest, you must use at least one sponsor's product.

SOUTHERN DESSERTS

GRAND PRIZE WINNER

SOUTHERN DESSERTS
Category Winner

PHILADELPHIA Cream Cheese *Brand Winner*

CHOCOLATE-COFFEE CHEESECAKE WITH MOCHA SAUCE

Prep: 20 min.; Bake: 1 hr., 10 min.; Stand: 30 min.; Chill: 4 hrs.

Top each serving with a dollop of whipped cream, fresh raspberries, and fresh mint sprigs, if desired. *(pictured on page 301)*

- 3 cups crushed chocolate graham crackers (about 20 sheets)
- ½ cup butter or margarine, melted
- PAM Original No-Stick Cooking Spray
- 4 (8-ounce) packages PHILADELPHIA Cream Cheese, softened
- 1 cup DOMINO Granulated Sugar
- ¼ cup coffee liqueur
- 1 teaspoon instant coffee granules
- 1 teaspoon vanilla extract
- 4 large eggs
- 4 (1-ounce) bittersweet baking chocolate squares
- Mocha Sauce

Stir together crushed graham crackers and butter; press mixture into bottom and up sides of a 9-inch springform pan coated with cooking spray.

Bake at 350° for 10 minutes. Cool on a wire rack. Reduce oven temperature to 325°.

Beat cream cheese and sugar at medium speed with an electric mixer until blended. Add liqueur, coffee granules, and vanilla, beating at low speed until well blended. Add eggs, 1 at a time, beating just until yellow disappears after each addition.

Remove and reserve 1 cup cream cheese mixture. Pour remaining batter into prepared crust.

Microwave chocolate squares in a medium-size glass bowl 1 minute or until melted, stirring after 30 seconds; let cool slightly. Stir reserved 1 cup cream cheese mixture into melted chocolate, blending well. Spoon chocolate mixture in lines on top of batter in pan; gently swirl with a knife.

Bake at 325° for 1 hour or until almost set. Turn oven off. Let cheesecake stand in oven, with door closed, 30 minutes. Remove cheesecake from oven, and gently run a knife around edge of cheesecake to loosen from sides of pan. (Do not remove sides of pan.) Cool on wire rack. Cover and chill at least 4 hours.

Remove sides of springform pan. Serve cheesecake with Mocha Sauce. **Makes** 8 servings.

Note: For testing purposes only, we used Kahlúa coffee liqueur.

MOCHA SAUCE:

Prep: 5 min., Cook: 3 min.

1 (12-ounce) package semisweet
   chocolate morsels
½ cup whipping cream
1 tablespoon butter or
   margarine
¼ cup strong brewed coffee

Cook first 3 ingredients in a small heavy saucepan over low heat, stirring often, 2 to 3 minutes or until smooth. Remove from heat, and stir in coffee. Serve warm. **Makes** 1½ cups.

SHARON COLLISON
NEWARK, DELAWARE

DOMINO Sugar *Brand Winner*

DECADENT BANANA CAKE WITH COCONUT-CREAM CHEESE FROSTING

Prep: 15 min., Bake: 30 min., Stand: 10 min.

Serve slices of this cake with a little coconut sprinkled on the side, if desired.

2½ cups plus 5½ tablespoons
   cake flour
1 tablespoon baking soda
Pinch of salt
½ cup unsalted butter, softened
1 cup DOMINO Granulated
   Sugar
¾ cup firmly packed DOMINO
   Light Brown Sugar
2 large eggs
4 large ripe bananas, mashed
   (about 2 cups)
⅔ cup buttermilk
Coconut-Cream Cheese
   Frosting

Sift together first 3 ingredients.
Beat butter at medium speed with an electric mixer until creamy. Add sugars, and beat until light and fluffy. Add eggs, 1 at a time, beating until blended after each addition. Beat in bananas at low speed. Increase speed to medium, and gradually add flour mixture to butter mixture alternately with buttermilk, beginning and ending with flour mixture. Pour batter into 2 greased and floured 9-inch round cakepans.
Bake at 350° for 30 minutes or until a wooden pick inserted in center comes out clean.
Cool in pans on wire racks 10 minutes. Remove from pans, and cool completely on wire racks.
Spread Coconut-Cream Cheese Frosting between layers and on top and sides of cake. **Makes** 8 servings.

COCONUT-CREAM CHEESE FROSTING:

Prep: 10 min.

1 (8-ounce) package
   PHILADELPHIA Cream Cheese,
   softened
2 tablespoons butter, softened
3½ cups DOMINO 10X
   Confectioners Sugar, sifted
2 teaspoons MILK
½ teaspoon vanilla extract
1¼ cups sweetened flaked
   coconut

Beat cream cheese and butter at medium speed with an electric mixer until creamy. Gradually add confectioners sugar, beating at low speed until blended. Beat at high speed until smooth. Stir in milk and vanilla. Stir in coconut. **Makes** about 3 cups.

AMANDA MOORE
ATHENS, GEORGIA

Grand-Prize Winner

Sharon Collison is a registered dietitian who loves to experiment with food. She particularly likes to make full-fat recipes lighter and healthier. She admits with some embarrassment that while she does make a lower fat version of the cheesecake, she intentionally left her contest entry full fat. Sharon thinks of a true Southern dessert as being "really rich and decadent, not an everyday thing, but something you serve on special occasions." Her pairing of chocolate with coffee was a natural match that easily fulfilled her "rich and decadent" criteria.

Sharon says she's still pinching herself in disbelief over her success. "During the contest, my husband and Pam Lolley (Test Kitchens professional and Cook-Off hostess) had to hear me complain for hours, worrying that I had used the wrong pan, and if I had left the cheesecake out long enough. They calmed me down, but I was not confident at all until my name was called. Then I started crying and shaking. I thought, 'There is no way this is happening.' I was completely overwhelmed." Obviously, so were the judges.

SOUTHERN PEACH-AND-BLUEBERRY SHORTCAKES

Prep: 30 min., Chill: 1 hr., Bake: 15 min.

You can find coarse sugar at specialty baking shops.

4 cups all-purpose flour
6 tablespoons DOMINO Granulated Sugar
4 teaspoons baking powder
1 teaspoon baking soda
1½ teaspoons salt
PAM Original No-Stick Cooking Spray
7 tablespoons cold CRISCO Shortening
6 tablespoons cold unsalted butter
2 cups cold buttermilk
All-purpose flour
1 egg yolk
¼ cup buttermilk
Coarse sugar
4 cups sliced fresh peaches
1 pint fresh blueberries
½ cup DOMINO Granulated Sugar
Pinch of ground nutmeg
1 cup whipping cream
3 tablespoons DOMINO 10X Confectioners Sugar
3 tablespoons almond liqueur (optional)
Garnishes: DOMINO 10X Confectioners Sugar, coarsely chopped toasted pecans, fresh mint sprigs

Sift together first 5 ingredients in a large bowl. Chill 1 hour.

Line a baking sheet with parchment paper. Lightly coat parchment paper with cooking spray. Set aside.

Cut shortening and butter into cold flour mixture with a fork or pastry blender until crumbly. Add 2 cups cold buttermilk, stirring just until dry ingredients are moistened. (Dough will be light and crumbly.)

Turn dough out onto a floured surface. Pat dough into a 1-inch-thick circle, and cut with a floured 3-inch round cutter. Place shortcakes 2 inches apart on prepared baking sheet. Repeat procedure once with remaining scraps of dough.

Stir together egg yolk and ¼ cup buttermilk. Brush mixture onto shortcake tops, and sprinkle evenly with coarse sugar.

Bake at 425° for 12 to 15 minutes or until lightly browned. Remove baking sheet to wire racks to cool.

Stir together peaches and next 3 ingredients; cover and chill.

Beat whipping cream and 3 tablespoons confectioners sugar at medium speed with an electric mixer until soft peaks form. Stir in liqueur, if desired.

Split shortcakes in half. Spoon fruit mixture on bottom halves of shortcakes; top with remaining halves and a dollop of whipped cream. Garnish, if desired. **Makes** 9 servings.

CLIFTON HOLT
BIRMINGHAM, ALABAMA

HEALTHY & GOOD FOR YOU

HEALTHY & GOOD FOR YOU
Category Winner

DOLE All Natural Fruit *Brand Winner*

CUBAN MOJO CHICKEN WITH MANDARIN-BLACK BEAN SALAD

Prep: 10 min., Cook: 15 min., Stand: 20 min.

Mix up the Mandarin-Black Bean Salad while the chicken marinates. *(pictured on page 303)*

¼ cup fresh orange juice
¼ cup fresh lime juice
2 garlic cloves, minced
1 teaspoon ground cumin
½ teaspoon dried oregano, crushed
½ teaspoon paprika
½ teaspoon salt
4 (5-ounce) PILGRIM'S PRIDE Boneless, Skinless Chicken Breasts
PAM for Grilling No-Stick Spray
Mandarin-Black Bean Salad
Garnishes: fresh mint sprigs, lime wedges

Combine first 7 ingredients in a zip-top freezer bag or shallow dish; add chicken. Seal or cover, and let stand 20 minutes.

Remove chicken from marinade, reserving marinade. Pat chicken dry with paper towels.

Coat a large nonstick skillet with cooking spray; heat skillet over medium-high heat. Add chicken, and cook 4 to 5 minutes on each side or until done. Remove chicken from skillet, and keep warm.

Wipe skillet clean. Add reserved mari-

Judges' Notes

The judges unanimously chose the Chocolate-Coffee Cheesecake With Mocha Sauce as the grand prize winner. "As soon as you tasted it, you just knew," stated judge and *Southern Living* Associate Foods Editor Mary Allen Perry. "It delivered big for its simplicity of ingredients and technique." Chief Cook-Off judge and *Southern Living* Foods Editor Scott Jones commented, "It was as close to perfect as I've seen since I've been a judge. It was perfectly baked, the texture was just right, and it looked terrific. It wasn't that we were looking for a cheesecake or dessert, she simply had the best recipe and did the best job on the day of competition."

Judges' Notes

Cuban Mojo Chicken With Mandarin-Black Bean Salad was a big hit with our judges. The presentation was "stunning," but what won them over was the combination of ingredients. Says Cook-Off judge and *Southern Living* Foods Editor Shirley Harrington, "There were three unexpected flavors in the salad that worked so well together and made this recipe a standout to me: the crunch of jícama; the fresh, clean taste of mint; and the slight heat from jalapeño. There was no oil, yet the chicken was amazingly juicy and flavorful; this was a clear Healthy & Good for You winner to me."

nade, and bring to a boil. Boil 2 minutes, stirring often.

Cut chicken diagonally into ½-inch-thick slices. Spoon Mandarin-Black Bean Salad in center of 4 serving plates. Arrange chicken slices around salad, and drizzle chicken evenly with warm marinade. Garnish, if desired. **Makes** 4 servings.

MANDARIN-BLACK BEAN SALAD:

Prep: 10 min.

> 2 cups DOLE All Natural Mandarin Orange Segments, well drained
> 1 cup canned black beans, rinsed and drained
> ¾ cup diced jícama
> 2 tablespoons chopped red onion
> 2 tablespoons seeded, minced jalapeño
> 2 tablespoons shredded fresh mint leaves
> ¼ teaspoon salt

Stir together all ingredients in a large bowl. Let stand until ready to serve, tossing occasionally. **Makes** about 4 cups.

GLORIA DUKE
TOMBALL, TEXAS

KRAFT 100% Grated Parmesan Cheese
Brand Winner

WHITE BEAN SOUP WITH GREMOLATA

Prep: 20 min., Cook: 50 min.

Gremolata, a fragrant topping or garnish containing garlic, lemon rind, and fresh parsley, adds fresh flavor to many dishes.

> 4 celery ribs, diced
> 1 red onion, diced
> 1 white onion, diced
> 4 garlic cloves, minced
> 1 teaspoon CRISCO Canola Oil
> 4 cups chopped seeded ALABAMA Tomatoes
> ¼ teaspoon DOMINO Granulated Sugar
> 4 (16-ounce) cans cannellini beans, rinsed and drained
> 4 cups chicken broth
> ¼ cup loosely packed fresh flat-leaf parsley leaves
> 2 fresh thyme sprigs
> 1 bay leaf
> Salt and pepper to taste
> Dash of hot sauce (optional)
> Gremolata

Sauté first 4 ingredients in hot oil in a Dutch oven over medium-high heat 5 to 10 minutes or until tender. Add tomatoes and sugar; cook, stirring occasionally, 5 minutes. Add beans and next 4 ingredients. Bring to a boil. Cover,

reduce heat, and simmer, stirring occasionally, at least 30 minutes. Remove and discard thyme and bay leaf. Stir in salt and pepper to taste, and if desired, hot sauce. Top each serving with a spoonful of Gremolata. **Makes** 4 to 6 servings.

GREMOLATA:

Prep: 10 min.

> ¼ cup loosely packed fresh flat-leaf parsley
> 4 garlic cloves
> 2 tablespoons KRAFT 100% Grated Parmesan Cheese
> 1 tablespoon grated lemon rind
> 1 tablespoon water
> 1 teaspoon herbes de Provence
> ½ teaspoon salt
> ½ teaspoon pepper

Process all ingredients in a food processor or blender until well blended or to desired consistency, stopping to scrape down sides. **Makes** ¼ cup.

CAROLINE HARRIS
LEXINGTON, GEORGIA

NATURE'S OWN Bread and Buns
Brand Winner

TOASTED PECAN, CRANBERRY, AND GORGONZOLA TURKEY BURGERS

Prep: 15 min., Bake: 8 min., Cook: 12 min.

Make the Cranberry Mustard right after you warm the buns.

- **6 NATURE'S OWN Honey Wheat Hamburger Buns**
- **½ cup coarsely chopped pecans**
- **1½ pounds JENNIE-O TURKEY STORE Lean Ground Turkey**
- **⅔ cup crumbled Gorgonzola cheese**
- **1 teaspoon onion powder**
- **1 teaspoon garlic salt**
- **½ teaspoon pepper**
- **PAM Original No-Stick Cooking Spray**
- **Cranberry Mustard**
- **2 cups fresh baby spinach**

Wrap buns in aluminum foil; place pecans on a baking sheet.

Bake buns and pecans at 350° for 8 minutes. Remove pecans from oven, leaving buns in oven.

Combine ground turkey and next 4 ingredients in a large bowl. Shape into 6 (¾-inch-thick) patties.

Cook patties in a large skillet coated with cooking spray over medium heat 6 minutes on each side or until done.

Remove buns from oven. Spread 2 heaping teaspoons Cranberry Mustard on each side of bun halves. Arrange half of spinach leaves evenly on bottom halves; top with turkey patties, toasted pecans, remaining spinach leaves, and remaining bun halves. Serve with remaining Cranberry Mustard, if desired. **Makes** 6 servings.

CRANBERRY MUSTARD:
Prep: 5 min.

- **½ cup whole-berry cranberry sauce**
- **⅓ cup Dijon mustard**
- **⅛ teaspoon dried crushed red pepper**

Stir together all ingredients. **Makes** about ¾ cup.

ANNA GINSBERG
AUSTIN, TEXAS

EASY ENTRÉES

EASY ENTRÉES
Category Winner

PILGRIM'S PRIDE Chicken *Brand Winner*

HERB-GRILLED CHICKEN WITH WATERMELON-FETA SALAD

Prep: 20 min., Chill: 30 min., Grill: 12 min.
(pictured on page 302)

- **3 tablespoons fresh lemon juice**
- **3 tablespoons CRISCO Vegetable Oil**
- **¼ cup chopped fresh flat-leaf parsley**
- **1 teaspoon dried oregano**
- **¾ teaspoon salt**
- **½ teaspoon ground cumin**
- **½ teaspoon pepper**
- **4 PILGRIM'S PRIDE Boneless, Skinless Chicken Breasts**
- **PAM for Grilling No-Stick Spray**
- **Watermelon-Feta Salad**
- **Garnish: fresh parsley sprigs**

Whisk first 7 ingredients in a shallow dish; remove and reserve 2 tablespoons marinade for Watermelon-Feta Salad.

Add chicken to dish; cover and chill 30 minutes.

Spray cold grill cooking grate with grilling spray; place on grill over medium heat (300° to 350°). Place chicken on grate.

Grill 6 minutes on each side or until done. Serve with Watermelon-Feta Salad. Garnish, if desired. **Makes** 4 servings.

WATERMELON-FETA SALAD:
Prep: 10 min.

- **1½ cups diced seedless watermelon**
- **¾ cup diced English cucumber**
- **¼ cup coarsely chopped pitted Kalamata olives**
- **¼ cup diced red onion**
- **2 tablespoons reserved marinade**
- **¼ cup crumbled feta cheese**

Place first 5 ingredients in a large bowl; gently toss. Sprinkle with feta cheese. **Makes** 3 cups.

PRISCILLA YEE
CONCORD, CALIFORNIA

PANÉ CHICKEN WITH SWEET-'N'-SPICY RED PEPPER SAUCE

Prep: 15 min., Chill: 15 min., Cook: 16 min.

- **4 PILGRIM'S PRIDE Boneless, Skinless Chicken Breasts**
- **1 cup fine, dry breadcrumbs**
- **1 teaspoon granulated garlic**
- **1 teaspoon dried oregano**
- **1 teaspoon seasoned salt**
- **1 large egg**
- **2 tablespoons water**
- **½ cup CRISCO Vegetable Oil, divided**
- **Sweet-'n'-Spicy Red Pepper Sauce**
- **Garnishes: fresh chives, parsley sprigs**

Place chicken between 2 sheets of heavy-duty plastic wrap; flatten to ¼-inch thickness, using a rolling pin or flat side of a meat mallet.

Combine breadcrumbs and next 3 ingredients in a shallow dish.

Whisk together egg and 2 tablespoons water. Dip chicken in egg mixture; dredge in breadcrumb mixture. Arrange chicken in a single layer on a baking sheet; chill 15 minutes.

Heat ¼ cup oil in a 12-inch nonstick skillet over medium heat. Add 2 chicken breasts, and cook 4 minutes on each side or until done. Remove from skillet, and keep warm. Repeat procedure with remaining oil and chicken. Serve with Sweet-'n'-Spicy Red Pepper Sauce. Garnish, if desired. **Makes** 4 servings.

SWEET-'N'-SPICY RED PEPPER SAUCE:
Prep: 10 min., Cook: 25 min.

- ⅔ cup drained, seeded, and diced jarred roasted red bell peppers
- ½ cup DOMINO Granulated Sugar
- ½ cup white vinegar
- ½ cup ketchup
- 1½ teaspoons dried crushed red pepper
- 1 teaspoon garlic powder
- 1 teaspoon paprika

Stir together all ingredients in a 2-quart saucepan. Bring to a boil over medium heat; reduce heat to medium-low, and cook, stirring often, 25 minutes. **Makes** about 1 cup.

DENISE TOWNSEND
SHELTON, WASHINGTON

SOUTHWESTERN CHICKEN-CORN CAKES
Prep: 20 min., Fry: 8 min.

- 1 (11-ounce) can Mexican-style corn, drained
- 1 (4.5-ounce) can chopped green chiles, drained
- 1 cup fine, dry breadcrumbs, divided
- 2 large eggs, divided
- 4 cups chopped cooked chicken
- ⅓ cup jarred roasted red bell peppers, drained and chopped
- ⅓ cup chopped red onion
- ¼ cup HELLMANN'S or BEST FOODS Real Mayonnaise
- 2½ teaspoons Dijon mustard
- 2 teaspoons salt-free herb-and-spice seasoning
- 2 teaspoons chopped fresh basil
- 2 teaspoons chopped fresh cilantro
- 2½ tablespoons olive oil
- Romaine lettuce leaves
- Tomato, Basil, and Corn Relish
- Yogurt Sauce

Remove ¼ cup corn, and place in a large bowl, reserving remaining corn in can for Tomato, Basil, and Corn Relish. Remove 1 teaspoon chiles, and place in bowl with corn, reserving remaining chiles in can for Tomato, Basil, and Corn Relish.

Add ½ cup breadcrumbs, 1 egg, chicken, and next 7 ingredients to corn and chiles in bowl. Combine chicken mixture until well blended; shape mixture into 8 patties.

Beat remaining egg in a small bowl. Dip patties in egg, and dredge in remaining ½ cup breadcrumbs, shaking to remove any excess.

Fry patties in hot olive oil in a large skillet over medium heat 4 minutes on each side or until golden brown. Drain on paper towels. Arrange patties on lettuce; top with Tomato, Basil, and Corn Relish, and drizzle with Yogurt Sauce. **Makes** 8 servings.

TOMATO, BASIL, AND CORN RELISH:
Prep: 15 min.

- Reserved Mexican-style canned corn
- Reserved chopped green chiles in can
- 1½ cups seeded and chopped plum tomatoes
- ⅓ cup chopped red onion
- ¼ cup chopped jarred roasted red bell peppers
- 2 tablespoons chopped fresh basil
- 1 tablespoon chopped fresh cilantro
- 1½ tablespoons red wine vinegar
- 1 tablespoon olive oil
- Salt and pepper to taste

Stir together first 9 ingredients; add salt and pepper to taste. **Makes** about 3½ cups.

YOGURT SAUCE:
Prep: 5 min.

- 1 (6-ounce) container Plain YOGURT
- ⅓ cup HELLMANN'S or BEST FOODS Real Mayonnaise
- 1 tablespoon Dijon mustard
- 1 teaspoon Worcestershire sauce
- Salt and pepper to taste
- Sugar to taste

Whisk together first 4 ingredients; add salt, pepper, and sugar to taste. **Makes** about 1 cup.

GEORGE R. YATES
DALLAS, TEXAS

Judges' Notes

The basis for this category was to present a dish that delivered taste and ease, all within a 30-minute hands-on prep time limit. Herb-Grilled Chicken With Watermelon-Feta Salad did all that, and much more. The cool, crisp watermelon countered the salty, creamy feta cheese to create a perfectly balanced, beautiful complement to the marinated grilled chicken.

YOUR BEST RECIPE

YOUR BEST RECIPE
Category Winner

CHOCOLATE CAKE IV

Prep: 30 min., Bake: 30 min., Cool: 10 min.
(pictured on page 304)

- **PAM Original No-Stick Cooking Spray**
- **CRISCO Vegetable Shortening**
- **½ (4-ounce) semisweet chocolate baking bar, chopped**
- **½ (4-ounce) bittersweet chocolate baking bar, chopped**
- **½ cup butter, softened**
- **2 cups firmly packed DOMINO Light Brown Sugar**
- **3 large eggs**
- **2 teaspoons vanilla extract**
- **2¼ cups cake flour**
- **2 teaspoons baking soda**
- **½ teaspoon salt**
- **¼ teaspoon ground cinnamon**
- **½ cup buttermilk**
- **1 cup boiling water**
- **Coffee Liqueur Ganache Icing**
- **Mocha-Chocolate Cream Filling**
- **Garnish: chocolate curls**

Coat 3 (8-inch) round cakepans with cooking spray. Line bottoms of pans with wax paper; grease wax paper with shortening, and set aside.

Melt chocolate in a small saucepan over low heat, stirring until smooth; set aside.

Beat butter at medium speed with an electric mixer until creamy. Gradually add sugar, beating until light and fluffy. Add eggs, 1 at a time, beating just until yellow disappears after each addition. Stir in melted chocolate and vanilla.

Sift together flour and next 3 ingredients; add to butter mixture alternately with buttermilk, beating at low speed just until blended, beginning and ending with flour mixture. Stir in boiling water. Pour batter evenly into prepared pans.

Bake at 350° for 28 to 30 minutes or until a wooden pick inserted in center comes out clean. Cool in pans on wire racks 10 minutes; remove from pans, and cool completely on wire racks.

Place 1 cake layer on a serving plate; spread top with 4 tablespoons Coffee Liqueur Ganache Icing. Spread half of Mocha-Chocolate Cream Filling evenly over ganache on cake layer. Top with second cake layer; spread top with 4 tablespoons Coffee Liqueur Ganache Icing, and remaining Mocha-Chocolate Cream Filling. Top with remaining cake layer. Spread remaining Coffee Liqueur Ganache Icing on top and sides of cake. Garnish, if desired. **Makes** 12 to 14 servings.

COFFEE LIQUEUR GANACHE ICING:

Prep: 10 min.; Cook: 5 min., Stand: 45 min.

- **3 (4-ounce) bittersweet chocolate baking bars, finely chopped**
- **1¼ cups whipping cream**
- **1 tablespoon butter**
- **2 tablespoons coffee liqueur**

Place chocolate in a bowl.

Heat cream in a small saucepan over medium heat just until cream begins to boil. Pour over chocolate in bowl, stirring until smooth. Stir in butter and liqueur. Let stand 45 minutes or until spreading consistency. **Makes** 2 cups.

Note: For testing purposes only, we used Kahlúa coffee liqueur.

MOCHA-CHOCOLATE CREAM FILLING:

Prep: 10 min., Cook: 5 min., Stand: 30 min.

- **5 tablespoons all-purpose flour**
- **2 tablespoons unsweetened cocoa**
- **2 tablespoons instant coffee granules**
- **1 cup half-and-half**
- **1 cup butter, softened**
- **1 cup DOMINO 10X Confectioners Sugar**
- **1 teaspoon vanilla extract**

Whisk together first 4 ingredients in a small saucepan. Cook over medium heat, whisking constantly, 5 minutes or until thickened. Spoon mixture into a small bowl; cover surface of mixture with plastic wrap, pressing wrap onto surface, and let stand 30 minutes or until cool.

Beat butter and sugar at medium speed with an electric mixer until light and fluffy. Gradually add cooled cocoa mixture, 1 tablespoon at a time, beating until blended after each addition. Add vanilla, beating until mixture is consistency of whipped cream. **Makes** 1½ cups.

FLORENCE NEAVOLL
SALEM, OREGON

HELLMANN'S or BEST FOODS
Real Mayonnaise *Brand Winner*

PIMIENTO CHEESE-STUFFED FRIED CHICKEN

Prep: 10 min., Cook: 20 min., Bake: 3 min.

- **4 PILGRIM'S PRIDE Boneless, Skinless Chicken Breasts**
- **1 teaspoon salt**
- **½ teaspoon pepper**
- **½ cup MILK**
- **1 large egg**
- **1½ to 2 cups Japanese breadcrumbs (panko)**
- **Vegetable oil**
- **1⅓ cups Pimiento Cheese**
- **Garnish: chopped fresh chives**

Sprinkle chicken evenly with salt and pepper.

Whisk together milk and egg. Dip chicken in milk mixture, and dredge in breadcrumbs.

Pour oil to a depth of ⅛ inch in a large skillet over medium-high heat.

Cook chicken in hot oil about 10 minutes on each side or until done.

Transfer chicken to a baking sheet. Hold chicken with tongs, and carefully cut a slit in 1 side of each chicken breast to form a pocket. Spoon ⅓ cup Pimiento Cheese into each pocket.

Bake at 350° for 2 to 3 minutes or until cheese is melted. Garnish, if desired, and serve immediately. **Makes** 4 servings.

PIMIENTO CHEESE:

Prep: 15 min.

- 2 (8-ounce) blocks Sharp Cheddar Cheese, shredded
- 1 (4-ounce) jar diced pimiento, rinsed and drained
- ½ cup HELLMANN'S or BEST FOODS Real Mayonnaise
- 2 tablespoons finely chopped onion
- 1 tablespoon Worcestershire sauce
- ¼ teaspoon salt
- ⅛ teaspoon pepper

Stir together all ingredients just until blended. Cover and chill leftover cheese mixture up to 1 week. **Makes** about 3 cups.

BETH ANN BARRINEAU
MURRELLS INLET, SOUTH CAROLINA

PAM No-Stick Cooking Spray *Brand Winner*

DOUBLE WHAMMIE YEAST ROLLS

Prep: 25 min., Cook: 5 min., Stand: 5 min., Rise: 2 hrs., Bake: 18 min.

The double whammie comes from using beer and potato buds in the recipe.

- ⅔ cup DOMINO Granulated Sugar, divided
- ⅓ cup butter
- 1 cup MILK
- ¼ cup dried instant potato buds
- 1¼ teaspoons salt
- 2 (¼-ounce) envelopes active dry yeast
- ¼ cup beer at room temperature
- 1 large egg, lightly beaten
- 4½ cups bread flour, divided
- PAM Original No-Stick Cooking Spray
- Butter (optional)

Remove and reserve 1 tablespoon sugar. Cook remaining sugar, ⅓ cup butter, and next 3 ingredients in a medium saucepan over medium-low heat, stirring constantly, until butter melts. Cool to 110°.

Stir together yeast, beer, and reserved 1 tablespoon sugar in a 2-cup liquid measuring cup; let stand 5 minutes.

Combine milk mixture and yeast mixture in a large bowl; stir in egg. Gradually stir in 4 cups flour to form a dough. (Dough will be very stiff.)

Turn dough out onto a lightly floured surface, and knead, adding additional flour (up to ½ cup) as needed, until smooth and elastic (about 6 to 8 minutes). Place in a bowl coated with cooking spray, turning to coat top of dough. Cover and let rise in a warm place (85°), free from drafts, 1 hour or until doubled in bulk.

Coat muffin pans with cooking spray. Punch dough down, and shape dough into 36 (1-inch) balls, and place 3 dough balls in each muffin cup.

Cover and let rise in a warm place, free from drafts, 1 hour.

Preheat oven to 350°.

Bake for 15 to 18 minutes or until rolls are golden. (Place a small pat of butter on top of each roll after baking 5 minutes, or brush rolls with melted butter after baking, if desired.) **Makes** 1 dozen.

AMY HILL
MUNCIE, INDIANA

Judges' Notes

Chocolate Cake IV, so named for the four types of chocolate used, will surely go down as one of the best cakes you've ever tried. "Absolutely beautiful," one judge remarked. For a moist cake, it cuts extremely well, and the interesting chocolate flavors and textures within the layers of fluffy filling and thick ganache make this cake definitely worth the time and effort.

KIDS LOVE IT!

KIDS LOVE IT!
Category Winner

CRISCO Oils, Shortening, and Sprays
Brand Winner

CRISPY COCONUT CHICKEN DIPPERS WITH WOWEE MAUI MUSTARD

Prep: 15 min., Fry: 3 min. per batch

Flaked coconut makes a surprisingly delicious crust for these crispy chicken fingers. It takes just 3 ingredients to make the tangy dipping sauce. *(pictured on page 303)*

4 PILGRIM'S PRIDE Boneless, Skinless Chicken Breasts
1 cup all-purpose flour
1 teaspoon salt
1 teaspoon ground ginger
½ teaspoon pepper
¾ cup lime-flavored seltzer water
2 cups sweetened flaked coconut
1 cup fine, dry breadcrumbs
CRISCO Vegetable Oil
Salt (optional)
Wowee Maui Mustard
Garnish: lime wedges

Cut each chicken breast into 4 to 6 (1-inch) strips.
Whisk together flour and next 4 ingredients in a bowl. Combine coconut and breadcrumbs in a large shallow dish. Dip chicken pieces in flour mixture, and dredge in coconut mixture.
Pour oil to a depth of 2 inches in a deep skillet or Dutch oven; heat to 350°.
Fry chicken, in batches, 2 to 3 minutes or until golden. Drain on paper towels. Sprinkle lightly with salt, if desired. Serve with Wowee Maui Mustard. Garnish, if desired. **Makes** 4 servings.

WOWEE MAUI MUSTARD:
Prep: 5 min.

1 (8-ounce) can crushed pineapple, drained
½ cup red pepper jelly
3 tablespoons whole-grain mustard

Stir together all ingredients. **Makes** about 1½ cups.

LISA KEYS
MIDDLEBURY, CONNECTICUT

ENOVA Brand Oil *Brand Winner*

SLOPPY JOSÉ SANDWICHES WITH CILANTRO SLAW

Prep: 10 min., Cook: 19 min.

1 medium onion, finely chopped
1 tablespoon ENOVA Oil
1 pound lean Ground BEEF
2 (8-ounce) cans no-salt-added tomato sauce
1 tablespoon ground cumin
1 tablespoon dried oregano
1 tablespoon chili powder
½ teaspoon pepper
¼ teaspoon salt
4 NATURE'S OWN Honey Wheat Hamburger Buns
Cilantro Slaw

Cook onion in hot oil in a cast-iron or large skillet over medium heat about 4 minutes or until onion is soft and tender. Stir in ground beef and next 6 ingredients, and cook, stirring occasionally, 15 minutes or until beef crumbles and is no longer pink.
Spoon beef mixture on bottom halves of toasted buns; top each with about 3 tablespoons Cilantro Slaw and remaining bun halves. Serve with remaining Cilantro Slaw. **Makes** 4 servings.

CILANTRO SLAW:
Prep: 10 min.

¼ cup finely chopped fresh cilantro
¼ cup Dijon mustard
3 tablespoons HELLMANN'S or BEST FOODS Real Mayonnaise
1 tablespoon white wine vinegar
1 (12-ounce) package broccoli slaw mix

Whisk together first 4 ingredients in a large bowl; add broccoli slaw, tossing to coat. **Makes** 4 cups.

AMANDA KEEN-ZEBERT
SAN MARCOS, TEXAS

Judges' Notes

Sometimes frying coconut can be a very difficult thing to do, especially under the pressure of a $100,000 contest. But the Crispy Coconut Chicken Dippers With Wowee Maui Mustard were perfectly fried a beautiful golden brown. The mustard sauce is extremely inventive and so versatile; you'll want to try it on sandwiches, over cream cheese with crackers, or at parties. Kids of all ages will love this recipe, and it's sure to become one of your favorites, too.

BRAND WINNERS

CRISPY GINGER-AND-GARLIC ASIAN TURKEY LETTUCE WRAPS

Prep: 15 min., Cook: 15 min.

- ½ cup finely chopped carrot
- ½ cup water
- 1 (20-ounce) package JENNIE-O TURKEY STORE Lean Ground Turkey
- 1 cup chopped shiitake mushrooms
- 1 (8-ounce) can water chestnuts, drained and chopped
- 3 garlic cloves, minced
- 2 tablespoons minced fresh ginger
- ⅓ cup teriyaki sauce
- 3 tablespoons creamy peanut butter
- 1 tablespoon sesame oil
- 1 tablespoon rice vinegar
- ¼ cup hoisin sauce
- ½ cup sliced green onions
- 1 head iceberg lettuce, separated into leaves
- Hoisin sauce (optional)
- Garnishes: sliced green onions, carrots

Cook carrots in ½ cup water in a large nonstick skillet over high heat, stirring occasionally, 3 to 5 minutes or until carrots are softened and water is evaporated. Remove from skillet.

Reduce heat to medium. Cook turkey in skillet about 5 minutes, stirring until turkey crumbles and is no longer pink. Add carrots, mushrooms, and next 8 ingredients. Increase heat to medium-high, and cook, stirring constantly, 4 minutes. Add green onions, and cook, stirring constantly, 1 minute. Spoon warm mixture evenly onto lettuce leaves, and roll up. Serve with hoisin sauce, and garnish, if desired. **Makes** 4 to 5 servings.

SUSAN RILEY
ALLEN, TEXAS

HEARTY HEALTHY BREAKFAST CASSEROLE

Prep: 15 min., Cook: 4 min., Bake: 45 min.

Egg substitute can be used in place of the 4 eggs.

- ½ cup diced red bell pepper
- ½ cup chopped Vidalia onion
- 4 large eggs
- 1 cup HOOD'S CARB COUNTDOWN Fat Free Dairy Beverage
- ¾ cup shredded Cheddar CHEESE
- ¼ cup KRAFT 100% Grated Parmesan Cheese
- ¼ teaspoon pepper
- PAM Original No-Stick Cooking Spray
- 4 COBBLESTONE MILL 100% Whole Wheat Bread slices, cut into 1-inch pieces
- 6 tablespoons reduced-fat bacon bits

Sauté bell pepper and onion in a nonstick skillet over medium heat about 4 minutes or until tender.

Whisk together bell pepper mixture, eggs, and next 4 ingredients in a large bowl.

Coat a 2-quart baking dish with cooking spray. Layer bread cubes evenly in dish; pour egg mixture over bread, and sprinkle with bacon bits.

Bake at 350° for 30 to 45 minutes or until a knife inserted in center comes out clean. Serve immediately. **Makes** 6 to 8 servings.

DEBRA SCHRAMM
AMERICUS, GEORGIA

TEX-MEX CHICKEN-AND-BACON PIZZA

Prep: 20 min., Bake: 19 min.

- PAM All Natural Olive Oil Cooking Spray
- 1 (13.8-ounce) can refrigerated pizza crust
- ½ teaspoon ground cumin
- 1 cup black bean-and-corn salsa
- 1 cup (4 ounces) shredded Sharp Cheddar CHEESE
- 1 cup diced cooked PILGRIM'S PRIDE Chicken Breasts
- 4 OSCAR MAYER Ready To Serve Bacon Slices, diced
- ½ red onion thinly sliced and separated into rings
- ½ cup diced seeded plum tomatoes
- 1 cup (4 ounces) shredded Mexican FOUR-CHEESE BLEND
- 2 small jalapeño peppers, sliced and seeded
- 1 ripe avocado
- 1 lime, halved
- Sour cream
- Chopped fresh cilantro

Coat a 14-inch pizza pan lightly with cooking spray.

Unroll pizza crust; press or pat onto prepared pan. Lightly coat dough with cooking spray; sprinkle with cumin.

Bake at 425° for 7 minutes or just until crust begins to brown. Remove from oven, and reduce oven temperature to 375°.

Spread salsa evenly over crust; sprinkle evenly with Cheddar cheese. Layer with chicken and next 5 ingredients.

Bake at 375° for 9 to 12 minutes or until cheese melts.

Slice avocado. Squeeze lime over slices. Arrange slices in a spoke design on pizza; dollop with sour cream, and sprinkle evenly with cilantro. **Makes** 6 servings.

JIM BRADLEY
CHICAGO, ILLINOIS

VELVEETA Shells and Cheese
Brand Winner

SOUFFLEETA

Prep: 25 min., Cook: 15 min., Bake: 1 hr.

- **1 tablespoon margarine**
- **¼ cup fine, dry breadcrumbs**
- **2 quarts water**
- **1 (12-ounce) package VELVEETA Shells & Cheese**
- **¼ cup margarine**
- **¼ cup grated KRAFT 100% Parmesan Cheese**
- **1½ cups MILK, divided**
- **6 extra-large eggs, separated**
- **1 teaspoon paprika**
- **½ teaspoon dry mustard**
- **½ teaspoon salt**
- **⅛ teaspoon ground red pepper**

Grease a 2-quart soufflé dish with 1 tablespoon margarine; coat bottom and sides with breadcrumbs. Set aside.
Bring 2 quarts water to a boil in a 3-quart saucepan. Stir in shell macaroni from package; set cheese aside for later use. Cook 15 minutes. Drain. (Do not rinse.) Return to pan. Stir in ¼ cup margarine, Parmesan cheese, and ½ cup milk, stirring until cheese melts. Let cool slightly.
Process macaroni mixture in a food processor, adding remaining 1 cup milk in a slow, steady stream, processing until almost smooth. Add cheese sauce, egg yolks, and next 4 ingredients; process 30 seconds, stopping to scrape down sides.
Beat egg whites at high speed with an electric mixer until stiff peaks form. Gradually stir about one-fourth of cheese mixture at a time into egg whites. Spoon into prepared dish; place on baking sheet. Bake at 350° for 1 hour. Serve immediately. **Makes** 6 servings.

HAL SHUGART
BARBOURSVILLE, VIRGINIA

POST Selects Cereals *Brand Winner*

SOUR CREAM-BLUEBERRY MORNING PANCAKES WITH WILD BLUEBERRY-AND-PEACH TOPPING

Prep: 15 min., Cook: 5 min. per batch

You can toss the warm peaches with the blueberry sauce, or leave them separate for a beautiful presentation.

- **1 cup all-purpose flour**
- **¼ cup firmly packed DOMINO Light Brown Sugar**
- **4 teaspoons baking powder**
- **¾ teaspoon ground cinnamon**
- **½ teaspoon baking soda**
- **¼ teaspoon salt**
- **2 large eggs, beaten**
- **½ cup CRISCO Canola Oil**
- **½ cup 1% low-fat MILK**
- **½ cup sour cream**
- **½ teaspoon vanilla extract**
- **1¼ cups crushed POST Selects Blueberry Morning Cereal**
- **CRISCO Shortening**
- **Wild Blueberry-and-Peach Topping**
- **Whipped cream, fresh mint sprigs, DOMINO 10X Confectioners Sugar (optional)**

Sift together first 6 ingredients in a large bowl. Whisk together beaten eggs and next 4 ingredients; stir in cereal. Add to flour mixture, stirring just until dry ingredients are moistened. (Batter will be thick.)
Pour about ¼ cup batter onto a hot (350°), greased griddle or a greased nonstick skillet over medium heat; spread batter into a circle with back of a spoon. Cook pancakes 2 minutes or until tops are covered with bubbles and edges look cooked; turn and cook 2 to 3 minutes or until done. Top each serving evenly with Wild Blueberry-and-Peach Topping, and, if desired, whipped cream, mint sprigs, and confectioners sugar. **Makes** 14 pancakes.

WILD BLUEBERRY-AND-PEACH TOPPING:
Prep: 5 min., Cook: 5 min.

- **½ cup DOMINO Granulated Sugar**
- **¼ cup water**
- **1 tablespoon cornstarch**
- **2 cups blueberries**
- **1 (24.5-ounce) jar DOLE All Natural Sliced Peaches, drained**

Whisk together first 3 ingredients in a medium saucepan; stir in blueberries. Cook over medium-high heat, stirring constantly, until thickened and bubbly. **Heat** peaches in a small saucepan over medium heat until warm. Stir into blueberry mixture, and serve immediately. **Makes** 3 cups.

LAURA FISHER
FORT COLLINS, COLORADO

JELL-O *Brand Winner*

THE ULTIMATE NO-BAKE CHEESECAKE BANANA PUDDING WITH CARAMEL SYRUP

Prep: 30 min.; Chill: 6 hrs.

- **3 (8-ounce) packages PHILADELPHIA Cream Cheese, softened**
- **1 (14-ounce) can sweetened condensed milk**
- **1 (5.1-ounce) package JELL-O Vanilla Instant Pudding & Pie Filling**
- **2 cups MILK**
- **1 teaspoon vanilla extract**
- **1 (8-ounce) container frozen whipped topping, thawed**
- **½ cup caramel syrup**
- **4 large ripe bananas, sliced**
- **1 (12-ounce) package vanilla wafers**

Beat cream cheese and condensed milk at medium speed with an electric mixer 2 minutes.
Beat dry pudding mix and milk in a large bowl at medium speed with an

electric mixer 2 minutes; add vanilla, beat 30 seconds. Add cream cheese mixture, beat 1 minute. Fold in whipped topping.

Spoon one-third of pudding mixture into a 4-quart bowl; drizzle with 2½ tablespoons caramel syrup. Layer with one-third each of bananas and vanilla wafers. Repeat layers twice with pudding mixture, caramel syrup, and bananas, ending with vanilla wafers placed in a single ring, flat sides down, around edge of bowl. Cover and chill at least 6 hours. **Makes** 16 servings.

SUSAN RODGERS
ROUND ROCK, TEXAS

WILD AMERICAN SHRIMP *Brand Winner*

Texas Best Fried Shrimp

Prep: 40 min., Cook: 3 min. per batch

Make sure your bread is a few days old before you process it; this will give you perfectly dry breadcrumbs. Texas Best Fried Shrimp feeds a small army, so feel free to halve the main recipe as well as the sauces.

- 1 (16-ounce) loaf day-old very thin white bread slices
- 5 pounds frozen Certified WILD AMERICAN Shrimp, thawed
- 2 cups half-and-half
- ¾ cup sugar
- 1 large egg
- 2 cups all-purpose flour
- CRISCO Canola Oil
- Red Sauce
- Tartar Sauce

Process day-old bread slices, in batches, in a food processor or blender until medium-fine crumbs form.

Peel shrimp, leaving tails on. Butterfly shrimp by making a deep slit lengthwise down the back from the large end to the tail, cutting to, but not through, the inside curve of shrimp. Remove vein from shrimp. Pat shrimp dry with paper towels.

Whisk together half-and-half, sugar, and egg until sugar dissolves.

Dredge shrimp in flour; shake off excess, and dip in egg mixture. Coat with breadcrumbs, and arrange on baking sheets.

Pour oil to a depth of 3 inches into a Dutch oven; heat to 300°. Fry shrimp, in batches, 3 minutes; drain on wire racks over paper towels. Serve with Red Sauce and Tartar Sauce. **Makes** 18 servings.

Red Sauce:

Prep: 10 min.

- 2 cups chili sauce
- 2 cups ketchup
- 3 tablespoons fresh lemon juice
- 3 tablespoons grated fresh horseradish*

Whisk together all ingredients; cover and chill, if desired. **Makes** about 4 cups.

*Substitute 3 tablespoons prepared horseradish, if desired.

Tartar Sauce:

Prep: 10 min.

- 4 cups HELLMANN'S or BEST FOODS Real Mayonnaise
- 1½ cups finely chopped onion
- ¾ cup sweet pickle relish
- ⅓ cup plus 1 tablespoon fresh lemon juice
- 2 tablespoons dried parsley flakes
- ¾ teaspoon hot sauce
- 1 teaspoon Worcestershire sauce

Whisk together all ingredients; cover and chill until ready to serve. **Makes** about 6 cups.

JIM RUSSELL
DENISON, TEXAS

MARIE'S Refrigeraed Salad Dressing
Brand Winner

Southern-Style Fish Tacos

Prep: 20 min., Cook: 3 min. per batch

- 3 large limes, divided
- 4 (6-ounce) catfish fillets, cut into 1-inch-thick strips
- 1½ cups yellow cornmeal
- 2 tablespoons dried parsley flakes
- 2 tablespoons paprika
- 2 teaspoons ground red pepper
- 2 teaspoons lemon pepper
- 2 teaspoons salt
- 1 teaspoon garlic powder
- CRISCO Canola Oil
- 8 (6-inch) MISSION Corn or Flour Tortillas, warmed
- 1 cup thinly shredded green cabbage
- 1 cup thinly shredded purple cabbage
- MARIE'S Refrigerated Ranch Salad Dressing
- Salsa
- Toppings: ripe avocado slices, seeded and diced; ALABAMA Fresh Tomatoes, chopped; fresh cilantro

Squeeze juice of 1 lime over fish.

Combine cornmeal and next 6 ingredients in a large zip-top freezer bag. Pat fish dry with paper towels, and place in bag, shaking to coat.

Pour oil to a depth of 1½ inches in a large deep skillet; heat to 325°. Fry catfish in batches, in hot oil, 2 to 3 minutes or until crispy and golden brown. Drain on paper towels.

Place catfish in warmed tortillas; top evenly with cabbage, desired amount of salad dressing, salsa, and toppings. Cut remaining 2 limes into wedges, and serve with tacos. **Makes** 4 servings.

CARLA WHITFIELD
TALLASSEE, ALABAMA

MARGARITA MARINATED CHICKEN WITH MANGO SALSA

Prep: 10 min., Chill: 2 hrs., Grill: 12 min.

- 2 large limes
- 2 cups liquid margarita mix
- 1 cup CRISCO Vegetable Oil
- 1 cup chopped fresh cilantro
- 2 teaspoons salt
- ½ teaspoon ground red pepper
- 3 tablespoons tequila (optional)
- 6 PILGRIM'S PRIDE Boneless, Skinless Chicken Breasts
- 2 cups uncooked MAHATMA Long Grain White Rice
- PAM For Grilling No-Stick Spray
- Mango Salsa
- Garnish: fresh cilantro sprigs

Cut limes in half. Squeeze juice into a shallow dish or large zip-top freezer bag; add squeezed lime halves to juice. Add margarita mix, next 4 ingredients, and, if desired, tequila. Whisk (or seal bag and shake) to blend. Add chicken; cover or seal, and chill at least 2 hours or up to 6 hours. Remove chicken from marinade, discarding marinade.

Prepare rice according to package directions.

Spray cold grill cooking grate with cooking spray; place on grill over medium heat (300° to 350°). Place chicken on grate.

Grill chicken, covered with grill lid, 6 minutes on each side or until done. Serve over hot cooked rice. Serve with Mango Salsa, and garnish, if desired. **Makes** 6 servings.

MANGO SALSA:
Prep: 10 min.

- 2 mangoes, peeled
- 2 avocados
- 1 red bell pepper
- ½ red onion
- 1 tablespoon chopped fresh cilantro
- 1 tablespoon CRISCO Vegetable Oil
- Juice of 1 large lime (about 1 tablespoon)

Chop first 4 ingredients; place in a medium bowl. Add cilantro, oil, and lime juice. Cover and chill, if desired. **Makes** about 2½ cups.

DINAH VANHOOK
EL DORADO, ARKANSAS

SPICY BAKED BEANS

Prep: 15 min.; Bake: 45 min.

- 1 pound JIMMY DEAN Ground Pork Sausage
- 1 onion, chopped
- 2 (28-ounce) cans bold-and-spicy baked beans
- 1 (15-ounce) can black beans, drained
- 1 (15-ounce) can light or dark kidney beans, drained
- 3 cups bottled barbecue sauce
- ½ cup firmly packed dark brown sugar
- ¼ cup yellow mustard
- 1 teaspoon black pepper
- ½ teaspoon ground red pepper
- 1 teaspoon garlic powder (optional)

Cook pork sausage in an ovenproof Dutch oven over medium-high heat, stirring until sausage crumbles and is no longer pink. Drain, reserving 2 teaspoons drippings in Dutch oven.

Return sausage to Dutch oven, and stir in onion, next 8 ingredients, and if desired, garlic powder.
Bake at 350° for 45 minutes or until thick and bubbly. **Makes** 12 servings.

KELLY BLACK
CROWNSVILLE, MARYLAND

MY BEST TUNA SALAD

Prep: 20 min.; Chill: 1 hr.

- 1 (9-ounce) can solid white tuna in spring water, drained and flaked
- 1 medium-size Red Delicious apple, peeled and finely chopped
- 2 hard-cooked eggs, grated
- 1 small carrot, grated
- ½ cup finely chopped green onions
- ¼ cup diced celery
- ¼ cup mayonnaise
- ⅛ teaspoon salt
- ⅛ teaspoon coarsely ground pepper
- 12 COBBLESTONE MILL 100% Whole Wheat Bread Slices
- 6 lettuce leaves

Stir together first 9 ingredients. Cover and chill 1 hour.

Cut and discard crusts from bread slices, if desired. Spread 6 bread slices evenly with tuna salad. Top with lettuce and remaining bread slices. Cut each sandwich in half. **Makes** 6 servings.

GLENDA TATOM
STAMPS, ARKANSAS

CUBAN PULLED PORK TORTILLA PIE WITH SNAPPY MANGO SALSA

Prep: 25 min.; Chill: 3 hrs., Bake: 4 hrs., Cook: 5 min.

- 1 (2-pound) pork shoulder roast
- ½ cup orange juice
- ¼ cup fresh lime juice (about 4 large limes)
- 2 garlic cloves, minced
- 1 tablespoon lemon pepper
- 1 tablespoon chipotle peppers in adobo sauce, minced
- 1½ teaspoons dried oregano
- 1 teaspoon salt
- ½ teaspoon ground cumin
- PAM Original No-Stick Cooking Spray
- 1 (15-ounce) can black beans
- 4 cups coarsely crushed MISSION Tortilla Chips
- 2 cups (8 ounces) shredded Monterey Jack CHEESE with peppers
- Snappy Mango Salsa
- 1 cup light sour cream

Rinse pork, and pat dry. Combine orange juice and next 7 ingredients in a large zip-top freezer bag; add pork, and seal. Chill at least 3 hours, turning occasionally. Coat an ovenproof Dutch oven with cooking spray. Place pork in Dutch oven, and pour marinade over pork.

Bake, covered, at 300° for 4 hours or until meat shreds easily with 2 forks. Remove pork, and cool slightly. Shred pork, and keep warm.

Cook beans in a small saucepan over medium heat until thoroughly heated; drain.

Place 1 cup crushed tortilla chips on each serving plate. Layer each with ¾ cup shredded pork, ¼ cup black beans, ½ cup shredded cheese, ½ cup Snappy Mango Salsa, and ¼ cup sour cream. Serve with remaining salsa. **Makes** 4 servings.

SNAPPY MANGO SALSA:

Prep: 15 min.

- 2 cups diced mango
- 1 medium-size red bell pepper, diced
- ½ cup chopped green onions
- 1 tablespoon diced shallots
- 2 tablespoons chopped fresh cilantro
- 2 tablespoons fresh lime juice
- ½ teaspoon salt
- ¼ teaspoon ground red pepper
- ¼ teaspoon ground cumin

Combine all ingredients in a large bowl; cover and chill, if desired. **Makes** about 2½ cups.

JENNIFER BRUMFIELD
BELLINGHAM, WASHINGTON

TEX-MEX GRILLED BEEF "TENDERS," CORN AND TOMATOES WITH CHIPOTLE-LIME CREAM

Prep: 15 min., Grill: 18 min.

A beef chuck tender steak can also be used in this recipe.

- 1 tablespoon CRISCO Vegetable Oil
- 1 teaspoon chili powder
- 1 teaspoon ground cumin
- ½ teaspoon salt
- 2 (8- to 10-ounce) BEEF Shoulder Tender Petite Roasts
- 2 ALABAMA Green Tomatoes, cut into ½-inch-thick slices
- 4 ears fresh corn, husks removed
- CRISCO Vegetable Oil
- ¼ teaspoon salt
- ¼ teaspoon pepper
- PAM for Grilling No-Stick Spray
- Chipotle-Lime Cream

Stir together first 4 ingredients; rub both sides of roasts with oil mixture.

Brush tomato slices and corn with vegetable oil. Sprinkle tomato slices evenly with ¼ teaspoon salt and ¼ teaspoon pepper.

Coat cold grill cooking grate with grilling spray; place on grill. Grill, covered with grill lid, over medium heat (300° to 350°). Grill roasts 7 to 9 minutes on each side; sliced tomatoes 5 to 7 minutes on each side or until tender; and corn 15 to 18 minutes or until tender. Let beef stand 5 minutes; cut into thin slices. Serve with Chipotle-Lime Cream. **Makes** 4 servings.

CHIPOTLE-LIME CREAM:

Prep: 10 min.

- 1 cup sour cream
- 2 tablespoons chopped fresh cilantro
- 2 teaspoons grated lime rind
- 1 tablespoon fresh lime juice
- 1 teaspoon seeded, chipotle pepper in adobo sauce, minced
- ½ teaspoon sugar
- ¼ teaspoon salt

Stir together all ingredients; cover and chill, if desired. **Makes** about 1 cup.

PRISCILLA YEE
CONCORD, CALIFORNIA

SARA LEE Bakery Breads *Brand Winner*

Fried Green Tomato Po' Boys

Prep: 20 min., Fry: 4 min. per batch,
Broil: 2 min.

- 2 cups self-rising flour
- 3 tablespoons Cajun seasoning
- 2 cups CRISCO Canola Oil
- 3 large green tomatoes, cut into ¼-inch-thick slices
- 1 cup buttermilk
- 9 slices OSCAR MAYER Ready To Serve Bacon
- 3 SARA LEE Center Split Deli Rolls
- 6 tablespoons HELLMANN'S or BEST FOODS Real Mayonnaise
- 1 ripe avocado, sliced
- 1½ cups shredded iceberg lettuce
- Hot sauce (optional)

Combine flour and Cajun seasoning in a shallow dish.

Heat oil in a large nonstick skillet over medium-high heat to 360°.

Dip tomato slices in buttermilk, and dredge in flour mixture. Fry tomatoes, in batches, 2 minutes on each side or until golden. Drain on a wire rack over paper towels.

Heat bacon slices according to package directions.

Split rolls, and arrange, split sides up, on a baking sheet. Broil 5 inches from heat 2 minutes or until lightly toasted; remove from oven.

Spread cut sides of rolls with mayonnaise; place fried green tomatoes on bottom halves. Top evenly with bacon, avocado, and lettuce; sprinkle with hot sauce, if desired. Top with remaining roll halves, and serve immediately.

Makes 3 servings.

KELLY BAXTER
OLYMPIA, WASHINGTON

U.S. BEEF *Brand Winner*

Maple-Mustard-Glazed Balsamic Steaks With Blue Pecan Confetti

Prep: 5 min., Chill: 2 hrs., Cook: 3 min.,
Grill: 10 min.

- ⅓ cup balsamic vinegar
- ⅓ cup pure maple syrup
- 4 tablespoons Dijon mustard, divided
- 3 tablespoons chopped fresh thyme
- 2 (1-pound) BEEF Flat-Iron Steaks
- 1 tablespoon olive oil
- ⅓ cup chopped pecans
- 2 tablespoons maple syrup
- 1 teaspoon kosher salt
- ½ teaspoon pepper
- 3 ounces crumbled blue cheese
- Garnish: fresh thyme sprigs

Combine vinegar, ⅓ cup maple syrup, 2 tablespoons mustard, and thyme in a shallow dish or large zip-top freezer bag; add steaks, turning to coat. Cover or seal, and chill 2 hours, turning steaks occasionally.

Heat olive oil in a large heavy skillet over medium-high heat; add pecans, stirring to coat. Stir in 2 tablespoons maple syrup, and cook, stirring constantly, 1 minute. Remove pecans from pan, and spread on wax paper to cool.

Remove steaks from marinade, reserving marinade. Sprinkle steaks evenly with salt and pepper. Grill, without grill lid, over medium-high heat (350° to 400°) 4 to 5 minutes on each side or to desired degree of doneness. Keep warm.

Whisk together reserved marinade and remaining 2 tablespoons mustard in a small saucepan. Bring to a boil, and cook at least 2 minutes. (Sauce should be thick and syrupy.)

Cut steaks into ½-inch-thick slices; sprinkle with pecans and blue cheese. Serve with sauce. Garnish, if desired.

Makes 4 servings.

DIANE SPARROW
OSAGE, IOWA

More Brand-Winning Recipes

Crisco Oils, Shortening, and Cooking Spray: Crispy Coconut Chicken Dippers with Wowee Maui Mustard, page 324

Dole All Natural Fruit: Cuban Mojo Chicken With Mandarin-Black Bean Salad, page 318

Domino Sugar: Decadent Banana Cake With Coconut-Cream Cheese Frosting, page 317

Enova Brand Oil: Sloppy José Sandwiches With Cilantro Slaw, page 324

Hellmann's or Best Foods Real Mayonnaise: Pimiento Cheese-Stuffed Fried Chicken, page 322

Jennie-O Turkey Store: Crispy Ginger-and-Garlic Asian Turkey Lettuce Wraps, page 325

Kraft 100% Grated Parmesan Cheese: White Bean Soup With Gremolata, page 319

Nature's Own Breads and Buns: Toasted Pecan, Cranberry, and Gorgonzola Turkey Burgers, page 320

Pam No-Stick Cooking Spray: Double Whammie Yeast Rolls, page 323

Philadelphia Cream Cheese: Chocolate-Coffee Cheesecake With Mocha Sauce, page 316

Pilgrim's Pride Chicken: Herb-Grilled Chicken With Watermelon-Feta Salad, page 320

Christmas bonus
our editors' favorites

Molasses Pork Tenderloin With Red Wine Sauce

Garlic-Orange Roast Pork

Breakfast Enchiladas

Broccoli With Pimiento Cheese Sauce

Pepper Jelly-Glazed Carrots

Creamy Leek Mashed Potatoes

Cranberry Congealed Salad

Two-Seed Bread Knots

Basic Buttery Biscuits

Cranberry-Orange Glazed Biscuits

Coconut Cake

Mama's Fudge

Brunch Punch

Our Holiday Favorites

For many of our staff, Christmas wouldn't be the same without these recipes.

Mix & Match Menus

Easy Christmas Dinner
Serves 6

Molasses Pork Tenderloin With
Red Wine Sauce

Creamy Leek Mashed Potatoes
(page 334)

Broccoli With Pimiento
Cheese Sauce (facing page)

Cranberry Congealed Salad (page 334)

Two-Seed Bread Knots (page 334)

Coconut Cake (page 335)

Down Home Supper
Serves 6

Garlic-Orange Roast Pork

Pepper Jelly-Glazed Carrots (page 334)

Basic Buttery Biscuits or
Cranberry-Orange Glazed Biscuits
(page 335)

Mama's Fudge (page 335)

Make-Ahead Breakfast
Serves 6 to 8

Breakfast Enchiladas

fresh fruit

Brunch Punch (page 335)

Continental Breakfast
Serves 8 to 10

Cranberry-Orange Glazed Biscuits
(page 335)

fresh fruit

Brunch Punch (page 335)

MOLASSES PORK TENDERLOIN WITH RED WINE SAUCE

Prep: 10 min., Chill: 8 hrs., Grill: 20 min., Stand: 10 min.

Executive Foods Editor Susan Dosier says Red Wine Sauce adds an extra layer of flavor.

> 1 cup reduced-sodium soy sauce
> 1¼ cups molasses
> ¼ cup fresh lemon juice
> ¼ cup olive oil
> 3 tablespoons minced fresh ginger
> 2 large garlic cloves, minced
> 3 (¾-pound) pork tenderloins
> Red Wine Sauce (optional)

Combine first 6 ingredients in a shallow dish or zip-top freezer bag; add tenderloins. Cover or seal, and chill 8 hours.

Remove tenderloins from marinade, discarding marinade.

Grill tenderloins, covered with grill lid, over medium-high heat (350° to 400°) 20 minutes or until a meat thermometer inserted into thickest portion registers 160°, turning occasionally. Let stand 10 minutes before slicing. Serve with Red Wine Sauce, if desired. **Makes** 6 to 8 servings.

RED WINE SAUCE:
Prep: 5 min., Cook: 12 min.

> ½ small sweet onion, minced
> 2 tablespoons butter
> ½ cup dry red wine
> 1 (14½-ounce) can beef broth
> ¼ cup water
> 2 tablespoons cornstarch

Sauté onion in butter in a saucepan over medium-high heat 3 minutes. Add wine; cook 3 minutes. Add beef broth; bring to a boil, and cook 5 minutes.

Stir together ¼ cup water and cornstarch; add to broth mixture, stirring constantly, 1 minute or until mixture thickens. Remove from heat, and serve over tenderloin. **Makes** about 1¼ cups.

GARLIC-ORANGE ROAST PORK

Prep: 30 min.; Bake: 3 hrs., 55 min.; Stand: 20 min.; Cook: 1 min.

Former staffer Editor Kim Sunée, now at *Cottage Living,* combines the vibrant flavors of her childhood growing up in New Orleans.

> 2 cups chopped fresh parsley
> ¼ cup herbes de Provence
> 2 tablespoons grated lemon rind
> ¼ cup fresh lemon juice
> 1 (5- to 6-pound) Boston butt pork roast
> 1 tablespoon salt, divided
> 1 tablespoon pepper, divided
> 10 garlic cloves, divided
> 2 large oranges, sliced
> 2 tablespoons olive oil
> 2¼ cups orange juice, divided
> 4 pints cherry tomatoes
> 1 tablespoon cornstarch

Combine first 4 ingredients. Set aside.
Butterfly roast by making a lengthwise cut down center of 1 flat side, cutting to within 1 inch of bottom. Open roast; sprinkle with 1 teaspoon each of salt and pepper. Chop 2 garlic cloves, and sprinkle evenly over pork. Rub half of parsley mixture over pork; fold pork over to close, and tie at 1-inch intervals with string. Sprinkle with remaining 2 teaspoons each of salt and pepper on outside of pork.
Place orange slices in a roasting pan with remaining 8 garlic cloves; drizzle with oil. Place pork on top of orange slices; pour 2 cups juice over pork.

Christmas Bonus Section

Bake at 450° for 15 minutes; reduce heat to 325°, and bake, basting every 20 minutes, for 1 hour and 30 minutes. Add tomatoes to pan, and bake 2 more hours or until a meat thermometer inserted into thickest portion registers 150°, basting occasionally with pan drippings. Remove pork from oven, and coat with remaining parsley mixture.

Bake 10 more minutes or until meat thermometer registers 155°. Remove pork, orange slices, and tomatoes; cover with aluminum foil, and let pork stand 20 minutes for temperature to rise to 160° and juices to settle. Reserve drippings in pan.

Combine cornstarch and remaining ¼ cup orange juice; stir into drippings. Bring mixture to a boil, and cook, stirring constantly, 1 minute or until thickened. Pour sauce through a wire-mesh strainer, if desired. Serve pork with tomatoes, orange slices, and sauce. Makes 8 to 10 servings.

Breakfast Enchiladas

Prep: 20 min., Cook: 10 min., Bake: 30 min.

Associate Foods Editor Mary Allen Perry likes the make-ahead ease of this casserole. Prepare it, without baking, and refrigerate overnight. She lets it stand at room temperature 30 minutes; then bakes as directed. Tip: Make the Cheese Sauce before scrambling the eggs so the sauce will be ready at the proper time.

- 1 (1-pound) package hot ground pork sausage
- 2 tablespoons butter or margarine
- 4 green onions, thinly sliced
- 2 tablespoons chopped fresh cilantro
- 14 large eggs, beaten
- ¾ teaspoon salt
- ½ teaspoon pepper
- Cheese Sauce
- 8 (8-inch) flour tortillas
- 1 cup (4 ounces) shredded Monterey Jack cheese with jalapeños
- Toppings: halved grape tomatoes, sliced green onions

Cook sausage in a large nonstick skillet over medium-high heat, stirring until sausage crumbles and is no longer pink. Remove from pan; drain well, pressing between paper towels.

Melt butter in a large nonstick skillet over medium heat. Add green onions and cilantro, and sauté 1 minute. Add eggs, salt, and pepper, and cook, without stirring, until eggs begin to set on bottom. Draw a spatula across bottom of pan to form large curds. Continue to cook until eggs are thickened but still moist; do not stir constantly. Remove from heat, and gently fold in 1½ cups Cheese Sauce and sausage.

Spoon about ⅓ cup egg mixture down center of each tortilla; roll up. Place seam side down in a lightly greased 13- x- 9-inch baking dish. Pour remaining Cheese Sauce evenly over tortillas; sprinkle evenly with Monterey Jack cheese.

Bake at 350° for 30 minutes or until sauce is bubbly. Serve with desired toppings. Makes 6 to 8 servings.

Cheese Sauce:

Prep: 10 min., Cook: 8 min.

- ⅓ cup butter
- ⅓ cup flour
- 3 cups milk
- 2 cups (8 ounces) shredded Cheddar cheese
- 1 (4.5-ounce) can chopped green chiles, undrained
- ¾ teaspoon salt

Melt butter in a heavy saucepan over medium-low heat; whisk in flour until smooth. Cook, whisking constantly, 1 minute. Gradually whisk in milk; cook over medium heat, whisking constantly, 5 minutes or until thickened. Remove from heat, and whisk in remaining ingredients. Makes about 4 cups.

Broccoli With Pimiento Cheese Sauce

Prep: 15 min., Cook: 5 min., Bake: 20 min.

"Use any leftover sauce, along with your leftover turkey, to make a delicious open-faced sandwich," recommends Test Kitchens Director Lyda Jones.

- 2 pounds fresh broccoli, cut into spears
- Pimiento Cheese Sauce
- 1 cup soft white breadcrumbs
- 2 tablespoons butter, melted
- ⅓ cup shredded Parmesan cheese

Arrange broccoli in a steamer basket over boiling water. Cover and steam 5 minutes or until crisp-tender.

Arrange broccoli in a greased 11- x 7-inch baking dish. Pour Pimiento Cheese Sauce evenly over broccoli.

Combine breadcrumbs, melted butter, and Parmesan cheese; sprinkle evenly over cheese sauce.

Bake at 375° for 20 minutes or until thoroughly heated. Makes 8 servings.

Pimiento Cheese Sauce:

Prep: 5 min., Cook: 7 min.

- ¼ cup butter
- ¼ cup all-purpose flour
- 2 cups milk
- ¼ teaspoon salt
- 1 teaspoon Worcestershire sauce
- 2 cups (8 ounces) shredded sharp Cheddar cheese
- 1 (4-ounce) jar diced pimiento, drained

Melt butter in a heavy saucepan over medium heat; add flour, stirring until smooth. Cook, stirring constantly, 1 minute.

Add milk gradually, stirring constantly, until mixture is thickened and bubbly. Stir in salt and remaining ingredients. Makes 3½ cups.

Christmas Bonus Section

PEPPER JELLY-GLAZED CARROTS

Prep: 5 min., Cook: 14 min.

"In Texas, everyone has some type of pepper jelly on hand," says Vanessa McNeil Rocchio Test Kitchens Specialist/Food Styling.

- 1 (2-pound) package baby carrots
- 1 (10½-ounce) can condensed chicken broth, undiluted
- 2 tablespoons butter or margarine
- 1 (10½-ounce) jar red pepper jelly

Combine carrots and chicken broth in a skillet over medium-high heat. Bring to a boil, and cook, stirring often, 6 to 8 minutes or until carrots are crisp-tender and broth is reduced to ¼ cup. **Stir** in butter and pepper jelly, and cook, stirring constantly, 5 minutes or until mixture is thickened and carrots are glazed. **Makes** 6 servings.

CREAMY LEEK MASHED POTATOES

Prep: 35 min., Cook: 30 min.

Former Assistant Foods Editor Cybil Brown Talley gives this potato recipe a delightful tang by adding buttermilk.

- 4 pounds baking potatoes, peeled and quartered
- 1½ teaspoons salt, divided
- 3 or 4 large leeks
- 2 tablespoons butter
- ½ cup butter
- ½ teaspoon ground white pepper
- ½ to ¾ cup milk
- 3 tablespoons buttermilk

Bring potatoes, 1 teaspoon salt, and water to cover to a boil in a Dutch oven; boil 20 to 25 minutes or until potatoes are tender. Drain and keep warm.
Remove root, tough outer leaves, and tops from leeks, leaving 2 inches of dark leaves. Thinly slice leeks; rinse well, and drain.

Melt 2 tablespoons butter in a large skillet over medium-high heat; add leeks, and sauté 5 minutes. (Do not brown.)
Mash potatoes with a potato masher; stir in remaining ½ teaspoon salt, ½ cup butter, and next 3 ingredients. Stir in leeks. **Makes** 6 servings.

CRANBERRY CONGEALED SALAD

Prep: 30 min.; Chill: 8 hrs., 30 min.

For a special presentation, Associate Editor Mary Allen Perry chills the salad in individual teacups. "This works well for holiday luncheons," she says.

- 1 (12-ounce) package fresh cranberries
- ½ cup sugar
- 3 (3-ounce) packages raspberry gelatin
- 2 cups boiling water
- 2 cups cranberry juice, chilled
- 1 (8-ounce) can crushed pineapple, undrained
- 2 celery ribs, diced (1 cup)
- ⅔ cup chopped pecans, toasted
- Lettuce leaves
- Pickled peaches
- Fresh mint sprigs
- Garnish: chopped pecans, toasted

Process cranberries in a food processor 30 seconds or until coarsely chopped, stopping to scrape down sides. Stir together cranberries and sugar in a bowl; set aside.
Stir together gelatin and 2 cups boiling water in a large bowl 2 minutes or until gelatin dissolves. Add cranberry juice, and chill 30 minutes or until consistency of unbeaten egg white.
Stir in cranberry mixture, pineapple, celery, and ⅔ cup pecans. Spoon into a lightly greased 10-cup Bundt pan; cover and chill 8 hours or until firm.
Unmold onto a lettuce-lined platter. Fill center of ring with pickled peaches and fresh mint sprigs. Garnish, if desired. **Makes** 12 servings.

TWO-SEED BREAD KNOTS

Prep: 30 min., Stand: 5 min., Rise: 20 min., Bake: 17 min.

Test Kitchens Professional Rebecca Kracke Gordon serves these delicate rolls with honey butter.

- 1 (¼-ounce) envelope rapid-rise yeast
- 1 cup warm water (100° to 110°)
- 3½ cups bread flour
- 2 tablespoons sugar
- 1½ teaspoons salt
- 3 tablespoons olive oil
- 1 egg yolk
- 1 tablespoon water
- 1 tablespoon sesame seeds
- 1 teaspoon poppy seeds

Preheat oven to 200°. Combine yeast and 1 cup warm water in a 1-cup liquid measuring cup; let stand 5 minutes.
Combine flour, sugar, and salt in a heavy-duty mixing bowl. Add yeast mixture and oil. Beat at low speed with an electric mixer 1 minute; beat at medium speed 5 minutes.
Divide dough into 20 equal portions. Shape each portion into a 7-inch rope, and shape into a knot. Combine egg yolk and 1 tablespoon water; brush over rolls.
Sprinkle with seeds; place on parchment paper-lined baking sheets. Turn oven off, and cover rolls loosely with plastic wrap; place in oven, and let rise 15 to 20 minutes or until doubled in bulk. Remove from oven, and preheat oven to 400°. Discard plastic wrap.
Bake at 400° for 15 to 17 minutes or until golden. **Makes** 20 rolls.

Note: These rolls are named for their unique shape and a sprinkling of sesame and poppy seeds. To create this distinct look, roll each ball of dough into a 7-inch rope, then form into a knot. A pastry scraper makes cutting and working with dough much easier. Cover dough with plastic wrap or a clean towel to keep dough from drying out.

Christmas Bonus Section

BASIC BUTTERY BISCUITS

Prep: 10 min., Bake: 9 min.

Rebecca Kracke Gordon of our Test Kitchens keeps a dozen or two of these tasty gems in the freezer for drop-in company.

- 2¼ cups all-purpose baking mix
- ⅓ cup buttermilk
- 6 tablespoons unsalted butter, melted and divided

Stir together baking mix, buttermilk, and 5 tablespoons melted butter just until blended.
Turn dough out onto a lightly floured surface, and knead 1 or 2 times. Pat to ½-inch thickness; cut with a 1½-inch round cutter, and place on greased baking sheets.
Bake at 450° for 7 to 9 minutes or until lightly browned. Brush tops evenly with remaining 1 tablespoon melted butter. **Makes** about 2 dozen.

Note: For testing purposes only, we used Bisquick all-purpose baking mix.

To make ahead: Freeze unbaked biscuits on a lightly greased baking sheet 30 minutes or until frozen. Store in a freezer bag up to 3 months. Bake as directed for 8 to 10 minutes.

Cranberry-Orange-Glazed Biscuits: Decrease baking mix to 2 cups plus 2 tablespoons. Add ½ cup chopped dried cranberries to baking mix. Prepare dough, and bake as directed. Omit 1 tablespoon butter for brushing biscuits after baking. Stir together 6 tablespoons powdered sugar, 1 tablespoon orange juice, and ¼ teaspoon grated orange rind. Drizzle evenly over warm biscuits.

COCONUT CAKE

Prep: 20 min., Bake: 30 min., Chill: 1 day

"I never remember a Christmas without my mother's coconut cake," says Creative Development Director Valerie Fraser Luesse, who thinks this one is so easy because it starts with a mix. The frozen flaked coconut provides the cake's moist texture.

- 1 (18.25-ounce) package butter cake mix
- ½ teaspoon almond extract
- 3 (6-ounce) packages frozen flaked coconut, thawed
- 2 cups sugar
- 1 (8-ounce) container sour cream
- 1 (8-ounce) container frozen whipped topping, thawed
- Flaked coconut
- Garnish: halved kumquats

Prepare cake mix batter according to package directions, adding almond extract to cake batter.
Pour batter into 2 greased and floured (8-inch) round cakepans.
Bake at 375° for 28 to 30 minutes or until a wooden pick inserted in center comes out clean. (Do not overbake.) Cool in pans 10 minutes. Remove from pans, and cool completely on wire racks. Slice each cake layer in half horizontally. Set aside.
Combine 3 packages coconut, sugar, and sour cream, reserving 1 cup mixture.
Spread remaining mixture evenly between 3 cake layers. Fold whipped topping into reserved 1 cup mixture, and spread on top and sides of cake. Sprinkle top and sides of cake evenly with flaked coconut. Cover and chill 1 to 3 days before serving. Garnish, if desired. **Makes** 8 to 10 servings.

Note: For testing purposes only, we used Duncan Hines Moist Deluxe Butter Recipe Golden.

NANNETTE FRASER
HARPERSVILLE, ALABAMA

MAMA'S FUDGE

Prep: 10 min., Cook: 20 min., Cool: 30 min.

"My grandmother taught my mother how to make this fudge, and my mother, in turn, taught me," says Rebecca Kracke Gordon of the Test Kitchens.

- 2 cups sugar
- ⅔ cup milk
- ¼ cup unsweetened cocoa
- 1 tablespoon corn syrup
- ¼ teaspoon salt
- 3 tablespoons butter
- 1 teaspoon vanilla extract

Stir together first 5 ingredients in a 2-quart saucepan. Bring mixture to a boil over medium-high heat, and cook until a candy thermometer registers 240° (soft ball stage). Remove from heat; add butter, and let melt. (Do not stir.) Let cool 10 to 15 minutes or until pan is cool to the touch. Stir in vanilla.
Beat mixture at medium-low speed with an electric mixer 2 to 3 minutes or until mixture begins to lose its gloss. Working quickly, pour fudge onto a buttered 11- x 7-inch platter. Let cool 15 minutes. Cut into 1-inch pieces. **Makes** about 20 (1-inch) pieces.

ANNE KRACKE
BIRMINGHAM, ALABAMA

BRUNCH PUNCH

Prep: 5 min., Chill: 2 hrs.

Test Kitchens Professional Angela Sellers chills the juices before stirring together, eliminating the need for additional time in the refrigerator.

- 1 (46-ounce) can pineapple juice
- 3 cups orange juice
- 2 cups cranberry juice
- ¾ cup powdered sugar
- ¼ cup lime juice
- Garnish: fresh mint leaves

Stir together first 5 ingredients. Cover and chill 2 hours. Stir before serving. Garnish, if desired. **Makes** 3 quarts.

menu index

This index lists every menu by suggested occasion. Recipes in bold type are provided with the menu and accompaniments are in regular type.

>> menus for special occasions

Progressive Dinner
Serves 8
(page 47)
Butternut Squash-Parsnip Soup
Festive Pork Roast
Roasted Baby Vegetables
brown rice
dinner rolls
Dark Chocolate Mousse With
    Raspberry Sauce

Spring Holiday Menu
    (Passover)
Serves 6
(page 72)
Roasted Red Pepper Soup
Peppered Tuna With
    Mushroom Sauce
Dill-and-Almond Green Beans
Flourless Chocolate Torte
    or **Matzoh-and-Honey Fritters**

Luncheon Party Menu
Serves 8
(page 96)
Apricot Bellinis
Cheese Wafers
Cucumber-Dill Rounds
Smoked Turkey Tetrazzini
assorted fresh fruit
bakery rolls

A Cooking Party Menu
Serves 8
(page 122)
Sunset Vodka-Orange Sipper
Easy Spicy Caesar Salad
Grilled New York Steaks
Coffee-Onion Jam
Potato-Stuffed Grilled Bell Peppers
Mint Nectarines With
    Pineapple-Coconut Ice Cream

Breakfast in Bed
    (Mother's Day)
Serves 6 to 8
(page 136)
Southwest Breakfast
    Strata
fresh fruit
bakery muffins
Coffee-Ice Cream Punch

Cocktail Supper
Serves 8
(page 172)
Grilled Crostini With Olive
    Tapenade
Sewee Preserve's Seafood Salad
    with **Dill Vinaigrette**
Spicy Cheese Cocktail
    Biscuits
Citrus Bars
wine and beer

Football Fan Fare
Here's an idea for setting up a
    hot dog and salsa bar for
    hungry football fans.
(page 212)
Southwestern Salsa
    Dip
warm queso dip
hot dogs
tortilla and potato chips,
    pretzels
celery and carrot sticks
broccoli florets
purchased caramel corn
    and snack mixes
Margarita Punch
assorted soft drinks

Holiday Dinner
Serves 10
(page 248)
Rosemary-Thyme Rib Roast
Potato-and-Gruyère Casserole
Strawberry-Cranberry-Orange
    Salad

A Dazzling Dinner
Serves 10
(page 258)
Baked Honey-Raisin Brie
Spiced-and-Stuffed Pork Loin
    With Cider Sauce
Caramelized Onions
Cranberry-and-Toasted Pecan
    Couscous
Balsamic-Browned Butter
    Asparagus
Berry Bread Pudding With
    Vanilla Cream Sauce

A Casual, Comfortable
    Buffet
Serves 10 to 12
(page 276)
Whiskey Punch, wine, and
    assorted soft drinks
ham with rolls or muffins
Broccoli Casserole
Squash Casserole
Broccoli Slaw (double the
    recipe)
Nutty Wild Rice (double the
    recipe)
homemade bread
banana bread
pimiento cheese sandwiches
peanut butter-and-jelly
    sandwiches for children
macaroni and cheese for children
pound cake

>> menus for special occasions (continued)

Fabulous New Year's Menu
Serves 6 to 8
(page 280)
appetizer—host's choice
Peppered Beef Tenderloin With Portobello-Marsala Sauce
Potato-Leek Gratin
Autumn Salad With Maple-Cider Vinaigrette
white wine: Red Bicyclette Chardonnay
red wine: Yellow Tail Shiraz
sparkling wine: Domaine Ste. Michelle Cuvée Brut
Chocolate Fondue

Healthy Holiday Supper
Serves 8
(page 289)
Molasses-Coffee Turkey Breast
Roasted Potato-and-Bacon Salad
Sugar-and-Spice Acorn Squash
Gingered Green Beans
Mocha-Pecan Mud Pie

Beautiful Buffets
Adapt this menu for a Fabulous Affair for 24, a Smaller Gathering for 12, or an Intimate Party for 8.
(page 296)
Black Bean-and-Mango Salsa
Zucchini-Carrot Salsa
Avocado-Feta Salsa
Tuscan Pork Loin
Herbed Roast Beef
Golden Buttermilk Mashed Potatoes
Roasted Asparagus
Mama Dip's Carrot Cake
Mascarpone Pecan Pie
Chocolate-Dipped Cookies

Deck the Halls With Appetizers
Serves 8 to 10
(page 300)
Chicken Fingers With Honey-Mustard Sauce
Sausage-Stuffed Mushrooms
Pinecone Cheese Ball
Spicy Chipotle-Barbecue Sausage Bites
Bourbon-Mustard Glazed Sausage Bites
Sweet-and-Sour Sausage Bites
Asian Snack Mix

Easy Christmas Dinner
Serves 6
(page 332)
Molasses Pork Tenderloin With Red Wine Sauce
Creamy Leek Mashed Potatoes
Broccoli With Pimiento Cheese Sauce
Cranberry Congealed Salad
Two-Seed Bread Knots
Coconut Cake

>> menus for company

Taste of Texas
Serves 8
(page 58)
Fiesta Salad
Mini-Doughnut Stacks
margaritas

Flavor-Packed Supper
Serves 6
(page 68)
Salmon With Almonds and Parsley
Rice With Fresh Herbs
Tomato-and-Cucumber Salad
Accompaniments (optional): plain low-fat yogurt, pickled peaches, fresh radishes, green onions

Seaside Menu
Serves 6
(page 130)
Broiled Mahi-Mahi With Parsleyed Tomatoes
Greek Pasta Salad
French bread slices
Almond Sand Dollar Cookies
ice cream

Summer Supper
Serves 8
(page 158)
Pickled Shrimp
Shredded Flank Steak Mini-Sandwiches
Tangy Bean Salad with chips
Key Lime-Coconut Mini-Cheesecakes

Brunch for a Bunch
Serves 8
(page 169)
Confetti Omelet Casserole
Breakfast Turkey Sausage Patties
Brown Sugar-Baked Pineapple
Sparkling Orange Punch

Backyard Picnic
Serves 6
(page 188)
Honey-Pecan Chicken Strips
Old Bay Shrimp Salad
Bacon 'n' Onion Potato Salad
bakery cookies

>> menus for company *(continued)*

Vineyard Menu
Serves 8
(page 200)
Grilled Shrimp With Bacon and Jalapeños
Avocado Soup
Grilled Pork Loin With Rosemary-Breadcrumb Crust
Mixed Greens With Toasted Almonds and Apple Cider Vinaigrette
Pecan Fudge Pie With Raspberry Sauce

Italian Menu
Serves 8
(page 214)
Baked Ziti *or* **Rigatoni With Sausage and Bell Peppers**
tossed salad
Garlic Bread
Splendid Strawberries

Fun With Friends
Serves 6
(page 219)
Tomato-Basil Dip
Balsamic-Marinated Chicken
Orange Rice Pilaf
Gingerbread

Simple Sandwich Supper
Serves 8 to 10
(page 309)
Beef Tenderloin With Horseradish Cream
Blue Cheese Biscuits
vegetable and relish tray
Mulled Pomegranate Cider

Christmas Cocktails
Serves 8 to 10
(page 310)
Mushroom Turnovers
Cranberry Meatballs
Creamy Olive Spread with pita chips
wine and beer

Company's Coming Supper
Serves 4
(page 312)
Baked Pecan Chicken With Creamy Mushroom-Artichoke Sauce
Rosemary Baked Vegetables
romaine lettuce salad with Red Delicious apple slices
Apricot Vinaigrette
bakery brownies

>> menus for family

Chili Night
Serves 6
(page 20)
Chunky Beef 'n' Tomato Chili
Quick Creamy Vegetable Dip with assorted vegetables
Parmesan Cheese Breadsticks

Breakfast for Supper
Serves 6
(page 26)
Cream Cheese Scrambled Eggs
bacon *or* sausage
fresh fruit
Easy Pan Biscuits
iced coffee

Two Slow-Cooked Meals
(page 36)
Cowboy Pot Roast
creamy-style deli coleslaw
Texas toast *or* **Cheese-and-Onion Cornbread**
apple and pear slices sprinkled with cinnamon and sugar

Italian Pot Roast
green salad *or* Caesar salad
buttery garlic bread
apple and pear slices sprinkled with cinnamon and sugar

Take-Out Lunch
Serves 8
(page 142)
Bacon-Pimiento Cheese with crackers
Chinese Cabbage Salad
Favorite Chocolate Chip Cookies
iced tea

Five Budget-Friendly Menus
Serves 4
(page 42)
Meat Loaf With Green Chile-Tomato Gravy
Garlic Mashed Potatoes
Sautéed Squash and Carrots

Lemon-Garlic Roast Chicken With Sautéed Green Beans
Cornmeal Pudding

Baked Chicken Breasts
Pasta Pancakes and Gravy
steamed fresh broccoli

Pan-fried Pork Chops With Onions
Cheddar Cheese Grits
Fresh Spinach-and-Apple Salad With Cinnamon Vinaigrette

Cornmeal-Crusted Catfish Nuggets
Oven-Roasted Potatoes
Lemon-Apple Coleslaw

>> menus for family *(continued)*

Summer Supper
Serves 4
(page 170)
Quick Pan-fried Catfish
Broccoli-Squash Slaw
Lemon-Garlic Toast

Italian Tonight
Serves 4
(page 202)
One-Pot Pasta
Italian Tossed Salad
Basil-Garlic Bread

Weeknight Roast
(Serves 4)
(page 202)
Ginger-Glazed Pork
    Tenderloin
Sweet Carrots and Rice

Picnic Supper
Serves 4
(page 204)
Giant Ham-and-Pepper
    Salad Sandwich
Mixed Fruit Pilaf
Praline Bars
Cranberry Lemonade

Cajun Supper
Serves 6
(page 205)
Cajun Shrimp-and-Crab Sauce
    with grits, pasta, or rice
Sautéed Green Beans
Lemon-Blueberry Layered
    Dessert

Easy Greek Supper
Serves 4 to 6
(page 206)
Quick Hummus Dip
Easy Greek Flank Steak
Sour Cream Cucumber Sauce
Tomato-Feta Salad

Dinner for Four
(page 256)
Crispy Oven-Fried Catfish
Ranch Potatoes
Pecan Broccoli
Rosemary-Roasted Cherry
    Tomatoes
S'mores Sundaes

Cookin' With Kids
Serves 6
(page 282)
Crispy Brown Sugar Bacon
Cheddar Cheese Grits Casserole
Fruitini
Overnight Oven-Baked French
    Toast
orange juice

Down Home Supper
(Serves 6)
(page 332)
Garlic-Orange Roast Pork
Pepper Jelly-Glazed
    Carrots
Basic Buttery Biscuits *or*
Cranberry-Orange Glazed
    Biscuits
Mama's Fudge

Make-Ahead Breakfast
Serves 6 to 8
(page 332)
Breakfast Enchiladas
fresh fruit
Brunch Punch

Continental Breakfast
Serves 8 to 10
(page 332)
Cranberry-Orange Glazed
    Biscuits
fresh fruit
Brunch Punch

>> menus for grilling outdoors

Dinner Fast and Fresh
Serves 6
(page 16)
Shredded Grilled Tilapia Tacos
    with **Fruity Black Bean Salsa**
    and **Sweet-and-Spicy Slaw**
Ginger-and-Lemon Fruit Salad
Lemon-and-Dill Green Beans
Lime-Grilled Portobello
    Mushrooms
Two-Color Rosemary Roasted
    Potatoes

Laid-Back Dinner Menu
Serves 8 to 10
(page 54)
Three-Cheese Pasta Bake
Lexington-Style Grilled Chicken
Spinach-and-Strawberry Salad
Oven-Roasted Asparagus
Double Citrus Tart
iced tea
bread or rolls

Backyard Barbecue
    Menu
Serves 6 to 8
(page 166)
Tabb's Barbecue Pork
Honey-Mustard Barbecue Sauce
Creamy Carolina Coleslaw
Tomato-and-Onion Salad
Barbecue Deviled Eggs
Peach-Cinnamon Ice Cream

>> menus for grilling outdoors (continued)

Backyard Cookout
Serves 8
(page 180)
Italian-Style Burgers with
    Tomato-Basil Mayonnaise
Slow Cooker Barbecue Beans
chips and salsa
sliced watermelon

Smart Supper
Serves 6
(page 194)
Jerk Turkey Tenderloin
    With Raspberry-Chipotle
    Sauce
Easy Grilled Veggies
Romaine Salad With Cashews
Whole Wheat Popovers
Super Fast Strawberry
    Shortcake Parfaits
Iced Green Tea

Dinner off the Grill
Serves 4
(page 197)
Saucy Pork Chops With Orange
    Slices
Basil Rice Pilaf
Grilled Asparagus

Grill It
Serves 4
(page 202)
Raspberry-Barbecue Chicken
Sautéed Squash and Zucchini
Quick Parmesan Couscous

>> menus with local flavor

Dinner on the Chesapeake
Serves 4
(page 104)
Sweet Potato-Peanut Soup
Currant-Glazed Ham
Maryland Crab Cakes
Marinated Asparagus
Memmie's Spoonbread
Maryland Black Walnut Cake

Cajun Supper
Serves 6
(page 118)
Crawfish Jambalaya
Blackened Fish
mixed salad greens
crusty French bread
Pineapple-Apple Bread Pudding
    With Bourbon Sauce

Fiesta With Flair
Serves 6
(page 138)
Meaty Empanadas
Cinco de Mayo Shrimp Cocktail
Armadillo Eggs
chips and salsa
margaritas and Mexican beer

Southwest Supper
Serves 6
(page 202)
Tex-Mex Salisbury Steak
Cheesy Mashed Potatoes
Zesty Green Beans

Carolina Celebration
Serves 8 to 10
(page 244)
Grilled Oysters
    With Paul's Cocktail Sauce
Roasted Turkey
Barbecued Pork Tenderloin
Maple-Sweet Potato Casserole
Creamy-and-Crunchy
    Green Bean Casserole
steamed carrots
Cranberry Relish Salad
Coconut Layer Cake

South Beach Supper
Serves 8
(page 278)
Grilled Sweet Guava Chicken
The Ultimate White Rice
mixed salad greens
Rum Cake

Cuban Celebration
Serves 8
(page 294)
Ham With Garlic and Orange
Yuca With Garlic-Lime Mojo
Cuban Black Beans
Mojito
Buñuelos

recipe title index

This index lists every recipe by food category and/or major ingredient.
All microwave recipe page numbers are preceded by an "M."

Almond Sand Dollar Cookies, 130
Almond-Toffee Chocolate Chip Cookies, 87
Angel Cookies, 308
Apple Bread, 210
Apple Brown Betty, 232
Apple Cider Vinaigrette, 201
Apple-Ginger Vinaigrette, 230
Applesauce Gingerbread, 231
Applesauce Turnovers, 231
Apple Spice-Raisin Snack Mix, 222
Apple Stack Cake, 108
Apple Tea, 24
Apricot Bellinis, 96
Apricot-Glazed-and-Spiced Pork Loin, 259
Apricot Vinaigrette, M312
Armadillo Eggs, 139
Aromatic Curry-and-Spice Chicken, 238
Asian Snack Mix, 306
Au Gratin Potato Casserole, 250
Autumn Salad With Maple-Cider Vinaigrette, 281
Avocado Butter, 159
Avocado-Feta Salsa, 298
Avocado Soup, 159, 200

Bacon-and-Egg Quesadillas, 88
Bacon-Cheddar Grits Bread, 83
Bacon 'n' Onion Potato Salad, 188
Bacon Pasta, 224
Bacon-Pimiento Cheese, 142
Bacon Potato Salad, 171
Baked Beans and Ham, 45
Baked Brie With Blueberry-Ginger Topping, 179
Baked Chicken Breasts, 43
Baked Honey-Raisin Brie, M258
Baked Lemon-Dill Catfish, 216
Baked Pecan Chicken, 312
Baked Pineapple, 160
Baked Whole Sweet Potatoes, 108
Baked Ziti, 214
Balsamic-Blue Cheese Portobello Burgers, 53
Balsamic-Browned Butter Asparagus, 260
Balsamic Garlic-and-Herb Chicken Thighs, 19
Balsamic-Marinated Chicken, 219
Balsamic Onion Stacks, 141
Banana-Berry Smoothie, 24
Banana-Berry Split, 193
Banana-Mocha Shake, 45
Barbecue Deviled Eggs, 167
Barbecued Pork Tenderloin, 245
Barbecue Rub, 166
Barley-Pine Nut Salad, 126
Barley, Vegetable, and Fruit Medley, 127
Basic Buttery Biscuits, 335
Basil-Cheese Roulade, 143
Basil-Garlic Bread, 202

Basil Pesto-Cheese Grits Bread, 83
Basil Rice Pilaf, M197
Béarnaise Mayonnaise, 144
Beef Ravioli in Basil-Cream Sauce, 293
Beef Tenderloin With Horseradish Cream, 309
Beefy Pizza Casserole, 217
Benne Seed Pita Triangles, 97
Benne Seed Wafers, 111
Berry-and-Spice Whole-Wheat Muffins, 25
Berry Bread Pudding With Vanilla Cream Sauce, 260
Berry Delicious Summer Salad, 179
Berry Freeze, 220
Big "D" Smoked Baby Back Ribs, 174
Big "D" Smoked Chicken, 175
Bistro Grilled Chicken Pizza, M131
Black Bean-and-Corn Salsa, 297
Black Bean-and-Mango Salsa, 297
Black Bean-Chicken-Spinach Enchiladas, 95
Black Bean 'n' Spinach Enchiladas, 95
Black Beans and Rice, 214
Black Bean Soup, 120
Blackberry-Buttermilk Sherbet, 133
Blackberry Curd Filling, 182
Blackberry Juice, 182
Blackened Fish, 119
BLT Potato Salad, 213
BLT Wraps, 224
Blueberry-Buttermilk Sherbet, 133
Blueberry-Rum Marinated Pork Tenderloin, 178
Blueberry Salsa, 179
Blue Cheese-Bacon Slaw, 91
Blue Cheese Biscuits, 309
Blue Cheese Iceberg Wedges, 160
Blue Cheese Vinaigrette, 233
Boston Butt Roast With Gravy, 90
Bourbon-Mustard Glazed Meatballs, 305
Bourbon-Mustard Glazed Sausage Bites, 305
Bourbon Sauce, 119
Braised Red Cabbage, 236
Breakfast Burritos, 204
Breakfast Enchiladas, 333
Breakfast Turkey Sausage Patties, 169
Broccoli Casserole, M276
Broccoli Slaw, 278
Broccoli-Squash Slaw, 170
Broccoli With Almond-Lemon Dip, 292
Broccoli With Pimiento Cheese Sauce, 333
Broiled Mahi-Mahi With Parsleyed Tomatoes, 130
Brown Rice-Pine Nut Salad, 126
Brown Sugar-Baked Pineapple, 170
Brown Sugar Bananas, 45
Brown Sugar Bread Pudding With Crème Anglaise, 239
Brunch Punch, 335
Buffalo Wings, 64
Buñuelos, 295
Buttercream Frosting, 308

Buttermilk Baked Chicken, 213
Buttermilk Corn Sticks, 218
Buttermilk 'n' Honey Pancakes, 137
Butternut Squash Bake, 234
Butternut Squash-Parsnip Soup, 36
Butter Pecan Ice-Cream Sandwiches, 62
Butter Sauce, 124
Buttery Dijon Deviled Eggs, 93
Buttery Parmesan Topping, 277

Cabbage-Apple Salad With Sugared Pecans, 91
Caesar Iceberg Wedges, 160
Cajun Shrimp and Andouille Alfredo Sauce Over Pasta, 57
Cajun Shrimp-and-Crab Sauce, 206
Cajun Shrimp Casserole, 237
Candied Walnuts, 60
Caper Sauce, 105
Caramel-Apple Coffee Cakes, 210
Caramel-Apple Muffins, 210
Caramel-Apple Quesadillas, 223
Caramel-Coconut-Pecan Brownies, M288
Caramelized Onions, 259
Caramel-Pecan Cheesecake Bars, 210
Caramel-Pecan Pie, 269
Carrot Soufflé, 66
Celery Seed Dressing, 291
Chalupa Dinner Bowl, 238
Champagne-Chocolate Sauce, M282
Checkerboard Cheese Sandwiches, 18
Cheddar Cheese Cream Sauce, 277
Cheddar Cheese Grits, 43
Cheddar Cheese Grits Casserole, 283
Cheddar Crescents, 70
Cheese-and-Onion Cornbread, 35
Cheese Ring, 33
Cheese Sauce, 333
Cheese Wafers, 97
Cheesy Chicken Curry Casserole, 311
Cheesy Grits Bread, 83
Cheesy Mac 'n' Chicken Soup, 292
Cheesy Mashed Potatoes, 204
Cherry-Tarragon Chicken Salad, 275
Chicken-and-Artichoke Olé, 59
Chicken-and-Black Bean Soup, 102
Chicken and Bow Tie Pasta, 49
Chicken-and-Slaw Wraps, 222
Chicken-and-Strawberry Salad, 132
Chicken-and-Vegetable Stew, 235
Chicken Breasts With Artichoke-Pepper Sauce, 139
Chicken Filling, 117
Chicken Fingers With Honey-Mustard Sauce, 300
Chicken-Fried Steak, 67
Chicken Pudding, 22
Chicken Salad, 65, 94

Chile-Cheese Logs, 64
Chilled Blueberry Soup, 178
Chimichangas, 290
Chinese Cabbage Salad, 142
Chipotle-Lime Cream, 329
Chive-Tarragon Deviled Eggs, 93
Chocolate and Mint Cookies, 308
Chocolate-Bourbon Pecan Pie, 134
Chocolate Cake IV, 322
Chocolate-Caramel Sheet Cake, 210
Chocolate-Cherry Surprise Cheesecake, 273
Chocolate-Cinnamon Biscotti, 30
Chocolate-Coffee Cheesecake With Mocha
    Sauce, M316
Chocolate Cookies on a Stick, 63
Chocolate-Covered Cherry Pie, M216
Chocolate-Dipped Cookies, M299
Chocolate-Dipped Pecans, M269
Chocolate Filling, M307
Chocolate Fondue, M281
Chocolate Fudge Brownies, M288
Chocolate Fudge Cheesecake, M288
Chocolate Glaze, 221, M287
Chocolate Icebox Pie, 157
Chocolate Milk Shake, 193
Chocolate-Peanut Butter Pizza, 193
Chocolate-Red Velvet Cake Batter, 286
Chocolate-Red Velvet Layer Cake, 287
Chocolate-Walnut Pie, 134
Chunky Beef Chili, 235
Chunky Beef 'n' Tomato Chili, 20
Chunky Cherry-Double Chip Cookies, M87
Chunky Chicken Parmesan Salad, 209
Cider Sauce, 259
Cider Vinegar-Honey Dressing, 41
Cilantro-Lime Sour Cream Dip, 247
Cilantro Slaw, 324
Cinco de Mayo Shrimp Cocktail, 138
Cinnamon Crisp-Topped Cream Cheese-Banana-Nut
    Bread, 27
Cinnamon-Pecan Crumb Cakes, 287
Cinnamon Vinaigrette, 133
Citrus-and-Garlic Pork Roast, 294
Citrus Bars, 173
Citrus Cider Sipper, 23
Citrus-Pear Honey, 230
Citrus-Pear Honey Cobbler, 230
Citrus Rémoulade, 69
Cocoa Bread With Stewed Yard Peaches, 23
Coconut Cake, 335
Coconut-Cream Cheese Frosting, 317
Coconut Cream Pie, 110
Coconut Crust, 157
Coconut Layer Cake, M246
Coconut-Macadamia Chunk Cookies, 87
Coconut-Pecan Filling, 107
Coffee Concentrate, 136
Coffee-Ice Cream Punch, 136
Coffee Liqueur Ganache Icing, 322
Coffee-Onion Jam, 123
Collard, Raisin, and Pecan Sauté, 292
Columbia's Flan, 120
Confetti Omelet Casserole, 169
Confetti Pasta Salad, 242
Cookies on a Stick, 63
Cornbread Croutons, 45

Cornmeal-Crusted Catfish Nuggets, 44
Cornmeal Dough, 112
Cornmeal Pudding, 43
Country-Fried Steak With Creamy Salsa Gravy, 67
Country Ham Sauce, 109
Cowboy Pot Roast, 35
Cranberry-and-Toasted Pecan Couscous, M259
Cranberry-Apple Salad, 65
Cranberry-Apple Sparkler, 61
Cranberry Chicken, 272
Cranberry Congealed Salad, 334
Cranberry Lemonade, 205
Cranberry Meatballs, 310
Cranberry Muffins, 313
Cranberry Mustard, 320
Cranberry-Orange-Glazed Biscuits, 335
Cranberry-Orange Sauce, 218
Cranberry-Pecan Cake Batter, 287
Cranberry-Pecan Chicken Salad, 284
Cranberry-Raspberry Herb Tea, 61
Cranberry Relish Salad, 245
Cranberry Vinaigrette, 247
Cranberry-White Chocolate Cookies, 308
Crawfish Jambalaya, 118
Cream Cheese-Banana-Nut Bread, 27
Cream Cheese-Banana-Nut Muffins, 27
Cream Cheese Filling, 251
Cream Cheese Frosting, 232, 287, 299
Cream Cheese Ladybugs, 211
Cream Cheese-Pumpkin Bread, 251
Cream Cheese Scrambled Eggs, 26
Cream Sauce, 248
Creamy-and-Crunchy Green Bean Casserole, 245
Creamy-and-Sweet Coleslaw, 125
Creamy Bell Pepper 'n' Tomato Soup, 293
Creamy Berry Ladyfingers, 36
Creamy Carolina Coleslaw, 167
Creamy Chipotle-Black Bean Dip, 247
Creamy Dijon Lamb Chops, 82
Creamy Leek Mashed Potatoes, 334
Creamy Mac and Cheese, 208
Creamy Mushroom-Artichoke Sauce, 312
Creamy Olive Spread, 311
Creamy Pimiento Cheese Soup, 254
Creamy Raspberry Bites, 36
Creamy Shrimp-and-Spinach Pasta, 239
Creamy Tomato Soup With Crispy Croutons, 207
Crème Anglaise, 239
Creole Rémoulade Sauce, 69
Crescent Roll Apples, 231
Criolla Rémoulade, 69
Crispy Brown Sugar Bacon, 283
Crispy Coconut Chicken Dippers With Wowee Maui
    Mustard, 324
Crispy Croutons, 207
Crispy Ginger-and-Garlic Asian Turkey Lettuce
    Wraps, 325
Crispy Oven-Fried Catfish, 256
Croissant French Toast With Fresh Strawberry
    Syrup, 132
Crunchy Oat 'n' Cereal Cookies, 181
Cuban Black Beans, 295
Cuban Mojo Chicken With Mandarin-Black Bean
    Salad, 318
Cuban Pulled Pork Tortilla Pie With Snappy Mango
    Salsa, 329

Cucumber-Dill Rounds, 96
Currant-Glazed Ham, 104
Curried Butternut Squash Soup, 234

Dark Chocolate-Almond Crisps, M30
Dark Chocolate Chip Cookies, 87
Dark Chocolate Mousse With Raspberry Sauce, 31
Dark Chocolate Sauce, 31
Decadent Banana Cake With Coconut-Cream Cheese
    Frosting, 317
Deviled Eggs With Capers, 93
Dill-and-Almond Green Beans, 81
Dilled Potato Salad With Feta, 128
Dill Vinaigrette, 173
Domino Cookies, 19
Double Chocolate Chunk Cookies, 181
Double Citrus Tart, 55
Double-Stuffed Barbecue Potatoes, 162
Double Whammie Yeast Rolls, 323
Dried Apple Filling, 108
Dried Cherry-and-Pecan Oatmeal, 126

Easy Brunswick Stew, 292
Easy Chocolate-Mint Ice-Cream Sandwiches, 62
Easy-Does-It Mashed Sweet Potatoes, 250
Easy Greek Flank Steak, 207
Easy Grilled Veggies, 194
Easy Microwave Frosting, M63
Easy Pan Biscuits, 26
Easy Spicy Caesar Salad, 122
Easy Spinach, Pear, and Blue Cheese Salad, 41
Eggplant Fritters, 128
Egg Rolls, 50
Egg Salad, 209

Favorite Chocolate Chip Cookies, 142
Festive Pork Roast, 46
Feta-Stuffed Tomatoes, 148
Field Greens With Roasted Bacon-Wrapped Pears, 230
Fiesta Cabbage, 236
Fiesta Chicken Salad, 223
Fiesta Salad, 58
Fiesta Taco Lasagna, 140
Fizzy Raspberry Lemonade, 61
Fizzy Strawberry Lemonade, 61
Florentine Stuffed Onions, 141
Flourless Chocolate Torte, 81
Fluted Chocolate-Red Velvet Cakes, 287
Fresh Apple Upside-Down Cake, 231
Fresh Cherry Tart, 168
Fresh Fruit With Lime Syrup, 220
Fresh Herb Mayonnaise, 144
Fresh Lemon Vinaigrette, 242
Fresh Spinach-and-Apple Salad With Cinnamon
    Vinaigrette, 44
Fresh Strawberry Syrup, 132
Fresh Vegetable Penne, 101
Fried Apples, 109
Fried Buffalo Oyster Po'Boys, 48
Fried Buffalo Oysters, 48
Fried Green Tomato Po' Boys, 330
Fried Rice 101, 50
Frogmore Stew, 111

Frozen Blueberry Margaritas, 179
Frozen Hawaiian Pie, 157
Fruitini, 283
Fruit Salad With Honey Dressing, 137
Fruity Black Bean Salsa, 16
Fudgy Bittersweet Brownies, 253

Garden Eggplant Pizza, 127
Garlic Bread, 215
Garlic Butter Sauce, M253
Garlic Croutons, 247
Garlic French Bread, 57
Garlic-Herb Mashed Potatoes, 218
Garlic-Herb Two-Bean Salad, 209
Garlicky "Fried" Vegetables, 177
Garlic Mashed Potatoes, 42
Garlic-Orange Roast Pork, 332
Garlic Shrimp and Grits, 111
German Chocolate Cake, 107
Giant Ham-and-Pepper Salad Sandwich, 204
Ginger-and-Lemon Fruit Salad, 17
Gingerbread, 219
Gingered Green Beans, 290
Ginger-Glazed Pork Chops, 203
Ginger-Glazed Pork Tenderloin, 203
Ginger-Marinated Flank Steak, 216
Golden Buttermilk Mashed Potatoes, 298
Granny's Pound Cake, 269
Great Northern Beans With Tomatoes, 23
Greek Chicken Rollups, 128
Greek Iceberg Wedges, 160
Greek Pasta Salad, 130
Greek-Style Chicken, 220
Green Beans With Blue Cheese, 177
Green Chile-Tomato Gravy, 42
Green Onion Fans, 271
Gremolata, 319
Grilled Asparagus, 197
Grilled Balsamic Pork Tenderloin, 241
Grilled Cheese-and-Ham Sandwiches, 293
Grilled Cheese Sandwiches With Tomato, Avocado, and Bacon, 213
Grilled Chicken Thighs, 163
Grilled Corn on the Cob With Red Chile Paste, 118
Grilled Crostini With Olive Tapenade, 172
Grilled Lamb Chops With Pineapple-Mint Salsa, 52
Grilled New York Steaks, 123
Grilled Oysters With Paul's Cocktail Sauce, 244
Grilled Pork Loin With Rosemary-Breadcrumb Crust, 200
Grilled Shrimp With Bacon and Jalapeños, M200
Grilled Steaks Balsamico, 84
Grilled Stuffed Potatoes, 123
Grilled Sweet Guava Chicken, 278
Ground Beef-Tomato Sauce, 290
Guava Glaze, 279

Ham-and-Bean Soup, 45
Ham With Garlic and Orange, 294
Harvest Crunch Salad, 291
Hearty Ham-and-Collard Stew, 236
Hearty Healthy Breakfast Casserole, 325
Hearty Mac and Cheese, 208
Helena Tamales, 112

Herb-and-Garlic Goat Cheese Truffles, 143
Herb-and-Veggie Meat Loaf, 161
Herb-and-Veggie Turkey Loaf, 161
Herbed Roast Beef, 297
Herb-Grilled Chicken With Watermelon-Feta Salad, 320
Holiday Herb Butter, 284
Holiday Pork Chops, 313
Homemade Applesauce, 231
Homemade Salsa, 59
Honey-Apple Punch, 23
Honey Mustard, 203
Honey-Mustard Barbecue Sauce, 167
Honey-Mustard Dressing, 185
Honey-Pecan Chicken Strips, 188
Honey-Spice Butter, 274
Honey-Sweet Cornbread, 137
Hoover's Picnic Salad With Honey-Mustard Dressing, 184
Hoppin' John, 21
Horseradish Cream, 309
Horseradish Sauce, 177, 203
Hot Crab Dip, 124
Hot Fudge Sauce, 193
Hot Pecan Peas, 85
Hot Spiced Lemon-Appleade, 23
Hot Tomato Salad, 129
Huguenot Torte, 98
Hush Puppies, 99

Ice-Cream Bread, 252
Iced Green Tea, 196
Irish Strawberry-and-Cream Cheesecake, 273
Italian Caramelized Oranges, 101
Italian Parmesan Herb Mix, 284
Italian Pot Roast, 34
Italian-Style Burgers, 180
Italian Tossed Salad, 202

Jalapeño Hush Puppies, 99
Jerk Turkey Tenderloin With Raspberry-Chipotle Sauce, M194

Key Lime-Coconut Mini-Cheesecakes, 159

Lapsang-Poached Chicken Salad, 135
Layered Catfish Dip, 55
Layered Cornbread-and-Turkey Salad, 147
Layered Fruit Congealed Salad, M146
Layered Green Bean-Red Potato Salad, 146
Layered Lebanese Salad, 148
Layered Southwest Cornbread-and-Turkey Salad, 147
Layered Sun-dried-Tomato-and-Basil Spread, 275
Lemon-Almond Green Beans, 218
Lemon-and-Dill Green Beans, 17
Lemon-Apple Coleslaw, 44
Lemon-Basil Snaps, 275
Lemon-Blueberry Layered Dessert, 206
Lemon-Garlic Roast Chicken With Sautéed Green Beans, 43
Lemon-Garlic Toast, 171
Lemon-Orange Rolls, 70
Lemon-Pineapple Salad, 65
Lemon-Poppy Seed Cake Batter, 287

Lemon-Poppy Seed Muffins, 33
Lemon-Rosemary Mayonnaise, 144
Lemon-Walnut Tea Bread, 59
Lemon Whipped Cream, 255
Lemony Apple Salad, 241
Lexington-Style Grilled Chicken, 54
Light and Crispy Pan-fried Catfish, 198
Lightened Texas-Style Enchilada Casserole, 247
Light Pimiento Cheese-Stuffed Celery, 161
Lime-Goat Cheese Cheesecakes, 176
Lime-Grilled Portobello Mushrooms, 18
Linguine With White Clam Sauce, 49
Loaded Turkey Melt, 159
Low-Cal Dilled Yogurt Dressing, 128

Main Dish Turkey Salad With Cranberry Vinaigrette and Garlic Croutons, 246
Make-Ahead Spoon Rolls, 221
Mama Dip's Carrot Cake, 299
Mama's Fudge, 335
Mama's Mexican Minestrone, 254
Mandarin-Black Bean Salad, 319
Mandarin Orange-and-Almond Salad, 291
Mango Salsa, 328
Mango Upside-Down Cake, 120
Maple-Cider Vinaigrette, 281
Maple-Mustard-Glazed Balsamic Steaks With Blue Pecan Confetti, 330
Maple-Sweet Potato Casserole, 245
Margarita Marinated Chicken With Mango Salsa, 328
Margarita Pork Tenderloin, 85
Margarita Punch, 212
Marian's Iced Tea, 135
Marinated Asparagus, 105
Marinated Dill Green Beans, 129
Marinated London Broil, 84
Marinated Potato-Apple Salad, 41
Marinated Squash, 129
Marinated Vegetable Salad, 129
Maryland Black Walnut Cake, 106
Maryland Crab Cakes, 105
Mascarpone Pecan Pie, 299
Matzoh-and-Honey Fritters, 81
Meat Loaf With Green Chile-Tomato Gravy, 42
Meaty Cheese Manicotti, 34
Meaty Empanadas, 138
Mediterranean Antipasto Salad Platter, 220
Mediterranean Cheese Ball, 143
Mediterranean Pasta Salad, 220
Memmie's Spoonbread, 105
Millionaire Shortbread, M94
Mini-Doughnut Stacks, 58
Mini Sour Cream Coffee Cakes, 212
Mint Nectarines With Pineapple-Coconut Ice Cream, 123
Mint Peaches With Pineapple-Coconut Ice Cream, 123
Mint Truffle Brownie Squares, M254
Minute Steak With Mushroom Gravy, 67
Mixed Fruit Granola, 240
Mixed Fruit Pilaf, 205
Mixed Greens With Toasted Almonds and Apple Cider Vinaigrette, 201
Mocha-Almond-Fudge Ice-Cream Sandwiches, 62
Mocha Café au Lait, 306
Mocha-Chocolate Cream Filling, 322

Mocha-Pecan Mud Pie, 290
Mocha Sauce, 317
Mocha Shortbread, M307
Mojito, 295
Mojo-Marinated Chicken, 163
Molasses-Coffee Turkey Breast, M289
Molasses-Glazed Chicken Thighs, 85
Molasses-Grilled Rib-Eye Steaks, 218
Molasses Pork Tenderloin With Red Wine Sauce, 332
Mozzarella, Avocado, and Tomato Salad, 41
Mulled Pomegranate Cider, 309
Mushroom Turnovers, 310
My Best Tuna Salad, 328

Next-Day Turkey Dinner Bake, 246
No-Bake Ice-Cream Angel Food Cake, 107
No-Bake Peanut Butter Clusters, M211
Nutmeg-Molasses Cream, 104
Nutty Wild Rice, 278

Oatmeal-Raisin Chocolate Chip Cookies, 87
Oatmeal-Rum-Raisin Ice-Cream Sandwiches, 62
Okra Soup, 98
Old Bay Shrimp Salad, 188
Old-Fashioned Meat Loaf, 95
One-Pot Pasta, 202
Open-Faced Monte Cristo Sandwiches, 222
Open-Faced Philly Sandwiches, 32
Orange-Date Muffins, 215
Orange 'n' Jellied Cranberry Sauce Stacks, 270
Orange-Pecan-Topped Cream Cheese-Banana-Nut
    Bread, 27
Orange Rice Pilaf, 219
Orange Syrup, 240
Orange Tea Cooler, 216
Oven-Grilled Loaded Turkey Melts, 159
Oven-Roasted Asparagus, 55
Oven-Roasted Potatoes, 44
Overnight Oven-Baked French Toast, 283
Overnight Slaw, 208
Oyster Stew, 48

Pané Chicken With Sweet-'n'-Spicy Red Pepper
    Sauce, 320
Pan-fried Pork Chops With Onions, 43
Parmesan Cheese Breadsticks, 20
Pasta Pancakes and Gravy, 43
Paul's Barbecue Sauce, 175
Paul's Chicken Rub, 174
Paul's Cocktail Sauce, 244
Paul's Pork Ribs Rub, 174
Peach-Cinnamon Ice Cream, 168
Peanut Butter-Banana Pudding, 44
Peanut Butter-Chocolate Chip Cookies, 87, 222
Peanut Butter Streusel-Topped Cream Cheese-
    Banana-Nut Bread, 27
Peanutty Ice-Cream Sandwiches, 62
Pear Crisp, 214
Pecan Broccoli, 257
Pecan Catfish With Lemon Sauce, 56
Pecan-Chocolate Chip Cookies, 87
Pecan Fudge Pie With Raspberry Sauce, 201
Pecan-Honey Butter, 137

Penne With Greek-Style Tomato Sauce, 187
Peppered Beef Tenderloin With Portobello-Marsala
    Sauce, 280
Peppered Tuna With Mushroom Sauce, 72
Pepper Jelly-Glazed Carrots, 334
Peppermint Brownie Tarts, M288
Pesto Focaccia Sandwich, 131
Pickled Shrimp, 158
Pig Pickin' Cake, 63
Pimiento Cheese, 323
Pimiento Cheese Sauce, 333
Pimiento Cheese-Stuffed Fried Chicken, 322
Pineapple-Apple Bread Pudding With Bourbon
    Sauce, 119
Pineapple-Orange Herb Tea, 61
Pineapple Salsa, 86
Pinecone Cheese Ball, 300
Pinto Beans, Ham Hocks, and Rice, 46
Polynesian Pork, 90
Pomegranate-Champagne Cocktail, 282
Pork-and-Black Bean Soup, 32
Pork Saté, 53
Portobello-Marsala Sauce, 280
Potato-and-Gruyère Casserole, 248
Potato-Leek Gratin, 281
Potato-Stuffed Grilled Bell Peppers, 123
Praline-Apple Pie, 251
Praline Bars, M205
Praline-Pecan Brownies, M288
Praline-Pecan Cakes, 286
Praline Pecans, 286
Pronto Pork Fajitas, 223
Pumpkin Bread, 232
Pumpkin Crisp, 269
Pumpkin Fudge, 232
Pumpkin Spice Cake, 232

Quick Broccoli Skillet, 86
Quick Caramel-Coconut-Pecan Frosting, 211
Quick Caramel Frosting, 211
Quick Caramel-Pecan Frosting, 211
Quick Coconut-Pineapple Cake, 106
Quick-Cook Rice With Fresh Herbs, 69
Quick Cranberry-Apple Chutney, 231
Quick Crawfish Étouffée, 57
Quick Creamy Vegetable Dip, 20
Quick Herbed Turkey Gravy, 270
Quick Hummus Dip, 206
Quick Orange-Cranberry Sauce, 270
Quick Pan-fried Catfish, 170
Quick Parmesan Couscous, 203
Quick Parmesan Spinach, 292

Ranch-Barbecue Sauce, 163
Ranch Potatoes, 256
Ranch-Seasoned French Fries, 93
Raspberry-Almond Pear Tart, 230
Raspberry-Barbecue Chicken, 203
Raspberry-Barbecue Sauce, 203
Raspberry-Buttermilk Sherbet, 133
Raspberry Sauce, 31, 201
Raspberry-Tomato Aspic, 65
Raspberry Vinaigrette, 91
Red Beans and Rice With Sausage, 125

Red Chile Paste, 118
Red Pepper Hummus, 97
Red Sauce, 327
Red Wine Sauce, 332
Red Wine-Tomato-and-Steak Pasta, 140
Red Wine-Tomato Pasta, 140
Refreshing Lemon Sherbet, 133
Refreshing Lime Sherbet, 133
Reuben Quesadillas, 131
Rice With Fresh Herbs, 68
Rigatoni With Sausage and Bell Peppers, 215
Roast Beef-Cheddar Panini Sandwiches, 223
Roasted Acorn Squash With Cranberry Relish, 234
Roasted Asparagus, 298
Roasted Baby Vegetables, 47
Roasted Butternut Squash Salad With Blue Cheese
    Vinaigrette, 233
Roasted Camp Corn, 174
Roasted Corn-and-Black Bean Salad, 209
Roasted Fall Vegetables, 217
Roasted Potato-and-Bacon Salad, 289
Roasted Red Pepper-Caesar Tortelloni, M186
Roasted Red Pepper Soup, 72
Roasted Turkey, 244
Roasted Vegetable-and-Goat Cheese Pizza, 176
Roasted Winter Squash, 233
Romaine Salad With Cashews, 195
Rosemary Baked Vegetables, 313
Rosemary-Crusted Lamb With Tzatziki Sauce, 82
Rosemary-Roasted Cherry Tomatoes, 257
Rosemary-Thyme Rib Roast, 248
Rum Cake, 279
Rum-Coconut Key Lime Pie, 157
Rum Syrup, 279

Salad with Red Grapefruit-Lemon Vinaigrette, 161
Salmon With Almonds and Parsley, 68
"Salsafied" Sour Cream Dip, 247
Sara's Grilled Chicken-Cornbread Salad, 184
Satin Icing, 246
Saucy Pork Chops With Orange Slices, 197
Sausage-and-Chicken Cassoulet, 237
Sausage-and-Scrambled Egg Pizza, 88
Sausage-Egg Soft Tacos, 26
Sausage-Stuffed Mushrooms, 300
Sautéed Green Beans, 206
Sautéed Green Beans With Bacon, M160
Sautéed Squash and Carrots, 42
Sautéed Squash and Zucchini, 203
Savory Ham-and-Swiss Breakfast Pie, 240
Sawmill Gravy, 110
Scalloped Cabbage, 236
Scalloped Oysters, 47
Sesame-Poppy Seed Dressing, 55
Sewee Preserve's Seafood Salad, 173
She-Crab Soup, 98
Shortbread Thumbelinas, 307
Shortcut Greek Shepherd's Pie, 238
Shredded Flank Steak Mini-Sandwiches, 158
Shredded Grilled Tilapia Tacos, 16
Shrimp and Pasta With Creole Cream Sauce, 49
Shrimp Paste, 98
Shrimp Pitas, 188
Shrimp Rolls, 188
Shrimp Salad, 65, 95

Shuck Beans, 109
Simple Creole Sauce, 203
Simple Mashed Potatoes, 271
Simple Potato Latkes, 272
Simple Syrup, 135
Sloppy José Sandwiches With Cilantro Slaw, 324
Slow Cooker Barbecue Beans, 180
Slow-Cooker Barbecue Beef Sandwiches, 64
Slow-Cooker Beef Stew, 235
Slow-Cooker Cornbread Dressing, 270
Slow-Grilled Pork With Ranch-Barbecue Sauce, 163
Smoked Turkey Tetrazzini, 96
Smoked Turkey Tetrazzini with Artichokes and Red
    Bell Peppers, 97
Smoky Chicken Thighs, 184
S'mores Sundaes, 257
Smothered Enchiladas, 59
Snappy Fruit Salad Dressing, 160
Snappy Mango Salsa, 329
Souffleeta, 326
Sour Cream-Blueberry Morning Pancakes With Wild
    Blueberry-and-Peach Topping, 326
Sour Cream Cake Batter, 286
Sour Cream Coffee Cakes, 212
Sour Cream-Cucumber Sauce, 207
Sour Cream-Pecan Cake Batter, 286
Southern Peach-and-Blueberry Shortcakes, 318
Southern-Style Fish Tacos, 327
Southern-Style Turkey Cobb Salad, 214
Southwest Breakfast Strata, 136
Southwest Cheesecake, 249
Southwestern BBQ Chicken Pizza, 33
Southwestern Chicken-Corn Cakes, 321
Southwestern Fettuccine Alfredo, 186
Southwestern Salsa Dip, 212
Southwestern Squash Casserole, M217
Southwest Fried Oysters, 48
Southwest Mashed Sweet Potatoes, 271
Southwest Pork in Black Bean Sauce, 139
Spaghetti Squash Sauté, 234
Spaghetti With Mint-and-Garlic Tomato Sauce, 100
Sparkling Orange Punch, 170
Speedy Lasagna, M252
Speedy Rosemary Green Beans, 241
Spiced-and-Stuffed Pork Loin With Cider Sauce, 258
Spiced Applesauce, 231
Spiced Coffee, 307
Spiced-Glazed Carrots, 274
Spiced Soufflés With Lemon Whipped Cream, 255
Spice Rub, 259
Spicy Baked Beans, 328
Spicy Cheddar-Stuffed Burgers, 163
Spicy Cheese Cocktail Biscuits, 173
Spicy Chipotle-Barbecue Meatballs, 305
Spicy Chipotle-Barbecue Sausage Bites, 305
Spicy Huevos Rancheros, 221
Spicy Sparkling Punch, 24
Spiked Strawberry-Lime Ice-Cream Pie, 89
Spinach-and-Strawberry Salad, 55
Spinach-Endive Salad With Warm Vinaigrette, 291
Spinach Madeleine, 95
Spinach Soufflé, 66
Splendid Strawberries, 215
Spring Salad With Raspberry Vinaigrette, 91
Squash Casserole, 277
Steak-and-Spinach Salad With Hot Pan Dressing, 19

Stewed Yard Peaches, 23
Stir-fried Asparagus With Garlic, 86
Stir-fried Cabbage, 86
Stir-fry Pork, 241
Strawberry-Balsamic Vinaigrette, 84
Strawberry-Citrus Chicken Salad, 84
Strawberry-Cranberry-Orange Salad, 249
Strawberry-Lime Ice-Cream Pie, 89
Strawberry-Rhubarb Pie, 132
Strawberry Salad With Cinnamon Vinaigrette, 133
Strawberry Smoothie Ice-Cream Pie, 89
Stuffed Jumbo Shrimp, 124
Succotash Rice Toss, 218
Sugar-and-Spice Acorn Squash, 289
Sugar-and-Spice Nuts, 274
Sugared Curried Walnuts, 281
Sun-dried Tomato-Herb Bread, 252
Sunset Vodka-Orange Sipper, 122
Super Fast Strawberry Shortcake Parfaits, 196
Sweet-and-Sour Meatballs, 305
Sweet-and-Sour Sausage Bites, 305
Sweet-and-Spicy Slaw, 17
Sweet-and-Tart Red Cabbage Coleslaw, 125
Sweet Broccoli Slaw Salad, 91
Sweet Carrots and Rice, 203
Sweet Corn Pudding, 66
Sweetened Whipped Cream, 132
Sweet-Hot Asian Noodle Bowl, 187
Sweet-Hot Honey Mustard, 284
Sweet-'n'-Spicy Red Pepper Sauce, 321
Sweet Pepper-Mango Salsa, 148
Sweet Potato Biscuits, 22
Sweet Potato Cornbread, 252
Sweet Potato-Peanut Soup, 104
Sweet Potato Salad, 171
Sweet Potato Soufflé, 110
Sweet Spice Blend, 274
Swiss Cheese Cream Sauce, 277

Tabb's Barbecue Pork, 166
Taco Dinner Mac and Cheese, 208
Tangy-and-Sweet Roast Beef Wraps, 92
Tangy Bean Salad, 158
Tangy Cabbage Salad, 162
Tartar Sauce, 327
Tea-Thyme Grilled Chicken, M52
Texas Best Fried Shrimp, 327
Texas Rockets, 175
Texas-Style Enchilada Casserole, 247
Tex-Mex Chicken-and-Bacon Pizza, 325
Tex-Mex Grilled Beef "Tenders," Corn and Tomatoes
    With Chipotle-Lime Cream, 329
Tex-Mex Lasagna, 58
Tex-Mex Popcorn, 204
Tex-Mex Salisbury Steak, 204
Thai Pork Chops With Caramelized Onions, 85
The Ultimate No-Bake Cheesecake Banana Pudding
    With Caramel Syrup, 326
The Ultimate White Rice, 279
Three-Cheese Pasta Bake, 54
Three-Potato Mash, 271
Toasted Coconut-Topped Cream Cheese-Banana-Nut
    Bread, 27
Toasted Pecan, Cranberry, and Gorgonzola Turkey
    Burgers, 320

Toffee-Topped Cream Cheese-Banana-Nut Bread, 27
Tomato-and-Cucumber Salad, 69
Tomato-and-Onion Salad, 167
Tomato-and-Sweet Onion Salad, 141
Tomato, Basil and Corn Relish, 321
Tomato-Basil Dip, 219
Tomato-Basil Mayonnaise, 180
Tomato-Black Olive Grits Bread, 83
Tomato Casserole, 22
Tomato-Feta Lettuce Salad, 207
Tomato-Feta Salad, 207
Tom's Roasted Chicken With Wilted Salad
    Greens, 185
Traditional Crawfish Étouffée, 56
Triple-Chocolate Cake, 221
Turkey, Bacon, and Havarti Sandwich, 92
Turtle Cake Squares, M211
Tuscan Pork Loin, 296
Two-Color Rosemary Roasted Potatoes, 18
Two-Seed Bread Knots, 334
Two Tomato Linguine, 187
Tzatziki Sauce, 82

Ultimate Chocolate Chip Cookies, 87
Uncle Frank's Crab Cakes, 124
Uptown Collards, 21

Vanilla Cream Sauce, 260
Vanilla Glaze, 287
Vanilla-Jasmine-Sour Cream Tea Cake, 135
Vanilla-Scented Fruit Salad, 209
Verla's Hot Tea, 257
Vietnamese Fajitas (Bo Nuong Xa), 117

Waffle Taco Sundaes, M62
Watermelon-Feta Salad, 320
Wayne's "French 75," 282
Whipped Cream, 269
Whipped Cream Frosting, 107
Whiskey Punch, 276
White Barbecue Sauce, 196
White Bean-and-Asparagus Salad, 100
White Bean Soup With Gremolata, 319
White Grape-and-Orange Cooler, 61
White Wine-Tomato-and-Clam Pasta, 140
Whole Wheat Popovers, 195
Wild Blueberry-and-Peach Topping, 326
Wild Rice-and-Chicken Bowl, 127
Wilted Greens and Red Beans, 21
Wilted Salad Greens, 185
Wowee Maui Mustard, 324

Yogurt Sauce, 321
Yuca With Garlic-Lime Mojo, 294

Zesty Fried Pork Bites, 90
Zesty Green Beans, 204
Zesty Lemon Pie, 157
Zesty Poblano-and-Cheese Casserole, 311
Zesty Vinegar Coleslaw, M125
Zucchini-Carrot Salsa, 298

month-by-month index

This index alphabetically lists every food article and accompanying recipes by month. All microwave recipe page numbers are preceded by an "M."

January

A Cozy Breakfast, 26
Cream Cheese Scrambled Eggs, 26
Easy Pan Biscuits, 26
Banana-Nut Bread, 26
Cream Cheese-Banana-Nut Bread, 27
Chili Tonight, 20
Chunky Beef 'n' Tomato Chili, 20
Parmesan Cheese Breadsticks, 20
Quick Creamy Vegetable Dip, 20
Down-Home and Delicious, 22
Chicken Pudding, 22
Cocoa Bread With Stewed Yard
Peaches, 23
Great Northern Beans With Tomatoes, 23
Stewed Yard Peaches, 23
Sweet Potato Biscuits, 22
Tomato Casserole, 22
Everyday Choices, 24
Banana-Berry Smoothie, 24
Berry-and-Spice Whole-Wheat Muffins, 25
Family Friendly, 16
Fruity Black Bean Salsa, 16
Ginger-and-Lemon Fruit Salad, 17
Lemon-and-Dill Green Beans, 17
Lime-Grilled Portobello Mushrooms, 18
Shredded Grilled Tilapia Tacos, 16
Sweet-and-Spicy Slaw, 17
Two-Color Rosemary Roasted Potatoes, 18
Family Game Night, 18
Checkerboard Cheese Sandwiches, 18
Domino Cookies, 19
Fast Meat-and-Sauce Meals, 19
Balsamic Garlic-and-Herb Chicken
Thighs, 19
Steak-and-Spinach Salad With Hot Pan
Dressing, 19
From Our Kitchen, 28
All about panini sandwiches, 28
Greens Made Simple, 21
Uptown Collards, 21
Wilted Greens and Red Beans, 21
Hoppin' John, 21
Hoppin' John, 21
The Comfort of Cider, 23
Apple Tea, 24
Citrus Cider Sipper, 23
Honey-Apple Punch, 23
Hot Spiced Lemon-Appleade, 23
Spicy Sparkling Punch, 24

February

Banana Bonanza, 44
Banana-Mocha Shake, 45
Brown Sugar Bananas, 45
Peanut Butter-Banana Pudding, 44
5 Money-Saving Menus, 42
Baked Chicken Breasts, 43
Cheddar Cheese Grits, 43
Cornmeal-Crusted Catfish Nuggets, 44
Cornmeal Pudding, 43
Fresh Spinach-and-Apple Salad With
Cinnamon Vinaigrette, 44
Garlic Mashed Potatoes, 42
Lemon-Apple Coleslaw, 44
Lemon-Garlic Roast Chicken With Sautéed
Green Beans, 43
Meat Loaf With Green Chile-Tomato Gravy, 42
Oven-Roasted Potatoes, 44
Pan-fried Pork Chops With Onions, 43
Pasta Pancakes and Gravy, 43
Sautéed Squash and Carrots, 42
From Our Kitchen, 50
Egg Rolls, 50
Fried Rice 101, 50
Good-for-You Chocolate, 30
Chocolate-Cinnamon Biscotti, 30
Dark Chocolate-Almond Crisps, M30
Dark Chocolate Mousse With Raspberry
Sauce, 31
Dark Chocolate Sauce, 31
Ham and Beans, 45
Baked Beans and Ham, 45
Ham-and-Bean Soup, 45
Pinto Beans, Ham Hocks, and Rice, 46
Keep It Casual, 36
Butternut Squash-Parsnip Soup, 36
Creamy Raspberry Bites, 36
One Dressing, Three Salads, 41
Cider Vinegar-Honey Dressing, 41
Easy Spinach, Pear, and Blue Cheese Salad, 41
Marinated Potato-Apple Salad, 41
Mozzarella, Avocado, and Tomato Salad, 41
Oysters, 47
Oyster Stew, 48
Scalloped Oysters, 47
Southwest Fried Oysters, 48
Pasta Suppers Ready in Minutes, 49
Chicken and Bow Tie Pasta, 49
Linguine With White Clam Sauce, 49
Shrimp and Pasta With Creole Cream Sauce, 49

Pot Roasts, 34
Cheese-and-Onion Cornbread, 35
Cowboy Pot Roast, 35
Italian Pot Roast, 34
Table-to-Table Dinner, 46
Festive Pork Roast, 46
Roasted Baby Vegetables, 47
The Kitchen: Recipe for Style, 32
Cheese Ring, 33
Lemon-Poppy Seed Muffins, 33
Meaty Cheese Manicotti, 34
Open-Faced Philly Sandwiches, 32
Pork-and-Black Bean Soup, 32
Southwestern BBQ Chicken Pizza, 33

March

Add Zest With Lemon, 59
Lemon-Walnut Tea Bread, 59
Bake These Southern Sides, 66
Carrot Soufflé, 66
Spinach Soufflé, 66
Sweet Corn Pudding, 66
Entertaining That's Simple, 60
Candied Walnuts, 60
Family-Favorite Casseroles, 58
Chicken-and-Artichoke Olé, 59
Smothered Enchiladas, 59
Tex-Mex Lasagna, 58
Freshen a Menu With Herbs, 68
Rice With Fresh Herbs, 68
Salmon With Almonds and Parsley, 68
Tomato-and-Cucumber Salad, 69
From Our Kitchen, 70
Cheddar Crescents, 70
Lemon-Orange Rolls, 70
Fruity Thirst Quenchers, 61
Cranberry-Apple Sparkler, 61
Fizzy Raspberry Lemonade, 61
Pineapple-Orange Herb Tea, 61
White Grape-and-Orange Cooler, 61
Good for the Soul, 56
Cajun Shrimp and Andouille Alfredo Sauce
Over Pasta, 57
Garlic French Bread, 57
Quick Crawfish Étouffée, 57
Traditional Crawfish Étouffée, 56
Hooked on Catfish, 55
Layered Catfish Dip, 55
Pecan Catfish With Lemon Sauce, 56

Irresistible Ice-Cream Sandwiches, 62
Easy Chocolate-Mint Ice-Cream
Sandwiches, 62
Peanutty Ice-Cream Sandwiches, 62
Waffle Taco Sundaes, M62
Laid-back Sunday Dinner, 54
Double Citrus Tart, 55
Lexington-Style Grilled Chicken, 54
Oven-Roasted Asparagus, 55
Spinach-and-Strawberry Salad, 55
Three-Cheese Pasta Bake, 54
Lollipop Cookies, 62
Cookies on a Stick, 63
March Madness, 64
Buffalo Wings, 64
Chile-Cheese Logs, 64
Slow-Cooker Barbecue Beef Sandwiches, 64
Ready, Set, Serve, 64
Cranberry-Apple Salad, 65
Lemon-Pineapple Salad, 65
Raspberry-Tomato Aspic, 65
Rémoulade Sauce, 69
Creole Rémoulade Sauce, 69
Criolla Rémoulade, 69
Season's First Grilling, 52
Balsamic-Blue Cheese Portobello Burgers, 53
Grilled Lamb Chops With Pineapple-Mint
Salsa, 52
Pork Saté, 53
Tea-Thyme Grilled Chicken, M52
Speedy Steaks Fried Right, 67
Chicken-Fried Steak, 67
Country-Fried Steak With Creamy Salsa Gravy, 67
Minute Steak With Mushroom Gravy, 67
Tex-Mex Tonight, 58
Fiesta Salad, 58
Mini-Doughnut Stacks, 58
You'll Love This Easy-Does-It Cake, 63
Pig Pickin' Cake, 63

April

Cut Up a Pineapple With Ease, 86
Pineapple Salsa, 86
Easy Menu for Passover, 72
Dill-and-Almond Green Beans, 81
Flourless Chocolate Torte, 81
Matzoh-and-Honey Fritters, 81
Peppered Tuna With Mushroom Sauce, 72
Roasted Red Pepper Soup, 72
Family Weekend Breakfast, 88
Bacon-and-Egg Quesadillas, 88
Sausage-and-Scrambled Egg Pizza, 88
Flavor Lamb With Fresh Herbs, 82
Creamy Dijon Lamb Chops, 82
Rosemary-Crusted Lamb With Tzatziki
Sauce, 82
From Our Kitchen, 102
Chicken-and-Black Bean Soup, 102

Good to the Last Bite, 89
Spiked Strawberry-Lime Ice-Cream Pie, 89
Strawberry Smoothie Ice-Cream Pie, 89
Grilling Smarter, 84
Grilled Steaks Balsamico, 84
Margarita Pork Tenderloin, 85
Marinated London Broil, 84
Molasses-Glazed Chicken Thighs, 85
Strawberry-Citrus Chicken Salad, 84
Thai Pork Chops With Caramelized
Onions, 85
Have a Deli-Style Dinner, 92
Ranch-Seasoned French Fries, 93
Tangy-and-Sweet Roast Beef Wraps, 92
Turkey, Bacon, and Havarti Sandwich, 92
Hush Puppies, 99
Hush Puppies, 99
Italian Made Fresh, 100
Fresh Vegetable Penne, 101
Italian Caramelized Oranges, 101
Spaghetti With Mint-and-Garlic Tomato
Sauce, 100
White Bean-and-Asparagus Salad, 100
Lunch in the Lowcountry, 98
Huguenot Torte, 98
Okra Soup, 98
She-Crab Soup, 98
Shrimp Paste, 98
Make Bread in the Mixer, 83
Cheesy Grits Bread, 83
Milk and Cookies Anytime, 87
Ultimate Chocolate Chip Cookies, 87
New-Fashioned Luncheon Party, 96
Apricot Bellinis, 96
Cucumber-Dill Rounds, 96
Smoked Turkey Tetrazzini, 96
Savor Easy Pork Roast, 90
Boston Butt Roast With Gravy, 90
Polynesian Pork, 90
Zesty Fried Pork Bites, 90
Speedy Appetizers, 97
Benne Seed Pita Triangles, 97
Cheese Wafers, 97
Red Pepper Hummus, 97
Start With Slaw Mix, 91
Blue Cheese-Bacon Slaw, 91
Cabbage-Apple Salad With Sugared Pecans, 91
Spring Salad With Raspberry Vinaigrette, 91
Sweet Broccoli Slaw Salad, 91
Stir Up Some Veggies, 85
Hot Pecan Peas, 85
Quick Broccoli Skillet, 86
Stir-fried Asparagus With Garlic, 86
Stir-fried Cabbage, 86
Stuff a Dozen (or Two), 93
Buttery Dijon Deviled Eggs, 93
Chive-Tarragon Deviled Eggs, 93
Deviled Eggs With Capers, 93
To Market, To Market, 94
Black Bean 'n' Spinach Enchiladas, 95

Chicken Salad, 94
Millionaire Shortbread, M94
Old-Fashioned Meat Loaf, 95
Spinach Madeleine, 95

Southern Living® Favorites

A Southern Sampler, 110
Coconut Cream Pie, 110
Sawmill Gravy, 110
Sweet Potato Soufflé, 110
A Taste of Sunshine, 120
Black Bean Soup, 120
Columbia's Flan, 120
Mango Upside-Down Cake, 120
Bayou Cooking, 118
Blackened Fish, 119
Crawfish Jambalaya, 118
Pineapple-Apple Bread Pudding With Bourbon
Sauce, 119
Comfort Food, Delta Style, 112
Helena Tamales, 112
Food You'll Yee-Haw Over, 117
Grilled Corn on the Cob With Red Chile
Paste, 118
Vietnamese Fajitas (Bo Nuong Xa), 117
Lowcountry Cuisine, 111
Benne Seed Wafers, 111
Frogmore Stew, 111
Garlic Shrimp and Grits, 111
Mid-Atlantic Flavors, 104
Currant-Glazed Ham, 104
Marinated Asparagus, 105
Maryland Black Walnut Cake, 106
Maryland Crab Cakes, 105
Memmie's Spoonbread, 105
Sweet Potato-Peanut Soup, 104
Mountain Country Recipes, 108
Apple Stack Cake, 108
Baked Whole Sweet Potatoes, 108
Country Ham Sauce, 109
Fried Apples, 109
Shuck Beans, 109
Short-Cuts to Top-Rated Cakes, 106
German Chocolate Cake, 107
No-Bake Ice-Cream Angel Food Cake, 107
Quick Coconut-Pineapple Cake, 106

May

A Taste of Honey, 137
Buttermilk 'n' Honey Pancakes, 137
Fruit Salad With Honey Dressing, 137
Honey-Sweet Cornbread, 137
Cheesy Bites, 143
Basil-Cheese Roulade, 143
Herb-and-Garlic Goat Cheese Truffles, 143
Mediterranean Cheese Ball, 143

May *(continued)*

Chillin' Out With Sherbets, 133
Raspberry-Buttermilk Sherbet, 133
Refreshing Lime Sherbet, 133
Chocolate-Nut Pies, 134
Chocolate-Bourbon Pecan Pie, 134
Chocolate-Walnut Pie, 134
Coleslaw Three Ways, 125
Creamy-and-Sweet Coleslaw, 125
Sweet-and-Tart Red Cabbage Coleslaw, 125
Zesty Vinegar Coleslaw, M125
Dill-icious Ideas, 128
Dilled Potato Salad With Feta, 128
Greek Chicken Rollups, 128
Low-Cal Dilled Yogurt Dressing, 128
Dish Up Pasta, 140
Fiesta Taco Lasagna, 140
Red Wine-Tomato Pasta, 140
Easy Beach Menu, 130
Almond Sand Dollar Cookies, 130
Broiled Mahi-Mahi With Parsleyed
Tomatoes, 130
Greek Pasta Salad, 130
Enjoy Fresh Strawberries, 132
Chicken-and-Strawberry Salad, 132
Croissant French Toast With Fresh Strawberry
Syrup, 132
Strawberry-Rhubarb Pie, 132
Strawberry Salad With Cinnamon
Vinaigrette, 133
Exceptional Eggplant, 127
Eggplant Fritters, 128
Garden Eggplant Pizza, 127
From Our Kitchen, 144
Béarnaise Mayonnaise, 144
Fresh Herb Mayonnaise, 144
Lemon-Rosemary Mayonnaise, 144
Keep That Knife Sharp, 124
Red Beans and Rice With Sausage, 125
Lunch on the Go, 142
Bacon-Pimiento Cheese, 142
Chinese Cabbage Salad, 142
Favorite Chocolate Chip Cookies, 142
Make Ahead and Marinate, 129
Hot Tomato Salad, 129
Marinated Dill Green Beans, 129
Marinated Squash, 129
Marinated Vegetable Salad, 129
Pamper Mom With Breakfast, 136
Coffee-Ice Cream Punch, 136
Southwest Breakfast Strata, 136
Ready-to-Assemble Meals, 131
Bistro Grilled Chicken Pizza, M131
Pesto Focaccia Sandwich, 131
Reuben Quesadillas, 131
Savor Sweet Onion Sides, 141
Balsamic Onion Stacks, 141
Florentine Stuffed Onions, 141
Tomato-and-Sweet Onion Salad, 141

Secrets to Great Seafood, 124
Butter Sauce, 124
Hot Crab Dip, 124
Stuffed Jumbo Shrimp, 124
Uncle Frank's Crab Cakes, 124
Skillet Suppers, 139
Chicken Breasts With Artichoke-Pepper
Sauce, 139
Southwest Pork in Black Bean Sauce, 139
Southwestern Starters, 138
Armadillo Eggs, 139
Cinco de Mayo Shrimp Cocktail, 138
Meaty Empanadas, 138
Start the Party in the Kitchen, 122
Coffee-Onion Jam, 123
Easy Spicy Caesar Salad, 122
Grilled New York Steaks, 123
Mint Nectarines With Pineapple-Coconut Ice
Cream, 123
Potato-Stuffed Grilled Bell Peppers, 123
Sunset Vodka-Orange Sipper, 122
Taste the Goodness of Grains, 126
Barley-Pine Nut Salad, 126
Barley, Vegetable, and Fruit Medley, 127
Dried Cherry-and-Pecan Oatmeal, 126
Wild Rice-and-Chicken Bowl, 127
Tea is the Key, 134
Lapsang-Poached Chicken Salad, 135
Marian's Iced Tea, 135
Vanilla-Jasmine-Sour Cream Tea Cake, 135

June

Avocados for Any Occasion, 159
Avocado Butter, 159
Avocado Soup, 159
Loaded Turkey Melt, 159
Barbecue Spuds, 162
Double-Stuffed Barbecue Potatoes, 162
Tangy Cabbage Salad, 162
Easy Icebox Pies, 157
Chocolate Icebox Pie, 157
Frozen Hawaiian Pie, 157
Rum-Coconut Key Lime Pie, 157
Zesty Lemon Pie, 157
From Our Kitchen, 164
Quick tricks with refrigerated piecrusts, 164
Great Time Get-together, 158
Key Lime-Coconut Mini-Cheesecakes, 159
Pickled Shrimp, 158
Shredded Flank Steak Mini-Sandwiches, 158
Tangy Bean Salad, 158
Growing Made Simple, 148
Feta-Stuffed Tomatoes, 148
Sweet Pepper-Mango Salsa, 148
Guilt-Free Comfort Food, 161
Herb-and-Veggie Meat Loaf, 161
Light Pimiento Cheese-Stuffed Celery, 161
Salad with Red Grapefruit-Lemon Vinaigrette, 161

Hot Off the Grill, 162
Mojo-Marinated Chicken, 163
Slow-Grilled Pork With Ranch-Barbecue
Sauce, 163
Spicy Cheddar-Stuffed Burgers, 163
Serve a Pretty Salad, 146
Layered Cornbread-and-Turkey Salad, 147
Layered Fruit Congealed Salad, M146
Layered Green Bean-Red Potato Salad, 146
Layered Lebanese Salad, 148
Take Five for Sides, 160
Baked Pineapple, 160
Blue Cheese Iceberg Wedges, 160
Sautéed Green Beans With Bacon, M160
Snappy Fruit Salad Dressing, 160

July

Barbecue Buddies, 166
Barbecue Deviled Eggs, 167
Creamy Carolina Coleslaw, 167
Honey-Mustard Barbecue Sauce, 167
Peach-Cinnamon Ice Cream, 168
Tabb's Barbecue Pork, 166
Tomato-and-Onion Salad, 167
Cherry Jewels, 168
Fresh Cherry Tart, 168
From Our Kitchen, 182
Blackberry Curd Filling, 182
Potato Salad Like You've Never Had, 171
Bacon Potato Salad, 171
Sweet Potato Salad, 171
Quick Catfish Tonight, 170
Broccoli-Squash Slaw, 170
Lemon-Garlic Toast, 171
Quick Pan-fried Catfish, 170
Simple and Fresh Brunch, 169
Breakfast Turkey Sausage Patties, 169
Brown Sugar-Baked Pineapple, 170
Confetti Omelet Casserole, 169
Sparkling Orange Punch, 170

Summer Living®
Add Flavor With Goat Cheese, 176
Lime-Goat Cheese Cheesecakes, 176
Roasted Vegetable-and-Goat Cheese Pizza, 176
Backyard Smokehouse in Dallas, 174
Big "D" Smoked Baby Back Ribs, 174
Big "D" Smoked Chicken, 175
Paul's Barbecue Sauce, 175
Paul's Pork Ribs Rub, 174
Roasted Camp Corn, 174
Texas Rockets, 175
Bake Up Some Fun, 181
Crunchy Oat 'n' Cereal Cookies, 181
Double Chocolate Chunk Cookies, 181
Casual Outdoor Get-together, 180
Italian-Style Burgers, 180
Slow Cooker Barbecue Beans, 180

Gather for a Blueberry Bash, 178
  Baked Brie With Blueberry-Ginger
    Topping, 179
  Berry Delicious Summer Salad, 179
  Blueberry-Rum Marinated Pork
    Tenderloin, 178
  Blueberry Salsa, 179
  Chilled Blueberry Soup, 178
  Frozen Blueberry Margaritas, 179
Savor a Sunset Supper, 172
  Citrus Bars, 173
  Grilled Crostini With Olive Tapenade, 172
  Sewee Preserve's Seafood Salad, 173
  Spicy Cheese Cocktail Biscuits, 173
Summer-Fresh Produce, 177
  Garlicky "Fried" Vegetables, 177
  Green Beans With Blue Cheese, 177

August

Cast-Iron Chefs, 184
  Hoover's Picnic Salad With Honey-Mustard
    Dressing, 184
  Sara's Grilled Chicken-Cornbread
    Salad, 184
  Tom's Roasted Chicken With Wilted Salad
    Greens, 185
Favorite Picnic Food, 188
  Bacon 'n' Onion Potato Salad, 188
  Honey-Pecan Chicken Strips, 188
  Old Bay Shrimp Salad, 188
From Our Kitchen, 198
  Light and Crispy Pan-fried Catfish, 198
It's on the Grill, 197
  Basil Rice Pilaf, M197
  Grilled Asparagus, 197
  Saucy Pork Chops With Orange Slices, 197
Pasta: Toss It and Love It, 186
  Penne With Greek-Style Tomato Sauce, 187
  Roasted Red Pepper-Caesar
    Tortelloni, M186
  Southwestern Fettuccine Alfredo, 186
  Sweet-Hot Asian Noodle Bowl, 187
  Two Tomato Linguine, 187
Smart Eating Starts With Good Taste, 194
  Easy Grilled Veggies, 194
  Iced Green Tea, 196
  Jerk Turkey Tenderloin With Raspberry-
    Chipotle Sauce, M194
  Romaine Salad With Cashews, 195
  Super Fast Strawberry Shortcake Parfaits, 196
  Whole Wheat Popovers, 195
Speedy and Scrumptious Desserts, 193
  Banana-Berry Split, 193
  Chocolate Milk Shake, 193
  Chocolate-Peanut Butter Pizza, 193
  Hot Fudge Sauce, 193
White Barbecue Sauce, 196
  White Barbecue Sauce, 196

September

Bake Sale Treats, 211
  Cream Cheese Ladybugs, 211
  No-Bake Peanut Butter Clusters, M211
  Sour Cream Coffee Cakes, 212
  Turtle Cake Squares, M211
Better Mac and Cheese, Please, 207
  Creamy Mac and Cheese, 208
  Hearty Mac and Cheese, 208
  Taco Dinner Mac and Cheese, 208
Blend the Easy Way, 207
  Creamy Tomato Soup With Crispy
    Croutons, 207
Casual Family Gathering, 200
  Avocado Soup, 200
  Grilled Pork Loin With Rosemary-Breadcrumb
    Crust, 200
  Grilled Shrimp With Bacon and
    Jalapeños, M200
  Mixed Greens With Toasted Almonds and
    Apple Cider Vinaigrette, 201
  Pecan Fudge Pie With Raspberry Sauce, 201
Easy Game Day Get-together, 212
  Margarita Punch, 212
  Southwestern Salsa Dip, 212
4 Speedy Suppers, 202
  Basil-Garlic Bread, 202
  Breakfast Burritos, 204
  Cheesy Mashed Potatoes, 204
  Ginger-Glazed Pork Tenderloin, 203
  Italian Tossed Salad, 202
  One-Pot Pasta, 202
  Quick Parmesan Couscous, 203
  Raspberry-Barbecue Chicken, 203
  Sautéed Squash and Zucchini, 203
  Sweet Carrots and Rice, 203
  Tex-Mex Popcorn, 204
  Tex-Mex Salisbury Steak, 204
  Zesty Green Beans, 204
From Our Kitchen, 224
  Bacon Pasta, 224
  BLT Wraps, 224
How Sweet It Is, 210
  Caramel-Apple Muffins, 210
  Caramel-Pecan Cheesecake Bars, 210
  Chocolate-Caramel Sheet Cake, 210
  Quick Caramel Frosting, 211
Menu With a View, 204
  Cranberry Lemonade, 205
  Giant Ham-and-Pepper Salad Sandwich, 204
  Mixed Fruit Pilaf, 205
  Praline Bars, M205
One Sauce, Three Meals, 205
  Cajun Shrimp-and-Crab Sauce, 206
  Lemon-Blueberry Layered Dessert, 206
  Sautéed Green Beans, 206
Simple Southern Salads, 208
  Chunky Chicken Parmesan Salad, 209
  Egg Salad, 209

Garlic-Herb Two-Bean Salad, 209
Overnight Slaw, 208
Roasted Corn-and-Black Bean Salad, 209
Vanilla-Scented Fruit Salad, 209

Southern Living® Cooking School
Dinner and a Movie, 214
  Baked Ziti, 214
  Garlic Bread, 215
  Rigatoni With Sausage and Bell
    Peppers, 215
  Splendid Strawberries, 215
Fruit and Spice Make It Nice, 215
  Baked Lemon-Dill Catfish, 216
  Chocolate-Covered Cherry Pie, M216
  Ginger-Marinated Flank Steak, 216
  Orange-Date Muffins, 215
  Orange Tea Cooler, 216
  Roasted Fall Vegetables, 217
Girls' Night Out, 219
  Balsamic-Marinated Chicken, 219
  Gingerbread, 219
  Orange Rice Pilaf, 219
  Tomato-Basil Dip, 219
Quick-and-Easy Favorites, 213
  Black Beans and Rice, 214
  BLT Potato Salad, 213
  Buttermilk Baked Chicken, 213
  Grilled Cheese Sandwiches With Tomato,
    Avocado, and Bacon, 213
  Pear Crisp, 214
  Southern-Style Turkey Cobb Salad, 214
Soccer Night Solutions, 222
  Apple Spice-Raisin Snack Mix, 222
  Chicken-and-Slaw Wraps, 222
  Open-Faced Monte Cristo Sandwiches, 222
  Peanut Butter-Chocolate Chip
    Cookies, 222
Southern Hospitality With an
* International Accent, 220*
  Berry Freeze, 220
  Fresh Fruit With Lime Syrup, 220
  Greek-Style Chicken, 220
  Make-Ahead Spoon Rolls, 221
  Mediterranean Pasta Salad, 220
  Spicy Huevos Rancheros, 221
  Triple-Chocolate Cake, 221
Tweens' Turn to Cook, 222
  Caramel-Apple Quesadillas, 223
  Fiesta Chicken Salad, 223
  Pronto Pork Fajitas, 223
  Roast Beef-Cheddar Panini
    Sandwiches, 223
Weeknight Wonders, 217
  Beefy Pizza Casserole, 217
  Buttermilk Corn Sticks, 218
  Cranberry-Orange Sauce, 218
  Molasses-Grilled Rib-Eye Steaks, 218
  Southwestern Squash Casserole, M217
  Succotash Rice Toss, 218

September *(continued)*

Try Greek for a Fresh Change, 206
Easy Greek Flank Steak, 207
Quick Hummus Dip, 206
Sour Cream-Cucumber Sauce, 207
Tomato-Feta Salad, 207

October

Cooking Up Cabbage, 236
Braised Red Cabbage, 236
Fiesta Cabbage, 236
Scalloped Cabbage, 236
Fast Asian Fare, 241
Stir-fry Pork, 241
From Our Kitchen, 242
Confetti Pasta Salad, 242
It's Great Pumpkin, 232
Pumpkin Bread, 232
Pumpkin Fudge, 232
Pumpkin Spice Cake, 232
Keep on Grilling, 241
Grilled Balsamic Pork Tenderloin, 241
Lemony Apple Salad, 241
Speedy Rosemary Green Beans, 241
Make a Batch of Texas Chili, 234
Chunky Beef Chili, 235
Oven-Roasted Goodness, 233
Butternut Squash Bake, 234
Curried Butternut Squash Soup, 234
Roasted Acorn Squash With Cranberry Relish, 234
Roasted Butternut Squash Salad With Blue
Cheese Vinaigrette, 233
Roasted Winter Squash, 233
Spaghetti Squash Sauté, 234
Savor a Fall Breakfast, 240
Mixed Fruit Granola, 240
Orange Syrup, 240
Savory Ham-and-Swiss Breakfast Pie, 240
Supper Tonight, 237
Cajun Shrimp Casserole, 237
Chalupa Dinner Bowl, 238
Sausage-and-Chicken Cassoulet, 237
Shortcut Greek Shepherd's Pie, 238
The Season's Best Spices, 238
Aromatic Curry-and-Spice Chicken, 238
Brown Sugar Bread Pudding With Crème
Anglaise, 239
Creamy Shrimp-and-Spinach Pasta, 239
Try a Taste of Fall, 230
Apple Brown Betty, 232
Citrus-Pear Honey, 230
Crescent Roll Apples, 231
Field Greens With Roasted Bacon-Wrapped
Pears, 230
Fresh Apple Upside-Down Cake, 231
Homemade Applesauce, 231
Raspberry-Almond Pear Tart, 230

Warm and Hearty Stews, 235
Chicken-and-Vegetable Stew, 235
Hearty Ham-and-Collard Stew, 236
Slow-Cooker Beef Stew, 235

November

Cook With Confidence, 250
Au Gratin Potato Casserole, 250
Easy-Does-It Mashed Sweet Potatoes, M250
Praline-Apple Pie, 251
Deep Chocolate Brownies, 253
Fudgy Bittersweet Brownies, 253
Mint Truffle Brownie Squares, M254
Easy, Elegant Dinner, 248
Potato-and-Gruyère Casserole, 248
Rosemary-Thyme Rib Roast, 248
Strawberry-Cranberry-Orange Salad, 249
Enjoy a Cup of Hot Tea, 257
Verla's Hot Tea, 257
From Our Kitchen, 284
Italian Parmesan Herb Mix, 284
Sweet-Hot Honey Mustard, 284
Gather Together, 244
Barbecued Pork Tenderloin, 245
Coconut Layer Cake, M246
Cranberry Relish Salad, 245
Creamy-and-Crunchy Green Bean Casserole, 245
Grilled Oysters With Paul's Cocktail Sauce, 244
Maple-Sweet Potato Casserole, 245
Roasted Turkey, 244
**Good News: Five-Ingredient Southern
Recipes, 256**
Crispy Oven-Fried Catfish, 256
Pecan Broccoli, 257
Ranch Potatoes, 256
Rosemary-Roasted Cherry Tomatoes, 257
S'mores Sundaes, 257

Holiday Dinners®
A Buffet Built on Comfort, 276
Broccoli Casserole, M276
Broccoli Slaw, 278
Nutty Wild Rice, 278
Squash Casserole, 277
Whiskey Punch, 276
At Play in the Kitchen, 282
Cheddar Cheese Grits Casserole, 283
Crispy Brown Sugar Bacon, 283
Fruitini, 283
Overnight Oven-Baked French Toast, 283
Bake the Best Cheesecake, 272
Chocolate-Cherry Surprise Cheesecake, 273
Irish Strawberry-and-Cream
Cheesecake, 273
Cheers to an Easy, Gorgeous Party, 280
Autumn Salad With Maple-Cider
Vinaigrette, 281
Chocolate Fondue, M281

Peppered Beef Tenderloin With Portobello-
Marsala Sauce, 280
Potato-Leek Gratin, 281
Gather Around the Table, 272
Cranberry Chicken, 272
Simple Potato Latkes, 272
Hats Off to This Celebration, 274
Cherry-Tarragon Chicken Salad, 275
Layered Sun-dried-Tomato-and-Basil
Spread, 275
Lemon-Basil Snaps, 275
Kitchen Shortcuts, 270
Orange 'n' Jellied Cranberry Sauce Stacks, 270
Slow-Cooker Cornbread Dressing, 270
Pack-and-Go Supper Club, 258
Baked Honey-Raisin Brie, M258
Balsamic-Browned Butter Asparagus, 260
Berry Bread Pudding With Vanilla Cream
Sauce, 260
Caramelized Onions, 259
Cranberry-and-Toasted Pecan
Couscous, M259
Spiced-and-Stuffed Pork Loin With Cider
Sauce, 258
Party Favors in a Flash, 274
Honey-Spice Butter, 274
Spiced-Glazed Carrots, 274
Sugar-and-Spice Nuts, 274
Sweet Spice Blend, 274
Pop the Cork, 282
Champagne-Chocolate Sauce, M282
Pomegranate-Champagne Cocktail, 282
Wayne's "French 75," 282
Three Yummy Desserts, 260
Caramel-Pecan Pie, 269
Granny's Pound Cake, 269
Pumpkin Crisp, 269
Ultimate Mashed Potatoes, 270
Simple Mashed Potatoes, 271
Southwest Mashed Sweet Potatoes, 271
Three-Potato Mash, 271
We're Glad You're Here, 278
Grilled Sweet Guava Chicken, 278
Rum Cake, 279
The Ultimate White Rice, 279
Love the Leftovers, 246
Main Dish Turkey Salad With Cranberry
Vinaigrette and Garlic Croutons, 246
Next-Day Turkey Dinner Bake, 246
Make-Ahead Appetizer, 249
Southwest Cheesecake, 249
Microwave Magic, 252
Garlic Butter Sauce, M253
Speedy Lasagna, M252
**Simple Southwestern Casserole Starts the
Fun, 247**
Cilantro-Lime Sour Cream Dip, 247
Creamy Chipotle-Black Bean Dip, 247
"Salsafied" Sour Cream Dip, 247
Texas-Style Enchilada Casserole, 247

Souffles: Here's the Trick, 255
Spiced Soufflés With Lemon Whipped Cream, 255
Soup for Supper, 254
Creamy Pimiento Cheese Soup, 254
Mama's Mexican Minestrone, 254
Stir-and-Bake Breads, 251
Cream Cheese-Pumpkin Bread, 251
Ice-Cream Bread, 252
Sun-dried Tomato-Herb Bread, 252
Sweet Potato Cornbread, 252

December

Can't-Miss Cakes, 286
Chocolate Fudge Brownies, M288
Chocolate-Red Velvet Layer Cake, 287
Cinnamon-Pecan Crumb Cakes, 287
Cream Cheese Frosting, 287
Fluted Chocolate-Red Velvet Cakes, 287
Praline-Pecan Cakes, 286
Praline Pecans, 286
Sour Cream Cake Batter, 286

Christmas All Through the House®
Beautiful Buffets, 296
Avocado-Feta Salsa, 298
Black Bean-and-Mango Salsa, 297
Chocolate-Dipped Cookies, 299
Golden Buttermilk Mashed Potatoes, 298
Herbed Roast Beef, 297
Mama Dip's Carrot Cake, 299
Mascarpone Pecan Pie, 299
Roasted Asparagus, 298
Tuscan Pork Loin, 296
Zucchini-Carrot Salsa, 298
Come Over for Coffee, 306
Mocha Café au Lait, 306
Spiced Coffee, 307
Garlands and Goodies, 300
Asian Snack Mix, 306
Bourbon-Mustard Glazed Sausage Bites, 305
Chicken Fingers With Honey-Mustard
Sauce, 300
Pinecone Cheese Ball, 300
Sausage-Stuffed Mushrooms, 300
Spicy Chipotle-Barbecue Sausage Bites, 305
Sweet-and-Sour Sausage Bites, 305
Have a Cookie, 307
Angel Cookies, 308
Chocolate and Mint Cookies, 308
Cranberry-White Chocolate Cookies, 308
Mocha Shortbread, M307
Shortbread Thumbelinas, 307
Comfort Foods Made Easy, 293
Creamy Bell Pepper 'n' Tomato Soup, 293
Grilled Cheese-and-Ham Sandwiches, 293
Crusted Baked Chicken, 312
Apricot Vinaigrette, M312
Baked Pecan Chicken, 312

Creamy Mushroom-Artichoke Sauce, 312
Rosemary Baked Vegetables, 313
Fast Dishes for Busy Days, 292
Beef Ravioli in Basil-Cream Sauce, 293
Cheesy Mac 'n' Chicken Soup, 292
Easy Brunswick Stew, 292
Fix and Freeze Ground Beef, 290
Chimichangas, 290
Ground Beef-Tomato Sauce, 290
Fresh Ways With Cranberries, 313
Cranberry Muffins, 313
Holiday Pork Chops, 313
From Our Kitchen, 314
Decorative and aluminum baking pans, 314
Hearty Casseroles, 311
Cheesy Chicken Curry Casserole, 311
Zesty Poblano-and-Cheese Casserole, 311
Lightened and Luscious, 289
Gingered Green Beans, 290
Mocha-Pecan Mud Pie, 290
Molasses-Coffee Turkey Breast, M289
Roasted Potato-and-Bacon Salad, 289
Sugar-and-Spice Acorn Squash, 289
Make-Ahead Appetizers, 310
Cranberry Meatballs, 310
Creamy Olive Spread, 311
Mushroom Turnovers, 310
Simply Splendid, 309
Beef Tenderloin With Horseradish Cream, 309
Blue Cheese Biscuits, 309
Mulled Pomegranate Cider, 309
Special-Occasion Salad, 291
Spinach-Endive Salad With Warm
Vinaigrette, 291
Spice Up Your Christmas, 294
Buñuelos, 295
Cuban Black Beans, 295
Ham With Garlic and Orange, 294
Mojito, 295
Yuca With Garlic-Lime Mojo, 294
Stir Up a Quick Side, 292
Broccoli With Almond-Lemon Dip, 292
Collard, Raisin, and Pecan Sauté, 292
Quick Parmesan Spinach, 292
Winter Fruit Salads, 291
Harvest Crunch Salad, 291
Mandarin Orange-and-Almond Salad, 291

Southern Living® Cook-Off 2005 Winners

Brand Winners, 325
Cuban Pulled Pork Tortilla Pie With Snappy
Mango Salsa, 329
Fried Green Tomato Po' Boys, 330
Hearty Healthy Breakfast Casserole, 325
Maple-Mustard-Glazed Balsamic Steaks With
Blue Pecan Confetti, 330
Margarita Marinated Chicken With Mango
Salsa, 328

My Best Tuna Salad, 328
Souffleeta, 326
Sour Cream-Blueberry Morning Pancakes
With Wild Blueberry-and-Peach Topping, 326
Southern-Style Fish Tacos, 327
Spicy Baked Beans, 328
Texas Best Fried Shrimp, 327
Tex-Mex Chicken-and-Bacon Pizza, 325
Tex-Mex Grilled Beef "Tenders," Corn and
Tomatoes With Chipotle-Lime Cream, 329
The Ultimate No-Bake Cheesecake Banana
Pudding With Caramel Syrup, 326
Easy Entrées, 320
Herb-Grilled Chicken With Watermelon-
Feta Salad, 320
Pané Chicken With Sweet-'n'-Spicy Red
Pepper Sauce, 320
Southwestern Chicken-Corn Cakes, 321
Healthy & Good for You, 318
Cuban Mojo Chicken With Mandarin-Black
Bean Salad, 318
Toasted Pecan, Cranberry, and Gorgonzola
Turkey Burgers, 320
White Bean Soup With Gremolata, 319
Kids Love It!, 324
Crispy Coconut Chicken Dippers With
Wowee Maui Mustard, 324
Crispy Ginger-and-Garlic Asian Turkey
Lettuce Wraps, 325
Sloppy José Sandwiches With Cilantro
Slaw, 324
Southern Desserts, 316
Chocolate-Coffee Cheesecake With Mocha
Sauce, M316
Decadent Banana Cake With Coconut-
Cream Cheese Frosting, 317
Southern Peach-and-Blueberry
Shortcakes, 318
Your Best Recipe, 322
Chocolate Cake IV, 322
Double Whammie Yeast Rolls, 323
Pimiento Cheese-Stuffed Fried Chicken, 322

Christmas Bonus: Our Editors' Favorites

Our Holiday Favorites, 332
Basic Buttery Biscuits, 335
Breakfast Enchiladas, 333
Broccoli With Pimiento Cheese Sauce, 333
Brunch Punch, 335
Coconut Cake, 335
Cranberry Congealed Salad, 334
Creamy Leek Mashed Potatoes, 334
Garlic-Orange Roast Pork, 332
Mama's Fudge, 335
Molasses Pork Tenderloin With Red Wine
Sauce, 332
Pepper Jelly-Glazed Carrots, 334
Two-Seed Bread Knots, 334

general recipe index

This index lists every recipe by food category and/or major ingredient.
All microwave recipe page numbers are preceded by an "M."

ALMONDS
Desserts
Cookies, Almond Sand Dollar, 130
Cookies, Almond-Toffee Chocolate
Chip, 87
Crisps, Dark Chocolate-Almond, M30
Ice-Cream Sandwiches, Mocha-Almond-
Fudge, 62
Shortbread Thumbelinas, 307
Green Beans, Dill-and-Almond, 81
APPETIZERS. *See also* **Salsas.**
Cheese
Baked Brie With Blueberry-Ginger
Topping, 179
Baked Honey-Raisin Brie, M258
Ball, Mediterranean Cheese, 143
Ball, Pinecone Cheese, 300
Biscuits, Spicy Cheese Cocktail, 173
Cheesecake, Southwest, 249
Logs, Chile-Cheese, 64
Ring, Cheese, 33
Sandwiches, Checkerboard Cheese, 18
Truffles, Herb-and-Garlic Goat Cheese, 143
Wafers, Cheese, 97
Chicken Fingers With Honey-Mustard
Sauce, 300
Crostini With Olive Tapenade, Grilled, 172
Cucumber-Dill Rounds, 96
Dips
Catfish Dip, Layered, 55
Chipotle-Black Bean Dip, Creamy, 247
Crab Dip, Hot, 124
Hummus Dip, Quick, 206
Hummus, Red Pepper, 97
Salsa Dip, Southwestern, 212
Sour Cream Dip, Cilantro-Lime, 247
Sour Cream Dip, "Salsafied," 247
Tomato-Basil Dip, 219
Vegetable Dip, Quick Creamy, 20
Egg Rolls, 50
Eggs, Armadillo, 139
Meatballs
Chipotle-Barbecue Meatballs, Spicy, 305
Cranberry Meatballs, 310
Glazed Meatballs, Bourbon-Mustard, 305
Sweet-and-Sour Meatballs, 305
Mushrooms, Sausage-Stuffed, 300
Mushroom Turnovers, 310
Nuts, Sugar-and-Spice, 274
Oysters With Paul's Cocktail Sauce, Grilled, 244
Pita Triangles, Benne Seed, 97
Sauce, Paul's Cocktail, 244
Sausage Bites, Bourbon-Mustard Glazed, 305
Sausage Bites, Spicy Chipotle-Barbecue, 305
Sausage Bites, Sweet-and-Sour, 305
Shrimp Cocktail, Cinco de Mayo, 138
Snack Mix, Apple Spice-Raisin, 222
Snack Mix, Asian, 306
Spreads and Fillings
Olive Spread, Creamy, 311
Shrimp Paste, 98

Sun-dried-Tomato-and-Basil Spread,
Layered, 275
Texas Rockets, 175
Wings, Buffalo, 64
APPLES
Beverages
Appleade, Hot Spiced Lemon-, 23
Cider Sipper, Citrus, 23
Punch, Honey-Apple, 23
Punch, Spicy Sparkling, 24
Tea, Apple, 24
Breads
Apple Bread, 210
Muffins, Caramel-Apple, 210
Coffee Cakes, Caramel-Apple, 210
Coleslaw, Lemon-Apple, 44
Desserts
Apples, Crescent Roll, 231
Betty, Apple Brown, 232
Cake, Apple Stack, 108
Cake, Fresh Apple Upside-Down, 231
Filling, Dried Apple, 108
Pie, Praline-Apple, 251
Torte, Huguenot, 98
Fried Apples, 109
Salad, Lemony Apple, 241
Snack Mix, Apple Spice-Raisin, 222
Vinaigrette, Apple Cider, 201
Vinaigrette, Apple-Ginger, 230
APPLESAUCE
Gingerbread, Applesauce, 231
Homemade Applesauce, 231
Spiced Applesauce, 231
Turnovers, Applesauce, 231
APRICOTS
Bellinis, Apricot, 96
Pork Loin, Apricot-Glazed-and-Spiced, 259
Vinaigrette, Apricot, M312
ARTICHOKES
Chicken-and-Artichoke Olé, 59
Sauce, Chicken Breasts With Artichoke-
Pepper, 139
Sauce, Creamy Mushroom-Artichoke, 312
ASPARAGUS
Balsamic-Browned Butter Asparagus, 260
Grilled Asparagus, 197
Marinated Asparagus, 105
Oven-Roasted Asparagus, 55
Roasted Asparagus, 298
Stir-fried Asparagus With Garlic, 86
ASPIC
Raspberry-Tomato Aspic, 65
AVOCADOS
Butter, Avocado, 159
Salsa, Avocado-Feta, 298
Soup, Avocado, 159, 200

BACON
Bread, Bacon-Cheddar Grits, 83
Brown Sugar Bacon, Crispy, 283

Pasta, Bacon, 224
Pears, Field Greens With Roasted Bacon-
Wrapped, 230
Pimiento Cheese, Bacon-, 142
Pizza, Tex-Mex Chicken-and-Bacon, 325
Quesadillas, Bacon-and-Egg, 88
Salad, Bacon 'n' Onion Potato, 188
Salad, Bacon Potato, 171
Salad, Roasted Potato-and-Bacon, 289
Slaw, Blue Cheese-Bacon, 91
BANANAS
Breads
Cream Cheese-Banana-Nut Bread, 27
Cream Cheese-Banana-Nut Bread,
Cinnamon Crisp-Topped, 27
Cream Cheese-Banana-Nut Bread, Orange-
Pecan-Topped, 27
Cream Cheese-Banana-Nut Bread, Peanut
Butter Streusel-Topped, 27
Cream Cheese-Banana-Nut Bread, Toasted
Coconut-Topped, 27
Cream Cheese-Banana-Nut Bread, Toffee-
Topped, 27
Muffins, Cream Cheese-Banana-Nut, 27
Brown Sugar Bananas, 45
Cake With Coconut-Cream Cheese Frosting,
Decadent Banana, 317
Pudding, Peanut Butter-Banana, 44
Pudding With Caramel Syrup, The Ultimate
No-Bake Cheesecake Banana, 326
Shake, Banana-Mocha, 45
Smoothie, Banana-Berry, 24
Split, Banana-Berry, 193
BARBECUE. *See also* **Grilled.**
Beans, Slow Cooker Barbecue, M180
Beef Sandwiches, Slow-Cooker Barbecue, 64
Chicken Pizza, Southwestern BBQ, 33
Chicken, Raspberry-Barbecue, 203
Deviled Eggs, Barbecue, 167
Meatballs, Spicy Chipotle-Barbecue, 305
Pork
Sausage Bites, Spicy Chipotle-Barbecue, 305
Tabb's Barbecue Pork, 166
Tenderloin, Barbecued Pork, 245
Potatoes, Double-Stuffed Barbecue, 162
Rub, Barbecue, 166
Sauces
Honey-Mustard Barbecue Sauce, 167
Paul's Barbecue Sauce, 175
Ranch-Barbecue Sauce, 163
Raspberry-Barbecue Sauce, 203
White Barbecue Sauce, 196
BARLEY
Medley, Barley, Vegetable, and Fruit, 127
Salad, Barley-Pine Nut, 126
BEANS
Baked Beans and Ham, 45
Baked Beans, Spicy, 328
Barbecue Beans, Slow Cooker, 180
Black. *See also* **Beans/Salads.**
Cuban Black Beans, 295

Dip, Creamy Chipotle-Black Bean, 247
Dip, Southwestern Salsa, 212
Enchiladas, Black Bean-Chicken-
    Spinach, 95
Enchiladas, Black Bean 'n' Spinach, 95
Rice, Black Beans and, 214
Salsa, Black Bean-and-Corn, 297
Salsa, Black Bean-and-Mango, 297
Salsa, Fruity Black Bean, 16
Sauce, Southwest Pork in Black Bean, 139
Great Northern Beans With Tomatoes, 23
Green. *See also* **Beans/Salads.**
    Blue Cheese, Green Beans With, 177
    Casserole, Creamy-and-Crunchy Green
        Bean, 245
    Dill-and-Almond Green Beans, 81
    Gingered Green Beans, 290
    Lemon-Almond Green Beans, 218
    Lemon-and-Dill Green Beans, 17
    Rosemary Green Beans, Speedy, 241
    Sautéed Green Beans, 206
    Sautéed Green Beans, Lemon-Garlic Roast
        Chicken With, 43
    Sautéed Green Beans With Bacon, M160
    Zesty Green Beans, 204
Hummus, Red Pepper, 97
Pinto Beans, Ham Hocks, and Rice, 46
Red Beans and Rice With Sausage, 125
Red Beans, Wilted Greens and, 21
Salads
    Black Bean Salad, Mandarin-, 319
    Black Bean Salad, Roasted Corn-and-, 209
    Green Bean-Red Potato Salad, Layered, 146
    Green Beans, Marinated Dill, 129
    Tangy Bean Salad, 158
    Two-Bean Salad, Garlic-Herb, 209
    White Bean-and-Asparagus Salad, 100
Shuck Beans, 109
Soups
    Black Bean Soup, 120
    Minestrone, Mama's Mexican, 254
    White Bean Soup With Gremolata, 319
Succotash Rice Toss, 218
BEEF. *See also* **Beef, Ground.**
Ravioli in Basil-Cream Sauce, Beef, 293
Reuben Quesadillas, 131
Roasts
    Chili, Chunky Beef, 235
    Herbed Roast Beef, 297
    Pot Roast, Cowboy, 35
    Pot Roast, Italian, 34
    Rib Roast, Rosemary-Thyme, 248
Sandwiches
    Barbecue Beef Sandwiches, Slow-Cooker, 64
    Flank Steak Mini-Sandwiches,
        Shredded, 158
    Panini Sandwiches, Roast Beef-Cheddar, 223
    Philly Sandwiches, Open-Faced, 32
    Sloppy José Sandwiches With Cilantro
        Slaw, 324
    Wraps, Tangy-and-Sweet Roast Beef, 92
Steaks
    Chicken-Fried Steak, 67
    Country-Fried Steak With Creamy Salsa
        Gravy, 67
    Fajitas (*Bo Nuong Xa*), Vietnamese, 117
    Flank Steak, Easy Greek, 207
    Flank Steak, Ginger-Marinated, 216
    Glazed Balsamic Steaks With Blue Pecan
        Confetti, Maple-Mustard-, 330
    Grilled Steaks Balsamico, 84

London Broil, Marinated, 84
Minute Steak With Mushroom Gravy, 67
New York Steaks, Grilled, 123
Pasta, Red Wine-Tomato-and-Steak, 140
Rib-Eye Steaks, Molasses-Grilled, 218
Salad With Hot Pan Dressing, Steak-and-
    Spinach, 19
Tenderloin With Horseradish Cream, Beef, 309
Stew, Slow-Cooker Beef, 235
Tenderloin With Portobello-Marsala Sauce,
    Peppered Beef, 280
BEEF, GROUND
Casseroles
    Enchilada Casserole, Lightened Texas-
        Style, 247
    Enchilada Casserole, Texas-Style, 247
    Enchiladas, Smothered, 59
    Lasagna, Fiesta Taco, 140
    Lasagna, Tex-Mex, 58
    Manicotti, Meaty Cheese, 34
    Pizza Casserole, Beefy, 217
    Ziti, Baked, 214
Chili, Chunky Beef 'n' Tomato, 20
Empanadas, Meaty, 138
Hamburgers
    Italian-Style Burgers, 180
    Stuffed Burgers, Spicy Cheddar-, 163
Meatballs, Cranberry, 310
Meat Loaf
    Green Chile-Tomato Gravy, Meat Loaf
        With, 42
    Herb-and-Veggie Meat Loaf, 161
    Old-Fashioned Meat Loaf, 95
Pasta, One-Pot, 202
Pie, Shortcut Greek Shepherd's, 238
Salad, Fiesta, 58
Salisbury Steak, Tex-Mex, 204
Sauce, Ground Beef-Tomato, 290
Taco Dinner Mac and Cheese, 208
BEVERAGES. *See also* **Tea.**
Alcoholic
    Bellinis, Apricot, 96
    Cocktail, Pomegranate-Champagne, 282
    "French 75," Wayne's, 282
    Margaritas, Frozen Blueberry, 179
    Mojito, 295
    Punch, Margarita, 212
    Punch, Sparkling Orange, 170
    Punch, Whiskey, 276
    Sipper, Sunset Vodka-Orange, 122
Appleade, Hot Spiced Lemon-, 23
Cider, Mulled Pomegranate, 309
Cooler, White Grape-and-Orange, 61
Freeze, Berry, 220
Lemonade, Cranberry, 205
Lemonade, Fizzy Raspberry, 61
Lemonade, Fizzy Strawberry, 61
Punch
    Brunch Punch, 335
    Coffee-Ice Cream Punch, 136
    Honey-Apple Punch, 23
    Spicy Sparkling Punch, 24
Shake, Banana-Mocha, 45
Shake, Chocolate Milk, 193
Sipper, Citrus Cider, 23
Smoothie, Banana-Berry, 24
Sparkler, Cranberry-Apple, 61
Syrup, Simple, 135
BISCUITS
Basic Buttery Biscuits, 335
Blue Cheese Biscuits, 309

Cheese Cocktail Biscuits, Spicy, 173
Cranberry-Orange Glazed Biscuits, 335
Pan Biscuits, Easy, 26
Sweet Potato Biscuits, 22
BLACKBERRIES
Filling, Blackberry Curd, 182
Juice, Blackberry, 182
Sherbet, Blackberry-Buttermilk, 133
BLUEBERRIES
Dessert, Lemon-Blueberry Layered, 206
Margaritas, Frozen Blueberry, 179
Muffins, Berry-and-Spice Whole-Wheat, 25
Pancakes With Wild Blueberry-and-Peach
    Topping, Sour Cream-Blueberry
    Morning, 326
Pork Tenderloin, Blueberry-Rum
    Marinated, 178
Salad, Berry Delicious Summer, 179
Salsa, Blueberry, 179
Sherbet, Blueberry-Buttermilk, 133
Soup, Chilled Blueberry, 178
Topping, Baked Brie With Blueberry-
    Ginger, 179
Topping, Wild Blueberry-and-Peach, 326
BREADS. *See also* **Biscuits; Cakes/Coffee
    Cakes; Cornbreads; Croutons; French
    Toast; Fritters; Hush Puppies;
    Muffins; Pancakes; Pies, Puffs, and
    Pastries; Rolls and Buns.**
Apple Bread, 210
Banana-Nut Bread, Cream Cheese-, 27
Basil-Garlic Bread, 202
Banana-Nut Bread, Cinnamon Crisp-Topped
    Cream Cheese-, 27
Banana-Nut Bread, Orange-Pecan-Topped
    Cream Cheese-, 27
Banana-Nut Bread, Peanut Butter Streusel-
    Topped Cream Cheese-, 27
Banana-Nut Bread, Toasted Coconut-Topped
    Cream Cheese-, 27
Banana-Nut Bread, Toffee-Topped Cream
    Cheese-, 27
Cocoa Bread With Stewed Yard Peaches, 23
Cream Cheese-Pumpkin Bread, 251
French Bread, Garlic, 57
Garlic Bread, 215
Gingerbread, 219
Gingerbread, Applesauce, 231
Ice-Cream Bread, 252
Lemon-Walnut Tea Bread, 59
Parmesan Cheese Breadsticks, 20
Popovers, Whole Wheat, 195
Puddings
    Berry Bread Pudding With Vanilla Cream
        Sauce, 260
    Brown Sugar Bread Pudding With Crème
        Anglaise, 239
    Pineapple-Apple Bread Pudding With
        Bourbon Sauce, 119
    Pumpkin Bread, 232
    Spoonbread, Memmie's, 105
    Sun-dried Tomato-Herb Bread, 252
Yeast
    Grits Bread, Bacon-Cheddar, 83
    Grits Bread, Basil Pesto-Cheese, 83
    Grits Bread, Cheesy, 83
    Grits Bread, Tomato-Black Olive, 83
BROCCOLI
Almond-Lemon Dip, Broccoli With, 292
Casserole, Broccoli, M276
Pecan Broccoli, 257

Broccoli (continued)

Pimiento Cheese Sauce, Broccoli
With, 333
Salads
Slaw, Broccoli, 278
Slaw, Broccoli-Squash, 170
Slaw, Cilantro, 324
Slaw Salad, Sweet Broccoli, 91
Skillet, Quick Broccoli, 86
BROWNIES. *See also* **Cookies/Bars and Squares.**
Bittersweet Brownies, Fudgy, 253
Caramel-Coconut-Pecan Brownies, M288
Chocolate Fudge Brownies, M288
Praline-Pecan Brownies, M288
Tarts, Peppermint Brownie, M288
Truffle Brownie Squares, Mint, M254
BURRITOS
Breakfast Burritos, 204
BUTTER
Avocado Butter, 159
Herb Butter, Holiday, 284
Honey-Spice Butter, 274
Pecan-Honey Butter, 137
Sauce, Butter, 124
Sauce, Garlic Butter, M253

CABBAGE. *See also* **Slaws.**
Fiesta Cabbage, 236
Red Cabbage, Braised, 236
Salad, Chinese Cabbage, 142
Salad, Tangy Cabbage, 162
Salad With Sugared Pecans, Cabbage-Apple, 91
Scalloped Cabbage, 236
Stir-fried Cabbage, 86
CAKES. *See also* **Cheesecakes.**
Angel Food Cake, No-Bake Ice-Cream, 107
Apple Stack Cake, 108
Apple Upside-Down Cake, Fresh, 231
Banana Cake With Coconut-Cream Cheese
Frosting, Decadent, 317
Black Walnut Cake, Maryland, 106
Carrot Cake, Mama Dip's, 299
Chocolate
IV, Chocolate Cake, 322
German Chocolate Cake, 107
Red Velvet Cake Batter, Chocolate-, 286
Red Velvet Cakes, Fluted Chocolate-, 287
Red Velvet Layer Cake, Chocolate-, 287
Sheet Cake, Chocolate-Caramel, 210
Triple-Chocolate Cake, 221
Turtle Cake Squares, M211
Cinnamon-Pecan Crumb Cakes, 288
Coconut
Coconut Cake, 335
Layer Cake, Coconut, M246
Pineapple Cake, Quick Coconut-, 106
Coffee Cakes
Caramel-Apple Coffee Cakes, 210
Sour Cream Coffee Cakes, 212
Sour Cream Coffee Cakes, Mini, 212
Cranberry-Pecan Cake Batter, 287
Lemon-Poppy Seed Cake Batter, 287
Mango Upside-Down Cake, 120
Pig Pickin' Cake, 63
Pound Cake, Granny's, 269
Praline-Pecan Cakes, 286
Pumpkin Spice Cake, 232
Rum Cake, 279

Shortcakes, Southern Peach-and-
Blueberry, 318
Sour Cream Cake Batter, 286
Sour Cream-Pecan Cake Batter, 286
Tortes
Chocolate Torte, Flourless, 81
Huguenot Torte, 98
Vanilla-Jasmine-Sour Cream Tea Cake, 135
CANDIES
Fudge, Mama's, 335
Fudge, Pumpkin, 232
CARAMEL
Bars, Caramel-Pecan Cheesecake, 210
Brownies, Caramel-Coconut-Pecan, M288
Cake, Chocolate-Caramel Sheet, 210
Cake Squares, Turtle, M211
Coffee Cakes, Caramel-Apple, 210
Frosting, Quick Caramel, 211
Frosting, Quick Caramel-Coconut-Pecan, 211
Frosting, Quick Caramel-Pecan, 211
Muffins, Caramel-Apple, 210
Pie, Caramel-Pecan, 269
Quesadillas, Caramel-Apple, 223
Syrup, The Ultimate No-Bake Cheesecake
Banana Pudding With Caramel, 326
CARROTS
Cake, Mama Dip's Carrot, 299
Glazed Carrots, Pepper Jelly-, 334
Glazed Carrots, Spiced-, 274
Rice, Sweet Carrots and, 203
Soufflé, Carrot, 66
CASSEROLES
Breakfast and Brunch
Enchiladas, Breakfast, 333
Grits Casserole, Cheddar Cheese, 283
Hearty Healthy Breakfast Casserole, 325
Omelet Casserole, Confetti, 169
Southwest Breakfast Strata, 136
Enchiladas, Black Bean-Chicken-Spinach, 95
Enchiladas, Black Bean 'n' Spinach, 95
Enchiladas, Smothered, 59
Meat
Beefy Pizza Casserole, 217
Enchilada Casserole, Lightened Texas-
Style, 247
Enchilada Casserole, Texas-Style, 247
Manicotti, Meaty Cheese, 34
Oysters, Scalloped, 47
Pasta Bake, Three-Cheese, 54
Pineapple, Baked, 160
Poultry
Chicken Curry Casserole, Cheesy, 311
Turkey Dinner Bake, Next-Day, 246
Turkey Tetrazzini, Smoked, 96
Turkey Tetrazzini with Artichokes and Red
Bell Peppers, Smoked, 97
Shrimp Casserole, Cajun, 237
Vegetable
Broccoli Casserole, M276
Butternut Squash Bake, 234
Green Bean Casserole, Creamy-and-
Crunchy, 245
Poblano-and-Cheese Casserole, Zesty, 311
Potato-and-Gruyère Casserole, 248
Potato Casserole, Au Gratin, 250
Potato-Leek Gratin, 281
Squash Casserole, 277
Squash Casserole, Southwestern, M217
Sweet Potato Casserole, Maple-, 245
Tomato Casserole, 22
Ziti, Baked, 214

CHEESE. *See also* **Appetizers/Cheese;
Cheesecakes.**
Breads
Biscuits, Blue Cheese, 309
Bread, Cheesy Grits, 83
Cornbread, Cheese-and-Onion, 35
Cream Cheese-Banana-Nut Bread, 27
Cream Cheese-Banana-Nut Bread,
Cinnamon Crisp-Topped, 27
Cream Cheese-Banana-Nut Bread, Orange-
Pecan-Topped, 27
Cream Cheese-Banana-Nut Bread, Peanut
Butter Streusel-Topped, 27
Cream Cheese-Banana-Nut Bread, Toasted
Coconut-Topped, 27
Cream Cheese-Banana-Nut Bread, Toffee-
Topped, 27
Crescents, Cheddar, 70
Muffins, Cream Cheese-Banana-Nut, 27
Pumpkin Bread, Cream Cheese-, 251
Burgers, Spicy Cheddar-Stuffed, 163
Casseroles
Grits Casserole, Cheddar Cheese, 283
Manicotti, Meaty Cheese, 34
Pasta Bake, Three-Cheese, 54
Potato Casserole, Au Gratin, 250
Couscous, Quick Parmesan, 203
Eggs, Cream Cheese Scrambled, 26
Grits, Cheddar Cheese, 43
Mac and Cheese, Creamy, 208
Mac and Cheese, Hearty, 208
Pasta, One-Pot, 202
Salads
Iceberg Wedges, Blue Cheese, 160
Mozzarella, Avocado, and Tomato
Salad, 41
Slaw, Blue Cheese-Bacon, 91
Sandwiches
Checkerboard Cheese Sandwiches, 18
Grilled Cheese-and-Ham Sandwiches, 293
Grilled Cheese Sandwiches With Tomato,
Avocado, and Bacon, 213
Sauces
Cheddar Cheese Cream Sauce, 277
Cheese Sauce, 333
Pimiento Cheese Sauce, 333
Swiss Cheese Cream Sauce, 277
Souffleeta, 326
Soup, Creamy Pimiento Cheese, 254
Spreads
Basil-Cheese Roulade, 143
Pimiento Cheese, 323
Pimiento Cheese, Bacon-, 142
Pimiento Cheese-Stuffed Celery, Light, 161
Topping, Buttery Parmesan, 277
Vegetables
Green Beans With Blue Cheese, 177
Mashed Potatoes, Cheesy, 204
Spinach Madeleine, 95
Vinaigrette, Blue Cheese, 233
CHEESECAKES
Chocolate-Cherry Surprise Cheesecake, 273
Chocolate-Coffee Cheesecake With Mocha
Sauce, M316
Chocolate Fudge Cheesecake, M288
Key Lime-Coconut Mini-Cheesecakes, 159
Lime-Goat Cheese Cheesecakes, 176
Pudding With Caramel Syrup, The Ultimate
No-Bake Cheesecake Banana, 326
Southwest Cheesecake, 249
Strawberry-and-Cream Cheesecake, Irish, 273

CHEF RECIPES
Desserts
Bread Pudding With Bourbon Sauce,
   Pineapple-Apple, 119
Flan, Columbia's, 120
Tea Cake, Vanilla-Jasmine-Sour Cream, 135
Dip, Hot Crab, 124
"French 75," Wayne's, 282
Jam, Coffee-Onion, 123
Main Dishes
Chicken Thighs, Smoky, 184
Crab Cakes, Uncle Frank's, 124
Fajitas (*Bo Nuong Xa*), Vietnamese, 117
Oysters, Southwest Fried, 48
Shrimp, Stuffed Jumbo, 124
Rémoulade, Criolla, 69
Salads and Salad Dressings
Chicken Salad, Lapsang-Poached, 135
Chicken With Wilted Salad Greens, Tom's
   Roasted, 185
Honey-Mustard Dressing, 185
Picnic Salad With Honey-Mustard Dressing,
   Hoover's, 184
Roasted Corn-and-Black Bean Salad, 209
Sara's Grilled Chicken-Cornbread
   Salad, 184
Wilted Salad Greens, 185
Sauce, Butter, 124
Soup, Black Bean, 120
Stew, Oyster, 48
Sweet Potato Soufflé, 110
CHERRIES
Cheesecake, Chocolate-Cherry Surprise, 273
Cookies, Chunky Cherry-Double Chip, M87
Oatmeal, Dried Cherry-and-Pecan, 126
Pie, Chocolate-Covered Cherry, M216
Salad, Cherry-Tarragon Chicken, 275
Tart, Fresh Cherry, 168
CHICKEN
Baked Chicken Breasts, 43
Baked Chicken, Buttermilk, 213
Baked Pecan Chicken, 312
Bowl, Wild Rice-and-Chicken, 127
Breasts With Artichoke-Pepper Sauce,
   Chicken, 139
Cakes, Southwestern Chicken-Corn, 321
Casserole, Cheesy Chicken Curry, 311
Cassoulet, Sausage-and-Chicken, 237
Coconut Chicken Dippers With Wowee Maui
   Mustard, Crispy, 324
Cranberry Chicken, 272
Curry-and-Spice Chicken, Aromatic, 238
Enchiladas, Black Bean-Chicken-Spinach, 95
Filling, Chicken, 117
Fingers With Honey-Mustard Sauce,
   Chicken, 300
Fried Chicken, Pimiento Cheese-Stuffed, 322
Greek-Style Chicken, 220
Grilled Chicken, Lexington-Style, 54
Grilled Chicken, Tea-Thyme, M52
Grilled Chicken Thighs, 163
Grilled Chicken With Watermelon-Feta Salad,
   Herb-, 320
Grilled Sweet Guava Chicken, 278
Honey-Pecan Chicken Strips, 188
Marinated Chicken, Balsamic-, 219
Marinated Chicken, Mojo-, 163
Marinated Chicken With Mango Salsa,
   Margarita, 328
Mojo Chicken With Mandarin-Black Bean
   Salad, Cuban, 318

Olé, Chicken-and-Artichoke, 59
Pané Chicken With Sweet-'n'-Spicy Red Pepper
   Sauce, 320
Pasta, Chicken and Bow Tie, 49
Pizza, Bistro Grilled Chicken, 131
Pizza, Tex-Mex Chicken-and-Bacon, 325
Pudding, Chicken, 22
Raspberry-Barbecue Chicken, 203
Roast Chicken With Sautéed Green Beans,
   Lemon-Garlic, 43
Rollups, Greek Chicken, 128
Rub, Paul's Chicken, 174
Salads
Cherry-Tarragon Chicken Salad, 275
Chicken Salad, 65, 94
Chunky Chicken Parmesan Salad, 209
Cranberry-Pecan Chicken Salad, 284
Fiesta Chicken Salad, 223
Lapsang-Poached Chicken Salad, 135
Picnic Salad With Honey-Mustard Dressing,
   Hoover's, 184
Roasted Chicken With Wilted Salad Greens,
   Tom's, 185
Spring Salad With Raspberry Vinaigrette, 91
Strawberry-Citrus Chicken Salad, 84
Strawberry Salad, Chicken-and-, 132
Smoked Chicken, Big "D," 175
Soup, Cheesy Mac 'n' Chicken, 292
Soup, Chicken-and-Black Bean, 102
Stew, Chicken-and-Vegetable, 235
Tamales, Helena, 112
Texas Rockets, 175
Thighs, Balsamic Garlic-and-Herb Chicken, 19
Thighs, Molasses-Glazed Chicken, 85
Thighs, Smoky Chicken, 184
Wings, Buffalo, 64
Wraps, Chicken-and-Slaw, 222
CHILI
Beef Chili, Chunky, 235
CHOCOLATE. *See also* **Brownies.**
Bars and Cookies
Almond-Toffee Chocolate Chip Cookies, 87
Biscotti, Chocolate-Cinnamon, 30
Cherry-Double Chip Cookies, Chunky, M87
Cranberry-White Chocolate Cookies, 308
Dark Chocolate-Almond Crisps, M30
Dark Chocolate Chip Cookies, 87
Dipped Cookies, Chocolate-, M299
Domino Cookies, 19
Double Chocolate Chunk Cookies, 181
Favorite Chocolate Chip Cookies, 142
Mint Cookies, Chocolate and, 308
Oatmeal-Raisin Chocolate Chip Cookies, 87
Peanut Butter-Chocolate Chip
   Cookies, 87, 222
Pecan-Chocolate Chip Cookies, 87
Praline Bars, M205
Shortbread, Millionaire, M94
Shortbread, Mocha, 307
Stick, Chocolate Cookies on a, 63
Ultimate Chocolate Chip Cookies, 87
Cakes and Tortes
Cheesecake, Chocolate-Cherry
   Surprise, 273
Cheesecake, Chocolate Fudge, M288
Cheesecake With Mocha Sauce, Chocolate-
   Coffee, M316
Flourless Chocolate Torte, 81
IV, Chocolate Cake, 322
German Chocolate Cake, 107
Red Velvet Cake Batter, Chocolate-, 286

Red Velvet Cakes, Fluted Chocolate-, 287
Red Velvet Layer Cake, Chocolate-, 287
Sheet Cake, Chocolate-Caramel, 210
Triple-Chocolate Cake, 221
Turtle Cake Squares, M211
Fudge, Mama's, 335
Fudge, Pumpkin, 232
Fondue, Chocolate, M281
Fillings and Toppings
Chocolate Filling, M307
Chocolate Glaze, M287
Coffee Liqueur Ganache Icing, 322
Glaze, Chocolate, 221
Mocha-Chocolate Cream Filling, 322
Ice-Cream Sandwiches, Easy Chocolate-
   Mint, 62
Ice-Cream Sandwiches, Mocha-Almond-
   Fudge, 62
Mousse With Raspberry Sauce, Dark
   Chocolate, 31
Pecans, Chocolate-Dipped, M269
Pies and Tarts
Bourbon Pecan Pie, Chocolate-, 134
Cherry Pie, Chocolate-Covered, M216
Icebox Pie, Chocolate, 157
Mocha-Pecan Mud Pie, 290
Pecan Fudge Pie With Raspberry Sauce, 201
Walnut Pie, Chocolate-, 134
Pizza, Chocolate-Peanut Butter, 193
Sauces
Champagne-Chocolate Sauce, M282
Dark Chocolate Sauce, 31
Hot Fudge Sauce, 193
Mocha Sauce, 317
CHUTNEY
Cranberry-Apple Chutney, Quick, 231
CLAMS
Pasta, White Wine-Tomato-and-Clam, 140
Sauce, Linguine With White Clam, 49
COCONUT
Cakes
Coconut Cake, 335
Layer Cake, Coconut, M246
Quick Coconut-Pineapple Cake, 106
Chicken Dippers With Wowee Maui Mustard,
   Crispy Coconut, 324
Cookies, Coconut-Macadamia Chunk, 87
Crust, Coconut, 157
Filling, Coconut-Pecan, 107
Frosting, Coconut-Cream Cheese, 317
Ice Cream, Mint Nectarines With Pineapple-
   Coconut, 123
Ice Cream, Mint Peaches With Pineapple-
   Coconut, 123
Pie, Coconut Cream, 110
Pie, Rum-Coconut Key Lime, 157
COFFEE
Jam, Coffee-Onion, 123
Turkey Breast, Molasses-Coffee, M289
COOKIES. *See also* **Brownies.**
Bars and Squares
Cheesecake Bars, Caramel-Pecan, 210
Citrus Bars, 173
Praline Bars, M205
Shortbread, Millionaire, M94
Benne Seed Wafers, 111
Biscotti, Chocolate-Cinnamon, 30
Chocolate-Dipped Cookies, M299
Drop
Almond-Toffee Chocolate Chip Cookies, 87
Cherry-Double Chip Cookies, Chunky, M87

Cookies, Drop (continued)

Chocolate and Mint Cookies, 308
Chocolate Chip Cookies, Dark, 87
Chocolate Chip Cookies, Favorite, 142
Chocolate Chip Cookies, Ultimate, 87
Chocolate Chunk Cookies, Double, 181
Coconut-Macadamia Chunk Cookies, 87
Cranberry-White Chocolate Cookies, 308
Oatmeal-Raisin Chocolate Chip Cookies, 87
Peanut Butter-Chocolate Chip
Cookies, 87, 222
Pecan-Chocolate Chip Cookies, 87
Ladybugs, Cream Cheese, 211
Oat 'n' Cereal Cookies, Crunchy, 181
Refrigerator
Almond Sand Dollar Cookies, 130
Lemon-Basil Snaps, 275
Shortbread Thumbelinas, 307
Rolled
Angel Cookies, 308
Dark Chocolate-Almond Crisps, M30
Domino Cookies, 19
Stick, Chocolate Cookies on a, 63
Stick, Cookies on a, 63
Shortbread, Mocha, 307
COOKING LIGHT. *See* **Healthy & Light Recipes.**
CORN
Cakes, Southwestern Chicken-Corn, 321
Cob With Red Chile Paste, Grilled Corn on
the, 118
Pudding, Cornmeal, 43
Pudding, Sweet Corn, 66
Relish, Tomato, Basil and Corn, 321
Roasted Camp Corn, 174
Salad, Roasted Corn-and-Black Bean, 209
Salsa, Black Bean-and-Corn, 297
CORNBREADS
Buttermilk Corn Sticks, 218
Cheese-and-Onion Cornbread, 35
Croutons, Cornbread, 45
Dressing, Slow-Cooker Cornbread 270
Honey-Sweet Cornbread, 137
Salad, Layered Cornbread-and-Turkey, 147
Salad, Layered Southwest Cornbread-and-
Turkey, 147
Salad, Sara's Grilled Chicken-Cornbread, 184
Sweet Potato Cornbread, 252
COUSCOUS
Cranberry-and-Toasted Pecan Couscous, M259
Parmesan Couscous, Quick, 203
CRAB
Cakes, Maryland Crab, 105
Cakes, Uncle Frank's Crab, 124
Dip, Hot Crab, 124
Soup, She-Crab, 98
CRANBERRIES
Beverages
Lemonade, Cranberry, 205
Sparkler, Cranberry-Apple, 61
Tea, Cranberry-Raspberry Herb, 61
Biscuits, Cranberry-Orange-Glazed, 335
Cake Batter, Cranberry-Pecan, 287
Chicken, Cranberry, 272
Chutney, Quick Cranberry-Apple, 231
Cookies, Cranberry-White Chocolate, 308
Couscous, Cranberry-and-Toasted
Pecan, M259
Meatballs, Cranberry, 310
Muffins, Cranberry, 313
Mustard, Cranberry, 320

Orange 'n' Jellied Cranberry Sauce
Stacks, 270
Relish, Roasted Acorn Squash With
Cranberry, 234
Salads
Apple Salad, Cranberry-, 65
Chicken Salad, Cranberry-Pecan, 284
Congealed Salad, Cranberry, 334
Relish Salad, Cranberry, 245
Sauce, Cranberry-Orange, 218
Vinaigrette, Cranberry, 247
CRAWFISH
Étouffée, Quick Crawfish, 57
Étouffée, Traditional Crawfish, 56
Jambalaya, Crawfish, 118
CROUTONS
Cornbread Croutons, 45
Crispy Croutons, 207
Garlic Croutons, 247
CUCUMBERS
Rounds, Cucumber-Dill, 96
Sauce, Sour Cream-Cucumber, 207
Sauce, Tzatziki, 82

DESSERTS. *See also* **Brownies; Cakes;**
Candies; Cheesecakes; Cookies;
Frostings; Ice Creams; Mousse; Pies,
Puffs, and Pastries; Puddings;
Sherbets.
Banana-Berry Split, 193
Bread With Stewed Yard Peaches, Cocoa, 23
Doughnut Stacks, Mini-, 58
Flan, Columbia's, 120
Fondue, Chocolate, M281
Fruitini, 283
Ladyfingers, Creamy Berry, 36
Lemon-Blueberry Layered Dessert, 206
Nectarines With Pineapple-Coconut Ice
Cream, Mint, 123
Oranges, Italian Caramelized, 101
Parfaits, Super Fast Strawberry Shortcake, 196
Peaches, Stewed Yard, 23
Peaches With Pineapple-Coconut Ice Cream,
Mint, 123
Raspberry Bites, Creamy, 36
Sauces
Bourbon Sauce, 119
Champagne-Chocolate Sauce, M282
Dark Chocolate Sauce, 31
Hot Fudge Sauce, 193
Mocha Sauce, 317
Raspberry Sauce, 31, 201
Vanilla Cream Sauce, 260
Soufflés With Lemon Whipped Cream,
Spiced, 255
Sundaes, S'mores, 257
Sundaes, Waffle Taco, M62
DOUGHNUTS
Stacks, Mini-Doughnut, 58
DRESSING. *See also* **Salad Dressings.**
Cornbread Dressing, Slow-Cooker, 270

EGGPLANT
Fritters, Eggplant, 128
Pizza, Garden Eggplant, 127
EGGS
Armadillo Eggs, 139
Casserole, Hearty Healthy Breakfast, 325
Huevos Rancheros, Spicy, 221

Quesadillas, Bacon-and-Egg, 88
Salad, Egg, 209
Scrambled
Cream Cheese Scrambled Eggs, 26
Pizza, Sausage-and-Scrambled Egg, 88
Tacos, Sausage-Egg Soft, 26
Stuffed
Deviled Eggs, Barbecue, 167
Deviled Eggs, Buttery Dijon, 93
Deviled Eggs, Chive-Tarragon, 93
Deviled Eggs With Capers, 93
EMPANADAS
Meaty Empanadas, 138
ENCHILADAS
Black Bean-Chicken-Spinach Enchiladas, 95
Black Bean 'n' Spinach Enchiladas, 95
Breakfast Enchiladas, 333
Casserole, Lightened Texas-Style
Enchilada, 247
Casserole, Texas-Style Enchilada, 247
Smothered Enchiladas, 59
ÉTOUFFÉE
Crawfish Étouffée, Quick, 57
Crawfish Étouffée, Traditional, 56

FAJITAS
Pork Fajitas, Pronto, 223
Vietnamese Fajitas (*Bo Nuong Xa*), 117
FAMILY FAVORITES
Apples, Fried, 109
Bacon, Crispy Brown Sugar, 283
Bacon-Pimiento Cheese, 142
Breads
Biscuits, Sweet Potato, 22
Cocoa Bread With Stewed Yard Peaches, 23
Cornbread, Cheese-and-Onion, 35
Cornbread, Honey-Sweet, 137
Cream Cheese-Banana-Nut Bread, 27
French Toast, Overnight Oven-Baked, 283
French Toast With Fresh Strawberry Syrup,
Croissant, 132
Grits Bread, Cheesy, 83
Hush Puppies, 99
Pancakes and Gravy, Pasta, 43
Pancakes, Buttermilk 'n' Honey, 137
Popovers, Whole Wheat, 195
Spoonbread, Memmie's, 105
Butter, Pecan-Honey, 137
Casserole, Cheddar Cheese Grits, 283
Desserts
Banana-Berry Split, 193
Bars, Citrus, 173
Cake, German Chocolate, 107
Cake, Granny's Pound, 269
Cake, Mango Upside-Down, 120
Cake, Quick Coconut-Pineapple, 106
Cookies, Almond Sand Dollar, 130
Cookies, Crunchy Oat 'n' Cereal, 181
Cookies, Domino, 19
Cookies, Double Chocolate Chunk, 181
Cookies, Favorite Chocolate Chip, 142
Cookies, Peanut Butter-Chocolate Chip, 222
Cookies, Ultimate Chocolate Chip, 87
Doughnut Stacks, Mini-, 58
Fruitini, 283
Oranges, Italian Caramelized, 101
Parfaits, Super Fast Strawberry
Shortcake, 196
Pie, Chocolate Icebox, 157
Pie, Chocolate-Walnut, 134

Pie, Coconut Cream, 110
Pie, Strawberry-Rhubarb, 132
Pie, Zesty Lemon, 157
Pizza, Chocolate-Peanut Butter, 193
Quesadillas, Caramel-Apple, 223
Sherbet, Raspberry-Buttermilk, 133
Sherbet, Refreshing Lime, 133
Tart, Double Citrus, 55
Tea Cake, Vanilla-Jasmine-Sour Cream, 135
Torte, Flourless Chocolate, 81
Torte, Huguenot, 98
Wafers, Benne Seed, 111
Gravy, Sawmill, 110
Grits, Cheddar Cheese, 43

Main Dishes
Boston Butt Roast With Gravy, 90
Casserole, Beefy Pizza, 217
Casserole, Texas-Style Enchilada, 247
Catfish Nuggets, Cornmeal-Crusted, 44
Chicken-and-Artichoke Olé, 59
Chicken and Bow Tie Pasta, 49
Chicken, Baked Pecan, 312
Chicken, Big "D" Smoked, 175
Chicken Breasts, Baked, 43
Chicken Breasts With Artichoke-Pepper
   Sauce, 139
Chicken, Buttermilk Baked, 213
Chicken, Cranberry, 272
Chicken-Fried Steak, 67
Chicken, Greek-Style, 220
Chicken, Lexington-Style Grilled, 54
Chicken, Mojo-Marinated, 163
Chicken Pudding, 22
Chicken, Raspberry-Barbecue, 203
Chicken Strips, Honey-Pecan, 188
Chicken, Tea-Thyme Grilled, M52
Chicken Thighs, Balsamic Garlic-and-
   Herb, 19
Chicken Thighs, Molasses-Glazed, 85
Chicken With Sautéed Green Beans, Lemon-
   Garlic Roast, 43
Country-Fried Steak With Creamy Salsa
   Gravy, 67
Enchiladas, Black Bean 'n' Spinach, 95
Enchiladas, Smothered, 59
Fajitas, Pronto Pork, 223
Ham, Currant-Glazed, 104
Lamb Chops, Creamy Dijon, 82
Lamb With Tzatziki Sauce, Rosemary-
   Crusted, 82
Lasagna, Fiesta Taco, 140
Lasagna, Speedy, M252
Lasagna, Tex-Mex, 58
Linguine With White Clam Sauce, 49
London Broil, Marinated, 84
Mac and Cheese, Creamy, 208
Mac and Cheese, Hearty, 208
Mac and Cheese, Taco Dinner, 208
Manicotti, Meaty Cheese, 34
Meat Loaf, Old-Fashioned, 95
Meat Loaf With Green Chile-Tomato Gravy, 42
Pasta, One-Pot, 202
Pizza, Bistro Grilled Chicken, M131
Pizza, Garden Eggplant, 127
Pizza, Sausage-and-Scrambled Egg, 88
Pizza, Southwestern BBQ Chicken, 33
Pork Bites, Zesty Fried, 90
Pork Chops With Caramelized Onions,
   Thai, 85
Pork Chops With Onions, Pan-fried, 43
Pork Chops With Orange Slices, Saucy, 197

Pork in Black Bean Sauce, Southwest, 139
Pork, Polynesian, 90
Pork Saté, 53
Pork, Tabb's Barbecue, 166
Pork Tenderloin, Margarita, 85
Pork With Ranch-Barbecue Sauce, Slow-
   Grilled, 163
Pot Roast, Cowboy, 35
Pot Roast, Italian, 34
Quesadillas, Bacon-and-Egg, 88
Quesadillas, Reuben, 131
Rib-Eye Steaks, Molasses-Grilled, 218
Salisbury Steak, Tex-Mex, 204
Shrimp and Grits, Garlic, 111
Shrimp and Pasta With Creole Cream
   Sauce, 49
Spaghetti With Mint-and-Garlic Tomato
   Sauce, 100
Steak With Mushroom Gravy, Minute, 67
Strata, Southwest Breakfast, 136
Tacos, Shredded Grilled Tilapia, 16
Tetrazzini, Smoked Turkey, 96
Turkey Dinner Bake, Next-Day, 246
Turkey, Roasted, 244
Wild Rice-and-Chicken Bowl, 127
Pasta Bake, Three-Cheese, 54
Pineapple, Baked, 160
Pudding, Cornmeal, 43
Rice Pilaf, Basil, M197

Salads and Salad Dressings
Cabbage Salad, Chinese, 142
Chicken-and-Strawberry Salad, 132
Coleslaw, Lemon-Apple, 44
Cornbread-and-Turkey Salad, Layered, 147
Fiesta Salad, 58
Fruit Congealed Salad, Layered, M146
Fruit Salad, Ginger-and-Lemon, 17
Fruit Salad With Honey Dressing, 137
Pasta Salad, Greek, 130
Potato Salad, Bacon, 171
Potato Salad, Sweet, 171
Slaw, Sweet-and-Spicy, 17
Spinach-and-Apple Salad With Cinnamon
   Vinaigrette, Fresh, 44
Spinach-and-Strawberry Salad, 55
Vegetable Salad, Marinated, 129
White Bean-and-Asparagus Salad, 100
Salsa, Fruity Black Bean, 16

Sandwiches
Burgers, Spicy Cheddar-Stuffed, 163
Melt, Loaded Turkey, 159
Mini-Sandwiches, Shredded Flank
   Steak, 158
Monte Cristo Sandwiches, Open-Faced, 222
Panini Sandwiches, Roast Beef-
   Cheddar, 223
Rollups, Greek Chicken, 128
Turkey, Bacon, and Havarti Sandwich, 92
Wraps, Chicken-and-Slaw, 222
Wraps, Tangy-and-Sweet Roast Beef, 92
Shake, Chocolate Milk, 193

Soups and Stews
Beef Stew, Slow-Cooker, 235
Chicken-and-Vegetable Stew, 235
Ham-and-Collard Stew, Hearty, 236
Jambalaya, Crawfish, 118
Minestrone, Mama's Mexican, 254
Okra Soup, 98
Pork-and-Black Bean Soup, 32
She-Crab Soup, 98
Tea, Marian's Iced, 135

Vegetables
Asparagus, Grilled, 197
Asparagus, Marinated, 105
Asparagus, Oven-Roasted, 55
Asparagus With Garlic, Stir-fried, 86
Beans With Tomatoes, Great Northern, 23
Bell Peppers, Potato-Stuffed Grilled, 123
Broccoli Skillet, Quick, 86
Carrot Soufflé, 66
Corn on the Cob With Red Chile Paste,
   Grilled, 118
Corn Pudding, Sweet, 66
Corn, Roasted Camp, 174
Eggplant Fritters, 128
French Fries, Ranch-Seasoned, 93
Green Bean Casserole, Creamy-and-
   Crunchy, 245
Green Beans, Lemon-and-Dill, 17
Green Beans With Bacon, Sautéed, M160
Green Beans With Blue Cheese, 177
Green Beans, Zesty, 204
Peas, Hot Pecan, 85
Portobello Mushrooms, Lime-Grilled, 18
Potato Casserole, Au Gratin, 250
Potatoes, Cheesy Mashed, 204
Potatoes, Double-Stuffed Barbecue, 162
Potatoes, Garlic Mashed, 42
Potatoes, Oven-Roasted, 44
Potatoes, Simple Mashed, 271
Potatoes, Two-Color Rosemary Roasted, 18
Potato Mash, Three-, 271
Spinach Madeleine, 95
Spinach Soufflé, 66
Squash and Carrots, Sautéed, 42
Squash Casserole, Southwestern, M217
Squash, Marinated, 129
Sweet Potato Casserole, Maple-, 245
Sweet Potatoes, Baked Whole, 108
Sweet Potato Soufflé, 110
Tomato Casserole, 22

FAST FIXIN'S
Appetizers
Cheese Wafers, 97
Crostini With Olive Tapenade, Grilled, 172
Cucumber-Dill Rounds, 96
Dip, Layered Catfish, 55
Dip, Quick Hummus, 206
Hummus, Red Pepper, 97
Oysters With Paul's Cocktail Sauce,
   Grilled, 244
Pita Triangles, Benne Seed, 97
Shrimp Paste, 98
Bacon-Pimiento Cheese, 142

Beverages
Appleade, Hot Spiced Lemon-, 23
Bellinis, Apricot, 96
Cider Sipper, Citrus, 23
Cocktail, Pomegranate-Champagne, 282
Cooler, White Grape-and-Orange, 61
Cranberry-Apple Sparkler, 61
"French 75," Wayne's, 282
Lemonade, Cranberry, 205
Lemonade, Fizzy Raspberry, 61
Margaritas, Frozen Blueberry, 179
Milk Shake, Chocolate, 193
Punch, Coffee-Ice Cream, 136
Punch, Honey-Apple, 23
Punch, Margarita, 212
Punch, Whiskey, 276
Shake, Banana-Mocha, 45
Smoothie, Banana-Berry, 24

Fast Fixin's, Beverages (continued)

> Tea Cooler, Orange, 216
> Tea, Iced Green, 196
> Tea, Verla's Hot, 257
> Vodka-Orange Sipper, Sunset, 122

Breads
> Biscuits, Easy Pan, 26
> Biscuits, Spicy Cheese Cocktail, 173
> Breadsticks, Parmesan Cheese, 20
> Cornbread, Honey-Sweet, 137
> Cornbread, Sweet Potato, 252
> French Bread, Garlic, 57
> French Toast With Fresh Strawberry Syrup, Croissant, 132
> Garlic Bread, 215
> Garlic Bread, Basil-, 202
> Muffins, Orange-Date, 215
> Pancakes, Buttermilk 'n' Honey, 137
> Toast, Lemon-Garlic, 171

Butter, Honey-Spice, 274
Butter, Pecan-Honey, 137
Chicken Filling, 117
Couscous, Quick Parmesan, 203
Cream, Nutmeg-Molasses, 104

Desserts
> Banana-Berry Split, 193
> Bananas, Brown Sugar, 45
> Blackberry Juice, 182
> Doughnut Stacks, Mini-, 58
> Filling, Coconut-Pecan, 107
> Filling, Cream Cheese, 251
> Fondue, Chocolate, M281
> Frosting, Cream Cheese, 232
> Frosting, Easy Microwave, M63
> Frosting, Quick Caramel, 211
> Frosting, Whipped Cream, 107
> Fruitini, 283
> Glaze, Chocolate, 221
> Icing, Satin, 246
> Nectarines With Pineapple-Coconut Ice Cream, Mint, 123
> Pecans, Chocolate-Dipped, M269
> Quesadillas, Caramel-Apple, 223
> Sauce, Bourbon, 119
> Sauce, Champagne-Chocolate, M282
> Sauce, Hot Fudge, 193
> Sauce, Raspberry, 31, 201
> Sauce, Vanilla Cream, 260
> Strawberries, Splendid, 215

Glaze, Guava, 279
Grits, Cheddar Cheese, 43
Herb Mix, Italian Parmesan, 284
Honey, Citrus-Pear, 230

Main Dishes
> Burritos, Breakfast, 204
> Catfish Nuggets, Cornmeal-Crusted, 44
> Catfish, Quick Pan-fried, 170
> Chicken Breasts With Artichoke-Pepper Sauce, 139
> Chicken, Raspberry-Barbecue, 203
> Eggs, Cream Cheese Scrambled, 26
> Linguine With White Clam Sauce, 49
> Mac and Cheese, Creamy, 208
> Oatmeal, Dried Cherry-and-Pecan, 126
> Pizza, Bistro Grilled Chicken, M131
> Pizza, Southwestern BBQ Chicken, 33
> Pork Chops With Onions, Pan-fried, 43
> Shrimp, Stuffed Jumbo, 124
> Steaks, Grilled New York, 123
> Tacos, Shredded Grilled Tilapia, 16

Mayonnaise, Tomato-Basil, 180
Orange 'n' Jellied Cranberry Sauce Stacks, 270
Peaches, Stewed Yard, 23
Rice Pilaf, Basil, M197
Rub, Barbecue, 166
Rub, Paul's Pork Ribs, 174
Rub, Spice, 259

Salads and Salad Dressings
> Apple Salad, Lemony, 241
> Autumn Salad With Maple-Cider Vinaigrette, 281
> Bean Salad, Tangy, 158
> Cabbage-Apple Salad With Sugared Pecans, 91
> Caesar Salad, Easy Spicy, 122
> Chicken Salad, Fiesta, 223
> Cider Vinegar-Honey Dressing, 41
> Field Greens With Roasted Bacon-Wrapped Pears, 230
> Fruit Salad, Ginger-and-Lemon, 17
> Fruit Salad, Vanilla-Scented, 209
> Fruit Salad With Honey Dressing, 137
> Iceberg Wedges, Blue Cheese, 160
> Mozzarella, Avocado, and Tomato Salad, 41
> Pasta Salad, Confetti, 242
> Red Grapefruit-Lemon Vinaigrette, Salad with, 161
> Romaine Salad With Cashews, 195
> Slaw, Blue Cheese-Bacon, 91
> Slaw, Broccoli, 278
> Slaw, Sweet-and-Spicy, 17
> Spinach-and-Apple Salad With Cinnamon Vinaigrette, Fresh, 44
> Spinach-and-Strawberry Salad, 55
> Spinach, Pear, and Blue Cheese Salad, Easy, 41
> Spring Salad With Raspberry Vinaigrette, 91
> Strawberry-Cranberry-Orange Salad, 249
> Strawberry Salad With Cinnamon Vinaigrette, 133
> Summer Salad, Berry Delicious, 179
> Tomato-and-Cucumber Salad, 69
> Tossed Salad, Italian, 202
> Turkey Salad With Cranberry Vinaigrette and Garlic Croutons, Main Dish, 246
> Vinaigrette, Apple Cider, 201
> Vinaigrette, Apple-Ginger, 230
> Vinaigrette, Blue Cheese, 233
> Vinaigrette, Cranberry, 247
> Vinaigrette, Dill, 173
> Vinaigrette, Maple-Cider, 281
> Vinaigrette, Raspberry, 91
> Vinaigrette, Strawberry-Balsamic, 84
> Wilted Salad Greens, 185

Salsa, Blueberry, 179
Salsa, Fruity Black Bean, 16
Salsa, Homemade, 59
Salsa, Sweet Pepper-Mango, 148

Sandwiches
> Burgers, Italian-Style, 180
> Cheese Sandwiches, Checkerboard, 18
> Focaccia Sandwich, Pesto, 131
> Grilled Cheese Sandwiches With Tomato, Avocado, and Bacon, 213
> Ham-and-Pepper Salad Sandwich, Giant, 204
> Monte Cristo Sandwiches, Open-Faced, 222
> Panini Sandwiches, Roast Beef-Cheddar, 223

Sauces and Gravies
> Barbecue Sauce, Raspberry-, 203

Barbecue Sauce, White, 196
Butter Sauce, 124
Butter Sauce, Garlic, M253
Caper Sauce, 105
Cider Sauce, 259
Cranberry-Orange Sauce, 218
Cream Sauce, 248
Green Chile-Tomato Gravy, 42
Horseradish Sauce, 177
Mushroom-Artichoke Sauce, Creamy, 312
Ranch-Barbecue Sauce, 163
Sawmill Gravy, 110
Tzatziki Sauce, 82

Snack Mix, Apple Spice-Raisin, 222
Soup, Chilled Blueberry, 178
Spice Blend, Sweet, 274
Syrup, Orange, 240

Vegetables
> Acorn Squash With Cranberry Relish, Roasted, 234
> Asparagus, Balsamic-Browned Butter, 260
> Asparagus, Oven-Roasted, 55
> Asparagus With Garlic, Stir-fried, 86
> Broccoli, Pecan, 257
> Broccoli Skillet, Quick, 86
> Cabbage, Stir-fried, 86
> Carrots, Spiced-Glazed, 274
> Celery, Light Pimiento Cheese-Stuffed, 161
> Cherry Tomatoes, Rosemary-Roasted, 257
> Corn on the Cob With Red Chile Paste, Grilled, 118
> Green Beans, Dill-and-Almond, 81
> Green Beans, Lemon-and-Dill, 17
> Green Beans, Speedy Rosemary, 241
> Green Beans, Zesty, 204
> Portobello Mushrooms, Lime-Grilled, 18
> Potatoes, Cheesy Mashed, 204
> Spaghetti Squash Sauté, 234
> Spinach Madeleine, 95
> Squash and Carrots, Sautéed, 42
> Squash and Zucchini, Sautéed, 203
> Sweet Potatoes, Southwest Mashed, 271
> Tomatoes, Feta-Stuffed, 148
> Vinaigrette, Apricot, M312
> Walnuts, Sugared Curried, 281
> Whipped Cream, 269

FETTUCCINE
> Alfredo, Southwestern Fettuccine, 186
> Shrimp and Andouille Alfredo Sauce Over Pasta, Cajun, 57

FILLINGS
> Chicken Filling, 117

Sweet
> Blackberry Curd Filling, 182
> Chocolate Filling, M307
> Coconut-Pecan Filling, 107
> Cream Cheese Filling, 251
> Dried Apple Filling, 108
> Mocha-Chocolate Cream Filling, 322

FISH. *See also* **Clams, Crab, Crawfish, Salmon, Seafood, Shrimp, Tuna.**
> Blackened Fish, 119

Catfish
> Baked Lemon-Dill Catfish, 216
> Dip, Layered Catfish, 55
> Nuggets, Cornmeal-Crusted Catfish, 44
> Oven-Fried Catfish, Crispy, 256
> Pan-fried Catfish, Light and Crispy, 198
> Pan-fried Catfish, Quick, 170
> Pecan Catfish With Lemon Sauce, 56
> Tacos, Southern-Style Fish, 327

Mahi-Mahi With Parsleyed Tomatoes, Broiled, 130
Tilapia Tacos, Shredded Grilled, 16

FONDUE
Chocolate Fondue, M281

FREEZEABLE RECIPES
Appetizers
Eggs, Armadillo, 139
Meatballs, Cranberry, 310
Mushroom Turnovers, 310
Spread, Creamy Olive, 311
Berry Freeze, 220
Breads
Coffee Cakes, Sour Cream, 212
Crescents, Cheddar, 70
French Bread, Garlic, 57
Muffins, Caramel-Apple, 210
Muffins, Cranberry, 313
Muffins, Lemon-Poppy Seed, 33
Pumpkin Bread, 232
Rolls, Lemon-Orange, 70
Desserts
Bars, Caramel-Pecan Cheesecake, 210
Cake, Chocolate-Caramel Sheet, 210
Cake, No-Bake Ice-Cream Angel Food, 107
Ice Cream, Peach-Cinnamon, 168
Ice-Cream Pie, Spiked Strawberry-Lime, 89
Ice-Cream Pie, Strawberry Smoothie, 89
Pie, Frozen Hawaiian, 157
Sherbet, Raspberry-Buttermilk, 133
Sherbet, Refreshing Lime, 133
Stack Cake, Apple, 108
Main Dishes
Casserole, Cajun Shrimp, 237
Casserole, Cheesy Chicken Curry, 311
Chili, Chunky Beef, 235
Étouffée, Quick Crawfish, 57
Étouffée, Traditional Crawfish, 56
Shrimp and Andouille Alfredo Sauce Over Pasta, Cajun, 57
Turkey Sausage Patties, Breakfast, 169
Sandwiches, Slow-Cooker Barbecue Beef, 64
Squash Casserole, 277
Walnuts, Candied, 60
FRENCH TOAST
Croissant French Toast With Fresh Strawberry Syrup, 132
Overnight Oven-Baked French Toast, 283
FRITTERS
Buñuelos, 295
Eggplant Fritters, 128
Matzoh-and-Honey Fritters, 81
FROM OUR KITCHEN
baking pans, 314
beans, canned
black bean dip, 102
blackberries, 182
recipe, Blackberry Curd Filling, 182
recipe, Blackberry Juice, 182
cakes, greasing pans, 314
caramel, 224
commercial food products
frozen cheese wafer dough, 144
cooking oils
infusing, 182
egg rolls, 50
recipe, Egg Rolls, 50
entertaining
presenting food, 102
sandwich bar for, 28
Web site, 314

fish
cooking, 198
freezing, 198
recipe, Light and Crispy Pan-fried Catfish, 198
selecting, 198
thawing, 198
frying foods
fish, 198
gifts of food, 284, 314
containers for, 314
recipe, Holiday Herb Butter, 284
recipe, Italian Parmesan Herb Mix, 284
recipe, Sweet-Hot Honey Mustard, 284
grits, leftover, 224
grocery shopping, 50
saving time and money, 50
leftovers, 50
grits, 224
mayonnaise
recipe, Béarnaise Mayonnaise, 144
recipe, Fresh Herb Mayonnaise, 144
recipe, Lemon-Rosemary Mayonnaise, 144
meats, 102
pastas
cooking, 242
salads, 242
piecrust
refrigerated dough, 164
recipe preparation
shortcuts in, 70
rice, 50
fried rice, 50
recipe, Fried Rice 101, 50
rolls
recipe, Cheddar Crescents, 70
recipe, Lemon-Orange Rolls, 70
salad dressing
recipe, Fresh Lemon Vinaigrette, 242
salads
recipe, Confetti Pasta Salad, 242
recipe, Cranberry-Pecan Chicken Salad, 284
sandwiches, 28
bar for entertaining, 28
fillings for, 28
grilled, 28
grill press for, 28
soups
recipe, Chicken-and-Black Bean Soup, 102
FROSTINGS
Buttercream Frosting, 308
Caramel-Coconut-Pecan Frosting, Quick, 211
Caramel Frosting, Quick, 211
Caramel-Pecan Frosting, Quick, 211
Coconut-Cream Cheese Frosting, 317
Coffee Liqueur Ganache Icing, 322
Cream Cheese Frosting, 232, 287, 299
Microwave Frosting, Easy, M63
Satin Icing, 246
Whipped Cream Frosting, 107
FRUIT. See also specific types.
Desserts
Bars, Citrus, 173
Bread Pudding With Vanilla Cream Sauce, Berry, 260
Cake, Pig Pickin', 63
Fruitini, 283
Pie, Frozen Hawaiian, 157
Split, Banana- Berry, 193
Tart, Double Citrus, 55
Dressing, Snappy Fruit Salad, 160
Freeze, Berry, 220

Fresh Fruit With Lime Syrup, 220
Granola, Mixed Fruit, 240
Medley, Barley, Vegetable, and Fruit, 127
Pilaf, Mixed Fruit, 205
Punch, Brunch, 335
Rémoulade, Citrus, 69
Salads
Congealed Salad, Layered Fruit, M146
Ginger-and-Lemon Fruit Salad, 17
Harvest Crunch Salad, 291
Honey Dressing, Fruit Salad With, 137
Vanilla-Scented Fruit Salad, 209
Salsa, Fruity Black Bean, 16

GARLIC
Asparagus, Marinated, 105
Asparagus, Oven-Roasted, 55
Asparagus With Garlic, Stir-fried, 86
Black Beans and Rice, 214
Boston Butt Roast With Gravy, 90
Casserole, Cajun Shrimp, 237
Chicken Breasts With Artichoke-Pepper Sauce, 139
Chicken, Grilled Sweet Guava, 278
Croutons, Garlic, 247
Étouffée, Quick Crawfish, 57
Étouffée, Traditional Crawfish, 56
French Bread, Garlic, 57
Gremolata, 319
Ham With Garlic and Orange, 294
Mashed Potatoes, Golden Buttermilk, 298
Mojo, Yuca With Garlic-Lime, 294
Pork, Garlic-Orange Roast, 332
Pork Loin With Rosemary-Breadcrumb Crust, Grilled, 200
Pork Roast, Citrus-and-Garlic, 294
Pork Roast, Festive, 46
Pork, Stir-fry, 241
Rib Roast, Rosemary-Thyme, 248
Rice With Fresh Herbs, 68
Sandwiches, Shredded Flank Steak Mini-, 158
Sauce, Paul's Barbecue, 175
Sauce, Spaghetti With Mint-and-Garlic Tomato, 100
Shrimp and Andouille Alfredo Sauce Over Pasta, Cajun, 57
Soup, Black Bean, 120
Soup, Roasted Red Pepper, 72
Soup With Gremolata, White Bean, 319
Vegetables, Rosemary Baked, 313
GARNISH
Green Onion Fans, 271
GLAZES. See also **Fillings, Frostings, Toppings.**
Chocolate Glaze, M287
Guava Glaze, 279
Vanilla Glaze, 287
GRANOLA
Fruit Granola, Mixed, 240
GRAVIES. See also **Sauces.**
Boston Butt Roast With Gravy, 90
Green Chile-Tomato Gravy, 42
Mushroom Gravy, Minute Steak With, 67
Pancakes and Gravy, Pasta, 43
Salsa Gravy, Country-Fried Steak With Creamy, 67
Sawmill Gravy, 110
Turkey Gravy, Quick Herbed, 270
GREENS
Collard, Raisin, and Pecan Sauté, 292
Collard Stew, Hearty Ham-and-, 236

Greens (continued)

Collards, Uptown, 21
Wilted Greens and Red Beans, 21

GRILLED. *See also* **Barbecue.**

Beef

Burgers, Italian-Style, 180
Burgers, Spicy Cheddar-Stuffed, 163
Fajitas (*Bo Nuong Xa*), Vietnamese, 117
Flank Steak, Easy Greek, 207
Flank Steak, Ginger-Marinated, 216
London Broil, Marinated, 84
New York Steaks, Grilled, 123
Rib-Eye Steaks, Molasses-Grilled, 218
Steaks Balsamico, Grilled, 84
Steaks With Blue Pecan Confetti, Maple-
Mustard-Glazed Balsamic, 330
Tenderloin With Horseradish Cream,
Beef, 309
"Tenders," Corn and Tomatoes With
Chipotle-Lime Cream, Tex-Mex Grilled
Beef, 329

Chicken

Guava Chicken, Grilled Sweet, 278
Herb-Grilled Chicken With Watermelon-
Feta Salad, 320
Lexington-Style Grilled Chicken, 54
Marinated Chicken, Mojo-, 163
Marinated Chicken With Mango Salsa,
Margarita, 328
Pizza, Bistro Grilled Chicken, M131
Salad, Sara's Grilled Chicken-
Cornbread, 184
Salad, Strawberry-Citrus Chicken, 84
Tea-Thyme Grilled Chicken, M52
Thighs, Grilled Chicken, 163
Thighs, Molasses-Glazed Chicken, 85
Thighs, Smoky Chicken, 184
Crostini With Olive Tapenade, Grilled, 172
Lamb Chops With Pineapple-Mint Salsa,
Grilled, 52
Oysters With Paul's Cocktail Sauce,
Grilled, 244

Pork

Chops With Caramelized Onions, Thai
Pork, 85
Chops With Orange Slices, Saucy
Pork, 197
Loin With Rosemary-Breadcrumb Crust,
Grilled Pork, 200
Saté, Pork, 53
Slow-Grilled Pork With Ranch-Barbecue
Sauce, 163
Tenderloin, Barbecued Pork, 245
Tenderloin, Blueberry-Rum Marinated
Pork, 178
Tenderloin, Grilled Balsamic Pork, 241
Tenderloin, Margarita Pork, 85
Shrimp With Bacon and Jalapeños,
Grilled, M200
Tilapia Tacos, Shredded Grilled, 16

Vegetables

Asparagus, Grilled, 197
Bell Peppers, Potato-Stuffed Grilled, 123
Corn on the Cob With Red Chile Paste,
Grilled, 118
Corn, Roasted Camp, 174
Easy Grilled Veggies, 194
Onion Stacks, Balsamic, 141
Portobello Mushrooms, Lime-Grilled, 18
Potatoes, Grilled Stuffed, 123

GRITS

Bread, Bacon-Cheddar Grits, 83
Bread, Basil Pesto-Cheese Grits, 83
Bread, Cheesy Grits, 83
Bread, Tomato-Black Olive Grits, 83
Casserole, Cheddar Cheese Grits, 283
Cheddar Cheese Grits, 43
Shrimp and Grits, Garlic, 111

HAM. *See also* **Bacon, Pork.**

Beans and Ham, Baked, 45
Country Ham Sauce, 109
Garlic and Orange, Ham With, 294
Glazed Ham, Currant-, 104
Mac and Cheese, Hearty, 208
Pie, Savory Ham-and-Swiss Breakfast, 240

Sandwiches

Focaccia Sandwich, Pesto, 131
Giant Ham-and-Pepper Salad Sandwich, 204
Grilled Cheese-and-Ham Sandwiches, 293
Monte Cristo Sandwiches, Open-Faced, 222
Soup, Ham-and-Bean, 45
Stew, Hearty Ham-and-Collard, 236

HEALTHY & LIGHT RECIPES

Barley, Vegetable, and Fruit Medley, 127

Desserts

Biscotti, Chocolate-Cinnamon, 30
Bread Pudding With Crème Anglaise, Brown
Sugar, 239
Crème Anglaise, 239
Crisps, Dark Chocolate-Almond, M30
Mousse With Raspberry Sauce, Dark
Chocolate, 31
Oranges, Italian Caramelized, 101
Parfaits, Super Fast Strawberry
Shortcake, 196
Pie, Mocha-Pecan Mud, 290
Pineapple, Brown Sugar-Baked, 170
Sauce, Dark Chocolate, 31
Sauce, Raspberry, 31
Sundaes, S'mores, 257

Main Dishes

Burgers, Balsamic-Blue Cheese
Portobello, 53
Casserole, Confetti Omelet, 169
Catfish, Crispy Oven-Fried, 256
Chicken, Aromatic Curry-and-Spice, 238
Chicken Bowl, Wild Rice-and-, 127
Chicken, Tea-Thyme Grilled, M52
Lamb Chops With Pineapple-Mint Salsa,
Grilled, 52
Oatmeal, Dried Cherry-and-Pecan, 126
Penne, Fresh Vegetable, 101
Pork Saté, 53
Sausage Patties, Breakfast Turkey, 169
Shrimp-and-Spinach Pasta, Creamy, 239
Spaghetti With Mint-and-Garlic Tomato
Sauce, 100
Turkey Breast, Molasses-Coffee, M289
Turkey Tenderloin With Raspberry-Chipotle
Sauce, Jerk, M194
Popovers, Whole Wheat, 195
Punch, Sparkling Orange, 170

Salads and Salad Dressings

Barley-Pine Nut Salad, 126
Bean Salad, Garlic-Herb Two-, 209
Brown Rice-Pine Nut Salad, 126
Chicken Parmesan Salad, Chunky, 209
Egg Salad, 209
Fruit Salad, Vanilla-Scented, 209

Potato-and-Bacon Salad, Roasted, 289
Roasted Corn-and-Black Bean Salad, 209
Romaine Salad With Cashews, 195
Slaw, Overnight, 208
White Bean-and-Asparagus Salad, 100
Tea, Iced Green, 196

Vegetables

Acorn Squash, Sugar-and-Spice, 289
Broccoli, Pecan, 257
Cherry Tomatoes, Rosemary-Roasted, 257
Green Beans, Gingered, 290
Grilled Veggies, Easy, 194
Potatoes, Ranch, 256

HUSH PUPPIES

Hush Puppies, 99
Jalapeño Hush Puppies, 99

ICE CREAMS. *See also* **Sherbets.**

Bread, Ice-Cream, 252
Cake, No-Bake Ice-Cream Angel
Food, 107
Peach-Cinnamon Ice Cream, 168

Pies

Mocha-Pecan Mud Pie, 290
Strawberry-Lime Ice-Cream Pie, 89
Strawberry-Lime Ice-Cream Pie, Spiked, 89
Strawberry Smoothie Ice-Cream Pie, 89
Pineapple-Coconut Ice Cream, Mint Nectarines
With, 123
Pineapple-Coconut Ice Cream, Mint Peaches
With, 123
Punch, Coffee-Ice Cream, 136
Sandwiches, Butter Pecan Ice-Cream, 62
Sandwiches, Easy Chocolate-Mint Ice-
Cream, 62
Sandwiches, Mocha-Almond-Fudge Ice-
Cream, 62
Sandwiches, Oatmeal-Rum-Raisin Ice-
Cream, 62
Sandwiches, Peanutty Ice-Cream, 62

JAM

Coffee-Onion Jam, 123

JAMBALAYA

Crawfish Jambalaya, 118

LAMB

Chops, Creamy Dijon Lamb, 82
Chops With Pineapple-Mint Salsa, Grilled
Lamb, 52
Rosemary-Crusted Lamb With Tzatziki
Sauce, 82

LASAGNA

Speedy Lasagna, M252
Taco Lasagna, Fiesta, 140
Tex-Mex Lasagna, 58

LEEKS

Gratin, Potato-Leek, 281
Mashed Potatoes, Creamy Leek, 334

LEMON

Beverages

Appleade, Hot Spiced Lemon-, 23
Lemonade, Cranberry, 205
Lemonade, Fizzy Raspberry, 61
Lemonade, Fizzy Strawberry, 61

Breads

Muffins, Lemon-Poppy Seed, 33
Rolls, Lemon-Orange, 70

Tea Bread, Lemon-Walnut, 59
Toast, Lemon-Garlic, 171

Desserts
Cake Batter, Lemon-Poppy Seed, 287
Layered Dessert, Lemon-Blueberry, 206
Pie, Zesty Lemon, 157
Sherbet, Refreshing Lemon, 133
Snaps, Lemon-Basil, 275
Tart, Double Citrus, 55
Green Beans, Lemon-Almond, 218
Green Beans, Lemon-and-Dill, 17
Catfish, Baked Lemon-Dill, 216
Chicken With Sautéed Green Beans, Lemon-
Garlic Roast, 43

Salads
Coleslaw, Lemon-Apple, 44
Fruit Salad, Ginger-and-Lemon, 17
Pineapple Salad, Lemon-, 65
Sauce, Pecan Catfish With Lemon, 56
Vinaigrette, Fresh Lemon, 242

LIGHT & EASY. *See* **Healthy & Light Recipes.**
LIME
Cream, Chipotle-Lime, 329

Desserts
Cheesecakes, Key Lime-Coconut Mini-, 159
Cheesecakes, Lime-Goat Cheese, 176
Pie, Rum-Coconut Key Lime, 157
Pie, Spiked Strawberry-Lime Ice-Cream, 89
Pie, Strawberry-Lime Ice-Cream, 89
Sherbet, Refreshing Lime, 133
Dip, Cilantro-Lime Sour Cream, 247
Mojo, Yuca With Garlic-Lime, 294
Portobello Mushrooms, Lime-Grilled, 18
Syrup, Fresh Fruit With Lime, 220
LINGUINE
Tomato Linguine, Two, 187
White Clam Sauce, Linguine With, 49
LIVING LIGHT. *See* **Healthy & Light Recipes.**

Macaroni
Cheese
Creamy Mac and Cheese, 208
Hearty Mac and Cheese, 208
Soup, Cheesy Mac 'n' Chicken, 292
Taco Dinner Mac and Cheese, 208
MAKE AHEAD RECIPES
Appetizers
Brie, Baked Honey-Raisin, M258
Buffalo Wings, 64
Cheese Ball, Mediterranean, 143
Cheesecake, Southwest, 249
Cheese Ring, 33
Cheese Wafers, 97
Deviled Eggs, Buttery Dijon, 93
Deviled Eggs, Chive-Tarragon, 93
Deviled Eggs With Capers, 93
Dip, Quick Creamy Vegetable, 20
Dip, Quick Hummus, 206
Dip, Southwestern Salsa, 212
Eggs, Armadillo, 139
Hummus, Red Pepper, 97
Logs, Chile-Cheese, 64
Meatballs, Cranberry, 310
Mushroom Turnovers, 310
Nuts, Sugar-and-Spice, 274
Pita Triangles, Benne Seed, 97
Shrimp Cocktail, Cinco de Mayo, 138
Spread, Creamy Olive, 311
Spread, Layered Sun-dried-Tomato-and-
Basil, 275

Truffles, Herb-and-Garlic Goat
Cheese, 143
Beans, Slow Cooker Barbecue, M180
Beverages
Berry Freeze, 220
Coffee Concentrate, 136
Punch, Sparkling Orange, 170
Punch, Spicy Sparkling, 24
Punch, Whiskey, 276
Sparkler, Cranberry-Apple, 61
Tea, Apple, 24
Tea Cooler, Orange, 216
Tea, Pineapple-Orange Herb, 61
Breads
Coffee Cakes, Sour Cream, 212
Crescents, Cheddar, 70
Muffins, Caramel-Apple, 210
Muffins, Cranberry, 313
Muffins, Lemon-Poppy Seed, 33
Pumpkin Bread, 232
Rolls, Lemon-Orange, 70
Rolls, Make-Ahead Spoon, 221
Toast, Lemon-Garlic, 171
Butter, Avocado, 159
Couscous, Cranberry-and-Toasted Pecan, M259
Croutons, Garlic, 247
Desserts
Angel Food Cake, No-Bake Ice-Cream, 107
Bars, Caramel-Pecan Cheesecake, 210
Blackberry Juice, 182
Cake, Chocolate-Caramel Sheet, 210
Cheesecakes, Key Lime-Coconut Mini-, 159
Cheesecakes, Lime-Goat Cheese, 176
Cookies, Domino, 19
Cookies on a Stick, 63
Cookies, Ultimate Chocolate Chip, 87
Crème Anglaise, 239
Crisps, Dark Chocolate-Almond, M30
Crust, Coconut, 157
Filling, Blackberry Curd, 182
Flan, Columbia's, 120
Ice Cream, Peach-Cinnamon, 168
Ice-Cream Pie, Spiked Strawberry-Lime, 89
Ice-Cream Pie, Strawberry Smoothie, 89
Ice-Cream Sandwiches, Easy Chocolate-
Mint, 62
Ice-Cream Sandwiches, Peanutty, 62
Lemon-Blueberry Layered Dessert, 206
Mousse With Raspberry Sauce, Dark
Chocolate, 31
Peanut Butter Clusters, No-Bake, M211
Pie, Chocolate-Covered Cherry, M216
Pie, Chocolate Icebox, 157
Pie, Coconut Cream, 110
Pie, Frozen Hawaiian, 157
Pie, Praline-Apple, 251
Pie, Rum-Coconut Key Lime, 157
Pie, Zesty Lemon, 157
Pudding, Peanut Butter-Banana, 44
Sauce, Hot Fudge, 193
Sundaes, S'mores, 257
Sundaes, Waffle Taco, M62
Tart, Double Citrus, 55
Tart, Fresh Cherry, 168
Dressing, Slow-Cooker Cornbread, 270
Fruit With Lime Syrup, Fresh, 220
Granola, Mixed Fruit, 240
Honey, Citrus-Pear, 230
Main Dishes
Casserole, Cajun Shrimp, 237
Casserole, Cheesy Chicken Curry, 311

Chicken, Lexington-Style Grilled, 54
Pork Roast, Festive, 46
Pork Tenderloin, Blueberry-Rum
Marinated, 178
Pot Roast, Italian, 34
Shrimp and Andouille Alfredo Sauce Over
Pasta, Cajun, 57
Shrimp, Pickled, 158
Strata, Southwest Breakfast, 136
Tetrazzini, Smoked Turkey, 96
Mayonnaise, Tomato-Basil, 180
Mustard, Sweet-Hot Honey, 284
Pasta Bake, Three-Cheese, 54
Pilaf, Mixed Fruit, 205
Rice Pilaf, Orange, 219
Roulade, Basil-Cheese, 143
Rub, Paul's Pork Ribs, 174
Salads and Salad Dressings
Aspic, Raspberry-Tomato, 65
Bean Salad, Garlic-Herb Two-, 209
Broccoli Slaw Salad, Sweet, 91
Chicken-and-Strawberry Salad, 132
Chicken Parmesan Salad, Chunky, 209
Chicken Salad, 94
Chicken Salad, Cherry-Tarragon, 275
Chicken Salad, Lapsang-Poached, 135
Cider Vinegar-Honey Dressing, 41
Coleslaw, Creamy-and-Sweet, 125
Coleslaw, Creamy Carolina, 167
Coleslaw, Lemon-Apple, 44
Coleslaw, Sweet-and-Tart Red Cabbage, 125
Coleslaw, Zesty Vinegar, M125
Cornbread-and-Turkey Salad, Layered, 147
Cranberry-Apple Salad, 65
Cranberry Relish Salad, 245
Egg Salad, 209
Fruit Congealed Salad, Layered, M146
Fruit Salad Dressing, Snappy, 160
Green Bean-Red Potato Salad, Layered, 146
Greens With Toasted Almonds and Apple
Cider Vinaigrette, Mixed, 201
Honey-Mustard Dressing, 185
Lebanese Salad, Layered, 148
Lemon-Pineapple Salad, 65
Overnight Slaw, 208
Pasta Salad, Confetti, 242
Potato-Apple Salad, Marinated, 41
Potato Salad, Bacon, 171
Potato Salad, Bacon 'n' Onion, 188
Potato Salad, BLT, 213
Potato Salad, Sweet, 171
Potato Salad With Feta, Dilled, 128
Roasted Corn-and-Black Bean Salad, 209
Seafood Salad, Sewee Preserve's, 173
Sesame-Poppy Seed Dressing, 55
Shrimp Salad, Old Bay, 188
Slaw, Broccoli, 278
Slaw, Broccoli-Squash, 170
Strawberry-Cranberry-Orange Salad, 249
Tomato-and-Onion Salad, 167
Tomato-Feta Salad, 207
Tomato Salad, Hot, 129
Vegetable Salad, Marinated, 129
Vinaigrette, Blue Cheese, 233
Vinaigrette, Cinnamon, 133
Yogurt Dressing, Low-Cal Dilled, 128
Salsa, Blueberry, 179
Salsa, Pineapple, 86
Salsa, Sweet Pepper-Mango, 148
Sandwiches
Barbecue Beef Sandwiches, Slow-Cooker, 64

Make Ahead, Sandwiches (*continued*)

Cheese Sandwiches, Checkerboard, 18
Turkey, Bacon, and Havarti Sandwich, 92
Wraps, Chicken-and-Slaw, 222

Sauces and Gravies
Barbecue Sauce, Honey-Mustard, 167
Barbecue Sauce, Paul's, 175
Caper Sauce, 105
Cocktail Sauce, Paul's, 244
Cranberry-Orange Sauce, 218
Horseradish Sauce, 177
Rémoulade, Criolla, 69
Sour Cream-Cucumber Sauce, 207

Soups and Stews
Avocado Soup, 159, 200
Beef Stew, Slow-Cooker, 235
Blueberry Soup, Chilled, 178
Butternut Squash-Parsnip Soup, 36
Chicken-and-Vegetable Stew, 235
Étouffée, Quick Crawfish, 57
Étouffée, Traditional Crawfish, 56
Ham-and-Collard Stew, Hearty, 236

Vegetables
Asparagus, Marinated, 105
Celery, Light Pimiento Cheese-Stuffed, 161
Green Beans, Marinated Dill, 129
Onions, Caramelized, 259
Potato Casserole, Au Gratin, 250
Squash Casserole, 277
Squash, Marinated, 129
Sweet Potatoes, Southwest Mashed, 271
Walnuts, Candied, 60
Walnuts, Sugared Curried, 281
Wild Rice, Nutty, 278

MANGOES
Cake, Mango Upside-Down, 120
Salsa, Black Bean-and-Mango, 297
Salsa, Mango, 328
Salsa, Snappy Mango, 329
Salsa, Sweet Pepper-Mango, 148

MANICOTTI
Meaty Cheese Manicotti, 34

MAYONNAISE
Béarnaise Mayonnaise, 144
Herb Mayonnaise, Fresh, 144
Tomato-Basil Mayonnaise, 180

MEATBALLS
Chipotle-Barbecue Meatballs,
  Spicy, 305
Cranberry Meatballs, 310
Glazed Meatballs, Bourbon-Mustard, 305
Sweet-and-Sour Meatballs, 305

MELON
Watermelon-Feta Salad, 320

MICROWAVE RECIPES
Brie, Baked Honey-Raisin, M258
Couscous, Cranberry-and-Toasted
  Pecan, M259

Desserts
Bars, Praline, M205
Brownies, Caramel-Coconut-Pecan, M288
Brownies, Chocolate Fudge, M288
Brownies, Praline-Pecan, M288
Brownie Squares, Mint Truffle, M254
Cake, Coconut Layer, M246
Cheesecake, Chocolate Fudge, M288
Cheesecake With Mocha Sauce, Chocolate-
  Coffee, M316
Clusters, No-Bake Peanut Butter, M211
Cookies, Chocolate-Dipped, M299

Cookies, Chunky Cherry-Double
  Chip, M87
Crisps, Dark Chocolate-Almond, M30
Filling, Chocolate, M307
Fondue, Chocolate, M281
Frosting, Easy Microwave, M63
Glaze, Chocolate, M287
Pecans, Chocolate-Dipped, M269
Pie, Chocolate-Covered Cherry, M216
Sauce, Champagne-Chocolate, M282
Shortbread, Millionaire, M94
Squares, Turtle Cake, M211
Sundaes, Waffle Taco, M62
Tarts, Peppermint Brownie, M288

Main Dishes
Chicken, Tea-Thyme Grilled, M52
Lasagna, Speedy, M252
Pizza, Bistro Grilled Chicken, M131
Shrimp With Bacon and Jalapeños,
  Grilled, M200
Turkey Tenderloin With Raspberry-Chipotle
  Sauce, Jerk, M194
Rice Pilaf, Basil, M197
Salad, Layered Fruit Congealed, M146
Sauce, Garlic Butter, M253
Tortelloni, Roasted Red Pepper-Caesar, M186

Vegetables
Broccoli Casserole, M276
Green Beans, Speedy Rosemary, M241
Green Beans With Bacon, Sautéed, M160
Squash Casserole, Southwestern, M217
Vinaigrette, Apricot, M312

MOUSSE
Dark Chocolate Mousse With Raspberry
  Sauce, 31

MUFFINS
Berry-and-Spice Whole-Wheat Muffins, 25
Caramel-Apple Muffins, 210
Cranberry Muffins, 313
Cream Cheese-Banana-Nut Muffins, 27
Lemon-Poppy Seed Muffins, 33
Orange-Date Muffins, 215

MUSHROOMS
Gravy, Minute Steak With Mushroom, 67
Portobello Burgers, Balsamic-Blue Cheese, 53
Portobello Mushrooms, Lime-Grilled, 18

Sauces
Artichoke Sauce, Creamy Mushroom-, 312
Portobello-Marsala Sauce, 280
Tuna With Mushroom Sauce, Peppered, 72
Stuffed Mushrooms, Sausage-, 300
Turnovers, Mushroom, 310

MUSTARD
Cranberry Mustard, 320
Dressing, Honey-Mustard, 185
Honey Mustard, 203
Honey Mustard, Sweet-Hot, 284
Maui Mustard, Wowee, 324

NECTARINES
Mint Nectarines With Pineapple-Coconut Ice
  Cream, 123

OATMEAL
Cookies
Cereal Cookies, Crunchy Oat 'n', 181
Chocolate Chunk Cookies, Double, 181
Raisin Chocolate Chip Cookies,
  Oatmeal-, 87

Dried Cherry-and-Pecan Oatmeal, 126
Ice-Cream Sandwiches, Oatmeal-Rum-
  Raisin, 62
Ice-Cream Sandwiches, Peanutty, 62

OKRA
Soup, Okra, 98

OLIVES
Spread, Creamy Olive, 311
Tapenade, Grilled Crostini With Olive, 172

ONIONS
Caramelized Onions, 259
Caramelized Onions, Thai Pork Chops
  With, 85
Green Onion Fans, 271
Jam, Coffee-Onion, 123
Pork Chops With Onions, Pan-fried, 43
Salad, Bacon 'n' Onion Potato, 188
Soufflé, Spinach, 66

Sweet
Balsamic Onion Stacks, 141
Salad, Tomato-and-Onion, 167
Salad, Tomato-and-Sweet Onion, 141
Stuffed Onions, Florentine, 141

ORANGES
Caramelized Oranges, Italian, 101
Muffins, Orange-Date, 215
Pork Chops With Orange Slices, Saucy, 197
Rice Pilaf, Orange, 219
Roast Pork, Garlic-Orange, 332
Salad, Mandarin-Black Bean, 319
Salad, Mandarin Orange-and-Almond, 291
Syrup, Orange, 240
Tart, Double Citrus, 55

OYSTERS
Fried Buffalo Oyster Po'Boys, 48
Fried Buffalo Oysters, 48
Fried Oysters, Southwest, 48
Grilled Oysters With Paul's Cocktail
  Sauce, 244
Scalloped Oysters, 47
Stew, Oyster, 48

PANCAKES
Buttermilk 'n' Honey Pancakes, 137
Pasta Pancakes and Gravy, 43
Sour Cream-Blueberry Morning Pancakes With
  Wild Blueberry-and-Peach Topping, 326

PARSNIPS
Soup, Butternut Squash-Parsnip, 36

PASTAS. *See also* **Couscous, Fettuccine,
  Lasagna, Macaroni, Manicotti,
  Ravioli, Spaghetti.**
Bacon Pasta, 224
Bake, Three-Cheese Pasta, 54
Bow Tie Pasta, Chicken and, 49
Minestrone, Mama's Mexican, 254
Pancakes and Gravy, Pasta, 43
Penne, Fresh Vegetable, 101
Penne With Greek-Style Tomato Sauce, 187
Red Wine-Tomato-and-Steak Pasta, 140
Rigatoni With Sausage and Bell Peppers, 215

Salads
Confetti Pasta Salad, 242
Greek Pasta Salad, 130
Mediterranean Pasta Salad, 220
Shrimp and Pasta With Creole Cream
  Sauce, 49
Shrimp-and-Spinach Pasta, Creamy, 239
Tortelloni, Roasted Red Pepper-Caesar, M186
Ziti, Baked, 214

PEACHES
Ice Cream, Peach-Cinnamon, 168
Mint Peaches With Pineapple-Coconut Ice
Cream, 123
Shortcakes, Southern Peach-and-
Blueberry, 318
Stewed Yard Peaches, 23
PEANUT BUTTER
Clusters, No-Bake Peanut Butter, M211
Cookies, Peanut Butter-Chocolate
Chip, 87, 222
Pizza, Chocolate-Peanut Butter, 193
Pudding, Peanut Butter-Banana, 44
PEARS
Cobbler, Citrus-Pear Honey, 230
Crisp, Pear, 214
Honey, Citrus-Pear, 230
Roasted Bacon-Wrapped Pears, Field Greens
With, 230
Tart, Raspberry-Almond Pear, 230
PEAS
Hoppin' John, 21
Pecan Peas, Hot, 85
PECANS
Broccoli, Pecan, 257
Brownies, Praline-Pecan, M288
Butter, Pecan-Honey, 137
Cakes
Cinnamon-Pecan Crumb Cakes, 288
Praline-Pecan Cakes, 286
Sour Cream-Pecan Cake Batter, 286
Catfish With Lemon Sauce, Pecan, 56
Chicken, Baked Pecan, 312
Chicken Strips, Honey-Pecan, 188
Chocolate-Dipped Pecans, M269
Cookies, Pecan-Chocolate Chip, 87
Ice-Cream Sandwiches, Butter Pecan, 62
Peas, Hot Pecan, 85
Pies
Caramel-Pecan Pie, 269
Chocolate-Bourbon Pecan Pie, 134
Fudge Pie With Raspberry Sauce, Pecan, 201
Mascarpone Pecan Pie, 299
Mocha-Pecan Mud Pie, 290
Praline Pecans, 286
Sugar-and-Spice Nuts, 274
Sugared Pecans, Cabbage-Apple Salad
With, 91
Wild Rice, Nutty, 278
PEPPERS
Chile
Chipotle-Barbecue Meatballs, Spicy, 305
Chipotle-Barbecue Sausage Bites,
Spicy, 305
Chipotle-Black Bean Dip, Creamy, 247
Chipotle-Lime Cream, 329
Green Chile-Tomato Gravy, 42
Logs, Chile-Cheese, 64
Poblano-and-Cheese Casserole, Zesty, 311
Red Chile Paste, 118
Jalapeño Hush Puppies, 99
Red
Hummus, Red Pepper, 97
Roasted Red Pepper-Caesar
Tortelloni, M186
Sauce, Sweet-'n'-Spicy Red Pepper, 321
Soup, Creamy Bell Pepper 'n' Tomato, 293
Soup, Roasted Red Pepper, 72
Stuffed Grilled Bell Peppers, Potato-, 123
Salsa, Sweet Pepper Mango, 148
Texas Rockets, 175

PIES, PUFFS, AND PASTRIES
Apples, Crescent Roll, 231
Cherry Pie, Chocolate-Covered, M216
Chocolate
Bourbon Pecan Pie, Chocolate-, 134
Icebox Pie, Chocolate, 157
Pecan Fudge Pie With Raspberry Sauce, 201
Walnut Pie, Chocolate-, 134
Cobblers and Crisps
Apple Brown Betty, 232
Citrus-Pear Honey Cobbler, 230
Pear Crisp, 214
Pumpkin Crisp, 269
Coconut Cream Pie, 110
Frozen Hawaiian Pie, 157
Ice Cream
Mocha-Pecan Mud Pie, 290
Strawberry-Lime Ice-Cream Pie, 89
Strawberry-Lime Ice-Cream Pie, Spiked, 89
Strawberry Smoothie Ice-Cream Pie, 89
Key Lime Pie, Rum-Coconut, 157
Lemon Pie, Zesty, 157
Main Dish
Ham-and-Swiss Breakfast Pie, Savory, 240
Pulled Pork Tortilla Pie With Snappy Mango
Salsa, Cuban, 329
Shepherd's Pie, Shortcut Greek, 238
Pastries
Buñuelos, 295
Coconut Crust, 157
Cornmeal Dough, 112
Pecan
Caramel-Pecan Pie, 269
Chocolate-Bourbon Pecan Pie, 134
Fudge Pie With Raspberry Sauce,
Pecan, 201
Mascarpone Pecan Pie, 299
Praline-Apple Pie, 251
Strawberry-Rhubarb Pie, 132
Tarts
Cherry Tart, Fresh, 168
Citrus Tart, Double, 55
Pear Tart, Raspberry-Almond, 230
Peppermint Brownie Tarts, M288
Turnovers, Applesauce, 231
Turnovers, Mushroom, 310
PINEAPPLE
Baked Pineapple, 160
Desserts
Baked Pineapple, Brown Sugar-, 170
Ice Cream, Mint Nectarines With Pineapple-
Coconut, 123
Ice Cream, Mint Peaches With Pineapple-
Coconut, 123
Pudding With Bourbon Sauce, Pineapple-
Apple Bread, 119
Salsa, Grilled Lamb Chops With Pineapple-
Mint, 52
Salsa, Pineapple, 86
PIZZA
Casserole, Beefy Pizza, 217
Chicken-and-Bacon Pizza, Tex-Mex, 325
Chicken Pizza, Bistro Grilled, M131
Chicken Pizza, Southwestern BBQ, 33
Chocolate-Peanut Butter Pizza, 193
Eggplant Pizza, Garden, 127
Roasted Vegetable-and-Goat Cheese Pizza, 176
Sausage-and-Scrambled Egg Pizza, 88
POMEGRANATE
Cider, Mulled Pomegranate, 309
Cocktail, Pomegranate-Champagne, 282

POPCORN
Tex-Mex Popcorn, 204
PORK. *See also* **Bacon, Ham, Sausage.**
Chops
Fajitas, Pronto Pork, 223
Glazed Pork Chops, Ginger-, 203
Holiday Pork Chops, 313
Pan-fried Pork Chops With Onions, 43
Saté, Pork, 53
Saucy Pork Chops With Orange Slices, 197
Southwest Pork in Black Bean Sauce, 139
Stir-fry Pork, 241
Thai Pork Chops With Caramelized
Onions, 85
Loin With Rosemary-Breadcrumb Crust,
Grilled Pork, 200
Ribs, Big "D" Smoked Baby Back, 174
Ribs Rub, Paul's Pork, 174
Roasts
Apricot-Glazed-and-Spiced Pork Loin, 259
Barbecue Pork, Tabb's, 166
Boston Butt Roast With Gravy, 90
Chalupa Dinner Bowl, 238
Citrus-and-Garlic Pork Roast, 294
Festive Pork Roast, 46
Fried Pork Bites, Zesty, 90
Garlic-Orange Roast Pork, 332
Grilled Pork With Ranch-Barbecue Sauce,
Slow-, 163
Polynesian Pork, 90
Pulled Pork Tortilla Pie With Snappy Mango
Salsa, Cuban, 329
Stuffed Pork Loin With Cider Sauce, Spiced-
and-, 258
Tuscan Pork Loin, 296
Salad, Fiesta, 58
Soup, Pork-and-Black Bean, 32
Stew, Easy Brunswick, 292
Tenderloin
Barbecued Pork Tenderloin, 245
Glazed Pork Tenderloin, Ginger-, 203
Grilled Balsamic Pork Tenderloin, 241
Margarita Pork Tenderloin, 85
Marinated Pork Tenderloin, Blueberry-
Rum, 178
Molasses Pork Tenderloin With Red Wine
Sauce, 332
POTATOES. *See also* **Sweet Potatoes.**
Casseroles
Au Gratin Potato Casserole, 250
Gratin, Potato-Leek, 281
Gruyère Casserole, Potato-and-, 248
French Fries, Ranch-Seasoned, 93
Latkes, Simple Potato, 272
Mashed
Buttermilk Mashed Potatoes, Golden, 298
Cheesy Mashed Potatoes, 204
Garlic-Herb Mashed Potatoes, 218
Garlic Mashed Potatoes, 42
Leek Mashed Potatoes, Creamy, 334
Ranch Potatoes, 256
Simple Mashed Potatoes, 271
Three-Potato Mash, 271
Roasted Potatoes, Oven-, 44
Roasted Potatoes, Two-Color Rosemary, 18
Salads
Bacon 'n' Onion Potato Salad, 188
Bacon Potato Salad, 171
BLT Potato Salad, 213
Dilled Potato Salad With Feta, 128
Green Bean-Red Potato Salad, Layered, 146

Potatoes, Salads (continued)

    Marinated Potato-Apple Salad, 41
    Roasted Potato-and-Bacon Salad, 289
  Stuffed Barbecue Potatoes, Double-, 162
  Stuffed Potatoes, Grilled, 123

PUDDINGS. *See also* **Mousse.**

Bread

    Berry Bread Pudding With Vanilla Cream
      Sauce, 260
    Brown Sugar Bread Pudding With Crème
      Anglaise, 239
    Pineapple-Apple Bread Pudding With
      Bourbon Sauce, 119
    Cheesecake Banana Pudding With Caramel
      Syrup, The Ultimate No-Bake, 326
    Peanut Butter-Banana Pudding, 4

Savory

    Chicken Pudding, 22
    Cornmeal Pudding, 43
    Corn Pudding, Sweet, 66

PUMPKIN

  Bread, Cream Cheese-Pumpkin, 251
  Bread, Pumpkin, 232
  Cake, Pumpkin Spice, 232
  Crisp, Pumpkin, 269
  Fudge, Pumpkin, 232

QUESADILLAS

Bacon-and-Egg Quesadillas, 88
Caramel-Apple Quesadillas, 223
Reuben Quesadillas, 131

QUICK & EASY RECIPES

Desserts

    Banana-Berry Split, 193
    Pizza, Chocolate-Peanut Butter, 193
    Sauce, Hot Fudge, 193
  Green Beans With Bacon, Sautéed, M160

Main Dishes

    Chicken and Bow Tie Pasta, 49
    Chicken Thighs, Balsamic Garlic-and-
      Herb, 19
    Lasagna, Speedy, M252
    Linguine With White Clam Sauce, 49
    Mac and Cheese, Creamy, 208
    Mac and Cheese, Hearty, 208
    Pizza, Bistro Grilled Chicken, M131
    Pizza, Sausage-and-Scrambled Egg, 88
    Pork, Stir-Fry, 241
    Quesadillas, Bacon-and-Egg, 88
    Quesadillas, Reuben, 131
    Ravioli in Basil-Cream Sauce, Beef, 293
    Shrimp and Pasta With Creole Cream
      Sauce, 49
    Steak, Chicken-Fried, 67
    Steak With Creamy Salsa Gravy, Country-
      Fried, 67
    Steak With Mushroom Gravy, Minute, 67
    Taco Dinner Mac and Cheese, 208
  Pineapple, Baked, 160

Salads and Salad Dressings

    Fruit Salad Dressing, Snappy, 160
    Iceberg Wedges, Blue Cheese, 160
    Iceberg Wedges, Caesar, 160
    Iceberg Wedges, Greek, 160
    Steak-and-Spinach Salad With Hot Pan
      Dressing, 19
  Sandwich, Pesto Focaccia, 131
  Sauce, Garlic Butter, M253
  Shake, Chocolate Milk, 193

Soup, Cheesy Mac 'n' Chicken, 292
Stew, Easy Brunswick, 292

RASPBERRIES

Aspic, Raspberry-Tomato, 65
Bites, Creamy Raspberry, 36
Chicken, Raspberry-Barbecue, 203
Lemonade, Fizzy Raspberry, 61

Sauces

    Barbecue Sauce, Raspberry-, 203
    Chipotle Sauce, Jerk Turkey Tenderloin
      With Raspberry-, M194
    Raspberry Sauce, 31, 201
  Sherbet, Raspberry-Buttermilk, 133
  Tart, Raspberry-Almond Pear, 230
  Vinaigrette, Raspberry, 91

RAVIOLI

Beef Ravioli in Basil-Cream Sauce, 293
One-Pot Pasta, 202

RELISHES. *See also* **Chutney, Salsas, Sauces,**
  Toppings.

Cranberry Relish, Roasted Acorn Squash
  With, 234
Tomato, Basil, and Corn Relish, 321

RICE

Beans and Rice

    Black Beans and Rice, 214
    Pinto Beans, Ham Hocks, and Rice, 46
    Red Beans and Rice With Sausage, 125
  Brown Rice-Pine Nut Salad, 126
  Fried Rice 101, 50
  Herbs, Rice With Fresh, 68
  Hoppin' John, 21
  Pilaf, Basil Rice, M197
  Pilaf, Orange Rice, 219
  Quick-Cook Rice With Fresh
    Herbs, 69
  Toss, Succotash Rice, 218
  White Rice, The Ultimate, 279
  Wild Rice-and-Chicken Bowl, 127
  Wild Rice, Nutty, 278

ROLLS AND BUNS

Lemon-Orange Rolls, 70

Yeast

    Crescents, Cheddar, 70
    Double Whammie Yeast Rolls, 323
    Spoon Rolls, Make-Ahead, 221
    Two-Seed Bread Knots, 334

SALAD DRESSINGS

Celery Seed Dressing, 291
Cider Vinegar-Honey Dressing, 41
Fruit Salad Dressing, Snappy, 160
Honey-Mustard Dressing, 185
Sesame-Poppy Seed Dressing, 55

Vinaigrette

    Apple Cider Vinaigrette, 201
    Apple-Ginger Vinaigrette, 230
    Blue Cheese Vinaigrette, 233
    Cinnamon Vinaigrette, 133
    Cranberry Vinaigrette, 247
    Dill Vinaigrette, 173
    Lemon Vinaigrette, Fresh, 242
    Maple-Cider Vinaigrette, 281
    Raspberry Vinaigrette, 91
    Red Grapefruit-Lemon Vinaigrette,
      Salad with, 161
    Strawberry-Balsamic Vinaigrette, 84
  Yogurt Dressing, Low-Cal Dilled, 128

SALADS. *See also* **Slaws.**

Antipasto Salad Platter, Mediterranean, 220
Apple Salad, Lemony, 241
Autumn Salad With Maple-Cider
  Vinaigrette, 281
Barley-Pine Nut Salad, 126

Bean

    Black Bean Salad, Mandarin-, 319
    Black Bean Salad, Roasted Corn-and-, 209
    Green Beans, Marinated Dill, 129
    Tangy Bean Salad, 158
    Two-Bean Salad, Garlic-Herb, 209
    White Bean-and-Asparagus Salad, 100
Broccoli Slaw Salad, Sweet, 91
Brown Rice-Pine Nut Salad, 126
Cabbage-Apple Salad With Sugared Pecans, 91
Cabbage Salad, Chinese, 142
Cabbage Salad, Tangy, 162
Caesar Iceberg Wedges, 160
Caesar Salad, Easy Spicy, 122

Chicken

    Cherry-Tarragon Chicken Salad, 275
    Chicken Salad, 65, 94
    Chunky Chicken Parmesan Salad, 209
    Cranberry-Pecan Chicken Salad, 284
    Fiesta Chicken Salad, 223
    Grilled Chicken-Cornbread Salad,
      Sara's, 184
    Lapsang-Poached Chicken Salad, 135
    Picnic Salad With Honey-Mustard Dressing,
      Hoover's, 184
    Roasted Chicken With Wilted Salad Greens,
      Tom's, 185
    Spring Salad With Raspberry Vinaigrette, 91
    Strawberry-Citrus Chicken Salad, 84
    Strawberry Salad, Chicken-and-, 132

Congealed

    Cranberry-Apple Salad, 65
    Cranberry Congealed Salad, 334
    Cranberry Relish Salad, 245
    Fruit Congealed Salad, Layered, M146
    Lemon-Pineapple Salad, 65
Cornbread-and-Turkey Salad, Layered, 147
Cornbread-and-Turkey Salad, Layered
  Southwest, 147
Egg Salad, 209
Field Greens With Roasted Bacon-Wrapped
  Pears, 230

Fruit

    Ginger-and-Lemon Fruit Salad, 17
    Harvest Crunch Salad, 291
    Honey Dressing, Fruit Salad With, 137
    Vanilla-Scented Fruit Salad, 209

Green

    Iceberg Wedges, Blue Cheese, 160
    Iceberg Wedges, Greek, 160
    Mixed Greens With Toasted Almonds and
      Apple Cider Vinaigrette, 201
    Romaine Salad With Cashews, 195
    Summer Salad, Berry Delicious, 179
    Wilted Salad Greens, 185
Layered Lebanese Salad, 148
Mandarin Orange-and-Almond Salad, 291

Meat

    Fiesta Salad, 58
    Ham-and-Pepper Salad Sandwich, Giant, 204
    Steak-and-Spinach Salad With Hot Pan
      Dressing, 19
Mozzarella, Avocado, and Tomato Salad, 41

Pasta

    Confetti Pasta Salad, 242

Greek Pasta Salad, 130
Mediterranean Pasta Salad, 220
Potato Salads, Cold
Bacon 'n' Onion Potato Salad, 188
Bacon Potato Salad, 171
BLT Potato Salad, 213
Dilled Potato Salad With Feta, 128
Green Bean-Red Potato Salad,
Layered, 146
Marinated Potato-Apple Salad, 41
Sweet Potato Salad, 171
Potato Salads, Hot or Warm
Roasted Potato-and-Bacon Salad, 289
Sweet Potato Salad, 171
Red Grapefruit-Lemon Vinaigrette, Salad
with, 161
Roasted Butternut Squash Salad With Blue
Cheese Vinaigrette, 233
Seafood Salad, Sewee Preserve's, 173
Shrimp Salad, 65, 95
Shrimp Salad, Old Bay, 188
Spinach
Apple Salad With Cinnamon Vinaigrette,
Fresh Spinach-and-, 44
Easy Spinach, Pear, and Blue Cheese
Salad, 41
Endive Salad With Warm Vinaigrette,
Spinach-, 291
Steak-and-Spinach Salad With Hot Pan
Dressing, 19
Strawberry Salad, Spinach-and-, 55
Strawberry-Cranberry-Orange Salad, 249
Strawberry Salad With Cinnamon
Vinaigrette, 133
Tomato
Cucumber Salad, Tomato-and-, 69
Feta Lettuce Salad, Tomato-, 207
Feta Salad, Tomato-, 207
Hot Tomato Salad, 129
Onion Salad, Tomato-and-, 167
Onion Salad, Tomato-and-Sweet, 141
Tossed Salad, Italian, 202
Tuna Salad, My Best, 328
Turkey Cobb Salad, Southern-Style, 214
Turkey Salad With Cranberry Vinaigrette and
Garlic Croutons, Main Dish, 246
Vegetable Salad, Marinated, 129
Watermelon-Feta Salad, 320
SALMON
Almonds and Parsley, Salmon With, 68
SALSAS. *See also* **Chutney, Relishes, Sauces,
Toppings.**
Avocado-Feta Salsa, 298
Black Bean-and-Corn Salsa, 297
Black Bean-and-Mango Salsa, 297
Black Bean Salsa, Fruity, 16
Blueberry Salsa, 179
Homemade Salsa, 59
Mango Salsa, 328
Mango Salsa, Snappy, 329
Pineapple-Mint Salsa, Grilled Lamb Chops
With, 52
Pineapple Salsa, 86
Sweet Pepper-Mango Salsa, 148
Zucchini-Carrot Salsa, 298
SANDWICHES
Beef
Barbecue Beef Sandwiches, Slow-Cooker, 64
Flank Steak Mini-Sandwiches, Shredded, 158
Panini Sandwiches, Roast Beef-Cheddar, 223
Philly Sandwiches, Open-Faced, 32

Sloppy José Sandwiches With Cilantro
Slaw, 324
Burgers, Balsamic-Blue Cheese
Portobello, 53
Cheese Sandwiches, Checkerboard, 18
Focaccia Sandwich, Pesto, 131
Grilled Cheese-and-Ham Sandwiches, 293
Grilled Cheese Sandwiches With Tomato,
Avocado, and Bacon, 213
Ham-and-Pepper Salad Sandwich, Giant, 204
Monte Cristo Sandwiches, Open-Faced, 222
Pitas, Shrimp, 188
Po' Boys, Fried Buffalo Oyster, 48
Po' Boys, Fried Green Tomato, 330
Rolls, Shrimp, 188
Rollups, Greek Chicken, 128
Turkey, Bacon, and Havarti Sandwich, 92
Turkey Melt, Loaded, 159
Turkey Melts, Oven-Grilled Loaded, 159
Wraps
BLT Wraps, 224
Chicken-and-Slaw Wraps, 222
Roast Beef Wraps, Tangy-and-Sweet, 92
Turkey Lettuce Wraps, Crispy Ginger-and-
Garlic Asian, 324
SAUCES. *See also* **Chutney; Desserts/Sauces;
Gravies; Relishes; Salsas; Toppings.**
Artichoke-Pepper Sauce, Chicken Breasts
With, 139
Barbecue
Honey-Mustard Barbecue Sauce, 167
Paul's Barbecue Sauce, 175
Ranch-Barbecue Sauce, 163
Raspberry-Barbecue Sauce, 203
White Barbecue Sauce, 196
Basil-Cream Sauce, Beef Ravioli in, 293
Black Bean Sauce, Southwest Pork in, 139
Butter Sauce, 124
Caper Sauce, 105
Cheese
Cheddar Cheese Cream Sauce, 277
Cheese Sauce, 333
Pimiento Cheese Sauce, 333
Swiss Cheese Cream Sauce, 277
Cider Sauce, 259
Cocktail Sauce, Paul's, 244
Country Ham Sauce, 109
Cream Sauce, 248
Creole Cream Sauce, Shrimp and Pasta
With, 49
Creole Sauce, Simple, 203
Fruit
Cranberry-Orange Sauce, 218
Lemon Sauce, Pecan Catfish With, 56
Raspberry-Chipotle Sauce, Jerk Turkey
Tenderloin With, M194
Garlic Butter Sauce, M253
Honey-Mustard Sauce, Chicken Fingers
With, 300
Horseradish Sauce, 177, 203
Mushroom-Artichoke Sauce, Creamy, 312
Mushroom Sauce, Peppered Tuna
With, 72
Portobello-Marsala Sauce, 280
Red Pepper Sauce, Sweet-'n'-Spicy, 321
Red Sauce, 327
Red Wine Sauce, 332
Rémoulade, Citrus, 69
Rémoulade, Criolla, 69
Rémoulade Sauce, Creole, 69
Shrimp-and-Crab Sauce, Cajun, 206

Sour Cream-Cucumber Sauce, 207
Tartar Sauce, 327
Tomato
Greek-Style Tomato Sauce, Penne
With, 187
Ground Beef-Tomato Sauce, 290
Mint-and-Garlic Tomato Sauce, Spaghetti
With, 100
Tzatziki Sauce, 82
White Clam Sauce, Linguine With, 49
Yogurt Sauce, 321
SAUSAGE
Appetizers
Bites, Bourbon-Mustard Glazed Sausage, 305
Bites, Spicy Chipotle-Barbecue Sausage, 305
Bites, Sweet-and-Sour Sausage, 305
Mushrooms, Sausage-Stuffed, 300
Casseroles
Breakfast Strata, Southwest, 136
Enchiladas, Breakfast, 333
Lasagna, Speedy, M252
Manicotti, Meaty Cheese, 34
Cassoulet, Sausage-and-Chicken, 237
Eggs, Armadillo, 139
Empanadas, Meaty, 138
Gravy, Sawmill, 110
Meat Loaf, Herb-and-Veggie, 161
Pizza, Sausage-and-Scrambled Egg, 88
Rigatoni With Sausage and Bell Peppers, 215
Salisbury Steak, Tex-Mex, 204
Stew, Frogmore, 111
Tacos, Sausage-Egg Soft, 26
Turkey Sausage Patties, Breakfast, 169
SEAFOOD. *See also* **Clams, Crab, Crawfish,
Fish, Salmon, Shrimp, Tuna.**
Salad, Sewee Preserve's Seafood, 173
SEASONINGS
Barbecue Rub, 166
Gremolata, 319
Herb Mix, Italian Parmesan, 284
Rub, Paul's Chicken, 174
Rub, Paul's Pork Ribs, 174
Rub, Spice, 259
Sweet Spice Blend, 274
SHERBETS
Blackberry-Buttermilk Sherbet, 133
Blueberry-Buttermilk Sherbet, 133
Lemon Sherbet, Refreshing, 133
Lime Sherbet, Refreshing, 133
Raspberry-Buttermilk Sherbet, 133
SHRIMP
Casserole, Cajun Shrimp, 237
Cocktail, Cinco de Mayo Shrimp, 138
Fried Shrimp, Texas Best, 327
Garlic Shrimp and Grits, 111
Grilled Shrimp With Bacon and Jalapeños, M200
Pasta
Cajun Shrimp and Andouille Alfredo
Sauce Over Pasta, 57
Creole Cream Sauce, Shrimp and Pasta
With, 49
Spinach Pasta, Creamy Shrimp-and-, 239
Paste, Shrimp, 98
Pickled Shrimp, 158
Pitas, Shrimp, 188
Rolls, Shrimp, 188
Salad, Old Bay Shrimp, 188
Salad, Shrimp, 65, 95
Sauce, Cajun Shrimp-and-Crab, 206
Stew, Frogmore, 111
Stuffed Jumbo Shrimp, 124

SLAWS
Blue Cheese-Bacon Slaw, 91
Broccoli Slaw, 278
Broccoli-Squash Slaw, 170
Carolina Coleslaw, Creamy, 167
Cilantro Slaw, 324
Creamy-and-Sweet Coleslaw, 125
Lemon-Apple Coleslaw, 44
Overnight Slaw, 208
Red Cabbage Coleslaw, Sweet-and-Tart, 125
Sweet-and-Spicy Slaw, 17
Vinegar Coleslaw, Zesty, M125

SLOW COOKER
Appetizers
Meatballs, Bourbon-Mustard Glazed, 305
Meatballs, Spicy Chipotle-Barbecue, 305
Meatballs, Sweet-and-Sour, 305
Sausage Bites, Bourbon-Mustard Glazed, 305
Sausage Bites, Spicy Chipotle-Barbecue, 305
Sausage Bites, Sweet-and-Sour, 305
Beans, Slow Cooker Barbecue, 180
Dressing, Slow-Cooker Cornbread, 270
Main Dishes
Chalupa Dinner Bowl, 238
Pot Roast, Cowboy, 35
Pot Roast, Italian, 34
Sandwiches, Slow-Cooker Barbecue Beef, 64
Stew, Slow-Cooker Beef, 235
Sweet Potatoes, Easy-Does-It Mashed, M250

SOUFFLÉS
Souffleeta, 326
Spiced Soufflés With Lemon Whipped Cream, 255
Vegetable
Carrot Soufflé, 66
Spinach Soufflé, 66
Sweet Potato Soufflé, 110

SOUPS. *See also* **Chili, Étouffée, Jambalaya, Stews.**
Avocado Soup, 159, 200
Bell Pepper 'n' Tomato Soup, Creamy, 293
Blueberry Soup, Chilled, 178
Butternut Squash-Parsnip Soup, 36
Butternut Squash Soup, Curried, 234
Chicken-and-Black Bean Soup, 102
Chicken Soup, Cheesy Mac 'n', 292
Ham-and-Bean Soup, 45
Minestrone, Mama's Mexican, 254
Okra Soup, 98
Pimiento Cheese Soup, Creamy, 254
Roasted Red Pepper Soup, 72
She-Crab Soup, 98
Sweet Potato-Peanut Soup, 104
Tomato Soup With Crispy Croutons, Creamy, 207

SPAGHETTI
Bowl, Sweet-Hot Asian Noodle, 187
Red Wine-Tomato Pasta, 140
Sauce, Spaghetti With Mint-and-Garlic Tomato, 100
White Wine-Tomato-and-Clam Pasta, 140

SPINACH
Florentine Stuffed Onions, 141
Madeleine, Spinach, 95
Parmesan Spinach, Quick, 292
Pork Loin, Tuscan, 296
Salads
Apple Salad With Cinnamon Vinaigrette, Fresh Spinach-and-, 44
Endive Salad With Warm Vinaigrette, Spinach-, 291
Pear, and Blue Cheese Salad, Easy Spinach, 41
Strawberry Salad, Spinach-and-, 55
Soufflé, Spinach, 66

SPREADS
Basil-Cheese Roulade, 143
Olive Spread, Creamy, 311
Pimiento Cheese, 323
Shrimp Paste, 98
Sun-dried-Tomato-and-Basil Spread, Layered, 275

SQUASH. *See also* **Zucchini.**
Acorn Squash, Sugar-and-Spice, 289
Acorn Squash With Cranberry Relish, Roasted, 234
Butternut
Bake, Butternut Squash, 234
Salad With Blue Cheese Vinaigrette, Roasted Butternut Squash, 233
Soup, Butternut Squash-Parsnip, 36
Soup, Curried Butternut Squash, 234
Casserole, Southwestern Squash, M217
Casserole, Squash, 277
Marinated Squash, 129
Roasted Winter Squash, 233
Sautéed Squash and Carrots, 42
Sautéed Squash and Zucchini, 203
Spaghetti Squash Sauté, 234

STEWS. *See also* **Chili, Étouffée, Jambalaya, Soups.**
Beef Stew, Slow-Cooker, 235
Brunswick Stew, Easy, 292
Chicken-and-Vegetable Stew, 235
Frogmore Stew, 111
Ham-and-Collard Stew, Hearty, 236
Oyster Stew, 48

STRAWBERRIES
Cheesecake, Irish Strawberry-and-Cream, 273
Ladyfingers, Creamy Berry, 36
Parfaits, Super Fast Strawberry Shortcake, 196
Pies
Ice-Cream Pie, Spiked Strawberry-Lime, 89
Ice-Cream Pie, Strawberry-Lime, 89
Ice-Cream Pie, Strawberry Smoothie, 89
Rhubarb Pie, Strawberry-, 132
Salad, Strawberry-Citrus Chicken, 84
Salad, Strawberry-Cranberry-Orange, 249
Salad With Cinnamon Vinaigrette, Strawberry, 133
Splendid Strawberries, 215
Syrup, Fresh Strawberry, 132
Vinaigrette, Strawberry-Balsamic, 84

SWEET POTATOES
Baked Whole Sweet Potatoes, 108
Biscuits, Sweet Potato, 22
Buñuelos, 295
Casserole, Maple-Sweet Potato, 245
Cornbread, Sweet Potato, 252
Mashed Potatoes, Golden Buttermilk, 298
Mashed Sweet Potatoes, Easy-Does-It, M250
Mashed Sweet Potatoes, Southwest, 271
Roasted Potatoes, Two-Color Rosemary, 18
Salad, Sweet Potato, 171
Soufflé, Sweet Potato, 110
Soup, Sweet Potato-Peanut, 104

SYRUPS
Caramel Syrup, The Ultimate No-Bake Cheesecake Banana Pudding With, 326
Lime Syrup, Fresh Fruit With, 220
Orange Syrup, 240
Rum Syrup, 279
Simple Syrup, 135
Strawberry Syrup, Fresh, 132

TACOS
Fish Tacos, Southern-Style, 327
Sausage-Egg Soft Tacos, 26
Tilapia Tacos, Shredded Grilled, 16

TAMALES
Helena Tamales, 112

TASTE OF THE SOUTH RECIPES
Chili, Chunky Beef, 235
Hoppin' John, 21
Hush Puppies, 99
Hush Puppies, Jalapeño, 99
Pie, Chocolate-Bourbon Pecan, 134
Pie, Chocolate-Walnut, 134
Sauces and Gravies
Barbecue Sauce, White, 196
Rémoulade, Criolla, 69
Rémoulade Sauce, Creole, 69

TEA
Cake, Vanilla-Jasmine-Sour Cream Tea, 135
Chicken, Tea-Thyme Grilled, M52
Hot
Apple Tea, 24
Verla's Hot Tea, 257
Iced
Apple Tea, 24
Cranberry-Raspberry Herb Tea, 61
Green Tea, Iced, 196
Marian's Iced Tea, 135
Orange Tea Cooler, 216
Pineapple-Orange Herb Tea, 61
Salad, Lapsang-Poached Chicken, 135

TOMATOES
Bread, Sun-dried Tomato-Herb, 252
Bread, Tomato-Black Olive Grits, 83
Casserole, Tomato, 22
Cherry Tomatoes, Rosemary-Roasted, 257
Dip, Tomato-Basil, 219
Fried Green Tomato Po' Boys, 330
Mayonnaise, Tomato-Basil, 180
Parsleyed Tomatoes, Broiled Mahi-Mahi With, 130
Pastas
Linguine, Two Tomato, 187
Red Wine-Tomato-and-Steak Pasta, 140
Red Wine-Tomato Pasta, 140
White Wine-Tomato-and-Clam Pasta, 140
Relish, Tomato, Basil and Corn, 321
Salads
Cucumber Salad, Tomato-and-, 69
Feta Salad, Tomato-, 207
Hot Tomato Salad, 129
Lettuce Salad, Tomato-Feta, 207
Mozzarella, Avocado, and Tomato Salad, 41
Onion Salad, Tomato-and-, 167
Onion Salad, Tomato-and-Sweet, 141
Salsa, Homemade, 59
Sauces
Greek-Style Tomato Sauce, Penne With, 187
Ground Beef-Tomato Sauce, 290
Mint-and-Garlic Tomato Sauce, Spaghetti With, 100
Soup With Crispy Croutons, Creamy Tomato, 207

Stuffed Tomatoes, Feta-, 148
Sun-dried-Tomato-and-Basil Spread,
    Layered, 275
TOPPINGS. *See also* **Frostings, Glazes,**
    Relishes, Salsas, Sauces.
Savory
    Apricot Vinaigrette, M312
    Blueberry-Ginger Topping, Baked Brie With, 179
    Blue Pecan Confetti, Maple-Mustard-Glazed
        Balsamic Steaks With, 330
    Chipotle-Lime Cream, 329
    Garlic-Lime Mojo, Yuca With, 294
    Horseradish Cream, 309
    Nutmeg-Molasses Cream, 104
    Parmesan Topping, Buttery, 277
    Red Chile Paste, 118
Sweet
    Bananas, Brown Sugar, 45
    Crème Anglaise, 239
    Lemon Whipped Cream, 255
    Oranges, Italian Caramelized, 101
    Peaches, Stewed Yard, 23
    Strawberries, Splendid, 215
    Walnuts, Candied, 60
    Walnuts, Sugared Curried, 281
    Whipped Cream, 269
    Whipped Cream, Sweetened, 132
    Wild Blueberry-and-Peach Topping, 326
TOP-RATED MENU RECIPES
Appetizers
    Cucumber-Dill Rounds, 96
    Dip, Quick Creamy Vegetable, 20
    Eggs, Armadillo, 139
    Logs, Chile-Cheese, 64
    Shrimp Cocktail, Cinco de Mayo, 138
    Wings, Buffalo, 64
    Bellinis, Apricot, 96
    Biscuits, Blue Cheese, 309
    Breadsticks, Parmesan Cheese, 20
    Cider, Mulled Pomegranate, 309
    Cream, Horseradish, 309
    Dessert, Lemon-Blueberry Layered, 206
    Granola, Mixed Fruit, 240
Main Dishes
    Beef Tenderloin With Horseradish
        Cream, 309
    Chicken Strips, Honey-Pecan, 188
    Chili, Chunky Beef 'n' Tomato, 20
    Empanadas, Meaty, 138
    Ham-and-Swiss Breakfast Pie, Savory, 240
    Rib Roast, Rosemary-Thyme, 248
    Roast, Festive Pork, 46
    Shrimp-and-Crab Sauce, Cajun, 206
    Tetrazzini, Smoked Turkey, 96
    Tetrazzini with Artichokes and Red Bell
        Peppers, Smoked Turkey, 97
Salads and Salad Dressings
    Potato Salad, Bacon 'n' Onion, 188
    Shrimp Salad, Old Bay, 188
    Strawberry-Cranberry-Orange Salad, 249
Sandwiches
    Barbecue Beef Sandwiches, Slow-Cooker, 64
    Pitas, Shrimp, 188
    Shrimp Rolls, 188
    Sauce, Cream, 248
    Syrup, Orange, 240
Vegetables
    Green Beans, Sautéed, 206
    Potato-and-Gruyère Casserole, 248
    Roasted Baby Vegetables, 47

TORTILLAS. *See also* **Burritos, Enchiladas,**
    Fajitas, Quesadillas.
    Chimichangas, 290
    Huevos Rancheros, Spicy, 221
    Pie With Snappy Mango Salsa, Cuban
        Pulled Pork Tortilla, 329
    Rolls, Shrimp, 188
    Strata, Southwest Breakfast, 136
TUNA
    Peppered Tuna With Mushroom Sauce, 72
    Salad, My Best Tuna, 328
TURKEY
    Bake, Next-Day Turkey Dinner, 246
    Gravy, Quick Herbed Turkey, 270
    Jerk Turkey Tenderloin With Raspberry-
        Chipotle Sauce, M194
    Loaf, Herb-and-Veggie Turkey, 161
    Molasses-Coffee Turkey Breast, M289
    Roasted Turkey, 244
Salads
    Cobb Salad, Southern-Style Turkey, 214
    Layered Cornbread-and-Turkey
        Salad, 147
    Layered Southwest Cornbread-and-Turkey
        Salad, 147
    Main Dish Turkey Salad With Cranberry
        Vinaigrette and Garlic Croutons, 246
Sandwiches
    Bacon, and Havarti Sandwich, Turkey, 92
    Burgers, Toasted Pecan, Cranberry, and
        Gorgonzola Turkey, 320
    Focaccia Sandwich, Pesto, 131
    Melt, Loaded Turkey, 159
    Melts, Oven-Grilled Loaded Turkey, 159
    Monte Cristo Sandwiches,
        Open-Faced, 222
    Sausage Patties, Breakfast Turkey, 169
    Tetrazzini, Smoked Turkey, 96
    Tetrazzini with Artichokes and Red Bell
        Peppers, Smoked Turkey, 97
    Wraps, Crispy Ginger-and-Garlic Asian
        Turkey Lettuce, 325

VANILLA
    Cake, Vanilla-Jasmine-Sour Cream
        Tea, 135
    Glaze, Vanilla, 287
    Salad, Vanilla-Scented Fruit, 209
    Sauce, Vanilla Cream, 260
VEGETABLES. *See also* specific types.
    Baked Vegetables, Rosemary, 313
    Dip, Quick Creamy Vegetable, 20
    "Fried" Vegetables, Garlicky, 177
    Grilled Veggies, Easy, 194
    Loaf, Herb-and-Veggie Turkey, 161
    Meat Loaf, Herb-and-Veggie, 161
    Medley, Barley, Vegetable, and Fruit, 127
    Noodle Bowl, Sweet-Hot Asian, 187
    Penne, Fresh Vegetable, 101
    Pie, Shortcut Greek Shepherd's, 238
    Pizza, Roasted Vegetable-and-Goat
        Cheese, 176
    Roasted Baby Vegetables, 47
    Roasted Fall Vegetables, 217
    Salad, Marinated Vegetable, 129
    Salad Platter, Mediterranean Antipasto, 220
    Yuca With Garlic-Lime Mojo, 294
VEGETARIAN
    Penne, Fresh Vegetable, 101

WALNUTS
    Cake, Maryland Black Walnut, 106
    Candied Walnuts, 60
    Sugared Curried Walnuts, 281
WHAT'S FOR SUPPER?
Breads
    Biscuits, Easy Pan, 26
    Cornbread, Cheese-and-Onion, 35
    Croutons, Garlic, 247
    Toast, Lemon-Garlic, 171
    Dip, Quick Hummus, 206
    Doughnut Stacks, Mini-, 58
Main Dishes
    Catfish, Quick Pan-Fried, 170
    Chicken, Baked Pecan, 312
    Eggs, Cream Cheese Scrambled, 26
    Flank Steak, Easy Greek, 207
    Lasagna, Fiesta Taco, 140
    Pasta, Red Wine-Tomato-and-Steak, 140
    Pasta, White Wine-Tomato-and-Clam, 140
    Pork Chops With Orange Slices, Saucy, 197
    Pork Tenderloin, Grilled Balsamic, 241
    Pot Roast, Cowboy, 35
    Pot Roast, Italian, 34
    Tacos, Sausage-Egg Soft, 26
    Turkey Dinner Bake, Next-Day, 246
    Pasta, Red Wine-Tomato, 140
    Rice Pilaf, Basil, M197
Salads and Salad Dressings
    Apple Salad, Lemony, 241
    Cabbage Salad, Tangy, 162
    Fiesta Salad, 58
    Slaw, Broccoli-Squash, 170
    Tomato-Feta Lettuce Salad, 207
    Tomato-Feta Salad, 207
    Turkey Salad With Cranberry Vinaigrette
        and Garlic Croutons, Main Dish, 246
    Vinaigrette, Cranberry, 247
    Sandwich, Turkey, Bacon, and Havarti, 92
    Sauce, Creamy Mushroom-Artichoke, 312
    Sauce, Sour Cream-Cucumber, 207
Vegetables
    Asparagus, Grilled, 197
    Baked Vegetables, Rosemary, 313
    French Fries, Ranch-Seasoned, 93
    Green Beans, Speedy Rosemary, 241
    Potatoes, Double-Stuffed Barbecue, 162
    Vinaigrette, Apricot, M312
    Wraps, Tangy-and-Sweet Roast Beef, 92

YOGURT
    Dressing, Low-Cal Dilled Yogurt, 128
    Sauce, Yogurt, 321
YUCA
    Buñuelos, 295
    Garlic-Lime Mojo, Yuca With, 294

ZUCCHINI
    Salsa, Zucchini-Carrot, 298
    Sautéed Squash and Carrots, 42
    Sautéed Squash and Zucchini, 203

favorite recipes journal

Jot down your family's and your favorite recipes for quick and handy reference. And don't forget to include the dishes that drew rave reviews when company came for dinner.

RECIPE	SOURCE/PAGE	REMARKS